THE COLLECT.
BENJAMIN HAWKINS, 1796–1810

Eng. by E. G. Williams & Bro. N.Y.

Benjamin Franklin

Pub'd by Van Nostrand, Publisher

THE COLLECTED WORKS OF BENJAMIN HAWKINS, 1796–1810

Edited by Thomas Foster

THE UNIVERSITY OF ALABAMA PRESS
Tuscaloosa and London

∞

The paper on which this book is printed meets the minimum requirements of
American National Standard for Information Science–Permanence of Paper
for Printed Library Materials, ANSI Z39.48-1984.

Library of Congress Cataloging-in-Publication Data

Hawkins, Benjamin, 1754–1816.
    [Works. 2003]
    The collected works of Benjamin Hawkins, 1796–1810 / Benjamin Hawkins ;
edited by Thomas Foster.
        p. cm.
    "The current volume contains a facsimile reprint of the original "Sketch" (1848)
and "Letters" (1916) as published by the G[eorgia] H[istorical] S[ociety]. In
addition, two previously unpublished journals are included . . . constitute the
complete works of Hawkins except for miscellaneous letters scattered in various
archives"—Introd. Includes index.
    ISBN 0-8173-1367-2 (cloth : alk. paper) — ISBN 0-8173-5040-3 (pbk. : alk. paper)
    1. Hawkins, Benjamin, 1754–1816—Correspondence. 2. Hawkins, Benjamin,
1754–1816—Diaries. 3. Creek Indians—History—Sources. 4. Indians of North
America—Government relations—1789–1869. 5. Indian agents—Southern
States—History—Sources. I. Foster, Thomas, 1970– II. Title.
    E99.C9H3 2003
    975.004'973—dc21   2003008305
British Library Cataloguing-in-Publication Data available

CONTENTS

INTRODUCTION

Benjamin Hawkins (1754–1816), a Revolutionary War soldier and former United States senator from North Carolina, lived among and wrote about the southeastern Indians during the late eighteenth and early nineteenth centuries. Born in colonial North Carolina into a landowning family, he became involved in politics when he was elected to the state's legislature in 1778 and to the U.S. Congress in 1789. Due to Hawkins's interest in Indians, President George Washington appointed him "Principal Temporary Agent for Indian Affairs South of the Ohio River" in 1796. Hawkins was a close confidant to Presidents Washington and Jefferson. His presence among the Creek Indians was a significant part of the presidents' plan to westernize them by converting them to European economic practices (Grant 1980).

Jefferson promoted Hawkins to "Principal Agent for Indian Affairs South of the Ohio River" in 1801, a position he held until 1816. Hawkins lived among the Indians, particularly the Creek (also known as Muscogee or Muskogee), for approximately thirty years. He wrote extensively about their geography, demographics, and culture. A more complete biography of Hawkins is included in the introduction to the "Letters of Benjamin Hawkins," which is reprinted in this volume.

For decades, the papers and writings of Benjamin Hawkins have been recognized for their value to ethnohistory, political history, and environmental reconstruction (Ethridge 1996; Pound 1951). Hawkins kept extensive notes regarding the Native populations and geographical landmarks of the Southeast. His journals are possibly the most detailed and useful written environmental accounts for the southeastern United States during the late eighteenth and early nineteenth centuries. His only rival is the renowned botanist William Bartram.

Hawkins's writings have been published in various forms over the last 150 years. In 1848 the Georgia Historical Society (GHS) published "A Sketch of the Creek Country, in the Years 1798 and 1799" in the *Collections of the Georgia Historical Society.* That manuscript is in the possession of the GHS and is similar to another copy of the "Sketch" that is in the Peter Force Collection at the Library of Congress. The "Sketch" is a brief summary of the major Creek towns and populations at the end of the eighteenth century. It includes important descriptions of the Creek landscape. Three other copies of the "Sketch" are known, but only the GHS version is complete. John Swanton (1922) published significant portions of the Library of Congress copy in his book about the history of the Creek. The GHS also possesses nine manuscripts that contain Hawkins's personal and public correspondence and a journal of Richard Thomas, an assistant to Hawkins. In 1916 the GHS published that collection of manuscripts as "Letters of Benjamin Hawkins," volume 9 of its *Collections of the Georgia Historical Society.* In 1938 the Americus Book Company reprinted the "Sketch" (Hodgson and Hawkins) for the unveiling of a monument near Americus, Georgia, by the Daughters of the American Revolution. The Reprint Company of Spartanburg, South Carolina, has twice reprinted facsimiles of the GHS volumes 3 (1974) and 9 (1982). Lastly, the Beehive Press in Savannah, Georgia, reset and reprinted the original "Sketch" and "Letters" and added a few of Hawkins's previously unpublished letters (Grant 1980). All of these publications are out of print.

The current volume contains a facsimile reprint of the original "Sketch" (1848) and "Letters" (1916) as published by the GHS. In addition, two previously unpublished journals are included. The new journals, combined with the previously published manuscripts from the GHS, constitute the complete works of Hawkins except for miscellaneous letters scattered in various archives.

The new journals in this publication contain field notes on observations and measurements Hawkins made during his trips throughout the Southeast. Between 1797 and 1810, Hawkins covered what is now central and northwestern Georgia, central and southwestern Alabama, and portions of Mississippi. Hawkins used his journals to record routes and to measure distances from one location to another. Hawkins traveled a total of 3,578 miles (5,758 km) throughout the Southeast (Figures 1 and 2) and occasionally traveled back over the same route in order to measure the distance between major and minor land features more accurately. He made extensive observations along the routes. Consequently, these journals of distances, or "viatories," provide de-

Figure 1. Hawkins's journeys in Georgia.

tailed microscale geographical and environmental data for the end of the eighteenth century and the first quarter of the nineteenth. Until now, however, these journals have not been published in their entirety and were available only through microfilm or the Library of Congress and the GHS. A section of one of the journals was published by the Valley Historical Association in the *Valley Historical Association Bulletin* (Fretwell 1954). Mark Fretwell's edited section focused on a

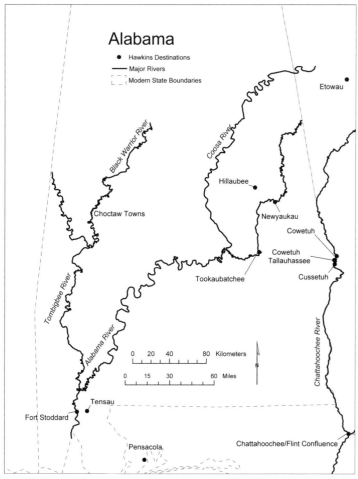

Figure 2. Hawkins's journeys in Alabama.

brief portion of the journal that relates to the Chattahoochee Valley in Georgia and Alabama. In addition, archaeologists have used parts of Hawkins's journals for the reconstruction of town locations. Wesley Hurt (1975) used the viatories (included in this volume) in his survey of the Lower Chattahoochee River valley for the Alabama Museum of Natural History. Harold Huscher (1959) used the viatories in his reconstruction of Creek Indian locations along the Lower

Chattahoochee River valley during his archaeological survey for the Smithsonian Institution.

The Viatories

Few other eighteenth-century sources provide the environmental and geographical detail as these journals by Benjamin Hawkins. When Hawkins first entered the Creek country, he traveled among the major towns in order to acquaint himself with the populations and the geography. These journeys were compiled and edited into the "Sketch of the Creek Country" described above. The viatories edited in this volume contain the field notes that Hawkins apparently used to construct the "Sketch." They contain his original data regarding cultural and physical geography and the distances between those features.

The viatories start in 1797 and end approximately in 1810. A generalization of his journeys described in the viatories is illustrated in Figures 1 and 2. These figures show each journey's starting point and ending point; a dotted line connects the two points. The figures are not topographically accurate because a detailed mapping of each journey is beyond the scope of this introductory chapter. (Mark Fretwell [1954] accomplished this type of detailed mapping in his publication of a portion of the viatory routes.) Rather, this introduction is intended to provide a brief summary of Hawkins's route as detailed in the viatories.

Before discussing Hawkins's journal entries, I need to address the issue of inconsistent spelling. The spellings of place names and common words used in this introduction are sometimes inconsistent. Furthermore, many of the words are English translations of Native American words, which can also result in inconsistent spellings. For consistency—and for the sake of preserving the journal's original text—I used Hawkins's original spellings. Hawkins was relatively consistent in his spelling and the justification behind his methodology is useful. He spelled *Muscogee* and other Native American words phonetically and separated syllables with commas. Since there are multiple spellings for almost every proper name and there is little, if any, consistent justification for each variation, I used Hawkins's phonetic spelling. Furthermore, I prefer to leave the interpretation of place-name identification to the reader. It is possible that two independent place names have similar spellings, and I did not want to erroneously label them as one location by giving them a common spelling. In the interest of clarity, I have included a table that compares the spelling variants of proper names used in the viatories and in my introductory chapter to the spellings John Swanton (1922) used in his book on the Creek and some common variants (Table 1).

TABLE 1

Hawkins Viatory Spelling	Swanton (1922)	Common Names
Aut,tos,see; auttossee	Atasi	Atasi; Otassee
Ca,hau,bau; Kahaba		Cahaba
Chat,to,ho,che; Chatt,o ,ho, che; Chatto hatchee	Chattahoochee	Chattahoochee
Chatto nogee		Chattanooga
Cheauhatche		Chiahatchee
Cherokee		Cherokee
Chicasau; Chicasaw; Chickasau		Chickasaw; Chickasa
Chick,au,mau,gau		Chickamauga; Chikamaga
Choctaw	Choctaw	Choctaw
Clonotis cau		Flint River
Co,chis,see		Ichisi?
Co,wag,gee		Cowagee
Cooloome	Kolomi	Kalumi; Colomi; Colomee
Coosau	Cosa; Coosa	Coosa; Kosa
Cow,e,tuh tal,lau,has,see; Cowetuh ta,lau,hass,ee; Cowetuh tallauhassee	Coweta Tallahassee	Coweta Tallahassee; Kawita Tallahassee; Coweta Old Town
Cowetuh	Coweta Tallahassee	Coweta; Kawita; Kawituh
Cussetuh	Kasihta	Cusseta; Kasita; Kasituh; Kashita
E,tow,ah; E,tow, who; e,taw,oh; Etau,wa; Etauweh; Etow,who	Itaba	Etowah
Ecun,hut,kee	Ecunhutke; Kanhatki	Ekunhutkee
Eit,cho,foo,ne		Hitchifoonee
Escambia; Escombia		Escambia
Eufau,lau,hat,chee	Eufaula Hatchee	Eufaula creek

Hawkins Viatory Spelling	Swanton (1922)	Common Names
Eufaulau	Eufaula	Eufaula; Yufaula
Fooscehatche	Fushatchee	Fusihatchee; Fusihatchi
Han,nau hat,che		Hannahatchee
Hatche Chubbau	Hatchee tcaba; Hatchechubbee	Hatchechubbau
Hill,au,bee	Hilibi	Hillabee; Hillaubee; Hilapi; Hillabi
Hit,che,too,che	Hitchetooche	
Hitchetee; Hitchitee	Hitchiti	Hichitee
Ho,ith,le,waule; Hoithle ti gau		Hothlewaulee; Hoithlewalee
Hookchoie	Okchai?	Oakchoy?
Hookoie	Okchai?	Oakchoy?
Hopewell		Hopewell
Kentucky		Kentucky
Kialijee	Kealedji	Kialigee
Kit,cho,foo,ne		Kitchefoonee
Koenecuh		Conecuh
Koo,loo, moo,kee		Kolomoki
Luchau Pogau	Loachapoka	Lochapoka; Lochapoga
Mississipi		Mississippi
Mook,laus,au	Muklasa	Muklasa
Nanihaba	Naniaba	
Natchez	Natchez	Natchez; Natchee
New,yau,cau	Nuyaka	New York
No,chil,lehatche		Nochilihatchee
Nucus,oe,sum,gau		bears hiding place
o,fuck,she	Okfuskee?	Okfuskee?
Oc fus koo chee Tal lau hassee	Okfuskutchi Tallhassee	Okfuskuche Tallahassee
Oc,mul,gee	Okmulgee	Okmulgee; Oakmulgee
Ocfus ke nena		Okfuskeneena; Burnt Village
Ocmulgee old fields	Okmulgee Old` Fields	Okmulgee Old Fields
Oconee	Okonee; Oconee	Oconee
oos,to,nau,lih; Oostenaule;		Oostenaula

Hawkins Viatory Spelling	Swanton (1922)	Common Names
Oostenaulih		
Pa,la,choo,cl,e	Pallachicola	Apalachicola
Pad,jee ligau; Padjaligau	Padgeeligau	Padgeeligo
Pasca o coola	Pascagoula	Pascagoola
Pensacola	Pensacola	Pensacola
Pin e,hoo,ta	Pinehoote	
Sa,le,quo,heh; Salequoheh;		Salenojah;
Sa,lequaheh; Soo,le,no juh;		Buzzard Roost
Su,lenojuh; Sule noj uh		Buzzard Roost
Salenojau nene		Path
Sau,woog,a,lo	Sawokli;	Sawokli
	Sauwoogelo	
Taensau; Tensau		Tensaw
Tal,la,poo,sau; Tallapoosa	Tallapoosa	Tallapoosa
Talauhassee; Tallauhassee	Tallahassee	Tallahassee
Tallasee; Tallassee	Talisi	Tallassee; Tulsa;
		Talisee
Tarrapin		Terrapin
Tellico	Tellico	Tellico
Thlotlogulgau	Thlotlogulgau;	
	Lalogalga	
Tomb igbe; Timbigby;		Tombigbee
Tombigbe;		
Took aub atche;	Tukabahchee;	Tukabatchee
Tookaubatche	Tookaubatche	
Tumassee		Tennessee
Tus cau,loo,sau		Tuscaloosa; black
		warrior
Tuskeegee	Tuskegee	Tuskeegee;
		Taskeegee
U,chee hat,che	Uche hatche	
Un,nut,te thluc,co		big swamp
we,tum,cau; Wetumcau	Witumka	Wetumka
Wewocau	Wiwohka	
witumcau hatche	Witumkahatchee	
Yauzau		Yazoo

Hawkins's Route

On December 6, 1797, Hawkins began his viatory entries with a trip from "Cussetuh," a Lower Creek town located at the present-day site of Lawson Army Airfield at Fort Benning, near Columbus, Georgia, (Willey and Sears 1952), to Fort Wilkinson, near the present-day site of Milledgeville, Georgia (Figure 1). He passed "No,chil,lehatchee" and "Ecun,hut,coo,chee" creeks along the way. Next, Hawkins traveled from "Etowau" to "Hillaubee" (Figure 2). Etowau was at or near the location of present-day Etowah, near Cartersville, Georgia; Hawkins's descriptions of the area's residents and geographical features are consistent with this interpretation. He wrote that the Cherokee who were living at "Etow,woh" had "increased their stock of hogs and cattle ... [and] appear well clothed and industrious." The Hillaubee town was situated among the Upper Creek Indian towns in east-central Alabama. On the way to Hillaubee, he passed the "remains of a hurricane" and a "conic mount." Since Hawkins noted the cardinal direction of the supposed hurricane's movement, he may have been observing the effects of a tornado instead.

Hawkins constantly noted the location and quality of reeds along the routes of his travels. For example, he noted during the trip from Etow,who to Hillaubee that at one point he crossed "a large bed of reeds on the left margin. on the right a flat, and between it and the high lands a thick bed of reeds." Hawkins departed from the Upper Creek town of "Newyaucau" on November 25, 1797, which is upstream from what is now Horseshoe Bend, Alabama, on the Tallapoosa River. From Newyaucau he traveled to "Cowetuh," the principal war town of the Lower Creek Indians. Cowetuh was situated south of Phenix City, Alabama, on the Chattahoochee River, upstream from Cussetuh (Figures 1 and 2). Along the way, he observed "6 houses on [the] right belonging to Eufau,lau,hatchee. They are well situated, the flats on the creek are rich and well cultivated." He also passed "the dividing ridge between Chat,to,ho,che and Tal,la,poo,sau," which marked the hydrological drainage units in east-central Alabama.

In 1798, Hawkins left the home of Timothy Barnard, a longtime trader and friend to Hawkins who lived on the Flint River near present-day Montezuma, Georgia (Figure 1). Hawkins traveled to the village of the Tussokiah Micco, who lived in the town of Upatoi near present-day Upatoi, Georgia, in Muscogee County (Elliot et al. 1996). Along

the way he "saw the Buffaloegrass So,we,nah" and passed the town of
Buzzard Roost, or "Soo,le,no juh." The route was "gravelly in places,
small oak blackjack, hickory saplins and grubs shortleaf pine. [S]ome
of the lands appear[ed] pretty good."

Previous to 1803, Hawkins had lived in various Creek towns, and
his travels usually departed from them. However, in 1803, Hawkins
settled permanently near the Flint River, not far from his friend
Barnard's house (Figure 1). This house became the Creek Indian
Agency (Hawkins Agency). Hawkins traveled from this location to
"Ocmulgee old fields" (Figure 1), an abandoned town and agricultural field near present-day Macon, Georgia, and probably at the
Ocmulgee National Park (Mason 1963; Waselkov 1994). There,
Hawkins observed that, "the lands rise into high waving land, the
growth mostly oak, the Ocmulgee old fields are below adjoining the
creek and river . . . the reserve should be 2 1/2 miles above the creek
and three back, the creek affords water for a saw mill, and there is a
convenient situation for one and the last mile includes some Longleaf
pine." After his stop there, Hawkins continued on to Fort Wilkinson.

His next entry, in 1798, picked up in the middle of a journey to
"Etauwah." Although he did not specify his origin, he was probably
coming from "Coweta Tallahassee," near present-day Phenix City,
Alabama. He "pass[ed] on the back of the Cowetuh Town on flat
lands . . . the buildings extend up for this distance on our right [east]."
During this journey he passed by "We,at,lo,tuc,kee" settlements, an
old square ground, and had breakfast at an isolated settlement where
he was fed "venison, ground peas, potatoes, and O sauf kee." After
continuing through a "neighborhood . . . devoted to hurricanes," he
passed through "Ocfuskoochee Talauhassee" and "Ocfuskenena." This
last town was burned by Georgian settlers just five years before
Hawkins passed through it. He noted "the remains of houses [and]
many peach trees which look well, some plum and Locust trees and
some cascine yupon of which their black drink was made." The town
of Ocfuskenena is presently under West Point Lake near West Point,
Georgia (Huscher 1972). He passed "Chattahochee Tallauhassee,"
which means "Chattahoochee Old Town" and may be the namesake
of the current Chattahoochee River. Next, he continued north and
arrived at the "E,tow,woh" (Etowah) town house near the
"Oostenaulih" (Oostenaula) and "Etawoh" rivers. Along the way, he
"saw a great number of muscadines [that] perfumed the air at the
distance of fifty yards."

On April 16, 1799, Hawkins traveled to Pensacola, Florida, from Cowetuh Tallauhassee (Figure 2). The latter town was the Coweta Old Town, located opposite Cusseta near Phenix City, Alabama. This route took him along the east-west trade route to the Upper Creek towns on the Lower Tallapoosa River and down the Alabama River and then over to the Pensacola Bay. From Pensacola, he traveled across land "strewed with Iron ore" and "pine barren[s] the pines some of them fit for plank" to the Tensaw Delta near Mobile, Alabama, and then up to Fort Stoddard near present-day Mount Vernon, Alabama. He wrote, "the Alabama [River] is 300 Y[ards] wide. . . . The Tombigby and Alabama make Mobile which is from 4 to 500." Hawkins then backtracked up to the Upper Creek towns on the Tallapoosa and ended at "Tookaubatchee" (Figure 2). Tookaubatchee was located near present day Tallassee, Alabama (Knight 1985). From there, he traveled back to Cowetuh Tallauhassee, passing "Weheint,lah a fine flowing little reedy creek."

Next, he traveled from Barnard's house on the Flint River to Cussetuh (Figure 1). Then, from Cowetuh Tallauhassee, across the river from Cussetuh, he traveled down the Chattahoochee for many days until he reached the confluence of the Chattahoochee and Flint rivers in present-day southwestern Georgia (Figure 1). During this route he passed "Oconee," "Sauwoogalo," and "Palachoocle." Palachoocle is near the historic Fort Apalachicola (1689–1691), east of Holy Trinity, Alabama (Kurjack and Pearson 1975). Hawkins noted along the way that the "land bordering on Uchee hatchee [wa]s poor pine land. . . . Pa,la,choo,cle is on the left ab.^t 15 minutes beyond Hitchitee on a poor pine flat . . . on the N[orth]. side of Oconee for near 30 minutes land level and some part thick set with dwarf small hickorys. . . . On the S[outh] there is some rich land tho' broken. This creek affords clay for potts." From the Chattahoochee–Flint River confluence, he traveled back up the Flint and over to Upatoi, which was situated on a tributary of modern-day Upatoi Creek (Figure 1). His next entry was from "Tallauhassee" to "Tookaubatchee," among the Upper Creek towns. He passed "Witumcau" Creek, individual houses, a natural bridge, and an "old ball ground" on the way.

His next entry was far to the east, on the east-west road that passed through the frontier trading town of Sulenojuh on the Flint River in Georgia. He continued west to Ocmulgee old fields and then returned to Cussetuh (Figure 1). Continuing on the east-west road he passed "Wetumcau," "Kialijee," "Thlotlogulgau town," and the path to the

"Hookoie town house" on his way from Tookaubatche to the "S. W. Point."

During 1802 and 1803, Hawkins traveled from the Mississippi Territory back to the Creek Territory and passed through Choctaw and Chickasaw land. He started this trip at the Kentucky (Chickasaw) Trace (later called the Natchez Trace) in present-day Mississippi. During this time, he traveled a significant distance without encountering any settlements except an "oblong square mound 50 by 33 feet and 8 feet high" (Figure 2). However, he passed "Cushtussau" and "Yauzau" in western Alabama. Cushtussau, a Choctaw town, had 34 settlements, while Yauzau was described as "miserable." He continued through west-central Alabama down the "Tombigbe" and passed the "Tuscauloosau River," which Hawkins wrote means "Black Warrior" in Choctaw. He passed Fort Tombigby and a number of individual Choctaw settlements on the way to central Alabama and the Upper Creek towns on the Tallapoosa and Alabama rivers. He passed through "Tuskeegee" at Fort Toulouse at Wetumka, Alabama, on his way to Daniel McGillivray's house "above Tuskeegee." The Coosa River was 150 yards at that point. He passed "Ecunhutkee," ten settlements, "Cooloome," "Fooscehatche," Nicolas White's house, "Hoithlewaule," Richard Bailey's house, and the "Auttossee" path, among other individual houses (Figure 2). All of these towns were situated along the Lower Tallapoosa River between modern-day Montgomery and Tallassee, Alabama. This entry concludes those from the viatory in the possession of the Library of Congress.

The Georgia Historical Society of Savannah, Georgia, has another field notebook that contains one entry regarding Hawkins's travels, a short trip from "Padjilagau" to Cussetuh (Figure 1). Padjilagau was a Yuchi settlement located on a tributary of the Flint River (Worth 1997).

The viatories were intended to be a field notebook, and Hawkins did not edit them for reading convenience. He intended to use them as raw data, most likely for his later writings as well to keep track of his travels among the towns. Besides early land-survey maps, these journal entries are the most detailed physical and cultural descriptions known for the late–eighteenth and early-nineteenth-century regions of Georgia and Alabama. They are biased, however, toward the area of east-central Alabama and west-central Georgia because that is where the Muscogee peoples congregated during Hawkins's time. The frequency of Hawkins's observations decreased when he traveled away from the Muscogee region.

Editorial Comments

The journals edited and reprinted here are located at the U.S. Library of Congress in Washington, D.C., and the Georgia Historical Society in Savannah. The first and longest journal is labeled on the outside "A Viatory or Journal of Distances and Observations by Col. Hawkins" (item 314b [series 8d, entry 66] of the Peter Force Collection, Manuscripts Division, Library of Congress). This edited version of this journal was created by viewing the microfilm copy from the Library of Congress and taking digital photographs. The entire journal except about ten blank pages was photographed by the editor under fluorescent light with tungsten slide film. The slides were scanned with a Nikon LS-2000 slide scanner. Both the microfilm and the digital images were consulted for this editing and transcription. The journal is undated but contains entries from 1797 to 1802.

The second journal included here is unlabeled and is in the possession of the Georgia Historical Society (item 14 of the Benjamin Hawkins Papers, Collection No. 373). It is a small "pocket notebook" and is mostly blank. Most of its text is a list of plants and items of unknown context. Approximately two pages appear to be English-Muscogee translations of a few phrases. The handwriting and the unknown Muscogee spellings make the text's transcription difficult. Consequently, I have included only the viatory, or distance-related matter, from the journal, which constitutes only one entry. The entry is undated but it is toward the beginning of the journal's three entries, which are dated between 1810 and 1813.

The strength of these journals is in the description of geographical features, place names, and town locations, which are at times unbelievably detailed. These viatories include a listing of the time, distance, and features from a variety of locations throughout what is now Georgia, Alabama, and Mississippi. Hawkins traveled on horseback with a group of individuals (Fretwell 1954) and recorded his observations and time as he traveled. He measured distance by observing the time: After measuring the time from location A to B, he then multiplied the time by a rate constant. He usually used three miles per hour as his traveling rate constant. However, as noted in the journal, sometimes his speed varied between three and a half and four miles per hour.

Notation in the journal is typical of Hawkins's organization. He recorded the time in minutes and recorded a key for commonly used words. The first number in his column system indicated the time, usually in minutes. Later in the journal he switched to a decimal format where the first number is the number of hours and the number after the decimal was the number of minutes. After the time, he recorded the water type with a "B" or "C." "B" indicates that he crossed a branch, and "C" indicates that he crossed a creek. Next, he indicated the direction of water flow, with an "L" for left flowing or "R" for right flowing. Water flow was measured from his traveling perspective. Next he recorded the width (in feet) of the water with a "forward slash" and a number. Finally he recorded environmental observations. He used these notations liberally throughout the journal and altered the format slightly while the journal was in use. For example, later in the journal, he recorded cardinal direction of his travels with "N," "S," "E," "W," and combinations of these symbols, which represent respectively, north, south, east, west, or some combination.

Since the layout, format, and notation of the journal is not always obvious, I will illustrate with a brief example. On November 13, 1798, Hawkins recorded:

13 Nov.ʳ course S45W.

1.10 + dry C. r. 6/.
12. + dry. C. r. 12/. here was the residence of the Tarrapin he is dead his house burnt but the heir to the estate lives well, The farm is manured and improved. The grand [unintelligible] with colewarts and shallots.
57 + dry C. r. 6/
41. The paths divide I take the left, The division just over a ridge, where there is some pine, the right is the largest, and the direct path to the Creeks.
6. + dry C. r. 6/ a flat of rich land, joins to one that is poor, and a conic mount caped and thick set with Limestone

These notes indicate that on November 13, Hawkins's direction of travel was south by 45 degrees west. After 1 hour and 10 minutes, he crossed a dry creek running to the right, which was 6 feet across. Twelve minutes later, he crossed a dry creek running to the right, which was 12 feet across. The "Tarrapin's" house was located there. The house was burned, but the heir to the estate still lived there. The farm was well manured and improved with colewarts and shallots. Fifty-seven minutes later, he crossed a dry creek running to the right, which was 6 feet across. After traveling for another 41 minutes, the path that he was traveling on divided in two at a ridge where there were pine trees. Hawkins took the left path. The path to the right was larger and led to the Creek Indian towns. After another 6 minutes of travel, he crossed a dry creek running to the right, which was 6 feet across. At that point, there was a flat of rich land that adjoined poorer land and a conic-shaped mound that was capped with limestone. Hawkins did not indicate how he judged land quality, although he often correlated it with vegetation.

I left editorial comments to a minimum. It is the intent of this volume to make Hawkins's viatories more accessible for environmental and cultural studies of the Southeast. Consequently, I did not comment extensively on the modern-day locations of Hawkins's travels, as Mark Fretwell (1954) did. While this endeavor would be valuable, I felt it more important to make the journals available and permit a wider audience to reconstruct his journeys with a variety of methods.

Since these viatories were field notebooks, they were written in a particular format. Hawkins used the layout of the journal entries to signify changes in topic, location, date, etc. Furthermore, it is sequentially laid out by time and geography. This means that information in a given entry is dependent on the entry that preceded it. Consequently, I have tried to reproduce the layout of the journal as closely as possible. I have also reproduced his spellings and misspellings as closely as possible. Hawkins's handwriting is generally good, and I was able to increase the resolution of the document's digital images; nevertheless, some text was illegible. Editorial comments are enclosed in brackets, [/] or marked in the endnotes. If a word was ambiguous but legible, I included it. Sometimes, a word did not make contextual sense but was included anyway. Words that are completely illegible are represented with the word *unintelligible* in brackets: [unintelligible].

Acknowledgements: John Ross, President of the Chattahoochee Valley Historical Society, granted permission to republish the portion of the viatory that was copyrighted by Mark Fretwell (1954). Miriam

Syler of the Cobb Memorial Archives in Valley, Alabama, was gracious and hospitable while I was there. Thank you to the Georgia Historical Society in Savannah for granting permission to publish portions of its Hawkins journal. Duke Beasley and two reviewers read portions of an earlier version of this document. Jerry Stephens, Director of the Mervyn H. Sterne Library at the University of Alabama at Birmingham, loaned us its copy of the *Collections of the Georgia Historical Society*, volume 9, for the reprint. Lastly, thank you to Kara Foster for helping with the transcription and interpretation of Hawkins's handwriting. This project would still be in preparation were it not for your help.

References Cited

Elliott, D. T., K. G. Wood, R. F. Elliott, and W. D. Wood
  1996 Up on the Upatoi: Cultural Resources Survey and Testing of Compartments K-6 and K-7, Fort Benning Military Reservation, Georgia. Submitted by Southern Research, Ellerslie, Georgia, for the Environmental Management Division, Directorate of Public Works, U.S. Army, Fort Benning, Georgia.
Ethridge, R. F.
  1996 A Contest for Land: The Creek Indians on the Southern Frontier, 1796–1816. Ph.D. dissertation, Department of Anthropology, University of Georgia, Athens.
Foster, H. T. II
  2001 Long-Term Average Rate Maximization of Creek Indian Residential Mobility: A Test of the Marginal Value Theorem. Ph.D. dissertation, Department of Anthropology, Pennsylvania State University, University Park.
Fretwell, M. E.
  1954 Benjamin Hawkins in the Chattahoochee Valley: 1798. Valley Historical Association *Bulletin* 1:1–30.
Grant, C. L. (editor)
  1980 *Letters, Journals, and Writings of Benjamin Hawkins, vols. 1 and 2.* Beehive Press, Savannah, Georgia.
Hawkins, B.
  1848 "A Sketch of the Creek Country, in the Years 1798 and 1799." *Collections of the Georgia Historical Society* 3(1). Georgia Historical Society, Savannah.

1916 "Letters of Benjamin Hawkins, 1796–1806." *Collections of the Georgia Historical Society* 9. Georgia Historical Society, Savannah.

1974 *A Combination of a Sketch of the Creek Country and Letters of Benjamin Hawkins, 1796–1806.* 1974 facsimile ed. Reprint Company, Spartanburg, South Carolina.

1982 *A Combination of A Sketch of the Creek Country and Letters of Benjamin Hawkins, 1796–1806.* 1982 facsimile ed. Reprint Company, Spartanburg, South Carolina.

Hodgson, W. B., and B. Hawkins

1938 *Creek Indian history: As comprised in "Creek Confederacy" by W. B. Hodgson, and "The Creek Country" by Col. Benjamin Hawkins Being a Reprint of Vol. Three, Part One of the Georgia Historical Society Publications to Which Is Added The Last Night of a Nation: Oration of J. E. D. Shipp at the unveiling of the Chehaw Monument Erected by the Daughters of the American Revolution.* Americus Book, Americus, Georgia.

Hurt, W. R.

1975 The Preliminary Archaeological Survey of the Chattahoochee Valley Area in Alabama. In *Archaeological Salvage in the Walter F. George Basin of the Chattahoochee River in Alabama,* edited by David L. DeJarnette. University of Alabama Press, Tuscaloosa.

Huscher, H. A.

1959 Appraisal of the Archaeological Resources of the Walter F. George Reservoir Area, Chattahoochee River, Alabama and Georgia. River Basin Surveys, Smithsonian Institution, Washington, D.C.

1972 Archaeological Investigations in the West Point Dam Area: A Preliminary Report. Department of Sociology and Anthropology, University of Georgia, Athens.

Knight, V. J., Jr.

1985 Tukabatchee: Archaeological Investigations at an Historic Creek Town, Elmore County, Alabama, 1984, Office of Archaeological Research, Alabama State Museum of Natural History, University of Alabama, Tuscaloosa.

Kurjack, E. B., and F. L. Pearson.

1975 Special Investigations of 1Ru101, the Spanish Fort Site. In *Archaeological Salvage in the Walter F. George Basin of the Chattahoochee River in Alabama,* edited by David L. DeJarnette, pp. 200–222. University of Alabama Press, Tuscaloosa.

Mason, C. A. I.

1963   The Archeology of Ocmulgee Old Fields, Macon, Georgia. Ph.D. dissertation, Department of Anthropology, University of Michigan, Ann Arbor.

Pound, M. B.
1951   *Benjamin Hawkins, Indian Agent.* University of Georgia Press, Athens.

Swanton, J.
1922   Early History of the Creek Indians and their Neighbors. Bulletin No. 73. Bureau of American Ethnology, Smithsonian Institution, Washington, D.C.

Waselkov, G.
1994   The Macon Trading House and Early European-Indian Contact in the Colonial Southeast. In *Ocmulgee Archaeology, 1936–1986.* Edited by D. J. Hally, pp. 190–196. University of Georgia Press, Athens.

Willey, G. R., and W. H. Sears
1952   The Kasita Site. *Southern Indian Studies* 4:3–18.

Worth, J. E.
1997   The Eastern Creek Frontier: History and Archaeology of the Flint River Towns, ca. 1750–1826. Paper presented at the 54th Annual Meeting of the Society for American Archaeology, Nashville, Tennessee.

A VIATORY OR JOURNAL OF DISTANCES AND OBSERVATIONS

Benjamin Hawkins

The following is a transcription of the journal entitled "A Viatory or Journal of Distances and Observations by Col. Hawkins" in possession of the Library of Congress.

A Viatory.

6 dec.[er] 1797 Left Cussetuh for the Oconee, Fort Wilkinson noting the distance in minutes 60 to 3 mile. + for crossing b. branch c creek l. r. left or right, the course they run. 2/ the width in feet

3.40 +. c. l. 25/ No,chil,lehatche
The lands poor broken pine, the range for stock very poor. within a mile of the c. + b. r waving oaky woods some reeds in patches pretty good. we encamp to the left of our path in the fork of 2 reedy bottoms, the ridge at the path has some coarse iron ore looking stone.

7 dec.[er]
50 + b. l. 2/ reeds and evergreens
6 + b. l 1/ reeds to the r. pretty good
6 + b. l. 1/.
7 + b. l. 1/.   There is between these two branches a small flat of poor pine barren called in creek Ecun,hut,coo,chee[1]
15. over poor broken land a large creek just under our left and reeds on r.
8 +. c. l. 8/. Hoc,[H]ilo,lā,ho,lo,che
The lands poor.

23 + c. l. 30/. a fall of 2/ to the l. there is no appearance of a
    water course on its borders no swamp, on the left margin
    the lands flat and poor, on the right high broken land.
    Yoc,pee.
28. over high stiff pine forest, pass a vale of reeds on the r.
38 a path to the right
3   the head of a small reedy bottom to be seen S. eastwardly
    to a considerable extent, and have fine affect viewed thro
    the pines.
50. reedy bottom l.
7. reeds to the r.
.6. black gum, large, spreading top with switch like limbs. reed to l.
    in a cove.
8. +. b. l. 3/. reeds on the sides of the hills
    The lands broken, and pineland rise up the hill, the stone
    black and appears to have iron ore

Our distance 3.2. or nine mile The course N.20E. The moun
tains are to Our right, parallel to our path, and within a mile of
us. The road level, the streams have good water and the lands fit
for culture, the growth post oak, and Hickory, all small.

57. cross Ska,le,co a creek 45 feet wide running to our left.
52. up the side of a creek on our right cross a fine running
    branch
32 cross an other.
36. join a path to our left
20. a Limestone spring on our right
1.40. cross a creek running to our left.
Our distance 4.55 or 15 mile, our cours N.10 E. We pass over
some Limestone dwarf post oak land, and the whole rout
generally poor The road fine and level.
2/ cross a creek to the left 10 feet wide
2. cross a creek to the left 20 feet
2.20 cross a branch running to our right from a fine spring on
our left.
1.12. cross a small creek to our right
33. the paths divide we take the right

1.12. cross Tellico 180 feet wide.
D. 45 arrive at Tuskeegee
Our cours N. 30. E. The distance 6.30 or 29$\frac{1}{2}$ mile. The road is good the land poor, limestone, postoak.

November 12 1798
I left Etow,woh this day for the Hill,au,bee There is a considerable change in the condition of the Cherokees of this town for the better since I visited on my first entering on the duties of my agency. All persons old and young appear to be happy Their little farms increased, vegetables to be had in plenty, I see bacon, colewarts, and turnips, at several houses, I met a sincere welcome, and The Children are no longer afraid of a white man they visit me the smallest of them when invited to do so with ease and gladness. They have increased their stock of hogs and cattle. appear well clothed and industrious.

X 1.10   arrive at John Vanns and pass the [warring?] his aged mother Mrs Roe, visited me, and informed me she had a side of bacon and some vegetables for me, for the path. She said
        X 40+.c.r. dry. Course to Vans 1V^2

The old cherokees would never forget At,tow, okee / the hawk a name given me at Hopewell the author of the beloved treaty of Hopewell, and who was now placed by Washington to take care of the red people.

        13 Novr course S45W.

1.10 + dry C. r. 6/.
12. + dry. C. r. 12/. here was the residence of the Tarrapin he is dead his house burnt but the heir to the estate lives well, The farm is manured and improved. The grand [unintelligible] with colewarts and shallots.
57 + dry C. r. 6/
41. The paths divide I take the left, The division just over a ridge, where there is some pine, the right is the largest, and the direct path to the Creeks.

6. + dry C. r. 6/ a flat of rich land, joins to one that is poor, and a
conic mount caped and thick set with Limestone
34 arrive at half breed Wills. near the large limestone spring, and
where I lodged

Their lives generally increased and caused attention paid to
them, and the cattle this family has twenty five hogs for market.

40.   [unintelligible] Limestone creek arrive at the first long leaf
and open land.
49.   encamp on the border of the creek the cane fine   14
[nov?]
1.13.+ d. c. 1   and enter a flat, the [hills] to the right
[thick] wet with limestone.
our course winds round to
38   the east and to the top of a mountain
43.   over the ridge broken land to our right and left, a vein of
reed to our left.
The cane and[?] with the creek [unintelligible] [unintelligible]
have past left.
28. +.b. 1. dry fine reed
28.+ c. 1. 8/ fine water and fine reed   I encamp
7.   and breakfast under a large [Peach or Beech]
near the creek in which I my same my name and the late.   opposite this branch on the other side of the Creek.
I encamped 4th december 1796
4. + [a, quo, re use,te?] 180/ flat pine land on the left
11. + c. r. 10/   fine water and reed the across the river S 20 E.
66. over a ridge of poor corse gravelly saplin land, the under
brush chesnut, a vein of reeds on the left
25. the remains of a hurricane the first from S.W The [wind?]
from W.
9 + c. b. 6/ fine water and fine reed to our right. The lands very
poor here
I encamp

15 [December?]

8. + c. r. 10/ [no?] reed
17. + c. r. 3/ small reed. over post oak broken land
31. + c. r. 30/ a flat of some large chesnut and
6. + c. r. 8/   beech between these two.[3]
    The lands on the right bank of the creek very broken and
    pooron the left of the small creek the
    lands level but poor and run into pine barren
47. + b. r. at its source reeds
6 + b. r. reeds
20. vein of reeds to the left, I stand on the right margin.
15. a conic mount on the left caped with [Horge?]
15 + this vein a branch r. And turns W.
6. over a flat of very tall large beach
+ c. r. 20/. and rise on a sharp ridge the creek makes a turn at the
point and the ascent is both up and down it at the same time
9. + d. b. r. 4

S20W
6 a vein of reeds on the right
11. + b. r . fine water below thick margined [unintelligible][4]
4 + d. b. r. 6/.

S.30W

12 + c. d. r. 4/ reeds
10. reeds to the left.
3. +. b. l. and here I breakfast

    For the last hour the lands are broken with coarse gravel,
the growth post oak red oak saplins and pine, some small
hickory, it is fit for cultivation, but is all poor land.

8 + c r. 8/ some reeds
21. + c. r. 12/. over highly broken land no reed
19 + b. r. 2/ this distance hilly and poor on the left bank of this
    branch it isbetter.
6 vein of reeds to the right

5. ditto

4 + c. r. 4/

15 + b. d. r. fine reed

11. + c. r 5/ fine reed

18 + d. b. r. no reed

7 + d. c. r.

13. + b. r. no reed.

3 + c. r. 6/ the lands broken and poor to

35. + c. r. 20/ fine cane and reed, and water only in holes, here I lodged.

     5 dec.ʳ 1796.

12. + c. d. r. 8/   reeds

10. + d. c. b 4/   very fine reed

29. + d. c. l. 8/.   no reed. I encamp on the north side to the right of the path, on a small reedy branch. The lands for the last 29 minutes very high ridges and poor, The course on the top of them, S.50.W

     16.

5. +. c. r. 5/ [below?] steep hills

9. a cane toped mountain a breast to the left a ridge extending from it parrallel to our course and a mountain in view in our [unintelligible]

26. +. b. r. This whole stage broken + stoney and the lands on the north part rich,

8. pass through the gap of a high ridge

8. + b. r. north front rich and well timbered.

12. vein of reed to our right

10 +. c. r. 10/.

19. + c. r. 10/ North front large poplars and rich broken stoney land

6 + b. r.

12 + 2. b. r

11 up one of these to the gap. The lands broken [rich?], the hill sides and bottoms the ridges poor stoney black jack and post oak dwarfs

10. +. b. l.

5. go over a high ridge, small chesnut saplins

8 reed to the left

4. +. c. r. 10/ lands good on the margins
4.   reeds to the left
18. ditto
6   a vein of reeds on the r. + l. I cross in the fork the junction
     a large bed of the small maiden reed
5. + a large hunting path its direction N.40W
     my course S.20.W
6. + b. l.   reeds
13   reeds r. and l.
12. reeds r.
7. + a vein of reeds
9.   a vein of reeds to the l.
6.   ditto. r.
7

X note that the [n? unintelligible] stream joins this 10 miles below, on the left.[5]
18.   The river Agus,na,use, ta. X 70 yards wide
The lands for two hours is very poor + stoney, the growth small, black oak saplins chestnut + post oak. The reeds the small low maiden reed. Here I breakfast and put my horses on a small island above the ford. The food is better below the ford.

12+ a small river 70 feet wide Kitchopultaugau.
16   reeds to the left
10. ditto left and r.
6   ditto l.
4. d. l
5 + c. l. 8/ a fine running stream + a large bed of reeds on the left
     margin.
     on the right a flat, and between it and the high lands a
     thick bed of reeds.
26. reeds. r.+. l. This whole stage over high broken oak land,
     the gravel dark, stiff red land
9.   reeds r. +. l.
10. The paths fork, at an old marked red oak I take the Right
6.   reeds to the l.
                    I go down a few minutes and within 50 yards of

the left, side, find on an other branch A fine spring. A
Holly at the head of it which I mark BH No. 16. 1798 and
here I encamp.

17.

15.   a vein of reed to the left
5 + d. b. l   a cluster of holly to the left
20.   a bed of reed to the left, red oak noll of black saplins to the right.
14 +. c. l. 15/ a vein of reeds parallel with the path joins the creek just below
6   a vein of reeds to the right
3   ditto. l.
13 +. d. b. l. a bed of reed our course S.10.W
24 + b. l.   through an extensive meadow of reed
7 +. d. b. l. ditto.
4. + vein of reed r.
10. ditto. l.
6 + c. l. 10/ water and reeds
21. + vein of reed.
9   vein reed r.
9 +   an extensive vein of reed. r.
11 + b. l.   through a bed of reed our course S.10.W
17.   reeds to the r.
8. +. c. l. 18/ fine flowing
    The lands from the last creek, more level, and less
stoney than before, The growth mostly black oak, and
small. The reed the low maiden reed. Here the lands more
uneven, yet fit for culture, and appear to be a soil that
would produce wheat.
14 +. c. l. 12 stoney land
7 + d. b. l   reeds and very fine
20.   reed r. +. l.
9. + d. b. l. reeds turn to the left and breakfast on a branch
parallel with the path.
    The whole of our path a good one the lands all
waving and hilly, the soil stiff with a coarse dark gravel the
growth mostly black oak and small

Take up the branch

5.+   the b. l. reeds
4   reeds to the r.
6.   reeds r. and. l.
7   reeds. l.
10.   reeds r.
6   reeds.l.

4. reeds l. and a cluster of holly at this [Line?]
12 reeds. r. an extensive view to the l. from a high chesnut oak
ridge. the lands on that side appear very broken
6 +. c. l. 4/ a fine reedy creek, Here I saw 16 fine hogs
12.   The longleaf pine on a stoney ridge
    a curiously variegated- rock, flowered or spoted, of lead
colour, white flint stone and a dingy red, the red seems to
have been spattered on.
7. The path is crossed by one at right angles to the r. reed
12. + b. l. reeds amidst very broken hills
10. d. b. l. and here ends these broken lands
8 vein of reed to the l.
        The paths fork take the right
16.   arrive at [lnnatte chepco?] on [Choofun,taulau,hatchee?].
+. the C. l. 10/.
14.   paths fork take the left.
14 + b. l. reeds and continue on up one that has fine winter reed
9. +   path
3. reed. l. + r.
6. + c. r. 8/
11 + c. l. 6/ fine winter reed below
9 + b. l.   ditto
6 + b. l.   reed
3 +   vein reed at the junction with a [larger] on[e] to the left.
8 reed to the r
3 + b. l.   reed
9 encamp on a branch of fine winter reed.

which I + /S
6 + b. l.   reed
6   reed on the left
22 +. c. l. 4/ fine water and the reeds above the food fine
17   vein of reed. l.
10 + d. c. l
10.+   Hill,au,bee hatche l. 40 feet wide and arrive at the house of
        Mr. Robert Grierson.

November 25.

The rout from New,yau,cau to Cowetuh ta,lau,hass,ee S.10.E

13 + the river 360/ it running to the right
20 +. c. r. 8/.
10 paths dive [divide?] take the r.
52. +. b. l. over high broken pine hills long leaf pine
6 + d. b. l. reeds
4 + b. l. broken stoney hills
19 + a path
15. + b. r. a bed of reeds. Over broken stoney oak land
6 + reeds
21 + b .l. reeds here I breakfast amidst flat reedy
glades, waving red oak saplin land stiff and good for wheat
10 + a vein of reed l.
3 + d. b. l. in a flat of reed. post oak land
7 + a large path E.20.S Our Cours S10.E open red and post oak
        land
3 + path . red oak and short leaf pine
10 + b. l. 4/ fine running with reeds the land good red oak land
10 path joins on the r. Oaky woods
7 a village, well situated on good lands in the neighbourhood of
        a large creek. Pin e,hoo,ta
5 + c. r. 20/ the land good hickory and oak
10 + b. r. this a bed of reed our course S20W
7 + b r. black oak and short leaf pine
20 + a path
3 + reeds r.

17. + b. r 3/ pine reed in oaky woods   hau[6]

6 + a river to the r 80 feet over a shoal Oc,tau,zauze.

26 vein of reed r. here I encamp Nov. 25 1798
    our course from the village S10W The lands near the river
    broken, no flat lands

16 + a path in flat oaky woods

15 + c. l.4/ fine water and reed. The lands broken and stoney, red
    oak and shortleaf pine.

10. some long leaf pine

7 a + path. we take the left E.30.S We find from our course of
    S.10.W. that we must have taken the rong path at the
    village.

14 the path forks we take the r.

6 a house of Tallasee people, well situated on a little creek the
    lands good. oak and hickory

4 + c. r. 8/ and resume the path we left

[9?] + path from the village

+ c. r. 10/ reeds   plantations on our right

34+b.r. reeds

4+ vein of reed r. in a pine barren long leaf pine and here I saw
    the salamander hillocks

5 + b. r. reed.

6 houses on our right, belonging to Eufau,lau,hat,chee. They are
    well situated, the flats on the creek are rich and well
    cultivated

5.+ Eufaulau hatchee 15/ r.

24. reeds to our l. in the midst of a hurricane from S.E. the lands
    poor hills

20 a path from or right

our course now N.80.E

36. a ball ground flat of oak and hickory

5. the head of a.b.r. thick set with reed, lands broken oak and
    hickory.

67 + c. r. 5 in a large bed of reed. The lands are broken stiff and
    stoney. red oak and small hickory, just above the path on
    the E side there is the appearance of a rich flat of level
    land. here I breakfast.

14 + c. r. 20/ over stiff land, oak hickory and shortleaf pine.

Lus,te hat,che

3 paths fork I take the left. The course E.

11 + d. b. l There is to the left of the path the appearance of flat low lands on the creek

7 + d. b. l. reeds The hill sides small hickory

7 + d. b. l fine reed the lands continue stiff and stony oak and hickory.

22. + b. r fine reed r. and l. some rock on the W. side land stiff and stony red oak and hickory

16 + b. r. lands of like quality

2+ d. c. l

25 + path.

3 + vein of reed r.

12 + b. r. fine reed and here I encamp. 26 nov.ᵣ 1798

The lands pretty good, oak small hickory chestnut and pine.

8 + c. r on a rocky bed

14 + d b. r. fine reed oak hickory and pine

5. + d. b. r. reed

28 + c.r. 20/ rocky bed oak and hickory. small

15 a vein of reed just after +ing a ridge of rock, hickory oak pine

7 + d. c. r. 8/ reed our course E.10.S

14 vein of reed l.

19 + vein of reed r. over poor saplin land

18 + b. r. fine reed

1 + d. b. r. The lands good on the E. oak, chestnut

7 a vein of oaky wood reed

3 + vein reed r

8 a ridge of poor blackjack. I take this to be the dividing ridge between Chat,to,ho,che and Tal,la,poo,sau course continues E.10.S

28 a + path

9 + b. r. just below the spring

26 + path our course E 15 S

5 + d. b. l broken lands

10 long leaf pine forest

8+d.b.r over a high pine nole

22 + d. c 8/r good land on the margin

6 + d. b. r fine reed

4 + d. b. r

2 + d. b. r

15 breakfast on a small branch to the r.

6 + d. c. r. 6/ reed and rich flats some large white oak our course
   E.40.S

4 path joins from l.

3. d. b. r

7. d. b. r The lands to the right a red oak flat

<u>15</u>. + d. b. r. near thick vein of reed on r.

4 + d. b. r. reed

16. + b. r. water

4 + c. l. 38/ dry {reed or sand} and palmetto

14 + c. l.30/ we,tum,cau on a rocky bottom

4 path forks to the right

4 + d. c. r.

3 a path + houses r. and fields l.

8. through rich highland to long leaf pine

17 + b. r fine reeds

2 + d b r reed and evergreens

20 old houses to the left, plum and peach trees

7 + c. r. 90/ We,tum,cau. land broken

20 down it to We,tum,cau

10 + c. d. r.10/ and here encamp 27 nov.ʳ 1798

10 + r. reed

29 + d. c. r 12/ large flat and cane

12. The path from Timothy Barnards to the E,fau,
   Tustun,nug,gee and Tussokiah Micco village.

15. + a saplin ridge to l. and reeds

2. +. c. l. 8/ a fine clear running bold stream margined with reeds.
   proced over poor and a little waving a cove of reed to the l.
   and a string of them to the r.

16. + c. l. 25/. Oc,e,le,ba,de flat on both sides the left margin
   with reeds below, some evergreen on its margin, no
   [unintelligible] a fine clear bold stream.

46. The dogwarriors path joins on our left.
   at a small stream in clining. r.

<u>N.45E</u>   <u>6.+c</u>.r. 4/ little food on it, the bottoms have

A reeds we turn up one to r. and
  encamp.
    8 dec.[r]
7. reed to r. and l.
10. The top of a nole and ridge much higher.
38. + a reedy slash r.
<u>5</u> a bed of reed to r.
13. a cove of reed to the r. our course N.70.E.
  on a sand hill ridge
8.l. reed. N30.E
18. l. r. reed.
10. l. reed post oak on the north front of the hill
6. pine nole from the largest cluster of pine one with large
  limbs there are four beds of reeds, 2 to the r. and 2
  to the l.
6. a flat reeds to the l. and an open pine to the right.
12. l. reeds flat poor land to r. The reeds are like the T the top
  parallel with the path the stem N.30.W
5. a large view of reed to the r.
8. l. reeds those on the r. hid by a small ridge The reeds are
  parallel with the path for 2 minutes then project out.
10. [unintelligible] small run, in the courner of the path to the r
<u>8</u>. + c. r.15/ Pad,jee ligau, rocky bottom
104[7] but little water. The lands broken
  on the right bank, pretty level
  and good on the left.

18. a pine nole course N.70.E.
8. r. small oak and hickory, Evergreens
5.r. the bed of a run, reed + white oak and hickory.
17. + c. r. dry oaky woods and pretty good, some reed.
9. up a vale to r. land good
10. +. c. r. 3/. dry some reed stoney on the left.
9 + a bottom of reed up a vale of oakey land reed
12. r. a hollow to the l. pine and oak.
  here I saw the Buffaloegrass So,we,nah.
3. a bottom the l. hickory and oak, the r. a large chesnut.
3. an oak hickory and pine ridge a fine view of reed to the r.

4. a path to the left.

3 + b .r. reeds

2. + b. r. reeds and near the head

4 a bottom reeds and large Holly. N.76.E.

17. a bottom a reedy vein joins an other just below.

<u>6</u> the paths divide I take the r. E

130⁸ The left is the Buzzard roost/ Soo,le,no juh

19 r. l. reeds

6. r. reeds and a cluster of dwarf saplins l

5. r. vein of reed

8. l. reed

3. r. reed

5. r. reed

4. r. reed willow leaved hickory on the left and on the right some oak and hickory.

29 l. steep bottom oak hickory and pine, the ridge stoney. to the r. dwarf saplins and through them some reeds are perceptable. small pine blackjack and oak soil poor

10. r. reed.

10. l. a hollow of oakland. l. reed

11. steep oakey bottom to. l.

2. ditto r

1. ditto cove of reed r.

10.+.c.r. 15/. down a long sloping hill pass a pond. On the r. descending Based on the creek the land good.

10 encamp on a small [drain?] to or r.

From a defect in my compass and traveling some in the night

I could not ascertain by it the course, till this day the course from this to Cussetuh is about S60.W. The lands generally long leaf pine except where otherwise noted. The course first noted on the sand hill ridge N.70.E. is on the dividing ridge between flint river and Chatt,o ,ho, che 9th dec.ʳ

41.+ the river to the r. Flint river/ Clonotis cau/ at the islands there is three channels, it is at a fall, the bottom rocky, covered with moss the ford a good one the river below appears about 150/ wide.

      The lands on the r bank and for 4/. back, are stiff and of a quality good enough for wheat but too broken.

27.+b.r. 2/

2+b.r. 3/

23.+.c.r. 8/ no water but in holes

5+.c.r. 8/ water in holes the hills steep on the l.

35.+.c.r. 10/ water in holes

6+.c.r. 8/

<u>16</u>. To a ridge of longleaf pine course N.80.E.

114⁹

      The whole of this [course?] from the river is hilly, gravelly in places, small oak blackjack, hickory saplins and grubs shortleaf pine. some of the lands appears pretty good. At the entrance into N.80.E the pine forest there is reeds to the r.

24. + b. r. small a few reed and evergreens

12. + b. r. small and reedy

7 +. c. r. 5/ to it go down a reedy branch oaky woods and short
    leaf pine

4 + a reedy bottom oaky wood and evergreens

3 a path joins from the r. a cluster of small saplins to the r.

6 + c. r. 8/ oaky land some reed.

10 +. b. r. a reedy one just above the fork

3. + the other fork.

8 + c. r. 4/ reedy

6. +. b. small

6 + c. r. 5/ large reed to the r.

5. + c. r. 6/. rocky bottom.

      Between these two creeks the lands are rich, and from their junction an extensive bed of reed, this the best place I have seen for a cow range.

30. + a bottom reeds to our right

30. l. a flat of pines two veins of reed on each side

10.+b.l. small and reedy here I encamp and here I breakfasted
    the 22 Feby last and here I join my rout from Cussetuh by
    Timothy Barnards to the fort.

      10.ᵗʰ

A[10] Correction of this rout by a better time piece
    22 June 1800. From the dog warriors path
N.50.E.
    4 + c. r. 4/.
    52 + b. r.
    15 a cove of reed to r
    6 a cove of reed to l
    21 coves of reed to r. called weciuwau
    32 reed to the left
    <u>21</u> + c. r.10/. padjee ligau
    151[11].
    19 + b r
    <u>22</u> + b r fine food in oakwoods <u>breakfast</u>
    11 + b r
    10 + b r
    4 + b. r
    22. path to the left N40E
N45E.   3 + b r
    2 + b r
    5 + d b r
N.70.E.19 path divides
  E. 22

[This next installment written sideways alongside of writing from
the N50E down to the bottom of the page which is the E. 22. From
this last letter **A** on, Hawkins seems to have added this next section
later.]

    From Tussekiah Micco. to A[12]
N80E.   9 + c r 10/
    20 + c. r 8/
    17 + c. r 15/
    47 + c. r 6/. good land and food
    12 path from r.
N70E.   9 + c r 20/ rich flat[s?]
    17. + b. l. reeds
    12 + vein of reed
    <u>15</u> path from r. the Cussetuh path

158[13]
N70E.   26 reed l
        1.7 + c. r 15/ New,fau pul,gau
N45E.   50 + Flint river leave the path and make one
        241[14].   Encamp 24 June 1800. have fish in plenty

N. 7+br. a small one good water and good [unintelligible] food to
   the left
   1 path an old one up the river
N.10E.36+d b. l. }post oak lands
   16+b l   }post oak lands
   3+b l   }post oak lands
N20E   31+b l   }post oak lands
   19+c l 10/   }land good
   13+c l 10/   }land good
   20 path from on left the Salenojau nene
   + c r 10/. In tach cooche
N.40E. 20 + b. r   }pretty good land
   14+c r 4/ good summer food   }pretty good land
N.45E 3+b. r   }pretty good land
   8+c. r 8/ co,hauthluc,ulgee }pretty good land
   22 + c. r. 6/
   3.33 breakfast
   16 + c r 4/ oak woods good summer food
   24 + d. b r
   16 + d c r
   14 + s b r
   9 + b r
   10 +s. b r
   6 + b r large rocks on the hills of the right bank
   10 + b r. good land
   49 + d b r. over post oak hills
A 8 + b l poor black jack [noals?]
   9 + b l
   10 + c. r. 25/ Itcho cummau rich land
   181[15] on the left bank good for fish
        Encamp

A[16] 14 minutes more than the half way from Flint to Oc,mul,gee

N50E 5 + c r
      26 + b l
      9 + s b r
N60E 27 + b r muddy slash
      21 + b l [provine?]
      4 + c r. 60/. on a bed of rock To,be,sauk,ke.
      92 breakfast.- Fine for fish
N30E. 55 + s b r   }The lands good
      6+ c r. 8/ on a bed of rock }The lands good
      2 + b l
N60E 28 + b l
N20E 6 + c r 4/
      5 + b l. called by the traders boggy branch
      18 + b r
      19 + b r
N30E 72 + c r 8/
      4 the path on our left to the high shoals of Chattohoche
E   5 along that path to the river Ocmulgee
      220[17] Encamp

           From Col.° Hawkins's at Flint river to Ocmulgee
      old fields.
      4 miles to the hour[18].
N.65.E.
      10. +. c. r. 10/. the mill creek at [Col.° H.?]
      50. + c. r. 7/. [stamp?] creek
      20. + b. r. sweet water
      11. + c. r} Deep small creeks join just below
      4. +. c. r. } and form large cane flats rich land in the fork.
      95.
N.75.E.
      70. + b. l a branch of Itcho cunna
      13. Barnards path from the right
      83[19]
N.50E.
      21. +. c. l. small

22. +.b. 1
8 +. c. r. 50/. Itcho cunna.

___
51²⁰

N.45.E
  15+.b.r.
N60.E
  15 [unintelligible].+. b. r
  9. large vein reeds to the right, which we cross
N.65.E
  11. + b. r
  5. + b. r
  8 +. b. r
  4 +. b. r
  17. + c. r. 75/. To,be,sau,kee
  16.+c.r. small
  8+b.r
  28 + c. r. 25/
  26. path to the flat at Ocmulgee
N.
  25. to a [point?]
  27. the river at the ford 600/.
  4 crossing the river
N.60.E.-
  34. + c. r. 30/.- [oak choncoolgau?]
            The mouth of this creek is the point of [lying?]
      for the reserve contemplated on the late agreement with
      the indians and this course comes thro it. Then is a narrow
      flat of cane brake on the [unintelligible] and thence the
      lands rise into high waving land, the growth mostly oak,
      the Ocmulgee old fields are below adjoing the creek and
      river. [I had c/ 2.?] the reserve should be 2 1/2 miles above
      the creek and three back, the creek affords water for a saw
      mill, and there is a convenient situation for one and the
      last mile includes some Longleaf pine.
            the flat is just above the mouth of the creek and
      the path to it is just beyond the creek²¹

continued to Fort Wilkinson Hawkins's Waggon road
60. a path to the right old rock landing path
N.20.E.
    70 + b. r. the new blazed path   }only light enough to take the
                                       [corner?] at the [bying?]
N.60.E.
    50.+ c. r. 30/ [unintelligible proper name] creek on a high pine
shoal
N.45.E.
    17. +. b. r.
    22. +. p. r.
    5. path from the left. The [terms foard?]
N.60.E
    108. +. C r small   }all branches of camp creek
    15. +. b. r.   }which joins oconee river
                                        [receve?]
    25. +. b. r.- path to Milledgeville the [fort?].
    19. +. b.
N.80E.
    7. + c. r.
    12 +. b. r
    20. to F.W.

       October the 5.th 1798
N10.E I continue on to Etau,wah
 48   I cross the small creek $_+$ at John Tarvins and arrive at his
       house. The whole of this distance is on a flat of rich land
       the soil dark the growth small hard shell hickory small
       oaks and some pines. This is the third rise from the river
       the first is under culture rich and low The second rises
       about 20f and continues back to this which rises about 20
       feet more then ponds and high pine forest
+ Cotes,ka,le,jau[22]

    1.57[23].Course N10W. cross a creek running to the right 20f over
    O,cow,o,cuh hat,che This creek emties itself into the river
    at the falls the lands bordering on it are hilly poor pine
    land. The first 50 minutes we pass on the back of the

Cowetuh Town on flat lands, the soil light the growth small the buildings extend up for this distance on our right bordering on the river here commences the broken piney hills of the falls. From this to the Creek, I saw no land fit for culture.

1.18 a path to the right, and continuing on some small distance an old path joins onthe left. The lands continue poor broken and unfit for culture.

35. Cross a branch running to the right 3 feet wide the water good.

12. We arrive at We,at,lo,tuc,kee some settlements on our right bordering on the river here was formerly an old square The lands are rich and fit for culture the timber a mixture of oak and hickory.

58 Cross a creek runing to the right. hat,che Canāne. The lands continue of good quality, the growth oak hickory poplar.

39. Cross Chatto hatchee running to the right 10 feet wide
The lands for the last 39 broken and poor we pass one settlement on the path and here is an other at this creek andhere I encamp. having traveled 6.29 or 19 1/2 mile
The average course N.25.W
All the creeks we have cross are stoped by the drought and water is only to be found in holes.

49 Over broken lands, pine willow leaved hickory scrub oak. Cross a creek running to the right 40 feet wide, Woc,coo,che. The lands bordering on the creek are rich. There is no water in the creek. There is one plantation on the north side under a worm fence with peach trees around the house.

41 Cross a creek inclining to the left. 4 feet wide. No water, but fine winter reeds.

55 Cross Hal, le, woc, kee 60 feet over. No water but in holes. One settlement on the north side where I saw some Indians who gave me breakfast of venison, ground peas, potatoes and O sauf kee. For this last hour there is chesnut,

and the nuts are now falling. The lands broken, a mixture of chesnut, pine, post oak, hickory, red oak.

20   Cross a path

7   Cross a dry branch to the right. Fine reeds.

8   Cross a dry branch to the right.

3   Cross a dry reedy branch to the right.

11   Cross a dry reedy branch to the right.

17   Cross a creek running to the right 60 feet wide.
O,sun,nup,pau. The lands broken of mixed growth, not rich, the bottom of the creek rocks with moss. The distance for this forenoon 3 hours 31 minutes, or 10 mile and a half. N 25. W.

N.20.W.

42.   The path to Tallassee. W. 20. S

10.   cross large path to the same town

18.   cross a branch running to the right dry and reedy

2   a small running meadow branch

22.   a fine little branch running to the right. rocky hills west.

13   Cross a creek running to the right 20 feet wide,
As,soon,au,wau,hatchee well watered.

14   a path to the right and a view of the river.
To this point one description serves for all the lands. They are stiff, gravelly and broken, fit for culture. The growth a mixture of post and red oak, hickroy, and pine

33   cross a dry branch to the right, some reeds and saplins.

20   Cross a vein of reeds with the appearance of a pond to the left the surrounding growth thic set and small post and red oak. Evidin a hurricane

7   cross a branch dry of [thick?] reedy The course of the hurricane N 25 E.

6   cross a branch of fine water to the right through a glade of dwarf reed
This neighbourhood seems to have been devoted to hurricanes. there is the appearance of five in the course of a mile in different directions and at some years differ ence from each other.

11   a high knol to the left from whence we can see the high

lands on the left bank of the river.

8   cross a reedy branch and encamp.
           Our distance is 3.24 or 10 1/2 miles the course
           N20.W.
           The lands bereft of trees by the hurricanes are
     poor and gravely. passing through them they are better.
     The river here is $^1/_4$ of a mile on our right the lands good
     bordering on it.
     The wild geese arrive this morning[24]
           7 of October

22   Cross a creek running to the right 40 feet wide, O,so,li,jee
10   Cross a creek running to the right 8 feet wide. Oc fus koo
     chee Tal lau hassee lies to our right bordering on the river,
     and in the approach to this creek we pass through a flat of
     long grass
28   cross a branch 2 feet wide
18   cross a creek 5 feet
34   cross c[25] running to the right 4 / old fields below.
5.   cross a branch to the right 3/. Old settlements in the
     north. Faint traces of plum, peach, locust. pass on through
     Ocfus ke nena a town taken by some volunteers from
     Georgia, 27 Sept. 1793. There is the remains of houses
     many peach trees which look well, some plum and Locust
     trees and some of the cascene yupon of which their black
     drink was made. This path from Oc fus koo chee Tal lau
     hassee is on the river bank. The lands are some of them
     low ground of good quality
29. cross a creek to the right 4 feet wide
12   over stiff land with dark gravel and a dwarf growth of
     hickory. cross
     Hoithle ti gau 100 ft wide running to the right
12. o cfus kee path on our left
58   cross a creek running to our right 4 feet wide. The lands
     from Hoithletigau are broken, stiff gravelly of good quality
     for wheat the growth small mixed pine shortleaf hickory,
     post and black oak and chesnut

The whole distance 3.55 or 12 mile. our course N. 20. W. The river appears fordable at the falls and its width 400 yards

19.   To the top of a ridge paved with small white flintstone.

8.   cross Hatchee soff, ke / deep creek running to our right 20 feet wide our course alters to the east of N.

32.   cross a branch running to the right margined with oakey woods reed. our course N 40 E

5   cross a vein of oaky woods and They are materially different from those of the piney woods. They are of a pale green these a very deep green with broad leaves

1.20   cross a creek running to the right but little water the lands good. For one hour back the lands are broken and gravelly with small stone the growth small and a hurricane had blowed down many trees it came S.W.

[10?] a small spring on our right at the head of a steep rich bottom covered with pea vine and I on a hill about one hundred yards north of it among some pine encamp.

The distance 3.24 or 10 1/2 mile The course N.10.E

The lands more broken than any below some of the hill sides rich. The whole has the appearance of River hills.

8 of october

4   cross a small branch running to the right The bottom rich covered with pea vine, The growth tall poplar red and white oak and hickory

7   Cross a creek running to the right 4 feet wide a fine running spring. The bottom rich.

12   cross a fine little branch running to our right

34   cross a creek running to our right 20 feet wide, and pass through the remains of the settlements, at Chau ke thlucco. Those several huts remaining uninhahited There are a number of thriving peach trees, some young from the stones ofthe last year and plums and locusts The falls here appear fordable at several places. And in passing up them

beyond the settlements, our course is N.70W.

26. cross a small bottom above the falls

10 over rich hills bordering on the river bank I cross a creek running to our right 5 feet wide the water in holes and here I saw cane.

13 a small branch

10. cross a rocky creek 3 feet wide running to our right

<u>15</u>. cross a branch to our right 2 feet wide

7 enter an old field on the river bank where we gather some large red haws

16 cross Luchau Pogau 80 feet wide with very little water.

22 a very extensive view to the westward

3 a path to our right to Chatto ho chee Tallauhassee from whence that river has its name

39 cross a creek of fine water running to our right

19. cross Pithlo hatchee, 4 feet wide running to our right.

    Our distance 3.57 or 12 miles The course has varied much in this distance it is about N.30.W. The lands are all broken stiff and gravelly or stoney, the growth mixed pine post oak chestnut some small red oak and hickory

58^{26} cross a dry creek to the right 6 feet wide the growth pine hickory post and black oak The lands hilly stiff and gravelly

26 cross a dry branch to the right 2 feet wide

4 a vein of reeds to the right

13 a dry branch to the right 3 feet wide

4 a dry creek in view of the river, and we pass near its banks

11 cross a creek 8 feet wide water in holes.

14. cross a creek 15 feet wide running to the right and pass through a flat of rich land low land abounding with holly poplar black scaly bark red and white oak.
Nucus,oe,sum,gau / The bears hiding place

28 cross a fine reedy branch running to the right.

39. over a high ridge cross Pochuse hatchee, 20 feet. running to the right. Here I saw a great number of muscadines they perfumed the air at the distance of fifty yards. Here the paths fork and I take the left.

21   cross a dry branch to the right
12.   cross a dry branch to the right
6   cross a creek running to the right 8 feet wide [unintelli-
        gible] water, and excellent pea vine and reed for the horses,
        The Lands very rich and level, Here I encamp.
                The distance 3.4.6. or 11 miles the course
        N.10.E.

                    9th of October
19   cross a branch runing to the right 3 feet a flat of good land
        on the left bank
12   cross a creek runing to the right 40 feet wide high broken
        poor stoney hills on each side above where I crossed.
        [Iassand?] one to the ridge
1.47   cross a dry branch of good food
3   cross a reedy dry branch
3   cross a fine reedy branch with water
27.   cross a creek running to our right, margined with cane the
        lands broken on its sides but fit for culture, the poplars
        large
3   cross a branch to the right 2 feet wide
12   cross a branch to the right 1 foot
8.   cross a creek to our right 30 feet wide the lands broken and
        gravelly, the Timber small
15   cross a branch to the left and go up
2   one, on the left, 2, And cross it running
        to the left,
45   cross a branch to our right 3 feet wide
19   cross 2 branches running to our right
                The lands generally are poor. stiff gravelly, with a
        mixt growth, Chestnut post oak, small pine, + red oak our
        path is generally on the ridges The course N.20E. The
        distance 4.33 or 13 1/2 mile
35   cross a creek running to the left 6 feet wide
50   over poor stoney chestnut ridges cross a creek running to
        the left 2 feet wide
4   cross a branch to the left 2 feet wide
1.   cross a branch to the left 1 foot

27   cross a creek 45 feet wide o,ke,hau hatche The lands poor on the margins its course uncertain as the water was [stale] and no sign on its banks to the right

8.   cross a branch to the left 2/ fine reeds

15   cross a reedy creek 4 feet wide

23   crossing a vein of reeds to a flat rock on a poor ridge of saplin land

17   cross 2 small branches and encamp.

         The lands generally this day poor stoney Chestnut hills some of the bottoms bordering on the water courses good, but the hill sides thick set with coarse gravel. Our distance 3.00 or 9 mile and course N.20.E[27]

         11 [October]

16   cross a dry creek to the left the bottoms rich and the food good, the hills poor chestnut post oak stoney land, we pass between two high stoney [rocks?]

8   cross a dry branch to the right

11   cross a dry branch to the right

16   pass a vein of reeds to the left and through some open land to a poor ridge

19   descending a steep stoney bottom by the side of a [purling mill?] cross a branch to the left 3 feet wide, the lands good but stoney

12.   cross a creek 8 feet wide, large rocks on the hill sides

21   cross a creek 16 feet wide [unintelligible] with reeds

35   cross a creek to the right 10 feet wide

50   cross a branch to the right 2 feet

9   cross a creek 6 feet wide the Veins in the direction of the creek

3   cross a branch to the right

13   cross a creek 8 feet wide

31   cross a branch to our right

21   cross a branch to our right

9   cross a branch to our right

8   cross a creek to our right 4 feet

51.   cross a creek to our right

1 . 5.   cross a creek 4 feet left

6.   cross [over?] 3 feet left

3   cross a creek 10 left
      Our distance to day 6.45. or 20 mile
            The lands generally poor but in the
      neighbourhood creeks they are rich
                  12.th
14   up a rich flat on the branch side and cross it running to the
      left
3   cross it again runing to the right.
17   The paths fork, the left a small blazed path we take the
      course of here N 10 W.
27.   cross a dry branch to the right after continuing on a ridge
28   cross a creek to the right 4 feet wide The land good but
      stoney.
11   cross a branch to the right 1 foot wide
4   cross a creek to the right 8 feet wide
26   cross a branch to the right with peavine
22   cross a branch to the right
38   arrive at a Cherokee hut
4   cross a creek to the right 60 feet wide
18   cross a branch to the right 2 feet wide
11.   cross a branch to the right
3   cross a branch to the right
33   cross a branch to the right
46   cross a creek to the right 6 feet wide
36   the bed of a Creek to the right
30   Cross a creek 10 feet wide to the right and arrive opposite
      Etauweh[28]
            Our distance 6.21 or 19 mile The course varied,
      The first half N.10 W. The remainder worse to the west
      winding down the river hills N.45.W.
      The hills are poor broken and stoney The flat lands on the
      river are rich.
                  14^{of} October
15.   cross the river and arrive E,tow, woh Town house.
1. 51. The paths fork the right to Sa,lequaheh I take the left
17.   cross a creek to the left, the land rich on the north. This
      creek joins E,tow,ah river at the town. There is a settle
      ment prettily situated on the south side of the creek to the

        left of our path.

22.   Limestone and the first I have seen on the path.

4   cross e,taw,oh creek again

9   cross a creek to the left 5 feet

28   cross a branch to the left on a poor flat

1. 3   cross a boggy branch

17.   the path to our right goes to [unintelligible word crossed out]

36.   a high chesnut knoll on a ridge

11.   houses on our right The bottom lands rich

7.   cross a creek to our left which goes to oos,to,nau,lih

46.   cross a fine bold stream 60/ runing to the left and to oos,te,nau,lih Sa le quo heh[29]

40   minutes a naked ridge and from it a view of the mountains beyond Oostenaulih

20.   crossing a dry creek we encamp on the bank of Salequoheh
         The lands generally to the first chesnut ridge are level The timber small mostly post oak gravelly, and rocky. adjoining the water courses in coves it is rich.
        Our course is to [unintelligible][30] path and to the first ridge is N. we incline then to the west and wind over poor hills
            The distance 7.26. or 23 1/2 mile

57.   Sa,le,quo,heh path
        Salequoheh to our righ

64.+ Oostenauleh[31] The lands rich bordering on the river

13   cross a creek runing to the right 40 feet wide.

1. 7   cross a creek runing to the right 6 feet wide

10.   arrive at Oos,te,nau,leh

40.   arrive at the house of Charles Huks a public interpreter.
           The distance 4.11 or 12 mile

        The course N 40 W. The Flat lands on this river are some of them rich, the hills all stoney, The width of the river 120 feet. it appears shoally and hence it takes its name Oos,te,nau,leh, shoal or Shoally.
                 16[32]

1.30.   cross a dry creek 8 feet wide

28	cross a branch to the left
38.	cross a creek to our right 8 feet
x 10.	cross a creek to our left 45 feet
1.11.	take the left hand path
36	Robert Browns.
1.16.	cross a creek to our left 50 feet

our distance 5.49 or 17 mile Course N.
The path is a pretty good one and Level, The lands stiff
and gravelly on the 45 foot creek there is an extensive flat
on the north side stiff an low, the growth Holly and beech.
In the neighbourhood of Robert Browns the lands stiff
gravelly the growth principally Hickory and red oak, he
has a good farm his fences well made and strait he has
good wheat and turnips.

x [oosekuste?] The Holly There is a great deal of this
growing on the right bank[33]

17.

+ 1.52.	cross a creek at [Shew inake?] 50 feet over runing to the left.
30.	cross a branch running to our right
13.	branch to our right
11.	up a Caney creek on the right cross a branch runing to the right
26	cross a branch to our right
6.	cross a branch to the left
14.	cross 2 small creeks to the left
21.	cross a creek to the left 5 feet
33.	cross a dry creek 10 feet
13.	cross a branch of oos,te,nau,leh 100 feet wide. Con,nuh,sau,gee. /slave/ + qual,lo,kuh,ka,ie, literally, big [shoesnake?][34]

The road pretty good, the lands generally rich
enough for culture in the neighbourhood of the two last
creeks the lands hilly, The flat land on this river rich with
fine cane. Our distance 4.49. or 14 miles. cours N.20.E

Below this about four miles Will Huks who lives here informs me, that these are large cane brakes, the lands very rich, and that in general the lands are rich on both sides of the river, that there are no settlements, on the river but his.

2.09. cross a creek to the left
38. a large spring to our left.
13 to Peggy Megeer oo,ac,co,he /may cocks/.
The road good, our course N20E. the distance 3.
or 9 mile

18

+ 8 cross Au,mo,he 300 feet runing to our left.
64 cross a creek to our left 6 feet wide
45. cross a creek to our left 15 feet wide
21. cross a creek to our left, 5 feet
18 . cross a creek to our left 4 feet
26. cross Hi,n,wos,sa, 360 feet over to our left, abounding with salt. Au,muh, is salt.[35]
9 + d. b. r. hilly pine land
5 + d b. r
11. + d. c. r 4/ reed
3. + d. b. r
11 + vein reed r
5. + d. b. r evergreens and reed
30 + b .r. fine water evergreens and reed
8 + d. b. r
6 + b. r. fine reed and some water
10 + c. r. 4/ water and evergreens
25 + .c. r. 4. land good
5 + d b. r
8 + path from left
5. tuft of evergreens to the r. [unintelligible] pine hills on left
10. tuft of evergreens on the r. near the top of a high ridge
20.+c.l.5/. at Talauhassee house Over a very high ridge which I enter and and continue and desend to the creek
Rout to Pensacola 16 april 1799
From Cowetuh tallauhassee cours S.25.W

7.   to The Pensacola path S.45.W
9. +   2 reedy branches running to the left
17. + c. l. 3/. a beech flat and oaky lands this creek called/ Water melon/.
47. c. l. 6/. Hatche Chubbau /middle creek/
15. + b. l. reeds
8 + b l. 3/.
11. + c. l. 8/ pine flat.
7. + c. l. 5/.
34. + c. l. 4/
7. + b. l. reeds
5. +   Tal,e,see path S.10.E. our course S.20W
            These creeks form the Oconee
10. + b. l
18. + b. l
24. + c. l. 12/. Co,wag,gee
23. + c. l. 15/. Cowaggee
48. + b. l.   Some good oak land to our left, This stage over
                  oak and blackjack land 1.8. over blackjack ridges
                  oaky botoms to Ecun hut ke nene
18 + b l.   reeds
42. + a creek 4/ left.
23 + c. l.   }The lands good
28. + b. l   }The lands good
10. + b. l
45. + b. l. The path to Benjamin Head hom *
9 + b. l
32. + c. l. 12/. The main fork of pea creek Tellaugue ehat,che
11. + b. l. reedy glade in a pine forest
10. + a path. Itchu haujos
17 + c. l. 15/. the lands broken and rich on the right bank
15. + c. l. 8/
31. + b. l.
+   The lands waving oak land fit for culture the bottoms and
     hill sides rich red oak hickory white oak shortleaf pine.
     Long moss.
23.   McQueens path N.10. E our cours S.W
15. + b. l. in a rich vale of land. at the angelica hills.

1.6   Tallahass soo che path on pea creek

10 + b. r Koenecuh

28.   To stoney hill.   }This is a high

1.26 to the end of the ridge   }ridge the whole
extent, with beautiful flats on the top a view very extensive
to the right and left. The waters of / Eoenscuh rise out
from the West side and those of Pea creek, on the East side

5. + b. r.   2 feet.

31. + c. r. 8/

1.   a path to the left,   }on a ridge of light land

1.6 + b. r 3/   }willow leaved hickory black
jack + oak. The land on the left bank of the branch broken
and rich

40.   path on our right from Aut,tos,see

1.25. breakfast on the right

14.   path to the left

28 + c. l. 4/. pea creek

5 + b. l.   reedy poor pine land

40. + c. l. 3/

40 + c. l. 8/

4 + b. l. 3/

1.3. + c. l. 3/

<u>25</u>.   encamp on the right in pine barren

43. + c. l. 4/ broken hill sides and rich this over high blackjack
ridge

11.   path from the right

7.   path to the left

43 + b. l   fine water a branch of [Yellow?] water

12+b.l

1. 14. path from the right

33   path to the left.

1.   breakfast near the Uchee Spring

45 + b. l.

2 + c. r. 20/

1.14. the path to the upper towns joins on the right its course is
S. ours S30W.

30.   to the ponds

<u>15</u>.   encamp on the right

27. + b. r. dead mans branch
7. + b. r.   reeds and good land
9. + c. r. 8/.
32   the path divides take the right
1.17. + c. r. 5/
13.   we approach near the river its 40 yards wide
5. + c. r. 5/
17. + c. r. 10/
11. + b. r.
21. + c. r. 5/
11. + c. r. 5/
6 + b. r
<u>24. + c. r. 15/</u>
6. + b. r
<u>9.</u>   breakfast.
4. + c. r 20/
10. + c. r. a natural bridge under the ground
24. + b. r
18. + b. r
4 + c. r
2 +   a drain, ponds to the left
10 + c. r. 6/ a magnolia among pines
48.   the ridge path and a pine flat
12. + b.   of evergreens
50. + b. r. There is a path sound [unintelligible] to the left
<u>30.</u>   encamp.
1.30. path to the left
16. + c. r 3/ in broken pine forest dogwood clumps among the
        pines
11 + b. r. 3
7 + b r
18 + b. r   pen branch
5 + b r
6   }+2.b.   evergreens to the left
1   }+2.b.   evergreens to the left
<u>1.32.</u>
 1.7.   the cold water path
1.16.   the narrow passage a ridge between the waters of

Koenecuh and Cold water
20.   spring to the r. pond to the left
20.   the paths divide the r. to millers S.20W the bay S
21.   Magnolia Spring
1.24. a pond to the left.
22.   path from the right
55. + b. r
30.   John Millers
39 + c. r. 10/ Baileys branch
1.48. the trading path
51.   12 mile Spring
1.12. 4 mile spring
54 + b. r.
20.   The Bay
S 44

Pensacola to Tensau
N.20W

1.38 + b. r
1.8 + c. r
16 + b r
47 + c. r. 10/ saw mill creek
19 + c. r
32 + c. r
26 + c. r
3³⁶.   paths fork take left.

N.W

2.34. path joins on the left
47 + path
3.4   pine barren Creek
For the last three hours the land is strewed with
Iron ore
13.   path fork take the left
1.44
45.   dry branch
40.   path forks take the right
1.08 path fork take the left
11.   path fork take the right
7.   Richard Baileys

20.   path fork take r
43 +   path
50.   John Randons Cowpen
                    S.20W
13   path fork r
32. + c. r. 4/. in a large vein of reed
1.50. path forks take the r
1.9.   John Randons on Tensau
                21 hours 59 minutes or 66 miles
            The first four hours poor pine barren the pines
        small curled top, not valuable for lumber. The streams fine
        flowing The remainder a pine barren the pines some of
        them fit for plank. The whole country thick set with them,
        and mostly a flat with ponds.

                        20 June 1799
            From John Randons to Fort Stodard
35.   to the cut off thence down the Alabama
3.13.   to Tombigby
1.5.   Fort Stodard:
            The swamp is low, though some of it under
        cultivation, it is subject every Spring to be overflowed, and
        this year so late that they are now planting their corn
        The Alabama is 300 Y.^{ds} wide The Tombigby and Alabama
        make Mobile which is from 4 to 500. In assending the
        Tombigby there is a fine bluff 26 minutes up the river on
        the right bank

            From John Randons to the Upper towns
                        24 June 1799.
                            N.
1.20+.c.l. 10/. Hollow creek
1. + c. l. 15/ Turkey creek
46. + c. l. 6/   N.E
51. + l. 30/ little river
1.7+c.l. 10/
1.35   some coarse rock
17.   path from the right

35.   fine curve of reed to the left

2.24. + c. l. 8/.

26^{37}

4. + c. l 20/

54. + c. r. 4

10 + c. r. 3 oaky bottoms high sharp stoney knobs.

1.52. + c. r. 4 dry The head of Scambia

50. + c. r. 3/. oaky hill sides

30 + c. l 15/. fine flowing lands on each side waving and rich, red oak dogwood

7 + c. l. 10/.

5. + c. r. 4/.

5   The pine barren hills

1.27 + c. l. 50/ This is limestone, the land on the left bank is broken butrich, red oak dogwood, ash poplar umbrella, on the hills and the flats canebrake large magnolia The right bank has poor pine hills,

14 + b. l. 3/. pine barren

25. + b. l.

22. + c. r. 10/. on the left bank high bluff of Limestone

25.   a small branch.

27th

1.37. + b. l

6. + b. r

10. + b. r

2. + c. r. 3/ a fine little stream

E. 15. +   a reedy branch

36   to the trading road.

N.E.

44 + b. r. dry deadmans branch

6. + c. r. 5/. [murder?] creek   }stiff red pine

1.35. a spring to our right.   }forest.

17.   path to the left

E.

32 + c. r. 15/ oak woods on the right bank chue,pul,gau

22 + b. r. dry

14. + c. l. 5/

2. + b. r. 2/

N.E.   53. + b. 1 oaky woods
 40. + b. 1
 <u>30</u>.   oakwoods and good land to the left
                28th
 1.40. path from the right /Wolf path/
 3.   springs to the left.
             The last 4 hours through pine forest no water but
        in the season of rains.
 18   spring to the left oaky woods deep hollow
 1.36   a high ridge, and from it a view of the hills beyond
        Alabama
  2.0. a spring to the left.
 25.   The path divides I take the left.
                N.
 35.   a high noll to the left.
 4   a spring to the right, the ridge high
        the lands good, bottoms steep
 1.30   The Savannas commence three [bare or lari?] are nolls
        with clumps of post oak, and veins of trees in the hollows
 12.   [Urmotte Thlucco?].
 29.   The width of the swamp crossing three dry creeks, The
        swamp is stiff and rich, white oak beech holly, cane. it is
        very flat and bordered with good oak land.
 2.0. + c. l. 10/. a fork of Pith,thlau,le
             This whole stage through the savannas, They are
        waving hill and dale, the hills, bare of wood and no under
        growth, among the clumps of post oak, which are large
        and beautifuly set in clumps. The lands appear whitish on
        the surface, the whole a dark clay, and under it a yellowish
        clay within the [unintelligible] of the ants. the clumps
        covered with long grass and weeds which indicate a rich
        soil the bare parts the grass is short and the whole stiff,
        clay soil, dry, without waters,
        N20E
 50.   through the glades. / hi,que,pul,gee /
 15. + c. l. 40/ eet Pith,thlau,le   }The lands rich on these
 50.   path to the left   }creeks and their margins
 27 + c. l. dry to the left   }bordering on

31 + c. l. 40/. /Sit,to,me   }the glades.
    N.10W
52.   path to the left
16 + path
30   arrive at Sehoys
              The glades / he,que,pul,gee commence 1 hour 30
      minutes south of Un,nut,te thluc,co / bigswamp / and
      continue to the north side of Kit,toma bordering on that
      creek. The creeks have all flat broad margins of stiff land
      rich and well wooded, the waving lands between, have
      glades, margined with clumps of post oak, large and
      abundant.

                    Took aub atche to Cowetuh tallauhasse
52.   a high poor [red?] hill. E.20.S
40 + d b. r   reed
35.   path to the left. E.20.N.
16.   path from the left
7.   path to the right pond on left.
48   path r.
28 + c. l. 4 /. Weheint,lah a fine flowing little reedy creek
17. + c. l. 20/. Opil,thluc,co
3.00 +   ditto r   E.20.S
1.30. East
14.   path to pensacola
30.   the Springs   N.E
36.   path to the left   N.30.E
6.00 Cow,e,tuh tal,lau,has,see
13.53[38]

              Timothy Barnards to Cussetuh
1.52 + b. l.
16. + b l
17 + b. l
2.3 + c. r.   4 feet wide fine flowing reedy creek rich hillsides
      oaky woods on the margins
57 + b. l. oak and hickory land
7. + b. l.   dry large reeds

1.0.   spring to the right, a flat of oaky woods with iron ore
45. + b. l. 3/ fine reedy branch
7 + c. l. 8/.
42. + b. l. fine reeds and poor land
1.0. + c. l
45. + c. l. 40 feet wide /Eit,cho,foo,ne
1.6. + c. l. 8/. dry
10. + b. l. dry
41. + b. l. dry
50   vein of reed to right
33.   breakfast on the left, among reeds in [unintelligible] pine
      barren
8 +   [this vein?]
11   Ecun hutkee nene
1. 33 + c l. mistake the path, turn to the right
22 + c. l. rich flat of land
23. + b. l.   }pine flat
39 + c. l.   }pine flat
18 + c l
13 + b. l
15 + c. l
6+   a path
17.+ path at the ponds
8 + b. l
2   road from left
31 + b. l
<u>13</u>.   Cussetuh hothouse
18.30[39]

            From Cowetuh tallauhassee to the confluence of
      Flint and Chattohoche At 4 miles the hour Course S.
      [16?] W.
1. 20 + c. l. 60/. U,chee hat,che
1. 50. pass a village on our right in a poor pine barren, Ful,lot
      who,e,jee's
15 cross c. l. 15 /. Hitchetee hatche au,hiqu
2. 0. + c. l. 60/. Oconee
1. 40 + c. l. 20/. Co,chis,see

15. Benjamin [Headhams?]
7 20⁴⁰

29 1/3 miles

The land bordering on Uchee hatche is poor pine land. On this side of [Fallotwho ejeu?] village there a flat mixed with oak and some hickory- Pa,la,choo,cl,e is on the left ab.ᵗ 15 minutes beyond Hitchitee on a poor pine flat. on the N. side of Oconee for near 30 minutes land level and some part thick set with dwarf small hickorys On the S. there is some rich land tho' broken. This creek affords clay for potts.

The Course

20. pass Sau,woog,a,lo a small town in the pine barren on the right bank of Chattohoche

1. 7. over a flat on the margin of the river fit for culture at the mouth of We, lau,ne + the river. The large creek Cowaggee is below in sight ab.ᵗ 15 minutes

21. + c. r. fine flowing 10/.

24 + ridge an extensive view on the right

21. + c. r

10. the top of a high noll

46. + c. r.

1. 0. + b. r. good water

1. 2 + p. to r. to Eufaulau course W

___
2

18 + c. r. 10/. this joins the river just below Eufaulau

28 + c. r. 100/. Tut,tau,lau a rapid stream the courses are rich and fine for cattle.

1. 15. + c. r. 8/. O,ke,te,yoc,en,ne.

___
3

30. settlement on the river to the right

30 + c. r. 40/. Sum,mo,che,cho.

10. settlement on the right Noah Harrod

1. 10. + b. r.

20. + c. r. 10/ Kalmia on its borders.

32. + c. r. 60/. Koo,loo, moo,kee   v
24.   path to the left to James Burges.

___
4

32.   Rorks on the left.
50 + c. r. 15/. fine flowing
1.18. + c. r. 6/
34. + c. r. 3/.
48. +. c. r. 45/
29 + b. r.

___
12.00
53 + a hurricane
10.   a pond to the right with live oak and first I have seen so
       high up the river.
5
1.13. large path from the right.
5. +. b. r
30. +. c. r. 25/
1.12. Thomas Perrimans

___
6 1.13. + c. r. under ground.- Here I saw
___   Limestone mills, the lands good on the river.
7
3.45. an Indian settlement on the bluff bordering on the river
1.0. + the river at Wills-
15.   W + ing the river
1.45. to a point opposite the encampment.
30   to the river E.
                        12.31
                        12.10
                        3.25
                        7.20
                        35.25   142 mile

            Rout from James Burges's
4.10 Encamp on the river
1.20. high bluff river on the left, limestone

1.20. the river on our left.
1.30. Encamp on the left near a pond.
                The lands from the pond to the river a poor flat
                some good reed on the river
1.10. the river on our left.
20.   the river close on our left.
30.   lake on the left
44.   river on the left
30.   falls, highpine bluffs on the left
35.   Augustine path.
6. + c. l. 10/. There is just above this creek a natural bridge over which
12.15   our pack horses passed.

12.15[41]
27.   Encamp on the river
40.   Hit,che,too,che
13.22   This whole path up flint river from Burges's is on
                pine lands, poor, with wire grass, there is a swamp below
                this Village bordering on the river, of land fit for culture
                with some cane and oak woods, but generally it is pine
                barren bluffs on both sides of the river
                The course is N20E the distance 13 hours 22 minutes at 3
                1/2 Mile to the hour. From Hit,che,too,che to Hitchetee
                course nearly W. 40 N. 4 mile the hour
12 + the river at Tustun,nuggee Micco
1.14 + c. r. 4/ Land level pine and some oak
2.   houses on our Right. The land for this stage is good oak
                hickory and dogwood, rather stiff, it [lies?] well
15 + c. r. 20/ Tul,lal,lose hat,che
10.   The square of the Village
                The lands on this creek are good, and the farms
                well fenced, the people attentive to Stock.
1.40. + c. r. 10/.
20.   W. Kinards. just on Kit,cho,foo,ne
                his brother Jack lives on the other side of the Creek, has
                several slaves and a large stock. This creek is 100 feet wide.
                From Jack Kinard.s
1.12. + b.

2.16. path from the left, this is from the village
44.   path from the right
4 + c. l. 4/
24.   a ridge of Iron ore
1.20 on an oak flat
1.30. Encamp. water to our right
            This oak flat continues [in all?] near two hours
        and are half the groth black and post oak the Land strewed
        over with Iron ore.
1.10. a spring to our left, a steep bottom, and rock.
16.   poor black jack broken land a spring to the left, and an
        extensive view to the N. West.
19.   Rock on left deep bottoms on right and left, the land good
        but too broken
33.   steep bottoms right and left the ridge good land, the whole
        broken. I take this 2 be the ridge dividing the waters of
        Flint and Chat,to,ho,che
20 + dry c. r. 8/
27 + c. l 25/ Han,nau hat,che
            broad flats on its margin of good land.
26. b. l. 3/ reed flats in poor land
24. + b. l 3/. reed flats
25.   black rock poor ridges
6. + b. r. 2/
46. b. r. under ground
30.   the Town house, to which we decend steep hills

Tallauhassee to Tookaubatche
S30W.
37 + 2. b. l.
50 + c. l. 30/. witumcau hatche
S.50.W.
12. + c. l. 20/. three houses
S.70.W
22. + b. r. house
S45W   17 path from left
        38 the springs a natural bridge.
        <u>176</u> minutes or 10 mile

S.45.W. 16. uche path from left
  W 3 + path
  46. spring to the r. called pot in the branch
  12 old ball ground
  32 path to Tom Millers
  32 path to Tom Millers[42]
S.45.W <u>36</u> spring to the right
  <u>167</u> minutes[43]
  25 pensacola path
  W14 the course continued to the ridge
  43 + b. l
  6 + b. l
  <u>1.36</u> + c. l. 10/ opilthucco
  3 04

  Left path crossing Flint river above Sule noj uh.

2.0. + c. r. encamp in the fork. over waving post oak land.
32. a creek on our right
28 + the river 150/. the food a good one some flat land on the
  right and a good flat on the left, some old field.
2.55. + c. r. Chumcau hatche, the path divides just out from the
  river take the old one to the right
1.5. + b. r. In,tack,coo,chee over waving post oak land, post
  oak hills
1.16. + c. r. 4/. in the fork
42. + b. r. oaky woods
34. + c. l 8/ broken rich land
45. + It,cho,cun,na
21. + c. r. Rocky
1.45. Tobesauk,kee 15/.r.
17. + c. r. 8/.
43. + c. r. 8/
13 +. c. r. 20/
19 +c. r
1. 38 Lick to the right
44. + b. r.
12. + c. l. 8/

1.27. path from r. This path + Flint river just below Su,lenojuh
5   Chau,ke,thlucco. on Ocmulgee

5.11[44]

5 1/4 + the river 400 yards.
13 + d. c. r. 8/
55 + d. b. r. 3 poplars left
34 + b. r.
23 + c. r. 8/
16 + b r.   level good land small growth timber
15 + b. r.   a flat rock
1 + d. b. r.
9 + c. d. r.
28 + d. c. r. 6/
26 + c. r.   Chatto thlucco
36 + b. r.
17 + c. r. 3/
19 + b. r.   in the fork
24.   a pine ridge.
20 + c r. 5/ oaky woods.
10 +. c .r.
6. + b. r.   paths fork take 1[45]
4 + b. r
16. + c. r
55.   spring to r
38 + c. r. 8/
39. + c. r.
22.   path down fishing creek

       From Ocmulgee towards Cussetuh
1. 15 +   chatto hatche l
35 + b. l
40. + Tobesauh,kee l.
20 + b. l
12 + b. l
8 + b. l
8 +   reed [unintelligible] l.
7.   rocks to the left

7 + d. c. 1
13. + d. b. 1
13. + c. 1
18 +   It,cho,cun,na
12 + b. r
24 + c. r
18.   path to the left.
       course continued to Tookaubatche
W. 20. N. 8 + d. c. 1. 4/
6 + c. 1. 5/
55 + d c. 1 10/
13 + d. c. 1. 4/
25 +   path.
33.   a spring to the right not good
<u>1.7</u> + c. r. 10/ opilthucco

S. 20 W. 17 + r [weheintle?] a fine little creek the best water for
       several hours
1.28 + a. s. b. r. Walige
10 + b. 1.
9   path from left. a pond on r
9

Rout from Tookaubatche to SW. Point
N 20 W
       minutes
80   60 + c. r 8/
40.   30 + c r. 8/
15.
N.30 W.
       80.   paths fork take r.
N
       30+cr 30/ Aucherauhatche
N10W
___   72.
N20W
       22 + c r 6/ some good land
N45W

8 + b r 3/
15 + b r
7 + b r
10.   to a path

N20W

10 + c r 8/ Wetumcau
10 + c r 10/ Kialijee
20 + c r 20/. Hookchoie creek and up the [river?]
10 + b r. Encamp.
35.   to Hookoie town house
40   broken stoney hills
50 + b r 2/
17 + b r 3/
3.   Thlotlogulgau town, on a branch of
           Ulkahatche
<u>22.</u>   to the traders.-

N.1   566

9.26 or 38 mile
       The path from Kialijee is up Hookchoie creek
which it crosses frequently, and passes thro' cornfields-
The land poor stoney and broken, all pine from
the Tookaubatche flats to the small creeked worked good.[46]

6 + c r 70/
16 + b r   The land good the black oak large
18 + c r. 4/
10 + c r. 8/
70 + c r 3/. The land good
60 + c r 4/
15.   the paths +
15

N

7.5 + b. l
10 + b l   From the cross path
20   view of mountains to l   much hill and
20 + c l 8/ pochusehatche   some mountain
45 + c l 4/   land good on the margins
50 + b r   of the streams, but
10   mountains in view   paved with small stone
10   down one + c l 8   on the mountains and

<u>15 + c</u> l.   encamp   hills.

2. 465 -7.45. or 31 mile

very little land for this stage of value all broken and stoney, in some places very poor hills, the streams have narrow flats and some of the hollows rich. no reed or cane, and a corse grass.

x The lands to the + path broken stoney well timbered in the hollows and [unintelligible] all strewed over with small stone[47]

N.   28th July

20 + b. l.

4 + c l 15/

60 + c l. 10/ some blackjack glades the land paved. with stone white slate

55 + c r. s/ and a small branch

4 + b r.   a fine spring

2.   the gap between two stoney mountains

75 + c l 90/ Eu,fau,lau,hat,che

<u>140</u> + c l 60/ Cheauhatche

3   <u>360</u>. 6 or 24 mile the land this stage is generally good the first part post red oak flat then small hickory then blackjack then a rise in black oak + hickory thick set with grass the land stiff and redish strewed over with iron ore. One settlement on the richest of the land. The land on this creek level and poor pine blackjack and postoak

N.10.E.

35.   a high stoney ridge the land to ridge stiff black oak and hickory thick set with fine grass

28 + c l 120/ Chaukethlucco

the land from the stoney ridge stiff and level oak hickory some gravel the flats of the Creek saplin growth hickory post oak and pine on the left bank, hickory and black oak on the right side thick set with grass

25. + c. l 15/ the land to the creek thick set with grass small hickory

N.10.W

40   a fine limestone spring to the left. The land stiff half of this stage hickory the remainder post oak and pine.

N.10E

25 + b. l.   in a glade. from the spring fine grass hickory saplins winding round N.E. to N.10W. and down a creek

44 + c l 8/ the land poor and paved with stone.

13.   the paths fork take the right

N.30E

<u>35.</u>   to a small creek here encamp in poor land

4   245[48] 4 hours or 16 miles

N.15E

17 + c l 45/

The land poor waving, post oak pine small hickory

69 + c l 8/

60 minutes the land poor then rich black oack bordering on this creek

8. + c l 60/. land good on the left branch, low and slashy on the right

57. + b. r

N.20E.

15   long path from our right

27 + c l 8/ right flat on the right side poor the left

<u>42. c</u> + l 10/.

5   <u>235</u>[49] The land for this half day or poor post

3.55 or   oak pine sower wood gum bushes

16 miles   except a little on the streams the hills all thick strewed over with small stone

N.

10 + c l 6/. The flat land on both sides good

51.   To the top of a mountain north front rich

N.10W.

28. + c. r then l poor land

55.   The [licks?] in poor pine flats, and here some cattle

41.   some settlements of Cherokees. Tun,whe,e.

<u>10 +</u> river l 750/. Coosau

6   195[50] 3.15 or 13 mile

The land from the mountain to the town poor level pine land trees small the land stiff pipe clay, and

generally the whole of this rout from Tookaubatche poor
broken + stoney except the margins of the creeks and some
hills about [Thltlogulgau?]. with The small vines between-
            Eufaulau hatche and Choauhatche and at the
Limestone spring on the N. of Chauko thlucco
            Stops
            1. 38
            2. 31
            3. 24
            4. 16
            5. 16
            <u>6. 13</u>
            <u>138</u> miles to Coosau river[51]

N. 30. E
    20. c. r. 6/. plantation
    60.   The land for 90 stiff oak
    17. + c. r. 4/   poplar and chestnut in the
    16. The [licks?].   valleys, pea vine no grass.
N. 40 E.   at the [lakes?] poor flats.
    12+br. 3/.   some distance after some
    <u>120</u>+c.r. 20/.   rich land Chestnut oak poplar
1   245- 4.5. or 16 mile   pea vine no grass- then
                               poor pine post oak to this creek
    34 + c r. 90/ shoal small saplin land
            Two settlements well fenced on the left bank of
            the Creek
    15 + b. + c r 3/
    28   a creek on our right 90/
    75   a Limestone spring on our right
N 60 E
    75   a river to our right 150

            an error in our course to correct which
W 10 S
    100/ To the path we left
N.
    30.+ c r 10/ rich flat

26. + c. r. 18/.
22. + a natural bridge 40 feet wide
30 + c r. 8/
95 + c r. 8.   The flats on these creeks and in the
2 530. 8.50. or 34 mile   course of the path rich
N 20 W
40. The top of a mountain
N. 70 W
70 + b.   right
N 30 W
43. here are very large rocks and we have passed them for
     some distance on our right in a grove of Chestnut Oak
N 10 E
107 to the north side of the mountain
35   to the flat below +c.r.
N. W
30   path from l.   The flat land to the N.
N 10 W   of the mountain rich
55. + c r 40/   and several indian
12 + c r 20/.   settlements under good
20   plantations   farms their corn plantings large.
60 + c r 4/
3 472. 7.52. or 30 mile

N10W
85. to Jack Sivills
N.E
90. + c. l. 60/. near Browns a trader
35. Chatto nogee here the Tumassee is just under this in view.
210. 3.30. or 13 1/2.
55. + c. l. 20
120+ b. l. 150/ Chick,au,mau,gau
95 + c l 10
4 480. 8. or 32 mile.
                    from Coosau,
          N.1.   16
          2.   34
          3.   30

4.   13.1/2
93.1/2
138
231.1/2 miles

From Tookaubatche to Chattonogee 231. $^{1}/_{2}$ miles

From Mobile to Taensau on the line of [Limits?] Lot. 31. 1st line miles 2.nd tallies 16 to the mile 3.rd 2 pole chain 10 of which make one tally. 4.th remarks

miles	Tal	ch	
215.			from Mississippi to the East side of Taensau. on the N. of Mr Byrans plantation
	2	3	open pine wood
	3	7	[unintelligible]
	5		top of a hill
	6	7	swamp
	7	6	open
	11		road
16^{52}	2		open woods descent
	8		open
17			open pines
	1	7	b. south
18			open pines low ground
	3		a path
	10		path
19			swamp
	3		pines open
	9		swamp
20			open
	2		swamp
	13		a remarkable hill
21			open
	2	5	a road
22			pines level and open
23			swamp
24			Low ground.
	1	4	a creek S.W

2	6	open woods
225		descent
26		open
6		a reedy swamp
13	7	a creek S.
27		open woods.
3		swamp
10	2	a creek 2 poles wide S
13		open woods
29		ditto
6		laurel swamp
8		open woods
30		open
4		reedy bottom
8		open
14	3	a creek N. 2 pole wide
31		open
32		open
33		Low ground open
34		Level
9		reeds
11	7	a creek S.
35		open woods
9		a run south
36		open
10		a pond
37		level pines
5	9	trading road to Pensacola
10		reeds.
38		level and open
39		hollow
	6	a run
40		open and level.
6	8	a cypress swamp
41		open and level
8	6	little branch
42		open
	3	trading road

	11	3	reeds a run	
43			level and open	
44			ditto	
45			ditto	
	8	5	a branch	
46			open	
	1	2	reedy a run	
47			open and level	
	12	8	an indian path	
48			uneven ground	
	3		reeds	
	8	5	a spring N.	
49			uneven ground	
50			ditto	
	1	6	a little run S.E	
	[4?]		a pond	
51			a swamp and run bearing N.	
	13		Escombia river S.W. 6 pole wide	
52			asscent	
	2		Wolf trading road from Tookaubatche to pensacola.	
	9	5	from this 10 - 57 mile thicket and swamp	
56	12		Koenecuh S.W. 16 pole	
57			open pine woods	

variation here 7°.45.E.

2.57[53]	1	6	open pine woods	
	11	2	top of an hill	
58			open pines	
	2	5	a rivulet	N.
	4	9	ditto.	N. W.
	11	7	path.	S. E
59			asscent	
		7	rivulet	N. W.
	9	7	a rivulet.N	
	12	5	a rivulet[54]	
		7	top of a hill[55]	
60			reeds asscent	

7	4	a rivulet N
12	5	a rivulet.
	7	top of a hill
61		descent
	7	a rivulet N.W
10	5	ditto. N.W
62		
63		open level
14		Trading path to pensacola S.W.
64		open and level
65	3	rivulet S.
7		descent
9	3	b. S.
66	9	b. S.W
67	2	5	b. S.W
68		descent open
69	5	8	c. S.
6	7.	c. S.W
7	7	open
2.70		
71.	4	4	c. S.E
10	7	c. S.W
13	4	b. S.W
72		ascent open
73		level
3	8	road S. to pensacola
5	8	b. S
8	9	b. S.
74	15	3	b. S.
75		top of a hill
11	5	b. N.
76	5		c. S.E.
14	8	b. S.E
9	b. N.
15		b. S.W
77		open asscent
78		nearly level
79		open level

	6	9	c. S.W
	8	8	a thicket
	9	9	open woods
	14	5	top of a hill
80		5	reeds
81			open pines
	5	2	thicket
82			low and open
	4	2	c. S.W. 11 yards
	8		open asscent
83	2		thicket
		5	c. S.
284			
85			
86	14	7	road to Pensacola
87		13	b. S.E
90	7	2	c. N.E
	8	6	b. N.W
91	1		b. N.W
92	1	8	c. S.E. 44 yards
	6		yellow river bearing W.
93	2	5	b. S.W
	8	6	c. N
95	14	4	c. S.W
96	4		c. S.E. 11 yards
98	3	1	road S.W
	13	2	b. S.E
		6	b. S.W
300	6		c. S.W
1	10		c. S.
6			swamp
7	10	5	path S.W
12		4	c. large N.W
13	11		c. N
16			c. N.W
	12		c. S.W
17		9	c. S.E
21			near a pond

22			near pea river
23			near the swamp of ditto
24			swamp of pea river
	15	4	c. S.
25			swamp of pea river
	13		c. S.E. steep banks
327	10	4	path S.
28	10	4	path
29		8	c. S.W
30	14		c. S.
33			west side of pea river
34			pea river low ground
36	8		c. S.W.
37	6		b. N
	8	3	c. S
	15	5	c. S
41	15	2	c. N
42	7	5	c. S
43	7	3	c. S.W
45	15	3	c. S
46	4	3	c. S
	5	8	road to pensacola
48	9	2	b. S.
50	13	6	b. N
	15	5	c. S
51	9	5	c. S
53			swamps
54			swamps
55			swamps and creek
57			
59			swamps creeks and level land
67	13		c. S.W
73			prarie
79	9	7	c. S.E
380	13	4	a road S.
81			bottom close to the river Chat,to,ho,che S.E. 22 pole.

varation of compass 7°.30.E.

From this point to the confluence of the rivers. 20
miles 316 poles S. Lat.

8.   42.   E. Longitude.

Rout from the Mississipi territory to Tookaubatche
commenced at the supposed boundary.

27 [dec.ᵗ?] 1801.

N.20E.

60.   whetstone spring the supposed boundary on the Kentucky
trace. The first of this course from the blacksmiths shop
the last settlemᵗ. N.70.E. lands broken steep bottoms
narrow ridges oak timber, land stiff, small cane-
There are several rocks of whetstone grit where
the Indians sharpen their knives and hatchets which gives
name to the spring the land around it broken, some fine
cane below a good camping place. Here is a [unintelligible]
raised hut and a small lying for a field but the indians
objected its being on their land, and the proprietor
deserted. Here I encamp.

28ᵗʰ

20. +. c. r. thick set with cane, the land broken

4. + c. l   timber oak hickory some poplar.

30 + c. l

11. +. c. l. 3/.

82. + c. l. 10 pine mixed with oak and hickory

6 + b. l.

4 + c. l. 15/

15. branch to the right here we breakfast.

172⁵⁶ low waving black oak, hickory and pine the pine tall and
large, all the shortleaf

N.30.E.

58. + b. l.
Land broken and rich cane in all the bottoms. Timber red
and white oak, hickory pine, gum hornbeam, + beach

17 + c. l. 30/. cane on the flats and large white oak

10 + c l 10/. cane. One the hills red and white

5 + b. r.   oak
go up and + this b. twice more

15. Encamp.

Tuesday 29.th

3. The top of a ridge

30. on the ridge, which is crooked high and the land on the right and left broken steep bottoms, set with cane.

Hickory, black oak thick hung with long moss. a good encampment at the end of the ridge on the right.

19. The land waving, and good black oak hickory pine and dogwood, the first large.

N50E.

29 +. c. l.10/ This stage black oak hickory post oak and pine. large cane on the creek.

4 + b. l.   post oak black oak pine hickory

4 + c l 8/ post oak and hickory saplins

N.30.E

18   post oak and pine saplin flats.

N60E.

8   The paths divide. The Kentucky or as it is here called the Chicasaw path is N.50E. our path is E. The land is poor post oak slashes E.

13. + c l 20/ large cane

The land flat post and black oak and pine all small

N.80E

47. + c l. 8/ large cane

3 + c l. 20/.

The land black oak blackjack hickory and pine, his well, the margins on the creeks, is the best and here the black oak the most abundant.

N.70.E

51. + c. r. 4/

The land waving, black oak hickory pine, black jack.

21 + c r 6/

The land waving post oak black oak hickory blackjack.

53 + c l 10/. cane

Land waving post oak, blackjack, black oak, hickory. a black jack glade on the left bank of the creek. The land flat bordering on the creek and the black oak the most abun-dant

30.   a blackjack knoll, and grind stone   grit rock

25. + c l. 8/. The land from the other creek is broken the ridges blackjack post oak and pine.- all the creeks are muddy or of whey colour. and from appearances are dry in autumn. They have steep banks from 6 to 15 feet

Wednesday 30.th

N.60.E

21 +. b. l. blackjack ridges, the slopes near the water courses, black oak and small hickory

7 + c. l. 20/.

a flat of cane, a little higher than swamp.   post oak flat on the right bank.

N.40.E.

17. + b. r. black oak

28. + c. l. 8/.   This stage over blackjack ridges, the growth large, the slopes have some black oak and near the creek some dwarf hard shelled hickory, the land open, with broom grass. The cane large and spread out on the right bank of the creek

4 + b r.   This four minutes on a black oak flat,

N.70.E

30   This stage over bold black jack woods the land a little undulated, the bold places have dwarf hardshelled hickory sparsely set. the bottoms have some black oak and small hickory the Land appears darkish

N.50.E

26 + c. r. 6/. this water is stagnant the course [unintelligible] blackjack woods continue. cane in all the nearest [unintelligible]

26.   holt and breakfast on the right- This course three tall black oaks on flat land.

N.60.E

14 + c r 8/.

N40E.

21. + c r 8/ no cane black oak, hickory blackjack

16 + b. r.   thin black oak flat, hickory blackjack post oak.

N.20E

40

N.60.E

    19 + b. 1 black jack hickory, bald uneven land the bald plains like old fields the Land darkish, underneath yellow.

E.

    15.   glade to the right creek and cane to the left

    14   paths divide take the left

    6 + c r 20/. black and post oak flats.

N.70.E

    32 + c r. 20/ good cane. black oak flats. Here encamp.

            Thursday 31.st

N.20.E

    19. +. c. r. 8/ flats of dwarf hickory

N.30.E

    30 + c r   large cane, oak flats

N.

    25 a post oak ridge

N.10W

    14 +. c. r 10/ deep banks

    2.   an oblong square mound 50. by 33 feet and 8 feet

N60E   high in oak and hickory land

    3 + c. r. 6/. post oak hickory black oak

    25.   to the edge of the [swamp?]

E   down the river flats thro' a cane brake

    9.   the river to our left

    8. + river r 120/. an oak and pine flat on the left bank.

N30E

    15.   flat of hickory and pine, shashes on our right and left.-

S80E.   flats, oak, hickory pine, slashes with

    18.   palmetto

N.60.E

    28.   flats post oak black jack and pine, the soil pipe clay. a small rise to red and post oak, then plains-

N.50.E

    15.   thro' the plains of 1200 acres, margined with post oak, they are a little waving no, wood, or shrubbery.

    20.   post oak and pine flat

N.40.E

    12.   thro' the plains

E.

23.   over oak flats to pine hills

38. + c. r. 8/. over post oak, blackjack red and spanish oak hills
         Jany 1.st 1802.

N.70.E

8 + c. r. 8.

N.60.E.

30 + c. r. 8. post oak black jack, pine red oak hickory

20. + c. r. 10/. flats of Holly and dwarf evergreens, these flats
    margined with hickory, oak pine.

N70E

70.   to the plains, pine post oak black jack, lies well but poor.

9.   thro' the plains ab.^{r} 1000 acres margined with post oak.

N.60.E.

23+c. l. 5/. post oak, pine, the flats of the creek open, hickory
    scaley bark, white oak red oak pine small cane.-

N.45.E

18.   a plain on the right of 600 acres margined with post oak,
    The growth generally post and black oak blackjack and
    hickory

20.+c. l 15/. good land white oak black oak and   hickory

17+cl 5/ pine post and white oak flats

N70E

34   flat post oak pine spanish oak

21+ a bed of a creek 20/. cypress, white pine beach hickory white
    oak- Land poor on the west, good oak and hickory on the
    East

17. + c l. 8/

N. 40 E.

24. + c l 8/ post oak black jack black oak saplins, lies well but
    poor

N 70 E.

34.   a small plain on our right post oak blackjack spanish oak
    lies well but poor.

9. + c. l. 8/ white oak flats on the creek

52. + c. l. 10/. Land bordering on the creek good hickory, black
    oak black jack
          2.nd January

N.70.W

 16. dark gravel blackjack ridge

 31. + c.   dry and large in a thick cane brake cypress white and red oak gum beach scaly bark hickory

N40W.

 25 + b. l. reed land uneven dwarf hickorys on the hill sides and bottoms, post oak and black oak and blackjack on the tops

 20. + b. l   red bay, white bay and reeds bottoms and hill sides hickory black oak post oak, light but good

 9   paths divide take the left

N.20.E

 40. a large dry creek and swamp

N.40E.

 33. + c. r.

 4 + c l. 30/. full flowing cane large on the path 40 minutes thro

 25. halt and breakfast. land a little hilly white oak hickory small pine

 20. + c r. 15/. fine swamp

 10. To Enoch Nelsons, a trader from Pensylvania 16 years in this nation.

    3.rd

N.70E

 6 + c r. 6/

 10 + b r.

 21. + c. r. dry 6/. flat white oak beach the lands of this stage post oak spanish oak hickory

24 + c r. 8/ post oak hickory, light land

N.40.E

 24. + c. r. 15/ white oak flat, cane beach white pine

 18 + c + b. r. reeds   post oak flat hickory spanish oak

 10 Longleaf pine

N.60E

 7. + c r 15/ The land poor on the right, holly and slashes on the flats, black oak and dwarf hickory on the left.

N.20.E.

 38. To Brashiers a traders, three settlements slashes, post oak pine.

N.40.E

6. + c r.
5. + c. r.   fine flowing little creek
20. + b r   poor land
11. + c. r. 8/ fine flowing
N70E
12   an old field some peach trees poor blackjack hills and reeds
       in the hollows some post and spanish oak all small
20 + b r.   just at the branch an old field and some
       fornignious stone, the hills poor, post oak blackjack in the
       bottoms dwarf hickory- on the East of the branch on a
       small hill to the left rich iron ore, the land begins to show
       very red at the roots of trees blown down
14   a ledge of rocks poor dwarf trees and black jack hills
8 + c. r.   at some small fields, the flats narrow but good the
       hillsides white oak and spanish oak, the tops of the ridges
       black jacks
10.   Encamp in the fork of 2 reedy branches to the left.
                          4.th

N.70.E
25.   Iron ore on a poor ridge
8. + c. r. 4/. settlements to the right and left, poor black jack land
12.   houses on the right, poor black jack hills
20. + c. l. 20/. rich flats.
14 + b l. reeds.
4.   a ridge with freestone, land poor.
14.   a large path from our right
N.40E   black jack post oak pine ridge
11   a ledge of rock at the grey freestone on a small pine poor
       ridge, blackjack hickory spanish oak in the bottoms and on
       the hill sides
7+cl. 6/
5+bl. and a dry creek an old field on the right bank and opposite
       to it reed in the swamp
10.   paths fork right to Mook,laus,au we take the left
9 + b l.   reeds land poor
11 + 2 b. ˢl. spanish oak post oak pine dwarf hickory
N70E
9 + b l.   reeds, spanish oak post oak red oak pine iron ore

on the hills of the right.

10 + c l. 8/ poor land

38 + path.

N10E

8. over hill poor black jack hills, + a path two settlements to the left.

N70E

10 houses to our left.

7 + c l 5/. flat land and slashy

6 + c l 10/. flat swamp adjoining land poor saplins oak and dwarf hickory and pine

8. Encamp- a house just ahead of us

Tuesday 5th

N.70E.

21 + c r. reeds in Cushtussau a Choctaw town on poor hills dwarf blackjack, oak and hickory, no pines. 34 settlements in view of our path

27 + b r. The end of the town, a reedy branch

28 + b r poor blackjack and dwarf hickory hills this is the land of pass ougoulau, a reedy branch

18 + b r. reeds, enter Yauzau, a poor miserable looking town on poor blackjack dwarf hickory and red oak saplin hills-

N.40E.

46 + b. r. open swamp poor flat, oak saplins

24 + c. l. 8/ oak flat.-

1 paths fork take the right

N80E.

20 + b l. red oak saplin land,

10 + path

4 + b l. The land of good quality, hickory oak pine, all small

E.

29. paths fork take the left, blackjack land,

N.70E.

12 + b l. adjoining a small creek on our left, cane on the flats, adjoining lands broken, we go down the creek. waters of Tomb igbe

3 + c. r.   a house on our left, we go down the creek on our
                 right, cane in all the coves and the flats have been or are
                 under Indian cultivation
E.
12 + c r.   near the creek on our right, one house on the
                 right
33   still down on the creek, cane in all the coves
                 The land becomes more level, and better red oak
                 large enough for rails and pine
7+br. three houses on the left side
13.+br.   reeds to our left
10.+br.   reeds right and left, here we encamp
                 in some old fields thick set with old field pine. we are now
                 on the waters of Tombigbe
                             Wednesday 6.th
N.70E.
30 + path and a fork to the right
13. + a wide reed slash running to our right
       poor black jack hills, small pines
E
31.   [au,b a,tub,poog,loo,se?] a town on our right
7 + path. poor blackjack hills, small pines
8.   pass houses, and a glade of reed on our right poor black
       jack hills, some small pines
40 + c. r. 10/. Tuck,fin,in,che,uh fine flowing reedy creek,
N.70E.
53 + c r 5/ fine little creek and good reed
       Land this stage broken, oak hickory blackjack pine. veins
       of reeds on the right and left at several bottoms iron ore on
       the hills near the creek
72 black rock, on the right
6 + b r.   hickory red oak pine on the hills some gravel
10.   Iron ore strewed over the hills, post oak spanish oak pine,
       some dwarf hickory and red oak on the hill sides
1+   the Chickasau trading path to mobile
N50E
41.+ c. r. 50/. sook,hin,ne,chuh
       Lands poor, this stage blackjack hills dwarf hickory and

black oak hillsides and bottoms. the flats of the Creek wide, white and red oak not rich, large cane in the coves of the creek.

N40E.

28 + b l.　　the flats and hillsides oak and cherry hickory the stage post oak, spanish oak blackjack small pine and hickory

N80E.

17 + c l　　　}

5 + b l.　　　}a swamp on the left, and high cane in view upland, post oak blackjack small hickory and pine, poor

N60E.

48 + c l.　　post oak blackjack red oak saplin land- cane on the left here we encamp

Thursday 7.th

N75.E

30.

S80E

20.　　a settlement to the left oak and hickory land bordering on a creek

S30E.

18　　old fields to the left oak and hickory, the lands with the plough fine for wheat.

E

7 + c l 10/. wide flats low and slashy saplins oak hickory pine ashe small cane in the coves of the creek

S70E.

8 + b r　　　　　　one house on the left open hickory wood

28 + b l.　　in a plain surrounded with open wood oak hickory blackjack, these last two stages open dwarf hickory land, rising into small hills, white Limestone in the bank of the creek to the right.-

22.

N.60E

12. + b r.　　open woods, hickory red and post oak blackjack. cane in the branch. The flat of the swamp rich white oak ash gum scaly bark hickory

N70.E.

32   over hilly good land hickory spanish and red oaks scaly bark hickory. some low cane in the hollows. The path a crooked one, winding on the hills, the bottoms thick set with rail timber. This is scarce on the path the timber is generally short bodyed and small

N.50.E

30.   a path from our left, our path crooked winds on the hills, land broken and rich well timbered in the bottoms ashe white and red oak scaly bark hickory. the tops blackjacks oaks and dwarf hickories, small cane on the hill sides and flats.- Plains at the junction of the paths and blackjack knolls. In these plains oyster shells, small shells of clams, [unintelligible] barnacles.

E.

16 + c l. [s?]. cane in the flats, plains, blackjacks on the hills, white and red oak and ashe on the flats.-

15.   encamp on a plain, to the left, bordering on a large creek.-
Friday 8.th Jan$^{y.}$

13. + c. l. flats rich, red and white oak post oak scaly bark hickory.

5 + b l.   late oak saplins a plain of 1500 acres, black jack ridges, on the north of the plains oak timber large and fine for rails.

18.   small cedar in the plains to the left, poor blackjack heights to our right.

6.   cedar on the left some of it tall, an white Limestone, our right a poor blackjack.

N.70E

15.   thro' the plains having them on the right, and into a flat of tall oaks fine for rails

5   Long moss on our right, a flat of oak saplins

3 + c l 8

E.

30   poor blackjack

19 + b l.   some palmetto

13.   The residence of Benjamin James 1 $^{1}/_{2}$ mile above The old fort Tombigby. we came here between Tombigby creek, and half way creek.- These two meete just before their junction with the river.

15. + c. r. 20/.

N.   Saturday the 9.th

30 + Tombigbe. r. 300/. The land between the creek and the river
     flat, oak and hickory

N.30E

14 + a pond 8 wide, land level hickory oak and pine

N80E

18   a creek

5 +   it and the swamps under water

12 + c. l.   a small one, oak hickory and pine

10 + c. 1 5/ black and white oak hickory and pine Land good,
     and lies well

N30E

14 + c l.   in a flat, in this flat, from high waters or from
     their sources are 1 b. and 2. c.
                This stage black oak hickory chestnut thin post
     oak, hickory small pine

N70E

18   black oak hickory

N.80E a path from our left

17   plains broken, blackjack knolls post oak these plains have
     much the likeness of old fields, a knoll on the right covered
     with gravel.

5 + b l.   some cedar to our right on the right side

5   path from our right, which gos to Timbigby

32.   Some of this slope post oak black jack and dwarf hickory,
     all level,

N30E.

35.   a plain of 1500 acres of land, bordered with post oak
     blackjack and dwarf hickory

13. + drain to the r. on the plain, cedar to the right on the left
     side

10 + b r.   still in the plain

153.

12 + c r. 8. This stage post oak- cane in the creek

        This plain has much the likeness of an old field
     bordered with post oak some large black jack and dwarf

hickory, the drains have flats, of swamp growth, the only thing opposed to this being formerly cultivated is that there is during the summer, no water near them. and the natives have no wells

N70E

25. + c r. 8. This stage post oak and blackjack and pine The flat of this creek rich, scaly bark hickory ash hickory sugar maple

N.30.E

23.   a path from the left

2.   a new blazed way N.85.E. which gos in to the path, to Kahaba village our direct path.

15 + c r. 6/

11 + b. r.   over a poor myrtle flat, Here formerly was a Buffalow lick, it is perceptable flat

7 + c r. 6/. Here the timber is tall, pine and hickory

N.30E

10 + c r. 4/.

20 + c r. 20/. pine oak hickory waving good land.

31 + c. r. 6/ hickory oak pine, good land

10 + c r. 3/. reed to the right.

8. +   a river to r. 150/.

a bluff on the right bank, and cane flat on the left, cane large, some of them 32 feet long. This river is called Tus cau,loo,sau /black warrior/ by the Choctaws, and [Sipre?] or Pat tau cauhatche by the Creeks

We with much difficulty cross the river in two small Indian canoes, it was very high, and we had to swim our horses we went a mile above the landing of the hunters and swam them down the river and across.-

Wednesday 13.th Jan[y].

S70E.

38. + a slash 60 yards wide, fed from the overflowing of the river. r[57]

9. +   a slash and creek 200 yards wide, The lands flat, white oak hickory red and post oak.-

43. + slash 60 yards wide The whole of this stage low and flat. white and red oak, hickory dogwood and swamp pine

holly, palmetto, some low cane,

N.30E.

30. still low flat and slashy the white

120^{58} oaks large, here is a rise of rich land, white oak, vines, dogwood.

S50E

20. swamp continues; The whole is valuable the Timber large and fine, particularly the white and red oak, it appears now to a disadvantage, as there has been for sometime days past great rains in the summer it is high enough for cultivation. The swamp ends with this stage

N60E.

20 + c. l. 5/. fine reeds. Upland rich white, red oak tall pine, dogwood chestnut and hickory, it lies well,

2 here we encamp

Thursday the 14.th Jan[y]

S70E

30. + b l. small black oak and pine

60. over a broken thicket bereft of the trees by a Hurricane

35.

S60E.

18 + c r. broken lands, oak pine chestnut

S.45E 13 + 2 b s. r. broken land oak pine and small cane

20 + c r.4. broken land oak and pine on the hills- small cane

208^{59}

5 + c. r. 6/. oak hickory chestnut dogwood pine, broken, cane on the creek and on the hill sides- we have been without a path from the river, and are moving this course to fall in with one on our right

13 + b r. saplin land pine and oak

13 + b r. reed, broken land oak chesnut hickory pine

14 + b r. reeds oak hickory pine, waving

18 + c r reeds oak hickory poplar chestnut, good land, the best upland we have seen

12 + c r. 8/ a wide swamp, low level, well set with oak some beach, and thick clustered with yellow leaf.

12 thro' the swamp rich and level the high lands wavy rich oak red and white, large, hickory and dogwood

5 + b r.   reed

14 + b r.   good land oak hickory chesnut beach

10 + c r   reed rich swamp

17 + c r. 8/ wide swamp

139^{60} 6   a path

N.20E   we take the path

20.   Encamp.

      The lands we have passed are good, the swamp, wide and very rich the cane is small, the oaks large and the whole thick clustered with the yellow leaf, some palmetto, and beach, take the whole together a drainable country

Friday 15th

N.20E

8.   The path is [unintelligible]

S70E.

10 + b r.   recede cane on the hillsides, [unintelligible] and vine

10 + b r.   low cane on the upland

5 + c r. 20/. fine flowing, a wide swamp, but little cane, ever greens, bay and yellow leaves

20 +   the swamp of the creek to a high chestnut hill beach oak, cucumber chestnut, umbrella

S45E.

14 + b r

3 + b r

5 + c. r.12

15   [The other swamp?]

125^{61} 15 + c r. 25/ [flat?] swamp

20 + b l.   broken rich land

12.   The path to Ka,hau,lau, on high pine hills some large red oak and chesnut

N70E

4+   reeds to our right

10 b on our left- we go down it

S45E.

5 + b. r.

4 + b. r. 3/ tall pine chesnut, oak, poplar thro the hills, fine reed in the branches

19 + drain to the left over hills

3 + b. r.　　　pine red and white oak post oak, then land ever greens in the branch

4　　drain to the right reed

3 +　a slash to the right

2 +　slash to the right flat thin land

3 + c r. 8/ reeds, soft stone in the bottom, water oak holly [unintelligible] bay on the creek right bank poor, the left, a wide rich flat, large white oaks The hills on this side high, the sides oak hickory souer wood and dogwood The top oak and pine.

<u>13</u>　path from our right the land. of a

102⁶²　　　　branch on the right, clustered with reed

N.80E

10　vein of reed to the left the land high red oak pine chesnut

N.60E

14　Salamander hillocks

11.　post, red oak pine small hickory reed to the right and in all the hollows

20　reeds to the right

E

13 + b r. 3/ flowing fine reed waving oak hickory pine and scattering chesnut reed in the bottoms

N.70.E.

8.　path from r.

7 + b. r　　　reed

N.60E

16. + b. r

2. + b. r

55 + c. r.

<u>30.</u> + c. r. 10/ acorn creek, the lands bordering on the creek oak, hickory, mixed on the hills with pine, cane on the flat margins of the creek and small cane on the hill sides
　　　　Saturday 16.ᵗʰ

12 + b r.　　　[unintelligible] reed on the flats post oak hickory dogwood small growth

16 + b r.

221⁶³　<u>7 + b</u> r.　reeds

8 + b r   reed

6-   Ca,hau,bau village, a small settlement of Creeks on the high lands of the right bank of that river, oak, hickory pine, good broken land, the timber small except on the Creeks and the pines on the hills.

<u>4 +</u>   Ca,hau,bau 60 yards wide

18^{64}

N.10.E.

20.   up the river thro' the low grounds, thick set with cane and bordering on the river Coy cypress on this side they have their fields

N.70.E

60.   thro flat swamp, intersected by drains, the whole rich, the oaks large, the point next the high land has beach and evergreens holly, bay yellow wood.

35 + b l.   This stage an a long leaf pine flat. crossing three little slashes

Sunday 17 Jan^y.

N.60.E

9   The top of the pine hills, a high broken country all long leaf pine

<u>34 +</u>. b. r   reed This stage over high longleaf pine

158^{65} hills, some iron ore on the west front of all the hills, and yellow ocre

15. + b. r   no reed

6 + c. r. 5/.

8.   The top of a little mountain, the west front iron ore; the whole covered with long leaf pine

16.+c.r. 8/. [wheyish?], thick set with reeds, Iron ore on the hills of the left side

N.80E.

32 + b r.

10   pine flat

8 + c. r. 15/. rapid in a poor pine flat

N.50.E

14   a high red pine hill, iron ore on the west front, and smoothe redish pebble stones

9.   over a poor red gravel pine ridge to a bottom of oaky land,

one poplar, chesnut and Chessnut oak

11. + c. r. 6/ small reed

10   pine flat of reeds to the right

5 + 2. b. r. reeds, they make a small island spring from a bed of
      reed to the left,

3 + b r.   reeds

2 + b r reed to the left

4 + c. r. 25/. rapid the right side a poor flat the left a rich and
      wide on

8.   Thro the rich swamp of the creek, reed and evergreens,
      some beach and oak

10   reeds to the right

15. + b. r. reeds. Here we breakfast

186[66]

      The high lands on this side of Ca,hau,bau are stiff and
      broken, thick set with long leaf pine, the hollows have
      some reed.-and are deep and frequent to the right and left

S70E

18 + b. r.   reeds and holly, thro this stage post and red oak
      hickory and pine sapling

3 + b r.   fine reeds some oaks on its borders and pines on
      the hills

20   winding round and on a ridge to a high pine ridge, from
      this an extensive vein right and left, of high broken long
      leaf pine lands Steep hollows right and left and reed in
      them.

N.60.E   on this high ridge, some blackjack and oak with
the pine

24   path from our right

30.

E.

7 + b. r   fine reed to the right and here [unintelligible] the
      long winding hill

7 + b. r   this course winds round S40E[67] to E

109[68] over hills covered with iron ore and here to the right is a
      high one covered with it.

20 + b r.   fine flowing branch thick set with reed to our
      right, which are seen at a great distance thro the pine

forest

20 +. a Hurricane trace, its course NE

15 + b. 1   fine reed

3 + c. r. 12/ full flowing wide low grounds thick set with reed

4   thro' the swamp

N.70E

10 + b r.

30 + c r. 60/. owl creek a wide rich swamp

102[69] This creek is a branch of Alabama

The lands from Ca,hau,bau is broken and stiff, covered
with long leaf pine, and abounding with iron ore, very little
oak to be seen, and that only in the steep hollows except
where noted The pine are strait bodyed, and small gener
ally from 8 to 18 miles diameter and thick set. The ship
hollows have reed- a country not fit for cultivation. The
swamp of owl Creek is wide rich and well timbered cane
near the creeks.

18 Jan[y].

E.

50 + c l. 5/ reeds. This stage a gravel ridge, long leaf pine
blackjack, the gravel coarse smoothe white amber redish
greyish and brown

N70E.

50. + b r.   reeds. This stage a poor blackjack longleaf pine
gravelly ridge

12   a vein of reeds to the right

7   a vein of reeds to the right

10 +   a bed of reeds spreading out on our right

2 + c r. 12/ Wat,tu,lau,hau,gau full flowing on a gravelly pebble
bed. The right side flat with reeds and pine, The left gentle
rise to a pine ridge the rise hickory and black jack, the
ridge gravel

N.50.E

53.   gravel pine land some small blackjacks the ridge flattens

E.

20 + b r.   reeds, pinewoods

10 + b r.

2 + c r. 10/. full flowing on a pebble bottom banks low- Here I

breakfast

N80E   16   vein of reed to the right
248[70]
E.
  7. + b. r.   a large bed of reed to the right just before we
come to the branch

4+c.r. 15/ on a pebble bottom evergreens on its margin bordered
with reeds.

N.80E
  24   path from our left. The Chickasaw path pine and blackjack
N.70E
  19.   Wewocau to the left.
E.
  10.   high pine blackjack flat
S.45E   }
  90.   }
N.80E   }on poor pine and blackjack
  15   }ridge. hollows to the right
N.80.E15   }and left. reed seldom in veins
N.50E.   }
  10
194[71]   This day the whole of the land is pine and blackjack., poor,
and much of it strewed over with gras + smoothe pebble
stones, the whole fit only for stock

Tuesday 19.th Jan[y].

S.45.E
  22   reeds to our right
  5 + b r   pine gravel hills
  7
E
  10
S60E
  17.
N.80E
  3.   vein of reeds the right and left. the narrow gap between
Mortar creek and Samballoh
  10.
S.50E.

5.   small hickory flat- on a ridge
15.   flat on a ridge of post oak blackjack pine
5   path from our right
S.70.E
20   cattle to our right
8.   a flat on the ridge oak hickory short leaf pine chesnut
45   path to the right to Tuskeegee
<u>38.+</u> b l.
199[72]
9.   reed right and left
23. + c. r. 15/. flat swamp on both sides
             The whole of this stage pine land except where
             otherwise noted. the hollows to the right and left not
             steep, and some have reed.
S.60.E
47.   over a pine flat.
S80E.
10 + swamp
27 + b r.   slashy in a pine flat
17.   pine flat, we turn out of the path for water and food
S.45.W.
38.   a creek on our front, and reeds.
S.30.E.
<u>38. +</u> Coosau 150 yards wide runing to the right
209[73] We cross at the residence of Daniel McGillivray. 3 miles
             above Tuskeegee.
S70E.
10 + path to the hickory ground.
10.
S40E
9   path to the left.
1 + b r.   steep bottom
10.   river swamp on our right, river hills
             to the left.
10.   plantation to the right.
S70E
10 + b r.
33 + b. r.   evergreens and reeds at its [source?]

This stage over high hills, sloping to the east hickory and oak.

10 + b r.   rich low ground

10 +. b. r

2 + c r. 15/ rich flats some cane on the creek. The hills high on the left bank,

15.   down a steep gravel hill reedy coves right and left, black jack post oak gravel

7 + b. r   evergreens and reeds.

S50.E

22   a flat small dwarf oak and black jack. a swamp to the left of bay and grass

10   path to the right

4.   an indian town Ecun,hut,kee on the bank of Tallapoosa

S.70.E

12 + c. r. 10/ settlements on the left bank to our left

9.   and Indian town Cooloome on the bank of Tallapoosa

2 + b r

12.   and Indian town Fooscehatche on the river bank

16   Nicolas White a Trader

S.30.E

8 +   Tallapoosa 60 yards wide to our right

20. +. b. r.

20   path to Pensacola

E

5.

N.50E

20.   a village to the left, of Ho,ith,le,waule

5 + c l 8/

N.20E.

50 + c l. 45/. o,fuck,she

9   path fork take the left.

N.

13.   houses to our left.

N.50.E

5.   river on our left. we go up

N.80E

12 + c l. 20 feet Kebihatche

N.20.E
   10.   river on our left
   13.   a settlement. Richard Baileys a half breed
S80E.
   13 +   path
S20E
   8 + b r.   slashy
   3 +   path
   4   reed to the left.
   12   path fork take the left
S70E
   5   path fork take the left.
   15.   a settlement on a pine oak and hickory flat, a good spring
        and reed branches-   Fishers.
  E.
   7+   path
   8   auttossee path
S50E.
   24   path to the right
  E
   9.   The residence of the agent.

General Wilkinson will thank Mr. Purcell for all information he may possess respecting the concession of Territory made by the Choctaws and Creeks to the British government, within the Limits of West Florida on the East as well as west of Mobile and Tombigbee rivers, to comprehend the places and periods of the several Treaties had with those natives, the terms & conditions of creek treaties and the lying course and termination of the several lines by which the concessions [unintelligible] were Limited. The General is desirous to receive this information as early as may comport? with M^r. Purcells convenience for which he will be happy to render to M^r. Purcell every requisite consideration and proper acknowledgement.-

Mr. Purcell in answer to General Wilkinson note begs leave to inform him that the line between the lands ceded by the Indians to the white people on the mississippi and east wardly to Escambia river.
   Begins at the mouth of Yazoo river from a gum and Sycamore

marked X3. and runs N.84.E 12 miles 60 chains[74] to a post marked
X3. from thence S.9.E. 17 miles 60 cha.ˢ to Lussa chitto or big black
river; ₍ thence from the said river one mile, thence up the said river
S.9.E. 16 miles 45 chains, thence S.30.W. 10 chains; thence S.6.E 7
miles 60 cha.s thence S.39.W one mile 55 chains; thence S.6.E 15
mile 5 cha.ˢ to the ford of Hoom a Chitto river, where the road from
the Choctaws to the Natchez crosses the said river; from thence S.6.E.
7 miles 15 chains; thence S.16.E. 19 miles to the Amet. river; thence
across the said river S61.E. 20 chains; thence S16E. 14 miles to a pine
and red oak marked X3. near Hau,it,hat,che;from thence N.84E. 24
miles to Bogue Chitto.thence E 53. M. 50 chains to Bogue Hooma
thence N.84.E. 27 miles 30 chains to a pine and chinquopin marked
X3. on the west bank of Pasca,Ocoola river. From thence up the
PascaO,coo,la river and Hatcho Comesa to the confluence of Chicasau
bay and Buck,hatamee rivers, thence up Buck,ha,tannee river to Bogue
Hooma, thence up the said Bogue to where it crosses the trading path
from Mobile to the Choctaws. Thence upon a Southeastern course to
the fork of Sontee bogue; thence down the said bogue to Tombigbee
river; down the said river to the mouth of Tallan bogue; thence across
the said river East wardly to the upper end of Nanihaba Island. Thence
across to the east side of Alabama, thence upon a South Eastern direction to the mouth of muddy creek on the west side of Escambia.
river; thence to the head of clear water creek, down the said creek to
Middle river, thence East to Yellow water river, and from there Eastwardly along the coast the boundary is regulated by the flowing of the
tide.

No the courses mentioned above were taken by the magnetic needle
at the time of the Survey. The Line from the mouth of Yazoo River
to Pasca Ocoo,la river is agreeable to the cession made by the Choctaws
in may 1777 and a talk held with the Chiefs of the O,coo,la Fu,ly,ha
tribe of the said nation in January 1779 and laid out and marked in
Feby and april 1779. And the Line from Pasca o coola to Yellow water river and East wardly is according to treaties held with the Choctaws
and Creeks in 1765 and 1770 and was in part laid out and marked in
1774.

The conditions on which the Indians made the said Concessions
were for goods to a certain amount which were delivered soon after
and the titles given by the Indians for the land so ceded are perpetual.

Charleston July 31.ˢᵗ 1802

Daniel McGillivray states that he was with Mʳ. Pursell when he assertained and marked the line for the Natchez district, they left Mobille in Nov.ʳ 1777 and they went to the ford of Homochitto and in Feby. 1778 began the line at the ford where the old Choctaw path from Yanzo to Natchez crossed that river, Then N. chained and mile marked the line every 3.ʳᵈ mile marked with a X and the initials of Joseph Pursell and Dan McGillivray, and [relay?] the line, and of the encampments, and at every 3 mile blazed several. They run N. to the neighbourhood of Bayone Pierre and there the Indians stoped line, a dispute arose about the line being in the opinion of the indians too far to the E. - The Indians insisted at this point, that the survey or should go N.W which could not be agreed to, owing to this difference they were oblidged to quit They went from thence to the Yacezoo water they made canoes, and went to the mouth of the river, Joseph Pursell the [artist?], there took his observations, and came 4 or 5 miles by water, and then thro' the hills and canebrake 10 miles E from the mouth of the river; the mouth of the river and this ten mile point was ascertained by celestial observations; and the line not marked from this 10 mile point they run due S. to big black, went down that / the waters being too high / to cross at the settlements 18 miles, crossed there, and returned up the edge of the swamp. 16 miles. there pursell commenced the line again, and continued it, they then went on until they discovered the line first commenced; -and found themselves ab.ʳ 200 yards East of it.- There was then a talk with the indian guides and they were satisfied. This line is mile marked and at 3 mi.s marked with a X- JP. and D.MG the mg joined- DMG

From here they went to the ford where they first commenced; and continued the line due S. to the Nit,to al,oon,ne path, from thence they run due E. to the Pas go goola river.- at this corner they marked as usual a X and the letters of their name, they finish the line at the mouth of a creek called by the Indians Fo,itch,ke / the mother of the bee /. nearly 60 miles west from Mobille. David McGillivrey was Interpreter and guide- Hardy Perry he went from the land of Bayone Pierre, with Pursell to the mouth of the Yazoo, and he and the Indians packed their provisions on their backs, Macgillivray he went round with the baggage and waited their return.-

The following is a transcription of a "viatory" from a field notebook in the possession of the Georgia Historical Society.

Road to Cussetuh

minutes

60. +. c. l. 40/.   Padjaligau
20. +. b. left.   at the [luad?]
35.   black rocks on a ridge
10.   swamp to left, open land, near the road
30.   take the left
49. +. b. l.
17. +. c. l. 20/
54. + c. l. 15/
20   The red hills, just before coming to the hills there is a small [drain?] from the left
7.   a clump of hickory trees
62.   a hammock of half an acre, on the left, a spring - Just beyond this the path forks, take right
71. + b. l.   reeds
9. + b. l. the fork of two reedy branches, water in the [unintelligible]
21.   head of a branch to the left
34.   a dry pond to the left
29. +. b. l.   reeds
6. +. c. r. 20/   fine reeds
21. +. c. r. 8.   fine reeds
21. +. c. r. 6/. fine reeds
84. +. c. r. 20/.
7. +. b. l. adjoining one parrallel with path
5. +. b. l. one above
68. +. b. r.
35.   Cussetuh town house

Notes

1. This statement is describing the land between this entry (7 + b. l.. 1/.) and the previous entry (6 + b. l.. 1/.).

2. Written sideways in the top margin.

3. This statement is describing the land between this entry (31. + c. r. 30/) and the previous entry (6. + c. r. 8/).

4. This statement is describing the land between this entry (11. + b. r .) and the next entry (4 + d. b. r. 6/.).

5. This is written sideways in the margin and is intended as an addition to the next line at the "X."

6. "hau" here may refer to an alternate spelling of the word below it in the journal, Oc,tau,zauze, and is unrelated to the line on which "hau" appears.

7. Hawkins starts summing his travel times. This is marked with a blue line over the summation. At this point 104 is sum of $13+8+18+10+6+6+12+5+8+10+8$.

8. $18+8+5+17+9+10+9+12+3+3+4+3+2+4+17+6=130$

9. $27+2+23+5+35+6+16=114$

10. This "A" seems to stand for addition and is a correction for a previous measurement also marked with an "A."

11. $4+52+15+6+21+32+21=151$

12. These measurements and observations were written in the margin and were apparently added later.

13. $9+20+17+47+12+9+17+12+15=158$

14. 241 here may be a mistaken summation. Hawkins may have intended to write 251 if the "1.7" above it is seventeen minutes. $158+26+17+50=251$. However, he clearly wrote "1.7" in the journal which indicates that it is NOT seventeen. If "1.7" is one minute and seven tenths of a minute, then the summation should be 235.7. If "1.7" is supposed to represent one hour and seven minutes, then the summation should be 301.

15. $16+24+16+14+9+10+6+10+49+8+9+10=181$

16. Written sideways in the margin. This appears to be an addition at the point indicated by an "A" above it.

17. $55+6+2+28+6+5+18+19+72+4+5=220$. This seems to be the end of a correction that started above at note 11.

18. Note that his speed has increased since the beginning of the journal. This affects distance measurements.

19. 70+13=83

20. 21+22+8=51

21. Written in the left margin of this page.

22. Written in the margin near the paragraph above it.

23. Hawkins seems to switch to a decimal system for recording time here. The first number is the number of hours and the second number is the number of minutes. He does not explain it, however.

24. Written in the margin.

25. creek

26. 39+19=58. Since Hawkins did not underline the "19," the "58" may not be a summation.

27. Note that Hawkins has switched back to a three-mile-per-hour calculation for distance here. He does not note this in his journal.

28. Etowah

29. Written sideways in the margin.

30. This unintelligible word was crossed out.

31. The word "Oostenauleh" is crossed out.

32. Of October?

33. Written sideways in the margin. Hawkins intended this as a footnote to the "x."

34. Written sideways in the margin. Hawkins intended this as a footnote to the "+."

35. Written sideways in the margin. Hawkins intended this as a footnote to the "+."

36. "1" inserted between 26 and 3

37. June 26, 1799?

38. This appears to be a summation of the time above.

39. Summation.

40. Summation of time is seven hours and twenty minutes. This totals twenty nine and 1/3 miles at four miles per hour.

41. This "12.15" may be a distance measurement that was carried over from the previous journal page for ease in summation.

42. This is written twice in the journal.

43. This adds up to 177 minutes.

44. The total time from here up to the beginning of "Left path crossing Flint river above Sule noj uh" is eighteen and one-half hours. The significance of the 5.11 is unknown.

45. left

46. Written in the margin.
47. Written in the margin.
48. 35+28+25+40+25+44+13+35=245
49. 17+69+8+57+15+27+42=235
50. 10+51+28+55+41+10=195
51. Written sideways in the margin. These figures apparently refer to the number of stops indicated in the left margin above.
52. In this column, Hawkins is recording miles. He notes the first entry as 215 miles and each entry after, he only records the second and third digit of the mileage. This "16" for example represents the 216th mile.
53. This "2.57" probably represents the 257th mile
54. line crossed out
55. line crossed out
56. 20+4+30+11+82+6+4+15=172
57. right
58. 38+9+43+30=120
59. 20+20+2+30+60+35+18+13+20=218. The original text records this sum as 208, but if the addition pattern follows the previous additions, this number should be 218. Hawkins either miscalculated or deviated from his normal summations here.
60. 5+13+13+14+18+12+12+5+14+10+17+6=139
61. 20+8+10+10+5+20+14+3+5+15+15=125
62. 20+12+4+10+5+4+19+3+4+3+2+3+13=102
63. 10+14+11+20+13+8+7+16+2+55+30+12+16+7=221
64. 8+6+4=18
65. 20+60+35+9+34=158
66. 15+6+8+16+32+10+8+14+9+11+10+5+3+2+4+8+10+15=186
67. "S4" crossed out in original.
68. 18+3+20+24+30+7+7=109
69. 20+20+15+3+4+10+30=102
70. 50+50+12+7+10+2+53+20+10+2+16=232. The original text records this sum as 248, but if the addition pattern follows the previous additions, this number should be 232. Hawkins either miscalculated or deviated from his normal summations here.
71. 7+4+24+19+10+90+15+15+10=194
72. 22+5+7+10+17+3+10+5+15+5+20+8+45+38=210. The original text records this sum as 199, but if the addition pattern follows the previous additions, this number should be 210. Hawkins either miscalculated or deviated from his normal summations here.

73. 9+23+47+10+27+17+38+38=209
74. One chain is 66 feet.

A SKETCH OF THE CREEK COUNTRY IN THE YEARS 1798 AND 1799

INTRODUCTION.

The Georgia Historical Society having, for some years, been in possession of several manuscript volumes of the late Colonel Benjamin Hawkins, the earliest agent of the United States for Indian Affairs, their examination and publication by the Society, became an object of interest. Accordingly, they were referred to a committee, whose report attested their value, as materials for the early history of Georgia, and especially for that of the confederacy of the Creek or Muscogee Indians, who formerly owned and swayed, the southwestern portion of the State. That report recommended the immediate publication of one of these manuscripts, which the author has called " *A Sketch of the Creek Country in the years* 1798 *and* 1799." As a member of the Society, I proposed to superintend this publication, and to defray its expense, as the resources of the Society were already anticipated by the erection of a Library and Historical Hall. The Society did me the honor to accept my proposition.

The Georgia Historical Society has now been in existence for nine years. During that period, it has published two volumes of Collections and Transactions, and the present publication will constitute the first part of the third volume.

The introduction to the first volume, thus alludes to these manuscripts of Mr. Hawkins : " In relation to the department of Indian history, a department so interesting in itself, and so intimately blended with the early settlement of this State, the Society has obtained some very rare and valuable manuscripts, which contain long and minute accounts of the manners and customs of the Indians ; proceedings of Indian agents ; treaties with various tribes ; all greatly augmenting the materials of aboriginal history."

The eight volumes of manuscripts, in possession of the Society, attest the industry and enlightened zeal of the author. He has preserved and transmitted to us, his *talks* and treaties, made with various Indian tribes; his correspondence with the General Government and with State authorities; vocabularies of aboriginal languages, and invaluable records of the manners, customs, rites and civil polity of the tribes.

It is reported, that many valuable papers of Mr. Hawkins have been irreparably lost to the world, by the burning of his residence in the Creek country. The present manuscripts, it is supposed, have been preserved by their having been submitted to the Governor of the State, at Milledgeville, for his perusal. Colonel Hawkins was still living in the year 1825. In that year, these volumes were in Savannah, under the charge of Mr. Joseph Bevan, who had been appointed by the General Assembly "to collect, arrange and publish, all papers relating to the original settlement or political history of the State." I learn this fact from a published report of his, made to Governor Troup. At the decease of Mr. Bevan, they were probably returned to the executive department at Milledgeville. At the institution of the Historical Society, a fortunate accident brought these valuable papers to the knowledge of J. K. Tefft, Esq., the corresponding secretary of the Society, and the actual cashier of the Bank of the State of Georgia, at Savannah. At his pressing instance, in favor of the Society, they were solicited and obtained, for the Society's library.

It is a singular fact, unparalleled in this age of printing, that there are five copies existing, of this "Sketch of the Creek Country." The most plausible motive for this curious multiplication of written copies, was the desire of speculators in Indian lands, to learn the topography, resources and character of the Creek country.

In this publication I have used the original manuscript of Mr. Hawkins, which has been attested by Mr. Tefft, who has a wide reputation for his collection of autographs, and for his admirable tas.e in that department of æsthetics. The writing and condition of the volume, give evidence of its having been written as early as the year 1800.

THE AUTHOR.

COLONEL BENJAMIN HAWKINS, was for more than thirty years, employed by the Government of the United States, in its intercourse with Indian tribes. The influence which he obtained and exercised among these tribes, is forcibly stated by Mr. Gallatin : " Mr. Hawkins, under the modest name of '*Beloved Man of the Four Nations*,' did govern, or, at least, exercise during his life, a considerable influence over the Creeks, Choctaws, and even the Chicasaws and Cherokees." A legitimate curiosity prompts me to trace the public career of a man, who, on the highest authority, rendered efficient and valuable services to his country, for a long series of years.

The first official notice of Mr. Hawkins, presents him as joint commissioner with Andrew Pickens, Joseph Martin, and Lachlan McIntosh, to negotiate with the Creek Indians, in the year 1785. They concluded the treaty of *Galphinton.* In the same year, the treaty of *Hopewell* was concluded with the Cherokees. By the treaty of New York, in 1790, the Creek Indians placed themselves under the protection of the United States, and of no other Power. By the treaty of Galphinton, they had acknowledged themselves to be within the limits of Georgia, and *members of the same.* These two inconsistent states of political relationship, and which are the origin of all subsequent controversies between the State of Georgia and the Indian tribes, led to the appointment, by General Washington, of three commissioners to treat with the Creek confederacy. Accordingly, he nominated to the Senate, in June, 1795, Benjamin Hawkins, of North Carolina, George Clymer, of Pennsylvania, and Andrew Pickens, of South Carolina, as commissioners for that object.

Mr. Hawkins was at this time, a Senator of the United States, from North Carolina.

In the year 1801, he was appointed by Mr. Jefferson, "principal agent for Indian affairs south of the Ohio," and as joint commissioner with General Wilkinson and Andrew Pickens, he negotiated treaties with the Chicasaws, Choctaws and Natchez.

From that period, he remained as agent of the United States among the Creek Indians, till the year 1816, when at his own request, as shown by his official letters, he was succeeded in that office, by David Brydie Mitchell, of Georgia. Colonel John Crowell succeeded this last agent; and from a letter of complaint against Crowell, written to the War Department in 1825, by Mr. Hawkins, it appears that he was then living in the Creek nation. I have not been able to learn the time of Mr. Hawkins's decease.

From the several volumes of correspondence, official and private, of Colonel Hawkins, I have made some extracts which very forcibly pourtray the high qualities of his mind, for the government and control of unlettered, semi-civilized tribes. This demands sound judgment and inflexible justice. An apparent indifference towards the women of the tribes, who are the objects of great jealousy, is not an unimportant quality. I have been assured from high authority, that this was one of the sources of Mr. Hawkins's extraordinary influence. In another part of the world, I have witnessed a like influence acquired by an agent of the United States, over a semi-civilized people. To their minds, it implies a moral superiority over other men, when accompanied by ordinary manly energies. It is a self-control, the more respected by such people, as it is the object of their chief indulgence, and of their liveliest jealousies.

Extract of a letter from Mr. Hawkins to a friend.

CUSSETUH, Nov. 25, 1797.

A few days ago, whilst I was sorely afflicted with rheumatism, so as not to be able to turn in my blanket, the arrival of the Queen of Tuckabatchee was announced to me. That town is sixty miles distant. I invited herself and her friends, to spend two or three days with me, which they did. Early one morning, she came to my bed side and sat down. I awoke, and she accosted me thus:

My visit is to you; I am a widow; I have a son so high; (holding her hand three feet from the ground;) I have a fine stock of cattle, and I wish them secured for my use and for my son. I know you are the *Isle-chate-lige-osetat-chemis-te-chaugo*, (the beloved man of the Four Nations,) and my relations are not careful of my interests. If you will take the direction of my affairs, the chiefs have told me you may settle my stock where you please, and it shall be safe. When you go to Tuckabatchee, you will have a home. Perhaps I am too old for you, but I'll do any thing I can for you. I shall be proud of you if you will take me. If you take a young girl into the house I shall not like it, but I will not say one word; may be I can't love her, but I won't use her ill. I have brought some *aus-ce* (cassine yupon) for you. I want some clothes for my boy and for myself. You can give them to me, and make the traders take cattle for pay. If you direct them they won't cheat me. I was taken prisoner by the Chickasaws, with my boy, when he was so high (about two feet.) I ran off from them, and was seventeen days in the woods, getting to my nation. I had no provisions when I set out, and was like to perish. When you were in the upper towns last year, I went twice to see you, and dressed myself. You took me by the hand and asked me to sit down. I wanted to speak to you then, but I could not. I said then I would never have an *Isle-chate* (red man.)

I replied to her, you shall be gratified; you may return home. I will have your cattle put out at a proper place, and I will take care of them and of your son. If you have any desire to call me *cha-e-he*, (my husband,) do so! But you must not forget, I have not yet determined to set up in that capacity in either of the Four Nations. But you are at liberty, as you already have one child, and know the trade, to carry it on under my name, and to choose any assistant you may deem suitable. The children will be mine and I will take care of them and of you.

It is not customary among the Creeks to associate with
the women ; and it is a curious fact, that there are white
men in the nation who have been here five years, without
ever entering an Indian house. I visit them, take them
by the hand, talk kindly to them, and eat frequently with
them. This day I had four Indian women to dine with
me, with some chiefs and white men, a thing, they tell me,
unknown before, to either of them. One thing I have noticed, in all I have conversed with, they have a great propensity to call every thing by its name. And, if the con-
current testimony of the white husbands may be relied
on, the women have much of the temper of the mule, except when they are amorous, and then they exhibit all the
amiable and gentle qualities of the cat.

Extract of a letter to William Faulkner, Esq.

CUSSETUH, NOVEMBER 25, 1797.

I am now, and have been in this town, which is on the
Chattahoche, among the lower Creek towns, (an hundred
and sixty miles from Fort Wilkinson, the residence of
Colonel Gaither on the Ocenee,) for more than a month,
and much engaged in the duties enjoined on me by my
office. It is not necessary to detail to you the difficulties
I have encountered daily, in adjusting with these people
the differences in the way of a friendly intercourse between them and their neighbors. The men are bred in
habits proudly indolent and insolent ; accustomed to be
courted, and to think that they conferred a favor when
they were naked, by receiving clothes and comforts from
the British agents ; and they will reluctantly and with
great difficulty, be humbled to the level of rational life.
I spend the day at their public places, in conversation ; or
at my hut, where I entertain a number ; and the evenings
I devote till midnight at the town house, to see their dancing and amusements, or at my hut, studying their language, or making arrangements to decide on disputed
property, and adjusting the misunderstandings between
the Four Nations. As business increased on me, I found
my mind and exertions always ready to rise above it ; or
as it would be better expressed, to be equal to my wishes,
and even beyond my expectations. In this situation I

had one visiter sorely afflictive, a severe attack in my left
leg and foot of the gout or rheumatism, for eight or ten
nights, sometimes not able to turn in my blankets, yet
constantly crowded with visiters, and obliged to attend to
the head men and warriors of twelve towns, invited to
convene at Cowetuh, a neighboring town.

I have one faithful assistant in Mr. Barnard, one of the
interpreters. The white and red men are much indebted
to his constant, persevering and honest exertions to do
justice to all applicants. It sometimes falls to the lot of
one man, though apparently in the humble walks of life,
to render more effectual service to his fellow creatures,
than thousands of his neighbors. This has been the case
with Mr. Barnard. He was a trader in this nation before
the war, and remained in it during the whole progress of
it, constantly opposing the cruel policy which pressed
these people to war with the Americans, and urged their
being neutral. He repeatedly risked his life and fortune
in the cause of humanity, and he remains to witness that
the purity of his actions has given him a standing among
the red people, which could not be purchased with
money.

I have, since I left you, seen much of the western country, witnessed the downfall of a character whom I highly
valued, when I first had the pleasure of knowing you, and
seen a check given, I hope an effectual one, to a base
system for the destruction of the Four Nations by the
E-cun-nau-nux-ulgee, (people greedily grasping after all
their lands,) and I have the happiness to know, that I
have contributed much to the establishment of the well
grounded confidence which the Four Nations have in the
justice of the United States ; and this confidence is so
well grounded, that the malice or wickedness of the enemies of our Government cannot destroy it.

I may here introduce some of the appellations and epi-
thets applied by the Creek Indians to white men, one of
which is used in the foregoing letter.

*E-cun-nau-nux-ulgee : People greedily grasping after the
lands of the red men,* against the voice of the United States.

Tucke-mico: The Dirt King, applied to Governor Blount
of Tennessee. The Cherokee name of this gentleman is

2

Dirt Captain ; and in both nations it arose from their opinion of his insatiate avidity to acquire Indian lands.

Chesse-cup-pe-tun-ne : The *Pumpkin Captain ;* a name given to Captain Chisholm.

E-cun-nau-au-po-po-hau : Always asking for land. This name was given to Governor Clark of Georgia.

Iste-chate-lige-osetate-chemis-te-chaugo : The beloved man of the Four *Nations ;* a name given to Colonel Hawkins.

Iste-chate : Red man.

Istc-hut-ke : White man.

Iste-semole : Wild man ; a Seminole.

Extract of a letter to James Burgess, Creek Interpreter.

CUSSETUH, NOVEMBER 27, 1797.

I have received your letter of the 14th of this month, in answer to mine of the 30th October. It is the first I have had from you. This letter you send me, I have read with attention ; and if you had not informed me you were sick, I should have supposed you were deranged in mind. Perhaps it is a delirium arising from sickness ; in that case it is a misfortune, not a fault. If I did not believe something of this sort really to affect you, I would let you know, that if you do not know *your* duty, I know *mine.*

Whoever heard of your being talked of about what was done at Coleraine? Nobody but your own imagination! You were only an interpreter, and I know the Indians never fault them, for doing their duty faithfully. I can tell you another thing. You overrate your standing, when you say the Indians blame you. The fact is they have not blamed you, and for a very obvious reason. The Indians do not suffer the white men in their land even to mention, much less to influence them in their treaties.

Another thing. You talk of Chulapockey, and the complaint of the Indians about it, and the trifle of goods; that these things must be settled before I leave the land. What do you mean by this stuff? Do you not know the Chulapockey line was settled by Mr. Gillivray and the Indians who went to New York? Don't you know that this nation appointed agents to go and run the line, and that

Bowles's* coming, prevented it? Did you not hear the chiefs tell me this publicly at Coleraine; and did you not know they told the truth?

What do you mean when you say if the Indians suffer you must suffer? Have you not, as it was your duty to do, told them boldly and plainly, what all the interpreters at Coleraine were ordered to do, that the Indians have now nothing to fear. The United States have guarantied their country to them. Did you not hear the plan of government explained at Coleraine, to better the condition of the Indians? And don't you know I am here to carry that plan into execution? Don't you know the Indians took part with Great Britain against the United States, and did us much injury; and that the retaliation on our part is to forgive them, because they were a poor, deluded people; to enlighten their understandings and to better their condition, by assisting them with tools and implements of husbandry, and teaching them the use of them, by furnishing them with blacksmiths, and spinning wheels, cards, looms and weavers. Where have you been that you have forgotten these things? Don't you know that we have placed an army, at great expense, to protect the Indians in the enjoyment of their rights, and that we established two stores, to supply the Indians at cost and charges?

You want me to clear you. Of what? Can you clear yourself, if you have not explained these things faithfully to the Indians? You cannot. You ask me to send you a certificate of what is done here, signed by two or three chiefs. What do you mean by this? Must Iste-chate-lige-osetat-chamis-te-chaugo have a certificate from three Indians? You are surely dreaming.

One piece of information I can give you. The Indians have appointed seven commissioners to see the line run, agreeably to the treaty of New York, and it will be run just after the new year.

You must visit me about the 25th of next month, at the store on Oconee, there to explain your conduct, and receive you salary.

BENJAMIN HAWKINS.

* This man Bowles, was at one time a portrait painter in Savannah.

THE CREEK CONFEDERACY.

ALL tradition among the Creeks points to the country west of the Mississippi, as the original habitat of those tribes. This universal tradition is confirmed by Du Pratz, Bernard Romans, Adair, Bartram and Hawkins. Our author asserts their migration, on the authority of Tusseloiah Micco, from the forks of Red river, *Wcchate-hatche Aufuskee.* We may entirely defer to the result of Mr. Gallatin's investigation of this subject, as the most correct. His comprehensive research and powerful analysis, have presented to the scientific world, all that can be known, perhaps, of that which is involved in the cimmerian darkness of ante-historical periods. In the second volume of the "Archæologia Americana," he says : "In the year 1732, when Georgia was first settled, the territory of the Creek Confederacy, including at that time the Seminoles, was bounded on the west by Mobile river, and by the ridge that separates the waters of the Tombigbee, from those of the Alabama ; on the north by the Cherokees, on the northeast by the Savannah, and on every other quarter by the Atlantic and the gulf of Mexico. It is believed, that at the end of the seventeenth century, the Creeks occupied south of the 34th degree of north latitude, the eastern as well as western banks of the Savannah.

" It is not possible to ascertain, when the Confederacy was consolidated to that extent. It now consists of several tribes, speaking different languages. The Muskhogees are the prevailing nation, amounting to more than seven-eights of the whole. The Hitchittees who reside on the Chattahoochee and Flint rivers, though a distinct tribe, speak a dialect of the Muskhogee. The Seminoles or *Isty-Semole*, ('wild men,') who inhabit the peninsula of Florida, are pure Muskhogees, who have gradually detached themselves from the confederacy, but who were still considered as members of it, till the United States treated with them as an independent nation. The name of Seminoles was given to them, on account of their being hunters, and attending but little to agriculture. A vocabulary is wanted, in order to prove conclusively, the identity of their language with the Muskhogee.

" There is some diversity in the accounts given by the Muskhogees of their origin. The chiefs of the delegation, who attended at Washington, in the year 1826, agreed, that the prevailing tradition among them was, that the nation had issued out of a cave near the Alabama river. The Hitchittees said, that their ancestors had fallen from the sky. These modes of speaking, common to several of the tribes, only show that they have lost the recollection of any ancient migration, and that they consider themselves as aborigines.

" The Utchees and the Natchez, who are both incorporated in the confederacy, speak two distinct languages, altogether different from the Muskhogee. The Natchez, a residue of the well known nation of that name, came from the banks of the Mississippi and joined the Creeks less than one hundred years ago. The original seats of the Uchees were east of the Coosa, and probably of the Chattahoochee, and they consider themselves the most ancient inhabitants of the country. It appears certain, that at the beginning of the eighteenth century, they were, at least in part, seated on the western banks of the Savannah. It has already been seen, that in 1736, they claimed the country above and below Augusta. In the year 1715, was that of the signal defeat of the Yamassees (in South Carolina.) The Yamassees were driven across the river, (Savannah,) and it is probable that the Uchees were amongst their auxiliaries, and that weakened by this defeat, they found it safer to remove to a greater distance from the English settlements, towards Flint river," (and Florida.)

" These five languages, the Muskhogee, the Hitchittee, Uchee, Natchez and the Alabama or Coosada, are, it is believed, the only one spoken by the different tribes of the Creek confederacy. The Uchee is the most guttural, uncouth, and difficult to express with our alphabet and orthography, of any of the Indian languages within our knowledge.

" Although partial and transient collisions with the Creeks, occurred subsequently to the settlement of Georgia, no actual war with them took place for near fifty years. They took an active part in that of the Revolution, against the Americans, and continued their hostilities till the treaty concluded at Philadelphia, in 1795. They then remained at peace eighteen years ; but at the beginning of the last war with Great Britain, a considerable portion of the nation, excited, it is said, by Tecumseh, and probably receiving encouragement from other quarters, took arms, without the slightest provocation, and at first committed great ravages. They received a severe chastisement; and the decisive victories of General Jackson, at that time and some years later, over the Seminoles, who had renewed the war, have not only secured a permanent peace with the southern nations, but have placed them all under the absolute control of the United States. The Creeks and Seminoles, after some struggles among themselves, have ceded the whole of their territory, and accepted in exchange, other lands beyond the Mississippi."

Such is the succinct, but comprehensive account of the Creek Confederacy, by Mr. Gallatin. Bernard Romans, who wrote his book in 1770, says that, " this confederacy, of remnants of tribes, are very cunning fellows. They are a mixture of Cowittas, Talepoosas, Corsas, Apalachias, Conshaes or Coosadas, Oakmulgees, Oconees, Okchoys, Alibamons, Natchez, Wetumkas, Pakanas, Taensas, Chacsihomas, Abekas, and other tribes." Classifying these numerous tribes by the science of philology, they must be reduced to the number of five, as Mr. Gallatin has shown.

They are jealous, says Romans, of their lands, and endeavor to enlarge their territories by conquest, and claiming large tracts from the Cherokees and Choctaws. They have forced these two tribes into alliance, and they wish to unite all tribes and languages under one general confederation or commonwealth. As an instance of their jealous policy, it may be related, that in 1764, Messrs. Rea and Galphin, having contracted to supply Pensacola with beef, the Creeks would not allow any other cattle than *oxen* to pass through their territory.

To my mind, it is evident, that the whole Atlantic coast, from the Mississippi to the country of the Six Nations, in the north, has for centuries past been the theatre of constant revolutions among the aborigines of the soil. Wars, conquests, subjugations, extinctions and productions of new races, migrations and new settlements, I do not doubt, have marked the life of western as well as of eastern nations. On this continent there are no Persepolitan, Etruscan, Egyptian or Runic inscriptions, to attest the rise and decay of nations, their wars, conquests and migrations; and where no records have been made of such movements among races and tribes, the modern science of comparative philology has detected, by speech, the far distant emigration of tribes of men, with as great certainty, as the comparative anatomist detects congeners, among fossil mammals. Thus, the Anglo-Saxon derives his origin through Teutonic and Zend, to Sanscrit in central Asia, with positive certainty.

The historians of Carolina and Georgia, have preserved some slight vestiges of the original inhabitants. The Shawnees appear to have been a peculiarly roving, romantic race. Lawson reports that the Catawbas in Carolina, drove back the Shawnees from the Pedee and Santee rivers. At one time, they were repelled by the Six Nations and retired to the valley of the Ohio. At another, they were found on the Savannah river, which was called *Chisketalla fau hatche;* and sometimes *Sauvannogee*, the name for *Shawanoe.* This is the report of Mr. Hawkins. It was called *Isundiga*, by the Carolina tribes. My own opinion is, that the river was so called, from the tribe of Savannahs occupying its banks; who belonged to the great Uchee family. There are many indications however, which favor the settlement of Shawnees on this river.

Hawkins says, that " the village of Sauvanogee, on the waters of Coosa and Tallapoosa, is inhabited by Shawanee. They retain the language and customs of their countrymen to the northwest, and aided them in their late war with the United States. Some Uchees have settled with them."

Entertaining the suspicion, that these Shawanee were in reality Uchees, I found confirmation in Bartram. He says, " their (Uchees) own national language is radically different from the Muscogulgee tongue ; and is called Savanna or Savannuca, Savanogee. I was told by the traders, that it was the same as the dialect of the Shawanese. The Uchees are in confederacy with the Creeks, but do not mix with them."

The language of the Shawnese is most certainly not like Uchee; and this contradiction of the traders I cannot well explain. Yet I have the conviction, that the tribe of Savannahs were Uchees. All travellers concur in assigning to the Uchees great influence in the confederacy ; and Bartram asserts that " they excite the jealousy of the whole Creek union." Palachoocla or *Parachoocla*, the capital of the confederacy, with two thousand inhabitants, on the waters of the Chattahoochee, is a very ancient Uchee town. There is at this day an old Indian station in Carolina, on the Savannah river, called Parachoola, which is Uchee. *Saukechuh*, (saltketchers,) where Governor Craven defeated the Yamassees, is most likely to be a Uchee word. Indeed, until the contrary shall be proved by comparative vocabularies, I shall think that the Savannahs, Sevannahs and Uchees, who conquered and expelled the Westos and Stonos, were one people with the Yamassees.

The Yamassees were, in turn, expelled from Carolina by the English, and took refuge in Florida. The Yamacraws belonged to this tribe. The Uchees seem to have been a conquering people, whose tide of success having been checked, flowed back towards the west, and there met the advancing waves of the Muscogee emigration from the west, rolling eastwardly. Policy and self-preservation combined to suggest a coalition. And thus, from these principles, acting upon other nomadic or migrating tribes, may have sprung the powerful Creek or Muscogee confederacy.

The existence of the numerous aboriginal tribes within the borders of the United States will, ere long, belong only to history. The generations of Indians that have passed away since the first English settlements in Amer-

3

ica, have left no monuments to attest their dominion. There exist in the valleys of the great west, striking evidences of an anterior civilization, which are objects of wonder to the Indians of our day as well as to ourselves. The only vestiges of their creation, that will be left to posterity, are the books of missionaries printed in their idioms, and vocabularies, unsatisfactory but invaluable to science. Too much honor and praise cannot be accorded to those enlightened men, who have devoted themselves to the preservation of these vestiges which are to become the fossil, organic remains of intellectual humanity. Du Ponceau and Gallatin are the two names which stand pre-eminent in this department of scientific labor. The one has closed his honorable career; the other still devotes, with advancing years, his philosophic mind to these subjects of human and scientific interest. At this moment he is preparing for press a volume of ethnographic investigations in California and New Mexico. The labors of the scholar and historian, will beautifully close the career of the benevolent and disciplined statesman.

WM. B. HODGSON.

June 20, 1848.

A SKETCH OF THE CREEK COUNTRY,

IN THE YEARS 1798 AND 1799.

THE origin of the name Creek is uncertain. The tradition is, that it was given by white people, from the number of Creeks and water courses in the country. The Indian name is Muscogee.*

The Creeks came from the west. They have a tradition among them, that there is, in the fork of Red river, west of the Mississippi, two mounds of earth; that at this place, the Cussetuhs, Conetuhs and Chickasaws, found themselves; that being distressed by wars with red people, they crossed the Mississippi, and directing their course eastwardly, they crossed the falls of Tal-lapoo-sa, above Took-au-bat-che, settled below the falls of Chat-to-ho-che, and spread out from thence to Oc-mul-gee, O-co-nee, Savannah, and down on the seacoast, towards Charleston. Here, they first saw white people, and from hence they have been compelled to retire back again, to their present settlements.

The country lying between Coosau, Tallapoosa and Chat-to-ho-che, above their falls, is broken. The soil is stiff, with coarse gravel, and in some places, stone. The trees are post oak, white and black oak, pine, hickory and chesnut, all of them small. The whole is well watered, and the rivers and creeks have rocky beds, clad in many places with moss greatly relished by cattle, horses and deer, and are margined with cane or reed, on narrow strips or coves, of rich flats. On the Coosau, sixty miles above its junction with Tallapoosa, there is limestone, and it is to be found in several places from thence up to Etowwoh, and its western branches.

---

* G is always hard in Creek. Mus-co-gee, a Creek Indian; Mus-co-gul-gee, the Creeks. Che-lo-kee, a Cherokee. Che-loc-ul-gee, the Cherokees.

The country above the falls of Oc-mul-gee and Flint rivers, is less broken than that of the other rivers. These have their sources near each other, on the left side of Chattohoche, in open, flat, land, the soil stiff, the trees post and black oak, all small. The land is generally rich, well watered, and lies well, as a waving country, for cultivation. The growth of timber is oak, hickory, and the short leaf pine ; pea-vine on the hill sides and in the bottoms, and a tall, broad leaf, rich grass, on the richest land. The whole is a very desirable country. Below the falls of these two rivers, the land is broken or waving. The streams are, some of them, margined with oak woods ; and all of them with cane or reed. The upland of Oc-mul-gee is pine forest ; the swamp wide and rich ; the whole is fine for stock. On its right bank, below the old Uchee path, there is some light pine barren, with saw palmetto and wiregrass.

Flint river, below its falls, has some rich swamp, for not more than twenty miles. Its left bank is then poor, with pine flats and ponds, down within fifteen miles of its confluence with Chat-to-ho-che. These fifteen miles is waving, with some good oak in small veins. On its right bank there are several large creeks, which rise out of the ridge dividing the waters of Flint and Chattohoche. Some of them are margined with oak woods and cane ; and all the branches, for seventy miles below the falls, have reed ; from thence down there are bay galls and dwarf evergreens, and cypress ponds, with some live oak. Between these rivers, there is some good post and black oak land, strewed over with iron ore, and the ridge dividing their waters has a vein of it, extending itself in the direction with the ridge. Within twenty-five miles of the confluence of the rivers, the live oak is to be seen near all the ponds, and here are limestone rocks. The land here is good in veins, in the flats and on the margins of the rivers. The trees of every description are small. The range is a fine one for cattle.

That exclusive body of land between Flint river, O-ke-fi-no-cau, A-la-ta-ma-ha and the eastern boundary of the creek claims, is poor pine land, with cypress ponds and bay galls. The small streams are margined with dwarf evergreens. The uplands have yellow pine, with dwarf saw palmetto and wiregrass. The bluffs on St. Illas, are, some part of them, sandy pine barren ; the remainder is a compact, stiff, yellowish sand or clay, with large swamps; the growth is the loblolly bay, gum and small evergreens. The whole of these swamps is bogs. In the rainy season, which commences after midsummer, the ponds fill, and then the country is, a great part of it, covered with water ; and in the dry season it is difficult to obtain water in any direction, for many miles.

Bees abound in the O-ke-fin-a-cau and other swamps, eastward of Flint river. The wortleberry is to be found in the swamps, and on the poorest of the land bordering on the cypress ponds. When the woods are not burnt for a year or more, the latter are on dwarf bushes, grow larger, and in great abundance.

The dwarf saw palmetto, when the woods are not burnt, in like manner bears a cluster of berries on a single stem, which are eaten by bear, deer, turkeys and Indians. The berries are half an inch in diameter, covered with a black skin, and have a hard seed ; they are agreeable to the taste, sweet, accompanied with bitter, and when full ripe they burst, and the bees extract much honey from them. The China briar is in the flat, rich, sandy margins of streams. The Indians dig the roots, pound them in a mortar, and suspend them in coarse cloth, pour water on them and wash them. The sediment which passes through with the water is left to subside ; the water is then poured off, and the sediment is baked into cakes or made into gruel sweetened with honey. This briar is called *Coonte*, and the bread made of it, Coon-te-tuc-a-li-sa, and is an important article of food among the hunters. In the old beaver ponds, in thick boggy places, they have the bog potatoe (Uc-lau-wau-he-āhā) a small root, used as food in years of scarcity.

The O-ke-fin-o-cau is the source of the St. Mary's and Little St. Johns, called by the Indians Sau-wau-na. It is sometimes called E-cun-fin-o-cau, from E-cun-nau, earth; and Fin-o-cau, quivering. The first is the most common amongst the Creeks. It is from Ooka a Chactau word for water, and Fin-o-cau, quivering. This is a very extensive swamp, and much of it a bog ; and so much so, that a little motion will make the mud and water quiver to a great distance. Hence the name is given.

Ho-ith-lepoie Tus-tun-nug-ge-thluc-co, an Indian who resided in it many years, says that, " the Little St. John's may be ascended far into the swamp, and that it is not practicable to go far up the St. Mary's, as it loses itself in the swamp ; that there is one ridge on the west side of the St. John's, and three on the east. The growth is pine, live and white oak ; the soil good ; the lakes abound in fish and alligators. On the ridges and in the swamps there were a great many bear, deer, and tigers. He lived on the ridge west of the St. John's, and was, with his family, very healthy. Being unwilling to take part in the war between the United States and Great Britain, he moved there to be out of the way of it, was well pleased with his situation, and should have continued to reside there, but for the beasts of prey, which destroyed his cattle and horses. He could walk round the swamp in five days."

The land between Chat-to-ho-che and Alabama, bordering on the southern boundary of the United States, is better than that on the east side of Flint river. The Ko-e-ne-cuh rises between these two rivers, and makes the bay Escambia at Pensacola. Between Ko-e-ne-cuh and Chat-to-ho-che, the land is broken or waving. The ridge dividing their waters, has high flats of light land, well set with willow-leaved hickory, and iron ore in places, and all the streams have reed or cane on their margins.

This country has the appearance of being a healthy one, and the range is fine for cattle, hogs, and horses. The pine flats have the wiregrass, and in some places, the saw palmetto. The soil of the waving land is, some of it, stiff and red, with stones on the ridges. The pine land is stiff, generally, and pretty good for corn.

The Tal-la-poo-sa from its falls to its confluence with the Coosau, about thirty miles, has some good flat land. The broken land terminates on its right bank, and the good land spreads out on its left. There are several pine creeks on this side, which have their source in the ridge dividing these waters from Ko-e-ne-cuh. The land bordering on them is rich ; the timber large, and cane abundant. This good land extends to the Alabama, and down it for thirty miles, including the plains, (Hc-guc-pul-gee.)

These are seventeen miles through, going parallel to Alabama south 20° west. They are waving, hill and dale, and appear divided into fields. In the fields the grass is short, no brush; the soil in places is a lead color, yellow underneath, within the abode of the ants, and very stiff. In the wooded parts the growth is generally post oak, and very large, without any under brush, beautifully set in clumps. Here the soil is a dark clay, covered with long grass and weeds, which indicate a rich soil. One observation applies to all the fields; in the centre the land is poorest, the grass shortest, and it rises gradually to the wooded margins, where it is tall, and the land apparently rich. Four large creeks meander through the plains to the Alabama. They all have broad margins of stiff, level, rich land, well wooded and abounding with cane. There is, notwithstanding these creeks, a scarcity of water in the dry season, and all the creeks were dry in 1799, and not a spring of water was to be found.

The Alabama is margined with cane swamps, and these, in places, with flats of good land or poor pine flats. The swamps at the confluence with the Tombigby and below on the Mobile, is low and subject to be overflowed every spring. Above, it is of great width, intersected with lakes, slashes, and crooked drains, and much infested with musketoes. The people who cultivate this swamp, never attempt to fence it, as the annual freshes, always in the spring, rise from three to ten feet over it. The land, bordering on the swamp, and for a mile back, is a poor, stiff clay; the growth is pine and underbrush, back of this broken pine barren, there are cypress ponds, and veins of reeds in the branches. The range is said to be a fine one for cattle. The settlement of Ta-en-sau borders on the Mobile and Alabama, on the left side. On the same side of Alabama, fifty miles above its confluence with the Tombigby, the high broken lands commence and extend for sixty or seventy miles upwards, and abound in places with large, fine, tall cedar.

The land between Alabama and Ko-o-ne-cuh, below the plains, is broken or waveing; the soil is stiff, very red in places, and gravelly; for thirty miles then succeeds stiff pine barren. Limestone, a creek which enters the Alabama, has some good broken land, with limestone, which gives name to the creek. At its sources there is a fine body of land called the " dog woods," the growth is oak, chesnut, poplar, lind and dogwood. This vein of land is nearly twenty miles in length, and eight wide. The dogwood is very thick set, and some of them large, ten inches diameter. The whole is finely watered.

The Coosau has its source high up in the Cherokee country. E-tow-woh and Oos-te-nau-lih, are its main branches. The land on these rivers is rich, and abounds with limestone. Sixty miles above the confluence of the Coo-sau with Tallapoosa, there is a high, waving, limestone country settled by the Indians of Coo-sau, Au-be-coo-che nau-che and Eu-fau-lau-hat-che. The settlements are generally on rich flats of oaks, hickory, poplar, walnut and mulberry. The springs are fine ; there is cane on the creeks, and reed on the branches. The surrounding country is broken and gravelly. The land fit for culture, is generally the margins of the creeks, or the waving slopes from the high broken land.

Throughout the whole of this country, there is but little fruit of any kind ; in some of the rich flats there are fox grapes and muscadines ; the small cluster grapes of the hills is destroyed by fire, and the persimmon, haw and chesnut, by the hatchet ; there are a few blackberries in the old fields, red haws on the poor sand hills, and strawberries thinly scattered, but not a gooseberry, raspberry or currant, in the land.

The traveller, in passing through a country as extensive and wild as this, and so much in a state of nature, expects to see game in abundance. The whole of the creek claims, the Seminoles inclusive, cover three hundred miles square; and it is difficult for a good hunter, in passing through it, in any direction, to obtain enough for his support.

The towns, with a description of their position, and the lands of their neighborhood.

There are thirty-seven towns in the Creek nation ; twelve on the waters of Chat-to-ho-che, and twenty-five on the waters of Coo-sau and Tal-la-poo-sa. The small towns or villages belong to some one of these. The old towns have the exclusive right of governing the ceremony of the Boos-ke-tuh.*

The towns on Chat-to-ho-che.

1	Cow-e-tuh.	7	Hitch-e-tee.
2	Cow-c-tuh-tal-lau-has-see.	8	Pā-lā-chooc-la.
3	Cus-se-tuh.	9	O-co-nee.
4	U-chee.	10	Sau-woog-e-lo.
5	Oo-se-oo-che.	11	Sau-woog-e-loo-che.
6	Che-au-hau.	12	Eu-fau-lau.

The towns on Coo-sau and Tal-la-poo-sa.

1	Tal-e-see.	14	O-che-au-po-fau.
2	Took-au-bat-che.	15	We-wo-cau.
3	Aut-tos-see.	16	Puc-cun-tal-lau-has-see.
4	Hoith-le Waulee.	17	Coo-sau.
5	Foosce-hat-che.	18	Au-be-coo-chee
6	Coo-loome.	19	Nau-chee.
7	E-cun-hut-kee.	20	Eu-fau-lau-hat-che.
8	Sau-va-no-gee.	21	Woc-co-coie.
9	Mook-lau-sau.	22	Hill-au-bee.
10	Coo-sau-dee.	23	Oc-fus-kee.
11	Hook-choie.	24	Eu-fau-lau.
12	Hook-choie-oo-che.	25	Ki-a-li-jee.
13	Tus-ke-gee.		

The towns of the Simenolies deserve a place here, as they are Creeks. They inhabit the country bordering on the gulf of Mexico, from A-pa-la-che-co-la, including Little St. John's and the Florida point. They have seven towns.

1	Sim-e-no-le-tal-lau-haf-see	5	Oc-le-wau-hau thluc-co.
2	Mic-co sooc-e.	6	Tal-lau-gue chapco pop-cau
3	We- cho-took-me.	7	Cull-oo-sau hat-che.
4	Au-lot-che-wau.		

Sim-e-lo-le or Sim-e-no-le, means *wild.* These towns

* Hereafter described.

4

are made from the towns O-co-nee, Sau-woog-e-lo, Eu-
fau-lau, Tum-mault-lau, Pa-lā-chooc-le and Hitch-e-tee.
They are called *wild* people, because they left their old
towns and made irregular settlements in this country to
which they were invited by the plenty of game, the mild-
ness of the climate, the richness of the soil, and the
abundance of food for cattle and horses. The range is
equally fine for hogs, but they are raised with difficulty,
as the ponds and swamps abound with alligators.

*A description of the towns on Coosau and Tal-la-poo-sa, gen-
erally called Upper Creeks.*

1. *Tal-e-see*, from Tal-o-fau, a town, and *e-see*, taken.
Situated in the fork of Eu-fau-le on the left bank of Tal-
la-poo-sa, opposite Took-au-bat-che. Eu-fau-be has its
source in the ridge dividing the waters of Chat-to-ho-che
from Tal-la-poo-sa, and runs nearly west to the junction
with the river; there it is sixty feet wide. The land on it is
poor for some miles up, then rich flats, bordered with pine
land with reedy branches, a fine range for cattle and horses.
    The Indians have mostly left the town, and settled up
the creek, or on its waters, for twenty miles. The settlements are some of them well chosen, and fenced with
worm fences. The land bordering on the streams of the
right side of the creek, is better than that of the left; and
here the settlements are mostly made. Twelve miles up
the creek from its mouth it forks ; the large fork of the
left side has some rich flat swamp, large white oak, poplar, ash and white pine. The trading path from Cus-se-
tuh to the Upper Creeks crosses this fork twice. Here
it is called big swamp, (opil-thluc-co.) The waving land
to its source is stiff. The growth is post oak, pine and
hard shelled hickory.
    The Indians who have settled out on the margins and
branches of the creek, have, several of them, cattle, hogs
and horses, and begin to be attentive to them. The head
warrior of the town, Peter McQueen, a half breed, is a
snug trader, has a valuable property in negroes and stock
and begins to know their value.
    These Indians were very friendly to the United States,
during the revolutionary war, and their old chief, Ho-bo-

ith-le Mic-co, of the halfway house, (improperly called the Tal-e-see king,) could not be prevailed on by any offers from the agents of Great Britain, to take part with them. On the return of peace, and the establishment of friendly arrangements between the Indians and citizens of the United States, this chief felt himself neglected by Mr. Seagrove, which resenting, he robbed and insulted that gentleman, compelled him to leave his house near Took-au-bat-che, and fly into a swamp. He has since then, as from a spirit of contradiction, formed a party in opposition to the will of the nation, which has given much trouble and difficulty to the chiefs of the land. His principal assistants were the leaders of the banditti who insulted the commissioners of Spain and the United States, on the 17th September, 1799, at the confluence of Flint and Chat-to-ho-che. The exemplary punishment inflicted on them by the warriors of the nation, has effectually checked their mischief-making and silenced them. And this chief has had a solemn warning from the national council, to respect the laws of the nation, or he should meet the punishment ordained by the law. He is one of the great medal chiefs.

This spirit of party or opposition, prevails not only here, but more or less in every town in the nation. The plainest proposition for ameliorating their condition, is immediately opposed; and this opposition continues as long as there is hope to obtain *presents*, the infallible mode heretofore in use, to gain a point.

2. Took-au-bat-che. The ancient name of this town is Is-po-co-gee; its derivation uncertain; it is situated on the right bank of the Tallapoosa, opposite the junction of Eu-fau-be, two and a half miles below the falls of the river, on a beautiful level. The course of the river from the falls to the town, is south; it then turns east three-quarters of a mile, and short round a point opposite Eu-fau-be, thence west and west-by-north to its confluence with Coosau, about thirty miles. It is one hundred yards wide opposite the town house to the south, and here are two good fords during the summer. One just below the point of a small island, the other one hundred yards still lower.

The water of the falls, after tumbling over a bed of

rock for half a mile, is forced into two channels; one thirty, the other fifteen feet wide. The fall is forty feet in fifty yards. The channel on the right side, which is the widest, falls nearly twenty feet in ten feet. The fish are obstructed here in their attempts to ascend the river. From appearances, they might be easily taken in the season of their ascending the rivers, but no attempts have hitherto been made to do so.

The rock is a light gray, very much divided in square blocks of various sizes for building. It requires very little labor to reduce it to form, for plain walls. Large masses of it are so nicely fitted, and so regular, as to imitate the wall of an ancient building, where the stone had passed through the hands of a mason. The quantity of this description at the falls and in the hill sides adjoining them, is great; sufficient for the building of a large city.

The falls above spread out, and the river widens to half a mile within that distance, and continues that width for four miles. Within this scope are four islands, which were formerly cultivated, but are now old fields margined with cane. The bed of the river is here rocky, shoally, and covered with moss. It is frequented in summer by cattle, horses, and deer; and in the winter, by swans, geese and ducks.

On the right bank opposite the falls, the land is broken, stoney and gravelly. The hill sides fronting the river, exhibit this building rock. The timber is post oak, hickory and pine, all small. From the hills the land spreads off level. The narrow flat margin between the hills and the river is convenient for a canal for mills on an extensive scale, and to supply a large extent of flat land around the town with water. Below the falls a small distance, there is a spring and branch, and within five hundred yards a small creek; thence within half a mile, the land becomes level and spreads out on this side two miles, including the flats of Wol-lau-hat-che, a creek ten feet wide, which rises seventeen miles from its junction with the river, in the high pine forest, and running south-south-east enters the river three miles below the town house. The whole of this flat, between the creek and the river, bordering on the town, is covered with oak and the small hard shelled hickory. The trees are all small;

the land is light, and fine for corn, cotton or melons. The creek has a little cane on its margins, and reed on the small branches; but the range is much exhausted by the stock of the town.

On the left bank of the river, at the falls, the land is broken pine forest. Half a mile below there is a small creek which has its source seven miles from the river, its margins covered with reed or cane. Below the creek the land becomes flat, and continues so to Talesee on the Eu-fau-bee, and half a mile still lower, to the hills between this creek and Ca-le-bc-hat-che. The hills extend nearly two miles, are intersected by one small creek and two branches, and terminate on the river in two high bluffs; from whence is an extensive view of the town, the river, the flat lands on the opposite shore and the range of hills to the northwest; near one of the bluffs there is a fine spring, and near it a beautiful elevated situation for a set-tlement. The hills are bounded to the west by a small branch. Below this, the flat land spreads out for one mile. It is a quarter of a mile from the branch on this flat to the residence of Mr. Cornells, (Oche Haujo,) thence half a mile to the public establishment, thence two miles to the mouth of Ca-le-be-hat-che. This creek has its source thirty miles to the east in waving, post oak, hick-ory and pine land; in some places the swamp is wide, the beach and white oak very large, with poplar, cy-press, red bay, sassafras, Florida magnolia, and white pine. Broken piny woods and reedy branches on its right side; oak flats, red and post oak, willow leaved hickory, long and short leaf pine and reedy branches on its left side. The creek at its mouth is twenty-five feet wide. The flat between it and the river is fine for corn, cotton and melons, oak, hickory, and short leaf pine. From this flat to its source, it is margined with cane, reed, and palmetto. Ten miles up the creek, between it and Kebihatche, the next creek below and parallel with this, are some licks in post and red oak saplin flats; the range on these creeks is apparently fine for cattle; yet from the want of salt or moss, the large ones appear poor in the fall, while other cattle, where moss is to be had, or they are regularly salted, are fat.

They have 116 gun men belonging to this town; they

were formerly more numerous, but have been unfortunate in their wars. In the last they had with the Chickasaws, they lost thirty-five gun men ; they have begun to settle out in villages for the conveniency of stock raising, and having firewood ; the stock which frequent the mossy shoals above the town, look well and appear healthy ; the Indians begin to be attentive to them, and are increasing them by all the means in their power. Several of them have from fifty to one hundred, and the town furnished seventy good beef cattle in 1799. One chief, Toolk-au-bat-che Haujo, has five hundred, and although apparently very indigent, he never sells any ; while he seems to deny himself the comforts of life, he gives continued proofs of unbounded hospitality ; he seldom kil's less than two large beeves a fortnight, for his friends and acquaintances.

The town is on the decline. Its appearance proves the inattention of the inhabitants. It is badly fenced ; they have but a few plum trees, and several clumps of cassine yupon ; the land is much exhausted with continued culture, and the wood for fuel is at a great and inconvenient distance, unless boats or land carriages were in use ; it could then be easily supplied ; the river is navigable for boats drawing two and a half feet in the dry season, from just above the town, to Alabama. From the point just above the town to the falls, the river spreads over a bed of flat rock in several places, where the depth of water is something less than two feet.

This is the residence of Efau Haujo, one of the great medal chiefs, the speaker for the nation at the national council. He is one of the best informed men of the land, and faithful to his national engagements. He has five black slaves, and a stock of cattle and horses ; but they are of little use to him ; the ancient habits instilled in him by French and British agents, that the red chiefs are to live on presents from their white friends, is so riveted, that he claims it as a tribute due to him, and one that never must be dispensed with.

At the public establishment there is a smith's shop, a dwelling house and kitchen built of logs, and a field well fenced. And it is in the contemplation of the agent, to have a public garden and nursery.

The assistant and interpreter, Mr. Cornells, (Oche

Haujo,) one of the chiefs of the Creek nation, has a farm well fenced and cultivated with the plough. He is a half breed, of a strong mind, and fulfils the duties enjoined on him by his appointment, with zeal and fidelity. He has nine negroes under good government. Some of his family have good farms, and one of them, Zachariah McGive is a careful, snug farmer, has good fences, a fine young orchard, and a stock of hogs, horses and cattle. His wife has the neatness and economy of a white woman. This family and Sullivan's, in the neighborhood, are spinning.*

3. *Aut-tos-se*, on the left side of Tallapoosa, below and adjoining Ca-le-be-hat-che. A poor, miserable looking place, fenced with small poles; the first on forks in a line and two others on stakes hardly sufficient to keep out cattle. They have some plum and peach trees; a swamp back of the town and some good land back of that, a flat of oak, hickory and pine. On the right bank of the river, just below the town, they have a fine rich cove of land which was formerly a cane brake, and has been cultivated.

There is, below the town, one good farm made by the late Richard Bailey, and an orchard of peach trees Mrs. Bailey, the widow, is neat, clean and industrious, and very attentive to the interests of her family; qualities rarely to be met with in an Indian woman. Her example has no effect on the Indians, even her own family, with the exception of her own children. She has fifty *bee-hives* and a great supply of honey every year; has a fine stock of hogs, cattle and horses, and they all do well. Her son, Richard Bailey, was educated in Philadelphia by the Government, and he has brought with him into the nation so much contempt for the Indian mode of life, that he has got himself into discredit with them. His young brother is under the direction of the Quakers in Philadelphia. His three sisters promise to do well, they are industrious and can spin. Some of the Indians have cattle; but in general, they are destitute of property.

* January 1st, 1801. Mr. Cornells has a flock of sheep presented to him by the agent, of which he is very careful. His farm is in fine order, the fences well made and straight, his garden 150 feet square, well paled, laid off and planted with the variety usual in good gardens. He has a nursery of peach trees, and two bushels of peach stones to plant, by order of the agent, for a public nursery. He is very attentive to all improvements suggested to him, and has now pepared a field of two acres for cotton. He has a field of rye which looks well, and is about to sow a field of oats. He retains his Indian dress, but has the manners of a well bred man.

In the year 1766 there were forty-three gun men, and lately they were estimated at eighty. This is a much greater increase of population than is to be met with in other towns! they appear to be stationary generally, and in some towns are on the decrease; the apparent difference here, or increase, may be greater than the real; as formerly men grown were rated as gun men, and now boys of fifteen, who are hunters, are rated as gun men; they have for two years past been on the decline; are very sickly, and have lost many of their inhabitants; they are now rated at fifty gun men only.*

4. *Ho-ith-le Waule*, from Ho-ith-le, *war*, and wau-le, to *share out or divide.* This town had, formerly, the right to declare war; the declaration was sent first to Took-au-bat-che, and thence throughout the nation, and they appointed the rendezvous of the warriors. It is on the right bank of the Tallapoosa, five miles below Aut-tos-see. In descending the river on the left side from Aut-tos-see, is two miles across Ke-bi-hat-che; thence one mile and a half O-fuck-she, and enter the fields of the town; the fields extend down the river for one and a half miles; the town is on the right bank, on a narrow strip of good land; and back of it, under high red cliffs, are cypress ponds. It borders west on Autoshatche twenty-five feet wide.

These peeple have some cattle, and a few hogs and horses; they have some settlements up O-fuck-she; the increase of property among them, and the inconvenience attendant on their situation, their settlement being on the right side of the river, and their fields and stock on the left, brought the well-disposed to listen with attention to the plan of civilization, and to comment freely on their bad management. The town divided against itself; the idlers and the ill-disposed remained in the town, and the others moved over the river and fenced their fields. On this side the land is good and level, and the range out from the river good to the sources of O-fuc-she. On the other side, the high broken land comes close to the river. It is broken pine barren, back of that. The situation of the

* January 1st, 1801. Richard Bailey being dead, much of the Indian appears. The fifty bee-hives are reduced to one, and his son Richard is neither an Indian nor white man; yet he promises to mend, as the agent for Indian affairs is soon to reside in his neighborhood. The date to the calculation of numbers, is here noted from a British return, but it is probably erroneous.

town is low and unhealthy ; and this remark applies to all the towns on Tallapoosa, below the falls.

O-fuc-she has its source near Ko-e-ne-cuh, thirty miles from the river, and runs north. It has eight or nine forks, and the land is good on all of them. The growth is oak, hickory, poplar, cherry, persimon, with cane brakes on the flats and hills. It is a delightful range for stock, and was preserved by the Indians for bears, and called the beloved bear-ground. Every town had a reserve of this sort exclusively ; but as the cattle increase and the bears decrease, they are hunted in common. This creek is sixty feet wide, has steep banks, and is difficult to cross, when the waters are high.

Kebihatche has its source to the east, and is parallel with Ca-le-be-hat-che ; the margins of the creek have rich flats bordering pine forest or post oak hills.

5. *Foosce-hat-che ;* from foo-so-wau, a *bird,* and hat-che, *tail.* It is two miles below Ko-ith-le-wau-le, on the right bank of Tal-la-poo-sa, on a narrow strip of flat land ; the broken lands are just back of the town ; the cornfields are on the opposite side of the river, and are divided from those of Ho-ith-le-wau-le by a small creek, Noo-coose-chepo. On the right bank of this little creek, half a mile from the river, is the remains of a ditch, which sur-rounded a fortification, and back of this for a mile, is the appearance of old settlements, and back of these, pine slashes.

The cornfields are narrow, and extend down, bordering on the river.

6. *Coo-loo-me,* is below and near to Foosce-hat-che, on the right side of the river ; the town is small and com-pact, on a flat much too low, and subject to be overflowed in the seasons of floods, which is once in fifteen or six-teen years, always in the winter season, and mostly in March ; they have, within two years, begun to settle back, next to the broken lands ; the cornfields are on the oppo-site side, joining those of Foosce-hat-che, and extend to-gether near four miles down the river, from one hundred to two hundred yards wide. Back of these hills there is a rich swamp of from four to six hundred yards wide, which, when reclaimed, must be valuable for corn or rice,

5

and could be easily drained into the river, which seldom overflows its banks, in spring or summer.

They have no fences; they have huts in the fields to shelter the laborers in the summer season from rain, and for the guards set to watch the crops while they are growing. At this season some families move over and reside in their fields, and return with their crops into the town. There are two paths, one through the fields on the river bank, and the other back of the swamp. In the season for melons, the Indians of this town and Foosce-hat-che show in a particular manner their hospitality to all travellers, by calling to them, introducing them to their huts or the shade of their trees, and giving them excellent melons, and the best fare they possess. Opposite the town house, in the fields, is a conical mound of earth thirty feet in diameter, ten feet high, with large peach trees on several places. At the lower end of the fields, on the left bank of a fine little creek, Le-cau-suh, is a pretty little village of Coo-loo-me people, finely situated on a rising ground; the land up this creek is waving pine forest.

7. *E-cun-hut-ke;* from e-cun-nau, *earth,* and hut-ke, *white,* called by the traders *white ground.* This little town is just below Coo-loo-me, on the same side of the river, and five or six miles above Sam-bel-loh, a large fine creek which has its source in the pine hills to the north, and its whole course through broken pine hills. It appears to be a never-failing stream, and fine for mills; the fields belonging to this town, are on both sides of the river.

8. *Sau-wa-no-gee,* is on a pine forest, three miles below Le-cau-suh, and back from a swamp bordering on the river; their fields are on both sides of the river, but mostly on the left bank, between the swamp and the river, on a vein of rich canebrake land; they are the Shaw-a-nee, and retain the language and customs of their countrymen to the northwest, and aided them in their late war with the United States. Some Uchees have settled with them; they are industrious, work with their women and make plenty of corn; they have no cattle, and but few horses and hogs; the town house is an oblong square

cabin, roof eight feet pitch, the sides and roof covered with the bark of the pine; on the left side of the river.

9. *Mook-lau-sau*, is a small town one mile below Sau-va-noo-gee, on the left bank of a fine little creek, and bordering on a cypress swamp; their fields are below those of Sau-van-no-gee, bordering on the river; they have some lots about their houses fenced for potatoes; one chief has some cattle, horses and hogs; a few others have some cattle and hogs.

In the season of floods, the river spreads out on this side below the town, nearly eight miles from bank to bank, and is very destructive to game and stock.

10. *Coo-sau-dee*, is a compact little town situated three miles below the confluence of Coosau and Tallapoosa, on the right bank of Alabama; they have fields on both sides of the river; but their chief dependence is a high, rich island, at the mouth of Coosau. They have some fences, good against cattle only, and some families have small patches fenced, near the town, for potatoes.

These Indians are not Creeks, although they conform to their ceremonies; the men work with the women and make great plenty of corn; all labor is done by the oint labor of all, called public work, except gathering in the crop. During the seasen for labor, none are exempted from their share of it, or suffered to go out hunting.

There is a rich flat of land nearly five miles in width, opposite the town, on the left side of the river, on which are numbers of conic mounds of earth. Back of the town it is pine barren, and continues so westward for sixty to one hundred miles.

The Coo-sau-dee generally go to market by water, and some of them are good oarsmen. A part of this town moved lately beyond the Mississippi, and have settled there. The description sent back by them that the country is rich and healthy, and abounds in game, is likely to draw others after them. But as they have all tasted the sweets of civil life, in having a convenient market for their products, it is likely they will soon return to their old settlements, which are in a very desirable country, well suited to the raising of cattle, hogs and horses; they have a few hogs, and seventy or eighty cattle, and some horses. It is not more than three years since they had not a hog among them. Robert Walton, who was then the trader for the town, gave the women some pigs, and this is the origin of their stock.

There are four villages below this town on A-la-ba-ma, which had formerly a regular town ; they are probably the ancient A-la-ba-mas.

1st. *E-cun-chate ;* from E-cun-nā, *earth,* and chāte, *red.* A small village on the left bank of Alabama, which has its fields on the right side, in the cane swamp ; they are a poor people, without stock, are idle and indolent, and seldom make bread enough, but have fine melons in great abundance in their season. The land back from the settlement, is of thin quality, oak, hickory, pine and ponds. Back of this, hills, or waving. Here the soil is of good quality for cultivation ; that of thin quality extends nearly a mile.

2d. *Too-wos-sau,* is three miles below E-cun-chā-te, on the same side of the river, a small village on a high bluff; the land is good about, and back of the village ; they have some lots fenced with cane, and some with rails, for potatoes and ground nuts ; the corn is cultivated on the right side of the river, on rich cane swamps ; these people have a few hogs, but no other stock.

3rd. *Pau-woc-te ;* a small village two miles below Too-was-sau, on a high bluff, the same side of the river ; the land is level and rich, for five miles back ; but none of it is cultivated around their houses ; their fields are on the right bank of the river, on rich cane swamp ; they have a few hogs and horses, but no cattle ; they had, formerly, the largest and best breed of hogs in the nation, but have lost them by carelessness or inattention.

4th. *At-tau-gee ;* a small village four miles below Pau-woc-te, spread out for two miles on the right bank of the river ; they have fields on both sides, but their chief dependence is on the left side ; the land on the left side is rich ; on the right side the pine forest extends down to At-tau-gee creek ; below this creek the land is rich.

These people have very little intercourse with white people ; although they are hospitable, and offer freely any thing they have, to those who visit them. They have this singular custom, as soon as a white person has eaten of any dish and left it, the remains are thrown away, and every thing used by the guest immediately washed.

They have some hogs, horses and cattle, in a very fine range, perhaps the best on the river; the land to the east as far as Ko-e-ne-cuh, and except the plains, (Hi-yuc-pul-gee,) is well watered, with much canebrake, a very desirable country. On the west or right side, the good land extends about five miles, and on all the creeks below At-tau-gee, it is good; some of the trees are large poplar, red oak and hickory, walnut on the margins of the creeks, and pea-vine in the valleys.

These four villages have, in all, about eighty gun men; they do not conform to the customs of the Creeks, and the Creek law for the punishment of adultery is not known to them.

11. *Hook-choie;* on a creek of that name which joins on the left side of Ki-a-li-jce, three miles below the town, and seven miles south of thlo-tlo-gul-gau. The settlements extend along the creeks; on the margins of which and the hill sides, are good oak and hickory, with coarse gravel, all surrounded with pine forest.

12. *Hook-choie-oo-che;* a pretty little compact town, between O-che-au-po-fau and Tus-ke-gee, on the left bank of Coosau; the houses join those of Tus-ke-gee; the land around the town is a high, poor level, with highland ponds; the corn fields are on the left side of Tallapoosa, on rich low grounds, on a point called Sam-bel-loh, and below the mouth of the creek of that name which joins on the right side of the river.

They have a good stock of hogs, and a few cattle and horses; they formerly lived on the right bank of Coosau, just above their present site, and removed, lately, on account of the war with the Chickasaws. Their stock ranges on that side of the river; they have fenced all the small fields about their houses, where they raise their peas and potatoes; their fields at Sam-bel-loh, are under a good fence; this was made by Mrs. Durant, the oldest sister of the late General McGillivray, for her own convenience.

13. *Tus-ke-gee;* this little town is in the fork of the two rivers, Coo-sau and Tal-la-poo-sa, where formerly stood the French fort Toulouse. The town is on a bluff

on the Coo-sau, forty-six feet above low water mark; the rivers here approach each other within a quarter of a mile, then curve out, making a flat of low land of three thousand acres, which has been rich canebrake; and one-third under cultivation, in times past; the centre of this flat is rich oak and hickory, margined on both sides with rich cane swamp; the land back of the town, for a mile, is flat, a whitish clay; small pine, oak and dwarf hickory, then high pine forest.

There are thirty buildings in the town, compactly situated, and from the bluff a fine view of the flat lands in the fork, and on the right bank of Coosau, which river is here two hundred yards wide. In the yard of the town house, there are five cannon of iron, with the trunions broke off, and on the bluff some brickbats, the only remains of the French establishment here. There is one apple tree claimed by this town, now in possession of one of the chiefs of Book-choie-oo-che.

The fields are the left side of Tal-la-poo-sa, and there are some small patches well formed in the fork of the rivers, on the flat rich land below the bluff.

The Coosau extending itself a great way into the Cherokee country and mountains, gives scope for a vast accumulation of waters, at times. The Indians remark that once in fifteen or sixteen years, they have a flood, which overflows the banks, and spreads itself for five miles or more in width, in many parts of A-la-ba-ma. The rise is sudden, and so rapid as to drive a current up the Tal-la-poo-sa for eight miles. In January, 1796, the flood rose forty-seven feet, and spread itself for three miles on the left bank of the A-la-ba-ma. The ordinary width of that river, taken at the first bluff below the fork, is one hundred and fifty yards. This bluff is on the left side, and forty-five feet high. On this bluff are five conic mounds of earth, the largest thirty yards diameter at the base, and seventeen feet high; the others are smaller.

It has been for sometime a subject of enquiry, when, and for what purpose, these mounds were raised; here it explains itself as to the purpose; unquestionably they were intended as a place of safety to the people, in the time of these floods; and this is the tradition among the old people. As these Indians came from the other side of the Mississippi, and that river spreads out on that side for a great distance, it is probable, the erection of mounds originated there; or from the custom of the Indians heretofore, of settling on rich flats bordering on the rivers, and subject to be overflowed. The name is *o-cun-li-ge*, mounds of earth, or literally, *earth placed.* But why erect these mounds in high places, incontestably out of the reach of floods? From a superstitious veneration for ancient customs.

The Alabama overflows its flat swampy margins, annually; and, generally, in the month of March, but seldom in the summer season.

The people of Tuskogee have some cattle, and a fine stock of hogs, more perhaps than any town of the nation. One man, Sam Macnack, a half breed, has a fine stock of cattle. He had, in 1799, one hundred and eighty calves. They have lost their language, and speak Creek, and have adopted the customs and manners of the Creeks. They have thirty-five gun men.

14. *O-che-au-po-fau;* from Oche-ub, a *hickory tree,* and po-fau, *in, or among,* called by the traders, *hickory ground.* It is on the left bank of the Coosau, two miles above the fork of the river, and one mile below the falls, on a flat of poor land, just below a small stream; the fields are on the right side of the river, on rich flat land; and this flat extends back for two miles, with oak and hickory, then pine forest; the range out in this forest is fine for cattle; reed is abundant in all the branches.

The falls can be easily passed in canoes, either up or down; the rock is very different from that of Tallapoosa; here it is ragged and very coarse granite; the land bordering on the left side of the falls, is broken or waving, gravelly, not rich. At the termination of the falls there is a fine little stream, large enough for a small mill, called, from the clearness of the water, We-hemt-le, *good water.* Three and a half miles above the town are ten apple trees, planted by the late General McGillivray; half a mile further up are the remains of Old Tal-e-see, formerly the residence of Lochlan McGillivray and his son, the general. Here are ten apple trees planted by the father, and a stone chimney, the remains of a house built by the son, and these are all the improvements left by the father and son.

These people, are some of them, industrious. They have forty gun men, nearly three hundred cattle, and some horses and hogs; the family of the general belong to this town; he left one son and two daughters; the son is in Scotland, with his grandfather, and the daughters with Sam Mac-nac, a half breed, their uncle; the property is much of it wasted. The chiefs have requested the agent for Indian affairs, to take charge of the property for the son, to prevent its being wasted by the sisters of the general, or by their children. Mrs. Durant, the oldest sister, has eight children. She is industrious but has no economy or management. In possession of fourteen working negroes, she seldom makes bread enough, and they live poorly. She can spin and weave, and is making some feeble efforts to obtain clothing for her family. The other sister, Sehoi, has about thirty negroes, is extravagant and heedless, neither spins nor weaves, and has no government of her family. She has one son, David Tale, who has been educated in Philadelphia and Scotland. He promises to do better.

15. *We-wo-cau;* from we-wau, *water* and wo-cau, *barking or roaring*, as the sound of water at high falls. It lies on a creek of the same name, which joins Guc-cun-tal-lau-has-see, on its left bank, sixteen miles below that town. We-wo-cau is fifteen miles above O-che-au-po-fau and four miles from Coosau, on the left side; the land is broken, oak and hickory, with coarse gravel; the settlements are spread out, on several small streams, for the advantage of the rich flats bordering on them, and for their stock; they have cattle, horses and hogs. Here commences the moss, in the beds of the creeks, which the cattle are very fond of; horses and cattle fatten very soon on it, with a little salt; it is of quick growth, found only in the rocky beds of the creeks and rivers north from this.

The hills which surround the town are stoney, and unfit for culture; the streams all have reed, and there are some fine licks near the town, where it is conjectured salt might be made. The land on the right side of the creek, is poor pine barren hills, to the falls. The number of gun men is estimated at forty.

16. *Puc-cun-tal-lau-has-see ;* from E-puc cun-nau, a *may-apple,* and tal-lau-has-see, *old town.* It is in the fork of a creek which gives name to the town ; the creek joins on the left side of Coosau, forty miles below Coosau town.

17. *Coo-sau ;* on the left bank of Coo-sau, between two creeks, Eu-fau-lau and Nau-che. The town borders on the first, above ; and on the other below ; they are a quarter of a mile apart at their junction with the river. The town is on a high and beautiful hill ; the land on the river is rich and flat for two hundred yards, then waving and rich, fine for wheat and corn. It is a limestone coun-try, with fine springs, and a very desirable one ; there is reed on the branches, and pea-vine in the rich bottoms and hill sides, moss in the river and on the rock beds of the creek.

They get fish plentifully in the spring season, near the mouth of Eu-fau-lau-hat-che ; they are rock, trout, buf-faloe, red horse and perch. They have fine stocks of horses, hogs and cattle ; the town gives name to the river, and is sixty miles above Tus-ke-gee.

18. *Au-be-coo-che,* is on Nau-che creek, five miles from the river, on the right bank of the creek, on a flat one mile wide. The growth is hard-shelled hickory. The town spreads itself out and is scattered on both sides of the creek, in the neighborhood of very high hills, which descend back into waving, rich land, fine for wheat or corn ; the bottoms all rich ; the neighborhood abounds in limestone, and large limestone springs ; they have one above, and one below the town ; the timber on the rich lands is oak, hickory, walnut, poplar and mulberry.

There is a very large cave north of the town, the en-trance of which is small, on the side of a hill. It is much divided, and some of the rooms appear as the work of art ; the doors regular ; in several parts of the cave saltpetre is to be seen in crystals. On We-wo-cau creek, there is a fine mill seat ; the water is contracted by two hills ; the fall twenty feet ; and the land in the neighbor-hood very rich ; cane is found on the creeks, and reed on the branches. From one or two experiments, tobacco grows well on these lands.

6

This town is one of the oldest in the nation; and sometimes, among the oldest chiefs, it gives name to the nation, Au-be-cuh. Here some of the oldest customs had
their origin. The law against adultery was passed here,
and that to regulate marriages. To constitute legal marriage, a man must build a house, make his crop and gather
it in, then make his hunt and bring home the meat; putting all this in the possession of his wife, ends the ceremony
and they are married, or as the Indians express it, the
woman is bound, and not till then. This information is
obtained from Co-tau-lau, (Tus-se-ki-ah Mic-co,) an old
and respectable chief, descended from Nau-che. He lives
near We-o-coof-ke, has accumulated a handsome property, owns a fine stock, is a man of much information,
and of great influence among the Indians of the towns
in the neighberhood of this.

They have no fences, and but a few hogs, horses and
cattle; they are attentive to white people who live among
them, and particularly so to white women.

19. *Nau-chee;* on Nauchee creek, five miles ahove Au-
be-coo-che, below the fork of the creek, on a rich flat
of land, of a mile in width, between two small mountains.
This flat extends from the town three-quarters of a mile
above the town house. The settlements are scattered on
both sides of the creek for two miles; they have no worm
fences, and but little stock. One chief, a brother of
Chin-a-be, has a large stock of hogs, and had ninety fit
for market, in 1798.

This town is the remains of the Nat-chez who lived on
the Mis-sis-sip-pi. They estimate their number of gun
men at one hundred; but they are, probably, not more
than fifty. The land, off from the mountains, is rich; the
flats on the streams are large and very rich; the high,
waving country is very healthy and well watered; cane
grows on the creeks, reed on the branches, and pea-vine
on the flats and hill sides. The Indians get the root they
call tal-e-wau, in this neighborhood; which the women
mix with bears' oil, to redden their hair.

20. *Eu-fau-lau-hat-che,* is fifteen miles up that creek,
on a flat of half a mile, bordering on a branch. On the
left side of the creek, the land is rich and waving; on
the right sides are steep hills sloping off, waving, rich

land; hickory, oak, poplar and walnut. It is well watered, and the whole a desirable limestone country; they have fine stocks of cattle, horses and hogs.

21. *Woc-co-coie;* from woc-co, a *blow-horn*, and coie, a *nest*, these birds formerly had their young here. It is on Tote-pauf-cau creek, a branch of Po-chuse-hat-che, which joins the Coo-sau, below Puc-cun-tal-lau-has-see. The land is very broken, sharp-hilly and stoney; the bottoms and the fields are on the small bends and narrow strips of the creek; the country, off from the town, is broken.

These people have some horses, hogs and cattle; the range good; moss, plenty in the creeks, and reed in the branches. Such is the attachment of horses to this moss, or as the traders call it, salt grass, that when they are removed, they retain so great a fondness for it, that they will attempt, from any distance within the neighboring nations, to return to it.

22. *Hill-au-bee;* on Col-luffa-de, which joins Hill-au-bee creek, on the right side, one mile below the town. Hill-au-bee joins the Tallapoosa on its right bank, eight miles below New-yau-cau. One chief only, Ne-hau-thluc-co Hau-jo, resides in the town; the people are settled out in the four following villages.

1st. *Thlă-noo-che au-bau-lau;* from thlen-ne, a *mountain*, oo-che, *little*, and au-bau-lau, *over*. The name is expressive of its position. It is situated over a little mountain, fifteen miles above the town, on the northwest branch of Hill-au-bee creek; the town house of this village is on the left side of the creek.

2d. *Au-net-te ·chap-co;* from au-net-te, a *swamp*, and chapco, *long*. It is situated on Choo-fun-tau-lau-hat-che, which joins Hill-au-bee creek, three miles north from the town; the village is ten miles above the town.

3rd. *E-chuse-is-li-gau;* (where a young thing was found.) A young child was found here, and that circumstance gives it the name. This village is four miles below the town, on the left side of Hill-au-bee creek.

4th. *Ook-tau-hau-zau-see;* from ook-tau-hau, *sand*, and zau-see, *a great deal*. It is two miles from the town, on a creek of that name, a branch of Hill-au-bee, which it joins a quarter of a mile below Col-luffa-dee, at a great shoal.

The land on these creeks, within the scope of the four villages, is broken and stoney, with coarse gravel; the bottoms and small bends of the creeks and branches, are rich. The upland is generally stiff, rich and fit for culture. Post oak, black oak, pine and hickory, all small, are the growth. The whole abounds in veins of reeds, and reedy branches. They call this the winter reed, as it clusters like the cane.

The villages are badly fenced, the Indians are attentive to their traders; and several of them are careful of stock, and have cattle and hogs, and some few have horses. Four half breeds have fine stocks of cattle. Thomas has one hundred and thirty cattle and ten horses. Au-wil-au-gee, the wife of O-pi-o-che-tus-tun-nug-gee, has seven cattle. These Indians promised the agent, in 1799, to begin and fence their fields; they have one hundred and seventy gun men in the four villages.

Robert Grierson, the trader, a native of Scotland, has by a steady conduct, contributed to mend the manners of these people. He has five children, half breeds, and governs them as Indians, and makes them and his whole family respect him, and is the only man who does so, in the Upper Creeks. He has three hundred cattle and thirty horses; he has, on the recommendation of the agent for Indian affairs, set up a manufactory of cotton cloth; he plants the green-seed cotton, it being too cold for the black-seed. He has raised a quantity for market, but finds it more profitable to manufacture it; he has employed an active girl of Georgia, Rachael Spillard, who was in the Cherokee department, to superintend, and allows her two hundred dollars per annum. He employs eleven hands, red, white and black, in spinning and weaving, and the other part of his family in raising and preparing the cotton for them. His wife, an Indian woman, spins, and is fond of it; and he has a little daughter who spins well. He employs the Indian women to gather in the cotton from the fields, and has expectations of prevailing on them to take an active part in spinning.

Hill-au-bee creek has a rocky bottom, covered in many places with moss. In the spring of the year, the cattle of the villages crowd after it, and are fond of it. From thence they are collected together by their owners, to mark and brand the young ones.

The climate is mild ; the water seldom freezes ; they have mast every other year, and peaches for the three last years. The range is a good one for stock. The owners of horses have a place called a *stomp.* They select a place of good food, cut down a tree or two, and make salt logs. Here the horses gather of themselves, in the fly season. They have in the villages a few thriving peach trees, and there is much gravelly land, which would be fine for them.

23. *Oc-fus-kee ;* from Oc, *in,* and fuskee, *a point.* The name is expressive of the position of the old town, and where the town house now stands on the right bank of Tal-la-poo-sa. The town spreads out on both sides of the river, and is about thirty-five miles above Took-au-bat-che. The settlers on the left side of the river, are from Chat-to-ho-che. They once formed three well settled villages on that river. Che-luc-co ne-ne, Ho-ith-le-ti-gau and Chau-kethluc-co.

Oc-fus-kee with its villages, is the largest town in the nation. They estimate the number of gun men of the old town, at one hundred and eighty ; and two hundred and seventy in the villages or small towns. The land is flat for half a mile on the river, and fit for culture ; back of this, there are sharp, stoney hills, the growth is pine, and the branches all have reed.

They have no fences around the town ; they have some cattle, hogs and horses, and their range is a good one ; the shoals in the river afford a great supply of moss, called by the traders salt grass ; and the cows which frequent these shoals, are the largest and finest in the nation ; they have some peach trees in the town, and the cassine yupon, in clumps. The Indians have lately moved out and settled in villages, and the town will soon be an old field ; the settling out in villages, has been repeatedly pressed by the agent for Indian affairs, and with considerable success ; they have seven villages belonging to this town.

1st. *New-yau-cau ;* named after New York. It is on the left bank of Tallapoosa, twenty miles above Oc-fus-kee ; these people lived formerly at Tote-pauf-cau, (spunk-knot,) on Chat-to-ho-che, and moved from thence in 1777.

They would not take part in the war between the United States and Great Britain, and determined to retire from their settlements, which, through the rage of war, might feel the effects of the resentment of the people of the United States, when roused by the conduct of the red people, as they were placed between the combatants. The town is on a flat, bordering on the river; the adjoining lands are broken or waving and stony; on the opposite side they are broken, stony; the growth is pine, oak and hickory. The flat strips of land on the river, above and below, are generally narrow; the adjoining land is broken, with oak, hickory and pine. The branches all have reed; they have a fine ford at the upper end of the town; the river is one hundred and twenty yards wide. Some of the people have settled out from the town, and they have good land on Inn-nook-fau creek, which joins the right side of the river, two miles below the town.

2d. *Took-au-bat-che tal-lau-has-see;* this village received in part a new name in 1797. Tal-lo-wau mu-chos-see, (new town.) It is on the right bank of the river, four miles above New-yau-cau; the land around it is broken and stony; off from the river the hills are waving; and post oak, hard shelled hickory, pine, and on the ridges, chesnut is the growth.

3rd. *Im-mook-fau;* (a gorget made of a conch.) This village is four miles west from Tookaubatche Tal-lau-has-see, on Immookfau creek, which joins the right side of Tallapoosa, two miles below New-yau-cau. The settlers are from Thu-le-oc-who-cat-lau and Sooc-he-ah; they have fine rich flats on the creek, and a good range for their cattle; they possess some hogs, cattle and horses, and begin to be attentive to them.

4th. *Tooh-to-cau-gee;* from tooh-to, *a corn house,* and cau-gee, *fixed or standing.* The Indians of Oc-fus-kee, formerly built a corn house here, for the convenience of their hunters, and put their corn there for their support, during the hunting season. It is on the right bank of Tallapoosa, twenty miles above New-yau-cau; the settlements are on the narrow flat margins of the river, on both sides. On the left side the mountains terminate here, the uplands are too poor and broken for cultivation; the path from E-tow-wah, in the Cherokee country, over the tops of these mountains, is a pretty good one. It winds down the mountains to this village ;· the river is here one hundred and twenty yards wide, a beautiful clear stream. On the right side, off from the river flats, the land is waving, with oak, hickory and pine, gravelly, and in some places large sheets of rock which wave as the land. The grit is coarse, but some of it is fit for mill stones; the land is good for corn, the trees are all small, with some chesnut on the ridges ; the range is a good one for stock ; reed is found on all the branches ; on the path to New-yau-cau, there is some large rock ; the vein lies south-west ; they are in two rows parallel with each other, and the land good in their neighborhood

5th. *Au-che-nau-ul-gau ;* from Au-che-nau, *cedar ;* and ul-gau, *all ; a cedar grove.* These settlers are from Loo-chau po-gau, (the resort of terrapins.) It is on a creek, near the old town, forty miles above New-yau-cau. This settlement is the farthest north of all the Creeks ; the land is very broken in the neighborhood. West of this village a few miles, there are large reedy glades in flat land ; red, post and black oak, all small ; the soil is dark and stiff, with coarse gravel, and in some places stone ; from the color of the earth in places, there must be iron ore ; the streams from the glades form fine little creeks, branches of the Tallapoosa. The land on their borders is broken, stiff, stony and rich, affording fine mill seats, and on the whole it is a country where the Indians might have desir-able settlements ; the path from E-tow-woh to Hill-au-bee passes through these glades.

6th. *E-pe-sau-gee ;* this village is on a large creek which gives name to it, and enters the Tallapoosa, opposite Oc-fus-kee. The creek has its source in the ridge, dividing the waters of this river from Chat-to-ho-che ; it is thirty yards wide, and has a rocky bottom ; they have forty settlers in the village, who have fenced their fields this season, for the benefit of their stock, and they have all of them cattle, hogs and horses. They have some good land on the creek, but generally it is broken, the strips of flat land are narrow; the broken is gravelly, with oak, hickory and pine, not very inviting. Four of these vil-lages have valuable stocks of cattle. McCartney has one hundred ; E·cun-chā-te E-maut-lau, one hundred ; Tote-cuh Haujo, one hundred, and Tools Micco, two hundred.

7th. *Sooc-he-ah ;* from Sooc-cau, *a hog ;* and heah, *here,* called by the traders, *hog range.* It is situated on the right bank of Tallapoosa, twelve miles above Oc-fus-kee. It is a small settlement ; the land is very broken ; the flats on the river are narrow ; the river broad and shoally. These settlers have moved, and joined Immookfau, with a few exceptions.

24. *Eu-fau-lau ;* on the right bank of Tallapoosa, five miles below Oc-fus-kee, on that side of the river, and but two in a direct line ; the lands on the river are fit for cul-ture ; but the flats are narrow, joined to pine hills and reedy branches.

They have hogs and cattle, and the range is a good one ; they have moss in the shoals of the river ; there are, belonging to this town, seventy gun men, and they have begun to settle out for the benefit of their stock. This season, some of the villagers have fenced their fields. They have some fine land on Hat-che-lus-ta, and several settlements there but no fences ; this creek joins the right side of the river, two miles below the town. On Woc-cau E-hoo-te, this year, 1799, the villagers, five fami-lies in all, have fenced their fields, and they have prom-ised the agent to use the plough the next season. On black creek, Co-no-fix-ico has one hundred cattle, and makes butter and cheese. John Townshend, the trader of the town, is an honest Englishman, who has resided many years in the nation, and raised a numerous family, who conduct themselves well. His daughters, who are married, conduct themselves well, have stocks of cattle, are attentive to them, make butter and cheese, and prom-ise to raise cotton and learn to spin. The principal cattle holders are, Conofixico, who has one hundred ; Choc-lo Emautlau's stock is on the decline, thirty ; Well Geddis Taupixa Micco, one hundred ; Co Emautlau, four hun-dred, under careful management. John Townshend, one hundred and forty, and Sally, his daughter, fifty.

25. *Ki-a-li-jee ;* on the right side of Kialijee creek, two and a half miles below the junction with Hook-choie. This creek joins the right side of Tallapoosa, above the falls ; all the rich flats of the creek are settled ; the land

about the town is poor and broken; the fields are on the narrow flats, and in the bends of the creek; the broken land is gravelly or stony; the range for cattle, hogs and horses, is the poorest in the nation; the neighborhood of the town and the town itself, has nothing to recommend it. The timber is pine, oak and small hickory; the creek is fifteen feet wide, and joins Tallapoosa fifteen miles above Took-au-bat-che. They have two villages belonging to this town.

1st. *Au-che-nau-hat-che;* from au-che, *cedar;* and hat-che, *a creek.* They have a few settlements on this creek, and some fine, thriving peach trees; the land on the creek is broken, but good.

2d. *Hat-che chub-bau;* from hat-che, *a creek;* and chub-bau, *the middle,* or *half way.* This is in the pine forest, a poor, ill-chosen site, and there are but a few people.

The remaining villages of the towns on Coosau and Tallapoosa.

1st. *Sou-go-hat-che;* from sou-go, *a cymbal;* and hat-che, *a creek.* This joins on the left side of Tallapoosa, ten miles below Eu-fau-lau. It is a large creek, and the land on the forks and to their sources, is stiff in places, and stony. The timber is red oak and small hickory; the flats on the streams are rich, covered with reed; among the branches the land is waving and fit for cultivation.

They have thirty gun men in this village, who have lately joined Tal-e-see. One of the chiefs. O-fau-mul-gau, has some cattle, others have a few, as they have only paid attention to their stock within two years, and their means for acquiring them were slender.

Above this creek, on the waters of Eu-fau-lau-hat-che, there are some settlements well chosen. The upland is stiff and stony or gravelly; the timber is post and red oak, pine and hickory; the trees are small; the soil apparently rich enough, and well suited for wheat, and the streams have some rich flats.

2d. *Thlot-lo-gul-gau;* from thlot-lo, *fish;* and ul-gau, *all;* called by the traders fish ponds. It is on a small, pond-like creek, a branch of Ul-kau-hat-che, which joins Tallapoosa four miles above Ocfuskee, on the right side. The town is fourteen miles up the creek; the land about

7

it is open and waving; the soil is dark and gravelly; the general growth of trees is the small hickory; they have reed in the branches.

Hannah Hale resides here. She was taken a prisoner from Georgia, when about eleven or twelve years old, and married the head man of this town, by whom she has five children. This woman spins and weaves, and has taught two of her daughters to spin; she has labored under many difficulties; yet by her industry has acquired some property. She has one negro boy, a horse or two, sixty cattle, and some hogs; she received the friendly attention of the agent for Indian affairs, as soon as he came in the nation. He furnished her with a wheel, loom, and cards; she has an orchard of peach and apple trees. Having made her election at the national council, in 1799, to reside in the nation, the agent appointed Hopoithle Haujo to look out for a suitable place for her, to help her to remove to it with her stock, and take care that she receives no insults from the Indians.

3d. *O-pil-thluc-co;* from O-pil-lo-wau, *a swamp;* and thluc-co, *big.* It is situated on a creek of that name, which joins Puc-cun-tal-lau-has-see on the left side. It is twenty miles from Coosau river; the land about this village is round, flat hills, thickets of hickory saplins, and on the hill sides and their tops, hickory grub and grape vines. The land bordering on the creek is rich, and here are their fields.

4th. *Pin-e-hoo-te;* from pin-e-wau, a *turkey;* and choo-te, *house.* It is on the right side of a fine little creek, a branch of E-pee-sau-gee. The land is stiff and rich, and lies well; the timber is red oak and hickory; the branches all have reed, and the land on them, above the settlement, is good black oak, saplin and hickory. This, and the neighboring land, is fine for settlement; they have here three or four houses only, some peach trees and hogs, and their fields are fenced. The path from New-yau-cau to Cou-e-tuh-tal-lau-has-see passes by these houses.

5th. *Po-chuse-hat-che;* from po-chu-so-wau, a *hatchet,* and hat-che, *a creek.* This creek joins Coosau, four miles below Puc-cun-tal-lau-has-see, on its right bank; this village is high up the creek, nearly forty miles from its mouth, on a flat bend on the right side of the creek; the settlements extend up and down the creek for a mile. A mile and a half above the settlements there is a large canebrake, three-quarters of a mile through, and three or four miles in length.

The land adjoining the settlement is waving and rich, with oak, hickory, and poplar. The branches all have reed; the neighboring lands above these settlements, are fine; those below, are high, broken hills. It is situated between Hill-au-bee and Woc-co-coie, about ten miles from each town; three miles west of the town, there is a small mountain; they have some hogs.

6th. *Oc-fus-coo-che;* (little Ocfuskee;) is a part of the small village, four miles above New-yau-cau. Some of these people lived at Oc-fus-kee-nene, on the Chat-to-ho-che, from whence they were driven by an enterprising volunteer party from Georgia, the 27th September, 1793.

The towns classed, and a Commander appointed over each class.

At a meeting of the national council, convened by order of the agent for Indian affairs, at Tookaubatche, the 27th November, 1799, the chiefs, after a long and solemn deliberation, on the affairs of the nation, which were laid before them by the agent for Indian affairs, came to a resolution to adopt the plan of the agent, " to class all the towns, and to appoint a warrior over each class, denominated the warrior of the nation."

The towns thus classed, with the warriors for the nation, are :—

1st. Hook-choie, We-wo-cau, Puc-cun-tal-lau-has-see, O-pil-thluc-co and Thlot-lo-gul-gau. For these five towns they appointed Sim-mo-me-jee of Wewocau.

2d. Ki-a-li-jee and Eu-fau-lau. For these two towns, they appointed E-maut-lau Hut-ke.

3d. Hill-au-bĕe, Woc-co-coie and Pochusehatche. For these three towns they appointed Cussetuh Tus-tun-nug-gee, of Hill-au-bee, and Thle-chum-me Tustunnuggee, of Woc-co-coie.

4th. Au-bee-coo-che, Nau-che, Coosau and Eu-fau-lau-hat-che. For these four towns, they appointed Olohtau Haujo.

5th. Ho-ith-le-wau-le, Ecunhutke, Sauvanogee, Mook-lau-sau and Took-au-bat-che. For these five towns, they appointed O-poie E-maut-lau, of Ho-ith-le-wau-le.

These five classes comprise the towns called Ke-pau-yau, or warriors of the nation. But on the present occasion, when their existence as a nation depends on their ability to carry the laws into effect, the chiefs assembled unanimously agreed that the E-tall-wau, *white towns*, should be classed as warriors.

6th. Oc-fus-kee and its villages, Sooc-he-ah, New-yau-cau, Im-mook-fau, Took-au-bat-che, Tal-lau-has-see, Took-to-cau-gee, Au-che-nau-ulgau, Oc-fus-coo-che and E-pe-sau-gee. For this town and its villages, they appointed Hopoie Tus-tun-nug-gee, of Oc-fus-kee, and Tal-lo-wau-thlucco Tus-tun-nug-gee.

7th. O-che-au-po-fau and Tus-kee-gee. For these two towns, they appointed Ho-po-ithle Ho-poie.

8th. Tal-e-see, Aut-tos-see, Foosce-hat-che and Coo-loo-me. For these four towns, they appointed Foosce-hat-che Tus-tun-nug-gee, of Tal-e-see, and Eu-fau-lau Tus-tun-nug-gee, of Foosce-hat-che.

9th. Hook-choie-oo-che, Coo-sau-dee, E-cun-chá-te, Too-wos-sau, Pau-woc-te, and At-tau-gee. For these towns and villages, they appointed Ho-ith-le-poie Hau-jo and Tus-tun-nuc, of Hook-choie-oo-che.

6 and 8 are E-tall-wau, or white towns.

The towns on Chat-to-ho-che, generally called the Lower Creeks.

The name of this river is from Chat-to, *a stone;* and ho-che, *marked or flowered;* there being rocks of that description in the river, above Ho-ith-le-ti-gau, at the old town Chat-to-ho-che.

1. *Cow-e-tugh;* on the right bank of Chat-to-ho-che, three miles below the falls, on a flat extending back one mile. The land is fine for corn; the settlements extend up the river for two miles on the river flats. These are bordered with broken pine land; the fields of the settlers who reside in the town, are on a point of land formed by a bend of the river, a part of them adjoining the point, are low, then a rise of fifteen feet, spreading back for

half a mile, then another rise of fifteen feet, and flat a half a mile to a swamp adjoining the high lands; the fields are below the town.

The river is one hundred and twenty yards wide, with a deep steady current from the fall; these are over a rough, coarse rock, forming some islands of rock, which force the water into two narrow channels, in time of low water. One is on each side of the river, in the whole about ninety feet wide; that on the right is sixty feet wide, with a perpendicular fall of twelve feet; the other of thirty feet wide, is a long sloping curve, very rapid, the fall fifteen feet in one hundred and fifty feet; fish may ascend in this channel, but it is too swift and strong for boats; here are two fisheries; one on the right belongs to this town; that on the left, to the Cussetuhs; they are at the termination of the falls; and the fish are taken with scoop nets; the fish taken here are, the hickory shad, rock, trout, perch, cat fish, and suckers; there is sturgeon in the river, but no white shad or herring; during spring and summer, they catch the perch and rock with hooks. As soon as the fish make their appearance, the chiefs send out the women, and make them fish for the *square.* This expression includes all the chiefs and warriors of the town.

The land on the right bank of the river at the falls, is a poor pine barren, to the water's edge; the pines are small; the falls continue three or four miles nearly of the same width, about one hundred and twenty yards; the river then expands to thrice that width, the bottom being gravelly, shoal and rocky; there are several small islands within this scope; one at the part where the expansion commences is rich and some part of it under cultivation; it is half a mile in length, but narrow; here the river is fordable; enter the left bank one hundred yards above the upper end of the island, and cross over to it, and down to the fields, thence cross the other channel; at the termination of the falls, a creek twenty feet wide, (O-cow-ocuh-hat-che, *falls creek,*) joins the right side of the river. Just below this creek, and above the last reef of rocks, is another ford. The current is rapid, and the bottom even.

In ascending the river on this side, on the river path,

travelling at the rate of three miles the hour, the following distances are noted.

1h. 3um.   Cross a creek running to the right, three feet wide. The land, the whole distance, is poor, broken and unfit for culture.

12m.   Some settlements on the river bank, at We-at-lo-tuck-e. The land is stiff and rich.

58m.   Cross Hătche Cănănc, (crooked creek,) running to the right, ten feet wide; the land stiff and good; oak, hickory, and a few poplar.

39m.   Chat-to-hat-che, (stony creek,) running to the right ten feet wide; the land broken and poor. There is one settlement on the path, and one at the creek.

49m.   Woc-coo-che, (calf creek,) over broken land; pine, willow-leaved hickory, and post oak; the land bordering on the creek is rich; there is one plantation, on the left bank, under fence, and some peach trees around the houses. The creek is forty feet wide and runs to the right.

41m.   To a creek running to the right, bordered with fine winter reed.

55.   Hal-e-woc-ke, sixty feet wide, running to the right. One plantation on the left bank of the creek; the land broken, chesnut, pine, post oak, hickory, and red oak.

27m.   To a branch running to the right.

8m.   A reedy branch running to the right, the land rich.

3m.   A branch, reedy, running to the right.

11m.   A reedy branch running to the right.

17m.   O-sun-nup-pau, (moss creek,) sixty feet wide, running to the right. The bottom rocky with moss; the land for this stage is broken; a mixed growth of post and red oak, pine and hickory.

On the left bank of the river at the falls, the land is level; and in approaching them one is surprised to find them where there is no alteration in the trees or unevenness of land. This level continues back one mile to the poor pine barren, and is fine for corn or cotton; the timber is red oak, hickory and pine; the banks of the river on this side below the falls are fifty feet high, and continue so, down below the town house; the flat of good land continues still lower to Hat-che thluc-co, (big creek.) Ascending the river on this bank, above the falls, the the following stages are noted in miles.

2½ miles, the flat land terminates; thence

3½ miles, to Chis-se hul-cuh running to the left; thence

4 miles, to Chusse thluc-co twenty feet wide, a rocky bottom.

5 miles, to Ke-tã-le, thirty feet wide, a bold, shoally, rocky creek, abounding in moss. Four miles up this creek, there is a village of ten families, at Hat-che Uxau, (head of a creek.) The land is broken with hickory, pine and chesnut; there is cane on the borders of the creek and reed on the branches; there are some settlements of Cowetuh people made on these creeks; all who have settled out from the town, have fenced their fields, and begin to be attentive to their stock.

The town has a temporary fence of three poles, the first on forks, the other two on stakes, good against cattle only; the town fields are fenced in like manner; a few of the neighboring fields, detached from the town, have good fences; the temporary, three pole fences of the town, are made every spring, or repaired in a slovenly manner.

Mr. Marshall, the trader here, has set up a manufactory of cotton cloth, at the recommendation of the agent; the cotton raised by him the last season, is fine; it is the green-seed; the experiment was commenced with the green-seed, and this year the black-seed of the seacoast has been tried; it is very good, but the season too short for it, although there was no frost this year, 1799, till the 13th of November. In light, rich, sandy land it will certainly succeed. The traders here adopted with spirit, the plan of the government; they have made gardens, fenced their fields, and they have this year raised wheat, rye, and barley.

2. Cow-e-tuh Tal-lau-has-see; from Cow-e-tuh, Tal-lo-fau, *a town;* and hasse, *old.* It is two and a half miles below Cowetuh, on the right bank of the river. In going down the path between the two towns, in half a mile cross Kotes-ke-le-jau, ten feet wide, running to the left is a fine

little creek sufficiently large for a mill, in all but the dry seasons. On the right bank, enter the flat lands between the towns. These are good, with oak, hard-shelled hickory and pine ; they extend two miles to Che-luc-in-te-getuh, a small creek five feet wide, bordering on the town. The town is half a mile from the river, on the right bank of the creek ; it is on a high flat, bordered on the east by the flats of the river, and west by high broken hills ; they have but a few settlers in the town ; the fields are on a point of land three-quarters of a mile below the town, which is very rich, and has been long under cultivation ; they have no fence around their fields.

Here is the public establishment for the Lower Creeks ; and here the agent resides. He has a garden well cultivated and planted, with a great variety of vegetables, fruits and vines, and an orchard of peach trees. Arrangements have been made, to fence two hundred acres of land fit for cultivation, and to introduce a regular husbandry to serve as a model and stimulus, for the neighboring towns who crowd the public shops here, at all seasons, when the hunters are not in the woods.

The agent entertains doubts, already, of succeeding here in establishing a regular husbandry, from the difficulty of changing the old habits of indolence, and sitting daily in the squares, which seem peculiarly attractive to the residenters of the towns. In the event of not succeeding, he intends to move the establishment out from the town, and aid the villagers where success seems to be infallible.

They estimate their number of gun men at one hundred ; but the agent has ascertained, by actual enumeration, that they have but sixty-six, including all who reside here, and in the villages belonging to the town.

They have a fine body of land below, and adjoining the town, nearly two thousand acres, all well timbered ; and including the whole above and below, they have more than is sufficient for the accommodation of the whole town ; they have one village belonging to the town, We-tumcau.

We-tum-cau ; from we-wau, *water ;* and tum-cau, *rumbling.* It is the main branch of U-chee creek, and is twelve miles northwest from the town. These people have a small town house on a poor pine ridge on the left bank of the creek below the falls; the settlers extend up the creek for three miles, and they cultivate the rich bends of the creek; there is cane on the creek and fine reed on the branches; the land higher up the creek, and on its branches is waving, with pine, oak, and hickory, fine for cultivation, on the flats and out from the branches; the range is good for stock, and some of the settlers have cattle and hogs, and begin to be attentive to them; they have been advised to spread out their settlements on the waters of this creek, and to increase their attention to stock of every kind.

3. *Cus-se-tuh;* this town is two and a half miles below Cow-e-tuk Tal-lau-has-see, on the left bank of the river. They claim the land above the falls on their side. In descending the river path from the falls, in three miles you cross a creek running to the right, twenty feet wide; this creek joins the river a quarter of a mile above the Cowetuh town house; the land to this creek, is good and level, and extends back from the river from half to three-quarters of a mile to the pine forest; the growth on the level, is oak, hickory and pine; there are some ponds and slashes back next to the pine forest, bordering on a branch which runs parallel with the river; in the pine forest there is some reedy branches.

The creek has its source nearly twenty miles from the river, and runs nearly parallel with it till within one mile of its junction; there it makes a short bend round north, thence west to the river; at the second bend, about two hundred yards from the river, a fine little spring creek joins on its right bank; at the first bend north there is a mill seat; the water might here be stopped with a dam, and taken across by a canal, at a little expense of labor, to the river, and the mills might be either here or at the river. About one mile up from the bend, there is another good mill seat in the neighborhood of the pine forest.

The flat of good land on the river continues two and a half miles below this creek, through the Cussetuh fields to Hat-che-thluc-co. At the entrance of the fields on the right, there is an oblong mound of earth; one quarter of a mile lower, there is a conic mound forty-five yards in diameter at the base, twenty-five feet high, and flat on the

8

top, with mulberry trees on the north side, and evergreens on the south. From the top of this mound, they have a fine view of the river above the flat land on both sides of the river, and all the field of one thousand acres; the river makes a short bend round to the right, opposite this mound, and there is a good ford just below the point. It is not easy to mistake the ford, as there is a flat on the left, of gravel and sand; the waters roll rapidly over the gravel, and the eye, at the first view, fixes on the most fordable part; there are two other fords below this, which communicate between the fields, on both sides of the river; the river from this point comes round to the west, then to the east; the island ford is below this turn, at the lower end of a small island; from the left side, enter the river forty yards below the island, and go up to the point of it, then turn down as the ripple directs, and land sixty yards below; this is the best ford; the third is still lower, from four to six hundred yards.

The land back from the fields to the east, rises twenty feet, and continues flat for one mile to the pine forest; back of the fields, adjoining the rise of twenty feet, is a beaver pond of forty acres, capable of being drained at a small expense of labor; the large creek bounds the fields, and the flat land to the south.

Continuing on down the river from the creek, the land rises to a high flat, formerly the Cussetuh town, and afterwards a Chickasaw town. This flat is intersected with one branch. From the southern border of this flat, the Cussetuh town is seen below, on a flat, just above flood mark, surrounded with this high flat to the north and east, and the river to the west; the land about the town is poor, and much exhausted; they cultivate but little here of early corn; the principal dependence is on the rich fields above the creek; to call them rich must be understood in a limited sense; they have been so, but being cultivated beyond the memory of the oldest man in Cussetuh, they are almost exhausted; the produce is brought from the fields to the town in canoes or on horses; they make barely a sufficiency of corn for their support; they have no fences around their fields, and only a fence of three poles, tied to upright stakes, for their potatoes; the land up the river, above the fields, is fine for culture, with oak, hickory, blackjack and pine.

The people of Cussetuh associate, more than any other Indians, with their white neighbors, and without obtaining any advantage from it; they know not the season for planting, or if they do, they never avail themselves of what they know, as they always plant a month too late.

This town with its villages is the largest in the Lower Creeks; the people are and have been friendly to white people, and are fond of visiting them; the old chiefs are very orderly men and much occupied in governing their young men, who are rude and disorderly, in proportion to the intercourse they have had with white people; they frequently complain of the intercourse of their young people with the white people on the frontiers, as being very prejudicial to their morals; that they are more rude, more inclined to be tricky, and more difficult to govern, than those who do not associate with them.

The settlements belonging to the town, are spread out on the right side of the river; here they appear to be industrious, have forked fences, and more land enclosed than they can cultivate. One of them desires particularly to be named, *Mic E-maut-lau.* This old chief has with his own labor, made a good worm fence, and built himself a comfortable house; they have but a few peach trees, in and about the town; the main trading path, from the upper towns, passes through here; they estimate their number of gun men at three hundred; but they cannot exceed one hundred and eighty.

Au-put-tau-e; a village of Cussetuh, twenty miles from the river, on Hat-che thluc-co; they have good fences, and the settlers under the best characters of any among the Lower Creeks; they estimate their gun men at forty-three. On a visit here the agent for Indian affairs was met by all the men, at the house of Tus-se-kiah Mic-co. That chief addressed him in these words : " Here, I am glad to see you; this is my wife, and these are my children; they are glad to see you; these are the men of the village; we have forty of them in all; they are glad to see you; you are now among those on whom you may rely. I have been six years at this village, and we have not a man here, or belonging to our village, who ever stole a horse from, or did any injury to a white man."

The village is in the forks of Hatche thlucco, and the situation is well chosen; the land is rich, on the margins of the creeks and the cane flats; the timber is large, of poplar, white oak and hickory; the uplands to the south, are the long-leaf pine; and to the north waving oak, pine and hickory; cane is on the creeks and reed in all the branches.

At this village, and at the house of Tus-se-ki-ah Mic-co, the agent for Indian affairs has introduced the plough; and a farmer was hired in 1797, to tend a crop of corn, and with so good success, as to induce several of the villagers to prepare their fields for the plough. Some of them have cattle, hogs and horses, and are attentive to them. The range is a good one, but cattle and horses require salt; they have some thriving peach trees, at several of the settlements.

On Ouhe-gee creek, called at its junction with the river, Hitchetee, there is one settlement which deserves a place here. It belongs to Mic-co thluc-co, called by the white people, the " bird tail king." The plantation is on the right side of the creek, on good land, in the neighborhood of pine forest; the creek is a fine flowing one, margined with reed; the plantation is well fenced, and cultivated with the plough; this chief had been on a visit to New York, and seen much of the ways of white people, and the advantages of the plough over the slow and laborious hand hoe. Yet he had not firmness enough, till this year, to break through the old habits of the Indians. The agent paid him a visit this spring, 1799, with a plough completely fixed, and spent a day with him and showed him how to use it. He had previously, while the old man was in the woods, prevailed on the family to clear the fields for the plough. It has been used with effect, and much to the approbation of a numerous family, who have more than doubled their crop of corn and potatoes; and who begin to know how to turn their corn to account, by giving it to their hogs. This Micco and his family, have hogs, cattle and horses, and begin to be very attentive to them; he has some apple and peach trees, and grape vines, a present from the agent.

The Cussetuhs have some cattle, horses and hogs ; but they prefer roving idly through the woods, and down on the frontiers, to attending to farming or stock raising. The three towns just described, have had a powerful stimulus to their industry, in the regulations adopted by the agent for his supplies. Heretofore, there was no market for provisions. The wants of the traders were few, and those procured with beads, binding, thread or needles. There is now a regular market, and weights and measures are introduced. To call the supply of a single table a regular market, requires some explanation. The annual expenses of the agent's table, for the two last years, has been 2,750 dollars ; and for 1799, the articles were paid for in money and merchandise ; 1000 dollars of the former, and 1,750 of the latter ; this was more than would be supplied by the three towns. The prices established were :

Pork, gross, per cwt.	$3	00	Capons, per pair .	0	25
Pork, net, per hundred	4	00	Fowls, 4 for . .	0	25
Bacon, do	10	00	Eggs, per dozen .	0	12½
Beef, do	3	00	Butter per lb. in the		
Corn, per bushel . .	0	50	spring . . .	0	25
Potatoes, ...	0	50	During summer .	0	17
Pumpkins, ...	0	18	Cheese, ...	0	17
Ground Peas, . . .	0	50	Oil of hickory nut per		
Field Peas, . . .	1	00	bottle . . .	0	75

4. *U-chee ;* is on the right bank of Chat-to-ho-che, ten and a half miles below Cow-e-tuh-tal-lau-has-see, on a flat of rich land, with hickory, oak, blackjack and long-leaf pine ; the flat extends from one to two miles back from the river. Above the town, and bordering on it, Uchee creek, eighty-five feet wide, joins the river.* Opposite the town house, on the left bank of the river, there is a narrow strip of flat land from fifty to one hundred yards wide, then high pine barren hills ; these people speak a tongue different from the Creeks ; they were formerly settled in small villages at Ponpon, Saltketchers, (Sol-ke-chuh,) Silver Bluff, and O-ge-chee, (How-ge-chu,) and were

---

* The two forks eight miles up ; on the right, We-tum-cau ; the left, Hosa-po-li-gee.

continually at war with the Cherokees, Ea-tau-bau and Creeks.

In the year 1729, an old chief of Cussetuh, called by the white people Captain Ellick, married three Uchee women, and brought them to Cussetuh, which was greatly disliked by his towns people; their opposition determined him to move from Cussetuh; he went down opposite where the town now is, and settled with his three brothers; two of whom, had Uchee wives; he, after this, collected all the Uchees, gave them the land where their town now is, and there they settled.

These people are more civil and orderly than their neighbors; their women are more chaste, and the men better hunters; they retain all their original customs and laws, and have adopted none of the Creeks; they have some worm fences in and about their town, and but very few peach trees.

They have lately begun to settle out in villages, and are industrious, compared with their neighbors; the men take part in the labors of the women, and are more constant in their attachment to their women, than is usual among red people.

The number of gun men is variously estimated; they do not exceed two hundred and fifty, including all who are settled in villages, of which they have three.

1st. *In-tuch-cul-gau;* from in-tuch-ke, a *dam across water;* and ul-gau, *all;* applied to *beaver dams.* This is on Opil-thluc-co, twenty-eight miles from its junction with Flint river. This creek is sixty feet wide at its mouth, one and a half miles above Timothy Barnard's; the land bordering on the creek, up to the village, is good. Eight miles below the village the good land spreads out for four or five miles on both sides of the creek, with oaky woods; (Tuck-au-mau-pa-fau;) the range is fine for cattle; cane grows on the creeks, and reed on all the branches.

They have fourteen families in the village; their industry is increasing; they built a square in 1798, which serves for their town house; they have a few cattle, hogs and horses.

2d. *Pad-gee-li-gau;* from pad-jee, a *pidgeon;* and li-gau, sit; *pidgeon roost.* This was formerly a large town, but broken up by Benjamin Harrison and his associates, who murdered sixteen of their gun men in Georgia; it is on the right bank of Flint river, and this creek, adjoining the river; the village takes its name from the creek; it is nine miles below the second falls of the river; these falls are at the Island's ford, where the path now crosses from Cussetuh to Fort Wilkinson; the village is advantageously situated; the land is rich, the range good for cattle and hogs; the swamp is more than three miles through, on the left bank of the river, and is high and good cane-brake; on the right bank, it is one mile through, low and flat; the cane, sassafras and sumach, are large; this extensive and valuable swamp extends down on one side or the other of the river, for twelve miles.

They have but a few families there, notwithstanding it is one of the best situations the Indians possess, for stock, farming and fish. Being a frontier, the great loss they sustained in having sixteen of their gun men murdered, discourages them from returning.

3d. *Toc-co-gul-egau;* (tad pole;) a small settlement on Kit-cho-foone creek, near some beaver dams on branches of that creek; the land is good but broken; fine range, small canes and pea vines on the hills, and reeds on the branches; they have eight or ten families; this establishment is of two years only, and they have worm fences. U-che Will, the head of the village, has some cattle, and they have promised to attend to hogs, and to follow the direction of the agent for Indian affairs, as soon as they can get into stock.

Some of the Uchees have settled with the Shaw-a-nee, at Sau-va-no-gee, among the Creeks of the upper towns.

5. *Oose-oo-chee;* is about two miles below Uchee, on the right bank of Chat-to-ho-chee; they formerly lived on Flint river, and settling here, they built a hot house in 1794; they cultivate with their neighbors, the *Che-au-hau,* below their land in the point.

6. *Che-au-hau;* called by the traders Che-haws, is just below, and adjoining Oose-oo-che, on a flat of good land. Below the town, the river winds round east, then west, making a neck or point of one thousand acres of canebrake, very fertile, but low, and subject to be overflowed; the land back of this, is level for nearly three miles, with red, post, and white oak, hickory, then pine forest.

These people have villages on the waters of Flint river; there they have fine stocks of cattle, horses and hogs, and they raise corn, rice and potatoes, in great plenty.

The following are the villages of this town :

1st. *Au-muc-cul-le ;* (pour upon me ;) is on a creek of that name, which joins on the right side of Flint river, forty-five miles below Timothy Barnard's. It is sixty feet wide, and the main branch of Kitch-o-foo-ne, which it joins three miles from the river; the village is nine miles up the creek; the land is poor and flat, with limestone springs in the neighborhood; the swamp is cypress in hammocks, with some water oak and hickory; the pine land is poor with ponds and wire grass; they have sixty gun men in the village; it is in some places well fenced; they have cattle, hogs and horses, and a fine range for them, and raise corn, rice and potatoes in great plenty.

2d. *O-tel-le-who-yau-nau ;* (hurricane town;) is six miles below Kitch-o-foo-ne, on the right bank of Flint river, with pine barren on both sides; they have twenty families in the village, which is fenced; and they have hogs, cattle and horses ; they plant the small margins near the mouth of a little creek ; this village is generally named as belonging to Che-au-hau ; but they are mixed with Oose-oo-ches.

3. *Che-au-hoo-che ;* (little che-au-hau ;) is one mile and a half west from Hit-che-tee, in the pine forest, near Au-he-gee ; a fine little creek, called at its junction with the river, Hit-che-tee; they begin to fence and have lately built a square.

7. *Hit-che-tee ;* is on the left bank of Chat-to-ho-che, four miles below Che-au-hau ; they have a narrow strip of good land, bordering on the river, and back of this it rises into high, poor land, which spreads off flat. In approaching the town on this side, there is no rise, but a great descent to the town flat; on the right bank of the river the land is level, and extends out for two miles, is of thin quality; the growth is post oak, hickory, and pine, all small, then pine barren and ponds.

The appearance about this town indicates much poverty and indolence ; they have no fences ; they have spread out into villages, and have the character of being honest and industrious ; they are attentive to the rights of their white neighbors, and no charge of horse stealing from the frontiers, has been substantiated against them. The villages are,

1st. Hit-che-too-che, (Little Hit-chetee,) a small village of industrious people, settled on both sides of Flint river, below Kit-cho-foo-ne; they have good fences, cattle, horses, and hogs, in a fine range, and are attentive to them.

2d. *Tut-tal-lo-see ;* (fowl;) on a creek of that name, twenty miles west from Hit-che-too-che. This is a fine creek on a bed of limestone; it is a branch of Kitch-o-foo-ne; the land bordering on the creek, and for eight or nine miles in the direction towards Hit-che-too-che, is level, rich, and fine for cultivation, with post and black oak, hickory, dogwood and pine. The villagers have good worm fences, appear industrious, and have large stocks of cattle, some hogs and horses; they appear decent and orderly, and are desirous of preserving a friendly intercourse with their neighbors; they have this year, 1799, built a square.

8. *Pā-lā-chooc-le ;* is on the right bank of Chat-to-ho-che, one and a half miles below Che-au-hau, on a poor, pine barren flat; the land back from it is poor, broken, pine land; their fields are on the left side of the river, on poor land.

This was formerly the first among the Lower Creek towns; a peace town, averse to war, and called by the nation, Tal-lo-wau thluc-co, (big town.) The Indians are poor, the town has lost its former consequence, and is not now much in estimation.

9. *O-co-nee ;* is six miles below Pā-lā-chooc-le, on the left bank of Chat-to-ho-che. It is a small town, the remains of the settlers of O-co-nee ; they formerly lived just below the Rock landing, and gave name to that river; they are increasing in industry, making fences, attending to stock, and have some level land moderately rich; they have a few hogs, cattle and horses.

10. *Sau-woo-ge-lo ;* is six miles below O-co-nee, on the right bank of the river, a new settlement in the open pine forest. Below this, for four and a half miles, the land is flat on the river, and much of it in the bend is good for corn. Here We-lau-ne, (yellow water,) a fine flowing

9

creek, joins the river; and still lower, Co-wag-gee, (par-tridge,) a creek sixty yards wide at its mouth. Its source is in the ridge dividing its waters from Ko-e-ne-cuh, Choc-tau hatche and Telāgue hatche; they have some settle-ments in this neighborhood, on good land.

11. *Sau-woog-e-loo-che ;* is four miles below Oconee, on the left bank of the river, in oaky woods, which ex-tend back one mile to the pine forest; they have about twenty families, and plant in the bends of the river; they have a few cattle.

12. *Eu-fau-lau ;* is fifteen miles below Sau-woog-e-lo, on the left bank of the river, on a pine flat; the fields are on both sides of the river, on rich flats; below the town the land is good.

These people are very poor, but generally well behaved and very friendly to white people; they are not given to horse-stealing, have some stock, are attentive to it; they have some land fenced, and are preparing for more; they have spread out their settlements down the river, about eight miles below the town, counting on the river path, there is a little village on good land, *O-ke-teyoc-en-ne.* Some of the settlements are well fenced; they raise plenty of corn and rice, and the range is a good one for stock.

From this village, they have settlements down as low as the forks of the river; and they are generally on sites well chosen, some of them well cultivated; they raise plenty of corn and rice, and have cattle, horses and hogs.

Several of these Indians have negroes, taken during the revolutionary war, *and where they are, there is more industry and better farms.* These negroes were, many of them, given by the agents of Great Britain to the Indians, in payment for their services, and they generally call them-selves " *King's gifts.*" The negroes are all of them, at-tentive and friendly to white people, particularly so to those in authority.

Timothy Barnard's.

This gentleman lives on the right bank of Flint river, fifteen miles below Pad-je-li-gau. He has eleven children by a U-chee woman, and they are settled with and around him, and have fine stocks of cattle in an excellent range.

He has a valuable property, but not productive ; his farm is well fenced on both sides of the river ; he has a peach orchard of fine fruit, and some fine nectarines, a garden well stored with vegetables, and some grape vines presented to him by the agent. He is an assistant and interpreter, and a man who has uniformly supported an honest character, friendly to peace during the revolutionary war, and to man. He has forty sheep, some goats, and stock of every description, and keeps a very hospitable house. He is not much acquainted with farming, and receives light slowly on this subject, as is the case with all the Indian countrymen, without exception.

Government.

The Creeks never had, till this year, a national government and law. Every thing of a general tendency, was left to the care and management of the public agents, who heretofore used temporary expedients only ; and amongst the most powerful and persuasive, was the pressure of fear from without, and *presents.* The attempt, in the course of the last and present year, to establish a national council, to meet annually, and to make general regulations for the welfare of the nation, promises to succeed. The law passed at the first meeting, to punish thieves and mischief-makers, has been carried into effect, in a few instances, where the personal influence of the agent for Indian affairs, was greatly exerted. On a trying occasion, the chiefs were called on to turn out the warriors, and to punish the leaders of the banditti, who insulted the commissioners of Spain and the United States, on the 17th of September. After this was repeatedly urged, and the agent agreed to be responsible for all the consequences, the chiefs turned out the warriors, and executed the law on the leader and a few of his associates, in an exemplary manner. While this transaction was fresh in the minds of the Indians, the agent for Indian affairs convened the national council, and made a report on the state of the nation to them, accompanied with his opinion of the plan indispensably necessary, to carry the laws of the nation into effect.

The council, after mature deliberation, determined that

the safety of the nation was at stake; that having a firm reliance on the justice of the President of the United States, and the friendly attention of his agent for Indian affairs, they would adopt his plan.

1st. To class the towns, and appoint a warrior over each class, denominated the warrior of the nation, to superintend the execution of the law.

2d. To declare as law, that when a man is punished by the law of the nation, and dies, that it is the law that killed him. It is the nation who killed him; and that no man or family is to be held accountable for this act of the nation.

3d. That all mischief-makers and thieves, of any country of white people, shall be under the government of the agent for Indian affairs, and that he may introduce the troops of the United States to any part of the Creek country, to punish such persons; and that, when he calls in the troops of the United States, he is to call for such number of warriors as he may deem proper, to accompany them, to be under pay: that, in apprehending or punishing any white person, if Indians should interpose, the red warriors are to order them to desist; and if they refuse, the agent may order them to fire, at the same time ordering the troops of the United States to make common cause.

Government of the Towns.

The towns, separately, have a government and customs, which they derive from a high source. They have their public buildings, as well for business as pleasure; every town has a chief who presides over the whole; he is their *Mic-co,* called by the white people, " King." The grades from him are regular and uniform, throughout all the towns. In the description of the public buildings, these grades will be explained.

The Public Buildings.

Choo-co-thluc-co, (big house,) the town house or public square, consists of four square buildings of one story facing each other, forty by sixteen feet, eight feet pitch;

the entrance at each corner. Each building is a wooden frame, supported on posts set in the ground, covered with slabs, open in front like a piazza, divided into three rooms, the back and ends clayed, up to the plates. Each division is divided lengthwise, into two seats ; the front, two feet high, extending back half way, covered with reed-mats or slabs ; then a rise of one foot, and it extends back, covered in like manner, to the side of the building. On these seats, they lie or sit at pleasure.

The rank of the Buildings which form the Square.

1st. Mic-ul-gee in-too-pau, the *Mic-co's cabin.* This fronts the east, and is occupied by those of the highest rank ; the centre of the building is always occupied by the Mic-co of the town ; by the agent for Indian affairs when he pays a vist to a town ; by the Mic-cos of other towns, and by respectable white people.

The division to the right is occupied by the Mic-ug-gee, (Miccos, there being several so called in every town, from custom, the origin of which is unknown,) and the counsellors. These two classes give their advice, in relation to war, and are in fact the principal counsellors.

The division to the left, is occupied by the E-ne-hau Ul-gee, (people second in command, the head of whom is called by the traders, *second man.*) These have the direction of the public works appertaining to the town, such as the public buildings, building houses in town for new settlers, or working in the fields. They are particularly charged with the ceremony of the ā-ce, (a decoction of the cassine yupon, called by the traders *black drink,*) under the direction of the Mic-co.

The Mic-co of the town superintends all public and domestic concerns ; receives all public characters ; hears their talks ; lays them before the town, and delivers the talks of his town. The Mic-co of a town is always chosen from some one family. The Mic-co of Tuck-au-bat-che is of the eagle tribe, (Lum-ul-gee.) After he is chosen and put on his seat, he remains for life. On his death, if his nephews are fit for the office, one of them takes his place as his successor ; if they are unfit, one is chosen of the next of kin, the descent being always in the female line. They have, in this town, a Mic-co of another family, the Is-po-co-gee Mic-co, the ancient name of the town.

When a Mic-co, from age, infirmity, or any other cause, wants an assistant, he selects a man who appears to him the best qualified, and proposes him to the counsellors and great men of the town, and if he is approved of by them, they appoint him as an assistant in public affairs, and he takes his seat on this cabin accordingly.

The Micco of a town generally bears the name of the town, as *Cussetuh Mic-co*. He is what is called by the traders the Cussetuh King.

2d. Tus-tun-nug-ul-gee in-too-pau, the *warriors' cabin*. This fronts the south; the head warrior sits at the west end of his cabin, and in his division the great warriors sit beside each other. The next in rank sit in the centre division, and the young warriors in the third. The rise is regular, by merit, from the third to the first division. The Great Warrior, for that is the title of the head warrior. He is appointed by the micco and counsellors, from among the greatest war characters.

When a young man is trained up and appears well qualified for the fatigues and hardships of war, and is promising, the Mic-co appoints him a governor, or as the name imports, a *leader*, (Is-te-puc-cau-chau,) and if he distinguishes himself, they give him a rise to the centre cabin. A man who distinguishes himself, repeatedly, in warlike enterprises, arrives to the rank of the Great Leader, (Is-te-puc-cau-chau thlucco.) This title, though greatly coveted, is seldom attained; as it requires a long course of years, and great and numerous successes in war.

The second class of warriors is the *Tusse-ki-ul-gee*. All who go to war, and are in company, when a scalp is taken, get a war name. The leader reports their conduct, and they receive a name accordingly. This is the Tus-se-ki-o-chif-co, or *war name*. The term leader, as used by the Indians, is the proper one. The war parties all march in Indian file, with the leader in front, until coming on hostile ground; he is then in the rear.

3d. Is-te-chaguc-ul-gee in-too-pau, the *cabin of the beloved men*. This fronts the north.

There are great men who have been war leaders, and

who although of various ranks, have become estimable in a long course of public service. They sit themselves on the right division of the cabin of the Mic-co, and are his cousellors. The family of the Mic-co, and great men who have thus distinguished themselves, occupy this cabin of the beloved men.

4th. Hut-te-mau-hug-gee in-too-pau, the *cabin of the young people and their associates.* This fronts the west.

The Convention of the Town.

The Micco, counsellors and warriors, meet every day, in the public square; sit and drink ā-cee, a strong decoction of the cassine yupon, called by the traders, *black drink ;* talk of news, the public and domestic concerns, smoke their pipes, and play Thla-chal-litch-cau, (roll the bullet.) Here all complaints are introduced, attended to, and redressed. They have a regular ceremony for making, as well as delivering the ā-cee, to all who attend the square.

5th. Chooc-ofau thluc-co, the *rotunda* or *assembly room,* called by the traders, " *hot-house.*" This is near the square, and is constructed after the following manner : Eight posts are fixed in the ground, forming an octagon of thirty feet diameter. They are twelve feet high, and large enough to support the roof. On these, five or six logs are placed, of a side, drawn in as they rise. On these, long poles or rafters, to suit the height of the building, are laid, the upper ends forming a point,. and the lower ends projecting out six feet from the octagon, and resting on posts five feet high, placed in a circle round the octagon, with plates on them, to which the rafters are tied with splits. The rafters are near together, and fastened with splits. These are covered with clay, and that with pine bark ; the wall, six feet from the octagon, is clayed up ; they have a small door into a small portico, curved round for five or six feet, then into the house.

The space between the octagon and the wall, is one entire sopha, where the visiters lie or sit at pleasure. It is covered with reed, mat or splits.

In the centre of the room, on a small rise, the fire is made, of dry cane or dry old pine slabs, split fine, and laid in a spiral circle. This is the assembly room for all people, old and young; they assemble every night, and amuse themselves with dancing, singing, or conversation. And here, sometimes, in very cold weather, the old and naked sleep.

In all transactions which require secrecy, the rulers meet here, make their fire, deliberate and decide. When they have decided on any case of death or whipping, the Micco appoints the warriors who are to carry it into effect; or he gives the judgment to the Great Warrior, (Tustunnuggee thlucco,) and leaves to him the time and manner of executing it.

War.

This is always determined on by the Great Warrior. When the Micco and counsellors are of opinion that the town has been injured, he lifts the war hatchet against the nation which has injured them. But as soon as it is taken up, the Micco and counsellors may interpose, and by their prudent councils, stop it, and proceed to adjust the misunderstanding by negotiation. If the Great Warrior persists and goes out, he is followed by all who are for war. It is seldom a town is unanimous, the nation never is; and within the memory of the oldest man among them, it is not recollected, that more than one half the nation have been for war at the same time; or taken, as they express it, the war talk.

The Great Warrior, when he marches, gives notice where he shall encamp, and sets out sometimes with one or two only. He fires off his gun and sets up the war whoop. This is repeated by all who follow him, and they are sometimes for one or two nights marching off.

Peace.

This is always determined on and concluded, by the Mic-co and counsellors; and peace talks are always addressed to the cabin of the Mic-co. In some cases, where the resentment of the warriors has run high, the Micco and council have been much embarrassed.

Marriage.

A man who wants a wife never applies in person; he sends his sister, his mother, or some other female relation, to the female relations of the woman he names. They consult the brothers and uncles on the maternal side, and sometimes the father; but this is a compliment only, as his approbation or opposition is of no avail. If the party applied to, approve of the match, they answer accordingly, to the woman who made the application. The bridegroom then gets together a blanket, and such other articles of clothing as he is able to do, and sends them by the women to the females of the family of the bride. If they accept of them the match is made; and the man may then go to her house as soon as he chooses. And when he has built a house, made his crop and gathered it in, then made his hunt and brought home the meat, and put all this in the possession of his wife, the ceremony ends, and they are married; or as they express it, the woman is bound. From the first going to the house of the woman, till the ceremony ends, he is completely in possession of her.

This law has been understood differently, by some hasty cuckolds, who insist, that when they have assisted the woman to plant her crop, the ceremony ends, and the woman is bound. A man never marries in his own tribe.

Divorce.

This is at the choice of either of the parties; the man may marry again as soon as he will; but she is bound, till all the *Boosketau* of that year are over; excepting in the cases of marriage and parting in the season when there is no planting, or more properly speaking, during the season the man resides at the house of the woman and has possession of her, during the continuation of the marriage ceremony; in that case the woman is equally free to connect herself as soon as she pleases.

There is an inconsistency in the exception above; since in fact, in such season, there can be no marriage; but the chiefs, on their report on this article, maintained it as an exception, and this practice, in these cases of half

10

marriage prevail universally. As soon as a man goes to the house of his bride, he is in complete possession of her, till the ceremony ends; and during this period the exception will apply.

Marriage gives no right to the husband over the property of his wife; and when they part she keeps the children and property belonging to them.

Adultery.

This is punished by the family or tribe of the husband. They collect, consult and decree. If the proof is clear, and they determine to punish the offenders, they divide and proceed to apprehend them. One half goes to the house of the woman, the remainder to the family house of the adulterer; or they go together, as they have decreed. They apprehend the offenders, beat them severely with sticks, and then crop them. They cut off the hair of the woman, which they carry to the square in triumph. If they apprehend but one of the offenders, and the other escapes, they then go and take satisfaction from the nearest relation. If both the offenders escape, and the tribe or family return home, and lay down the sticks, the crime is satisfied. There is one family only, the "Wind," (Hotul-ul-gee,) that can take up the sticks a second time. This crime is satisfied in another way, if the parties offending absent themselves till the Boos-ke-tuh is over. Then all crimes are done away except murder. And the bare mention of them, or any occurrence which brings them in recollection, is forbidden.

Murder.

If murder is committed, the family and tribe alone have the right of taking satisfaction. They collect, consult and decide. The rulers of the town, or the nation, have nothing to do or to say in the business. The relations of the murdered person consult first among themselves, and if the case is clear, and their family or tribe are not likely to suffer by their decision, they determine on the case definitively. When the tribe may be effected by it, in a doubtful case, or an old claim for satisfaction, the family then consult with their tribe; and when they have deliberated and resolved on satisfaction, they take the guilty one, if to be come at. If he flies, they take the nearest of kin, or one of the family. In some cases, the family which has done the injury promise reparation; and in that case are allowed a reasonable time to fulfil their promise; and they are generally earnest of themselves, in their endeavors to put the guilty to death, to save an innocent person.

This right of judging, and taking satisfaction, being vested in the family or tribe, is the sole cause why their treaty stipulations on this head, never have been executed. In like manner, a prisoner taken in war, is the property of the captor and his family, it being optional with his captor, to kill or save him at the time. And this right must be purchased, and it is now the practice, introduced within a few years, for the nation to pay. The practice has been introduced by the agent for Indian affairs, and he pays on the orders of the chiefs, out of the stipend allowed by the United States to the Creeks. Claims of this sort of seventeen years standing, where the prisoner has been delivered to the order of the chiefs, have been revived, allowed and paid.

*Boos-ke-tau.**

This annual festival is celebrated in the months of July or August. The precise time is fixed by the Mic-co and counsellors, and is sooner or later, as the state of the affairs of the town, or the early or lateness of their corn, will suit for it. In Cussetuh, this ceremony lasts for eight days. In some towns of less note, it is but four days.

FIRST DAY.

In the morning, the warriors clean the yard of the square, and sprinkle white sand, when the a-cee, (decoction of the cassine yupon,) is made. The fire-maker makes the fire as early in the morning as he can, by friction. The warriors cut and bring into the square, four logs, as long each as a man can cover by extending his

* See page 25.

two arms ; these are placed in the centre of the square,
end to end, forming a cross, the outer ends pointed to the
cardinal points; in the centre of the cross, the new fire
is made. During the first four days, they burn out these
four logs.

The pin-e-bun-gau, (turkey dance,) is danced by the
women of the turkey tribe ; and while they are dancing,
the possau is brewed. This is a powerful emetic. The
possau is drank from twelve o'clock to the middle of the
afternoon. After this, the Toc-co-yule-gau, (tadpole,) is
danced by four men and four women. (In the evening,
the men dance E-ne-hou-bun-gau, the dance of the people
second in command.) This they dance till daylight.

SECOND DAY.

This day, about ten o'clock, the women dance Its-ho-
bun-gau, (gun-dance.) After twelve, the men go to the
new fire, take some of the ashes, rub them on the chin,
neck and belly, and jump head foremost into the river,
and they return into the square. The women having prepared the new corn for the feast, the men take some of it
and rub it between their hands, then on their face and
breasts, and then they feast.

THIRD DAY.

The men sit in the square.

FOURTH DAY.

The women go early in the morning and get the new
fire, clean out their hearths, sprinkle them with sand, and
make their fires. The men finish burning out the first
four logs, and they take ashes, rub them on their chin,
neck and belly, and they go into the water. This day
they eat salt, and they dance Obungauchapco, (the long
dance.)

FIFTH DAY.

They get four new logs, and place them as on the first
day, and they drink a-cee, a strong decoction of the cassine yupon.

They remain in the square.

Is spent in like manner as the sixth.

They get two large pots, and their physic plants, 1st. Mic-co-ho-yon-e-juh. 2. Toloh. 3. A-che-nau. 4. Cup-pau-pos-cau. 5. Chu-lis-sau, the roots. 6. Tuck-thlau-lus-te. 7. Tote-cul-hil-lis-so-wau. 8. Chofeinsuck-cau-fuck-au. 9. Cho-fe-mus-see. ·10. Hil-lis-hut-ke. 11. To-te-cuh chooc-his-see. 12. Welau-nuh. 13. Oak-chon-utch-co. 14. Co-hal-le-wau-gee. These are all put into the pots and beat up with water. The chemists, (E-lic-chul-gee, called by the traders physic makers,) they blow in it through a small reed, and then it is drank by the men, and rubbed over their joints till the afternoon.

They collect old corn cobs and pine burs, put them into a pot, and burn them to ashes. Four virgins who have never had their menses, bring ashes from their houses, put them in the pot and stir all together. The men take white clay and mix it with water in two pans. One pan of the clay and one of the ashes, are carried to the cabin of the Mic-co, and the other two to that of the warriors. They then rub themselves with the clay and ashes. Two men appointed to that office, bring some flowers of to-bacco of a small kind, (Itch-au-chu-le-puc-pug-gee,) or, as the name imports, the old man's tobacco, which was prepared on the first day, and put in a pan on the cabin of the Mic-co, and they give a little of it to every one present.

The Micco and counsellors then go four times round the fire, and every time they face the east, they throw some of the flowers into the fire. They then go and stand to the west. The warriors then repeat the same ceremony.

A cane is stuck up at the cabin of the Mic-co with two white feathers in the end of it. One of the Fish tribe, (Thlot-lo-ul-gee,) takes it just as the sun goes down, and goes off towards the river, all following him. When he gets half way to the river, he gives the death whoop; this whoop he repeats four times, between the square and the water's edge. Here they all place themselves as thick as they can stand, near the edge of the water. He sticks up the cane at the water's edge, and they all put a grain of the old man's tobacco on their heads, and in each ear. Then, at a signal given, four different times, they throw some into the river, and every man at a like signal plunges into the river, and picks up four stones from the bottom. With these they cross themselves on their breasts four times, each time throwing a stone into the river, and giving the death whoop; they then wash themselves, take up the cane and feathers, return and stick it up in the square, and visit through the town. At night they dance O-bun-gau Haujo, (mad dance,) and this finishes the ceremony.

This happy institution of the *Boos-ke-tuh*, restores man to himself, to his family and to his nation. It is a general amnesty, which not only absolves the Indians from all crimes, murder only excepted, but seems to bury guilt itself in oblivion.

The Ceremony of initiating Youth into Manhood.

At the age of from fifteen to seventeen, this ceremony is usually performed. It is called Boos-ke-tau, in like manner as the annual Boosketau of the nation. A youth of the proper age gathers two handsfull of the Sou-watch-cau, a very bitter root, which he eats a whole day; then he steeps the leaves in water and drinks it. In the dusk of the evening, he eats two or three spoonfulls of boiled grits. This is repeated for four days, and during this time he remains in a house. The Sou-watch-cau has the effect of intoxicating and maddening. The fourth day he goes out, but must put on a pair of new moccasins (Stil-la-pica.) For twelve moons, he abstains from eating bucks, except old ones, and from turkey cocks, fowls, peas and salt. During this period he must not pick his ears, or scratch his head with his fingers, but use a small stick. For four moons he must have a fire to himself, to cook his food, and a little girl, a virgin, may cook for him ; his food is boiled grits. The fifth moon, any person may cook for him, but he must serve himself first, and use one spoon and pan. Every new moon, he drinks for four days the possau, (button snakeroot,) an emetic, and abstains for these days, from all food, except in the evening, a little boiled grits, (humpetuh hutke.) The twelfth moon, he performs for four days, what he commenced with on the first. The fifth day, he comes out of his house, gathers corn cobs, burns them to ashes, and with these, rubs his body all over. At the end of this moon, he sweats under blankets, then goes into water, and this ends the ceremony. This ceremony is sometimes extended to four, six, or eight moons, or even to twelve days only, but the course is the same.

During the whole of this ceremony, the physic is administered by the Is-te-puc-cau-chau thluc-co, (great leader,) who in speaking of a youth under initiation, says, " I am physicing him," (Boo-se-ji-jite saut li-to-mise-cha,) or " I am teaching him all that is proper for him to know," (nauk o-mul-gau e-muc-e-thli-jite saut litomise cha.) The youth, during this initiation, does not touch any one except young persons, who are under a like course with himslf, and if he dreams, he drinks the possau.

War Physic, Ho-ith-le Hil-lis-so-wau.

When young men are going to war, they go into a hothouse of the town made for the purpose, and remain there for four days. They drink the Mic-co-ho-yon-e-jau and the pos-sau, and they eat the Sou-watch-cau. The fourth day, they come out, have their bundle ready, and march. This bundle or knapsack, is an old blanket, some parched corn flour, and leather to patch their moccasins. They have in their shot bags, a charm, a protection against all ills, called the war physic, composed of chitto gab-by and Is-te-pau-pau, the bones of the snake and lion.

The tradition of this physic is, that in old times, the lion, (Is-te-pau-pau,) devoured their people. They dug a pit and caught him in it, just after he had killed one of their people. They covered him with lightwood knots, burnt him and reserved his bones.

The snake was in the water, the old people sung and he showed himself. They sung again, and he showed himself a little out of the water. The third time he showed his horns, and they cut one; again he showed himself a fourth time, and they cut off the other horn. A piece of these horns and of the bones of the lion, is the great war physic.

The opinion of Efau Haujo, great Medal Chief of Took-au-bat-che, and Speaker for the Nation in the National Council, on these Ceremonies, given in answer to some queries put to him.

1st. What is the origin of the new fire, and of the Boosketau? Answer. I have been taught from my infancy, that there is an E-sau-ge-tuh E-mis-see, (master of breath,) who gave these customs to the Indians, as necessary to them and suited to them; and that to follow them, entitles the red people to his care and protection, in war and difficulties. It is our opinion that the origin of the Boosketau and our physics, proceeds from the goodness of Esaugetuh E-mis-see; that he communicated them in old times to the red people, and impressed it on them to follow and adhere to them, and they would be of service to them.

2d. Do the red people believe in a future existence? Answer. The old notion among us, is, that when we die, the spirit, (po-yau-fic-chau,) goes the way the sun goes, to the west, and there joins its family and friends, who went before it.

3rd. Do the red people believe in a future state of rewards and punishments? Answer. We have an opinion that those who behaved well, are taken under the care of E-sau-ge-tuh E-mis-see and assisted; and that those who have behaved ill, are left there to shift for themselves; and that there is no other punishment.

4th. What is your opinion of retaliation, as practised among the Indians; can it be just to punish the innocent for the guilty; and do you believe that this custom of the Indians proceeded from E-sau-ge-tuh E-mis-see? Answer.

I believe our custom did not proceed from E-sau-ge-tuh E-mis-see, but from the temper of rash men, who do not consider consequences before they act. It is a bad custom.

5th. What is your opinion of the custom of the red people, to punish for accidental death, with the same severity, as where there has been a manifest intention to kill? Answer. This custom of ours is a bad one, blood for blood; but I do not believe it came from E-sau-ge-tuh E-mis-see, but proceeded from ourselves. Of a case of this sort, I will give you my opinion, by my conduct. Lately, in Tookaubatche, two promising boys were playing and slinging stones. One of them let slip his sling, the stone flew back and killed his companion. The family of the deceased took the two boys, and were preparing to bury them in the same grave. The uncles, who have the right to decide in such cases, were sent for, and I was sent for. We arrived at the same time. I ordered the people to leave the house, and the two boys to remain together. I took the uncles to my house, raised their spirits with a little rum, and told them, the boy was a fine boy, and would be useful to us in our town, when he became a man; that he had no ill will against the dead one; the act was purely accidental; that it had been the will of E-sau-ge-tuh E-mis-se to end his days, and I thought that the living one should remain, as taking away his life would not give it to the other. The two uncles, after some reflection, told me, as you have advised us, so we will act; he shall not die, it was an accident.

The Opinion of Tus-se-kiah Mic-co, on the Origin of the Creeks, and the New Fire.

" There are in the forks of Red river, (We-chä-te-hat-che Au-fus-kee,) west of Mississippi, (We-o-coof-ke, *muddy water*,) two mounds of earth. At this place, the Cussetuh, Cowetuh and Chickasaws found themselves. They were at a loss for fire. Here they were visited by the Hi-you-yul-gee, four men who came from the four corners of the world. One of these people asked the Indians, where they would have their fire, (tote-kit-cau.) They pointed to a place; it was made; and they sat down

11

around it. The Hi-you-yul-gee directed, that they should pay particular attention to the fire, that it would preserve them and let E-sau-ge-tuh E-mis see, (master of breath,) know their wants. One of these visitors took them and showed them the pas-sau; another showed them Mic-co-ho yon-ejau, then the Au-che-nau, (cedar,) and Too-loh, (sweet bay.) [There are one or two other plants, not recollected. Each of these seven plants was to belong to a particular tribe,] (E-mau-li-ge-tuh.) After this, the four visiters disappeared in a cloud, going from whence they came."

"The three towns then appointed their rulers. The Cussetuhs chose the Noo-coose-ul-gee, (bear tribe,) to be their Mic-ul-gee, (mic-cos,) and the Is-tau-nul-gee, to be the E-ne-hau-thluc-ul-gee, (people second in command.) The Cowetuhs chose the Thlot-lo-ul-gee, (fish tribe,) to be their Mic-ul-gee, (miccos.")

"After these arrangements, some other Indians came from the west, met them, and had a great wrestle with the three towns; they made ball sticks and played with them, with bows and arrows, and the war club, (Au-tus-sau.) They fell out, fought, and killed each other. After this warring, the three towns moved eastwardly, and they met the Au-be-cuh at Coosau river. Here they agreed to go to war for four years, against their first enemy ; they made shields, (Te-po-lux-o,) of Buffalo hides, and it was agreed that the warriors of each town, should dry and bring forward, the scalps (E-cau halpe) of the enemy and pile them ; the Aubecuh had a small pile, the Chickasaws were above them, the Cowetuhs above them, and the Cussetuhs above all. The two last towns raised the scalp pole, (Itlo chäte, *red wood*,) and do not suffer any other town to raise it. Cussetuh is first in rank."

"After this, they settled the rank of the four towns among themselves. Cussetuh, called Au-be-cuh and Chickasaw cha-chu-see, (younger brothers.) The Chickasaws and Aubecuhs, called Cussetuh and Cowetuh, chat-la-hau, (oldest brothers.) Au-be-cuh, called Chickasaw, Um-mau-mau-yuh, (elders, or people a head of them.) Chickasaws sometimes use the same expression to Aubecuh."

This being done, they commenced their settlements on Coo-sau and Tal-la-poo-sau, and crossing the falls of Tallapoosa above Tool-cau-bat-che, they visited the Chat-to-hoche, and found a race of people with flat heads, in possession of the mounds in the Cussetuh fields. These people used bows and arrows, with strings made of sinews. The great physic makers, (Au-lic-chul-gee,) sent some rats in the night time, which gnawed the strings, and in the morning, they attacked and defeated the flats. They crossed the river at the island, near the mound, and took possession of the country. After this, they spread out eastwardly, to O-cheese-hat-che, (Ocmulgee,) Oconee, O-ge-chee, (How-ge-chuh,) Chic-ke-tal-lo-fau-hat-che, (Savannah,) called sometimes Sau-va-no-gee, the name for Shaw-a-nee. They met the white people on the sea-coast, who drove them back to their present situation."

" Cussetuh and Chickasaw consider themselves as people of one fire, (tote-kit-cau humgoce,) from the earliest account of their origin. Cussetuh appointed the first Micco for them, directed him to sit down in the big Savanna, where they now are, and govern them. Some of the Chickasaws straggled off and settled near Augusta, from whence they returned and sat down near Cussetuh, and thence back to their nation. Cussetuh and Chickasaw have remained friends ever since their first acquaintance."

During the late war between the Creeks and Chickasaws, Cussetuh refused her aid, and retained her long established friendship for the Chickasaws; and when the Creeks offered to make peace, their offers were rejected, till Cussetuh interposed their good offices. These had the desired effect, and produced peace.

State of the War Party in September, 1813.

| Oc-fus-kee, | Aut-tos-see. |
| Tal-e-see, | |

These towns formed a front of observation towards Cowetau.

| Ho-ith-le-wau-lee, | Coo-loo-me, |
| Foosce-hat-che, | E-cun-hut-kee, |

Sau-van-no-gee,
Mook-lau-sau,
A-la-ba-mo,
Hook-choie-oo-che,
O-che-ub-e-fau,

We-wo-cau,
Puc-cun-tal-lau has-see,
Woc-co-coie,
Po-chuse-hat-che.

These towns furnished the warriors for the expedition against Tensau. They did not intend an expedition against the white people till they compelled Cowetau and Tookaubatchee to join or fly the nation, and every town to join with them. But being attacked by the half breeds and whites, at Burnt Corn, in their own land, they determined to retaliate, and planned the expedition accordingly.

Thlot-lo-gul-gau,   Ki-a-li-je,
Eu-fau-lau,

These are neutral. Ho-bo-kei-eth-le Haujo, hearing that the war party intended to cut off Kialije, sent word he had warriors, and would fight for Kialijee. This last town has taken the war club, and dance the prophets dances, and are used as spies on the war party.

Too-to-gau-gee,   Au-che-nau ulgau.

These are at Tookaubatche Tal-lau-has-see. Chattuck-so-cau is above Oc-fus-kee and with it.

This settlement is on the east of Tallapoosa, on a wide creek which gives name to it, twelve miles nearly from the river.

From Burges's 30 miles above the mouth of the river Flint,
To We-thluc-coo-chee, 16 miles, 20 yards wide.
O-ke-lock-ei-me, 18 miles,   30 yds wide, and deep.
St. Marks, 40 miles,   half a mile wide.
Aussille, 40 miles,   50 yards wide, shallow.
Sawaune, 70 miles,   120 yards wide.
Picaulata, 130 miles,   two miles wide.
St. Augustine,   26 miles.

Information relative to the waters and country on the post road, commencing at Ka-le-be, near the agency on that creek.

	Miles.	Width in feet.	
Ka-le-be,		30	
Ke-bi-hatch-e,	4	30	lands post oak, clay, good range for stock.
O-fuk-she,	2	60	post oak, small hickory, clay, red oak.
Noo-coose Chepo,	2	8	post oak, plains, clay, red oak.
Kit-to-me,	14	60	post, black oak, plains, clay.
Pilth-lau-le,	7	20	do. do.
Pinchunc,	2	20	do. do.
In-tuck-kee,	4	10	do. do.
Opil-thluc-co,	6	10	do. do.
1st Fork of,	3	10	do. do.
2d do	3	15	do. do.
Us-se-wau-sau,	4	4	oak, hickory, chesnut, water Ko-ne-cau.
	10		first pine land, left 4 by 5 miles, clay.
Suck-pul-gau,	23	15	oak, hickory, walnut.
	3		pine ridge to Ko-ne-cau, wide in places, 10 to 15 miles level clay land.
Murder Creek,	8	20	a belt of pine land 5 by 4 miles, clay.
Burnt Corn,	12	10	between these creeks on the left.
Limestone,	5		a small branch of Alabama.
Little Escambia,	4	20	waters of Ko-ne-cau.
Big Escambia,	9	90	do. do.

(The rows from Pilth-lau-le through 2d do are grouped by a brace: "All waters of A-la-ba-ma.")

The pine lands commence near Burnt Corn, around the head of Limestone, to the two Escambias, and to Ko-ne-cau. Half way from Burnt Corn to Little Escambia, the pine land loses the quality of clay, and is sandy, the pine tall and large.

APPENDIX

INDIAN TREATIES.

TREATY AT AUGUSTA, JUNE 1, 1773.

By Sir James Wright and John Stewart, with the Cherokees and Creeks.

This treaty fixes the eastern bounds of the Cherokees to be from the tree marked by the Cherokees, near the head of a branch falling into the Oconee river, and from thence to Savannah river.

TREATY AT HOPEWELL, NOVEMBER 28, 1785.

From Tugalo river, "thence a direct line to the top of Currohe mountain ; thence to the head of the South fork of Oconee river."
In 1803, at the treaty near Fort Wilkinson, this boundary admitted by the Creeks, and that a line from the High Shoals of Apalatche, along the old path to Sauwanna, on Chat-to-ho-che, bounds the Creek claims on this quarter.

TREATY AT NEW YORK, AUGUST 7, 1790.

Article III.

" The Creek Nation shall deliver, as soon as practicable, to the commanding officer of the troops of the United States, stationed at the Rock-landing on the Oconee river, all citizens of the United States, white inhabitants or negroes, who are now prisoners in any part of said nation. And if any such prisoners or negroes should not be so delivered on or before the 1st day of June ensuing, the Governor of Georgia may empower three persons to repair to the said Nation in order to claim and receive such prisoners and negroes."

TREATY AT COLERAIN, JUNE 29, 1796.

ARTICLE VII.

" The Creek Nation shall deliver, as soon as practicable, to the Super-intendent of Indian affairs, at such place as he may direct, all citizens of the United States, white inhabitants and negroes, who are now prisoners in any part of the said Nation, agreeable to the treaty of New York, and also all citizens, white inhabitants, negroes and property taken since the signing of that treaty. And if any such prisoners, negroes or property should not be delivered, on or before the first day of January next, the Governor of Georgia may empower three persons to repair to the said Nation, in order to claim and receive such prisoners, negroes, and property, under the direction of the President of the United States."

LETTERS OF BENJAMIN HAWKINS,
1796–1806

INTRODUCTION

This volume contains the writings of Col. Benjamin Hawkins, the United States Agent for Indian Affairs South of the Ohio River, covering a period from 1796 to 1806. The original manuscripts have been in the possession of the Georgia Historical Society for about three-quarters of a century, and as a contribution to the history of Georgia and of the United States the Society now gives them to the public. There are, in all, nine of these volumes, written by Hawkins himself, and one by his secretary, Richard Thomas. They are in the form of bound journals, and the writing is distinct and well preserved.

One of these volumes, entitled **A Sketch of the Creek Country,** was published for the Georgia Historical Society in 1848, by Mr. Wm. B. Hodgson, and it forms Part I of Volume III of the Society's collections. This is not included in the present volume. The letters of Richard Thomas, who seems to have been the secretary of Hawkins for a time, are included, as they pertain to the affairs of the Indian Agency.

How these manuscripts came into the possession of the Georgia Historical Society is best told by Mr. Wm. B. Hodgson in his introduction to **A Sketch of the Creek Country,** written in 1848. He says:

"It is reported that many valuable papers of Mr. Hawkins have been irreparably lost to the world by the burning of his residence in the Creek country. The present manuscripts, it is supposed, have been preserved by their having been submitted to the Governor of the State, at Milledgeville, for his perusal. Colonel Hawkins was still living in the year 1825.* In that year these volumes were in Savannah, under the charge of Mr. Joseph Bevan, who had been appointed by the General Assembly to collect, arrange and publish all papers relating to the original settlement or political history of the state. I learn this fact from a

---

* This date is in error. Colonel Hawkins died on June 6, 1816.

published report of his made to Governor Troup. At the decease of Mr. Bevan they were probably returned to the executive department at Milledgeville. At the institution of the Historical Society a fortunate accident brought these valuable papers to the knowledge of I. K. Tefft, Esq., the Corresponding Secretary of the Society, and the actual Cashier of the Bank of the State of Georgia at Savannah. At his pressing instance, in favor of the Society, they were solicited and obtained for the Society's library."

The portrait and biographical sketch of Colonel Hawkins have been reproduced from the **Biographical History of North Carolina,** by the courteous permission of the publisher, Mr. Charles L. Van Noppen, of Greensboro, N. C., to whom the thanks of the Society are due.

In the body of the work no attempt has been made to correct errors common to writers of that time, but the aim has been to present the matter as it appears in the manuscript.

While much of the matter contained herein has but little value, there is still much that will throw additional light upon the obscure history of the Indians in the South, and with the hope that the future historian may find in these pages valuable material for a larger history of our state and country, the Georgia Historical Society offers this volume with its unselfish motto, *Non Sibi, Sed Aliis.*

OTIS ASHMORE.
J. F. MINIS.   Committee on
W. W. MACKALL.   Printing and Publishing.
DR. T. J. CHARLTON.

BENJAMIN HAWKINS

BENJAMIN HAWKINS, public servant in many capacities,
was born August 15, 1754, in what was then Granville, later Bute,
and now Warren County, North Carolina. He was the son of
Philemon and Delia (Martin) Hawkins and came of a family which
has been well known in the State and has filled many positions of
trust and honor. His father's life forms the subject of a separate
sketch in the present work. Benjamin Hawkins, the son, was
reared in what is now Warren County, and like his neighbor, Nat
Macon, was sent, along with his younger brother, Joseph, to
Princeton and was a student in the senior class when the war
of the Revolution began. Having acquired a knowledge of French,
he left Princeton, was appointed on the staff of General Washington, and acted as his interpreter. But his duties as a member of
Washington's military family did not cease with translating. He
braved the rigors of the campaign, participated in the Battle of
Monmouth, and won the respect of his superiors.

He soon returned to North Carolina, and in February, 1779,
the State commissioned him as agent to obtain at home and abroad
supplies of all kinds for the prosecution of the war, including
arms and ammunition, blankets, hats, clothing, tent cloth, corn,
salt, pork, etc. He was instructed to visit Holland, France and
Spain (State Rec. XIII. 605-6) and did make a trip to St. Eustatia,
a neutral island of the West Indies and a sort of Nassau of that
day. Tobacco was used as a basis for purchases. It was bought
in North Carolina and shipped to the West Indies and there exchanged. Hawkins loaded a merchant ship and sent her to North
Carolina with supplies, chiefly munitions of war, but she was
captured by the British on the home trip, and her owner, John
Wright Stanly, of New-Bern, failing to recover from the State,
sued Hawkins in his personal capacity. The Courts decided that
the purchases and contracts of the State's agent did not bind him
personally (1st Haywood's Reports). His efforts at importa-
tion from foreign ports were not entirely without success, for in
February, 1780, he had imported 878 stands of arms from St.
Eustatia, but adds: "I could not procure anything on the faith
of the State, or by barter for provisions or tobacco, as was expected." (State Rec. XV., p. 337.) At home he was also employed
in procuring food supplies, especially corn, salt and pork, and met
with more success than in his foreign enterprises, for there were
fewer obstacles to overcome.

He early impressed the Assembly with his fitness for activity
on a wider field, for as early as February 3, 1779, he was nominated for, and on July 14, 1781, was elected a delegate to the
Continental Congress in place of Charles Johnson, declined (State
Rec. XIII. 585; XVII. 872). He first appears in the journals of
that body on October 4, 1781; was re-elected May 3, 1782; again
in May, 1783, and served until 1784. He was chosen December
16, 1786, for the remainder of the year, which had begun November 1st, to supply a place then vacant and was again elected in
December, 1787, but seems not to have served this last appointment. While in the Continental Congress he was particularly interested in the navigation of the Mississippi, in the protection of
the frontiers from the Indians, in a southern post route, in trade
and commerce, etc. In December, 1787, along with Robert Bur-
ton and William Blount he gives a gloomy but accurate picture
of the state of the Union. It was then on the eve of bankruptcy;
little had been paid on the foreign debt, and the Government was
on the verge of dissolution. He resigned his post the same month.

Hawkins had served in the North Carolina Assembly as early
as the April and August sessions, 1778, and January session,
1779. He was again in the Assembly in April, 1784, as a representative from Warren. He played here a conspicuous part,
being often on the floor and serving on such committees as that
on the tax to be levied by the Continental Congress and on the
Continental Line, and on such special committees as those on confiscated estates, civil list, duties, Martinique debt, etc. He was
nominated for membership in the Council of State this year, and
it is known that he opposed the wholesale condemnation of Tories,
acting in this connection with the conservatives and opposing
such radicals as Bloodworth, Rutherford and Martin (State Records XVII. 145).

During the years immediately following the war the State was
very much oppressed by the want of a fixed circulating medium.
The paper money had depreciated till it was worth only 800 to 1;
there was practically no gold and silver in circulation, and as a
result the State was hard put to meet its current obligations, pay
its officers, and raise its proportion of the foreign debt of the Confederation. To meet this emergency State buyers of tobacco were
appointed in various towns, who gathered and stored such amounts
of merchantable tobacco as were available. This was then sold
to the best advantage and the proceeds used in payment of the
foreign debt. In 1787 Hawkins and William Blount, in addition
to their other duties as delegates in the Continental Congress, were
charged with the sale of this tobacco, which work was successfully
accomplished.

In December, 1788, Hawkins was nominated along with Hugh Williamson and Abishai Thomas as agent to settle the accounts of North Carolina with the United States; the last two were chosen. In November of that year he was also nominated as a delegate to the proposed convention, whose work it was to be to further revise and democratize the new Federal Constitution. In November, 1789, he represented Warren County in the Fayetteville Convention. He served on its committee on order and voted for the adoption of the Federal Constitution.

After the State entered the new Federal Union there was another struggle between the two parties of the day, conservatives and radicals, or Federalists and anti-Federalists, later Republicans, over the senators to the new Federal Congress. The struggle began in the Assembly three days after the ratification of the Constitution. The nominees for senators were Samuel Johnston, Benjamin Hawkins, James White, Joseph McDowell, Timothy Bloodworth, Thomas Person, William Blount, John Williams, William Lenoir, John Stokes, Richard Dobbs Spaight and William Polk, a goodly company, where the rankest Federalist was crowded and jostled by the extreme Radical. The Federals were in power, and it was proper that Samuel Johnston, the leading exponent of that party's political principles, should be chosen the first senator in Congress from North Carolina (November 27, 1789). After some skirmishing Hawkins was chosen on December 9th as the second senator. He was the first to enter upon his duties, having qualified January 13, 1790, and winning the long term, served till March 3, 1795. Johnston drew the short term and served from January 29, 1790, to March 2, 1793. In the meantime the political tide changed in North Carolina, and the Federalist and ultra-conservative Johnston was succeeded in 1793 by the more liberal Alexander Martin, while in 1795 Hawkins, aristocratic, conservative, proud and wealthy, gave way for the ultra-radical Bloodworth, who had begun life as a blacksmith and by sheer force of native intellect had worked his way to the front in public life.

It is of interest to make note here, merely as a sign of the times, that in 1790 the "alarming secrecy" of the Senate caused the North Carolina Assembly to instruct its senators to use their influence to make the debates of the Senate public when sitting in its legislative capacity; "to correspond regularly and constantly with the executive during the recess of the Legislature" and at other times with the Legislature itself, and to secure the publication of the journals of the Senate.

Hawkins had been appointed a commissioner on March 21, 1785, to treat with the Cherokees and "all other Indians southward of them" in accord with the act of Congress of March 15, 1785.

The other commissioners were Daniel Carroll, William Perry, Andrew Pickens and Joseph Martin (q. v.). Carroll and Perry did not serve and their place was taken by Lachlan McIntosh. They were instructed to give due notice to the Governor of North Carolina. They were to treat with the Cherokees, and also with the Creeks, Chickasaws and Choctaws, and were authorized to draw on Virginia, North Carolina, South Carolina and Georgia for funds, and warned the executives of those States that funds must be forthcoming if the treaties were to be held. Caswell writes back that, while North Carolina was hard pressed, he would furnish one-third of the total sum asked for. The commissioners spent 1785 in making preparations; goods were purchased and sent to Charleston to go overland to Koowee. The Indians were slow in coming; the Creeks failed them entirely and the Continental commissioners did not sign the treaty of Galphinton, which was the work of the agents of Georgia alone. On November 28, 1785, Hawkins signed at Hopewell on Koowee with the Cherokees the treaty of Hopewell, than which perhaps no other Indian treaty was more roundly denounced by the whites. The object of this treaty was to define the claims of the whites and Indians respectively and so prevent encroachments of the former. William Blount was present as agent for North Carolina, and agents for Georgia were also in attendance. The treaty was mainly the work of Martin; the chief question was that of boundaries, and the Indians drafted a map showing their claims. They were induced to give up Transylvania, to leave out the Cumberland section and the settlements on French Broad and Holston. The boundaries thus fixed were the most favorable it was possible to obtain without regard to previous purchases and pretended purchases made by private individuals and others. The Indians yielded an extensive territory to the United States, but on the other hand the commissioners conceded to them a considerable extent of territory that had been purchased by private individuals, though by methods of more than doubtful legality. The commissioners agreed to remove some families from the Indian lands, but they did not agree to remove those between French Broad and Holston. This angered the Indians, who said that they had never sold those lands. The whites were angry because some favors had been shown the Indians and because there had not been further curtailment of territory, and the States were angry because the commissioners had encroached on their reserved rights. William Blount, as agent of North Carolina, protested, and efforts were made in Congress to destroy the treaty (State Rec., XVII. 578-9; XVIII. 49, 591-2, 490-1; XX. 762). Encroachments continued; orders were issued by North Carolina and by the Continental Congress that settlers should leave the Indian lands. These settlers were even threatened with the army; but treaties, proclamations and threats were alike in vain, for the terms of the treaty were never fully executed. Hawkins, Pickens and Martin signed treaties with the Choctaws on January 3rd, and with the Chickasaws January 10, 1786, at the same place.

With this preliminary experience Hawkins was somewhat prepared to undertake the difficult and dangerous work of an Indian agent. His term as senator expired March 3, 1795. In June of that year Washington appointed him along with George Clymer, of Pennsylvania, and Andrew Pickens, of South Carolina, to treat with the Creek Confederacy and to investigate the anomalous political relationship caused by the treaty of Galphinton in 1785, where the Creeks had acknowledged themselves as within the limits of Georgia and members of the same, and the treaty of New York, signed August 7, 1790, where they placed themselves under the protection of the United States alone and bound themselves not to enter into any treaty with any other individual, State or power.

In 1796 Washington appointed Hawkins agent of the United States among the Creeks and general superintendent of all the tribes south of the Ohio River (Chappell's "Miscellanies;" his commission was renewed by Jefferson in 1801). From this time, 1796, the remainder of the life of Benjamin Hawkins was devoted entirely to the Indian. It is said that his family opposed this determination, for it was ambitious and wealthy. It is possible that there was an element of pique at the change in the political tide in North Carolina, but it is certain that Hawkins had already been much among the Indians; he had penetrated the mighty forests and had tasted the freedom that comes with life in the woods; he had felt what a modern novelist has keenly denominated the "call of the wild," and when this spirit has once entered into and mastered the soul of man it is seldom that he again willingly submits to the restraints of civilization. When Hawkins accepted this position as Indian agent he practically quit civilized society, buried himself in the remote and savage woods and among a still more savage people, with whom the remainder of his days were spent.

On June 29, 1796, Hawkins negotiated with the Creeks the treaty of Colerain which served as a useful supplement to the treaty of New York and by which the boundaries of the earlier treaty were confirmed. From this time for twenty years Colonel Hawkins as United States agent among the Creeks wielded a proconsular sway over a scope of country regal in extent: Beginning at St. Mary's the Creek boundary ran across to the Altamaha; thence it turned up and along the west bank of that river and of the Oconee to the High Shoals of the Appalachee, where it inter-

sected the Cherokee line; thence through Georgia and Alabama
to the Choctaw line in Mississippi; thence south down the Choctaw line to the 31st parallel; thence east to the Chattahoochee,
and then down that river to its junction with the Flint; thence
to the head of St. Mary's River, and thence to the beginning.

Hawkins began his work as agent by a careful study of the
people and of their country. He did much to initiate and encourage
them in the lower forms, the basal elements, of civilization; pastur-
age was brought into use; agriculture was encouraged by example
as well as precept, for he brought his slaves from North Carolina
and at the agency on Flint River cultivated a large plantation and
raised immense crops of corn and other provisions, thus setting
a high example of how to do by doing. He owned great herds
of hogs and cattle and practised towards the Indians a profuse
hospitality which always wins their friendship and esteem. Other
treaties were negotiated with the Creeks at Fort Wilkinson,
Georgia, in 1802, and at Washington, D. C., in 1805; also with the
Chickasaws and Choctaws in 1801, 1802, 1803, and 1805, in which
Hawkins was more or less of a participant and all of which meant
a further cession of lands to the United States by the Indians who
were under his control. But peaceful and friendly relations were
generally maintained by Hawkins between advancing white and
retreating Amerind for about sixteen years. With the war of
1812 the times changed. It was no longer possible for him to
control the Creeks, who fell under the influence of British emissaries. Tecumseh had visited them in 1811 on a mission of war.
Hawkins met the great warrior of the north at Tuckabatchee, the
Creek capital, while holding a great council of the nation, but
Tecumseh kept silent as to the object of his mission till the departure of Hawkins. Then, through that fierce Indian eloquence
of which he was master and by the fanatical religiosity of his
brother, the Prophet, a great Indian war was kindled, which
spread far and wide over the frontier. But that part of the Creek
country bordering on Georgia and extending west from the Ocmulgee, to the Chattahoochee, never became the seat of actual
warfare, and hence the eastern frontier was spared its horrors.
This was due very largely to the fact that Hawkins's seat was on
the Ocmulgee, opposite the present Macon, and afterwards on the
Flint at the place since known as the Old Agency, and that his
influence was naturally greater on the eastern than on the western
border of the Creek country. The eastern Creeks were actually
organized into a regiment of defence of which Hawkins became
titular colonel, the actual command devolving on the halfbreed
chief, William McIntosh.

The uprising of the Creeks was crushed in fire and blood by
Jackson early in 1814; by the treaty of Fort Jackson their limits

were greatly reduced and their strength broken forever. This treaty was the death-knell of the nation; even the friendly chiefs withered under its influence, and the passing of the people for whom he had so long and faithfully labored perhaps hastened the death of Hawkins himself, which occurred at the Old Indian Agency on the Flint River, now Crawford County, Georgia, on June 6, 1816, where he was buried. Wheeler states in his "Reminiscences" that Hawkins married and left one son, Madison, and three daughters.

Colonel Hawkins was a man of liberal education, high attainments and much experience. He was far above the average Indian agent of that day and of this in general culture and grasp of affairs. Further, he was a man of approved honesty, and his life, as seen in his published letters, shows clearly that he was devoted to the material upbuilding of the Indians under his care and to their intellectual advancement. The eminent position that the Creeks, Cherokees, Chickasaws and Choctaws now occupy among the civilized tribes of the Indian Territory is to be traced beyond question in part to the fostering and fatherly care shown them a hundred years ago by one who sought not to exploit his proteges for his own material benefit, but strove rather, by example as well as precept, to lift them to a higher life, and whose efforts they recognized and rewarded in the significant title Iste-chate-lige-osetat-chemis-te-chaugo—Beloved Man of the Four Nations.

Colonel Hawkins also devoted much time to the study of Indian history, especially that of the Creeks. Much of his material was destroyed by fire, but eight manuscript volumes escaped and are in possession of the Georgia Historical Society. These volumes relate to the history of the various tribes with whom he treated and are filled with details of treaties, his correspondence on behalf of the Indians with the State and General Governments, vocabularies of Indian languages, records of the manners and customs, religious rites, civil polity, etc. His "Sketch of the Creek Country in 1798 and 1799" was published in 1848 as Part 1 of Volume 3 of the Historical Collections of the Georgia Historical Society. It is filled with matters relating to the life, manners and customs of the Creeks and to the natural features of their country. His journal of a "Tour Through the Creek Country," November 19, 1796, to May 21, 1797, is still in manuscript and is owned by the same society. While in many respects Hawkins's studies have been superceded by later and more scientific ones, they are in others still of great value, and if published would serve as a valuable picture of Creek Indian life at a time when that powerful nation had come little in contact with the English-speaking world by whom they were to be in part destroyed, in part absorbed.

This sketch is based on the sketch of Hawkins in his "Creek Country," on that in Chappell's "Miscellanies of Georgia," on the "North Carolina State Records" and on Royce's "Indian Land Cessions in the United States."

STEPHEN B. WEEKS.

Reproduced by permission from the Biographical History of North Carolina. Charles Van Noppen, Publisher, Greensboro, N. C.

LETTERS

OF

BENJAMIN HAWKINS

How many were killed?
Hungau humgot humgotcan istornin acunnan wocgiegescan.
How many were wound?
Iste unnutulgee natchomau.
Are you wounded?
Achenuttau.

South Carolina, 19th Nov., 1796.

I this day arrived at Hopewell on the Koowee, the seat of Maj. General Andrew Pickins, on my way to the Creeks as principal temporary agent for Indian affairs south of the Ohio.

November 22.

Having consulted the General on the objects of my mission, and obtained the requisite information on some points relative thereto, I wrote to the Secretary of War.

No. 1.   Hopewell on Koowee, 22nd Nov., 1796.

Sir:

I have been unwell since I left you, and unable to travel as fast as I intended when I sat out from Philadelphia. I arrived however, here, the seat of General Pickins, on the 19th inst., in better health than I have experienced for several years.

I have explained to the General the benevolent views of the government in relation to the Indians, with which he is much pleased; and situated as he is on this frontier, confided in and respected by the citizens and Indians, ne can and will do much in aid of our plan. We have fixed on the 10th of March to meet at the Currahee Mountain to run the boundary line between the Creeks and the United States agreeably to Treaty. The line must be run from Tugalo River over the Currahee Mountain to the source of the main south branch of the Oconee. The General supposes the distance to be from Tugalo to the Currahee Mountain 15 miles, and from thense to the termination 35 miles. In the neighbourhood of this line there is plenty of young cane and provisions. It may be necessary to order a company of cavalry to attend the runing of the line.

The Cherokee line may be commenced the 1st of April, and not sooner, as there is not any cane from the North Carolina line to Holston. There remains to be run about 15 miles in this State to the North Carolina boundary. There is some ambiguity in the part of the line from that boundary as expressed in the Treaty, "thense north to a point." How far north is this point?

There are several traders down from the Cherokees who have come to the Ocunna station with pack horses, and taken their skins and furs, about 30 waggon loads, from thense to Charleston; the price of waggonage 2 dollars, 12 cents per horse; the average price for some years past $2.50. There are at that station 20 militia, 4 of them mounted. The distance from the Ocunna to Hopewell 23, and from this to Charleston 240 miles.

I hope Mr. Dinsmoor has been able to give you the characters of the persons who have accompanyed the Chickasaws, Choctaws and Creeks. The latter cannot be too much discountenanced. This visiting did not originate among the Indians. I have been informed that Rogers & Chisholm have some connexion in land jobbing not favourable to the peace of the frontiers.

I shall leave this on the 24th, go over the Ocunna Mountain, through the upper Cherokee to the Tallapoosa and down that river among the Creeks. I shall devote all the time between my arrival and march, to visiting their towns to explain the objects contemplated in my mission, and return at the time appointed with some of the chiefs to the Currahee Mountains.

As the path over the Ocunna Mountain is the thoroughfare for this extensive frontier, I think it advisable for the present, that the President should appoint General Pickins to grant paper. He has a better knowledge of the people and their pursuits than any man I know. If you approve of this, you can send him some blanks, and request of him to postpone this session. He is in 4 miles of Pendleton Court House, a post town. I shall not mention the subject to him.

I have the honor to be with sincere regard and esteem, sir,

Your obedient servant.

The Honorable
    JAMES McHENRY,
        Secretary of War.

November 24th.

I this day sat out from General Pickins's, to the Ocunna station, after having been fited out with whatever was necessary by the most friendly hospitality of the General and his lady. I crossed the Theowee near his house and traveled W. N. W. up the river and through an uneaven broken country 11 miles to Cane Creek. Here I met with George Downing a trader from the Pine Log, and Notetsenschansaie with his brothers, halfbreeds; they have uniformly supported a fair character. He sent his nephew, Tom Pettit, a decent, orderly young man with me to Ocunna to provide a pilot and interpreter for me, 8 miles farther I crossed a small creek and 4 more arrived at William Richard's, a trader who lives at the station; he was from home, but Mr. Cleveland, his clerk, was there and furnished me with such accomodations as he had, being pretty good. There I added to my traveling stock a bear skin and some things necessary to procure provisions from the Indians on my way. Tom Pettit engaged as a pilot for me Richard Ratley, a native of Halifax district in North Carolina, an inhabitant for several years of the Creek Path, a town on the Tennessee.

25th.

This morning the hour 4. Mr. Mossley returned to the station. I sat out over the mountain and he accompanyed me, as far as the line. One mile and an half from the top of the mountain there is an extensive view of the country below and the surrounding mountains. The land just over on the Cherokee side of the line has been recommended as a fit site for a station to secure the execution of the law for regulating trade and intercourse among the tribes and as proper for a trading post. I believe a small post might be kept to advantage. The Lt. informs me he sends a scout every other day as far as Tugalo, and that it has had some effect in lessening the depredations on this quarter. I heard, notwithstanding, that hunting parties after bear and deer were going daily over on the Indian lands. I informed him of the law, and the necessity there was to cause it to be respected. He told me that altho' he had heard of the law, he had never seen it. I parted with him and continued on my journey 8½ miles to Chattuga River, the north fork of Tugalo, the lands broken and not furtile, crossed the river and went on thro' a vale between the mountains 1 mile to Warwoman's Creek, crossed it 2 miles further, traveling thro' better land, crossed it again and continued up 5 miles to a canebrake; here I encamped. In my neighbourhood were some camps of packhorsemen, waiting for the return of the goods from Charleston. The night was very clear and cold, and my encampment ill-chosen. My horses had strayed a mile from me, which induced me to remain here and breakfast.

26th.

My pilot arrived, and I sat out at 9 o'clock and continued up the creek to its source, crossing it in all nine times. This creek is called Falling Creek by Bartram. I met two Indian women on horseback, driving ten very fat cattle to the station for a market. I crossed a ridge which divides the waters of this creek from those of Sticcoa, and went down then to the main creek at the dividings, so called from the division of the path here. I take the left, the course W. This path is 8 miles from camp. There is on the creek in this neighbourhood fine cane in abundance, and here I saw encamped the remainder of the packhorsemen, with 60 or 70 horses. There passed me this day from Etowwah, 10 horses loaded with skins, this makes 31 waggon loads that have been brought down this path this season.

I traveled down this creek one mile and crossed a creek 8 feet wide runing to the left; in the forks of these creeks stood foremost the town Sticcoa, both creeks abound with cane. The course now was S. W. 4 miles to the Potato Hill Mountains, the lands in this vale, not rich, the timber small and mostly scruboak, there is in front a beautiful mountain, standing apparently alone, and of a conic form going round and rising S. from it the top of one of the Potato Hills. There is a very grand view of mountains to the N. and the whole scope from that point E. and W. I continue on 6 miles farther thro' broken hills, the valeys moderately rich, to Tooroora, a branch of the South Tugalo, is 15 yards wide. 5 miles farther I cross another creek, and 2 miles farther another, a branch of Chattahoochee, cross here a small branch, go down the creek half a mile and encamp. The Chattahoochee runs W. The lands are good in the valeys, the timber large, the cane abundant, about 15 feet high. I lodged in the canebrake on the border of the creek, the night very cold, clear and freezing, the creek 12 feet wide.

27th.

I sat out this morning before sun rise, and soon turned S. by W.; in two miles passed through Santa, formerly an Indian

---

Chattohoche, from chatto, a stone, and hoche, flowered—a place on the R.

town, there was one hut, some peach trees and the posts of the town house, the town was in the fork of Chattahoochee and a creek, 12 feet wide, which we crossed, both well stored with cane, the lands about the town poor, gravelly, covered with dwarf trees, a mountain to our left, very barron. 4 miles farther south we passed through Little Chota, a creek 35 feet wide run through the town, there remains one small field of corn, some peach, plumb and locust trees, the border of the creek covered with small cane. The lands in the neighbourhood poor. As I approached this town I had a fine view of a mountain to the S. The water which oozed from near its summit formed a sheet of ice of several acres. One mile farther I entered a savanna and passed thro' it E. cross a creek runing to the left 15 feet wide, leave the second town on that side, turn to the S. up a small river to its source 1½ miles, then passing over the ridge the mountain is again in view, exhibiting a long slope of it from its summit, with the appearance of a road, 2 miles cross a creek runing to the right, the paths divide and I take the left, the course for the last 3 miles W. One mile farther I cross a rocky creek after descending the whole way near its border: covered with ever-greens, the creek 15 feet wide, the fall 12 feet over rocks in the course of 60 feet, the lands poor, the creek runing to the right. In 2 miles I came to a large canebrake to the right, cross a small branch runing to the right and breakfast on its border, at its junction with one runing N. Thence up the latter, cross it; in 3 miles cross another rocky creek runing to the right, the fall 10 feet in 40 yards, the width 15 feet. Travel on through poor lands for 8 miles, cross a branch runing to the right and then one to the left, and down this 4 miles to the river, the hill sides steep and rich, the bottoms covered with cane. Cross the river runing to the left, 120 feet wide, the lands rich and level on both sides; continue 3 miles thro' pretty good land, the growth oak mixed with pine, and encamp on the margin of a creek runing to the left, 10 feet wide; the lands rich, the cane small but excellent for food, but not abundant.

28th.

Sat out at sun rise W.; in two miles cross a river 60 feet wide which I suppose to be Etowwah, travel over some poor, sharp hills, our course S. W. by W. In 4 miles came to a large and beautiful savanna, a creek runing thro' it stored with cane. After entering the savanna ¼ of a mile, enter a grove of dwarf hard shelled hickory trees, the ground covered with nuts, pass one mile over flat lands with small growth, cross a creek 15 feet wide runing to the left, stored with cane; one mile farther cross over 3 creeks within half a mile of each other, the site of a town which I take to be Newtown, the land very good, and all the creeks margined with cane, go down the richest vale of land I have yet seen, one mile to Etowwah, the timber white oak, poplar, and chesnut, very large, and tall cane on the river, cross the river 75 feet wide, runing to the right, continue thro' rich uneaven chesnut land for 5 miles and cross the Etowwah runing to the left, 120 feet wide, continue down the river W. by S. over steep poor hills for 5 miles and cross a creek 15 feet wide, the bottoms rich with cane. On the west side bordering on the river is the remains of some Indian settlement. Continue 2 miles down the river and cross Looccunna heat (Long Swamp), a creek 35 feet wide, turn down the creek and thro' the remains of the town of this name, there were some peach trees, cotton stalks and corn; continue down the river 3 miles and saw an Indian and his family from Pine Log, going out to hunt, he conducted me to the habitation of some Indian women, there were 3 families from Towe. I lodged at the hut of one who was a halfbreed. She treated me hospitably. She was poor, she said from trouble and difficulty not from want of industry. She had been greatly incommoded by the misunderstanding between the Red and White people. She knew not where to fix down, and this uncertainty continued until it was too late to make corn, she planted some, but too late. She showed me a wound in one of her arms which she got on a visit to some of her friends who lived in the neighbourhood when the town was attacked by some white people from Tugalo. I mentioned the plan contemplated by the government for bettering the condition of the Red people, she replied she had once made as much cotton as purchased a petticoat, that she would gladly make more and learn to spin it, if she had the opportunity. I went over the river to John Candry's and purchased from his wife some corn, potatoes and fodder. John was from East Florida since 1783, he uses the plough and has some fine cattle.

I was here informed of some of the difficulties and hardships which these poor people are subject to. They sell the fowls grown, 2 for 2½ yards of binding worth 2 cents, a bushel of corn for a quart of salt and sometimes a pint, and the woman had just returned from the settlements, a journey of 17 days. She carried a bushel and an half of chesnuts on her back and gave them for a petticoat. This little settlement is on the richest lands I have seen, the second low grounds about eighty feet above the first, with a gentle slope, the lands above by far the richest, the growth poplar and chesnut very large without any undergrowth, back of these rich lands about 500 yards are two hills which over-look the whole of the flat lands, and are beautiful sites for a dweling.

Wednesday, 29th.

I set out this morning after breakfast, went down the river
one mile, on these rich lands, then turned thro' the woods W.
2 miles to the path I left yesterday, took it S. W. I met an
Indian girl and a halfbreed servant, on horseback, who informed
me as the pilot understood, that we were near to the Pine Log,
and that the path turned to the right some small distance back.
I turned thro' the woods for half an hour N. W., found myself
housed in with hills and mountains, turned round to the right
until in one hour I fell in with the Indian girl again, found she
had been misunderstood, discharged my pilot at his request, and
set out with the girl who agreed to conduct to some Indians on
the path who were getting hickory nuts. From the place where
I first met them, in one mile I crossed a river 20 yards wide and
traveled up a steep and long hill, the lands poor, and continued on
5 miles cross a creek 4 feet wide, the creek runing to the left,
go up the branch to the left one mile; the lands on this branch
to its source were timbered with large white oak and some large
poplar near the source. Crossed a ridge and small branch where
gro some large poplars and go down the same 1½ miles to the
creek, the lands broken, stoney and rich. The growth chesnut,
poplar, white & red oak. Then down the creek ½ mile to an
old Indian settlement, deserted, the peach trees thriving, the
lands rich, the growth mostly hickory, tall and large. Here I
saw several Indian women from Etowwah, gathering hickory nuts,
and here this path divided and I was under some difficulty in
endeavoring to get into the right one, until one of the women
spoke to me in English and gave me the information I wanted.
There being plenty of cane on the borders of the creek, I determined to encamp altho' I was out of provisions, and the Indian
women unable to afford me any. The distance between here and
Etowwah is said to be one day's ride, and from here to Pine Log
3 hours. Bashel Pettit who spoke to a halfbreed daughter of
James Haws, she is the wife of Thomas Pettit, a nephew of
George Downing, she appears to be a very decent, good little
woman, has a little daughter with white hair and a beautiful
rosy complexion. Thomas Pettit her husband is the man who
came with me to Ocunna to provide me with a pilot. In the
course of the morning Christian Russel a Silician by birth, with a
young man from Georgia arrived. Russel has been for some time
in the nation and about to set up a tanyard at Etowwah, he has
taned some leather in the nation and taken it into the settlements.
I inform him of the Law, and the penalties annexed to the violations, he said he was pleased with it and should conform to it.

and aid in its execution, that he had already been at Oosetenale to see Mr. Dinsmoor who had been for some time to the northward. He gave me some testimonials of his character, which were favourable and I wanted him now to proceed in obtaining his licence. The weather continues cloudy and very cold.

Thursday, 30th Nov.

I sat out this morning early and took the right hand W. to Fine Log, in half a mile $\times$ a creek runing to the left, go one mile, take the left path, 2 miles $\times$ a creek 15 feet over, moving to the left, rise a steep hill and continue on over broken stony hills 8½ miles to Pine Log (Notetsenschansaie). Here I had a negro woman for my interpreter, I determined to spend the day here, it being rainy and cold. I lodged in the house of Mrs. Gagg the mother of the Downings. In the course of the evening and this morning the Indian women visited me, and Mrs. Downing, who had heard the president's talk interpreted, repeatedly informed them who I was, and the object of the government in sending me to them. They informed me that the men were all in the woods hunting, that they alone were at home to receive me, that they rejoiced much at what they had heard and hoped it would prove true, that they had made some cotton, and would make more and follow the instruction of the agent and the advise of the President. They exhibited to me a sample of their ingenuity in the manufacture of baskets and sifters, out of cane, the dies of the splits were good and workmanship not surpassed in the United States by white people. I recommended to them to be attentive to Mr. Dinsmoor.

Friday, 1st December.

Set out for Etowwah at 10 and arrived in 4 hours. The lands good in the neighbourhood of Pine Log, the way pretty level, the land poor from thense until I arrive in the neighbourhood of the town. Having been put a little out of the path of my direction, I was put to some difficulty in finding a person who could interpret for me. I was directed to two or three women, but they were at the opposite end of the town from that which I entered, and I had to apply to 8 or 10 persons before I could get one to direct me. At length I found Sally Waters, a halfbreed wife of Col. Waters late of Georgia, she speaks the tongue well, it being her mother tongue, and she speaks English well enough for common subjects within the sphere of domestic objects. She was on a visit to her aunt, the wife of Ogosatah (sowes much) and consented to remain with me while I continued in town, and I took up my abode in the house of this chief. Sally Hawes called to see me and assisted in interpreting for me. The chiefs and warriors were all out hunting. There were a few old men and some young ones only at home. The old people and many of the women and children who are unprovided with blankets and winter cloathing sleep in the hot houses. I visited them in the evening and conversed with them on the plan for bettering their conditions. Mrs. Waters and Sally Hughes took much pains to explain the whole. I remained for several hours with them. She told them that she had learnt to spin and weave while she was in the settlements, and that she would readily assist them. They expressed much satisfaction at the assurances given, that they might remain in their towns in peace and that the government meant seriously to assist them. They said they would follow the advise of their great father General Washington, they would plant cotton and be prepared for spining as soon as they could make it, and they hoped they might get some wheels and cards as soon as they should be ready for them, they promised also to take care of their pigs and cattle. They told me that they would make corn enough but that they never could sell it. That they were willing to labour if they could be directed how to profit by it.

Saturday, 2nd Dec.

This day being cold and cloudy, I determined to remain where I am. I applied to the women to supply me with provisions while I remained, and to provide some for the road. I applied to the old men to procure me a pilot for the nearest Creek town.

The women immediately brought some fowls which were very fat, and made the necessary provisions for me here and for the road. They asked a pint of salt a pair for fat hens, and a quart for a bushel of corn. I had a long conversation with them on the situation and circumstances as it respected their labour, and inquired to know what they made and what they wished, in aid of their own exertions. They informed me they performed almost all the labour, the men assisted but little and that in the corn. They generally made a plenty of corn and sweet potatoes and pumpkins. They made beans, ground peas, cymblins, gourds, watermelons, musmelons, collards and onions. They made great use of beans in their bread.

They wanted principally salt, that they used but little from necessity, and where they were able to supply themselves plentifully with meat, they were unable to preserve it for the want of salt. They raised hogs, some cattle, and a great many poultry.

If they could be directed how to turn their labour to account like the white people, they should be contented, they made sugar, had raised some cotton, and manufactured their baskets, sifters, pots and earthen pans. Their men hunted in the proper season and aided them with the skins in providing cloathes and blankets, such as I saw, but this was not sufficient to make them comfortable and the poor old men, women and children were under the necessity of sleeping as I saw them in their town house.

They in the morning told me that many men had been sent into their nation to their chiefs but I was the first who thought it worth while to examine into the situation of the women. I had addressed myself to them, and talked freely and fondly to them, and they were sure I meant to better their condition. They would follow my advise. They told me they were healthy, and lived to old age, some few had had the ague and fever, but that generally speaking they were never too unwell to labour, even when they bore children they were their own midwives and would most of them turn out the next day after delivering themselves and pursue their ordinary occupations.

Sunday, 3rd Dec.

This morning the women recommended two men, a young one and an old man to conduct me to the Creeks. They brought them prepared to set out, and they said that as I should soon be in a situation not so secure as I had been with my horses, the old man determined to take me by the hand and see me safe. I sat out X the river about 80 yards wide, moving W. N. W. went down for half a mile, then left it W. and passed thro' some very level land, not rich, in 2 miles X a small creek, in 1½ come to John Van's & David Roe living on a creek 10 feet wide (Raccoon). John Van bargained with my two guides to conduct me for a blanket each. I paid them. The blankets were 3 dollars each. Here old Mrs. Roe, near 80, the mother of these men, received me and treated me with great kindness.

I sat out X the creek accompanyed by David Roe, who very obligingly offered to walk to my next stage. We passed the house of Mrs. Waters, continuing on 6 miles to the old Tarrapins, X here a creek and passed thro' some good lands S. W. W. to his house, he was from home. I visited his wife, informed her who I was, and directed her to inform her husband of it, and to deliver him a present of paint which I brought him. The old fellow lives well, the land he cultivates is lined with small growth of saplins for some distance, his farm is fenced, his houses comfortable, he has a large stock of cattle, and some hogs. He uses the plow. I continued on through level open land for 2 miles, the growth tall young black oaks. Near the creek at the Tarrapins I saw some of the blue limestone, asked the name of the creek and was informed it was a branch of Lime Stone, a large creek on my right, which I was going up and should X in 8 miles. I saw some large holes on this flat land, 15 feet deep, 30 feet over, an inverted cone; continued on X another creek, the lands on the left mountainous. Here I saw much sign of turkies and the earth covered with acorns.

I was informed that at this place last summer the Indians had dug 3 bushels of the root of the buckeye, mixed 2 bushels of clay with it, pounded it in a mortar, and put it in Limestone Creek 4 miles above and that it poisoned the fish for eight miles, and 60 or 80 persons picked up as many as they could carry home.

4 miles farther thro' broken lands, passing a large hill of limestone rock on the left, I arrived at 3 Indian houses, and took up my abode in one belonging to halfbreed Will. The father and mother were out hunting, his daughters received me kindly and furnished plentifully. They gave me good bread, pork and potatoes for supper, and ground peas and dried peaches. I had corn for my horses. The hut in which I lodged was clean and neat. In the morning I breakfasted on corn cakes and pork. They had a number of fowls, hogs and some cattle, the field of 4 acres for corn fenced, and half an acre for potatoes. These huts and 2 others in sight of them are the fartherest south of any in the direction I am going to the Creeks. I asked the girls when they expected the return of their parents, they answered not till the last of February, or as they expressed it not till after 3 full moons.

In every hut I have visited I find the children exceedingly alarmed at the sight of white men, and here a little boy of 8 years old was especially alarmed and could not be kept from screaming out until I got out of the door, and then he run and hid himself. Yet as soon as I can converse with them, and they are informed who I am, they execute any order I give them with eagerness.

I inquired particularly of the mother what could be the reason of this; they said, this town was the remains of several towns who formerly resided on Tugalo and Koowee and had been much harrassed by the whites; that the old people remember their former situation and sufferings and frequently spoke of them. That those tales were listened to by the children, and made an impression which showed itself in the manner I had observed. The women told me, who I saw gathering nuts, that they had a sensation upon my coming to the camp, in the highest degree alarming to them, and when I lit from my horse, took them by the hand and spoke to them, they at first could not reply, although one of them understood and spoke English very well.

There is at this place a limestone spring that affords water enough for a mill. I visited it in the morning and found it warm.

Monday, 4th Dec.

This morning being very cold I could not set out so early as I wished. The Tarrapin came and breakfasted with me, he told me he was glad to see me. He knew me, and rejoiced when he was informed in the talk from the President that I was to superintend their affairs. That this nation had been under much embarrassment from the uncertainty of their existence as a nation, as the encroachments of the whites were constantly going against them, notwithstanding their treaties, and the repeated promises made them to the contrary, by the agents of the government. I was fortunate in having David Roe as an interpreter; the Indian is his native tongue and he speaks English accurately. I determined to explain the views of the government and my determination to use every effort in my power to carry them fully into effect, he heard me with great attention, and put many questions and then generally replied that the Act and the talk had been interpreted to him before, but not so satisfactorily as now, because he had the advantage of a conversation upon points which he did not clearly understand. He told me he had some cotton for market, and should soon send it to Tellico Block-house. He wished to know when they might expect plows, and such other implements as are contemplated in the President's talk, he intended that I should be satisfied with his co-operation with the agents of the government. He told me he had raised some cattle of 1,200 lbs. I sat out and he accompanyed me to Richard Roe's the last house on the path. I X Limestone Creek, 20 feet wide, the lands rich on its borders, and abounding with sugar maple, on this creek the sugar is made by the Indian women, they use small wooden troughs, and earthen pans to ketch the sap, and large earthen pots for boilers.

I continued on up this creek S. 2 miles and came to the long leaf pine and open land, here we saw 2 deer and much sign of turkies, in one mile the soil altered, to oak and short leaf pine, here we saw many turkies and one of my guides killed a fine one, the creek abounds with cane, and large trees, the hills are poor, the bottoms rich. One of my horses being disabled I was under the necessity of dismounting one of my attendants, and as my Indian guides were on foot, I divided the ride, turn about between the old Indian and myself, and between the two attendants. I walked two hours. 6 miles from the entrance into the long leaf pine I came to two high hills and went between them, and over some broken open lands, in 3 miles I came to a mountain and went round up to the top on my right. The view from N. W. round to N. E. extensive, and apparently a level country. Continue on 3 miles and came again over the tops of the mountains to the long leaf pine. 2 miles I came to a branch covered with reeds, my guide stoped and viewed it for some time, waved his hand up and down, said horse, pointed south, holding up two fingers, miles says he. I assented and away we went, we came to the creek 8 feet over, went down it until I saw good reeds, and here I encamped. The branches are a mile and an half apart, and I went half a mile down it, the reed abundant, the whole length, but ruined by a recent burning of the woods, except at the place where I halted.

My guides spoke their native tongue only. I gave them directions when I set off, and had the aid of an interpreter, which they follow with great exactness.

I observe that the reed here has the appearance of being an evergreen, the leaves nearly being as broad as the cane, and long in proportion. I am informed they shed their leaves in March and the cane in September.

Monday, the 5th December.

I sat out at nine down the creek and in half a mile X Aquonausete runing to the right, 75 feet wide. Since I left the mountains yesterday I find I am on the Creek waters. This river is the Tallapoosa. Continuing on S. by W., X a creek in ¾ of a mile, 10 feet wide, abounding with reeds, runing to the right, continue on 6 miles, the lands poor and broken, came to a poor hill bereft of all its trees by a whirlwind; at the bottom of it X a small branch from the right, some reed, continue on ¾ of a mile, X it again from the left, go up a long steep hill, and down a descent as long as 2 miles, X a creek runing to the right, 15 feet over, the lands on the hills poor, on the creek very rich, the growth chesnut of a large size and beech and cane and reed. Continue on over open piney broken land. X 2 little reedy branches and go down one on the left, in all 6 miles, the land stiff with sharp flint stone. X the last branch; on the left; one mile before I X it there terminates a mountain toped with stone. Turn W. as soon as I X this branch (at the approach of which the lands are of a good quality though broken and stoney) thro' some low rich bottom land, among some of the tallest and largest beech I ever saw, many of them 3 feet over, X the creek runing to the right, go upon a narrow ridge for half a mile, the lands rich on both sides. The creek makes so short a turn that it may be said one can go up and down the creek at the same time on this ridge, continue on 5 miles, Xing 3 little branches, the whole of the bottoms adjoining were covered with reed, the lands broken, but capable of cultivation, the growth pine scrub and black oak, the soil gravelly. Here I $\times$ a creek 8 feet, runing to the right, continue on S. W. W. 9½ miles farther, $\times$ing 3 little creeks, and 2 little branches, with but little cane, except the first, at 3 miles. The lands broken, but fit for cultivation, the growth pine, black, white and scrub oak, the bottoms mostly tall black oak. The streams fit for two mills. The last 2 miles of this stage, long leaf pine upon broken stiff flint stone land. I encamped on a creek margined with cane, runing to the right. All these waters empty into Aquonausete. My guide in the evening told me we had traveled 34 miles—here I saw a Creek Indian, near his hunting camp, he at first was a great distance from me and walked hastily on till he came up with me, gave me his hand, told me who he was and conversed for some time with my guide, who had been instructed to inform every one he saw on the path who I was. In the course if the evening it rained. I had prepared for a shelter in time which was covered with a blanket, bear skins and oilcloth cloak. I was surprised at the little effect the rain had on my two Indians, the old man had a leather shirt and legings, the young one leather legings and an old shirt, they had each a small halfworn blanket, the young man every evening pulled off his shirt and spread it under him. They both slept soundly the whole time it rained, got up once and ordered my attendants up twice to endeavor to preserve our fire by the addition of wood, but they never stired till daybreak; they are small eaters, use no salt, and but little bread. They carry their parched corn meal, Wissoetaw, and mix a hand full in a pint of water which they drink. Although they had plenty of corn and fowls they made no other provision than a small bag of this for the path. I have plenty of provisions, and give them some at every meal. I have several times drank of the Wissoetaw and am fond of it with the addition of some sugar. To make of the best quality I am told the corn should be first boiled, then parched in hot ashes, sifted, pounded and made into flour.

Tuesday, 6th December.

Sat out at 9, $\times$ the creek 10 feet, runing to the right, on the top of the hill the right path W. In 2 miles came on some hills, continue to the ridge from whence to the N. there is a very extensive view of the country. 2 miles $\times$ a creek 10 feet, runing to the right, stored with cane and reed, continue on up a branch to the left covered with cane to its source, 2 miles come to a $\times$ path take to the south, S. by W. 2 miles $\times$ a branch and come to another with cane, 1 mile and part of this thro' long leaf pine, ╳ a branch above the fork, take up the right for one mile between high hills, the land hitherto poor. ╳ the branch and passed thro' better land, the growth large, the land stoney. ╳ a branch and take up one prong, the lands rich tho' broken, the timber large, of poplar, white oak and chesnut, 1½ miles to a high ridge, from this S. E., the growth of timber appears large and for a mile or more. Then we turn W. by S. down one valey, ╳ a branch and go up it to its source, 1 mile, and on the ridge take our course S. by W. The lands broken, stiff and stoney, continue on to a branch thro' poor stoney lands, and down the same one mile to some fine reed where I rested for half an hour for my horses to eat some of the cane. Continued on ╳ the branch runing to the left, in half a mile, re╳ it and rise up a steep hill the north from very rich lands, the growth poplar and large chesnut. Here I observe as I have done for 12 miles past, that the repeated gusts of wind have blown down or torn to pieces a great many trees, some many years past, some but few and some the present year. The lands on the ridge are poor and continue so 4½ miles, broken, a mixture of pine and dwarf oaks. I have frequently observed at a distance on both sides reeds in all the moist parts of the hollows. At the termination of this ridge there is a very extensive slope from N. W. round southwardly to E. of the horison. I descend here a long and steep hill to broken descending hills, long leaf pine land, stoney and stiff, at 5 miles came to a considerable rise, and have an extensive view of the distant hills beyond the Oconee. Turn here on the top of the ridge W. S. W. 4 miles and encamp on the bank of the Oconee. The whole scope of these hills poor and stoney, and the whole land very broken. I observe reed in abundance in all the hollows—hills I call them, but they are mountains.

Wednesday, 7th.

I turned from the cove in which I lodged to the path, continued S. by E., 2 miles over broken stoney land, the growth oak, of various kinds, and some chesnut. I came to Aquonausete, ╳ it, its about 70 yards wide, the bottom covered with red moss on the north side and within a few yards of the opposite shore, where it is green. In front is a small mountain, the rocks projecting over the river. I land to the right and wind up to the top, continue S. W. 3 miles, ╳ a creek runing to the right, in 4 miles ╳ 3 branches all covered with reed, the first three miles on this side the river, long leaf pine, steep bottoms on both sides of the path, the remainder 4 miles the lands equally broken but a mixture of trees of various sorts, here rise up a mountain from which is distinctly to be seen the hills on the north side of the river. Continue on this mountain for one mile and rise to the summit of the Apaleniosa Mountains in this quarter, here the path divides, I take the left and continue on $\times$ the mountains for 3 miles and arrive at Toostecaugae on the banks of the Tallapoosa, $\times$ the river here which is 120 yards over, my horses were swam over by the side of a canoe. This river I find is the Tallapoosa of the Creeks. The Cherokees call it Aquonausete. The mountains here are not difficult to pass, the path is pretty good and direct, mostly on the slope of descending mountains until they terminate at the town.

Being without an interpreter I could not avail myself of the information I wished. One of my guides understood and spoke the Creek tongue, he looked out for a house, and the necessities I stood in need of. I was out of provisions when I arrived at the house. I discovered it belonged to a chief. His little daughter about 12 years old I had seen at the treaty at Colerain, she immediately came to me with her mother, brushed up the hut in which I was to lodge, gave me a basket of corn for my horses, a fowl, some sofkey (hommony) and ground peas. My guides in conformity with instructions, informed the women who I was. I gave them my hand, and contrary to the usual custom they received me without reserve. The men were all out hunting.

In the morning I visited the women in their hot house where they were apparently comfortably situated. They appear to be much poorer than their neighbours the Cherokees, they have but a few fowls and hogs.

In the morning I made the little girl and her mother some little presents and I sat out at sunrise.

Thursday, the 8th.

I resume my path and continue 3 miles, the lands more eaven than any I have seen for some days, the growth a mixture of oak and pine. I $\times$ a small creek at a flat rock, the quality of the rock suited for mill stones, tho' rather course, continue on 4 miles farther over uneaven lands, some times pine, and some a mixture of pine and oak. I arrive at a very extensive flat rock of 8 or ten acres, covered in some places with moss, then coat of gravelly earth, the growth dwarfs, of various trees, among them some cedar. I observe here that this rock varied as the hills. Here my guide discovered he had taken the rong path, he waited for his companion, and after a conversation, turned to me and pointed a course forming a triangle, we set out through the woods. For the four miles past we $\times$ed some fine little branches, and continued up some to their sources, stored with reeds. We continued on thro' the woods for four miles and came into our path and took it S. W. I continue on 1 mile, the paths divide. I take to the left, two miles, ✕ a small creek, and rise up a steep hill, the north front, exhibiting parallel rows of large rock, N. E., and the rows 40 yards apart. Continue on turning to the west 11 miles, ✕ing several small branches covered with reed, the lands hilly and stoney, a mixture of oak, hickory, and pine for 5 miles and mostly pine for the remainder, the lands very broken as I approach New York. At this town I arrived in the afternoon, at the house of James Sullivan a trader, he was from home, his assistant, David Hay received me and treated me with every possible mark of attention. The few Indian men at home visited me, I had a conversation with them, not very interesting, as my interpreter, a black woman, was not very intelligent. In the morning I crossed the river on a visit to the family of Tuskena Patki (white Lieutenant), this old man, one of the principal chiefs of the Creeks, and head of the Oakfuskies, was out hunting. I saw his young wife, her mother and family. I stayed half an hour with them. She said she had not any thing to offer me to eat. I told her I had breakfasted. She gave me saufkee and ground peas. Several of the women visited me. They appear not so well provided in their houses as the Cherokees, nor have as many poultry, hogs or cattle. I left them and re✕ed the river 120 yards wide. This river is here called the Oakfuskies, but the Cherokees call it Aquonausete (like a river).

Friday, the 9th.

Mr. Hay informed me that I was within 12 miles of the Hillabees, a town on a creek of that name, that in this town or its neighbourhood, lived Robert Grierson, a native of Scotland, who was intelligent, had lived many years in the nation as a trader, and had an Indian family; that he spoke the language well, and had large possessions, negros, cattle and horses. I determined to take this rout, Mr. Hay accompanyed me.

I sat out at 12, traveled 1 mile and ✕ creek N. W. 15 feet runing to the left, the lands fine for cultivation, continued on over uneaven lands, ✕ing several small creeks and over a small mountain, in 9 miles arrive at the Hillabees, 20 yards wide, ✕ it and over waving lands 4 miles to the house of Mr. Grierson.

The whole of the moist land on every branch finely covered with reed, the bottoms fit for culture, the uplands uneaven, stoney, gravelly and stiff, the timber a mixture of pine and oak, not furtile. The first ten miles of this path is W. by N., the remainder N. W. & N., the direct line N. W.

Mr. Grierson was at home and received me with a social hospitable frankness. He had his family around him ginning and picking cotton. I was much pleased to see it. He had made a considerable quantity and is preparing it to send to Tennessee, where he expects 34 cents the lb.

The old town Hillabees lies on the creek of that name 3 miles below Mr. Grierson's, at the junction of the Cullufadee Creek, about 4 miles still lower is the Oaktasazee. There is but one house in the town, here is the town house and here they have their husks and dances, the head man Opio Dockta; the other 2 chiefs are Ottasie Matlah, and Neclucko Hajo. The whole number belonging to the town are about 170 gun men, they are settled in four villages. One village below the old town on the creek is Tuscaslegah. The next, 13 miles from the old town, up the main creek, is Netachapco (long swamp). The third on the N. W. branch of Hillabee, 15 miles above, Claknucheeaballah (a village over the mountain).

They are attentive to raising cattle, and some few of them have hogs, and one or two have horses. There are four brothers, George, Thomas, James, Tiltlagee, they are halfbreeds, they live near Mr. Grierson, the two first have stocks of cattle and horses. Thomas has 130 cattle and ten horses.

Opioche Tustanwick Hajo, his wife, Auwillangee, has about 70.

Saturday, the 10th December.

I took a view of Mr. Grierson's farm, he had planted the last season two acres of cotton in drills, 4 feet asunder; the land apparently not very good, high, dry and gravelly, the cotton grew well, many of the stalks 8 feet high. I saw he had not thined it sufficiently, nor toped any part and that it was mixed with the Nankin. I viewed his cotton house, the staple of the cotton good, tho' not so much so as it would have been, had it been thined and toped. The bowls or pods would then have been larger. I advised him in the next season to pursue the proper course and to seperate the seed, and as from his information the black seed cotton will not do here, to plant only the green seed. The seasons being sufficient to bring that to perfection. He has a treadle gin, well made, sent him from Providence. I saw some defect in the puting it up, which I directed him how to remedy. He informs me he finds no difficulty in hiring the Indian women to pick out cotton, he hired them to pick by the basket of about a bushel, he gave half a pint of salt, or 3 strans of mock wampum beads a basket, or half a pint of taffra for 2 baskets; where the cotton was fully open, they could pick from two to three baskets the day. There is 30 acres in the farm, the product, corn, cotton, rice, peas, beans, squashes, pumpkins, watermelons, colewarts. Peaches grow well but he has but a few trees, and not any other fruit trees. The climate is mild, the water seldom freezes. There is mast every other year, and fruit, ffor the last 3 years it has been annual. The soil in villages of the Hillabees, gravelly, stoney and broken, the bottoms rich, the hills poor, the water abundant and salubrious, and every moist bottom covered with reed. The growth a mixture of pine, oak, and some hickory, the trees small, some of them tall.

I saw on the path as I came here some women picking up red oak acorns, for the purpose of making oil. They gather the acorns, dry them on reed mats, hull them, beat them fine in a mortar, mix them up in water and let them stand for an evening. The oil rises to the top, and they skim it off with a feather. This oil is used as food; one bushel of acorns makes about a pint of oil.

Sunday, 11th Dec., 1796.

I intended this day to set out for the Tuckabatchees, and Mr. Grierson obligingly promised to accompany me, but some person last evening stole his horses, and the day has been spent in searching after them. I have had much conversation relative to Indian affairs with this gentleman, he speaks the language well, and is intelligent, he was during the Revolution War attached to the armies of the U. S. and made some contributions in aid of them; he is now much attached to this country and means to spend his days here with his Indian family and connexions, he justly estimates his situation, and can, and will contribute his aid in furthering the views of the government.

The family of Robert Grierson are his wife, Sinnugee, of the family Spanalgee; their children, Sandy, Sarah, Walter, David, Liza, & William.

Sarah is married to Stephen Hawkins, their children Pinkey, & Sam.

> 40 negros.
> 300 cattle.
> 30 horses.

They have in the range a place called a stamp, where the horses have salt every spring, and here they gather of themselves at that season. The cattle at that season come to the creek for moss, the bottom being covered with it. And at this season all the stockholders make a gathering.

Monday, 12th Dec., 1796.

This day application being made to me by Robert Grierson, trader in the Hillabees, for permission to pursue some persons who had stolen two horses from him, and from information rec'd from some Indians it being probable that some Creeks had commited the theft—and Stephen Hawkins a resident trader in this town, consenting to pursue with four Indians, I thought proper to give him the authority following.

Hillabees in the Creeks, 12 Dec., 1796.

Complaint having been made to me by Robert Grierson trader, that he was on the 10th, inst. robed of two horses, by persons supposed to be Creeks, who will probably endeavor to convey them into some one of the neighbouring tribes, or into the settlements: and he having expressed an intention to cause the said offenders to be pursued and apprehended, and requested my aid in the premises;

I do hereby authorize Stephen Hawkins, a resident trader in this town to take with him such aid as he may deem necessary, and to pursue and apprehend the said offenders, wherever to be found within the agency South of the Ohio. And I do hereby require of the agent of the Cherokees, his assistants and all others in authority to be aiding and assisting in the premises.

BENJAMIN HAWKINS,
P. T. Agent for Indian Affairs South of the Ohio.

I inserted the discription of the horses on the back of this authority.

I this day sat out for the Tuckabatchees in company with Mr. Grierson, at 12. We traveled S. 4 miles, X a creek, turn a little to the W. 2 miles, X a creek both runing to the left; at the first is the site of the town of Hillabees, at the other one settlement, the creek margined with cane. At this hut I saw the Casseneyupon growing about 8 feet high, it had been brought from the seacoast, and did well. Continue on, X 2 small creeks runing to the left, and at the end of 6 miles come to some large rock to the left, they are in a direction N. E. S. W. The lands hitherto, broken, stoney, gravelly, the growth a mixture of pine and oak, with a few dwarf hickories. Continue on 3 miles, X a creek runing to the left, the creek rocky, 15 feet wide; continue over one branch and up and a✕ another and rise the top of a hill 1 mile. The lands very broken near the creek, and mountainous. Our course S. W. Continue on 5 miles, ✕ing 3 small creeks or branches, and arrive at Cuialegees Creek, 15 feet, ✕ it, pass the town on the left and arrive at the house of John O'Riley, he was from home. The lands broken, gravelly, and stoney, the growth pine, oak, and small hickory, the branches covered with small cane.

Tuesday, 13th Dec.

The Muscogueulgoes were at a meeting of the governors of Georgia, S. & N. Carolina, & Virginia, divided into five districts at Appalatchee, Pahachucalee, Alabama, on the Coosau, and up as far as the fork of the Tuskogees, Tallapoose and the Abbecoss.

The district of the Abbecoos have the following towns:

No. 1.		
	1.	Hillabees.
	2.	Euffaulics, N. W. 35.
	3.	Notchiss, W. N. W. 25.
	4.	Abbacoochee, W. N. W. 29.
	5.	Coosau, W. N. W. 43.
	6.	Woccocoies, W. 25.
	7.	Wocgufkee, W. S. 35.
Fish ponds.	8.	Thloclagulga, S. W. 12.
Big swamp.	9.	O'Pilkthlorcco, S. W. S. 30.
	10.	Wewocah, S. W. 37.
	11.	Pocuntallahope, S. W. 52.
Little Tallasu.	12.	Tallasuchee, S. W. 45.
	13.	Ockchoics, S. W. 20.
	14.	Kialigee, S. W. S. 23.
	15.	Euffaulau, S. 25.
	16.	Ocfuskees, S. 20.
Hog range.	17.	Soguspogase, S. 10.
	18.	New York, S. E. 15.
2 Corn houses.	19.	Tochlacaugee, N. E. 30.
	20.	Luchaossoguh, N. b. E. 40.

The wife of John O'Riley, treated us with kindness and hospitality, as soon as she was informed who I was, she got corn for my horses, and cooked some pork and potatoes for supper. She prepared her own lodging for me, a good one, of clean blankets, with a nice coverlid. She had some fine fowls and fat hogs.

I bade her adieu and set out for Tuckabatchee, 4 miles. I arrive at Achina Hatche (cypress creek), a village of Keolgee, there are 6 habitations and a small town house, some thriving peach trees. X the run, 2 miles cross another at the settlement of 3 families. The lands all poor, stoney and gravelly. Continue on 2 miles, cross a creek, the lands pretty good tho' broken. Rise up a steep hill, the lands piney; continue on 4 miles, they become bad; continue 3 miles down a steep, gravelly hill X a creek and rise on high broken hills, 1 mile further X a creek just above Tuckabatchee, enter the old fields, and in 4 miles arrive at the town house. Here obtain a pilot and continue through the town down the river 4 miles, arrive at the landing opposite Mr. Cornell's, the agent in this quarter. The description of the sites of the towns are numbered.

No. 2. On Euffaula Hatchee, which empties into the Coosau at the town on the upper side, James Lessle, the trader.

3. Natchew, on a creek of that name, it empties into Coosau, above the 3 Islands 6 miles, Joseph Stiggins trader, and just joining the Coosau town below, ¼ below Efaulauhatchee.

4. On Kiomulgee, this is the same creek before mentioned, but here the name is altered.

5. Coosau, on the left of the river of that name, 60 miles above the Alabama River. John O'Kelly a half breed, his father was a trader in the same town, Tucpaufcau.

6. On Pochuso Hatche (rabbet creek). This empties into the Coosau 4 miles below Puccewi Tallauhassee, 41 miles below Coosau, John Clark, a Scotchman.

7. Weocufkee, on a creek of the same name, which empties into the foregoing on the right bank, 4 miles below the town,—George Smith, an Englishman.

8. Thlotlogulgee, on Elka Hatche, which empties into the Oakfuskies, on the right bank just above the town. This town nearly 8 miles from the river, it runs E. John Shirley, and Isaac Thomas, the first an American, the latter of German parents.

9. On a creek of the same name which empties into Pocuntallahasse on the left. Trader, Hendrick Durgin.

10. Wewocah on a creek of that name, which empties into Pocuntallahassee, 16 miles below that town on the left.

11. Four miles above the mouth of Pochuse Hatche.

12. Upon the left of Coosau, 8 miles above the fork, Daniel McGillivray, the trader, Benjamin Crook.

13. On a creek of that name which empties into the Kiolijie, on the left 4 miles above Kiolijie has John O'Riley an Indian factor.

14. On a creek of that name which empties into the Tallapoosa 12 miles below Ocfuskee. 20 miles above, Alex Cornell, the trader John O'Kelley.

15. Euffauleis, on the right of the Tallapoosa, 5 miles below the Oakfuskee town, John Townshand an Englishman.

16. On the right bank of the river, Patrick Donnelly. One Indian factor, Kussatah Tuskeneah, a brother of the white Lieutenant.

17. Soockeah, on the right bank of the river 12 miles above Oakfuskie. One fire* with Ocfuskee.

Wednesday, 14th.

I took up my abode in the house of Alex Cornell, on the left bank of the river. He was at home and received and treated me with much attention. I had much conversation with him and Mr. Grierson on the subject of my mission, as they possessed and could give the best information now to be had in the nation. The result as to some important points was interesting.

The condition of the Indian is much bettered within 20 years, he is less cruel, more attached to a friendly intercourse with his neighbours, and mild in his manners. They have an increasing attachment to stock, & are more industrious, some few very careful and provident.

Since the treaty at Colerain the Indians have manifested a disposition for peace, unknown before, it is almost universal. Mr. Grierson says that he has seen many of the Indians in the district of the Abbecoos and they all spoke of the conduct of the U. S. as friendly and perfectly just and they were pleased with it. I asked this question.

What would most likely the soonest disturb this friendly disposition of the Indians?

Intrusion on the hunting grounds and horse stealing.

The latter was encouraged entirely by the whites in the nation, many of whom were more depraved than the savages, had all their vices without one of their virtues. The whites have reduced the stealing of horses to a system, their connections are extensive. Some in Cumberland, Georgia, Tennessee, and among the neighbouring tribes. This evil being now so deep-rooted that it would require much exertion and some severity to put an end to it. The whites who had Indian families took no care of them, neither to educate them or to teach them any thing useful. They were

---

* This word very uncertain in manuscript.

left with their mothers, who were always the slaves of the house and the fathers making money by any and every means in their power, however roguish, and using the children and the relations of the family as aids.

Mr. Grierson being about to leave me requested me to aid him in some concerns of his family in Georgia, he gave me this statement. There were of his family four brothers, James, Thomas, William & Robert.

James was a colonel of militia in the neighbourhood of Augusta. He was killed at the siege of Augusta, after his surrender to the American arms.

Thomas was an officer in the militia in the service of the U. States. He died on or about the year 1775. He left a son, a half-breed, in the Euffaulies. He had 500 acres of land on little river, 8 miles below Writesborough, on Upton Creek, adjoining the land of James Grierson and Joshua Saunders. Mr. Grierson requests to be informed of the situation of the property and the measures necessary to the securing it for the family.

Mrs. Anne Hopkins of Augusta, died in the year 1775 or 6. She gave by will her property to Jane Pettigrew, and the children of James Grierson, James Thomas and David. Jane Pettigrew was sister to three children on the maternal side. She married David Homes, a nephew of George Galphin. Homes died at Pensacola the year 1779.

After the siege of Augusta the Rev. James Seymore carried some of the negros to Savannah, and from thence to Augustine. He died on his passage from thense to Providence, and Mr. Thomas Forbes, partner of Mr. Panton, took possession of the negros. If this statement is true in substance Mr. William Panton will see the negros' fourthcoming to the children of their representatives.

The necessary information can be had in the neighbourhood of Augusta, and mostly from John Milledge, he took George, the youngest of the children to his house, where he died.

Thursday, 15.

There are 4 traders in this town and they are supplied by Mr. Panton at Pensacola.

Obediah Low has an Indian wife and 2 children. He is from the upper part of Georgia.

Patrick Laine, native of Ireland, has a wife, and Christian Hagel, called Huffle, a native of Germany has a wife, and Mrs. Cornell has four children and 4 grand children, she is a widow, the wife of Joseph Cornell, deceased, formerly interpreter.

George, her oldest son is a trader. James is a lad at school.
Lucy, her oldest daughter is a widow, her husband John Cane
died at Tensaw. She has 3 children.
Vica, the youngest has one little girl.

Halfbreed Billy.

I this day paid a visit to the old men at the town house and
partook with them of the black drink. I then visited the falls and
lands adjoining to the town. The falls are at 2½ miles above town
house, the river here is after tumbling over a bed of rock for half
a mile, formed into 2 narrow channels, one 30 the other 15 feet.
The fall is 30 feet in 50 yards, the first part nearly 20 feet in less
than 10, fish are here obstructed in their passage up the river.
The rock is a light gray, very much broken and divided, in
square blocks of various sizes, fine for building, the best I think I
ever saw. It requires very little labour to reduce it to any form,
for plain walls, large masses of it is so nicely fited, and regular
as to imitate the side of a square building where the stone has
passed through the hands of the mason. Above the falls the river
widens and within half a mile stretches out to near half a mile
in width and continues for near four miles. There are 4 islands
which have been cultivated, they are now old fields margined with
cane, the bed of the river shoal, rocky and covered with moss, it is
frequented in the spring and summer by horses, cattle and deer,
and in the winter by swans, geese and ducks.
The lands on the right bank opposite the falls is broken, stoney
& gravelly, the growth oak, hickory and pine, the sides of the
hills fronting the river exhibit this building rock, a small creek
and a branch enter in 300 yards of each other, on the right, the
lands half a mile below the falls become level and spread out on
this side to 2 miles in width, bordering on a creek, Wollawitatchee
which rising in the broken lands 17 miles from its mouth, runs
S. S. E. and empties into the Tallapoosa, 3½ miles below the
town house. The whole of this flat is covered with oak, and
hickory land, the latter altogether the large hard shelled nut, the
creek margined with cane. The course of the river from the
falls to the town house S. thence E. and winding round a point
to W. and W. & N. to its confluence with Coosau.
The lands on the left bank of the falls broken and piny, to
the bank of the river, half a mile below a creek empties in, it
rises 7 miles from the river, its course nearly N. W., its sides
covered with reed and cane. Below this creek the lands become
flat on the river and extend 3 miles to the Euffaulee, here the
Tallassee lies, on the banks of this creek, it is at the junction 60
yards wide. This is the most valuable creek known here for fish

in the spring and summer. Sturgeon, trout, perch, rock, red horse, the trout here is also called the chub. The Euffaulee is settled nearly 20 miles, the lands rich. 1½ miles below the flat lands terminate, there the hills commence, and continue 2 miles, one small creek and 2 branches intersect. From these hills there are two high bluffs, from whence there is an extensive view of the town, the river above and below the extensive flat lands on the opposite shore, and a range of hills to the N. W. At the termination of these hills is a small branch, and the flat lands commence and spread for one mile on the side of the branch. 140 yds. from the river is a house of the wife of George Cornell. Below, 300 yards is the habitation of Alex Cornell, and from this down the river is settled with Indian families. 2¾ miles below, Caleebe Hatchie empties into the river, it has its source near 20 miles to the east, it is 15 feet over.

The town of Tuckabatchee stands on the right bank of the river, in the bend, the town house opposite the Euffaulee. The number of gun men 116. They have lately begun to settle out in villages for the advantage of wood and raising stock.

Some few have stocks of cattle, they hold them high, being accustomed to sell fowls, bacon and beef at Pensacola, at an extravagant price, they ask at home the same, making no allowance for the expense of carriage or between the war and peace price of provisions..

Friday, 16.

I amused myself this day in riding thro' the neighbouring woods, visiting and conversing with the Indians. The lands every where covered with acorns and hickory nuts. Some of the women who saw and knew me at St. Mary's immediately recollected me, they expressed pleasure at seeing me among them, and at the same time said they were poor, and had not good things to give, their food being so different from what they saw at the table of the commissioners of the U. States. They were apprehensive I would find uncomfortable living among them. They sent me a present of bean bread and dumplins, some oil of hickory nuts, pleasant to the taste, and some milk of the same nuts.

The process is simple, they pick up the nuts, dry them, pound them in a mortar, fan them, to free the kernels as much as possible from the shells. They then apply water, mix up the mass with their hands, and work it something like the bakers neading their bread, as the oil rises they separate it from the remains which is the milk.

I had some oil and beans, the oil was not inferior to Florence oil. It was new, they find a difficulty in preserving it from becoming rancid.

Saturday, 17.

I repeat my visits to some of the Indians, and to view what remained yet to be seen in my neighbourhood. I examined into the state of commerce as carried on by George Cornell, the half-breed. His stock of trade is almost 1,000 dollars annually.

Old Mrs. Cornell and her family hearing of my being in town, they came to see me, this old lady is the mother of the man who was unfortunately killed at Colerain by the scout, as he went there bearing a flag with a message to the President of the U. States.

The old lady expressed much satisfaction at seeing me, assured me of her friendship for the white people, being her own blood as well as the red, and her personal regard for me, for my attentions to her at Colerain.

Sunday, 18 Dec.

I sat out this day on a visit to the towns down the river. Mr. Richard Bailey had called to see me, and promised to accompany me. I directed the agent here, Mr. Cornell, to attend me. I went down the river on the left bank, passing 5 separate Indian settlements, under fork fences, good against cattle only, the lands level and of good quality, the growth hard shelled hickory nut, oak, black oak, scrub, and some few white, not large. I crossed Caloobe Creek and enter the town of Auttossee, pass through the town, the gun men all from home, the buildings bordering on the river, the whole fenced with small poles, the first on forks, the other two on stakes, fit only to keep out cattle. X a small creek, the growth cypress. Here I was showed as a curiosity an oak on the side of the creek which had been struck with lightning, it penetrated the tree about 5 feet from the ground, went through and out two feet lower on the opposite side, entered the earth and plowed it up for some distance a foot deep, the tree remains with marks on both sides, and not otherwise injured. I continue on to the house of Mr. Bailey, in all 5 miles. Here I met a welcome reception, and here I remained for the knight. Mr. Bailey is a good farmer, has many conveniences about, with his lands fenced, stable, garden, lots for his stock, some thriving trees, and a small nursery to plant out. His stock of horses, cattle and hogs numerous; the lands where he lives rich, tho' the growth of timber is small. He informs me the product is 50 bushels of corn to the acre. He has an Indian woman, and 5 children, and as many grand children. His wife is of the Otalla (wine) family. She is neat, cleanly, provident and economical, as careful of her family concerns as a white woman.

On the opposite bank formerly stood the old town O Hassee, a beautiful rich level plane surrounded with hills, to the north, it was formerly a canebrake, the river makes a curve round it to the south, so that a small fence on the hill side across would enclose it.

In the year 1766 there were in this town 43 gun men, there are now 80. The women industrious, and some few of the men. The whole of them uneasy on the score of their white neighbours keeping stock among them, so much so, that Mr. Bailey finds his not safe, but as the property of his wife and children. The course of the river here is west, the creeks which empty in on the left side take their rise to the south at the ridge dividing the Pinsausta waters from them, about 25 miles, it is nearly the same distance to Kongeau, continuing on thense south. The lands rich to the source of the creeks, the growth of timber very large, and canebrakes on the ridges, which are none of them high. There are poplars of 4 and 5 feet through, large cherry trees and persimmon trees.

The stock is sometimes troubled with distemper; the mast hits every year, the whole country abounds with very troublesome flees and nats at some seasons.

I saw at Mr. Bailey's 20 bee hives, he says they do well, and that there are wild bees in the country in every direction. They are extending themselves west, and some hunters informed him they had lately discovered some, the west of Mississippi about 30 miles, that they had but recently arrived there, as the trees they fell had young comb only.

Mr. Bailey's 2 daughters are married to white men, they both spin cotton and the youngest, Elizabeth Fletcher, can read and write and is very industrious. This whole family are remarkable for being healthy and cleanly. This may be owing to a custom continued by Mrs. Bailey, she and her family every morning winter or summer bathe in cold water.

I have been much pleased in my visit here as well as at Mr. Grierson's; it being demonstrated to me that the Indian women from there too, are capable of and willing to become instrumental in civilising the men. Mrs. Bailey shares in all the toils of her husband when there was a necessity for it, she attended the pack horses to market, swam rivers to facilitate the transportation of their goods, is careful of the interest of her family and resolute in support of it. She presides at her table which is always neat and well supplied with coffee or tea, butter of her own make, meat and well made bread.

His stock of cattle 200, horses 120, hogs 150 and 7 slaves. He is a native of England, served in Savannah, to the carpenter and joiner business, has been 40 years in this country.

Monday the 19.

I sat out this day travelled down the river W. ✕ Kebihatche in 1½ mile, continued 1½ farther ✕ Ofeeckske, 20 feet over, this creek has its rise near Koenekuh, the main branch of Scambia. This creek has several forks, the lands good to their sources. We enter into the fields of the Hollewaulee (the shearer of the war), and continue on 2 miles. Just at the entrance of the fields, high red cliffs are to be seen to the north by the flat lands on the right of the river.

The town of Hollewaulee, is on the opposite bank of the river. Continue on still down the river in all 8 miles ✕ Noocooschepoo (bear ark). Here we enter the Toosahatche & Colooswe fields, (the towns being on the opposite side) and continue four miles through them, and ✕ a small creek Leecawsah, at the Colooswe, little village pritly situated on a rising ground to the left. Here commence large swamps and between them and the river are some rich flat canebrake land, where these Indians cultivate their corn, pulse, and melons. Continue on 2 miles ✕ a branch, rise a hill, where is the remains of a circular mound on the left, the lands thin, tho' level. To the right the descent 20 feet to the swamp land. From this bank arise several springs, particularly one, a large one, half a mile farther, the Uchee village, a remnant of those settled on the Chattahoochee, half a mile farther pass a Shawne village, they speak the language and retain the manners of their countrymen to the N. W. This town house differs from the Creek, it is an oblong square building 8 feet pitch roofed on the common mode of cabin building, the sides and roof covered with bark of pine. Continue on 2 miles ✕ a small creek, at Mucclassau, continue on in all 18 miles ✕ a creek 10 feet wide. 1½ mile further ✕ another small creek and in half a mile arrive at the house of Charles Weatherford.

I chose the river path that I might have a view of the Indian fields, their mode of culture and the quality of the lands. The first 4 miles were high and open sound low grounds, subject to inundations only in the seasons of floods which happen once in 15 or 16 years, the river is also subject to annual overflowings, but always in the winter season, generally in March; the next 8 miles is mostly canebrake land, very rich, much of it under cultivation, the corn planted in hills, not regular, about 5 feet from each other, and from 5 to 10 stalks in a hill, near every small division of corn they have a patch of beans stuck with cane. The margins on the river under cultivation is from one hundred to 200 yards wide, then the land becomes a rich swamp for 400 to 600 yards, this when reclaimed must be valuable for rice or corn, the river never subject to freshes in the spring or summer. I saw one conic mound in this low land 30 feet diameter, ten feet high, it stands near the river. The towns standing on the right bank of the river, there are at several places large peach trees, and a few summer huts to shelter the labourers in summer against rain, and the guards who watch the crops whilst it grows to protect it against every thing that may be injurious to it. Many of them move over their families, reside in the fields whilst the crop is growing and when it is made they gather the whole and move into town.

During this season, they show in a particular manner their hospitality, they call to all travelers, particularly white travelers and give them fruit, melons and food. If there is a necessity the women and children eat of the young corn before the husk, but the men do not.

Tuesday 20.

Mr. Weatherford showed me this morning some fine horses raised by him, on his plantation, they were blooded nearly full, 15 hands high, looked well, their feet somewhat too flat, owing to their being raised in flat swampy lands. The residence of this man is on a high bluff on the left bank of the Alabama one mile below the confluence of the Coosau and Tallapoosa, it is the first bluff below, here are to be seen near his house 5 conic mounds of earth, the largest 30 yards diameter, 17 feet high, the others all small, about 30 feet diameter and 5 feet high.

It has for some time been a subject of enquiry when and for what purpose these mounds were raised, but here it explains itself as to the purpose. The Alabama is not more than 150 yards over at low water, the banks high, yet subject to be overflowed in the season of **floods,** which happen once in 20 or 25 years.

The last flood was in January last, the river rose at the house where I am 47 feet high, it spread itself over the adjoining country for many miles, and the general width of the river was below the junction 6 to 7 miles, every thing within that scope was compeled to retire from it to the trees on rising grounds or were destroyed. The margin of the river is low swamp and canebrake, the up lands stiff level, pine and oak very open.

There are some mounds which I saw 2 miles from the river in this flat open country, and here they were covered with the water, and all others known in the neighbourhood except the largest, and on this Mr. Weatherford secured such of his stock of horses and cattle as he could collect in time, the remainder were lost.

I observed in examining into this curious phenomenon that the first range of flat swamp lands extends one quarter of a mile, 15 feet from the water, then arise in steep bank, 15 feet, the land then poor and flat for one mile, then another rise of 15 feet, and here and there a gradual rise to lands still higher.

This second flat which generally speaking is poor land has some very good land in small patches of 20 to one hundred acres. The growth generally small and on every place the hard shelled hickory nut, mostly dwarfs.

The flood rises the highest in the Coosau, and some times so sudden as to drive a rappid current up the Tallapoosa for 8 miles. Up the river from Weatherford's, half a mile is a large sand beach, here I saw collecting in the evening the greatest collection of crows I ever saw, and on examining I was informed that they collected there every night, entertained each other with their croaking, took a drink at the edge of the river and then rose and roosted on the canes. In the morning half an hour before sun rise, they began to move in large flocks of many thousand together, first in spiral and then irregular, constantly croaking and ultimately in a direction down the river, out of sight and out of hearing. I left this bluff, and set out on a visit to Mrs. Durant, the oldest sister of Mr. McGillivray, she has had eleven children, 8 are living; I found her poor, and dirty in a small hut, less clean and comfortable than any hut I have seen belonging to any Indian however poor. She is in possession of near eighty slaves, near 40 of them capable of doing work in or out doors. Yet from bad management they are a heavy burthen to her and to themselves, they are all idle. She told me her poverty arose from want of tools for her labourers and some misunderstanding between her and Mr. Panton. He had refused to supply her with any thing. Her husband is a man of good figure, dull and stupid, a little mixed with African blood. She and her sister Mrs. Weatherford keep the command absolute of every thing from their husbands. She can spin and weave, and has her cloth made. The last year she lost her cotton by worms, she asked me for some tools and goods, and said she had directed her sons to apply for them but she supposed they were ashamed to do so. The sister I am informed lives well in some taste, but expensively. Her negros do but little, and consume every thing in common with their mistress, who is a stranger to economy. She has been a trader for some time but is now out of credit with Mr. Panton. The lands near Mr. Durant are rich.

I crossed the river in a canoe, near this plantation turned down the river to the Tuskeegee, in the fork here formerly stood an old French fort Thoulouse, the flood of the last January flowed over this high ground, here I saw 5 iron cannon, the trunnions broke off; this is a beautiful high bluff, which overlooks the flat land in the fork and on the Tallapoosa, the Coosau, and the lands on its right bank, the river is near 200 yards over. I saw a few bunker beds and the cannon, the only remains of the French establishment. The town house stands near where the fort was, and the buildings, about 30, are compactly situated in the neighbourhood of it. Their fields for culture are the flat lands in the fork, the land where the town stands is level and poor, and continues so out for near a mile, the lands a whiteish clay, the growths small pine, oak and dwarf hickory; the bluff here is as high as at Weatherford's, or somewhat higher, perhaps 46 feet, yet not high enough for a town, if it was, the situation would be a beautiful one. I continued on up to the Coosau, 3 miles to the hickory ground, the lands poor all the way and level, passing the Little Oakchoies on the way, a neat compact little town. Most of the lands cultivated by these 2 towns lie on the right bank of the river; just above the hickory ground the falls commence, they can be passed with canoes, the lands to the right are broken and mountainous & gravelly, not rich, the rock at the falls very different from those at the Tallapoosa Falls, here it is ragged. Continue on 4 miles farther to the remains of the old Tallassu, formerly the residence of Mr. McGillivray and his son the general, here I saw some large apple trees, 10 of them planted by the former, and a stone chimney, the remains of a house built by the latter, I saw half a mile below 8 or 10 apple trees planted by the general, which were thriving. The hickory ground is inhabited by those who formerly lived at the Tallassu, and the old town is a desert, half a mile from this is the residence of Daniel McGillivray, a trader, a native of Scotland, formerly a trader among the Choctaws, but for 12 years a resident and trader among the Creeks, he has a Creek woman and a son 6 years old. He has been a medling troublesome man, talkative and capable of misrepresentations among the Indians. He seemed much pleased at the notice I took of him, to visit him and converse freely with him, and offered his aid to co-operate with me, and his services by day or night. I told him I expected a like conduct from every man in the department. His woman was very attentive and did every thing she could to render my situation comfortable. Mr. McGillivray cultivates a small field with the plow, lying on the river. He informed me that when he applied to the Indians for permission to settle out of town they brought him to this spot, marked the front on the river and permitted him to call all his that he could clear and cultivate. The river here is 250 yards wide and shallow. The poor, broken, gravelly, long leaf pine land close to his house, about 300 yards from the river. At the falls below his house half or ¾ of a mile a creek empties in on the left large enough for a mill.

Wednesday, 21.

I left Mr. McGillivray's at 12 for the Hickory Ground, by the path through the piny woods, the lands generally broken and gravelly, except near the branches, which were covered with reeds. ✕ 2 or 3 of them which unite below and form the creek at Old Tallassee Falls. I arrived at the Hickory Ground and spent one hour with the principal chief of the town, McFasshion, a cousin of Gen. McGillivray. I sat out for Cooborne, the land variegated, flat, hilly and mountainous, pass in four miles Pasabulluh, a beautiful flat ¾ of a mile, and ✕ a creek large and fine for a mill, at 10 miles arrive at the Cooborne leaving the White Ground to the right. The creek before mentioned, Sambulloh, entering the river still lower. Cooborne is a pretty little compact town, beautifully situated, but too low; the flood having covered it near 4 feet. The chiefs being all from home, I continued on to the Fusatchees, and took up my residence with the trader Nicholas White, a native of Mersailles, but resident in this nation 30 years; he has an Indian woman, and 4 children, 2 of each sex, 3 of them married to Indians; he lives comfortable, has stables, and a kitchen, and his wife appears, tho' old, healthy, industrious and pretty cleanly. I spent the evening with him agreeably, except the conduct of my deputy Alex Cornell, who, forgetting himself, got drunk, and was a little disorderly. This morning I began to correct the abuse in my own family. I told my deputy that he was a chief of the land and in the service of the United States, he knew well how to conduct himself, and I was surprised at the impropriety of his conduct, he must reform, and not give me the pain of seeing him again playing the part of the drunken Indian. Mr. White is the trader for these two towns, he informed me that the Cooborne people had always behaved themselves in such a manner towards the white traders, that none of them could reside there, that he kept an Indian factor there, who did the business with fidelity.

Thursday, 22.

I sat out this morning very cold, traveled 3 miles to Hochilliwallies, here I halted at the house of James Russel, a native of the United States; he has been 12 years in the nation, has a decent woman and one son. After one hour's conversation with him and eating some venison and beef, I continued on, passing some very rich level land, low cane swamp on the right, and some high red hills or mountains to the left. I pass over some level lands, ✕ Wehuarthy (sweet water) a beautiful little creek, in sight of a village of that name, belonging to the Tuckabatchee, come to and over the flat old canebrake of the Old Ottassue, pass thro' the old fields to the river opposite Mr. Bailey's, in all 5 miles, ✕ the river in a canoe, and send a person from his house to swim over our horses. The weather cold and freezing.

Friday, 23.

It is cold and cloudy, and snowed for 2 hours. I remain this day with Mr. Bailey, he informs me that the distemper which has for 3 or 4 years past destroyed the horses in the Southern States, and called there the yellow water, was introduced into this country from St. Antoine, and Appaluca. It raged here for two years, and has disappeared; the horses were drooping, the legs swelled, yellow water droped from the nose, a high fever, the sides beat like the thumps, when dead the entraiels were decayed, particularly the lites. Those which survived, on the recovery, if used were sure to relapse and die, but if left to themselves got well; it raged in the hotest part of the summer, abated in the fall and ceased in the winter. There has not been any cure discovered for it. The old horses sufferd most. It was a plague among them.

At some seasons and for a year or two the range is not much infested with flies, either in wet or very dry seasons, they do however come some years in such numbers as to destroy poor horses. In May they appear, June and July they are the most numerous and troublesome, and then they gradually disappear. About cleared land and in stables they are not troublesome. A large flie called the horse guard come at the same season, they continue in cultivated and open land, attack and destroy all the flies they meet with. The flie which is the most troublesome has a small green head. In the month of May on the small bushes, particularly the red root, there is to be seen all over the country more or less in patches, a white froth, and in every lump of it there is one or two flies. Here they are produced but he knows not how. Take a young flie out of the froth, clean it and put it on a leaf, it will soon be surrounded with another coat of froth, and then will be perfected.

The honey in this country is poisonous in the month of March, some negros and Indians have been killed at that season. At that season on the small branches, there is a plant in bloom called by the whites wolfs tongue, or fire leaves, by the Indians Hochkau, (oachfoe), it has a long stem with yellow blossoms, and bears around the stem, green berries, which altho' poisonous are eaten in years of scarcity by the Indians, they boil them in 2 or 3 waters, shifting them, and thus extract the posion from them, they are then pleasant to the taste, somewhat like the garden pea. The Indians are the authors of the discovery. Milk has been the only afficacious remedy discovered here for this poison. The last season a bee tree was taken in this neighbourhood and all who eat of the honey sickened instantaneously, they retired to the house, except a black boy, and took some milk which restored them, the boy was unable to get to the house, and altho' aid was sent him, in 2 hours he was dead.

Those who eat of the honey are first taken with a giddiness, then blindness accompanied with great pain and uneasiness, and thurst.

Saturday, 24.

The weather cold and cloudy, the ponds in the neighbourhood frozen over, which seldom ever happens in this climate.

Sunday, 25.

The weather still cold and freezing. I spend my Christmas in the hospitable house where I am. This good woman as cleanly as any of her sex, is very particular in cooking, altho' she has two black women to assist her, she does much of it with her own hands, has many conveniences about her, and is nice and clean in every thing. She governs her black people and shows much attention to the stock about the plantation. She some times beats the meal for bread, sifts it and bakes it herself. She is agreeable and jocose in conversation, kind to every body, yet firm enough to prevent any imposition on the part of her country people; she gives me daily, coffee, bread and butter, and a relish of some kind of meat, the butter of her own make, a dinner of fowls and pork, with rice, and a dish of tea in the evening.

Mr. Bailey keeps some good rum in his house, and it is remarkable in him that he neither drinks or smokes tobacco. By the former I mean, to excess; he every day takes a glass of grog or two and that's all. The Indians of the town where he lives are more orderly than any others in their neighbourhood, he keeps them at a proper distance, when he is at dinner they never enter the dining room, and even at times of drinking and when in their cups they show the same respect. When I was informed of this, I asked them both to account for it, they said they could attribute it only to the long standing of Mr. Bailey among them and his uniform perseverance in this plan which he adopted on his first settling among them. Some few years past they were under the necessity to remove to Tengau, on account of their stock, and the ill nature of the Indians, who always have been funny and are in the habit of distroying hogs or cattle whenever they tresspass on the fields under cultivation. By this removal the town was three years without a trader and the Indians sent several messages to them to return, but Mrs. Bailey said she would not unless their stock could be secure, and it should be left to Mr. Bailey to choose his place of residence near the town. The Indians sent their king to confirm this agreement, which they adhere to with some little murmuring, at the largeness and increase of his stock.

I applied particularly to Mrs. Bailey for her opinion of the practicability of carrying the benevolent views of the government into effect, explaining them fully to her; she replied it was uncertain; her daughter had learnt to spin among the white women, at Tanasau, were cleanly, neat and industrious. That many of the Indian women were industrious, but not cleanly, nor so provident and careful as the white women. This I replied might be owing to want of information, and the means of helping themselves. She said she did not know whether it was so or not, but of one thing she was certain, they all had water enough, and yet they never kept their husbands clean, even the white men, that this was really a source of vexation to her, and put her under the necessity of scolding the men whenever she saw them, for not making their wives wash their linen; and the women for their want of cleanliness.

I dined this day with Mr. Bailey and three Indian women, on pork and coleworts, a pair of fowls, and ducks; and the conversation related to the Indians and the practicability of bettering their condition. I should have added to my bill of fare some rice and potatoes—rum and water. Some incidents brought to my recollection that on Christmas, 1785, I dined at the public table at Hopewell on the Theowee, being one of the Commissioners for negotiating a peace with the Southern Indians, that the table was covered with a great variety of wild meat and fowls, the company large, that all of them are still living, and that the conversation then was the means of establishing a peace with these Indians, and of bettering their condition. I remember well that the sentiments I then entertained were the same I still possess, and am labouring to carry into effect.

I was this day visited by the negros from the towns above me, on their way to Mrs. Durant's to keep Christmas. I asked how this was done, they answered that at this season of the year they made a gathering together at Mrs. Durant's or her sister's, where there lived more of the black people than in any other part of the nation. And there they had a proper frolic of rum drinking and dancing. That the white people and Indians met generally at the same place with them and had the same amusement.

The black people here are an expense to their owners except in the house where I am. They do nothing the whole winter but get a little wood, and in the summer they cultivate a scanty crop of corn barely sufficient for bread.

Monday, 26.

The weather cloudy and freezing in the forenoon, and cold and clear in the afternoon. This day I had some provisions prepared for the road, and had every thing in readiness for my departure to-morrow for the lower towns.

Tuesday, 27.

I sent my attendants on the nearest road for Tuckabatchee, and set out myself to view the lands back of the Ottassee. For a mile the lands level, intersected with swamps, the growth a mixture of oak, pine, poplar and hickory, the dwarf hard shelled nut, free from stone yet not rich. The lands there on the right rise a little into hills, and flat, the branches stored with cane, the levels on the hills stiff red land, excellent for wheat, the growth black oak, scrub oak and hickory, and yellow pine, not large or abundant. There is to the left, back of the town, a swamp half a mile diameter, and on my right, one still larger, mostly a cane-brake. I pass the remains of an old settlement, formerly a part of the Ottassee, on the borders of Caloebee. descend to the flat land on the creek and up it one mile, the little drains which empty from my right, abound with reeds, the lands not rich. I cross the creek and turn to Tuckabatchee; I visited Mrs. Cornell and dined with her, on venison and pork stakes, and coffee. The old woman said she had expected me yesterday and had something good for me, but to-day she was unprovided.

Two old chiefs visited me and had much conversation on the affairs of their nation.

Wednesday, 28.

Emautle Hutke, white chief, one of those who visited me last evening, remained all night with me. He informed me he lived out of town about seven miles. That he moved out for the advantage of stock, and had now about one hundred head. This old man told me he had a great regard for the white people, that of his own knowledge or from his father knew that from an intercourse with them, the Indian had notwithstanding his obstinacy received much useful instruction.

That now they had many comforts, to which they were strangers to, cloathing, comfortable houses, and plenty of bread.

He remembered when the part of the nation where he lived had not a blanket or a hoe, and his father remembered the introduction of the knife and the hatchet. He remembered when there was not a horse in the nation and the rum used to be packed by the traders and sent down with the skins, he remembers the first horse and mare that was brought in the nation by a trader and that the Indians were afraid of them.

And now he said they had hoes, axes, knives, guns and other necessaries, and he was glad I intended to increase the number, and trade them other useful things. I promised to visit him.

Thursday, 29.

I sat out for the lower creeks, took the path up the Eufaube, thro' the Tallassee. I called at the house of James Moore, who accompanyed us, continued on 8 miles to James McQueens, an old trader, he was from home. I was very desirous of seeing this old man, he being the oldest white man in the nation, and trader, he has accumulated a considerable property. Continue on 2 miles farther and cross the creek, 30 feet wide, at Baskets one of the grandchildren of Mr. McQueen. The Indians are settled in plantations and villages upon the banks of this creek, many of them prittily situated and fenced. The huts neat and cleanly, the last one particularly so, the family remarkable industrious, the fields large and fenced. Continue on half a mile and call at the house of William Pound, here I dined; he has been four years in the nation, has a pretty little Indian woman, and one child. I saw a great number of fowls, and they gave me stewed fowls and pork. I continue on 2 miles farther and encamp. In 4 miles cross a creek, in 4 more cross another, and in 5 recross the Eufaube. The lands uneaven and gravelly, very good on the creeks, but poor on the hills, all the bottoms covered with reed, the first creek from the encampment has some cane. I call and breakfast with William Drew, a native of Virginia, at the half way house, Chowolle Hatche. He has an Indian woman who was kind, good natured and attentive. He is a trader, and silversmith, the latter he took up of himself by way of amusement a year of two ago. The chief of the business in this line is in making broches, rings and ear bobs. I continue on S. E., the route hitherto E. 9 miles, over high broken pine forrest, the pines large without any undergrowth. Cross Crane Creek (Wattooluhhaugau hatche); this creek is difficulty to pass, the margins on both sides covered with reed without any thing else, it is mirary, the channel of the creek 3 feet but deep, the little hollows above and below the ford exhibit the most beautiful and variegated bed of reed that I have seen. From the creek rise up a steep red hill and continue on 5 miles over uneaven lands, the growth pine, not large, with blackjack and willow leaved hickory. The land then more level for five miles, the growth the same as the preceding 5 miles, all the little drains to the right and left covered with reed. This Crane Creek is the first waters on the path of the Chattahoochee. Take the left hand path, the course E. N. 1 mile, encamp on and afterwards cross a small branch runing to the left, continue on ¼ of a mile, recross it runing to the right, and in half a mile cross the Wetumcau, 35 feet over, falling down a long slope of craggy rock, a small village on the hill; here I breakfast with George Clem, a trader. Continue on pass Wetumcau to the right, cross a creek in 2 miles runing to the right, continue on over high pine hilly land 2 miles, cross another creek runing to the right, 4 miles farther over high open pine forest, the trees large, come to and up a steep hill, from the top there is an extensive view S. and S. E. The tops of the ridges in the last direction rising gradually, and terminating in their blue cloudlike appearance 10 or 12 miles off, descend pass the broken rock on the right formed at the head of a bottom like a horse shoe. The lands very uneaven, some high hills, to the right and left, the pine smaller but more abundant, and fine for log huts, 4 miles over land descending, passing several reedy meadows and branches, I arrive at the flat lands adjoining the town, and in one mile over land moderately rich, I arrive at the town house. The course from Clem's generally S. E. I visited Mr. James Darouzeaux and dined with him and crossed over the river to Thomas Marshall's, where I arrived the 31st of December.

January the first, 1797.

This morning the weather cold, clear and frosty. Some young men called on me on their way from Tombigbee to Georgia on business, they produced passports signed by the commandant of the district in Spanish and requested me to sign them, after the necessary enquiry I did so, and directed them to take the rout by the Rock Landing, their names Hiram Monger, native of Georgia, and Flood Megrew, a native of South Carolina, both inhabitants of Tombigbee, and James Barrow their pilot, a native of the Red Banks on Tar River in North Carolina, at present Spawacta on the Alabama.

Barrow informed me had been at the Natches early in December, that the commissioners appointed to run the line had not arrived, owing to the impossibility of descending the rivers Ohio and Tennessee in dry season.

He says the inhabitants of that district are uneasy at the expected change in the government, they have obtained titles to their lands from the Spanish governor, and they are apprehensive of loosing them, as the whole country was covered with old British patents.

I rote by him a letter to Col. Gaither.

Coweta, January 1st, 1797.

Dear Colonel:

I came through the upper Cherokees to the Tallapoosa, and down that river to the Alabama. I have visited the towns in those rivers, and some of those on the Coosau, and I arrived here last evening. I was informed at the Tuckabatchee of the bad conduct of some of the young men of this town, who had murdered a negro woman on Chulapocca, this determined me to come immediately to examine into it. The chiefs and warriors are all of them out hunting and not expected to return till March.

I find the upper Creeks disposed for peace, and more friendly to the white people than they have ever been known to be. This information I have obtained both from the Indians and the white people resident among them.

From the unusual length of the time the traders have been down to Colerain I am apprehensive Mr. Price is not safe. I understood he was to leave Philadelphia in September with the full supply of goods. I expected my baggage to be sent round by him to the care of the agent of the War Department to be forwarded to me, as I shall reside a month or two on this river I shall be much in want of it.

If any opportunity offers pray let me hear from you and the agent of the War Department.

I have the honor to be, dear Colonel,

Your obedient servant,

HENRY GAITHER,
Lt. Col. Commandant Fort Fidins.

Monday the 2 January, 1797.

This day two Indians, Billy Wright and Badmouth, of the Tallassee on Tallapoosa, applied for permission to visit their friends on Ogeechee. I received at the same time satisfactory information of the friendly disposition and peaceable orderly conduct. I gave them each a passport.

Coweta, Lower Creeks, 2 January, 1797.

Billey Wright of the Tallassee on the Tallapoosa, a halfbreed Creek has applied to me for a passport to visit his friends and relations on Ogeechee in Georgia. He is a friend to the white people, peaceable and orderly, fond of strong drink. I recommend him to the protection of my fellow citizens, his rout is by Beard's Bluff.

At the same time to remove as far as possible all prospect of danger I wrote this note to the commanding officer at that post.

Sir:

The two Indians, the bearers of this, have a passport from me to visit their friends in Georgia. They are directed to your post, to show their passports and receive your directions; you will of course be pleased to give such directions to them as the existing state of things may require.

I have visited most of the towns of the upper Creeks, and on being informed of the bad conduct of some of the young men of this town in murdering a negro woman and doing other damage on the Tulpocca, I determined to come immediately to examine into it, I arrived on the 31st ultimo. The chiefs and warriors are all of them out hunting and not expected to return till March.

I find the upper Creeks inclined to peace and more friendly to the white people than they have ever been known to be. This information I have obtained from the Indians themselves and the white people resident among them.

I addressed a letter yesterday to Col. Gaither at Fort Fidins, being uncertain where he is.

I am, &c.,

The Officer in Command at Beard's Bluff.

Mr. Darouzeaux visited me; I had much conversation with him, Mr. Marshall, Alex Cornell and Mr. Thomas on the state of the Indians in this quarter, and recent murder on the Oconee. The chiefs of the town being out on a hunt I determined to visit the Cusseta, it being probable I shall there have an opportunity of meeting and conversing with some of the chiefs. Mr. Thomas gave me a copy of the talk sent to Mr. Seagrove disapproving this conduct of some of their giddy hotheaded mad young men. I permited Alex Cornell to return back to Tuckabatchee, and Mr. Moore accompanyed him.

Tuesday, 3 January.

I discover that the nights in this climate are much colder than any I have ever felt compared with the warmth of the day. The season continues still dry, and colder than is usual.

In the course of conversation to-day with Mr. Marshall on the domestic economy of the Indians, I was surprised at his want of information as he has resided twelve years in their towns, and has two Indian wives. He explained for himself, by saying that during the whole of his residence he had not entered 3 of the Indian houses, that whatever business he had with the men he went to their doors, mentioned it to him, said and did what was necessary and left them, or sat under their corn house.

This disposition of Mr. Marshall brings to my recollection, that David Hay informed me while I was at New York on a visit to the white Lieutenant's family, that he had been five years in the land, and that the house he then entered with me was the first and only Indian hut he had entered; he added that probably he should never enter another altho' he might remain as long again. I asked him if he had had no intercourse with the women, he answered no, nor with the men, except to look at them. He is a stout active young fellow, a native of Lancaster County in Pennsylvania. Seems well conditioned, decent and orderly.

Wednesday, 4th.

I sat out down the river on a visit to the Cusseta; the lands for 2½ miles level, pine, oak and hickory, black jack, the soil dark and apparently rich; enter here the cornfields belonging to the town, an oblong mound, to the right ¼ mile farther another mound near the river 25 feet high, flat at top, surrounded on the north with mulberry and on the south with evergreens, some of them large, the top flat, the diameter 40 yards at the base. This is the most beautiful I have ever seen, from the top is a view of the river above, the flat lands on the right bank, and all the fields, of about one hundred acres, these fields have been long under culture and yet they are rich, there is no where a stump to be seen. At the lower end of the fields a branch from the left, and a large beaver pond of 40 acres, capable of being drained at a small expense of labour. The lands back of these fields rise about 20 feet, continue on flat for one mile and then enter pine barron; continue on over the branch and broken rich land to Hatchee-thlucco (great creek), 60 feet over, a rappid current, rise up a steep bank, and continue on a high level flat, cross a small branch, Rookluggee Chiclowau Ocosecuh, this branch is between the town and the fields, and is so named from a practice in warm weather the women have of washing as they pass it. Pass thro' an old field formerly a Chickasaw town, from the lower border of which is seen at one view the Cusseta, on a flat 40 feet below, surrounded with this barron bank to the North and East and by the river to the West. The lands about the town are poorer than any I have ever seen, and could only have been selected from the beautiful flat on which the town is situated, just above the floods. Very little of corn or any thing else is cultivated in the town, every thing almost except the early corn being cultivated above Hatcheelemo and all brought to town either in canoes or on the backs of the women or horses. I arrived at the house of Thomas Carr, a trader; he is an old man, has resided many years in the nation, has suffered much by the uncertain and precarious situation of a trader among the Indians, during times of war. He received me and treated me hospitably. He apoligised for his situation, which he did not intend to alter until he knew the success of the mission intrusted to me. He has good butter, made by his people, and a plenty of pork and corn, he makes some rice, carries on his trade. I dined with him on stewed pork, and he gave me a can of good rum grog. The Indians expected I would be down in the morning and waited for me till 12 o'clock and then dispersed. As soon as I arrived they sent to inform me they would expect to see me in the morning at the ceremony of the black drink. I sent a message to Mr. Darouzeaux to request him to attend me as interpreter.

Thursday the 5th.

This morning I attended at the square and the Micos and chiefs received me in the most friendly manner. As soon as Mr. Darouzeaux arrived, at their request I informed them of my rout since I parted with them at Colerain.

I informed them of the disposition of the United States relative to the red people, and the plan for bettering their condition, told them of the happy accommodation of our political differences with all our neighbours red and white, and our fixed determination to be at peace with all the world. I informed them that I expected that Col. Gaither was before this fixed down on their lands at the places contemplated at Colerain; that the President, as soon as he saw what the commissioners had done, and the conversation between them and the chiefs, he directed the Secretary of War to augment the troops on the frontiers of Georgia, and give the necessary orders for the fixture of the posts. I gave them a particular account of my reception among the Cherokees at Etawwah, the information I gave them of the plan of the government, and the determination of the Cherokee women to accept of the benevolent offers of the government. I told them that I had visited the chief of that town at his place of residence six miles on this side of the town, that he was a good farmer, had a fine stock of cattle, hogs and horses, used the plow, made cotton and immitated the ways of the white people.

They all heard me with attentive silence, untill I mentioned the raising and spinning of cotton. One of them laughed at the idea, but the Fusatchee Mico assent to all and said it must be done.

The objection made to it by the men, is, that if the women can cloathe themselves, they will be proud and not obedient to their husbands.

I returned in the evening to Coweta.

No. 2.   Coweta, 6 January, 1797.

The Secretary of War.

Sir:

I left my letter, No. 1, of the 22 Nov. in the care of General Pickins to be forwarded to you, by post from Columbia. I have pursued the rout pointed out to you in that letter, and visited three of the Cherokee towns, thense to the Tallapoosa, and down that river to the Alabama, up the Coosau to two towns and from thense returning up the Tallapoosa to Tuckabatchee, and thro' the Tallassee to this town, down to the Cusseta, and back again.

I have in the course of this tour made on all occasions suitable efforts to impress on the minds of the Indians the benevolent views of the government, and to avail myself of the necessary information in aid of the plan contemplated in my mission. The season was not a very favourable one, as most of the chiefs were out hunting and there remained at home in the towns, the traders, the women and old men only, with some few exceptions.

I have through the whole of the upper Creeks obtained this interesting fact, from all the traders and Indians; that the Indians are inclined to peace and more friendly to the white people, than they have ever been known to be. This was to be expected, and it can readily be accounted for arrising out of the confidence they have in the justice of the U. S., accommodation of our political differences with Spain and Great Britain.

The Indians who were at Colerain have spoken highly of the candid, just and friendly conduct of the Commissioners of the

United States during the whole of the negotiations, and in every town I find some of them, who point me out as one of them.

Before my arrival I had been informed that there were some white people in the nation who's past conduct would not bear the strictest scrutiny. I have determined not to retrospect, and I have announced this determination in every town, with a requisition to all the white people to aid and assist me, and I am promised the co-operation of all the traders and their dependents.

I find myself surrounded with innumerable difficulties, the Indians are all of them beggars, and being accustomed for several years past to receive presents from the United States, Great Britain or Spain sufficient to cloathe all the idlers in the nation, they view with supprise their great beloved friend and father the agent of the four nations offering them cotton and flax seed, ploughs, spining wheels, cards and looms, with instructors in the useful branches of mechanics and agriculture. They are extremely jealous of their women, who are slaves and destined to every office of labour and fatigue. They will not suffer the least intercourse with them, fearing that by being able to cloathe themselves, they will attempt to break the chains which degrade them. The young women and the widows are exempt from these restrictions, with some few of the married women.

The traders, several of whom have amassed considerable fortunes, have almost all of them been as inattentive to their children as the Indians. It has not entered the head of one of them to attempt to better the condition of the Indian. I believe they look on such attempts as fruitless. They have no social intercourse with them, they pursue their profession steadily. They are all of them hospitable. Mr. William Panton has engrossed the greatest part of the trade of this nation, his establishment is at Pensacola; he supplies not only the white traders, but he has set up a number of Indian factors. They are both behind-hand with him, and the Indians are indebted to them to a considerable amount; the skin and fur trade is on the decline, and the wants of the Indians are increasing. I believe I shall find no difficulty in establishing a national council, to meet once a year, at the town of my residence, but the expense must be borne by the government, and I think it may be so conducted as not to exceed 700 dollars. An establishment of this sort appears to me indispensable, to enable the nation to fulfil it engagements with us, for except as to the government of the women, there is no law, it belongs to individuals to take personal satisfaction, or to the family of the person injured to avenge the rong—the chiefs may interpose, but their interposition is seldom of any avail,—there is here and there a solitary instance where the chiefs of a town have interposed all their authority, which could only prevail on the weldisposed of the relations to put their offending brethren to death. We must aid them to fulfil their engagements, and it will require much and patient instruction to enlighten their understandings.

I visited this town sooner than otherwise I intended to do expressly to examine into the recent murder of the negro woman at the Appalatche. The chiefs are from home but expected soon to return, I shall do what is proper on the occasion; I have visited at the Cussetas several of the chiefs, five of whom I was personally acquainted with, two of them Micos, one of them the Birdtail who was at New York. They are as friendly as I could wish.

From the unusual time the traders have been down at Colerain I am apprehensive Mr. Price, the full supply of goods, and my baggage are all lost. I am much in want of the baggage; and if the whole is lost, I must request of you to repeat the order for the articles mentioned in the list I left with you.

I shall soon write to you again. I beg you to assure the President of my sincere wishes for a long continuation of his health and happiness and to believe me yourself with the sincerest regard and esteem,

Sir,

Your obedient servant.

JAMES McHENRY,
Secretary of War.

Coweta, 7th January, 1797.

Col. H. Gaither.

Dear Sir:

I rote you on the 1st of this month, by James Barrow, since then I have visited the Cussetas; several of the chiefs were at home, and 3 of the Mico's, two of whom you know, Fusatchee Mico, and Tussekiah Mico. They are as friendly as I could wish.

I have directed Mr. Thomas to be the bearer of my letters to you and the Secretary of War. You will oblige me by communicating to me the progress you have made in fixing your posts, according to the new arrangement; and the state of the frontiers. He will return immediately to this town.

I shall probably visit you some time next month, as I have fixed the 10th of March for runing the line from the Apalatchee over the Currahee Mountain to Tugalo; something may intervene to enduce a postponement of the time to a more convenient season—of this I shall apprise you in due time.

Two Indians, Billey Wright and another of the Tallassee, applied to me for a permit to visit their friends on Ogeechee. I directed them to the station near Beard's Bluff,* and gave them a letter to the officer commanding there, requesting him to give them such directions as the existing state of things may require. It has been expressly enjoined on all the Indians now out not to cross the Oconee, on any account whatever. If you should see any of them you will oblidge me by repeating this prohibition to them.

I request you to mention me respectfully to the officers under your command, and to believe me with sincere regard and esteem,

Sir,

Your obedient servant.

HENRY GAITHER,
Lt. Col. Commandant.

Coweta, the 8th January, 1797.

Sir:

In September last there were packed up at Philadelphia implements of husbandry for the Creeks, and other things necessary to the Indian department. They were to be forwarded to the care of the agent for the Department of War at the intended establishment near Fort Fidins with orders for the quartermaster to cause them to be sent to the town up the river care of the agent. If you have received any of the articles, as discribed I wish you would send them to me at this place. I expected the things would have been sent round in the vessel with Mr. Price and the full supply of goods; as such a vessel has not yet arrived it is probable some accident has happened during the stormy season and the vessel is lost or missed her port. I enclose you a list of some articles belonging to the Indian Department in the possession of Mr. Price, who has as I expect an order from the Secretary of War to deliver them. If he has not received any such order, I request you notwithstanding to direct them to be sent and I in that case will be accountable for them.

If you in the course of your researches have found out the secret of making Indians fulfill their public engagements, where there is no law and it belongs to individuals to take personal

---

* Beard's Bluff is on the Altamaha River in Liberty County Ga.

satisfaction, and to the family of a person injured to avenge the
rong, and you will communicate that secret to me, I hereby bind
myself and successors in office to send you six princesses in full
dress.

I am with sincere regard,

Sir,

Your obedient servant.

MAJ. FREEMAN,
Agent for the Department of War.

8th January, 1797.

I this day signed passports for William Hunt, of Pawarta,
James McGraw and John Sheppard, of Tombigbee, to go into the
State of Georgia.

9th January.

The falls of this river are about 3 miles from this, the width
of the river opposite the town house 120 yards, and about the
same width to the falls, the current steady, the river up; the body
or bed of rocks over which the water falls rough, coarse and
vainey, and rising into small islands of ½ of an acre, the water
is formed into two channels, one on the right the other on the
left side of the river, both together about 40 feet over; at low
water, the fall about 15 feet in 150, the current in the left channel
rappid, but no where so steep but that fish may ascend. Here
are two fisheries, one on each side of the river, that on the left
belongs to the Cussetas, the other to the Cowetas, the fish are
taken in scoop nets. The lands on the left bank of the river flat,
and for some distance back, the timber pine, oak, hickory, the
soil stiff. On the right side from the lower end of the falls up the
river, a pine barron to the water's edge, the pines small. In
approaching this river on the left side, one is surprised at finding
the falls, without the least appearing of any change or uneaven-
ness of the surface of the earth, the whole level, and continues
so back for 1 mile. The banks of the river generally fifty feet
high down to the town house. A creek empties in half a mile
above, 15 feet over, and it descends with a rappid current, going
up this creek a small one joins it on the left, about 200 yards from
the river, continuing up one mile, the lands on both sides to the
margin, without any swamp; the banks steep enough any where
for mills. The course of this creek for this distance is nearly
north; here is the bend, it has its source near 20 miles from this,
and nearly north from the bend.

I saw several ponds on the flats which are dry most part of the year, but at this season full of water, and abounding with ducks and geese; which feed constantly on the acorns.

19th January.

I this day signed passports for James Lewis, Prior Hardiman and James Foster, of the district of Natches, to go into the State of Georgia. James Lewis is a native of North Carolina, born near the shallow ford of the Yadkin, he at present lives on Coles Creek 13 miles from the Mississippi, and 30 from the Natches.

James Foster is a native of South Carolina, and he has resided in the Natches since he was a boy.

I have been for several days confined to the house with dul cloudy rainy weather. Was only able to make short excursions up the river. I have been visited frequently by the few Indians who are in town or who arrive from the woods.

20th.

The falls of this river continue three or four miles nearly of the same width, then the river expands to thrice the width below, the bottom gravelly, rocky, and its shoally. There are several small islands, one of them at the part where the expansion commences, rich and some part of it under culture. Going up the river 2½ miles from the end of the falls the broken lands commence. 3½ miles farther Chisse Hulkuha, small creek joins the river. 4 miles farther Chusethlocco, a creek 20 feet wide joins the river, it is a rocky creek. 5 miles still higher Ketalee, a bold shoally rocky creek, its bed covered with moss joins the river, the creek 30 feet wide. 10 miles still higher a large creek enters.

On the opposite shore beginning below at the termination of the falls is Ocowaccoh Hatchee (Falls Creek), 15 feet over; 6 miles still higher up is Leader's Creek, a small one. One mile farther Hatchee Canawe (crooked creek) a small one. Thense up to Hollowockee, opposite Ketalee and of nearly the same size. 6 or 7 miles still higher is Mossy Creek, Assunoppa.

The island which is in part under culture is nearly 4 miles from the termination of the falls, its about ½ a mile in length and narrow, here the river is fordable, from the left bank of the river, go to within 100 yards of the uper end of the island, then down the island to the fields and then ✕ to the other shore.

There is a village on Chusethlocco, about 4 miles up from the river, of 8 or 10 families, the village is called Itatchee Uscaw (head of a creek). The lands broken, growth oak, hickory, pine, chesnut, cane on the creek and reed on the branches.

There is a village a mile below the mouth of Leader's Creek, on the river, and some settlements on most of the creeks. The growth on this side similar to that on the other, the lands broken, cane on the creeks and reed on the branches.

21 January.

In the year 1784 William Marshall a young man 17 years of age, a native of Ireland, was murdered at a Coweta village about 10 miles above the town, by an Indian of the Cowetas; Thomas Marshall his brother, applied to the chief of the town for satisfaction, and declared his determination of leaving the town if he did not obtain it, that he might have an opportunity of obtaining it for himself. The uncle of the murderer said he should have satisfaction, that either he himself or the guilty one should suffer, and he determined that the guilty should. The chiefs all immediately promised that justice should be done. The chiefs after consultation in the square, determined that the murderer should suffer death, and they directed two of his clan to carry the determination into execution. The two appointed went, one of them with the rifle of the deceased, and shot the murderer; he was on the top of a house helping to cover it when they came, and there were many Indians present house building. The executioners fired at him and missed him, he thought the balls which missed him had been fired at turkies. They then shot and wounded him, he fell to the ground, when they shot at and wounded him again, he lived about one hour and died. He had repeatedly made attempts to kill a white man before; and at one time, run a knife thro' the arm of Nicholas Miller. He said his father had been killed by a white man, and a white man he would have; after murdering William Marshall, he said he knew he must die for it, and he was determined to kill every white man he met with. While he was wounded and just before he died, he said a white man he had determined to have, and one he had got, that his heart was straight and that he was a man.

The family of Mr. Marshall have been so unfortunate, most of them, as to meet an untimely end; during the late war a party of Indians said to be Chekaws attacked the house of Mrs. Marshall the mother, and of her son-in-law Capt. David Stewart about one mile above Old Town on Ogeechee and killed Mrs. Marshall, Capt. Stewart, his wife and two children, the two brothers William and Henry were in the house with their mother, and defended themselves with their guns untill their mother was killed, and then they retreated; Henry was afterwards killed at Sappalo; a lad at school by Capt. Baker and his company, after he had surrendered himself wounded a prisoner. This action is mentioned as having been done in a manner shocking to humanity.

23 January.

Visited Tallauhassee, and dined with the old queen, the prince's mother, she had sent for me, she received me and treated me with much attention. Her brother an old man and three warriours were at home. I dined on stewed pork, fryed pork and eggs, with good bread, fried potatoes and saufkee. The young men informed me that they had been hunting towards Cumberland, that one of them saw Mr. Dinsmoor who gave them an order for ammunition in case they should want, but that after crossing the path from Knoxville to Nashville, they heard some white people hunting bear, and they determined to return. Another said he had been on the branches of Tulapocca, saw some white men who spoke kindly to him, that he and some others killed a hog high up on Little River, where they saw several cattle and hogs, and much sign of horses, some of them shod. They complained of the stocks of white people ranging on their lands, and requested that measures might be taken to cause them to be removed.

Tallauhassee is on a small creek, Chulucintigatuh, two miles below Coweta. They moved from Tlocorcau, (broken arrow). The lands level between the two towns, and pretty good, the growth pine, oak, and hard shelled hickory, all of them small. The town is surrounded on the North by the creek, on the East by the river, and a pond, and some high ground to the West, it is small, not compactly built; there are about 100 gun men, belonging to the town, tho' many of them reside in villages. I saw at three or four houses some peach trees planted around them, which appeared in a thriving state, and had been attended to by the owners. I was shown in an old field some stakes to which the Cherokees had been tied in the last war they had with the Creeks about 40 years past when taken prisoners. Three of the stakes remain. Here the captives were tied and here they received their doom, which with the exception of young lads and a few women was the tortue till death.

Near the river below the creek is a rich flat, there is a conic mound 17 or 18 feet high and near 40 over, it has some appearance of having been five sided, it is surrounded with the usual growth on the flat lands of the river, has some evergreens to the south, and an elm in the center. This mound is below the point of the river, about 600 yards, the one on the other side in the Cusseta fields is nearly opposite to the point.

Below the point, so called from the short turn of the river, there is a ford, pretty good in dry seasons. Still higher up the river and just above the oblong mound on the Cusseta side, there is a small oblong island in the river of one, or at most two acres, surrounded with ducks and geese during the winter season.

I returned through the Cabeta fields, they are in the point, the river forms two sides and a small fork fence with stakes and three rails, the other of the fields. Some years ago, the town was built here, and during the winter when the Indians were out hunting, a flood carried off the houses and all their corn. They then sat down at a rise a little back, and in a few years after removed to its present site.

The creek at Tallauhassee is large enough for a mill, with a pair of light stones to grind at all seasons. The creek adjoining the Coweta affords water sufficient for a saw mill. They both have their rise in the piney lands to the West, and the branches are all of them reedy.

24.

Some days past one of my mares proved sickly, and did not return as usual to be fed, I directed the servants to hunt for her. This day an old woman called to inform me she was stolen; that a man now out in the woods with his family had come expressly with the intention of doing it. Some of the young lads in town have turned out to recover her, and all of them express concern at the action, the man being known. I have informed them of my determination to demand of the chiefs the execution of their law upon him. He has long been at the habit of stealing horses, and is a fit subject for an example.

25.

I am this day informed that a lad has returned to the Cussetas, from the north side of the Oakmulgee, he had been hunting on the waters of Oconee, and had taken a mare and colt, which he saw on the Indian lands. The mare he says he took to bring the packs of skins, having 40 of them, and in retaliation for one taken from his brother nine years past. He was immediately informed by some of the Indians of my being here, and that he would be compelled to deliver her up. He replied if he was ordered he should do it, but he meant to keep her till he saw his brother.

26.

I had some conversation with the women, on this particular situation, their wants and the means of gratifying them. I found among them one, who is intelligent and speaks English well enough to be understood. I have promised her to cloathe her and her two children at the expense of the United States, annually and to furnish her with the means of living comfortably, on condition that she will have her daughter taught to spin, and assist herself, to interpret to the women, whatever may be devised for their benefit. She readily assented and has promised to be governed in all things by those who have the direction of Indian affairs.*

The trader's son arrived to-day from Flint River and brought me a letter from Mr. Barnard and one from Col. Gaither. The Col. writes from Fort St. Tammany of the 13; informs me of the arrival of Mr. Price at Savannah, on the 16, with public goods addressed to me, and that he had sailed for St. Marys after the 24 of December.

The Col. informs that the fort on the south side of the Altamaha is recently finished (called Fort James); that he shall leave Ensign Thomson and 25 men to compleat the inside work, and that he shall ascend the river in a few days to build the fort ordered near Fort Fidins on the Oconee.

The messenger informs me that there are some people settled on this side of the Oconee, and that Col. Gaither had given notice to the people to move from the Indian lands, and to drive their stock on the north side of the Oconee. He further informs that a body of cavalry had arrived from the northward, and that Col. Gaither intended to go up the river with them, destroy the plantations which are made, and collect such stock as remains on the Indian lands after the time allowed for their removal.

Yesterday evening he lodged with the Cusseta Mico, and brought a message to me, that chief has sent some young men out to take the mare and colt, brought in as mentioned on the 25, and hold them subject to my order, that the head warriour was out, or he should have directed him to go for her and whip the lad for bringing them off; that I might expect a man to call on me to-morrow for orders.

28 January.

Opocthe Mico of the Cussetas called on me to inform me that he had executed the orders of the Cusseta Mico; had taken the mare and colt that I had been informed of the day before yester-day, and carried them to that Mico, who would take care of them till my order; that they were taken by the lad on the south waters of Little River.

---

* August 1805, this promise she did not perform, nor could she be prevailed on to use any other means than lying whenever she saw a white man.

29 January.

Aron Harad Oketeqockenne and the second man of that town applied to me to give Harad an opportunity to defend his character for some injurious insinuations circulated against him. Harad is a native of Roanoke in North Carolina, about 30 miles below Halifax, he was attached to the British during the war, and has resided in the Creek nation ever since the evaculation of St. Augustine. He has an Indian wife and three children, has heretofore been a trader, has acquired some property and is desirous of trading again. After the necessary enquiry I informed him how he was to proceed to obtain a license to trade, and I wrote to Maj. Freeman.

Coweta, 31st January, 1797.

Sir:

Aron Harad of the Oketeqockenne has been with me, he says some reports have been circulated in the nation unfavourable to his character, and he requested that I would enable him remove them. He is desirous to obtain a licence to trade. The second man of his town accompanyed him and delivered me a talk from Kennard in his favour. I have not heard any thing which should preclude him from obtaining a license provided he can give the requisite security.

MAJ. COMMANDANT FREEMAN,
Agent for the War Department.

31st.

Mr. Barnard arrived last evening, he brought with him Cusseta Mico; Owlelo Mico of this town visited me, I had much conversation with them, and explained the plan of the government to them. I found that it would be disagreeable to many of the chiefs if I should cause the line to be run, before the meeting of the chiefs Coweta & Cusseta.

I received a letter from Mr. Price of the 14, informing me of his arrival at Colerain, with goods for the Indian department and that they were very much damaged by bad weather on the passage. He further says, "We have a number of Indians here continually importunning us for provisions and presents, the first

I have been oblidged to supply them with in moderate quantity; presents I cannot think myself justifiable in giving them, altho' considerable have been made up for them before my arrival, composed of factory goods and public goods under the charge of Mr. Seagrove and at his recommendation. I am in great hopes of hearing from you 'ere long, it will relieve me from a great deal of perplexity which I endure at present for want of a person to act in the department of Indian affairs."

There is something not readily to be accounted for, in the Indians crowding in the midst of the hunting season to Colerain; when they were invited here to the treaty, and assured that there was a plenty of every thing comfortable for them, the whole nation seemed unconcerned and not more than 4 or 5 hundred attended. When they are informed that there is not any thing for them there, either to eat or as presents, John Galphin, who says he is in the pay of the United States, by appointment of Mr. Seagrove, sets out with a long train of men, women and children, and go's to Colerain; and they were at the eve of obtaining considerable presents, but the arrival of Mr. Price puts a stop to it.

It is in vain for the executive to dijest and adopt plans for continuing the friendship of the Indians and preserving peace with them and the citizens, if they are thus intruded on. The Indians have repeatedly in my tour applied for presents, many of them in a stile rude and indelicate: "I want a paper to get a blanket, shirt flap and some things for my wife and children, you are come, and you are the man to get these things for us." Yes I am the man, and I intend you shall get them out of your own exertions, you must follow my advise and if you cannot get the things you want, I will then see that they are brought and delivered to you. If you will not follow my advise, you will get no presents of any kind. After repeated similar conversations, I was told at the Tuckabatchees of this troop of beggars being on the way to Colerain; the two Indians who informed me of them applied for an order for their presents, that they would then go and get them; I told them these Cowetas would be disappointed, that there were no presents there for them, and that they must return as they went. The two applicants assured me that they expected presents and would get them.

1st February.

Aron Harad applied to me again to aid him in obtaining the requisites to enable him to trade; Mr. Barnard and Mr. Marshall at his earnest request agreed to become security for his licence; they at the same time observed they were led to do it, knowing that he had heretofore been in trade, the Indians were indebted to him, and that it would be difficult if not impracticable to collect the debts unless he had some goods.

I filled up a bond with the security offered, and directed Mr. Harad to take it or send it to Maj. Freeman, who was the person appointed to grant the licence.

Having an opportunity by Mr. Harad, to send a letter to Mr. Burges, I wrote him.

———————

Coweta, 1st of February, 1797.

James Burges:

Measures calculated to insure a continuance of the friendship of the Indians and to preserve peace along the interior frontiers of the United States have been dijested and adopted by the President of the U. States. The plan in a considerable degree depends for its execution on my agency, south of the Ohio, and throughout the whole a rigid economy in the public expenditure is deemed indispensable.

In arranging the necessary assistants for the Creek department, I shall give a preference to those in service, and retain as many of them as may be necessary. I have therefore appointed you to be one of the assistants; your allowance will be 400 dollars per annum, paid quarterly, and this allowance will commence with the first of December 1796, as I suppose your former services have been paid by Mr. Seagrove up to that day.

I am &c.

———————

I this day received information from St. Augustine, St. Marks and the Semanoles, that war was actually commenced between the Spaniards and English; and that the Indians were pleased at it, and were circulating reports fabricated by some mischief makers among them tending to induce a belief that Col. Brown would very soon be in the nation from Providence to call on the Indians to take part with them. The king of the town, Owlelo Mico, informed me that from appearances at Pensacola, he expected they were hourly in expectation of hearing of a declaration of war. That he spoke to the governor, who informed him "that people were liable to unpleasant sensations from unforseen difficulties and perplexities, that their affairs were embarrassing."

I told the chiefs that they were not to take part on either side, that they had nothing to do, in a contest between the

Europeans. Let the people of the old world fight their own battles, and us mind our own affairs at home. They replied it was right, we will do so.

Coweta, 2 February, 1797.

Sir:

In the course of my tour through the Creeks, I find that you have a very extensive commercial intercourse with them, and that probably your present or future prospects may be materially affected by the political state of affairs in Europe. I do not know that I can in any way contribute any thing that may be of service to you, within my agency, but if you know wherein I can, and will do me the favour to call on me, I possess the decision, and will prove to you my readiness to assist you.

I am sir,

Your obedient servant.

MR. WILLIAM PANTON.

The second man of the town and Owlelo Mico visited me, the former with a request that I would permit Hardy Reed to reside and trade in their nation; that he had been to Colerain and obtained goods to the amount of 4 or 5 hundred dollars, part on credit from Mr. Price, that he had not obtained a licence.

I explained the law on this subject, and told them how Mr. Reed was to act. Mr. Reed attended and informed me that he had applied for a licence and could have given security, but he was refused by Maj. Freeman, he understood because he had not yet heard from the agent, or for some other cause unknown to him; that he applied to Mr. Price for goods, and was refused, but after some time, Mr. Price supplied him, some for cash and some on credit.

I directed Mr. Reed not to attempt to sell his goods in the town where he was as there were two traders long resident there, but to go to some place, where there was a vacancy, and there reside until he was informed where the agent of the War Department would reside and grant licence, and then to conform himself in future to the law.

I sat out this day on a visit to the village of the Tussekiah Mico, on the waters of Hatcheethlocco, the course E.; continue on

2 miles on flat land, thin, open, hilly, piney, the moist hollows covered with reeds; continue on 13 miles, very little alteration in the land, come to a creek runing to the right, and 5 miles farther arrive at the house of this Mico. He expected this visit, and the few men in the village were at his house and received me in a manner that did credit to the Mico and was highly pleasing to me.

Here I am he said, glad to see you, this is my wife and these are my children, they are glad to see you. These are some of the men in the village, there are 40 of them in all, they are glad to see you. You are now among those on whom you may rely. I have been 6 years at this place and there is not a man here or belonging to the village, who ever stole a horse or did any injury to a white man.

I suped on boiled eggs, pork, venison, potatoes and coffee. My horses were fed and carried to the canebrake by his sons. I lodged in the store house, comfortably, by myself, in some blankets, on a lodging prepared for me.

3rd of February.

This morning the Mico told me he was not well fixed to entertain me, but such as he had was mine. There were 5 settlements in view, and all surrounded with a worm fence. "These" says he, "are my relations, they and all of us will follow your advise. I am trading. I have paid off what I owe to Mr. Panton. I have goods on hand. I am indebted to Mr. Price; I shall have enough to pay him, and have 4 or 5 hundred skins to spare. I will continue my trade. I have given five mares to my boys; I have some pack-horses besides, they with my own exertions will do for me and my wife. The whole village have fenced their fields. The Dog Warrior first settled out here, this was our beloved bear ground, and reserved as such as long as it was of value for bear. I followed him, and we have made it a rule to admit no neighbours who will not make fences. We have most of us some cattle and hogs, and all of us hope to be able to get some. The creek which runs through my field is Ottasee Hatchee, and was formerly settled by the Ottasees; about 2 miles from this is the Uvachee Hatchee, the Dog Warrior has a field on the other side, in a large canebrake, and he lives on a high piney hill just beyond it."

I directed Mr. Barnard to accompany me to the houses in view. I had a friendly conversation with the women and returned.

I told the chief that I had determined to begin with him and his relations; he had been at New York, had seen much of the ways of the white people, and would understand the directions

I gave. He and his people must clean up their ground, and I would introduce the plough. He replied, "I will follow your directions, and will most willingly labour myself. We have had serious apprehensions for our safety, and been under the necessity to leave our homes and go into the town; you are now come; I rely entirely on the assurances given by you, that we may remain at home, and be under the protection of the United States."

This man, his wife and children all have the air and manners of well bred people, he saw to every thing himself, his wife cooked, the boys assisted in making fires and washing the cups, bringing water and taking care of my horses; they all, to the least came to me and took me by the hand and seemed much at their ease.

This man informed me that he'd always had an attachment to the white people; that this was left him as a legacy by his father, who, on his death had enjoined it on him to hold all white people by the hand, and to place entire confidence in the English, that he might put some little confidence in the French, but none in the Spaniards; at the same time he gave his pipe to Samuel Thomas, in the presence of his two sons, saying, my boys may make an ill use of the pipe, you are an old acquaintance and a white man, and I hope you will give them good advice. Thomas, he died afterwards and left his pipe to his half brother James Darouzeaux, and James sold this pipe at St. Augustine for two kegs of rum. From that day to this he had respected this solemn injunction of his father, and enjoined it on his children in like manner, to treat all white people well, and never to suffer one of them to be injured, if they could prevent it.

I am pleased to see that his boys bid fair to fulfill this injunction of their father, and that they are such worthy subjects, to have bestowed on them the benevolent care of the government.

The lands on the creek are rich, most of them a canebrake, the timber large poplar, white oak, beech, sycamore; on the hills pine. The situation fine for cattle and hogs.

4th of February.

I left this worthy family and sat out for Flint River, crossed the creek in the plantation, went through some level rich land, and over waving piney hills, passed a small plantation on the right and came to Usachee Hatchee, crossed the creek, went through a canebrake and a small field belonging to the Dog Warrior, crossed at the edge of the rising ground a small creek, ascended a steep hill and came to the habitation of this warrior and the Coosau Mico. They were both at home, received me and treated me with attention; they had ready for me some potatoes, hickory, milk, pumpkin and beans, with hickory nut oil, ground peas and chesnuts. The land on the side of the creek, where I first came to it is a bluff, 15 feet above the creek and very rich, a pleasant place for a farm. The lands on the other side are much lower, covered with tall cane, and a large growth of trees. I saw one sycamore 4 feet diameter. The N. W. front of the hill in ascending to the warrior's, is a mixture of oak and hickory, the tops of the hill a pine barron. There are 5 families settled on this hill, and they cultivate some things about their houses, but the product trifling. Their corn is made on the flat land, and the potatoes on the hillsides, where the soil is suited to them. I continue on half a mile cross another creek, here I parted with the Tussekiah Mico, the Coosau Mico accompanyed us two hundred yards farther, where I crosses another creek, and over all of them I had to swim my horses, and have the baggage carried on logs. The lands between these 2 creeks are low, not very rich; on the other side of this last creek for nearly one quarter of mile the whole mostly covered with water, the growth not large; come to the high grounds and continue on 4 miles over poor barron land and encamp on the side of a reedy branch, in all 7 miles.

5th of February.

Resumed my rout over poor pine barron, intermixed with small dwarf scrub oaks, 13 miles, the course E., come to the falling grounds of Okayhutkee; the lands are now some better, the bottoms oakey, the hills pine; in 9 miles cross a branch covered with reeds, come on the dividing ridge between the Creek and Opilthlucco, in 4 miles have on the left a view of some of the timber on Okayhutkee, covered with long moss; 4 miles farther cross Opilthlucco, 50 feet over, the swamp on the west side low, and covered with water; on the opposite side the lands rich and rise up to a high bluff, the top of the bluff less rich than the sides of the hills, and declines regularly and becomes a flat pine barron. In 2 miles cross a small creek runing to the left and in one mile, over flat piny pondy land, arrive at Mr. Barnard's, in all from camp 33 miles. 6½ miles from Tussekiah Mico's we crossed the path from Cusseta to the Buzzard Roost; 5 miles farther enter the white ground path and continue 200 yards, take the right, and in 7 miles cross the path from the Uchee village on Flint River to the main Uchee town, and 2½ miles cross the halfway ground path, from Flint River village, by a village on Opilthlucco to the Uchee town; 5 miles farther enter the path from the Uchee town which crosses the Flint 3 miles above Mr. Barnard's. Continue on and take the first, right.

Okauhutkee (okau, Choctaw for water) is entirely watered from springs, and from being clear and transparent is called hutkee or white; it enters Flint River about 3 miles above Mr. Barnard's. It is remarkable for being always full of water at all seasons, and for having great quantities of Rockfish at its mouth during the summer season; they are there to be seen in great numbers, being during the day, and it is conjectured they ascend the creek in the evening and return again to this place by the morning. The water being clear they are shy, and to take them with a hook, it is necessary to have a long line and fix it to float down the river, near them, in this way they are often taken.

The whole length of the creek is through a pine barron, with but a small exception of some oaky land, in small quantities. Above the entrance of this creek there is a large swamp on the river nearly 3 miles through, and it is itself 25 yards wide. Opilthlucco enters the river about 1¾ miles below, and is about 20 yards over. On this creek there is a good deal of oak land, very good, particularly at 18 miles up it, and just below the village. There is some cane on the swamp and reed in abundance on all the branches.

9th February, 1797.

Some Indians of the Cusseta returning from St. Mary's informed me that they had suffered much on the path with hunger, there being no game of any kind to be had, and provisions were scarce there. I told them they ought not to have gone without being previously asked; it was a place, where, as they knew, we could not make much provisions, and we only provided occasionally, as the necessities of those fixed there required; that in the spring, when the nation was invited, suitable provision was made to accommodate a great many, and then I was surprised to see but 4 or 5 hundred; and now when none were invited, and there were no provision made, I was surprised to hear when I was in the upper towns that a number who would not go when invited in the spring, had gone there at the time they ought to have been in the woods hunting. They replyed they blamed their own folly, only they heard some of their head men were going and they determined to follow in hopes of obtaining some presents. They said they had behaved well and had done no mischief going or returning. They called to see me, to talk with me, and as it was their duty, to inform me that some of those who were down did not conduct themselves as well as they ought to have done, that they had killed some beef, and that John Galphin had driven off 4 hogs and killed or otherwise made way with them as he returned; that two men,

Naubonelubby, of Coweta, and Stimmauketah, of Tallauhassee, asserting* having set out on their return, with some salt, complained that their horses were poor and would not carry them home; they left their camp declaring they would return and steal horses enough to bring them up, and they were to return by Kennard's.

I determined immediately to inform the chiefs of the two towns of what I had heard relative to these two fellows and wrote to them.

Mr. Barnard's on Flint, 9th February, 1797.

Benjamin Hawkins, principal agent for Indian affairs south of the Ohio, to Owlelo Mico, of Coweta, and the little Prince of Tallauhassee.

I have had some information relative to the conduct of two men of your towns which it is my duty to communicate to you. Naubonelubby Thlocco, of Coweta, and Stimmauketah, of Tallauhassee, who lately returning up from St. Mary's left their camp and went with a declared intention of stealing some horses from the white inhabitants, their neighbours, to bring their small packs to the nation. They are expected to return by Kennard's. I hope they have not been so wicked and foolish as to bring this disgrace on themselves; but if they should have succeeded, you will know what to do with them, and I must call on you both, and require of you to take the necessary measures as chiefs of the Creek land to punish these offenders, that we may prove to our white brethren that the promises of the Creeks may be relied on, and that we mean to put a stop to this accursed abominable practice.

With the sincerest wishes for the happiness of the Creeks, I am your friend.

With this letter I sent one to Mr. Carr, and one to Mr. Marshall, of Coweta, requesting Mr. Marshall and Mr. Darouzeaux to interpret my letter to the chiefs. I requested of Mr. Carr to inform his townsmen, that they had met their deserts, that as they would not go when invited and there was a plenty of good things for them, they deserved the disappointment they met with in going without an invitation, and at a season of the year when they ought to be in the woods.

---

* This word very uncertain in manuscript.

I am informed of a curious fact relative to this Naubonelubby Thlucco, he is a remarkable horse thief, and has been for many years in that practice. The chiefs of Coweta met to devise some measures for puting an end to this practice, and was agreed that they should all of them be answerable for the conduct of their young men, and that they should send for and talk with them; as this man was advanced in years, the leader was directed to go and give him a talk from the whole of them. He went and addressed the chief: "I am come from all the chiefs on a visit to you, we are determined to put a stop to this stealing from the white people, and all of us who have young men are to be answerable for them, but as you are yourself a man in years, and have no particular chief to answer for you, I am directed to talk to you, and to inform you, that if you cannot live without stealing, as you have been so long in the practice of it, you must steal from us, when you find that you must steal a horse or hog or cattle, come and steal from us, even if you want fowls, come and steal them from us and let the white people and their property alone." This address had for some time the desired affect, he almost quit his former ways, and began again to be in favour among his acquaintances.

I this day received a letter from Mr. Panton, at Pensacola, informing me that war was proclaimed there against Great Britain on the 22 January, and requesting me to give his messenger a passport through the Creeks, on his way to Savannah, with letters to his correspondent there, relative to the ensurance of his property. I gave Mr. Snell the following:

Mr. Snell having lawful business to transact in Savannah, within the State of Georgia, he is by these presents permitted to pass thro' the Creek land into that state; and I request the officer commanding at Fort James to facilitate his journey.

Given at Flint River, Lower Creeks, 9th of February, 1797.

Flint River, Lower Creeks, 9th February.

Sir:

The bearer of this, Mr. Snell, is on his way from Pensacola to Savannah on business of importance to a very respectable commercial gentleman there, Mr. Panton. At the request of that gentleman, I have given him a passport through the Creeks and directed him to your post, and I beg of you to facilitate his journey.

Mr. Panton writes me on the 24 ultimo that war against England was proclaimed there on the 22 of that month. You are, I suppose, informed of this before now, being so near our seaports.

I have heard that the post at Colerain has been pesstered with a troop of beggars from the Cusseta and Coweta towns. Some of them have returned and I have rebuked them for crowding down to our posts without an invitation, at the season when they should be hunting. It will require much firmness in the gentlemen commanding on the frontiers to resist their importunity. They have played the spoiled child so long with the British and others that many of them have ceased to do any thing useful for themselves. I shall be glad to hear from you from time to time, as opportunities occur to the nation.

ENSIGN THOMPSON,
Commanding at Fort James.

I wrote to Mr. Habershâm.

Sir:

I have just received a letter from Mr. William Panton at Pensacola, of the 24 ultimo, informing me that war against England was proclaimed there on the 22nd. The war, I suppose you have heard of before this, and I imagine it will materially affect the gentlemen concerned in commerce within my agency. I have visited most of the upper towns and some on the Chatto Hochee, and find the nation better disposed towards their neighbours and more inclined to peace than they have ever been known to be. There are some disorderly young men, that cannot well be restrained, yet I am not without hopes of curbing them; as the chiefs have assured me they will exert themselves in aid of my wishes on this head.

I have been particular in my endeavors to find whether these people have ever given satisfaction for murder committed by them, and I have received satisfactory proof that they have in five instances.

I shall be glad to hear from you by the return of Mr. Snell; he goes to your city on business for Mr. Panton, and will return through the Creeks.

I am with sincere regard and esteem Sir,
Your obedient servant,

MAJ. JOHN HABERSHAM.

Flint River, 10 February, 1797.

I received your favour of the 14 ultimo, by Mr. Walton, and it gave me sincere joy, for I had been under apprehension for your safety, as you were so much longer on your voiage than I expected you would be when I left you, and I had heard of the bad weather on the coast.

It is unfortunate that the goods have been damaged, but I hope you had them inspected and the damage ascertained, as I imagine they were ensured.

I heard while I was in the upper towns that a number of beggars had sat out from Cusseta and Coweta, to Colerain, and that others were going; the latter I stoped. I am glad you prevented their receiving any presents; had I been on the spot I should not have given them any thing. I saw some of them on their way home, and I rebuked them for crowding down to our posts without any business, and without an invitation, at the season when they should be hunting.

It will require much firmness in you and the gentlemen commanding the frontiers to resist their importunity; they have played the spoiled child so long with the British and others, that many of them are under no control, and have ceased to do any thing useful for themselves. I inquired of many of them why they did not go down in the spring when they were invited, and told that provision was made for them; they answered they did not want any thing.

I have been informed that they did not behave well on the return, and that they stole hogs, beef and horses. If the latter is true, I have taken measures already to detect them, as well as to know whence this visiting originated.

I have just received a letter from Mr. Panton, who informs me war was proclaimed against England in Pensacola, the 22 January, and that for the present it prevented any direct communication between him and his friends in England.

I have visited most of the towns of the upper Creeks and I find them more disposed for peace and more friendly to the whites than they were ever known to be.

I saw one man, Hardy Reed, of Coweta, who you had audited for goods without his having a licence. As soon as I leave where Maj. Freeman resides I shall take in concert measures to enable the traders to obtain them, and you will do well to be careful to know that all who apply are licenced, as otherwise they forfeit their goods, and it is my duty to see that the law is enforced.

I am with sincere regard Sir,

Your obedient servant.

MR. EDWARD PRICE.

Flint River, 10 February, 1797.

Alexander Cornell:

Measures calculated to ensure a continuance of the friendship of the Indians, and to preserve peace along the interior frontier of the United States, have been adjusted and adopted by the President. The plan in a considerable degree depends for its execution on my agency south of the Ohio, and throughout the whole a rigid economy in the public expenditure is deemed indispensable.

In arranging the necessary assistants for the Creek department, I shall give a preference to those in service, and retain as many of them as may be necessary. I have appointed you to be one of the assistants. Your allowance will be 400 dollars per annum, paid quarterly. Remember me to Mrs. Cornell and your children and accept of my sincere wishes for the prosperity of your nation.

Flint, the 10 February, 1797.

Mucclassee Hoopoi:

When I went down the Tallapoosa I expected the pleasure of seeing you, but I heard you had gone to amuse yourself in the woods. I hope successfully so. I have directed Mr. Walton to carry and present to you a token of my personal regard for you; accept it and be assured that I have a sincere regard for the Creeks and will contribute my mite to make them a happy people.

I addressed a similar letter to Efau Haujo, mad dog of Tuckabatchee, and Hopoithle Mico, Tallassee king of the halfway house, and sent to each of them a package of vermilion.

Flint River, 10th February, 1797.

Sir:

I have heard since my being here that your sons were well and placed in some Quaker families, who have taken them, and promised to treat them as their own family. You know the character of these people. Whether they are with them or remain yet with Major Hagg, they will be equally under the protection of the Secretary of War, and of course want for nothing. I have heard of the arrival of the garden seeds in the care of Mr. Price; the peas were damaged. As soon as I have it in my power, I shall send you some of each sort.

You are informed before this I imagine, that war has been proclaimed at Pensacola against England. A messenger from Mr. Panton, on his way to Savannah, called on me yesterday for the necessary passport. This, I am apprehensive, will be productive of some temporary inconvenience to him in his commercial pursuits, & I hope and wish they may me temporary only.

Recommend to your neighbours to make fences, attend to their cattle and hogs, and prepare in time to make a plenty of corn, and all will go well notwithstanding this rage for war among the white people. Let them fight if they chuse it, and my red brethren remain and enjoy peace at home.

Tell your wife I have often thought of her industry, cleanliness and good housewifery, and that I shall take care to let the people know where her sons are—what a worthy woman she is. Give my best wishes to her for her happiness and believe me, with due regard,

Your obedient servant,

RICHARD BAILEY, OHassee.

Having had some information of the execution of a white man by order of General McGillivray, for the murder of some white people who were trading through the Creeks, I applied to Mr. Walton for information and he gave me this narrative: On or about the year 1789, Col. Kirkland, his son, and another white man, with one John Linder and a black boy, were going through the Creeks to Tonsau. They were met at the Little Suppulgaws by John Catt, of Holston, a negro, Bobb, belonging to Stephen Sullivan, Catt's wife, an Indian woman of the fish ponds, and an Indian man called the murderer (this name he had for killing Mr. Scott's hireling). The travellers went about 10 miles to Murder Creek (Lucho Hatchee), and there encamped. The others continued on 2 miles to the Big Suppulgaws. After supper the murderers took their horses, and went in pursuit of the travellers. Col. Kirkland had drank freely and gone to sleep, the murderers had given him some to drink when they met him and a bottle to take with him. Sullivan's negro crept up to a tree, took the gun and put it to the head of the old man, and blowed his brains out. Catt and the Indian rushed in, the latter with his hatchet and the former with his club and knife. The son jumped up therefore on his hands and knees and said, I will tell you all about it, spare my life. Catt replyed we did not come to hear talks, and he was knocked down with the hatchet; Catt cut his throat with a knife; Linder had a tommahawk stuck in his head; he after set on his hams, and throwing his head back, Catt stuck him in the throat. The murderer killed the other one; he had the hatchet stuck in his head, and traveled in the knight about 50 yards and died with his head in a branch. They had a good many papers and letters; these were burnt. They then took every thing except the clothes on the ded bodies. The negro boy they took prisoner, and they slept there all knight and returned.

Flint River, 11th February, 1797.

Robt. Walton:

I have been arranging the necessary assistants on the plan dijested and adopted for the future conducting of Indian affairs south of Ohio. I have not judged it advisable to retain any of the express riders, as I shall reside for some time myself among the Indians. You have behaved well, and on any suitable occasion you may expect to be prefered.

You will take the letters intrusted to your care and deliver them to the persons to whom they are addressed, and your time of service is to expire on your arrival at your own house, and you may send the estimate up to that time and I will give a draft on the proper department for payment.

I have heard that there is a halfbreed in the savannas, Leonard Megee, who is òf an excellent character, speaks English well. He was at Colerain at the Treaty; I want a man of his character. If Mr. Walton should see him, or can contrive a message to him, I shall be glad to employ him.

Mr. Walton will write to me on all occasions, when an opportunity offers; I shall furnish him with some tools of husbandry, and rely on his following the directions I give him, to use them for himself, and to teach the use of them to his neighbours. I shall send him some garden seeds as soon as my pack arrives, and give directions how they are to be managed.

The murderer of Col. Kirkland came up to the nation. Sullivan's negro called at Mr. Weatherford's and told what had been done. Jourdan Morgan and John Brown went immediately and talked to Catt; he acknowledged he had done it. They then went over to Mr. McGillivray's and informed Robert Walton of it, and they all pursued fifteen miles, but did not come up with them; they returned and Walton sat out again with Bill Tally and a negro and pursued, and overtook them at Sullivan's. Mr. Walton entered the house and seised Catt, and took him down to the Hickory Ground in company with Mr. Grierson; there he got Red Shoes and another Indian to go with him, and he carried him within 15 miles of Pensacola, left him there and went into Mr. McGillivray's, who sent for Governor White. The governor told McGillivray as it was not done in the Spanish dominions he could not do any thing in it.

After one knight's reflection McGillivray said the man must die, and directed John Forbes and Lewis Melford to go out with Walton and hear the prisoner make his defences, and if he was guilty to execute him. Mr. Panton was desirous of a regular trial, and that the prisoner should have some time to repent. McGillivray said no, these evidences of his guilt was sufficient and they should hang him; when these men examined him, he acknowledged the whole, and they took him 10 miles back over the old English line, and hung him on the first convenient limb over the path. After he was sensible of his approaching end, he beged to be pardoned; said he was young and he would never do so again; if he must die he beged to be shot. When he came to the place where he was to be hung, he beged them to take his cloathes off, they were a suit taken from one of the murdered men. The answer to this request was, you die for the act by which you acquired them, and you have the least right to them. He asked if they intended to hang him; they said yes, by a rope in the air; he was silent and executed. His body remained 3 or 4 months without being touched by any thing; it hung by the rope for 6 or 8 days; was afterwards cut down & striped and so remained. The other bodies were soon devoured by the wolves and buzzards.

When Mr. Walton took him down to Pensacola, he carried him to the camp where the murdered bodies lay; the buzzards had picked out the eyes and eaten some of their breasts. Catt pointed out the two that he killed; he upon seeing of them could scarcely speak, his appearance was wretched, his countenance changed, and appeared black.

The negro still lives, and in possession of Mr. Sullivan. The Indian is also alive. When Walton entered the house and took Catt, the Indian was desirous of defending him, and would have killed Tally had not Sullivan prevented it. Sullivan's negro said that after the travellers passed them the Indian proposed to him to pursue and murder them, and he refused that. When they came to the camp he mentioned what had passed between him and the Indian, and that Catt instantly said, if the Indian had made the proposition to him, that he would have gone; to this the woman said, it is not yet too late, they have not gone far, and they agreed and sat out.

The negro boy is in possession of Robert Grierson.

Translation into Creek of the note sent on the 10th to Mucclassee Hoopoi.

Clonotiscau, otullahahsee auligot auttege nitta ispaule. Tallapoosahatchee aufopejit autliafoh hejoatlist checomiete. Ummomecunxcha. Ittoopoh auit faucun autleist mauhogun poiunx cha. Nauk comat attecot inhitchkin aufotchkit autlatist checomat chomuckelijiunxcha.

  Mr. Walton imbonoiet nauk chekiltlijiatte auemiete auchemofoh aunhisse ummiltlunx comitscatlits cha. Auchemofon essitscatlits cha, esitscofoh muscogetoitscat cheenhissee toiat chemaupoiejie emongin chahajits catlist cha.

BENJAMIN HAWKINS.

  Chinhissee toiat chemistechauco hawkiteistechate toitskee chimponuccuh amauthlocco osotat chimponauikine aupohijatitx cha.

Mr. Barnard's, Flint, 15 February, 1797.

Col. Gaither:

  Your favour of the 13th January, was delivered me by Mr. Barnard on the last of that month. I had addressed two letters to you, one on the 1st of January, the other of the 7, in the care of Mr. Thomas. I have expected his return daily for three weeks, and am apprehensive that some mishap has befel him, unless he should have gone to Colerain, and in that case probably he may arrive in the course of a few days. I have found it necessary to send the bearer to you, as I have not received any letters from the Secretary of War since I left him, or from any other person in that quarter, or from Georgia relative to the state of the frontiers.

  I have received a letter from Mr. Panton informing me that war was proclaimed at Pensacola against Great Britain on the 22 January. My red brethren have expected it for some time, and have already began to calculate how they can turn it to account. I have recommended to them to make fences, mind their cattle and hogs, and prepare in time to make a plenty of corn; to pay no regard to the war among the white people, let them fight if they choose it and we will mind our farming and hunting and enjoy peace and plenty at home.

  I am under the necessity for reasons not necessary to detail, to postpone the runing of the line between the State of Georgia and the Creeks, to some future day, tho' not distant. The Indians do not like to go and see it done unless I can give assurances that there will be a guard of regular troops, or be personally answerable for their safety. I did expect you would have had orders on this head er'e this, and informed me of them, but it is likely that a crowd of business on the War Department during a session of Congress may have retarded the order.

I have a smith who wants some iron; if you can lend me 50 lbs. from your stock, without injury to the public supply, and replace it from that which I have in care of Mr. Price, belonging to the Indian department, you will enable me to further the objects I have in view in this quarter. I am also in want of some nails and Mr. Barnard informs me there are 20 or 30 lbs. belonging to the Indian department in the care of John Whitney; I request you to direct him to send them to me.

I have not as yet any vacancy in my department that would suit a gentleman such as you describe Mr. Warfield to be. Whenever there is one, I shall with pleasure make him an offer. He is the first who has been recommended to me.

16 February.

The mother of Mrs. Barnard called at my lodgings and requested I would accept of her daughter, a young widow, during my residence here, or as much longer as I thought proper, recommending her for her cleanliness and attention to white people, and for being the mother of three beautiful children, and that she could speak Creek and Uchee.

This woman and most of these Creek women, being in the habit of assuming and exercising absolute rule, such as it was, over their children, and not attending to the advice of their white husbands, and taking part with them when they found it necessary to oppose any unjust pretentions of their families, I determined to address a note to the old woman, and to read it to her and daughter, in the Creek tongue. I wrote to her this note:

You have offered me your daughter. I take it kind of you. Your daughter looks well, is of a good family, and has some fine children, which I shant be pleased with. The ways of the white people differ much from those of the red people. We make companions of our women, the Indians make slaves of theirs. The white men govern their families and provide cloathing and food for them; the red men take little care of theirs, and the mothers have the sole direction of the children.

You know I am the principal agent of the four nations. I do not yet know whether I shall take one of my red women for a bedfellow or not, but if I do, if it is for a single night, and she has a child, I shall expect it will be mine, that I may cloathe it and bring it up as I please. If I take a woman who has sons or daughters, I shall look upon them as my own children. The wife must consent that I shall cloathe them, feed them and bring them up as I please, and no one of her family shall oppose my doing so. The red women should always be proud of their white husbands, should always take part with them and obey them, should make the children obey them, and they will be obedient to their parents, and make a happy family. The woman I take must beside all this be kind, cleanly and good natured, and at all times pleasing and agreeable when in company with me or with those who visit at my house. She must promise me this; her mother must promise it to me, and all her family.

The Translation.

Chechuseowoh aumitskeomen poast cha momitscotte chaufotchcosistcha. Chechuseowoh hejat chaufignoose omen hejuscha. Ehotulgee isteitthlaugee ome ummomus cha. Aupoattaucooche ilthlaugeeomen oppenhejiaut chaufotchcosistcha.

Istehutkee toie ummauhaugau etutscha. Istechate toitchkee chemauhaugau etutscha. Inhutkee toie hooktogee ihellijiet fullijiitchcha. Istechatee toitchkee sullufcoejatscuns cha. Inhutkee toie hooktogee umfullot ihethlijat fulllijeitch cha, opoetaugee umfullot imponoiat opothlingau immauhauiot nauk yeouchatle attecot inhopoiitchcha. Istechatee toitchkee opoautaucooche nauk immauhauetuhseco fullijatixtcha. Itchkulgee tulkosist aufaustunscha.

Chinkilcosistcha istechate toitchkee chincaugetah osetat chemistechago thlocco hawkite whoethline chauhejatixtcha. Kattoe unkillkecostcha istechate hooktogee opiatilaunihauks umfutchchecostcha. Mami aunomatlist nihle humgocist umwockesausot inqoupah hopoewoh inhitchcot aumitscomaulauniitchcha. Inqoupah atchejite naukeetice emauhauite chaufecomat aufustautlistcha. Hooktee opoat taugee imoje epauictomice chappoochetaugee mohhee omejito utchejite opothlingau immauhauatlischa. Itchkee umuccahsumatlistcha atchejite humbijite opothlingau omoihoeautlistcha. Ehotulgee atteut mohomauts chuckiochecostcha. Istechate hooktogee toitchkee istehutkee chiwoh haugitskeattocot equccohsaumosit fullacontomon noinatchkistcha. Nauk immomat attecot emaupoiejit chimponocaunomatlist immuccoh qummauheintling autligimtscha. Chechuseataugee mattaupomen immouhauitc ilcalgee imponoiet attecot ummuccohsummau heintling fullijicuntscha, humenomau immauhauitscaunomatlist. Ehotulgee attecot aufautchketuh heintling aupoho catlistcha. Hooktee opoinomatlist ephegeheintling aumatatlischa nauk atchau attecot ausutkeeheintling hauetlatischa. Isteunehucco pilthlijiaut attecot qumnau fotchkeit inqeamausit unligaultischa. Tepauget caugice aufotchkecheintling emligaullistcha. Hookee apoiaut ummomen ummuccah saumitlist. Itchcalgee haugco chotulgee attegin ummuccau saumatlistcha.

When I read this note, the old woman was much pleased with the first part of it, assented to it and acquiesced, but when I read the latter part, she remained silent, and could not be prevailed on to acquiesce in the conditions proposed. She would not consent that the women and children should be under the direction of the father, and the negotiation ended there.

18th.

Tustunnagau Haujo, of Chehaw, called to see me, and had much conversation on the affairs of his nation; he expressed much pleasure at our commercial establishment, had visited it, and traded, and met such treatment as would induce him to go there for all that he should want. I told him that Mr. Price would make no difference in the price with the Indians or traders, that they would all fare alike; he replyed he had experienced it, as he mentioned many inconveniencies attending the intercourse with the present establishment. I requested him to be particular and enumerate such as occured. He immediately gave the following narrative: I am as you see, a man in years; I have been a hunter and I know the situation of the ground from where I live to Clotthlo Coofcau (St. Mary's). I have hunted many years about Okefinacau (quivering water) or Akinfinocau (quivering earth), the first a Choctaw word Okewah. The wet season commences with the winter and then the whole country was covered with water, in many places 2 and 3 feet deep, particular in the ponds, which spread over most of the country; at this season it is difficult to find a dry place to encamp on, and where there were some risings, they bore but a small proportion to the ponds, through which a person going from his town must pass, and to this the whole country was a pine barron, with wiregrass and saw palmetto, without reed or cane for horses; and in the dry season, always in autum, the ponds dried up, and it was then difficult to find water anywhere; that he had often been under the necessity of hunting for aligator holes to get some, and been oblidged to put his moccasin on a stick and put it far under their caves to get it, and then it was muddy and very filthy; that in such a situation he had frequently lost his horses for the want of water; that he had several times seen aligators dead in their holes for want of water. I asked how had it happened that he who knew the country should be put to these inconveniences; he answered that he used to go towards St. Augustine and sometimes on St. Illas for his summer hunt, and it usually happened when he was returning from them. He continued: This part of the country is sometimes so infested with musquetoes as to destroy horses, by runing and heating of them, when water is not to be had for them, but by geting it out of aligator holes for them. He had seen most of the border of the Okefinacau, and once attempted with some young lads to pursue a bear he had wounded; they went in several hours, and were compelled to return. The whole earth trembled under them, and at several places, where the surface was pressed with the foot, the water would spout out. One of his lads sunk in so deep that he called for help, and they took him out. There are some large cypress, but the growth mostly dwarf. Some of the Tallassee people had been in much farther than he had; they saw some ponds, many aligators, turtles and snakes, particularly a small snake with a button at the end of the tail like the rattlesnake; they saw considerable number of them, and some times 20 or 30 in one view, coiled up on the small grassy nobs; two of these people were killed with the bites of them. He knew of one man who attempted a settlement near this swamp, but he gave it up because the tygers killed his hogs, cattle and sometimes horses.

21st February.

I sat out this day for Fort Fidins, Mr. Barnard and his son, Homanhidge, accompanyed me; we X the river at Mr. Barnard's and take up it N. Go one mile X a small reedy creek, here on the north side Mr. Barnard has begun to establish a dairy, the situation is fine for it, the ground high, an excellent spring surrounded with evergreens; and here two of Mr. Barnard's sons, Falope and Yuccohpee, have begun an establishment for themselves. They were here with their father's negros, at work clearing a field, and preparing logs of pine for their houses. The land good for corn, to the river swamp, and that and the swamp of the small creek good for rice. There is a margin on this river of oak, pine and hard shelled hickory, adjoining the swamp, and then back of this pine barron, the good land but a small strip. Continue on ¾ of a mile, come to a plantation of Mr. Barnard's; here some fine peach trees, the lands pretty good on the creek; here lives Tenpoeje, another son and his Cusseta wife, they were both of them clearing land with a small black boy. He has just finished a dweling house, mostly the labour of his own hands. We gave him some garden seeds and I promised to assist him with tools. X a creek at the plantation 30 feet over, and continue on over some land pretty good for corn, the timber a mixture, oak, pine and some hard shelled hickory, here and there some long moss. Most of the oakes, the scrub, very crooked, with many limbs and all of them with a green broad leaved fern moss. In 8 miles $\times$ a branch runing to the right; this is a branch of the creek I crossed at Tunpanejies, and the path has been on the ridge which divides its waters from the hollows making into the river. This is a small branch, but covered with reeds. Continue on 2 miles and there are 2 very steep heads of bottoms close to the left, and from the first is distant view of the lands on the other side of the river; here I saw an Indian encampment. One woman at the camp, without any other food than hickory nuts. There were several others but all of them out gathering these nuts; and I am informed they frequently take to the woods at this season, when there is a great hickory masst, and fatten on them and the cold potatoe uccollewauhohah. I saw under all the oakes great quantities of acorns. Continue on 2 miles farther and come to some reed patches, continue over the flat and cross a small creek runing to the left, abounding with reed, and rise up a steep hill, and have a very extensive view of a bed of reeds to the left, nearly ¾ of a mile through; continue on this ridge and soon arrive at Ecimna Chate (red hills); from these there is an extensive view S. W., and the bed of reeds continuing in that direction to the river, and appear surrounded with hills covered with pine, amidst them is distinctly marked the margin $\times$ the river, forming a vain wandering through the piney view, of growth usual on the swamp lands. 2 miles farther, passing over waving pine barron, come to the side of a large bed of reeds on the left, as extensive as those before described; continue on near a mile and $\times$ a small branch making into the bed, and this well stored with reeds. Continue on 4 miles farther and encamp on a small reedy creek runing to the left.

I saw this day the yellow jasmine, the plumb, may cherry, strawberry and sassafras in bloom. I have not any where seen less sign of game, although we have guns and dogs, we have not been able to get any thing. The ridge on this side the creek extends to the river and there forms a bluff 80 feet high, at the lower part of which, near low water mark, is a bed of oyster shells.

22.

We sat out this morning early and continue our course, one mile, leave the path which go's to the Uche village, and go through the woods, one mile and enter the Uchee path, continue on, take a small path to the left to facilitate the crossing of the beaver dam, the direct path being the nearest, but the passage of the creek nearly impracticable when the season is wet. In 5 miles $\times$ the beaver dam, and in 5 miles enter the old horse path, our course now E. N. E.; continue on 5 miles and $\times$ a small branch, here we breakfast. The first 2 miles pine barron, the trees large, the path in sight of the reedy bottoms which make into the river. The remainder of the way through broken pine barron, in several places the trees dwarf pine and black jack. Resume our journey, in 2½ miles X a small creek stored with reed; in 1 & ½ farther X a small branch, and in one mile X Itchocunnah (deer trap), 40 feet over, runing to the right; the whole of these 5 miles through a pine forest. This creek has its name from being covered with moss on its rocky bed, and the deer resorting to it, where they are killed by the hunters. Continue on one mile, X a small creek runing to the right, the hillsides steep, the growth poplar, oak, hickory and dogwood, the creek stored with reed; one mile farther another small branch of the like discription, and in 2 miles, X Horse Rosemerry, a small creek runing to the right; this is so named by the packhorsemen from the quantity of the rosemerry which grows near its borders. Continue on 2 miles farther over flat piney sloshy land, passing some fine reedy glades to the right, arrive at Tobosaufkee, 60 feet over, runing to the right. There is a little creek within a few yards of Tobosaufkee, the land is broken and stoney, and there are on the left of the path, and within view of the creek, some large rocks; X the creek, left the path and went up it 200 yards and encamped near a small branch, the north side of which was well stored with winter cane; still higher up, ¼ mile, is a small creek stored with small cane, the lands broken & gravelly, but rich, the growth a mixture of oak, pine and small hickory. At this camp the Indians have left a very convenient camp standing; it had been used during the winter's hunt; on a small beech at the mouth of the branch are marked the initials of my name and the date.

23.

Sat out early this morning, E. for one mile, X a small creek stored with reed, the lands broken and piney, continue N. E. on over lands of a similar quality, one mile, X two little small runs, and 2 miles farther, X Rockey Creek, the hillsides steep and stoney, or gravelly, a mixture of oak and pine, the creek 20 feet wide. Continue on over an open waving pine forest 2½ miles to the path which crosses the Ocmulgee ford; the path here intersects with the direct path to the Uchee village that crosses Tobosaufkee one mile below the junction with Stoney Creek. Continue on 1½ miles to the Ocmulgee, the lands poor and piney the whole way till we enter the flats on the river, which are pretty good, the timber small within half a mile, the old fields included; here I saw one mound about 60 feet at the base, 6 feet high, and one lower. The fields extend down the river for a mile; I rode through them.

I saw in two places the hills where corn had been planted, the whole grown up with old field pine, some of them a foot and an half diameter, thinly scattered; I saw some red haws and large patches of small winter cane (cohaumothluaku); I breakfasted in these fields on the river bank, and then × the river below the mouth of Oakchuncoolgau, a large creek which empties itself into the river on the E. side. Our canoe was a very bad one, scarcely fit to carry over two persons, made out of a decayed red oak, 10 feet long, and lanched with the bark on; this I find is prefered by the Indians, as being easily concealed; when they have passed over the river they take it to a convenient place, turn it over, and tie it; it then has the appearance of an old log. The land where I landed is a high bluff seldom if ever overflowed. We traveled 2 miles on this flat land N., sometimes within sight of the creek, the soil pretty good, tho' in some places sloshy, and the whole way covered with small winter cane about 4 feet high. Continue 1 mile over open poor land to the path, and took it N. E. Continue 4 miles over a high pine forrest, very open and hilly, saw on the left a vane of reeds and on the right a steep hollow with some reeds; pass in half a mile some rocks to the left, and in half a mile farther × Boxing Hill Branch, well stored with cane; there is on the S. W. side a high hill, here formerly the traders used to camp, and their packhorsemen frequently got drunk, and amused themselves with boxing. Continue on × a small branch and in 2 miles × Longslash, and encamp in the fork on a high nole. This slash looks beautiful covered with reed to a considerable extent.

24.

Sat out over hilly mixed piny and oak land, one mile × a reedy branch, one mile farther × a branch, 1½ another, wide and well stored with reed; half a mile × two small branches, ½ a mile × one, ½ mile × one, the lands about it oakey. 3½ × Commissioner's Creek, 40 feet over, the flat lands rich, but subject to be overflowed; the whole scope of this 8½ miles pine land, except on some of the branches. There is a beautiful bed of reeds on the right as I approached Commissioner's Creek. One mile × a branch, ½ mile × another, 1½ × Holly Run, 1¾ a reedy branch to the left, 1 mile a branch to the left, 1¾ branch to the right, half a mile a branch to the right, half a mile a branch to the right; continue on then 2 miles and leave the path through the woods 5 miles, ×ing a branch runing to the left, and then Camp Creek, and arrive at the encampment on the river.

28th February.

William Williams, of Handcock County, in the State of Georgia, exhibited to me a claim for a horse supposed to be stolen by the Creeks on the 8th of September; the claim properly attested. He gave me also the claim of Byron Marsh for a horse taken on the 8 September and supposed by the Creeks.

Fort Fidins, 28 February, 1797.

Sir:

I arrived here on the 25 of this month from the Creeks, after having been for three months among their upper and lower towns; and I am happy in being able to assure you that the nation are inclined to peace and more friendly to the white people than they have ever been known to be. They are taking measures to prevent predatory parties from plundering and killing their neighbours. They have promised me that if any of their hunters should steal any horses, on its being known they will cause them to be restored without delay. They have sent me two which were recently taken from Little River, and informed me of two others which will be sent here in 8 or 10 days.

I have the honor to be, Sir,

Your obedient servant,

His Excellency,
The Governor of Georgia.

Memorandom of Indian Justice.

Cary, three miles from Ogeechee old town, was murdered by a Choctaw Indian. Mr. Galphin sent a talk to the heads of the town on the subject, requesting satisfaction; Mr. Barnard carried the demand. The heads of the town ordered the murderer to be put to death, and they appointed two men, and ordered them to execute him in the ball ground; they did so, in the presence of 2 or 3 white men.

3 were killed and the Coweta leader outlawed, for killing Grant, a Scotchman, and Weatherford in Savannah.

Fort Fidins, 1st of March, 1797.

Received from the Department of Indian Affairs, under the direction of Benjamin Hawkins, one mare and 3 year old horse, returned by the Cusseta Indians. They were taken from the neighbourhood of Little River. My name is Joseph Wheat, I live on Oconee at the mouth of Little River, on Island Creek, and I have had these horses returned without any expence.

His

JOSEPH X WHEAT

Mark

HENRY GAITHER.

Fort Fidins, March 4th, 1797.

Received from the Department of Indian Affairs, under the direction of Benjamin Hawkins, one brown mare, 3 year old, one black mare 6 year old, and one 2 year old filley; they were taken from the Islands. My name is Isaac Hanby; I live on the Oconee, near the Islands, and I have had these horses returned without any expence.

His

ISAAC X HANBY,

Mark

RICHARD THOMAS.

Fort Fidins, 1st March, 1797.

My letter, No. 2, of 6 of January, I sent to this post to be forwarded to you by Col. Gaither. I remained among the Indian towns and villages till the 20 of February, and set out and arrived here on the 25 of that month. Here I received your letter of the 22 of October, accompanyed with some from the Society of Quakers, and yesterday I received your dispatches of the 2nd of February; they were sent to the commanding officer here by express from Louisville. I received a letter from Mr. Price since his arrival; the goods he informs me are much damaged, the stationary from report unfit for use. I hope he has had the damage asscertained and reported to you. I shall not give drafts for the Creek annuity until I have a meeting of the chiefs, and consult them upon the division. The other things I shall order up for the objects contemplated in my mission as soon as I can obtain packhorses, and the path is passable. There has been a vile attempt to prevail on the Indians to thwart the measures of the government, but they, more wise than the author of it, have refused their co-operation; I expect you will have received some information from the agent of the War Department on this subject; what I enclose authorises the assertion I have made.

I have persevered in endeavours to be useful, I have addressed myself freely to all classes within my agency that I could visit, and the result is favourable. I have received assurances from the Lower Creeks that they are desirous of peace, and that they will take measures in concert with me to carry the views of the government into effect. The chiefs told me that probably some of their young men might bring in horses from the settlements when they return from their winter hunt, but that I might rely on their efforts to restore them immediately. The promptness with which they have fulfilled this assurance do's them much credit; they have sent me six horses and I have restored five of them to their owners free of expence, which has given entire satisfaction.

The Indians on their part complain of the inexecution of the promises made to them, and charge their neighbours with tresspassing on their rights, driving their hogs, horses and cattle to range on their lands, going about in hunting parties, making pens for their cattle and hogs, and salt troughs for their stock, surveying their lands and cultivating some of them; that this is a source of vexation to the whole nation and keeps their young men unruly.

They have given unsatisfactory proof of their having executed five Indians and one white man for the murder of white people; this gives a hope that the right of revenge may be transfered from private hands to a public jurisdiction. I applied very gravely the other day to some influential chiefs to inform me who governed in their land, they or their boys, that I might know where to address myself for a violation of a Treaty. They replied, we understand you, you must help us, we mean well, but our people have been sadly corrupted in their intercourse with the whites.

I have judged proper to postpone the runing of the Creek line till we run the Cherokee line, that presses and this does not; intrusions there are most likely to be apprehended, and to such an extent as to give much embarrassment to the government. I shall execute this trust strictly in conformity with the wishes of the government, and I hope I shall be able to remove in concert with my colleagues any difficulty that may occur with the Indians. I have for another reason judged proper to postpone the Creek line. The people who have stock cannot support them, if they are compelled to drive them back, before there is grass in the woods, and this indulgence can be given them, without offence, until the line is closed. It will be a measure too, so conciliatory in its operation as that which it produces the good we aim at, takes off the odium which would attach itself to a rigid execution of our trust. The resident traders in the Creek country are most of them without a licence, their trade has hitherto been carried on by Mr. Panton at Pensacola. Some of them claim the right to trade without a licence, and urge that they are British subjects; I do not admit their claims. I have directed them to conform to our regulations, and they should not prejudice their claim thereby. It will require that you should make some additional regulations on this head, either to send me an authority to licence the resident traders, or to some person to whom they can apply in the absence of the agent for the War Department. The citizens who live in the Natches district pass through the Creeks to their state; several of them have called on me on their way, and have obtained, when they were suitable characters, passes to this post.

The report of a war between Spain and England has been circulated through the Creeks for some time before I heard of its being proclaimed, and some mischief makers have reported that Col. Brown (the last British Agent) was soon to arrive from Providence to call on the Indians to take part with them. I have explained to the Indians that we were bound by treaty to protect their rights, and to prevent their doing any injury to Spain; that they must be at peace and let the Europeans fight their own battles.

I shall send a young messenger with the necessary orders to the Cherokees, and information to General Pickins and I shall follow him on the 10th.

I have the honor to be with great respect, Sir,

Your obedient servant.

THE SECRETARY OF WAR.

Fort Fidins, 7th March, 1797.

Sir:

The President, with the advice and consent of the Senate, has appointed Benjamin Hawkins, Andrew Pickins and James Winchester, Commissioners to ascertain and mark the boundary lines, agreeably to treaties between the Indian nations and the United States, and we are directed to apply to you to furnish us with an escort of dragoons. I shall set out from this on the 10th towards the frontiers and request you to furnish an escort of one

Serjeant, one Corporal and 12 dragoons, 1 horseman's tent with a fly, 3 common tents, 3 packhorses, 2 fasceme hatchets and the necessary camp kettles. The horses must be all shod, and the Serjeant must be directed to receipt for these articles, and be held accountable under the directions of the Commissioners.

I believe I shall take the escort over the Ocunna Mountain, to Tellico Blockhouse; I give this information for your direction or advice as to the furnishing them with forage and provisions.

With great regard, I am Sir,

Your obedient servant,

HENRY GAITHER,
Lieut. Col. Commandant.

———

Fort Fidins, 7th March, 1797.

Dear General:

I arrived here on the 25 ultimo, and on the last of that month received dispatches from the war office of 2nd, informing me that you are appointed with James Winchester, Commissioners to ascertain and mark the boundary lines agreeably to treaties between the Indian nations and the United States.

As no time should be lost in establishing the Cherokee line, as every day adds to the number of intruders upon their land; I have for that and other reasons which I shall detail to you when I meet you, determined to postpone the intention we expressed of runing the Creek boundary in this month. I have sent Richard Williams to inform you that I shall set out for Tellico Blockhouse on the 10th of this month, and intend, if you approve of it, to go over the Ocunna Mountain, through the Cherokees, as being the nearest rout. I have applied and obtained an escort of dragoons, and I shall bring one horseman, but for our use; I shall call on you.

The enclosed letters I must request you to forward to Mr. Dinsmoor by care of the Cherokees in your neighbourhood, and to have one of the most intelligent of them in readiness to accompany us. I shall address a letter to the Governor of this State, to inform him of our giving the preference mentioned.

Scale the letters when you have red them.

With sincere regard, I am, dear General,

Your obedient servant,

ANDREW PICKINS.

Sir:

Fort Fidins on the Oconee, 7th March, 1797.

The Commissioners appointed to ascertain and mark the boundary lines agreeably to treaties between the Indian nations and the United States, will meet at Tellico Blockhouse the first of April, and will proceed thence to ascertain and mark the boundary between the Cherokees and the United States. You will be pleased to make this communication to the Cherokees, that the persons named by them may attend on their part. It is also deemed expedient to convene some of the Indians who were present at and agreed to the Treaty of Holston, as well as the interpreter, if to be found. You will take the necessary steps on this head. General Pickins will accompany me and we shall have an escort of dragoons, and I intend to take the direct rout from the Ocunna Station through your agency; you will inform the Indians of this and direct one of your interpreters to meet us, and you will go in yourself as soon as you can do so with convenience.

With sincere regard, I am Sir,

Your most obedient servant,

B. H.

SILAS DINSMOOR,
Temporary Indian Agent in the Cherokee Nation.

———————

Fort Fidins on Oconee, 7th March, 1797.

Sir:

Being informed by the Secretary of War that you are appointed a Commissioner with General Pickins and me to ascertain and mark the boundary line between the Indian nations and the United States, I take the earliest opportunity to apprize you that we purpose meeting at Tellico Blockhouse on the first of April, and to proceed from thense to ascertain and mark the Cherokee boundary first. I have given the necessary directions to Mr. Dinsmoor on the part of the Indians.

I am with due regard, Sir,

Your obedient servant,

JAMES WINCHESTER, ESQ.

One Other Instance of Indian Justice.

A Chickasaw, an Oakmulgee fellow, killed a woman and child near Midway; satisfaction was demanded of the nation, and two young men, of the party of murderers, went immediately and shot their uncle, saying that he had directed them to do the mischief, and he must die for it.

7 March.

Paid an Indian 5 dollars for keeping stolen horses.

Fort Fidins, 7th March, 1797.

Timothy Barnard:

Having appointed you assistant to me as Principal Temporary Agent for Indian Affairs South of Ohio, you will be attentive to the execution of the duties depending on you, and avail yourself of the proper time to address the Indians on the following points:

1st. Inform the Indians of the fixture of the posts on their lands in conformity with the arrangements made with them at Colerain.

2nd. That the chiefs must, as soon as they can get together, appoint three of their nation to attend and see the boundary run and marked from the Apalatchee over the Currahee Mountain; that I shall advise them through you of the time when I intend to have this line run.

3. Explain to the Indians the proceedings of the Choctaw, Chickasaw and Cherokee representatives, who have visited the President at Philadelphia, that Benjamin Hawkins, Andrew Pickins and James Winchester are appointed Commissioners to ascertain and mark the boundary between those Indians and the United States. That they shall begin with the Cherokee boundary, because there it is apprehended intrusions will the most likely be the soonest made on the lands of those Indians.

4. You will inform the Indians of the disposition of government relative to the Indians on this interesting point; that I set out as soon as I heard of my appointment and fixed the runing of the Cherokee line for the first of April; that as soon as I have seen justice done to the Indians on this quarter, I shall return round with General Pickins to fulfill our engagements with the Creeks; that I shall send to those whom the nation may appoint to see the line run and inform them of the time and place where I shall expect to meet them; that as soon as this business is done I shall return into the nation and there remain with

them; that the annuity for the last year is sent on to be delivered to the chiefs, and as soon as I arrive I shall give those who the nation may appoint orders to receive it.

5. Inform the Indians of the complaints sent in by the Governor of this State to the President, and that the whole nation ought to be under serious apprehensions for their future tranquility unless a stop can be put to such abominable proceedings on the part of their young men.

6. Inform the chiefs that the citizens on this frontier have some of them begun to remove their stock on their own lands, and that I expect by the last of April much of it will be removed.

7th. Mr. Counts is to be considered as in the pay of the United States, while he works at the smith's trade at your house, and I wish your first care would be to have good axes and hoes for the three young halfbreeds, your sons; I mean plough hoes; I have some of all sorts at Mr. Price's. Let Mr. Counts make a plough for each and one for the Tussekiah Mico.

8th. One thing above all others you are to be particularly attentive to: The Indians are, as you know, beggars, and have not the shadow of gratitude for any favours they receive, almost every thing is lost on them. Their annuity will be punctually paid, but they are not to be suffered to expect to obtain presents of any kind whatever when they visit our posts. They must in future be treated as men, and not as spoiled children. Those who are in the Indian department must expect to live on their sallaries, and for them to do the business assigned them, and must exhibit in their own conduct at all times, examples worthy of imitation to the Indians. I have come to correct abuses and to fix the management of Indian affairs in those who will zealously and steadily execute the orders of the government.

9. You will send to Mr. Price for the garden seed, and when you get it, send some to all the traders you can, particularly Mr. Marshall, Darouzeaux, Car, Grierson, More & Bailey, and you will send some to Mr. Burges and Mr. Alex Cornell. You can also order up axes, hoes, plough and weeding, plough lines, bridlebits, grubing hoes, hand saws, pruning knives, crosscutt saws, hand saws and other files.

You will retain some of these things and send some to the village of Tussekiah Mico. Send them there on loan; say half a dozen axes, half a dozen grubing hoes & weeding, half a dozen plough hoes, 1 hand saw, 1 drawing knife, 2 socket chisels, 2 inch screw augurs and 1 ✕cut saw with files. Give Nitta Hooktee's mother 2 hoes.

You will do the best you can till you see me, and let me hear from you if you have an opportunity. You will write by every opportunity to Col. Gaither.

10. I wish you to inform the chiefs that the Society of
Quakers in Philadelphia have sent to me a present for them,
which I have in care for them at Colerain; that I shall distribute
it as soon as I see the chiefs; and cause their address to be
interpreted to them expressive of the benevolent views of this
society.

                                    Fort Fidins, 8th March, 1797.
Alexander Cornell.

Sir:

Since I left you I have had frequent conversations with some
of your countrymen relative to the affairs of your nation, and
I am happy in being able to inform you that there appears to
be a disposition favourable to peace and good neighbourhood
among the Lower Creeks. Some of the unruly young men have
done mischief, but I hope in the course of the summer that you
and the other chiefs will take measures to govern the nation, and
when the hatchet is buried, to punish any unruly individual who
will lift it up against the voice of the nation. The chiefs of the
land ought to have the right of making peace and war, and any
man who acts contrary thereto must be taught to know he do's
rong. I actually had some doubts while I was at Coweta, whether
I ought to apply to the chiefs or the young men; as the latter
seem determined on mischief and the chiefs unable to control
them. There have been several horses stolen from this frontier,
and one from me while I was at Mr. Marshall's. The chiefs of
Cusseta have behaved well in causing 6 of them to be restored.
We must try and stop this business; if we do not, the day of
reckoning will come and we shall see another long roll which must
be paid.

The troops have arrived from the northward and are fixed
and fixing down to keep peace on these frontiers. Col. Gaither
will do every thing in his power that will lead thereto, but the
chiefs must help him, or all will be in vain.

I have just had sent on to me the conferences had with the
Choctaws, Chickasaws, Cherokees and the mad Spaniard in Philadelphia; the substance will be sent to you by Mr. Barnard. The
President, with the advice of the Senate, has appointed me, with
General Pickins and General Winchester, to ascertain and mark
the lines between the Indian nations and the United States; this
thing presses much, and we have determined to begin the Cherokee line first, and to finish that early the next month; we did intend
to run your line first, but we find that delay would be injurious to

the Cherokees, as intrusions are continually increasing on their lands.

I hope your people will appoint 3 men to see their line run, and have them ready as soon as we have done with the Cherokees and Chickasaws, that we may finish the whole and put an end to all incroachments. I believe this matter now will depend on the Cowetas, and that they are to appoint the 3 men.

The annual present of goods are arrived, and when I come into the nation, which I shall do as soon as I have run the lines, I shall consult the chiefs how they are to be distributed, and divide them accordingly, giving every man an order for his share.

I have had some information of a misunderstanding in your family, which I hope your prudent conduct has enabled you to accommodate so as not to disturb your friends.

I have sent you a draft on Mr. Price for your sallary from the 1st of December to the first of April ensuing. I suppose Mr. Seagrove has paid you up to that date, and in future I shall pay you regularly, every 3 months. You will be particularly careful, as you are an officer in the government, never to suffer anything to be said in the nation relative to public affairs without you have the directions of a superior officer. Remember me to your friends, and believe me, with sincere wishes for the happiness of your nation, to be,

Your friend.

Fort Fidins, 8th March, 1797.

Sir:

Your oldest son remains still under the care of the Secretary of War; the youngest is with the Quakers, as you will see by the following extract from a letter received of the 22nd October: "The two Indian boys which Mr. Price brought with him from Colerain have been placed with the Society of Quakers, who have promised me to superintend and be at the expense of their education, and to have them, if approved by their parents, taught such mechanical professions as they shall fix upon, and as the boys may show an aptitude to learn, you will be pleased therefore to consult the boys' parents and if they should like that one or both of them should be taught the turner's, carpenter's, or blacksmith's trade, to transmit me a proper authority to have them bound."

Mr. Henry Drinker, one of the Society of Quakers, writes to me: "The Secretary of War and Secretary of State signified their desire that some members of our religious society would undertake to place the boys in some sober exemplary family in the country, where they may be trained up in a good degree of innocence, and where endeavors would be used to ground them in some moral principals, to instruct them in useful and common branches of learning, such as reading, writing and figures, and particularly to lead them on in a gradual course of industry, and in the knowledge of husbandry. The proposals being considered by us, and feeling a real concern for our red brethren and their descendants, that they may be improved and encouraged in useful knowledge and in the habits tending to their comfort and benefit, it has been agreed to take the two boys, to-wit, Alexander Durant and James Bailey, under our care for the purpose of placing them in some suitable situation in the country, where they may be carefully and tenderly treated, and their advancement in school instruction and agriculture promoted. But in pursuing this plan, it is desired to have the concurrence of their parents; if they do not fully and freely assent thereto, and particularly that the lads may, as they advance in years, be accustomed to such moderate labour in the farming business as may be necessary for their safety, their health, and their right instruction therein, in the manner we train up our white children." You see in these two extracts that you are to give your advice respecting the future fate of your son; I think you will leave it entirely with the Secretary of War and Secretary of State, and the Quakers, to do what they may deem advisable, for then they cannot be in better hands. I wish you would read your letter to Mrs. Durant, and send me your and her determination.

I am appointed a Commissioner, together with General Pickins and General Winchester, to ascertain and mark the boundary lines between the Indian nations and the United States; and as there are intrusions daily increasing on the Cherokee lands, we have determined to begin there early in April; as soon as this business is finished I shall return into the nation, to reside there. I have received the annual stipend for the Creeks, and a present for them from the Society of Quakers, which I shall distribute as soon as I know the will of the nation. I wish you to mention this to your neighbour and particularly to your wife, for whom I have a sincere regard.

I wish you health & happiness.

RICHARD BAILEY,
    Of Ottassee.

———————

Joseph Hammond, a soldier of Captain Swaine's company, a gunsmith.

Fort Fidins, 9th March, 1797.

Sir:

I rote to you the 10th of last month, and sent the letter to the care of Ensign Thomson, at Fort James. This will be forwarded to you by Mr. Barnard. I wish you would send forward to his care, such of the implements of husbandry as can conveniently be packed upon the horses which he will address to you. The annuity and the present from the Quakers you will keep until I consult the nation and draw on you in conformity with such arrangement as I may make with them. I wish the whole of the business in my department to be so conducted as to explain itself, and be free from any ambiguity.

I have as yet made no new appointments; I have retained such of the persons in office as appeared best qualified to discharge such duties as I might assign to them, arising out of my mission. There being no occasion for express riders, they are of course discharged, and I have promised to pay Walton from the time of my coming into office up to the day of his return home, as soon as he sends in his appointment; this pay he intends for you, and I shall give you a draft accordingly. I have the following persons in service:

Timothy Barnard, Assistant and Interpreter, 700 dollars per annum.

James Burges, Assistant and Interpreter, 400 dollars per annum.

Alexander Cornell, Assistant and Interpreter, 400 dollars per annum.

Richard Thomas, Clerk to the Chiefs, 200 dollars per annum.

I have one at a less sum, but not fixed. I give you this information as your guide in case you should credit any of them, as I shall give drafts quarterly for that sum. The present quarter I shall draw on you for, altho' I am not authorised particularly to do so, because there can no injury arise to the public, as I am authorized to draw on the Secretary of War. It is an accommodation to these people, and it may be that you have amounts against some or all of them of trading.

As this new arrangement takes place the first of December, I include that month in the first quarter, and the drafts are:

No. 1. 9 March, 1797, Timothy Barnard, 233 1-3 dollars.
No. 2. 9 March, 1797, Alexander Cornell, 133 1-3 dollars.
No. 3. 9 March, 1797, James Burges,   133 1-3 dollars.
No. 4. 9 March, 1797, Richard Thomas,   66 2-3 dollars.

As I have been under the necessity of advancing forty dollars to Richard Thomas, and fifty to Mr. Barnard, I request you to make an entry to correspond therewith, that is, to open an account with me in your books and credit me for these sums.

There has been a vile attempt to prevail on the Indians to thwart the marker of the government, but the Indians, more wise than the authors of it, have refused their co-operation. They have sent me the whole procedure, unasked and unsuspected. I am appointed, with General Pickins and General Winchester, a Commissioner to ascertain and mark the boundary lines between the Indian nations and the United States. I leave this to commence the execution of this trust to-morrow; this draws me a little out of the line of direct communication with you, but I shall soon return, and in the well grounded expectations that the joint endeavors of all of us in this quarter will be productive of the good contemplated in our exertions by the government.

I am with much esteem, Sir,

Your obedient servant.

MR. EDWARD PRICE.

Mrs. Anne Vansant, widow of Isaac Vansant, who was murdered by the Indians at Old Bushes Fort, the morning they burnt Harrison's Stockade, informs me that after killing her husband, they took off 2 horses, the one a bay horse branded on the near buttock with a W. on the turn of his rump, a smart active horse, of £23 value; the other a sorrel mare, branded with I. V., a large smart mare, older than the horse; and three cows. She says she is informed the Indians killed one of the cows, and carried two of them into the nation. Mrs. Vansant says she lays the death of her husband to Harrison, that she has said so repeatedly, and that it has given offense to Harrison—he was a very peaceable, inoffensive man, and could never believe that the Indians, or anybody else, could do him an injury.

The doctrine in her neighbourhood was, let us kill the Indians, bring on a war, and we shall get land; her husband replyed, no, he would oppose anything of that sort, it being altogether rong and unjust; he would never be guilty of murder for property.

Martin Hardin, contractor for supplying the troops, is hereby permited to purchase within the district of Fort James, such articles of the Indians as are authorized in their traffic with the citizens of the United States by the Act for regulating trade and intercourse with the Indian tribes, and to preserve peace on the frontiers; conforming himself to the regulations in the said Act, and to such regulations as are or shall be made for the government of the said fort and district. This permit to remain in force until revoked by me, the agent for the Department of War, or the officer commanding the troops of the United States in the State of Georgia.

Given under my hand this 11th of March, 1797.

Fort Fidins, 11th March, 1797.

You will proceed from this to Mr. Barnard's on Flint River, and assist him and his halfbreed boys in fixing their ploughs; you will go from thense to the Tussekiah Mico's village and fix a plough or plows for him, and then you will show him how they are to be used; lay off his cornfield in a proper manner, five feet and a half square, quite true, the furrows or rows strait. You must plough the potato field before the hills are made; the women will make the hills. I wanted the peas to be planted half in the step, the other half in the hills. You must be careful to conduct yourself well, for on that your future fate depends. Mr. Barnard will give you some garden seeds as soon as they are sent up from Mr. Price. Your pay will be ten dollars per month, paid quarterly or monthly, as you may require. I want you to take half a bushel or more of cotton seed with you, to plant at the Tussekiah's.

Fort Fidins, 10 March, 1797.

Christian Russel, a Silician by birth, an inhabitant of Ogelthorp County, in the State of Georgia, is by these presents permited to remove some hogs, his property, from Hightower and Pine Log, to Tellico Blockhouse for market and to sell them under the direction of Silas Dinsmoor, Esq., the Indian agent in the Cherokee nation.

BENJAMIN HAWKINS,
P. T. A. for I. Affairs South of Ohio.

United States, 14th March, 1797.

Beloved Chickasaws:

I am informed by the bearer, Col. Mattews, that he is desirous of paying you a visit, and of being known to you. He has been one

104   *LETTERS OF*

of our old warriors, a Governor of one of the United States, and always deemed to be an honest man, and friendly to the rights of man. It will afford you pleasure to have such a man among you, that you may show him the Chickasaw hospitality and prove to him how worthy you are of being ranked among us as fellow citizens, natives of the same soil and joint defenders of our mutual interests.

Accept of my sincere wishes for the prosperity of your nation and believe me to be your friend.

———

Hopewell on Koowee, 19 March, 1797.

Sir:

I sat out from Fort Fidins on the 11th and arrived here on the 16 of this month. I applied to Col. Gaither for an escort, he had not received any orders from you on that head, but said your letter to me was quite sufficient. I asked only for a Serjeant, Corporal and 12 dragoons, and have them with me; they are bare of cloathing, and I have, at the request of Col. Gaither, purchased some linen for them, and a shirt for each will be made in this neighbourhood, and I shall furnish them with such other things as are indispensible and obtainable on the rout. General Pickins will be ready on the 23, and we shall set out on that day, go over the Ocunna Mountain, through the Cherokees to Tellico Blockhouse. I have made all the necessary arrangements in conformity with the intimations from you in yours of the 2nd of February. I have, with the concurrance of the General, appointed two discrete, honest men of this frontier, acquainted with surveying, to accompany us as surveyors. We give them two dollars each per day and feed them, they furnish their own horses and instruments. Some of the Cherokees, apprised of my intention of being here, have visited me; they will some of them accompany us through their nation.

After I wrote my last to you by trader Gillespie, I saw many of the citizens who live contiguous to Oconee, some of whom I was personally acquainted with; I saw also as I traveled through the State of Georgia, some of those who had embarked in the project of Zachariah Cox for settling the best of Tennessee. I conversed freely and in a friendly manner with them and explained the law to them, and hope that by a temperate President and firm line of conduct in the affairs of the government in this quarter, we shall be able to carry the laws into effect.

General Pickins, from some defect in the post office, has not received the original dispatches to him, and only got the duplicate on the 7, just before my messenger arrived.

I beg you to mention me respectfully to the President, to assure him of my sincere wishes for his happiness, and to believe me yourself, with sincere regard and esteem, Sir,

Your obedient servant,

JAMES McHENRY.

23 March, 1797.

I sat out this day from General Pickins's, from Tellico Block-house, accompanyed by the General and Joseph Whitner and John Clark Kilpatrick, surveyors appointed by us to assist in runing and marking the lines between the Indian nations and the United States. We went on to Timossa, a plantation of the General's adjoining the Cherokee boundary; this was an Indian town before the Revolution War, inhabited by 20 gun men. I saw some fine peach trees, which had been planted by the original inhabitants, and the remains of the square, and some locusts. The farm is pleasantly situated on Timossa Creek, and in the fork of that and the main branch of Little River. To the southward of E. there is a high and beautiful situation for a building, showing the whole Timossa Old Town in front, a majestic conic mountain to the S. W., the flat lands of the two creeks to the north and the serpentine course of the two creeks high up towards their source, and the mountains beyond. In the neighbourhood of this place, in the year 1776, the General had a sharp acting with some of the Chero-kees; he had been detached by General Williamson with a few men, about 35, and were attacked by a considerable body of Indians. The Indians lost 65, and left 14 on the field; the General had 6 killed dead and 5 died of their wounds. The dead were buried in some of the houses in the town and the houses burnt.

24.

Set out, called at the Ocunna Station, took Lieutenant Mosely, two of his men, made some arrangements for the journey, and continued on over the Ocunna Mountain 1½ miles to the boundary; continue on 2¼ miles farther and arrive at the village on Chauga, here is a beautiful situation for a military post, in the fork of the two main branches of Chauga is a high nole, easily to be made defensible; the lands on the creek rich, and those bordering thereon fine for wheat, the whole exhibiting all that is desired to designate this as a healthy position and neighbourhood; it is convenient for a trading establishment. The following is the distance of and position of the water courses in going from the boundary to this site, estimating the same in minutes, counting 3 miles to the hour: Begining at the boundary 2 minutes, cross a creek runing to the left, 4 feet wide, 5 minutes; X a branch runing to the left 2 feet wide, 6 minutes; X a branch runing to the left 1 foot 6 inches wide, 26 minutes; X a creek runing to the right, 3 feet over, 3 minutes; X a creek 15 feet over, runing to the left, and in 4 X a creek runing to the left, 8 feet wide; in the fork of these two is the site recommended in this note. The whole of the growth on this path scrub, black and small spanish oak, with a few pine.

To continue in like manner the distance to Chattuga is 6 minutes, X a branch runing to the left, 1 foot wide; 8 minutes X a creek runing to the left, 8 feet wide; 7 minutes X a branch runing to the right, 1 foot; 28 minutes a beautiful meadow, ¼ of a mile to the left of the path, the grass at this season very thick and eight inches high. This meadow was burnt the last of November, when I passed this to the Creek country. 15 minutes X a branch to the left, 2 feet wide; 6 minutes X a branch runing to the left, 3 feet wide; 5 minutes X a branch runing to the left, and in this direction a mountain of a conic form; 5 minutes X a branch to the left, and 9 minutes X 2 small branches, and over the ridge of Whetstone Mountain; this vale exhibits for some time back, marks of rich land; descend down 9 minutes and X a creek runing to the right, 3 feet wide, falling over for some distance below a bed of rock, margined with spruce, hemloc, pine, and some mountain laurel; 22 minutes X Chattuga, 40 yards over, just above the mouth of Warwoman's Creek.

On the side of the meadow before mentioned we encamp.

25.

This day I met John Martin, of Corn Creek, in Pendleton County, South Carolina; he had been to Cowe trading as a hireling of Ellis Harding, on examining him he seemed much confused, he had three loads of leather. I informed him I should examine into the truth of his statement and report his name for a violation of the law, and that I would not suffer any man to trade without a licence.

The course appears to be N. W. to the point where we cross Warwoman's Creek the second time, 3 miles from Chattuga; from thence to the dividings on Sticcoa 13 miles W. in ascending the creek for the first 5, in this comes X 3 creeks which enter from the right, and from just below Walnut Creek to the uppermost the feed in the moist places good.

From Sticcoa, at the dividing, we go over a hill west to the creek and continue on in that direction one hour 7 minutes to its source, the whole of this the path is good, there is at 30 minutes some cane on the creek and some good grass. From the source of Sticcoa over a ridge 9 minutes to a beautiful little branch tumbling out of the mountains to the left, we cross it runing to the right, it is margined with evergreens; we continue our course down the branch 15 minutes to a creek 15 feet wide, here the paths divide, we take the right N. W. and up the creek a rugged path, 18 minutes ✕ the creek 10 feet wide and up a branch of it to our left 22 minutes to the ridge, thense down 23 minutes to a branch and cross it runing to the right, 3 feet wide, the land now more level; in 10 minutes arrive at a creek runing to the left, here we encamp, the food not good, from the late burning of the woods. The Lieutenant Mossley left us here with his two dragoons, he seems to be an active deserving young officer; General Pickins furnished him with a copy of the intercourse law with the Indians, and I gave him verbal directions how to act in case he should apprehend any person violating the law.

26.

We ✕ the creek 25 feet wide, our course W.; 15 minutes ✕ a ridge and have an opening to S. W. and a view of distant mountains; 9 minutes ✕ a branch runing to the left, and over bad road 8 to the top of a ridge, then down 9 to a creek 45 feet over, go down and ✕ three minutes to an old field, here the grass being fine, we halt for 20 minutes and let our horses graze; here we saw some fine grass in bloom, the small winter grass common on the hills in bloom, the state of vegetation in the trees, the hickory a little smaller, the dogwoods not quite in full bloom; there is some cane below this field and this is a good camping place; the creek our guide calls Oloktah. Our course now N. W.; 17 minutes ✕ a branch runing to the right and up it 11 minutes to the ridge, and over and down 6 passing large timber on both sides which were steep; come to the creek we have passed runing to the right, continue up 19 minutes, ✕ and up it 40 minutes to the ridge, wind round down, have an opening to S. W., come to the western waters and go down one hour 42 minutes, ✕ the creek 10 feet wide just below the junction with one from the right, ✕ it again in a few yards, 45 feet wide, the land pretty level; 10 minutes come to a small branch and breakfast near a maple swamp, the grass pretty good, tho' in small patches; 31 minutes ✕ a creek 25 feet wide running to the left; in 32 a branch

runing to the left, near the creek here is some cane; in 9 minutes
a large creek called by our guide Etowwah, join the one we are
descending on the left side and nearly at right angles; the day
being very cloudy, we were a little out in our conjecture of the
course we were going, at breakfast we found it was W. and so
continued to this creek, now N. W.; we go down the right bank
8 minutes, X a creek 8 feet, 20 minutes come to the fork of the
path, continue our course and leave the left; 10 minutes come
opposite a large mound of earth near the creek on the flat land, 45
minutes to a ridge, our ascent N. and a grand view of mountains
in this direction. From the mouth of Etowwah down to the
mound the lands are good, a little waving on the left bank but
fine for culture.

From the ridge we descend 5 minutes X a creek runing to
the left 15 feet wide. In 67 minutes we X several small branches,
the soil poor, stoney, with glades, the growth dwarf, black jack,
oak and hard shelled hickory; there had been recently a hurrycane
which had twisted and broken the little trees. The glades, now
green, exhibit a beautiful contrast with the poor scrubby dwarf
trees; 7 minutes the soil alters for the better, X a creek runing
to the left 36 feet, Coqeentah, the banks formerly inhabited; 16
minutes X a creek runing to the left, 6 feet, near the river, and
go down the river 13 minutes and encamp near a branch on the
river bank; on the left bank of this was the town of Quanasee, for
many years the residence of Cornelias Daughtertu, an old Irish
trader; at present there is nothing remaining of the town except
the open flats where were formerly the corn fields; here we had
fine food, the grass abundant in the moist branches; the state of
vegitation in trees very backward, the dogwoods but just swollen
and the sassafras begining to bloom. At the point of the river
just above our encampment there are 2 rocks in the river and the
curve of the river from S. E. round to S. W. We had a heavy
shower of rain during the night and much thunder.

27.

Continue on 15 minutes, X a creek to the left, and in 4 minutes
arrive at the river and proceed down 14 minutes through Indian
old fields to a hill on the right and a large conic mound to the
left, just on the left bank of the river; this mound is large,
apparently 15 feet high and near 100 at the base. I saw on the
top a peach tree and I believe a large locust; the river being too
high to forde I could only judge of what I saw at the distance of
100 yards. The whole of the mound was covered with cane and
the margin of the river in the neighbourhood of it. On the left
bank of the river there is a very extensive old field. 21 minutes

lower there is a village; I saw five houses in view and there were several others in the neighbourhood; it is called Chewayqok; the river is of the same name. From appearances there must have been a very large town in the neighbourhood of our encampment last evening, and from thense down to this village. The lands on both sides of the river are now green and free from briars or shrubbery. In the neighbouring hills on either side are some beautiful situations for buildings, particularly on the left side just below the mound. After refreshing ourselves at the village and procuring some corn, we sat out, still down the river, 12 minutes and $\times$ Tujquatah 30 feet over, and soon enter the hills bordering on the river; 18 minutes $\times$ a branch, 3 feet, a rapid fall to the river, and large enough for an overshot mill. In 48 minutes $\times$ a creek runing to the left, 30 feet over; 10 minutes the paths divide; we take the right over the mountain and arrive at the top in one hour 10 minutes; from this there is an assemblage of mountains in every direction; to the S. W. we have a view of Little Hewossa, and to the S. E. the old fields of Chewayqok. We descend in 37 minutes, arrive at the first flat land and $\times$ a creek runing to the left, 8 feet; in 17 minutes arrive at a small rise in the fork of 2 branches and here encamp. There is on this side of the mountain a spring near the summit, and the water tumbles rapidly down near the path. This pass is a difficult one, ascending or descending, and I recommend to all travellers to take the other rout, unless they are pleased with mountain scenes and will exchange for the plague and fatigue of climbing for them as I have done.

It is to me worthy of remark, that where we are now encamped we have an abundance of fine grass for our horses, without the least show of vegetation in the trees anywhere in view except on the south front of the mountains.

28.

We sat out early from our encampment N. W.; in 16 minutes go thro' a narrow pass between two mountains, where probably in some former period the natives must have made a stand in defense of their country. In the center of the pass there is a large heap of stones, which must have been placed as covering to the warriors who lost their lives in defense of the pass; the pass is about 30 feet wide and the ascent on both sides very steep. In 45 minutes pass a creek runing to the left, 8 feet wide; in 19 the paths divide just before we arrive at a large creek, we cross a small one and go down the large one 14 minutes to Little Tellico; here I saw 28 gun men who collected on being informed that I should be here accompanyed with General Pickins. I addressed a short speach to them relative to our visit. They expressed pleasure at seeing us, and confidence in our exertions to restore order between the red and white people. One of them informed me that five of their hunters who went towards Cumberland were missing and he was apprehensive they had been killed. We procured some corn of the women and proceeded on, crossed the creek, 45 feet over, my guide calls it Ocunqustah; continue on pass some buildings to the right and in 40 minutes a bed of iron ore near a small glady branch runing to the left; in 7 minutes arrive at the river again and in 5 $\times$ it. There are two settlements on this side, the lowest surrounded with peach trees, which are very thriving. Cross the river again and in 20 minutes arrive at the Fort of Notly Mountain; ascended the mountain to the top in 45 minutes, and descended near a fine little creek, $\times$ing it 2 or 3 times, and in 58 minutes $\times$ the creek runing to the left; continue on over uneaven ground 28 minutes to 3 creeks, $\times$ 2 of them in the direction of the path and the third to encamp, rise a small ridge and encamp between the third and a 4 creek. There is a small island of cane and some good grass, the lands near the creeks just above the ridge we encamp on level.

29.

Some of our horses having strayed during the night, I had an opportunity of examining the land in the neighbourhood of the encampment. The 2 creeks I find forms an island and they are the same, called by my Cherokee guide Cautustuwoh. The flat extends for half a mile, and the grass good in all the moist places. We set out, 45 minutes pass between 2 mountains; 10 down and up to the next rise; 32 to a flat of 5 caves between 2 branches; 28 cross the Beaverdam Creek, 15 feet wide, runing to the left, 25 a gap, two mountains in front; 11 $\times$ a branch runing to the left; 3 meadow to the right, two holleys to the left of the path bending over the branch and a meadow to the left; wind round a hill on its border; 2 to a creek and ascend it, here the Notly path joins and there is cane on the right bank of the creek; 27 pass under a delightful grove of evergreens, $\times$ a creek runing to the left; 11 $\times$ a branch runing to the left, 4, flat land on both sides; 9 $\times$ a creek to the left; 15 cross two branches in 2 minutes; 6 $\times$ a branch; 9 $\times$ main branch and go up on the right bank; 11 $\times$ a small branch; 9 $\times$ the main branch, and in 3 arrive at the source near the gap; 4 minutes pass thro' the gap, a spring on the left, and $\times$ a creek running to the left; 4 and a branch, both clustered with evergreens; 11 $\times$ a branch to the left; 5 pass a gap, a small hill in front and the mountains beyond; descend 34, a small branch to the left; 5 a chain of rock to the right; 3 a small branch;

5 the gap, turn to the right and wind round the mountain and through a gap of rock; on the rise to the first gap there is an extensive view of mountains to the S. W.; 17 a cluster of rock on a piny nole; 16 wind round on a ridge to a gap, a small pine nole to the right; 7 to the termination of the ridge of pines; 30 to the small rocks on the ridge of oakes, from this the vale of mountains S. W. and N. E. are as extensive as the eye can reach; 15 the top of the ridge and pass of rocks, the ridge in the narrowest part is about 6 feet and the descent on other side 300. This pass has been represented as tremendious, but a person who has been for some days familiarized with mountain scenes passed it with care and without emotion; 20 pass Turnback Point and X a branch; 10 X a branch to the right; 12 arrive at main gap of the Unecoi Unacaqec. At Turnback Point there is the black slate. From this mountain there is the most extensive view westward of any known among the mountains, we had not a favourable time to see it. The evening was haisy and the morning equally so. We encamped near the gap, there is good water on both sides, that on the west nearest the summit. I have been informed that this spring was on the top of the mountain, and that springs are some times found on the tops of mountains, but it is not true; here it opens on both sides from near the ridge or gap, and it is always so in all cases within my view, and I have seen most of our southern mountains.

30.

This morning, after a boisterous night, we began to descend the mountain, no show of vegitation anywhere in view, every thing looking as in the dead of winter. We descend rapidly, winding over poor dwarf pine ridges one hour to a small branch and a creek 8 feet wide runing to the left, descend and cross the creek seven times in 12 minutes, here vegitation begins to show itself and here I saw the may cherry found; 23 minutes X a small branch to the left; in 14 minutes X a creek 20 feet wide runing to the right, the descent to it very steep and through evergreens; here are large pendent rocks of slate stone, its the grey striped; in 14 minutes X a branch to the left, and in 44 have a view of the old fields and river Tellico; here we perceive a great increase of vegitation; in 14 descend to the river, go down 5 minutes & X it, 50 yards over, a rocky bottom, two feet deep, the front of the mountain and the flat covered with grass fit for grazing; descend the river, in 12 minutes enter it a few feet for a road, the rocks to the right hanging over; in 32 arrive opposite the town and fields, and in 15 at the town house.

The town house is on a mound of earth 12 feet high, situated near a bend of the river in the midst of the old fields, the houses are all in a state of decay, and the whole has the appearance of a waste; the old fields very extensive above and below and covered with wild onion. There are four large and old apple trees. The chiefs and warriors received us in a very friendly manner; there were 18. I saw a number of children, and all smiling and healthy. We stayed and breakfasted and procured some corn. The lands in the neighbourhood of the town barron piny hills. The flats appear rich and capable of a high degree of culture. We continued on 45 minutes down, our course N.; 30 E. pass some lime stone near the town, some more old fields to the left, and have a view of a settlement over the river prittily situated on a rising ground surrounded with peach trees. In 45 minutes arrive at the river and wind round the bend over a mountain to our right, the sides stored with lime stone; in 15 minutes enter a beautiful flat, and in 4 minutes $\times$ a creek runing to the left, 25 feet wide, a large sheet of lime stone rock to the left of the ford. From the lower end of this flat, where we turn to $\times$ the creek, there is prittily situated on the opposite side of the river some Indian huts. The situation still farther back appears to me a more eligible one, if it has the advantage of the water prospect. In this flat my guide says the garrison of Fort Lowdon were attacked and destroyed. In 36 minutes, going thro' a vale of scrub oak and limestone land, $\times$ a branch to the left; in 16 pass a fine spring on the left in front of a mount of limestone toped with red cedar, here vegitation is far advanced, the hickory shows fine leaves, the honeysuckel and dogwood in full blow, and grass abounds for grazing; in 12 $\times$ a branch, down it 8 & $\times$ a creek 3 feet wide runing to the left, and in 15 minutes encamp on the side of a drain in the course of the path near its source; the lands hilly, the grass good on the sides of them.

31.

Set out, in 16 $\times$ the branch we encamp on, It, 3 feet wide, continue on, cross on the It 3 times where it becomes a considerable large creek, the lands rich, the growth of timber large; 30 $\times$ a creek to the left 3 feet wide near the river; in 18 arrive at the low ground where we saw on our right a poplar 22 feet in circumfrence, measured 3 feet from the ground, and the stem for a great height of the same sise; in 5 minutes $\times$ the creek Unnatotaqee, 25 feet over; in 14 cross a branch and continue on a blind tract thro' hilly loch timbered land and down a stream where the natives have been making sugar from the maple; in 49 arrive in flat lands; 20 to an old town, part of Tuskeegee, where we saw an apple and some peach trees, with 2 hills covered with limestone; in 30 pass through Tuskeegee fields thro' the remains of Fort Lowdon and arrive on the Tennessee opposite the blockhouse. This river is 160 yards wide opposite the landing. Tellico, Lat. 35° 15'.

3 April.

The Honble. David Campbell, one of the Commissioners to ascertain and mark the line between the State of Tennessee and Cherokees, commissioned 22 September, 1792. Letter of notification of same date from Geo. Blount, Charles McClun & John McKee for Dan Smith, Colonel Carlu Tellico.

<hr>

April the 3rd, 1797.

Benjamin Hawkins, Principal Temporary Agent for Indian Affairs South of Ohio, to Efau Tustunnagau:

I arrived here two days past, with General Pickins, to ascertain and mark the boundary line between the United States and the Indian nations, we shall mark the Cherokee boundary first and then the Chickasaw and Creek. Morgan, of Wewoca, will give you this, he has been waiting here for your presents, which are sent on to you under the care of Serjeant Thrap.

Mr. Rogers informs me you have collected some horses taken by your wild ungovernable young men from Cumberland, and that you wished for an opportunity to send them to their owners. The Serjeant is directed by Colonel Henley to receive them and bring them to this post from whence they will be forwarded as you desire. You will order as many of your young men as you may deem necessary to accompany the Serjeant to this post. If they have any skins or furs they can have an opportunity of disposing of them here.

You have had an opportunity to see the supreme executive of the United States, and many of my fellow citizens, and I hope you have formed just conceptions of the power as well as justice of our government, and that you will on all occasions impress on the minds of your countrymen the information you have received on these points, and how necessary it is to your existence as a nation to cultivate a friendly intercourse with us by a strict compliance with the terms of your treaty.

I hope soon the Creek chiefs will be able to do more than they have hitherto done to prevent horse stealing, by punishing the offenders, that we may prove to our white brethren that the promises of the Creeks may be relied on, and that we mean to put a stop to this accursed abominable practice.

Accept of my sincere wishes for the prosperity of your nation.

> BENJAMIN HAWKINS,
> P. T. Agent for I. Affairs S. of Ohio.

Tellico Blockhouse, 6th April, 1797.

Sir:

The letter you showed me from General Winchester, of 31st of March, makes it necessary that you should trace the letter from me to him of the 7 of that month from Oconee, inclosed in yours of the 23rd, and sent by express to him in care of a serjeant.

The idea of the General that General Pickins and I expected to meet him here the "first of April for the purpose of proceeding to the runing of the Creek lines," is pretty extraordinary. He says he has no acquaintance with the Creek nation, nor no geographical knowledge of that country. He appears, by his letter, to have some knowledge of his appointment and probably has seen by his instructions that the "Cherokees have been promised that the runing of their line would be commenced in April," and he certainly must know that Tellico Blockhouse is on the Tennessee near the Cherokee line, and that we could never be so absurd as to come from the Creek line two hundred and fifty miles here for the purpose merely of meeting him to accompany us back again.

I am with sincere regard & esteem, Sir,

> Your obedient servant.

SILAS DINSMOOR, ESQ.,
T. I. Agent in the Cherokee Nation.

Tellico, 6 April, 1797.

Sir:

I received your excellency's favour of the 17th of February on the 3rd of this month. I have in the course of the winter visited several of the towns of the Upper & Lower Creeks, and obtained from the Indians and traders this interesting fact, that the Indians are more inclined to peace and more friendly to the citizens, their neighbours, than they have ever been known to be.

This I attribute to the confidence they have in the justice of our government and to the accommodation of our political differences with Spain and Great Britain, the latter removing all interference in the management of Indian affairs.

The arrangements in train of execution will, I hope, increase the friendly disposition of the Indians and induce them to do justice to my fellow citizens. I rely with confidence on the agents in my department, and if my fellow citizens who inhabit the frontiers will co-operate with me, I presage that the open of my mission will be successful.

I have received information that there are some horses among the Upper Creeks supposed to be stolen from the frontier inhabitants, and I have given directions for them to be restored to a serjeant who is sent into that country. The negros you mention are, I believe, in the possession of Daniel Lessly, a halfbreed son of James Lessly. I heard some thing of them while I was among the Upper Creeks, but it was so vague that I could not then examine the case thoroughly. I shall return into that nation as soon as the lines are shaped and do what may be proper.

I have seen your excellency's proclamations of the 10th of August and 20th of March, they are well timed to prepare the citizens who may be affected by the "Act to regulate trade and intercourse with the Indian tribes and to preserve peace on the frontiers," to conform to it. The period is arrived when the line will be run, and the citizens who are intruders will have had time to remove, and if they should neglect the warning, painful as the task may seem to be, the officers intrusted with the execution of the law will faithfully execute the trust confided to them.

I shall be glad to hear from you on all occasions wherein I can be useful to the citizens of Tennessee for whose prosperity I have the sincerest wishes.

I have the honor to be, your Excellency's,

Most obedient servant.

His Excellency,
JOHN SEVIER,
Governor of Tennessee.

Tellico, 7th April, 1797.

The Commissioners for ascertaining and marking the boundary lines between the Indian nations and the U. S. will leave this to-day at 12 o'clock and encamp this evening on the dividing ridge between the waters of Little River and Tennessee; tomorrow they will visit the point at Fort Gavinger and from thence up the

Holston to Little River, on that and the next day, as soon as they receive a return from Mr. Dinsmoor to their letter of yesterday, which they will expect by Sunday evening, they expect to be able to decide on the manner how they are to proceed, and will give notice to Captain Sparks and Colonel Henley accordingly. The Captain will be ready to march at an hour's notice.

B. H.

Mr. Dinsmoor:

———————

The escort are much in want of some cloathing, if there are any jackets I wish Colonel Henley would send one for each.

This day 13 of the Cherokees visited General Pickins and me, and the speaker, Little Woman, holder of Highwassa, welcomed us on our arrival, said he and the Cherokees rejoiced at the expectation of having their lines closed, that the affair would meet with some difficulty, but he hoped the men chosen by the President would hear both sides and do justice, that there was much talk in the nation about the line and he supposed as much among the whites, but that when the line was fixed on and marked by the persons who were chosen, all this talk would subside and the parties acquiesce.

We replied, we should hear the red and white people and wished that they might agree among themselves, but if they could not we should do justice and we expected our red and white brethren would give up little points of difference and concur in our dicision; that it might be some days before their representation would be here, we should move on and encamp on the dividing ridge between the two rivers, and obtain such information of the whites as we could, relative to their opinion of the line, and when the Indian representation arrived we should know something of the ground we were on and would the better understand them.

The speaker replied: "Go see your people, hear what they have to say, and obtain all the information you can from them, but do not give them any opinion at all till you hear us. The Bark, one of the men appointed by us is here, you have taken him by the hand, he will be ready when the others arrive."

Lieutenant George Strather informed us that he had heard Colonel McKee say, the line called the experiment line had been run secretly, that the Indians had been notified of the time when it was to be run, but that they began before the time, and met the Indians in the woods, attempted to secrete the instruments, and upon their being discovered by the Indians, they invited the Indians to go and run it; they replied, we suppose you have done it, we need not go about it.

Colonel McKee further said that he was of opinion that when the line was run fairly it would take in Colonel Craik.

7 April.

Set out from Tellico Blockhouse to find and encamp on the ridge which divides the waters of Little River from those of the Tennessee. Took the road to Knoxville; one hour passed five small settlements near the road, and two large limestone springs; took the left road to Squire Wallace's, and in 15 minutes arrived at the creek near his house, turned off a small distance and encamped. The Honourable David Campbell accompanyed us. Here we were visited by Captain Henley and three others, his neighbours, they expressed some anxiety at their situation. I told them that I could inform them with certainty that the government were determined to fulfill their engagements and to carry their treaties into effect with the Indians. Captain Henley seems to be a very decent orderly man.

8th April.

This day being rainy we moved our encampment near the road to Knoxville in the neighbourhood of Captain Henry. We spend the day with Mr. Wallace and several of the neighbours who appear to show much anxiety on the apurtaining of the Indian boundary. We requested them to give us such information as they could, to enable us to be prepared on the hearing of the Indians, to do justice between the parties. Colonel David Craig replied, those present possessed and would give the best information and if we would meet them to-morrow at his house, or Mr. Bartlot McGee's, they would be there and ready to accompany us for that purpose. We promised to breakfast with Mr. McGee and accepted the offer.

9th.

We set out to breakfast with Mr. McGee, here we found several of the neighbours. We requested information on the following points: The course and distance to Tellico, 12 miles, W. S. W.; Tennessee, 8 direct, S. & W.; Little River, 15, N. & E.; Experiment Line, 4, S. & W.; Colonel Craig's, 1¼, N. E.; Head of 9 Mile C., 1½, N. E., it joins the Tennessee at Tellico; Baker's Creek, 2½, N., it joins Tennessee 3 miles below.

Pistol Creek has two branches, one heads opposite the source of 9 Mile Creek, the west fork opposite Baker's Creek; its junction with Little River 5 miles above the confluence of that with Holston. Crooked Creek has its source three miles below the mountain, and its junction with Little River 5 miles above Pistol Creek. The ridge between the sources of these four creeks is that which divides the waters runing into Little River from those runing into Tennessee, which they will demonstrate by our next point at Colonel Craigs. The next point we go to is to the ridge just above the plantation of Colonel Craig's, N. E. 1¼ miles. This the Colonel informed us was the ridge mentioned at Mr. McGee's. The point where we were was 20 miles south from Knoxville. There is a scope of mountains from N. E. round eastwardly to S. W.; Little River breaks through this chain in a direction N. 88 E.; Tennessee in S. 10 W. The experiment line crosses the mountain S. 10 E. at Chilhowe Path. The Unecahoe over the chain of Chilhowe Mountains, S. 41 E. This mountain is better known east of this by the name of Black or Smoky Mountain. In the direction of this Smoky Mountain it is 6 miles of flat lands to the Chilhowe Mountains; this flat is thickly settled, and here are the sources of the north fork of 9 Mile Creek. Mr. Patrick Salvidge, who is well informed, fixes the course to the source of Little Pigeon S. 24 E.; the source of Pistol Creek S. 83 E. From this to Captain Henry's 5½ miles to the line of experiment, the course S. 59 W.; the head of Baker's Creek North 15 W.

We sat out for the point on the ridge where the experiment line for fixing the courthouse of Blount County passes the ridge between Pistol Creek and Baker's Creek, due E. from a point in Tennessee 13½ miles, and this point is one and half miles S. from the point from whence a line W. joins the confluence of Holston and Tennessee; they run this line with much exactness. The point where we are is the point 2½ miles N. from McGee's.

In approaching it from the point at Colonel Craig's, we note these views, counting in minutes, 60 to 3 miles: 6, cross a bottom of Baker's and go down it west; 4 minutes, X another bottom of the same, a spring 200 yards to our left, said to be large and fine; 7, a ridge, and in front of us, there is a very high ridge crossing of us; 4, descend to another bottom of Baker's Creek; 6, cross a branch of the same at Jeremiah Alexander's; 8, cross a branch of the same: 7, come to a bottom of Pistol Creek; 3 minutes, to the point on the ridge in the experiment line run to ascertain the site for Blount Courthouse.

From this point the confluence of Little and Holston Rivers N. 21 E.; the distance 10 miles. The nearest point on the Holston at Colonel Alexander Kelley's at the mouth of Lackey's Creek, N. 5½ W.; the distance 6 miles. The source of this creek is the course to the Colonel's.

We sat out 8 minutes W. to a ridge dividing Pistol and Baker's Creeks, the bottoms steep to the right and left, and rise to a high ridge; turn south 6 minutes, to the top of a nole, the bottoms steep, to the right the falling grounds of Gallaher's Creek. The nole I am on we call it Iron Hill. Gallaher's Creek empties into Holston 7 miles below Lackey's Creek. 11 minutes I cross a small ridge and ascend a hill, 4 minutes S. S. W. and cross a path from Baker's Creek to the settlements on Holston. The ridge is now S. S. W. one mile, S. W. W. one mile, S. S. W. 3 miles, then N. W.

From the path before mentioned we go W. 36 minutes to the main source of Gallaher's Creek, Godfrey Fowler's half a mile below John Allison's, a mill.

Being satisfied with the statement made by the gentlemen who accompanyed us, that all the waters to our right run into Holston and those on the left into Tennessee, we determined to encamp at this spring and return to the Iron Hill to view the ridge bordering on Little River.

10th.

We returned this morning to Iron Hill, and proceeded thense to ascertain whether there was a ridge bordering on Little River of the discription mentioned in the treaty; we went on the ridge northwardly to John Cochran's, Esquire, at the source of Lackey's Creek, here we determined to correct our point from observation and we fixed this point to be from our point of departure, one hour and 20 minutes, about 5 miles, the course S. 27 W.; to the mouth of the creek N. 57 W., 3½ miles; to the mouth of Little River N. 7 E, 7 miles. The source of this creek is a spring thirty feet diameter, and of as much depth; it is limestone water, and affords enough for a mill.

We continued on the course of the ridge to a point we call Iron Mount, between 5 & 6 miles, high and covered with pine, here we made the following observations: The course to Chilhowe Gap S. 1 W.; to the termination of the chain of mountains S. 85 E., and to the right S. 3 W.; a mountain over the Holston, a vale exhibited which apparently extends to the river, suppose to be Clinch Mountain, Bull Run, N 17 E.; the course to Knoxville N. 33 E., distance 9 miles; the course to Little River N. 3 W., one mile; Major Singleton's house N. 51 E., one mile wanting 220 yards. Major Singleton met us here and accompanyed us to the mouth of Little River, on a very high and commanding ridge, which divides the waters of Little River from those of Holston; we arrive at the junction of the two rivers. The course of Little River at the junction N. 40 W. The view up or rather across the river at the point of the right side of Little River N. 20 E.; David Lovelau possesses the land.

We return through the plantation and up the ridge half a mile, and on the ridge ascertain the course to Colonel Samuel Wear's in Sevier County, S. 82 E.

Encampment on the dividing ridge between Little River and Tennessee, 11th of April 1797.

Sir:

We left General Pickins's on 23, and arrived at Tellico Blockhouse on the 31st of March; there we expected to meet General Winchester, and there we expected to make the necessary arrangements for ascertaining and marking the boundary from Clinch over Holston towards the North Carolina line first, as far as intrusions were the most likely to increase. The letter to the General was received at Knoxville and sent by express, and his reply to Mr. Dinsmoor (very extraordinary); I have not the reply, but you have the substance in our letter to Mr. Dinsmoor, a copy of which we enclose, with an extract from him in reply. If there is any real intention to postpone the runing of the line under the idea that the knowledge of the three Commissioners are indispensable, and thereby to give time to the intruders to plant their crops, we will frustrate it. We have, as far as we could, endeavored to comply with the expectations, "that all of us would be present at the runing of the Cherokee line," but as we see where the pressure is, we will mark a line here from Clinch to the mountains and then proceed to Cumberland.

We have been for three days endeavouring to obtain the requisite information to fix the point where the line is to cross Hoston, we visited all the necessary points ourselves, and obtained from a number of the neighbours who accompanyed us satisfactory information as to others, and are ready to decide on the boundary as expressed in the treaty as soon as we see the Indians. The gentlemen who accompanyed us, all of whom may be affected by the line, have conducted towards us, very satisfactorily, they express that they have been the dupes of misinformation. We have visited several of them in our rout and paid suitable attention to all. They express confidence in us; we have, by viewing every place with them, been able to let them decide in a manner for themselves the question. Their hope now is that some thing can be done for them with the Indians, all of whom arrived last evening, as we are informed at the blockhouse.

Although much caution was used to have a few of the principal chiefs only, who negotiated the treaty of Holston, we are informed that near three hundred are arrived or expected, arising in some degree out of the anxiety of the nation relative to their boundary, and an apprehension that we should attempt to acquire more land. Measures are taken to render this visit as little expensive as possible.

We beg you to assure the President of our sincere wishes for a long continuance of his health and happiness, and to believe me yourself, with great respect, Sir,

Your obedient servant,

BENJAMIN HAWKINS.
ANDREW PICKINS.

The Honorable
JAMES McHENRY,
Secretary of War.

---

12 of April, 1797.

Major John Singleton, Blount County on Little River, in Tennessee, has a note of Alexander Cornell's dated first day of September, 1795, due the 10th of October thense ensuing, for 280 dollars; Mr. Cornell gave with this note a power of attorney to James White to receive so much of his sallary as would discharge the same. The application has been made to Philadelphia and not on James Seagrove, the then agent for the Creeks.

Major Singleton requests that measures may be taken by the officers of government to obtain payment for him. He is directed to hold the note and power in possession till he receives information from the Superintendent, or until some opportunity presents to the nation, by whom he can send it and receive the returns in safety.

Tellico Blockhouse, 12 April, 1797.

Sir:

I have just received your letter of the 10th; it requires no comment from me, as I submit the propriety of your conduct to your own reflections.

I am with due regard, Sir,

Your obedient servant.

RICHARD SPARKS,
Captain 3rd Regiment.

Tellico Blockhouse, 14 April, 1797.

Sir:

The Commissioners appointed to ascertain and mark the boundary line between the Indian nations and the United States request that you would furnish them with a copy of the order you received from Captain Sparks relative to them, a few days past, by his express. It is necessary in the present state of things to be informed of this order, to the end that they may take eventual measures for the completion of the objects of their mission.

I am with due regard and esteem, Sir,

Your obedient servant,

B.

GEO. STROTHER,
Ensign Commandant.

Answer.

A copy of part of my orders, received from Captain Sparks, 11 April, 1797.

"You will please to be cautious about the Indians that come there and the inhabitants, perhaps there may be some desperate and you can't be too careful.

And you will observe that no order from the Commissioners you are to obey.

You are the commandant of that post and I expect you will give me a good account of it.

A copy.　　　　　　　　　　RICHARD SPARKS,
　　　　　　　　　　　　　　Captain Commandant.

GEO. STROTHER,
Ensign Commandant.

Tellico Blockhouse, 15th April, 1797.

Sir:

It being our duty to draw in the Indians under our agency as much as possible to a friendly intercourse with our fellow citizens, and to cement it by an interchange of good offices, I think we should by every means encourage all their legal attempts to acquire a living, and in cases like that of Vann, where, in your judgment, any of them possess skins or furs and would prefer any other market than the public one, that you would grant them a permit, expressing therein the articles, as near as may be, and the person employed to go to the market. You will affix all the necessary checks in the permit to prevent fraud, and require that the white person shall take an oth to "promote as far as in his power the execution of the Act passed the 19th May, 1796," entitled "An Act to regulate trade and intercourse with the Indian tribes and to preserve peace on the frontiers." In providing for the cases contemplated in this arrangement, care must be taken not to introduce white people into the nation so as to injure in any degree the plan of trade and intercourse, as established by law, which might be done under cover of their being agents to hunters. Temporary provision in this way can be made for James Vann, and as soon as his health will permit, he may be advised to make the requisite application to the Agent of War.

MR. SILAS DINSMOOR.

Tellico, 15th of April, 1797.

Sir:

The Indians who may convene here to meet the Commissioners appointed to ascertain and mark the boundary line between the Indian nations and the United States, on the invitation given in conformity with my communication to you of the 7th of March, must be provided with provisions. I request of you to make the necessary arrangements for this purpose, have the returns made as regularly as the Indian trade of doing business will admit, and sign all the provision returns yourself; these will serve as vouchers with the agent for the Department of War. The issues will be in the usual course. Let an Indian's ration be meat and meal, or corn; in particular cases you may add whiskey.

If you require any aid from the escort you shall have it, and if any additional aid is necessary apply to the officer commanding at this post, who is requested to furnish it.

I am Sir, your obedient servant,

B. H.,
P. T. A. I. South of Ohio.

MR. SILAS DINSMOOR,
T. A. for the Cherokee Nation.

Chohaddookoh or The Bark, nephew of the Tarrapin, of Etowwah, has my mare in possession, stolen from me at Coweta. He gave the thief for the mare, one gun valued 50 lbs. of leather, goods for the like value, 150 lbs. of skins.

Tellico, 15th of April, 1797.

I request you to pay to Chohaddookoh (The Bark) 15 dollars, upon his delivering of a sorrel mare, stolen from me, belonging to the Creek Department, and you will oblidge,
Your obedient servant,

15 dollars.   B. H.,
                                    P. T. A. for I. Affairs South of Ohio.

MR. JAMES BYERS,
Factor for the U. States.

Tellico, 16th of April, 1797.

Sir:

When we conversed with you on the objects of our mission, we told you that the Indians invited to convene here were under some apprehension for their safety in visiting us, and that there were some important objects to negotiate and adjust for the mutual interest of the Indians and of the United States; that to remove those apprehensions it would be advisable to concentrate as much of the force intrusted to your command as could, without injury to the service, be conveniently brought together; we recommended to you to order this force to be ready to march at a short notice, and we would advise you of the time and place we deemed proper for the object contemplated by us, and you promised us your co-operation.

We now Sir, inform you we believe it would be advisable to order the detachment to meet at this place. The Indians are soon expected to arrive, and this force will answer the double purpose of removing all causes of alarm on their part, as well as on the part of the citizens, whom the Governor seems to entertain an opinion, are much alarmed.

From this force we require you to furnish us as Commissioners for ascertaining and marking the boundary line between the Indian nations and the United States, an escort to consist of 30 privates with two commissioned officers, two serjeants, and two corporals, with the necessary camp equipage and packhorses; our plan may require a division of the escort, in which case we wish a commissioned officer with each division, if you can furnish that number; the officers to have orders to proceed with and under the orders of the Commissioners in the execution of the duties enjoined upon them, and to return the nearest rout to your command, when they may receive such orders from the Commissioners or either of them.

We are with due regard,

Your obedient servants,

BENJAMIN HAWKINS,
A. PICKINS.

RICHARD SPARKS,
Captain 3rd Regiment and Commander the forces of the United S. in Tennessee.

Tellico, 16 of April, 1797.

Sir:

Being desirous that you should possess all the information which comes to us interesting to the public while I am in this quarter, I have sent my young man up to you with this budget, and shall continue to do so as occasion offers. From the copy of the enclosed order and some other information we have received, I am of opinion that Captain Sparks has behaved himself as is unbecoming an officer and a gentleman; as he has remained in Knoxville you have probably learned more than I have; you will be able to judge whether you think the executive can safely trust the important command of this frontier to such a character. I have been informed that in your presence he said he did not care a dam for his commission.

I have directed Mr. Dinsmoor to have returns of the Indians made, and to sign the provision returns himself. The Indians are invited here in conformity with orders received from the Secretary of War; the invitation extended to a few only of the principal chiefs, who signed the treaty at Holston. The necessary measures have been taken to prevent a crowd. The rations will be of meat and meal only, or corn, except in some instances an addition of whiskey. The amount of the orders will be reported to you by Mr. Dinsmoor.

COLONEL DAVID HENLEY.

Art. 20. Whatever commissioned officer shall be convicted before a general courtmartial of behaving in a scandalous and infamous manner, such as is unbecoming an officer and a gentleman, shall be dismissed the service.

18 April, latitude of Tellico Blockhouse, taken by Mr. Dinsmoor:
35° 15'.
35° 17' the 19, the instrument changed end for end.
35° 15' the 20.

Tellico, 19th of April.

Captain John Garden, of Davidson, in Tennessee, informs that about 8 or 9 years past, a negro fellow, 5 feet 10 inches, bow legs, bushy hair, Sam, the property of Captain James Bassley, his neighbour, was taken by some Indians, supposed Creeks, within three or four miles of Nashville; he was driving a wagon at the time he was taken, and they cut out and took the horses with him. In the spring 90 or 91, he was in the possession of one of the Sullivan's, then living at New York.

Tellico, 19th of April, 1797.

Sir:

I received your favor of October 24 last, on my arrival the last of February at Fort Fidins on the Oconee. My rout through the Cherokees and Creeks had detached me from all intercourse with my friends from October to that date. On the 8 of March I wrote to the parents of the two boys, Mr. Bailey and Mrs. Durant; my letter contained a long extract from yours and one from the Secretary of War on the same subject. I subjoined: "You see in these two extracts that you are to give advise respecting the future fate of your son, I hope you will leave it entirely with the Secretary of War, the Secretary of State and the Quakers, to do what they may deem advisable, for they cannot be in better hands. I wish you would read your letter to Mrs. Durant and send me your & her determination." On the last of December, while I was on the Tallapoosa, I visited the parents of your boys, for so I call them, and told them of my having introduced their children to some members of your society, that it was uncertain when I left Philadelphia what would be the orders of the Secretary of War relative to them. Mrs. Durant replied she hoped her's would not be suffered to return till they were men, and she did not wish to see them short of eight years. I have no doubt but Mr. & Mrs. Bailey will readily and thankfully accept of the offer of your benevolent society. I have again addressed them both, but engaged as I now am in ascertaining and marking the boundary lines between the Indian nations and the United States, it is probable I shall not obtain an answer until I return to the frontiers of Georgia, altho' I keep up an intercourse with all the tribes.

I wish you would act on the expectation of a ready assent of the parents, I have no doubt but it has been given, or will be as soon as I can see them. Accept of sincerest wishes for your present and future happiness, and believe me to be,

Your friend & obedient servant,

BENJAMIN HAWKINS.

MR. DRINKER.

Tellico Blockhouse, Tennessee, 19th of April, 1797.

My worthy friend:

Received your favor of the 21st of October on my arrival at Fort Fidins the last of February. I will have your message or talk carefully and faithfully translated and will myself deliver it to the Creeks at their annual meeting, which will be in June or July. I had an opportunity on the day I received it to inform several influential chiefs of the benevolent views of your society, and that I should make the communication here promised, and present to them the articles sent as a testimony of your good will towards them.

I had been all the winter visiting the towns, hearing complaints, obtaining information, and removing difficulties in the way of the plan contemplated in my mission, and on my arrival on Oconee, fatigued, both in mind and body, I had the pleasure to receive your letter, talk and list of presents. The reflections which arose in my mind at the moment were such as the communication seemed calculated to inspire. Had you known my thoughts and endeavors to be useful since I left you, you could not better express your approbation of them. I will deserve success, be the issue what it may, and until I can convene my red charges, to impress upon them what you have authorised me to do, that they must speak for themselves, suffer me, as their agent, to return you thanks in the name of the whole Creek nation for your co-operation with the agents in carrying the benevolent views of the government into effect.

I shall send you a copy of the translation so pointed as that a Creek shall understand you if you were to read it to him yourselves. I have devoted all the leisure I had to learning their language, and not without success; I have already translated, with help, some talks and I mean in this way in future to address them.

Accept of my sincere wishes, and that of every member of your benevolent society, for your present and future happiness, and believe me to be your friend and obedient servant.

                                                                   B. H.

JOHN PARISH.
HENRY DRINKER.
THOMAS WISTAR.

Extract from my letter to Mr. Price, 9th March.

"The annuity and the present from the Quakers you will keep until I can consult the nation and draw on you in conformity with such arrangements as I may make with them."

Tellico, 22 April, 1797.

I have consulted with General Pickins on the relief sought for by Messrs. Crozier and McCarry; we are of opinion the contract covers the supplies for two of the districts only. We have recommended to the contractors to supply for the whole rout, and we proposed that the public should find the packhorses, debit them for two-thirds, and hold them accountable for a like portion of the cost. As it is uncertain whether the distance for supplies on the line bordering on the district of Mero is more or less than one-third, we have further proposed that this point should be left to us, and we would certify what we deemed to be reasonable. Mr. Crozier has, after hearing our observations on this subject, said he would act in conformity therewith, and upon the terms proposed.

To remove all ambiguity, we mean by the whole rout: The line to be run from Clinch to the South Carolina Indian boundary on the North Carolina line, and the line round from Clinch, as expressed in the treaties between the United States and the

Cherokee and Chickasaw nations of Indians. As the most of this line will be in the neighbourhood of the settlements, we have given as our opinion, that supplies can be had from them, and there will be no necessity to provide for the transportation of more than eight day's provisions at one time. If you approve of this opinion of ours, you can make an agreement to correspond with it.

I have the honor to be, with much and sincere regard, Sir,
Your obedient servant,

B. H.

COLONEL DAVID HENLEY.

Tellico, 16 April, 1797.

Sir:

Mr. Cowan handed us last evening your excellency's favour of the 13th, and we loose no time in reply. You have received on the 6th of this month, from Mr. Hawkins, principal agent for Indian affairs South of the Ohio, information that "the Indians are more inclined to peace and more friendly to the citizens, their neighbours, than they have ever been known to be, that the arrangements in train of execution will increase the friendly disposition of the Indians and induce them to do justice to our fellow citizens," "and that he relys with confidence on the agents in his department."

We think Sir, that this communication, and knowledge that the agents in the Indian department were here, ought to have been sufficient to remove all cause of alarm from the citizens of this state. The agents possess and can give the only information to be relied on; they are entitled to the confidence of your excellency, and we hope that on reflection you will see the impropriety of suspecting them to be capable of withholding any information from you whereby our fellow citizens can be in the least degree injured. The invitation sent to a few Indians to convene here was from the proper authority and for objects interesting to the U. S.

The assurance you give of the disposition of the executive to promote and cultivate peace and good understanding with the neighbouring tribes is pleasing to us and is what we had a right to expect; it would be in unison with the agents in the southern department, and there is no doubt, if our actions correspond with this avowed disposition, but that we shall have peace and a good understanding between our fellow citizens and the Indians.

We are appointed, together with James Winchester, Esq., "Commissioners to ascertain and mark the boundary lines agreeably to treaties between the Indian nations and the United States," and we are now here on that business; we in due time took measures to apprize General Winchester of our intention of being here the first of April; he is not arrived. We shall take care that in the execution of this trust our fidelity shall correspond with the confidence reposed in us by the appointment.

We have the honor to be,
            Your Excellency's obedient servants,

                                        B. H., A. P.
His Excellency,
      JOHN SEVIER,
            Governor of Tennessee.

                                  Tellico, 24 April, 1797.

I recollect that the Commissioners appointed to treat with the southern Indians at Hopewell in the winter 1785-6, did appoint John Pitchlynn interpreter to the Choctaws, that the appointment originated in part in a request made by the Choctaws, after the treaty was concluded, for an interpreter among them on whom they might rely, and from a knowledge of the character of Pitchlynn, who had testimonials of his being an honest sober man, attached to the U. States, and well acquainted with the Choctaw tongue. I do not believe that there was any sallary mentioned in the appointment; the sum charged by him appears not unreasonable.

                                        B. H.,
                              P. T. A. I. A. South of Ohio.
THE HON. JAMES McHENRY,
      Secretary of War.

                                  Tellico, 24th April, 1797.

We wrote to you on the 11th inst.; the information there given that the Indians had arrived was premature; they arrived only this day, and we are in the morning to meet them. Almost every town in the nation has sent 1, 2, or 3. Wats is here. Just after we wrote you we had very unexpectedly a misunderstanding with the officer commanding in this quarter; we did expect for a while we should be under the necessity to send to you on the subject. He has since visited us, had an explanation with us, and promised his co-operation, and appears to be disposed to fulfill the duties of his station as we have promised to overlook the past, and agreed with him that his statement we would respect, we deem it unnecessary to go into detail. As soon as we have had an explanation with the Indians we shall proceed; we have obtained an escort of 30 infantry. We have had conveyed to us from several persons, information of a determination expressed by lawless persons, of an intention not to insult the Commissioners of the U. States, but to attack the Indians who may accompany us; we shall be prepared against such an attempt.

We have just had a letter from General Winchester, of the 4; we do not expect him here. On reviewing our instructions, you will judge of the propriety of an alteration, so as to give authority to 2 of us, if from any accident we cannot all attend. It has been intimated to us that General Winchester deems the whole number indispensable, and that on this ground it has been in the contemplation of some persons to frustrate the intentions of the government. We have no expectations of visiting Duck River, nor has the General, who knows well that the line is to be continued on the ridge between the waters of Cumberland and Tennessee. Our correspondence with the Governor explains itself.

The officer intrusted with the command on this frontier should be a prudent, cautious, firm character.

We have the honour to be, with much and sincere regard, Sir,
Your obedient servants.

JAMES McHENRY,
Secretary of War.

Tellico, 24 April, 1797.

Under the expectation that I should be some time in this quarter, I made the necessary arrangements for all the assistants in the Creek department while I was at Fort Fidins and left instructions upon every important point with the principal assistant, Mr. Barnard, and I keep up with them a correspondence. I gave drafts on Mr. Price for the first quarter sallary dew the assistants; if you approve of my continuing to do so, or that I should do it in any other way, you will be pleased to direct.

I find the four nations a little alarmed, particularly the Chickasaws and Choctaws; at the late Georgia sales of land, some persons have industriously explained the whole of that project to them, and particularly the imprudent step of Zachariah Cox to attempt to settle a station or post on the Muscle Shoals; I am taking the necessary measures to quiet the minds of the Indians on this head, but the impression is made that our fellow citizens are eagerly grasping after their lands, and mean if they can, at some short period, to possess them. If encroachments cannot soon be stoped, and we should get involved in any difficulties with a European power who has or can obtain a footing in our neighbourhood, we shall have an Indian war.* Mr. Cox visited me with Colonel Henley the 23; he explained to me his object, applied to me for a licence to trade with the Chickasaws, and declared that he would not take any step but in concert with the agents of the government in this quarter. I spoke freely to him, on the impression his arrangements had made on the Indians, from the manner they had been communicated to them, and the embarrassment thrown on the Indian department on that account; he had been apprised of it, and was determined he said, to do it away, as much as lay in his power, every thing that should be disagreeable to the government. I requested him to write freely to me and to detail, as he had done in conversation, his plan, and I would give him an answer; he has promised this in 2 or 3 days, and in the meantime I have requested Colonel Henley not to grant a licence to any man, to trade with the Chickasaws, until we can have a further consultation on this subject. I send you a certificate of the appointment of John Pitchlynn interpreter to the Choctaws; he is well attached to the United States, and I am pleased at your having continued his appointment. The other objects in yours of 2 February I shall attend to, and I am of opinion that the military force destined for this frontier should be within the Indian line, and I expect the Indians will leave to us the choice of such sites as may be occupied to advantage.

Tellico, 25 April, 1797.

Gentlemen:

I received your favour of yesterday; I do not understand what you mean by this application, as from the tenor of the last paragraph it is quite uncertain now whether you will contract or not to supply the escort. We must require of you at all events

---

* The Indians readily distinguish between intruders on their rights and the government, and express on all occasions unbounded confidence in the justice of the latter, and in the measures in train of execution to fulfill our stipulations with them. If we fail in this that confidence falls.

to be ready to supply within the two districts covered by your contract; we shall expect to move from this by the 27, in the evening. You have misunderstood us altogether if you believe that we consented that the public should furnish horses to induce you to comply with your contract in the two districts which were covered. You may see the letter we sent to Colonel Henley, and which I showed to Mr. Crozier before I sealed it. I did not expect it necessary that any further application should be made to me other than what is contemplated in that letter.

I am with due regard, gentlemen,

Your obedient servant,

BENJAMIN HAWKINS.
MESSRS. CROZIER & McCARRY.

---

30 of April, 1797.

I gave a permit to David Jolly, of Ohio County, Virginia, to go into the Cherokee nation for his brother, supposed to be there, and a prisoner; he has leave to buy a horse if he should want one for his brother.

He succeeded and obtained his brother from the Little Turkey's town.

Tellico, 30th April, 1797.

Being, with General Pickins, authorized by special agreement entered into with the Cherokees at Tuskeegee, the 28 January, to chuse the proper sites and to fix the posts, in conformity with instructions to me of the 2 February to obtain this permission, if I should be of the opinion that a distribution of the military force destined for Tennessee within the Indian line would give the Indians more effectual protection than if stationed on its exterior, & being of the opinion aforesaid, and having agreed that I would provide that the establishment should be beneficial to a friendly intercourse between the red & white people, and when useful, manufactures shall be carried on;

I do hereby permit Nicholas Byers, a hatter, to remain at the trading post and carry on his trade, until I make the choice contemplated as aforesaid, and he shall then be permited to reside at one of the posts, to carry on his trade, conditioned on his part

to conform to such regulations as may be made, in execution of
the trust vested in me, and that he takes one Indian lad as an
apprentice, and that he uses his best endeavours to learn him
to make hats. The privilege of geting timber for the necessary
buildings is annexed hereto.

Given under my hand at Tellico, the 30th of April, 1797.

Knoxville, 4th of May, 1797.

Mr. Blun overtook us with your favour of the 25th April
in the woods between Little River & Tennessee, moving on to
ascertain some points necessary to be known in that quarter; I
could not then reply, but I promised him to be here last evening
& to give you an answer.

I had, before I saw you, received information from the 4
nations that they were alarmed by the information they had
received, particularly the Cherokees & Choctaws, of an attempt
soon to be carried into opporation to dispossess them of their
lands; I can only conjecture who give them information of the
Georgia sales, & the purchases, but I find that the narative has
been pretty accurately given, & the impression is made that some
of my fellow citizens are eagerly grasping after their lands, &
mean, if they can, at some short period to possess them. Since
I saw you the Cherokees have, in full council of representatives
from every town in the nation, expressed their apprehension on
this subject; I give you an extract from their address to the
President.

"Father:

We must mention to our father, the President, what we have
heard of Zachariah Cox and his followers; they are about to
settle the bend of Tennessee; we & the other nations are alarmed
at our situation, & apprehension that such people will some how
or other come at our lands, or lands of our neighbours." I may
add sir, that among all the tribes you are named as the precursor
of those who are represented as grasping after their lands, that
you are to make the first attempt to get possession & the rest are
to follow, with the train of evils so alarming to the Indians.

I am taking measures to quiet the minds of the Indians, to
remove improper impressions, & to free the department from
embarrassments which constantly result from such impressions.

At this period particularly, for reasons not necessary to detail,
it is unquestionably of the utmost importance that we should,
by every means in our power, prevent that unbounded confidence

which the Indians have in the justice of the government from being in the least degree impared.

I have made this statement to you, as an appeal to your own judgement, whether it would not be advisable for you to postpone for the present any further attempts to carry your views into opporation; we can in a short time receive information from the government which will serve as a guide to both of us.

MR. ZACHARIAH COX.

Knoxville, 4 of May, 1797.

Sir:

The enclosed are copies of the conference and other proceedings with the Indians at Tellico, the originals I leave in the care of Colonel Henley. There were representatives from every town in the nation, and the whole procedure was conducted conformable with their wishes; it explains itself. I have it in contemplation, as soon as we have fixed on the proper sites for military posts, to lay out a small town at each, and to establish there useful manufactures. I have had application made to me by some manufacturers to permit them to reside at the posts and carry on their trades, and one, a hatter, I have permited, conditioned on his part, to conform to such regulations as may be made in execution of the trust vested in me, and that he takes one Indian lad, as an apprentice, and that he uses his endeavours to teach him to make hats. The Indians are pleased at the idea of having tradesmen in their neighbourhood, and they request me not to suffer him to make corn on their lands. You would oblidge me by giving me your ideas of such an establishment, detailed so as to serve as the basis of it, and directing in the whole procedure; I want all the light I can get, and particularly your directions. I enclose you copies of letters between Mr. Cox and me, as expected from my communication of the 24 ult. I consulted with Colonel Henley and we are of opinion that a reference to you for information to serve as a guide to the parties concerned was the most delicate mode of procedure I could devise in an affair which may in its consequences involve the government in serious difficulties. If we should be fortunate enough to escape from being involved in difficulties with the European powers, there cannot much, if any, injury arise to the government in permiting Mr. Cox to trade. The agents will, I hope, at all times do their duty. You have his and my statement, and you must decide.

I left Tellico the 29 of April, and moved up the Holston. The surveys between that and Clinch are by this time completed so as to enable us to fix the point of departure from thence. I left General Pickins with the escort on the way to Cumberland. I arrived here last evening for the purpose of consulting with Colonel Henley, and to write to you. I shall leave this early in the morning and follow the General; we fix points as we go, and shall return with the line; this mode of procedure we have now judged to be indispensable.

The Cherokees are giving proofs of their approximation to the customs of well regulated societies; they did, in full council, in my presence, pronounce, after solemn deliberation, as law, that any person who should kill another accidently should not suffer for it, but be acquited; that to constitute it a crime, there should be malice and an intention to kill.

They at the same time gave up, of their own motion, the names of the great rogues in the nation, as well as those in their neighbourhood, and appointed some warriors expressly to assist the chiefs in preventing horse stealing, and in carrying their stipulations with us into effect. To him who exerts himself the most, to prevent horse stealing, I have rendered a premium annually, of a rifle gun, with the name of the person engraved thereon, and a certificate that he is an honest man.

I wish you would send me some testimonials of the discription you sent of those given to the Choctaws; I was of opinion twelve years past that the measure was a good one and recommended it highly to congress, and did not know till I came among the Indians that it had ever been approved. I shall want them at a meeting of the Creeks this summer.

I have thought it would be advisable to have a few Indians in the pay of the United States and under the direction of the agents, to enable them to help the chiefs to fulfill their engagements with us; without some such help, it will be difficult to put an effectual stop to their predatory parties. I would, as this is intended as an experiment, have the number limited to four for each nation of the Cherokees and Creeks, one to have the pay and cloathing of a serjeant, the others that of soldiers; the cloathing to be suited to the Indian mode of dress. If you should concur in opinion with me, I wish for your directions.

I have the honour to be, with much esteem & regard, Sir,

Your obedient servant.

The Honourable
    JAMES McHENRY,
        Secretary of War.

Tellico Blockhouse, 1st July, 1797.

Peter Becker and Godfried Friderici, natives of Germany, at present inhabitants of Pennsylvania, weavers by trade, are by these presents permited to visit the Cherokees and to reside among them. It is expected of them to set examples to their neighbours by their morals and industry, and that they will at all times conform to the regulations that are or shall be made "for the regulation of trade and intercourse with the Indian tribes, and to preserve peace on the frontiers." If they should want to purchase two or three cows, to furnish themselves milk, they are permited to do so.

B. H.,
P. T. A. for I. A. S. of Ohio.

21st May, 1797.

William Lamons lives on Mill Creek, 12 miles from Nashville; he married Mrs. Mayfield; her son George Mayfield is with John O'Kelly on the Coosa, and has been for 7 or 8 years, and was taken prisoner when his father was killed. I rote a letter of this date to Mrs. Lamons by her husband; on better information, he lives with Procter, at Pocuntallehope.

From Tuckabatchee going up Tallapoosa W.

Miles.
6, Scugohatche, a creek to the E.
6, Kialijee, creek to the W.
6, Wotohatche, creek on E.
4, Lusetehatche, E.
1, Eufaulau, old town, W.
4, Epesauge, E.
2, Ocfuskee, old town, W.
2, Chattucsocau, E.
2, Elcauhatche, W.
6, Hillaubeehatchee, W.
5, Immookfau, W.
3, Nuoqaucou, E.
5, Tuckabatchee Tallenihosse, W.
Going up Longohatche 8 miles, the town.
Still higher, Luchaupogau, 8.
Chattucsocau Town, 6, top the creek of that name.
Just above Immookfau the river bends round E., then west, and makes nearly an island below Theoqoucau.
Immookfau, a town on the creek, 1½ miles from Nuoqaucou.

Journal of the Proceedings of the Commissioners Appointed to Ascertain and Mark the Boundary Lines Agreeably to Treaties Between the Indian Nations and the United States.

Fort Fidins, on Oconee, 28 February, 1797.

Colonel Gaither handed me a packet which he received by express from Louisville, containing dispatches from the Secretary of War of the 2nd inst. As far as related to this object there was inclosed a commission and instructions to Benjamin Hawkins, General Pickins and General Winchester to establish and mark the lines, and a letter directing to Benjamin Hawkins on some interesting points connected with that business.

March 1st.

I this day wrote to the Secretary, from which this is an extract: "I have judged proper to postpone the runing of the Creek line till we run the Cherokee line; that presses and this does not. Intrusions there are the most likely to be apprehended, and to such an extent as to give much embarrassment to the government. I shall execute this trust strictly in conformity with the wishes of the government and I hope I shall be able to remove, in concert with my colleagues, any difficulty that may occur with the Indians. I have, for another reason, judged proper to postpone the Creek line. The people who have stock cannot support them, if they are compelled to drive them back before there is grass in the woods, and this indulgence can be given them without offence until the line is closed. It will be a measure too, so conciliatory in its operation as that which it produces, the good we aim at, takes off the odium that would attach itself to a rigid execution of our trust."

"I shall send a messenger with the necessary orders to the Cherokees and information to General Pickins, and I shall follow him on the 10th."

March 7th.

Sir:

The President, with the advise and consent of the Senate, has appointed Benjamin Hawkins, Andrew Pickins, and James Winchester Commissioners to ascertain and mark the boundary lines agreeably to treaties between the Indian nations and the United States, and we are directed to apply to you to furnish us with an escort of dragoons. I shall set out from this on the 10th towards the frontiers, and request you to furnish an escort of one Serjeant, one Corporal and twelve dragoons, one horseman's tent with a fly, three common tents, three pack horses, three fascine hatchets and the necessary camp kettles. The horses must be all shod and the Serjeant must be directed to receipt for these articles and be held accountable under the directions of the Commissioners. I believe I shall take the escort over the Ocunna Mountain to Tellico Blockhouse. I give this information for your direction or advise as to furnishing them with forage and provisions.

With great regard, I am, Sir,

Your obedient servant,

BENJAMIN HAWKINS.

HENRY GAITHER,
Lt. Col. Commandant.

The Colonel replyed to me: "I have not received any orders from the Secretary of War on the subject of your letter, but I have seen his letter to you, which is quite sufficient for me. I will do every thing I can to promote the execution of the plans of the government."

Fort Fidins, 1st March, 1797.

Dear General:

I arrived here on the 25th ult., and on the last of that month received dispatches from the War Office of the 2nd, informing me that we are appointed, with James Winchester, Commissioners to ascertain and mark the boundary lines agreeably to treaties between the Indian nations and the United States. As no time should be lost in establishing the Cherokee line, as every day adds to the number of intruders on their land; I have, for that and other reasons which I shall detail to you when I meet you, determined to postpone the intention we expressed of runing the Creek boundary in this month. I have sent Richard Williams to inform you that I shall set out for Tellico Blockhouse on the 10th of this month, and intend, if you approve of it, to go over the Ocunna Mountain through the Cherokees, as being the nearest rout. I have applied and obtained an escort of dragoons and I shall bring one horseman tent for our use. I shall call on you.

The inclosed letter I must request you to forward to **Mr.**
Dinsmoor by one of the Cherokees in your neighbourhood, and to
have one of the most intelligent of them in readiness to accompany us.

ANDREW PICKINS.

The inclosed are two letters, the first to Mr. Dinsmoor, **the**
2nd to General Winchester.

Sir:

The Commissioners appointed to ascertain and mark the
boundary lines agreeably to treaties between the Indian nations
and the United States will meet at Tellico Blockhouse the first
of April and will proceed thence to ascertain and mark the boundary between the Cherokees and the United States. You will be
pleased to make this communication to the Cherokees, that the
persons named by them may attend on their part. It is also
deemed expedient to convene some of the Indians who were
present at and agreed to the treaty of Holston, as well as the
interpreter, if to be found. You will take the necessary steps on
this head. General Pickins will accompany me and we shall have
an escort of dragoons, and I intend to take the direct rout from
Ocunna Station through your agency. You will inform the Indians of this and direct one of your interpreters to meet us, and
you will join us yourself as soon as you can do so conveniently.

SILAS DINSMOOR,
Temporary Indian Agent in the Cherokee Nation.

Fort Fidins, on Oconee, 7th March, 1797.
Sir:

Being informed by the Secretary of War that you are appointed a Commissioner, with General Pickins and me, to ascertain and mark the boundary line between the Indian nations **and**
the United States, I take the earliest opportunity to apprize **you,**
that we purpose meeting at Tellico Blockhouse on the first **of**

April, and to proceed from thence to ascertain and mark the Cherokee boundary first. I have given the necessary directions to Mr. Dinsmoor on the part of the Indians.

I am with due regard, Sir,

Your obedient servant.

JAMES WINCHESTER, ESQ.

9th March.

Closed the necessary arrangements for all the assistants in the Creek Department, and left instructions upon every important point with the principal assistant, Mr. Barnard.

Colonel Gaither informed me that the escort were ready, that they were badly cloathed and he wished I would get them some shirts wherever linen could be had, and such other things as I saw they wanted and could not do without; that they could take five days' provision with them, and unless I would take a man for the purpose, he advised that I would let the Serjeant obtain the necessary forage and provisions on the road, make the returns to me, and pay them myself; that when I arrived at the station on the frontiers of Tennessee the contractors would there supply, or the Commissioners make the proper arrangements. He informed that there were four dragoons at Knoxville, left by Captain Webbs, and five horses, which he wished the Commissioners to annex to the escort.

11th March.

I set out for the Ocunna Station; Colonel Gaither accompanied me for some distance and gave these orders for the serjeant:

Fort Fidins, March 11th, 1797.

Serjeant Greer will take command of one Coporal and twelve privates from the cavalry already furnished, with three pack horses and saddles, one horseman's tent and fly, three common tents, three camp kettles and three fascine hatchets, and proceed with them under the orders of Colonel Benjamin Hawkins, Commissioner of the United States for runing and marking the lines between the United States and the Creek and Cherokee Indians and Chickasaws.

He will constantly obey all orders from the Commissioners and return the nearest rout to this place whenever he may receive such orders from Colonel Hawkins, General Pickins, or General Winchester.

HENRY GAITHER,
Lt. Col. Commandant.

---

13 March.

Arrived at Washington and purchased of T. Maquen & Le Prostre some linen for the escort and necessaries for the Commissioners.

I was in the course of the evening informed of the preparations made and making by Mr. Zachariah Cox for taking possession of the best of Tennessee, and making an establishment there. One of the informants said he believed Mr. Cox intended to go on to Knoxville soon; that some goods and arms had been sent there, but that he would take no steps after his arrival there without the concurrence of the agents of government.

16 March.

I arrived this day at Hopewell, the seat of General Pickins; he was at home, had received and sent forward to Mr. Dinsmoor the letters for him and General Winchester. He informed me he had not received the original dispatches and that the duplicate came to hand just before the arrival of my messenger; that he would be ready to set out with me on the 23.

17 March.

I directed the Serjeant to get some person to make the shirts for the men and have their cloathes and boots or shoes mended.

Hopewell, on Koowee, 19 March, 1797.

Sir:

I set out from Fort Fidins on the 11th and arrived here on the 16th of this month. I applied to Colonel Gaither for an escort; he had not received any orders from you on that head, but said your letter to me was quite sufficient. I asked only for a Serjeant, Corporal and twelve dragoons, and have them with me. They are bare of cloathing and I have, at the request of Colonel Gaither, purchased some linen for them, and one shirt for each will be made in this neighbourhood, and I shall furnish them with such other things as are indispensable and attainable on the rout.

General Pickins will be ready on the 23 and we shall set out on that day, go over the Ocunna Mountain through the Cherokees to Tellico Blockhouse. I have made all the necessary arrangements in conformity with the intimations from you in yours of the second of February. I have, with the concurrence of the General, appointed two discrete honest men of this frontier, acquainted with surveying, to accompany us as surveyors. We give them two dollars each per day and feed them. They find their own horses and instruments.

Some of the Cherokees, appraised of my intention of being here, have visited me; they will some of them accompany us through their nation.

I saw after I wrote my last letter to you by Doctor Gillispie, many of the citizens who live contiguous to Oconee, some of whom I was personally acquainted with. I saw also, as I traveled through the State of Georgia, some of those who had embarked in the project of Zachariah Cox for settling the best of Tennessee.

I conversed freely and in a friendly manner with them and explained the law to them and I hope that by a temperate, prudent and firm line of conduct in the officers of the government in this quarter we shall be able to carry the laws into effect.

General Pickins, from some defect in the post office, has not received the original dispatches to him and only got the duplicate on the 7th inst., before my messenger arrived.

I beg you to mention me respectfully to the President, to assure him of my sincere wishes for his happiness, and to believe me yourself, with sincere regard & esteem, Sir,

Your obedient servant.

The Honourable
JAMES McHENRY,
    Secretary of War.

---

23 March.

Joseph Whitner, one of our surveyors, set out with us; we went on to Timossa, 20 miles, a plantation belonging to the General adjoining the Cherokee boundary. This was an Indian town at the commencement of the late war, inhabited by 20 gun men. There are some fine peach trees which had been planted by the original inhabitants, the remains of the square and some locusts. The farm is pleasantly situated on Timossa Creek and in the fork of that and the main branch of Little River.

24.

We set out and called at the Ocunna Station; here we met, by appointment, our other surveyor, John Clark Kilpatrick. Lt.

Mossley, who commands at the station, was ready to accompany us with two of his mounted militia. We proceeded on one and one half miles to the boundary, thence two and one-quarter of a mile to Chauga village; here is a beautiful situation for a military post. In the fork of the two main branches of Chauga there is a high nole capable easily of being made defensible. The lands on the creeks rich, and those bordering thereon fine for wheat; the whole exhibiting all that is desired to designate this as a healthy position and neighbourhood. It is convenient for a trading establishment; 266 miles from Charlestown. The following is the distance between, and position of the water courses in going from the boundary to this site, estimating the same in minutes and three miles to the hour: Begining at the boundary, 2 minutes cross a creek runing to the left, 4 feet wide; in 5 minutes cross a branch runing to the left, 2 feet wide; 6 minutes cross a branch runing to the left, eighteen inches wide; 26 minutes cross a creek runing to the right, 3 feet over; in 3 minutes cross a creek 15 feet over, runing to the left; and in 4 minutes cross a creek runing to the left, 8 feet over. In the fork of these creeks is the site recommended in this note; the whole growth on this path scrub, black and small Spanish oak, with a few pines.

To continue in like manner the path to Chattuga: In 6 minutes cross a branch runing to the left, one foot wide; 8 minutes cross a creek runing to the left, 8 feet wide; in 7 minutes cross a branch runing to the right, one foot wide; 28 minutes a beautiful meadow one-quarter of a mile to the left of the path, the grass at this season very thick and eight inches high; this meadow was burnt the last of November; in 15 minutes cross a branch to the left, 2 feet wide; in 6 minutes cross a branch runing to the left, 3 feet wide; in 5 minutes cross a branch runing to the left; there is on this side a mountain of a conic form; in 5 minutes cross a branch to the left, and in 9 minutes cross two small branches and over the ridge of Whetstone Mountain; the vale for some distance back exhibits marks of rich land.

From this ridge descend down 9 minutes and cross a creek runing to the right, 3 feet over; following over for some distance below a bed of rock, margined with hemloc and mountain laurel; in 22 minutes Chattuga, 40 yards over, just above the mouth of Warwoman's Creek; the course of the path N. W.

From this river to Tellico see the notes of the Principal Temporary Agent for Indians Affairs South of Ohio.

31st.

We arrived at Tellico Blockhouse and were informed that the letters sent to Mr. Dinsmoor and to General Winchester had been received by Mr. Dinsmoor and the necessary measures taken in conformity therewith.

1st of April.

Mr. Dinsmoor arrived and informed us that he had received our letter for General Winchester and that it had been sent to him express by a trusty Serjeant; that he had sent into the nation immediately on the receipt of the orders to apprize the chiefs of the intention of the Commissioners to be here this day, and had invited the interpreter, Mr. Thomson, and some of the principal chiefs to convene here, who were present at and signed the treaty of Holston.

2.

The gentlemen of the army came here and visited us; they informed us they were waiting our arrival, that the Secretary of War had directed Captain Sparks to consult us on the fixture of the military posts.

3.

Colonel Henley informed us that the express had returned from Cumberland; that Major Blackmore informed him he had received the packet for General Winchester; that the General had not returned from Philadelphia.

The Honourable David Campbell visited us and informed us that he had been appointed on the 22nd September, 1792, a Commissioner, with Daniel Smith and Colonel Landon Carter, to ascertain and mark the boundary line between the Cherokees and people of Tennessee, and that the two last mentioned gentlemen not attending, Governor Blount appointed Charles McClung & John McKee in their stead; that the Commissioners proceeded on and did in part ascertain and establish the boundary and report the same to the Governor; that so far as they had acted he would accompany us and show us, as well as give us, such information as he possessed.

4 April.

We had a long conversation with Captain Richard Sparks, commanding the forces in Tennessee, on the objects of our mission. We told him that the Indians invited to convene here were under some apprehensions for their safety in visiting us, and that there were some important objects to negotiate and adjust for the mutual interest of the Indians and of the United States; that to remove these apprehensions it would be advisable to muster as much of the force intrusted to his command as could, without injury to the service, be conveniently brought together. We recommended to him to order this force to be ready to march at a short notice and we would advise him of the time and place we deemed proper for the object contemplated by us, and he promised us his co-operation.

5 of April.

We received information from some of the principal chiefs that Colonel John Watts was unwell, and that the Indians had received some information tending to raise some apprehensions for their safety in visiting us; measures were ordered to be taken to counteract all fears of this sort.

We received information of a confidential nature as to the informants that General Winchester would not be here; that a postponement of the runing of the line by some means or other was in contemplation by some persons interested in intrusions on Indian rights.

6 of April.

Mr. Dinsmoor communicated to us a letter which he received from General Winchester in these words:

Cragfont, 31st of March, 1797.

Dear Sir:

Yesterday I returned from Philadelphia, and on my arrival received from Major Blackmore your favour of the 23rd instant, which mentions a letter from Colonel Hawkins to me, but I have not received it; Major Blackmore says the express delivered no such letter to him.

General Pickins and Colonel Hawkins, expecting to meet me at Tellico Blockhouse the first of April, must be for the purpose of proceeding to the runing of the Creek line now, as our appointment authorizes and empowers any one or two of the Commissioners to run that line. It is my intention not to be present, especially as I have no acquaintance with the Creek nation, nor no geographical knowledge of that country, but shall hold myself in readiness to attend the runing and establishing of the Cherokee and Chickasaw lines.

I am, with much respect, dear Sir,
Your obedient servant,

J. WINCHESTER.

SILAS DINSMOOR, ESQ.

The contents of this letter and a knowledge of the measures to insure the safe delivery of ours made the following necessary:

———

Tellico Blockhouse, 6 April, 1797.

Sir:

The letter you showed me from General Winchester of the 31st of March makes it necessary that you should trace the letter from me to him of the 7th of that month from Oconee, inclosed in yours of the 23rd and sent by express to him in care of a Serjeant.

The idea of the General that General Pickins and I expected to meet him here the "first of April for the purpose of proceeding to the runing of the Creek line," is pretty extraordinary. He says he has no acquaintance with the Creek nation, nor no geographical knowledge of that country. He appears, by his letter, to have some knowledge of his appointment and probably has seen by his instructions, that the "Cherokees have been informed that the runing of their line would be commenced in April," and he certainly must know that Tellico Blockhouse is on the Tennessee near the Cherokee line, and that we could never be so absurd as to come from the Creek line, two hundred and fifty miles, here, for the purpose merely of meeting him to accompany us back again.

I am, with sincere regard and esteem,
Your obedient servant,

B. H.

SILAS DINSMOOR,
T. I. Agent in the Cherokee Nation.

———

The Commissioners being informed that there was a mathematical instrument maker at Knoxville, requested Mr. Dinsmoor, as he would go there for the object expressed in the preceding letter, to superintend the construction of an instrument for taking the latitude and bring it down with him.

7th.

We determined to visit the ground between Little River and Tennessee to see if we could ascertain the dividing ridge between the waters of the first and the latter, and we requested Mr. Dinsmoor to inform Colonel Henley and Captain Sparks of the rout we had in contemplation.

A deputation of 13 Cherokees visited us and the speaker, the little woman holder of Hewossa, welcomed us on our arrival and said "he and all the Cherokees rejoiced at the expectation of having their line closed; that the affair would meet with some difficulty, but he hoped the men chosen by the President would hear both sides and do justice; that there was much talk in the nation about the line, and he supposed as much among the whites; that when the line was fixed on and marked by the persons who were chosen, all this talk would subside and the parties acquiesce."

We replyed we should hear the red and white people and wished that they might agree among themselves, but if they could not, we should do justice and we expected our red and white brethren would give up little points of difference and concur in our decision; that as it would be some days before their representation would be here, we should move on and encamp on the dividing ridge between the two rivers and obtain such information of the whites as we could relative to their opinion of the line, and when the Indian representation arrived we should know something of the ground we were on and would the better understand them.

The speaker replied: "Go see your people, hear what they have to say, and obtain all the information you can, but do not give them any opinion at all till you hear us; The Bark, one of the men appointed by us, is here, you have taken him by the hand, he will be ready when the others arrive."

We received information that the line run between the Indians and the white inhabitants by the Commissioners, mentioned on the 3 inst. by Mr. Campbell, was by order, for the express purpose of ascertaining a line of accommodation for the white settlers who were then over the treaty line.

We set out from Tellico to find and encamp on the ridge between the two rivers. We took the road to Knoxville, in one hour we passed five small settlements on the road, and two large limestone springs; took the road to the left for Squire Wallace's, and in fifteen minutes arrive at the .creek near his house and encamp. Mr. Campbell accompanyed us, and here we were visited by Captain Henley and some of his neighbours who expressed some anxiety at their situation. We told them that we could inform them of a certainty that the government were determined to fulfill their engagements and to carry their treaties with the Indians into effect.

8 of April.

This day being rainy we moved our encampment near the road to Knoxville in the neighbourhood of Captain Henry. We spend the day with Mr. Wallace and several of his neighbours, who appear to show much anxiety on the ascertaining of the

Indian boundary. We requested them to give us such information as they could, to enable us to be prepared on the hearing of the Indians to do justice between the parties. Colonel David Craig replied those present possessed and could give the best information, and if we would meet them to-morrow at his house, or Mr. Bartlet McGee's, they would be there and ready to accompany us for that purpose. We accepted the offer and promised to breakfast with Mr. McGee.

9 of April.

We set out and arrived at Mr. McGee's; here we found the gentlemen convened and we requested and obtained information on these points:

Tellico Blockhouse, 12 miles, W. S. W.

Tennessee, direct, 8 miles, S. by W.

Little River, 15 miles, N. by E.

Experiment Line, 4 miles, S. by W.

Colonel Craig's, 1¼ miles, N. E.

Head of Nine Mile Creek, 1½ miles, N. E.

Head of Baker's Creek, 2½ miles, N.

Nine Mile Creek Joins the Tennessee at Tellico and Baker's Creek joins three miles below. Pistol Creek has two branches, one begins opposite the source of Nine Mile; the west fork opposite Baker's. Its junction with Little River is five miles below the confluence of that with Holston. Crooked Creek has its source three miles below the mountain, and its junction with Little River five miles above Pistol Creek. The ridge between the sources of these four creeks is that which divides the waters runing into Little River from those runing into Tennessee; this they will demonstrate by our next point at Colonel Craig's.

The next point we go to is to the ridge just above the plantation of Colonel Craig's, N. E. 1¼ miles; this, the Colonel informed us, was the ridge mentioned at Mr. McGee's. The point where we were fixed was 20 miles south of Knoxville. There is a scope of mountain from N. E. round eastwardly to S. W.; Little River breaks through this chain in a direction N. 88 E.; Tennessee is S. 10 W. The experiment line crosses the mountain S. 10 E. at Chilhowe Path; the Uriccahee Mountain over this chain of Chilhowe Mountains S. 41 E. This mountain is better known E. of this by the Black or Smokey Mountain; in the direction of this Smokey Mountain there is six miles of flat lands to the Chilhowe Mountain. This flat is thickly settled and here are the sources of the north fork of Nine Mile Creek.

Mr. Patrick Salvedge, who is well informed, fixes the course to the source of Little Pigeon S. 84 E.; the source of Pistol Creek

S. 83 E.; the course from this to Captain Henry's S. 59 W. to the experiment line, 5½ miles; the head of Baker's Creek N. 15 W.

We set out for the point on the ridge where the experiment line for fixing the Courthouse of Blount County passes the ridge between Pistol Creek and Baker's Creek due E. from a point on Tennessee 13½ miles, and this point on the Tennessee is one and half miles south from a point from whence a line west joins the confluence of the Holston and Tennessee. They run the line with much exactness. This point of which we speak on the ridge is the point 2½ miles N. from McGee's.

In approaching of it from the one at Colonel Craig's we note these views, counting in minutes, 60 to 3 miles:

6 minutes cross a bottom of Baker's, go down it W.

4 minutes cross another bottom of the same, a spring 200 yards to our left said to be large and fine.

7 minutes a ridge and in front of us there is a very high ridge crossing of us. This cross ridge seems to point to Little River and Tennessee parallel with Holston, and the waters from it on the west side run into that river.

4 minutes descend to another bottom of Baker's.

6 cross a branch of the same at Jeremiah Alexander's.

8 minutes cross a branch of the same.

7 come to a bottom of Pistol Creek.

3 minutes come to the point on the ridge in the experiment line run to ascertain the site for Blount Courthouse.

From this point the confluence of Little and Holston Rivers N. 21 E., the distance 10 miles. The nearest point on the Holston at Colonel Alexander Kelley's, at the mouth of Lackey's Creek N. 5½ W., the distance 6 miles; the source of this creek in the course to the Colonel's.

We set out 8 minutes west to a ridge dividing Pistol and Baker's Creeks, the bottoms steep to the right and left, and we rise to a high ridge and turn south; S. 6 minutes to the top of a nole, the bottoms to the right the falling grounds of Gallaher's Creek; this nole iron ore, we call it Iron Hill. Gallaher's Creek empties into the Holston 7 miles below Lackey's Creek. We continue S. 11 minutes, cross a small ridge and ascend a hill; 4 minutes S. S. W. and cross a path from Baker's Creek to the settlements on Holston; the ridge level; now, S. S. W. one mile; S. W. by W. one mile; S. S. W. 3 miles, thence N. W.

From the path aforementioned we go west to the source of Gallaher's Creek at Godfrey Fisher's, half a mile below John Allison's; there is a mill just below the source of this creek, the spring affording water abundantly sufficient for one.

Being satisfied with the statement made by the gentlemen who accompanyed us, that all the waters to our right run into

Holston, and those to our left into Tennessee, we determined to encamp at this spring, return to Iron Hill and view the ridge bordering on Little River.

10th of April.

We returned this morning to Iron Hill and proceeded thence to ascertain whether there was a ridge bordering on Little River of the discription called for in the treaty. We went on a ridge northwardly to John Cochran's, Esq., at the source of Lackey's Creek; here we determined to correct our point from observation, and we fixed this point to be, from our point of departure, one hour and 20 minutes, about five miles; the course S. 27 W.; to the mouth of Lackey's Creek N. 57 W., 3½ miles; to the mouth of Little River N. 7 E., 7 miles; the source of this creek is thirty feet diameter and of as much depth; it is limestone water and affords enough for a mill.

We continued the course of the ridge to a high nole we call Iron Mount, between 5 and 6 miles from Cochran's, high and covered with pine. Here we make the following observations: The course to Chilhowe Gap S. 1 W.; to the determination of the chain of mountains S. 85 E., and to the right S. 3 W., a mountain over the Holston, a vale exhibited which apparently extends to the river; the mountain supposed to be Clinch Mountain; Bull Run N. 17 E. The course to Knoxville N. 33 E., distance 9 miles. The course to the mouth of Little River N. 3 W., one mile; Major Singleton's house N. 51 E., one mile wanting 220 yards. Major Singleton met us here to accompany us to the mouth of Little River. On a very high and commanding ridge which divides the waters of Little River from those of Holston, we arrive at the junction of the two rivers. The course of Little River at the junction N. 40 W.; the view up or rather across the river on the right side of Little River N. 20 E. David Lovelaw occpuies the lands at the junction of the rivers on the lower side of Little River. We return through his plantation and up the ridge half a mile, and on this ridge ascertain the course to Colonel Samuel Ware's, in Sevier County, S. 82 E. We returned to our encampment on the ridge dividing Little River from Tennessee.

11th of April.

We dispatched a messenger to Colonel Henley with letters to the Secretary of War and to the officer commanding at Tellico. We informed the Secretary that the gentlemen who accompanyed us, all of whom may be effected by the line, have conducted towards us very satisfactorily.

We on all occasions gave to these gentlemen answers to the numerous questions they continued to press upon us, and as we were here to part with them for a day or two, we invited them to visit us at Tellico, and⸍we would show them our commission and instructions; they would then know how to estimate the answers we gave to the numerous questions they put to us. We had read the treaty to them, they had viewed the ground with us, and could for themselves decide the point where the line would cross the Holston. They said their hope now was that something might be done for them with the Indians. We informed them that we had reason to believe that the Indians were now arrived at Tellico, and we should return there immediately. They said that they had been the dupes of misinformation. We set out and returned to Tellico.

12 of April.

We received information that there had been a train of misinformation circulated at Knoxville; that the Governor and several influential gentlemen had expressed themselves in terms of warmth in opposition to the measures of government in train of execution, and that Captain Sparks, who commands in this quarter, had imbibed some of this improper warmth, and would likely give some momentary opposition to expectations we had of his co-operation with us. We received a letter from him in terms very unbecoming an officer and a gentleman; to this we made this reply:

Tellico, 12 April, 1797.

Sir:

I have just received your letter of the 10th. It requires no comment from me, as I submit the propriety of your conduct to your own reflections.

I am, with due regard, Sir,
Your obedient servant,

BENJAMIN HAWKINS.

RICHARD SPARKS,
Captain 3rd Regiment.

13 of April.

We are informed that the Indians would not be here for some days to come; that they had been a little alarmed by information from their neighbours, and were apprehensive for their safety in visiting us. Measures were immediately taken to remove improper impressions, and to induce them to rely implicitly on the justice of the government and to have confidence at all times in the invitations of the agents.

15 of April.

The P. T. Agent for Indian Affairs South of Ohio gave orders to the agent for the Cherokees to make the necessary arrangements, to provide the Indians be supplied with provisions, to have the returns made as regular as the Indian mode of doing business will admit of, to sign all the provision returns himself, the issues to be in the usual course, and the ration to consist of meat and meal or corn, with, in particular cases, an addition of whiskey; that in the returns for provisions regard must be had to the communication of the 7th of March, and never be supplied but to those invited.

A deputation of the gentlemen visited us; we showed them as we promised, our appointment and instructions as far as was necessary, & conversed freely with them. The result of this conference was that they saw clearly the objects of the government, and did believe that the period had arrived when the citizens must respect the laws; that heretofore intrusions were always countenanced by the government in the provision made to give them a preference in all the land laws. They wished much that what had heretofore been usual as to persons in their situation, might apply to them, and that in future all persons should be made to conform to the new arrangement. They hoped and wished that in the conference with the Indians regard will be had to their wishes, and the line compromised to fit their case.

The Commissioners asked the gentlemen why the line run by former Commissioners, as mentioned by Mr. Campbell, had three names, that of experience, of experiment, & the treaty line with the Indians. They answered, it was not the treaty line, but a line run to see how the citizens could be covered, as they were then settled on the frontier. That they understood this to be the direction to the Commissioners and that they conformed to it, and run the line we had noticed in viewing the lands between the two rivers. They then requested of us to know if nothing could be done for them at the conference; whether they could be permited to make their crops now on hand. We answered that as to the small grain, we would see that they saved that and their fruit, but for any thing else, it did not depend on us; in case of doubtful settlement for want of the line, it would be reasonable to expect our indulgence, but where the intrusions were manifest violations of the treaty of Holston, no indulgence ought to be expected, as they had notice of the law in the proclamation of their Governor of the 7th of August. They said the law, as they were likely to be affected, had been incautiously worded; they understood from it that the line from Clinch to cross the Holston at the ridge would turn thence south to the South Carolina Indian boundary on the North Carolina line. We replied that their understanding of it was erronious, there was no such course in the treaty, and they should never suppose that the government would be capable of violating a solemn guarantee; that altho' the expression was thence south, yet it must be understood as meaning S. eastwardly, to the point next called for, as the point is in that direction and far to the east; that the lands in question had moreover, been expressly reserved by the State of North Carolina for the Indians, and the occupants had not, as some others had, even the plea of entry in the land office of that State.

We, after some deliberation, told them that the invitation given to the Indians to convene here was from Mr. Hawkins, by order, for purposes interesting to the United States; to call on the Indians to appoint Commissioners on their part, to attend us in runing the line, to convince them that the United States meant to take no undue advantage of them, and to obtain some points which we deemed important in the protection the government intended to afford the Indians; we were not authorized to open a negotiation for land; we could not then see any way of accommodation for them; if such presented, we might embrace it, and probably it would be in this way. We had now come to a resolution to deviate a little from our original intention; we should not report partially as we intended, but generally; this would give time for their small grain and fruit, as we could not close the line here till the last of June. The Indians were expected to arrive in a few days and we would then be glad to see them again.

Tellico, 16 of April, 1797.

Sir:

When we conversed with you on the objects of our mission, we told you that the Indians invited to convene here were under some apprehensions for their safety in visiting us, and that there were some important objects to regulate and adjust for the mutual interests of the Indians and of the United States; that to remove their apprehensions, it would be advisable to muster as much of the force intrusted to your command as could, without injury to the service, conveniently be brought together. We recommend to you to order this force to be ready to march at a short notice, and we would advise you of the time and place we deemed proper for the object contemplated by us, and you promised us your co-operation. We now, Sir, inform you we believe it would be advisable to order the detachment to meet at this place. The Indians are soon expected to arrive, and this force will answer the double purpose of removing all causes of alarm on their part, as well as on the part of the citizens, for whom the Governor entertains an opinion that they are much alarmed.

From this force we require you to furnish us as "Commissioners for ascertaining and marking the boundary line between the Indian nations and the United States," an escort, to consist of 30 privates with two commissioned officers, two Serjeants and two Corporals, with the necessary camp equipage and pack horses. Our plan may require a division of the escort, in which case we wish a commissioned officer with each division, if you can furnish that number; the officers to have orders to proceed with and under the orders of the Commissioners in the execution of the duties enjoined on them, and to return the nearest rout to your command when they may receive such orders from the Commissioners or either of them.

We are, with due regard,

Your obedient servants,

BENJAMIN HAWKINS.
ANDREW PICKINS.

RICHARD SPARKS,
Capt. 3rd Regiment and Commander the forces of the U. S. in Tennessee.

———

The Commissioners received, for several days past, information of an intention to prevent them from executing the trust reposed in them, either by the non-attendance of General Winchester, or by attacking the Indians, to bring on a war. They had been apprized of some strong expressions used by the Governor, as well as of some rude remarks on the conduct of the government towards the Indians, made by some influential gentlemen, as they deemed themselves, at Knoxville. We were apprized that this letter which we received late last evening from the Governor, had been shown by him, and copies circulated before we received the original.

State of Tennessee, Knoxville, 13th of April, 1797.

BENJAMIN HAWKINS AND ANDREW PICKINS, ESQ.:

Gentlemen:

It is with extreme pain I have to inform you that many of the citizens of this is much alarmed on being informed that a very large body of Indians is about to assemble on the frontiers. It must be recent in your memories that several murders have lately been commited on some of the citizens of this State by the Cherokees, as well as a number of roberies at various times since last autumn. It is also just to observe that two Indians was murdered by some people of this State. It must naturally and inevitably occur that outrages of such an inhuman nature is not easily and soon eradicated out of the minds of those who have been injured, either by the loss of their friends or property, and that retaliation is but too often attempted to be taken when opportunities are afforded by either party. It is no wonder that the citizens of the State feel themselves in danger at the approach of so large a body of Indians, who have so lately evinced a disposition for hostilities, being at no time secure from the murders and ravages of savage banditties.

It is reported that you are appointed Commissioners to ascertain and mark the boundary line between the United States and the Indians, and altho' the State of Tennessee is so materially and essentially interested in the event, no official information thereof has been communicated to its executives, neither by the Executive of the United States or the Commissioners, if they be such.

The Executive of the State of Tennessee has been at much pains to promote and cultivate peace and good understanding with the neighbouring Indian tribes, and still intends availing every favourable object and opportunity to procure and support harmony and permanent tranquility with the savage nations.

I have, without reserve, communicated to you the fears of the people and the conduct and intention of the executive with some observations.

I now beg leave to take the liberty to inform you unless I am satisfactorily informed, which I hope may be the case, the cause and intention of so numerous a party of Indians being about to assemble and embody on the confines of our State, I shall, from the due regard I have for the safety and protection of the citizens, the great desire I have to support and continue an uninterrupted peace, be obliged to order out a sufficient number of the militia for the purpose of observing and watching the movements of the Indians, and protecting the citizens from any insults that may unjustifiably be offered.

I have the honour to be, gentlemen, with due respect and regard,

Your obedient honourable servant,

JOHN SEVIER.

MESSRS. HAWKINS & PICKINS.

We determined to answer this note immediately and to send it by a special messenger to the Governor; we wrote this letter:

Tellico, 16 April, 1797.

Sir:

Mr. Cowan handed us last evening your Excellency's favour of the 13th, and we loose no time in reply. You have received on the 6th of this month, from Mr. Hawkins, Principal Agent for Indian Affairs South of Ohio, information that "the Indians are more inclined to peace and more friendly to the citizens, their neighbours, than they have ever been known to be; that the arrangements in train of execution will increase the friendly disposition of the Indians and induce them to do justice to our fellow citizens, and that he relys with confidence on the agents in his department.

We think Sir, that this communication and a knowledge that the agents in the Indian department were here, ought to have been sufficient to remove all cause of alarm from the citizens of this State. The agents possess and can give the only information to be relied on; they are entitled to the confidence of your Excellency, and we hope that on reflection you will see the impropriety of suspecting them to be capable of withholding any information from you whereby our fellow citizens can be in the least degree injured.

The invitation sent to a few Indians to convene here was from the proper authority and for objects interesting to the United States.

The assurance you give of the disposition of the executive to promote and cultivate peace and good understanding with the neighbouring tribes is pleasing to us and is what we had a right to expect it would be, in unison with the agents in the Southern Department, and there is no doubt, if our actions correspond with this avowed disposition, but that we shall have peace and a good understanding between our fellow citizens and the Indians.

We are appointed, together with James Winchester, Esq., "Commissioners to ascertain and mark the boundary lines agreeably to treaties between the Indian nations and the United States," and we are now here on that business. We in due time took measures to apprize General Winchester of our intention of being here the first of April; he is not arrived. We shall take care that in the execution of this trust our fidelity shall correspond with the confidence reposed in us by the appointment.

We have the honour to be,

Your Excellency's obedient servants,

BENJAMIN HAWKINS.
ANDREW PICKINS.

His Excellency
JOHN SEVIER,
Governor of Tennessee.

The Agent for Indian Affairs South of Ohio addressed a note to Colonel Henley to inform him of what had passed since they were together, particularly of the measures taken to provide for the Indians who were expected to convene here on his invitation.

18 of April.

Mr. Dinsmoor returned last evening with his semicircle for taking the latitude and this day commenced to ascertain the latitude of the place where we now are.

We are again informed of the fears of the Indians for their safety in visiting this place, as well as that they are apprehensive the object in inviting them, under pretence of runing their line, is to obtain more land from them to accommodate the intruders on their lands. Measures were taken in conformity to give the right impression.

19.

The Indians begin to arrive so as to induce an expectation that in a few days there will be a full representation; they say that their tardiness is to be attributed to two causes only, the first to excessive rains, the second to the fears of the nation for their safety, notwithstanding their confidence in the government, fearing that the number of troops on their frontier were not sufficient to insure to them what had been promised by the government.

The 24 of April.

Captain Sparks arrived last evening; we sent Captain Wade to him to call on us, to have an explanation of the misunderstanding between us for which we could not account. He came & we had a conference with him of some length, and we promised to overlook the past, and agreed with him that his statement we would respect. We deem it unnecessary to go into detail, as he promises us his co-operation in the business intrusted to us, and appears to be disposed to fulfill the duties of his station.

We addressed a letter of this date to the Secretary of War, and detailed as much of the existing state of things as we were in possession of. We had received another letter from General Winchester not more satisfactory than the one addressed to Mr. Dinsmoor of the 31st of March.

We are well aware of the speculative pursuits of the General, and if we were not, he seems determined to betray himself; he knows we are at Tellico, where the military force is now stationed, or in the neighbourhood of it, and he affects ignorance of every thing, offers his services to get an additional escort, surveyors, assistants, &c., to go to Duck River to save time. There are no troops in his neighbourhood, and he knows we are not going to Duck River.

The Indians applied to the P. T. Agent for Indian Affairs South of Ohio to indulge them with a little whiskey. He answered no, not one drop till the business they convened on was completely adjusted. They replyed this was not usual, they heretofore were indulged and expected a continuance. He rejoined he saw but little good in their past transactions, that he did not come to continue abuses, but to remedy the past, and he should, for himself, make a point of doing what he judged proper regardless of the past. After some hesitation, the chiefs agreed that this decision was just and they expected some good from it, as heretofore much injury had been done them when in a state of drunkenness.

They requested to know whether it would be agreeable for them to fix their council fires, and that the agent, General Pickins and Mr. Dinsmoor, their agent, should attend them only, with all the interpreters. Mr. Hawkins replyed they were on their own lands on either side of the river, and might determine every thing as they liked relative to the objects mentioned. He should meet them to-morrow at their own council fire.

25 of April.

The chiefs informed Mr. Hawkins that they were ready to receive him, General Pickins and Mr. Dinsmoor at their fire at Tuskeegee. He proceeded there with the two gentlemen.

A conference held at Tuskeegee between Benjamin Hawkins, Principal Temporary Agent for Indian Affairs South of Ohio, on the part of the United States, and the chiefs and warriors of the Cherokees in behalf of their nation, and an agreement entered into between the said parties to carry the treaty of Holston into effect, and for the fixture of military posts to afford more effectual protection to the Indians.

April 25.

The conference opened by Mr. Hawkins, present 147 chiefs and warriors, General Andrew Pickins, Mr. Silas Dinsmoor, Temporary Agent for the Cherokee Nation, John Thompson, one of the interpreters for the Treaty of Holston, Charles Hicks, James Carey and Arthur Cordy, sworn interpreters.

The commission was explained for ascertaining and marking the boundary lines between the Indian nations and the United States, and the object he had in view in inviting them to convene being to satisfy the nation that the United States have taken no advantage of them, and to obtain permission to fix and establish the military posts where they should give the most effectual protection to the Indians. He concluded by asking the chiefs to appoint Commissioners on their part to carry the treaty into effect.

The chiefs conversed for several hours on the subject, showed much reluctance at admiting of the construction given of the courses of the lines particularly bordering on Cumberland. They lamented that their efforts, thrice repeated, had been unsuccessful in obtaining an alteration in the treaty to correspond with what they intended when they made it. They lamented that from the language of the agent of the four nations, the treaty could not be altered after the President had signed it. They saw their own situation and would think of what had been said to them and give an answer to-morrow.

26th of April.

Present as yesterday, the chiefs and warriors replyed: We have come to a determination to run the line agreeable to the orders of the President and the meaning in the treaty. We will appoint men on our part and we rely upon the Commissioners of the United States and expect they will do justice to both sides. We have appointed two old men and two young ones on our part, if you approve of them. Mr. Hawkins, I do name them, Oolaqoah, Chunoheleek, Oohallukeh and Weelik.

A chief presented a string of white beads to the agent from Ummuctooqokuk, Principal Chief of the river towns, with the respects of that chief, and assurances of his reliance on the Great Spirit and the agent for a strait talk.

Mr. Hawkins stated to the chiefs that he wished they would permit him and General Pickins to chuse the proper sites for the military posts on the frontiers of Tennessee, mentioning that he believed three would be necessary, each to contain a garrison of about one company; that they could not now say where it would be proper to fix them, but they expected to obtain the necessary information on the line. He mentioned also that it might be deemed advisable to have one post at Chauga, near the South Carolina boundary.

The chiefs took one day to answer.

27 of April.

Present as yesterday.

The chiefs answer to the request of yesterday that they do not know the proper places for military posts for the protection of their rights, and they leave it in the power of the two Commissioners, Mr. Hawkins and General Pickins, and they hereby give them authority to chuse the proper sites and to fix the posts, and they hope care will be taken to prevent their being injurious to the nation.

Mr. Hawkins: Your decision is a wise one; I accept of the trust and I do hereby engage to secure your permission to establish the posts from being injurious to your nation, and I will provide that it shall be an establishment beneficial to a friendly intercourse between the red and white people, and where useful manufactures shall be carried on.

The chiefs: We claim the ferry on Clinch and wish the agent to do in that affair for us what he thinks just. We want John Rogers, who has one of our women and many children, to keep the ferry.

Mr. Hawkins: As to the ferry at Clinch, the man who keeps it shall be recommended annually by the chiefs and approved of by the agent of the four nations, or provisionally by the agent for the Cherokees. The agent may remove him at pleasure and appoint one provisionally until the nation can meet and recommend a fit character. The agents shall fix the rate of ferriage, make the necessary regulations for the government of the ferryman, and provide that the Indians at all times pass with their property free of expence, and he shall ascertain from year to year what rent shall be paid to the nation and take measures to secure the payment.

The chiefs then agreed to name other Commissioners on their part, and to divide the line between them, which being approved. they named Nonetooqa of Willtown, Sullacoocuhwoluh, Suquiltakeh and Coiucatee of Runing Water, Cloxanah, Ioannuhkiskeh, Cussooleatah and Jaunah of Cowee.

The chiefs requested that their Commissioners might attend four at a time, and that they might be paid out of the annuity. Mr. Hawkins agreed.

The chiefs then said: We hope every thing is done to the satisfaction of the agent of the four nations. Answer by Mr. Hawkins: Perfectly so. They then directed Keawotah or Little Turkey, and Ocunna, the Badger, to attend to the agent and give a speech to be sent to the President; the speech, after being drawn, to be approved to-morrow. They must mention to the President, we now appeal to the justice of the United States to protect us in the enjoyment of our lands solemnly presented to us by the Treaty of Holston.

28.

The speech read and interpreted in full council, and approved of by all the chiefs, and is to be considered an essential part of this agreement. The chiefs then said that one-half of the expence of their Commissioners was, by agreement, to be borne by the United States, agreed for the time they were actually attending.

Agreed to and signed by order of all the chiefs now present, on their part, at Tuskeegee, the 28 of April, 1797, and on the part of the United States.

> BENJAMIN HAWKINS.
> P. T. A. for I. Affairs South of Ohio.
>
> KEANOTAH, X His Mark.
>
> OCUNNA, X His Mark.

In the presence of

SILAS DINSMOOR, T. Agent to the Cherokees.

ANDREW PICKINS.

JOHN THOMPSON, One of the Interpreters of the Holston Treaty.

CHA. HICKS, Interpreter.

JAMES CARY, Interpreter.

A talk of the chiefs and warriors of all the Cherokees to the President of the United States:

Father:

On the invitation of Benjamin Hawkins, the agent of the four nations, we, the chiefs and warriors of the Cherokees, convened at Tellico to appoint suitable persons on our part to see the line ascertained and marked agreeably to the Treaty of Holston, and to adjust other points submitted to us by the agent. We have had some misunderstanding, but we could not help it; from the manner the treaty was made there was great cause of difference of opinion, and the nation has been embarrassed on that account, as we, their representatives here, are believing they never did assent to it.

Father: We are happy that we have been able to settle matters; we rejoice that the agent is come forward, and that we have come to a right understanding for the future. We hope that the agent for the four nations and the other Commissioners and our people who we have appointed will go together and mark the line so that it may never be removed. We wish to acquaint the President of the United States that we think our loss will be great on the side of Cumberland; there we did not expect we had parted with any more land than was expressed in the Treaty of Hopewell, and we hope, as we request, that the agent may report this fact to the President, as it appears to him, when he sees the line, and that our father will have regard to our poor women and children.

Father: We are happy the President of the United States has sent a man among us who respects our rights. We are no judges of proper places for military posts to protect us. We have come to the resolution to leave this matter entirely to the agents, Colonel Hawkins and General Pickins, to chuse and fix them, and we are happy that our father, the President, has sent men who are judges of such business, and on whom the nation so willingly rely. We are sure they will see justice done to the red and whites.

Father: We must mention to our father, the President, what we have heard of Zachariah Cox and his followers. They are about to settle the best of Tennessee. We and the other nations are alarmed for our situation and apprehensive that such people will some how or other come at our lands or the lands of our neighbours. We have most willingly granted every thing asked of us by the agent of the four nations, because we are satisfied he asked for our good, and we now look up to our father, the

President, to fulfill his promises and protect the little land we have left for our wives and our children.

Father: We are some of us very old, and have laboured under many difficulties in times past, but we now hope things are so arranged that we may go into our own woods and hunt to cloathe our naked women and children. We now hope to have some rest and that no one will be permited to disturb us again by intrusions on our rights.

Father: We have given away much of hunting lands, and that which is not valuable for any thing but hunting, and we hope that our father, the President, will take this into consideration and let us hunt among the white people, on such vacant lands, and others, where it may be convenient for us.

By order of all the chiefs.

KEANOTAH, X His Mark.
OCUNNA, X His Mark.

Tuskeegee, 28 April, 1797, in the presence of

BENJAMIN HAWKINS, P. T. A. I. Affairs South of Ohio.
SILAS DINSMOOR, T. Agent to the Cherokees.
JOHN THOMPSON, one of the Interpreters of Holston Treaty.
CHAS. HICKS, Interpreter.
JAMES CAREY, Interpreter.

We were visited during the conference by several of the gentlemen of our neighbourhood who were deputed to attend the conference on the part of the citizens. They were told that the mode prefered by the Indians and approved by the agent would not admit of their being present. Captain Henley replyed on the part of the deputation that it was expected that the conference would be in presence of the citizens, and that they and the Indians would be brought face to face and be heard. We told the Captain that it was not in contemplation to make a new treaty, but to carry the treaty of Holston in effect; that we did not expect much light on this subject from the Indians; that we should form our decision from the instrument itself and not from interested reports on either side; that all who were on the Indian lands could not be relieved by us, except in particular cases we had before mentioned to them; that he and most of the deputation lived on this side of the line of experiment, and that they had informed us that that line was merely to ascertain how the citizens could be accommodated, and on this side of the true line intended in the treaty; that to accommodate them a new treaty must be had, and a new line agreed on, and in our opinion at this time it could not be affected; that the Indians were much alarmed for their situation and viewed every attempt to acquire land as a violation of the solemn guarantee of the government; that we need not expect ever to obtain fairly their consent to part with their lands unless our fellow citizens would pay more respect than we saw they did to their treaties.

We find, from observation, the latitude here to be 35° 15.'

29th of April.

Closed all business with the Indians and set out from Tellico. Having found it necessary to order a survey from this ponit to ascertain some points more exactly than we had done on our first visit, the surveyors commenced a survey from the center of the hill near the river, where it is in contemplation to build one of the fortified posts.

They report the survey as follows: N. 62 chain to a branch runing to the left, 4 feet wide; two and half miles to Baker's Creek, runing to the left, 20 feet wide. Here we encamped.

30 of April.

Colonel David Henley, the agent for the Department of War, sent us some pack horses and information that we should soon have the contractor with us, who would accompany us, and make arrangements for provisioning the escort.

May the 1st.

Set out and continue our course N. one mile and 60 chain; thence N. 20 E., 61 chain, to a branch to the right; one mile, 21 chain, to Stinking Creek, runing to the left, 20 feet wide; 27 to a branch to the right, 4 feet wide; 36 to the same branch to the left; 39 to the same branch to the right, 2 feet wide; thence one mile to a point; thence E., 3 chain to the branch again; thence 43 chain to the valley; thence N. 30 E., 64 chain to a branch to the left, 4 feet wide; thence 66 to a point; thence N. 50 E., 5 chain to a creek, 8 feet wide, runing to the left; one mile to the main Gallaher's Creek, 8 feet wide, and 5 chain to the encampment.

May the 2nd.

We set out E., two miles to Deer Point; thence S. 65 E., 35 chain, to a part of Iron Ridge; thence S. 11 W., 14 chain, to the Iron Ridge. This is the point called Iron Hill during our former observations; the course of the ridge dividing the waters of Pistol and Baker's Creeks, S. 88 E.; the general course of this ridge westwardly, is S. 73 W.; from this on the ridge to the blazed tree on a path being the ridge dividing the waters of Holston from those of Tennessee, S. 27 W. The preceding course of S. 73 W., which appears to be a continuation of the main ridge, divides the waters of Gallaher's Creek from Lackey's Creek; the ridge bordering on Little River is from this point N. 17 E.

We returned to Deer Point and proceed for Holston, N. 25 W., 2 miles, 70 chain, to a spring to the left; 20 chain to a ridge, where we have a full view of the Warchile Mountain on Clinch; the junction of Clinch with the Tennessee supposed S. 38 W. We continue on our course one mile, 70 chain, to a branch to the left, and one mile, 57 chain, to the Holston River at Wm. Gillispie's, passing through his field.

3 May.

Mr. Hawkins went to Knoxville on public business and General Pickins crossed the river and proceeded on for Clinch, N. 25 W., 34 chain, to the river; thence N. 5 E., 64 chain, to a point; thence N. 45 W., 34 chain, to Campbell's ¼ of a mile from Holston; here the river makes a grand bend to the left, 1 mile and 8 chain to Montgomery's mill on Sinking Creek, runing to the left; 10 chain to a point; thence N. 70 W., 65 chain, to Turkey Creek and encamp on the ridge to the left.

4th of May.

Set out on the course, N. 70 W., one mile to Major Campbell's; thence 74 chain to a point; thence N. 82 W., 2 miles, 34 chain. to a point; thence N. 88 W., one mile, 27 chain, to a creek runing to the left, 10 feet wide; thence 42 chain to the same creek, runing to the right; thence continuing in all one to a point; thence S. 70 W., 1 mile, 16 chain, to a point; thence S. 49 chain to a point; thence N. 64 W., 12 chain, to Clinch; supposed from those informed to be three miles above Poppaw Foard.

5.

Mr. Hawkins visited the junction of Holston with the Tennessee, and received this information from Judge Campbell, who lives on the right bank of the river, near the confluence: That the lands in the fork are flat, and just above flood water mark; that the Experiment Line entered the river at the point of Holston and Tennessee and continued down the river some distance below before it touched the right bank; that this line was N. 62 or 63 W.

6.

The Commissioners met together at S. West Point, and took a view of this position; it is high, well watered, somewhat broken & rich, and may easily be made to command both rivers. Captain Wade is stationed here with the company he commands. We ordered a survey of the lands in part, in the fork of the rivers begining at the point of confluence. The course of Clinch on the right bank, N. 40 E.; that on the left, N. 68 E.; Tennessee, the left bank, S. 1 E.; the land on the right bank, S. 22 E.; Tennessee, below the junction, the curve of land on the left bank, W.; the rock on the right bank, N. 82 W.; the point opposite the curve, N. 67 W.

The course from the point, S. 56 E., 13 chain, 50 links; here is the gardens to the left, and from this we take these views: The gap between is two mountains, N. 21 E.; distance to Clinch, 15 chain; the nole to the left, N. 20 E.; the nole to the right, N. 22 E.; from this same point at the garden, S. 21 W., 9 chain, to Tennessee; thence continue the original course, S. 56 E., 9 chain, to a point; thence S. 30 W., 15 chain, to Tennessee; this course has a fine view of the river through a street cut by order of Captain Wade; the curve of the right bank of the river is in this direction, and in this street the troops are encamped.

At the first point near the gardens, there is within 20 paces to the right, a conic mound of earth, formerly the burying place of the antients, and here are the remains of bones; this is the highest ground in the neighbourhood, perhaps 80 feet high. The lands on the left bank of the Tennessee level, some of them formerly cultivated. Here the river makes a beautiful curve or circle of near five miles, and comes within half a mile of the begining of the curve; the whole capable of a high degree of culture; there are, a little back, two fine springs, and the neighbouring lands finely covered with grass. On the right bank of the Clinch the lands are low and rich. The ferry on this river is within 600 yards of the point.

Unthlaubee of Nauche.
Auwihejoe.
Elissiowau.
Uchee Billy at John Miller's old cowpen.
George, Mr. Barnard's wife's nephew; he killed Allen; his father was killed by Harrison; Tommojijee was his Indian and George his white name.
Tustunnuggee Clochucconee.
William Tannehill.
James Harris, a little pin out of the side of his nose.

Traders in the Upper Creeks.

The 26 towns are the mother towns:
1. Tallassee. James McQueen, a Scotchman; has property. The oldest white man in the nation; was a soldier under Oglethorp when he first came to Georgia, in the year 1732. He is healthy and active; has had a numerous family, but has outlived most of them.

William Powel, of little property and not desirous to accumulate much.

2. Tuckabatchee. Christopher Heickle, a very honest, industrious man; in debt to Mr. Panton. He has been 40 years in the nation. A native of Germany; was a good pack horseman, but not sufficiently intelligent for a trader.

Obadiah Lowe, a meddling, troublesome fellow; has some property.

3. Auttossee. Richard Bailey, a native of England. 33 years a resident among the Creeks; has property, but is in debt to Mr. Panton and to the public factory. He has two sons; they have been educated; the oldest by the U. S.; the youngest is now with the Quakers; he was banished the 28th of May by the national council at Tuckabatchee and has since been permited to return, and was killed by a fall from his horse.

Josiah Fisher, a cooper; an inoffensive man.

4. Hothlewaulee. James Russel, has the character of a good trader.

Abraham M. Mordecai, a Jew of bad character; in debt to Mr. Panton, Mr. Clark and the factory.

William McCart, his hireling, said to be honest.

5. Fuscehatchee. Nicholas White, a native of Marseilles, an old trader, a good trader, 30 years in the nation.

William Gregory, his hireling, of good character.

6. Cooloome.

7. Ecunhutkee.

8. Sauvanogee. John Haigue, commonly called Savannah Jack; much of a savage.

9. Mooklausau. Michael Elhart, an industrious, honest man; a Dutchman.

10. Coosaudee. Robert Walton, an active man; more attentive to his character now than heretofore.

Francis Tuzant, an idle Frenchman; in debt to Mr. Panton and to the factory.

John McLeod, of bad character.

11. Wetumcau.

12. Hookchoie.

13. Hookchoieoochee.

14. Tuskeegee.

15. Ocheubofau.

16. Wewocau.

17. Poccuntallauhassee. John Proctor, a halfbreed.

18. Coosuh. John O'Kelley, a halfbreed.

19. Aubecoochee.

20. Nauche. James Quarls, has the character of an honest man.

Thomas Wilson, a saddler.

21. Eufaulauhatche. James Lesley, appears to be a decent, respectable man. He died in the spring of 1799.

22. Woccocoie. James Clark, a Scotchman, a hard drinker; in debt to Mr. Panton.

John Gilliard, his hireling.

James Simmons, an indolent, careless man.

23. Hillaube. Robert Grierson, a Scotchman; has property.

David Hay, his hireling, a Pennsylvanian.

Stephen Hawkins, an active man, of weak mind; fond of drink, and much of a savage when drunk.

24. Ocfuskee. Patrick Donnally, formerly trickey, but reformed, and has property.

25. Eufaulau. John Townshend, a man of good character.

26. Kialijee. John O'Riley, an Irishman, who drinks hard.

Townlay Bruce, of Maryland, formerly a clerk in the Indian Department; removed for improper conduct. A man very capable of business; excessively attached to strong drink; an enemy to truth and his own character.

The following are villages belonging to the mother towns:

27. Newqaucau. On the left bank of Tallapoosa, 18 miles above Ocfuskee.

28. Tooktacaugee. On the right bank of Tallapoosa, 15 miles above Newqaucau.

29. Chuleocwhooatlee. On the left bank of Tallapoosa, 11 miles below Newqaucau.

30. Tuckabatchee Tallauhassee. On the right bank of Tallapoosa, 6 miles above Newqaucau.

These four towns are one fire with Ocfuskee.

31. Luchaupoguh. On a creek of that name.

32. Pauwockee. On the left bank of the Alabama, 7 miles below the fork.

Charles Weatherford, a man of infamous character; a dealer in stolen horses; condemned and repreaved the 28th May.

33. Succauputtoi. On a creek of that name, which empties into Pochusehatche; this creek empties into Coosau 4 miles below Puccuntallauhassee.

34. Weocuffke. On the creek of that name, 4 miles from its mouth. The towns 33 & 34 are one fire with Woccocoie.

George Smith.

35. Thlotloculgau. On Ulcauhatchee, which empties into Tallapoosa 4 miles above Ocfuskee. The town is 14 miles up the creek.

36. Opilthlucco. On a creek of that name which empties into Puccuntallauhassee on its left bank, 20 miles from Coosau River.

Hendrick Dargin, the trader.

37. Tallasooche.

38. Succaupogau—Soocheah. On the right bank of Tallapoosa, 12 miles above Ocfuskee, and one fire with that town.

40. Aubecoochee. The lands waving with rich flats, oak, hickory, poplar, walnut, mulbery. The country abounds in limestone and fine large limestone springs; one above the town, the other below. High up the creek cane; on the branches there is reed. There is, north of the town, a very large cave on the side of a high hill; the entrance small; it is much divided, and some of the rooms appear as the work of art; the doors regular. There is saltpeter in christals; 4 gun men. There is on Wewocau a creek, a fine well seat; the water contracted by two hills; the fall of water 20 feet, and the lands very rich.

70. Nauche.

60. Coosau.

40. Eufaulauhatche.

These four are on limestone land over Therennehollewee.

The 12 mother towns of the Lower Creeks, Tallowau unmaumauquh:

1. Coweta. Thomas Marshall, a steady trader, has accumulated considerable property.

John Tarvin, in debt to Mr. Panton; called Johnny Haujo by the Indians, a name expressive of the man; he is honest.

James Darouzeaux, an old residenter and interpreter in the nation.

Hardy Read, an illiterate trader.

Christian Russel, an active, honest Silisian; a tanner, shoemaker from choice, a doer by trade; a seaman; constantly in motion and trying every thing for an honest livelyhood.

2. Coweta Tallauhassee. James Lovet, a trader of some activity; illiterate, without much regard for truth.

3. Cusseta. Thomas Carr, of long standing in the nation; has property, cattle and negros; is in debt to Mr. Panton; appears to be an honest, funny seaman; says he is a Scotchman, but has the Irish dialect.

John Anthony Sandoval, a Spaniard; in debt to Panton, Clark & the factory, and out of credit.

4. Uchee. John Smithmoor, in debt to Mr. Panton.

5. Ooseuchee. Samuel Palmer, an honest old man, of little property.

6. Cheauhau.

7. Hitchetee. William Grey, an active, good natured man, of loose character, but more attentive to his character now than heretofore.

8. Palachooclee. Benjamin Steadham, an old man, a saddler; has an industrious, honest son at Tensaw, and one of halfbreed, and two daughters at Palachooclee, who live well; are industrious and have property; the girls are good spinners.

9. Oconee.

10. Sauwoogolo.

11. Sauwoogeloochee.

12. Eufaulau.

The following are villages belonging to the mother towns:

13. Padjeelegau. A Uchee village, formerly a large town, but broke up by Benjamin Harrison; he murdered 14 of their gun men; it is on Clonotiscauhatchee, on the right bank of the river, adjoining the river and the creek on the lower side of the creek. The town takes its name from the creek Padjeelegau (Pigeon Roost). 18 miles above Timothy Barnard's and 9 miles below the old horse path, the first rockfalls in the river, and these falls are 5 miles below the second falls, at which there are two small islands, and here a path now crosses from Cusseta to Fort Wilkinson. This village is advantageously situated, the range good for cattle, the land very rich, the swamp near three miles through, all of excellent quality for culture, the cane very large and the sassafras and shumake very large.

14. Intackculgau (Beaver Ponds). On Opilthlucco, 28 miles from its junction with Clonotiscauhatchee. Opilthlucco is a large creek; its junction, a mile and a half above Timothy Barnard's, 60 feet wide; the lands good on its margins up to the village; about 8 miles below the village the lands extend out for 4 or 5 miles;

are tucaumau pofau (oak lands). The adjoining lands are good pine; they are good for cattle; cane on the creeks and reed on the branches; the whole well watered. There are 14 families; their industry is increasing; they have built a square in 1798. They have cattle, hogs and a few horses. They are Uchees.

Aumuccullee. On a creek of that name, 60 feet wide, on the right bank of Thlonotiscauhatchee. The village is 15 miles up the creek, on the left bank; it is 45 miles below Timothy Barnard's. There are 60 gun men in the village; they belong to Cheauhau. The lands are poor; limestone springs in the neighbourhood. The swamps are cypress, in hammocs, some water oaks and hickory. The pine lands are poor, with ponds and wire grass. This creek is a main branch of Kitchofoone, which it joins 3 miles from its mouth.

Thlontiscauhatche—Flint River. It heads near Ocmulgee, and near Thennethlofkee, the southernmost mountain on the left of Chattahooche. It runs S. E. to within 12 miles of Chattahooche, thence S. to the junction. From Ocfuskenene upwards the water in the branches is fine, the margins of the creeks rich with cane, reed on the branches, the ridges poor and gravelly at the heads of the rivers, flats open, post oak and black oak.

8 miles below Ocfuskenene ford lands broken pine, post oak, small hickory. 9 miles, the lands continue broken, the river spreads out from half a mile to ¾, shoally, and moss fine for cattle; here the broken lands terminate.

Authlucco, 14 miles. This is a large, fine creek on the right bank of the river, the falls 30 feet, 3 miles from the river. This 14 miles the river contracts; the lands are level and fit for culture; the growth oak, hickory and some pine.

Aupiogee, 8 miles. On the right bank of the river; the lands on the river continue level and fit for culture.

Salenojuh, 8 miles. Here there was a compact town of Cusseta people, of 70 gun men in 1787, and they removed the spring after Colonel Alexander killed 7 of their people near Shoulderbone. Their fields extended 3 miles above the town; they had a hot-house and square, water, fields well fenced, their situation fine for hogs and cattle. Just above the old fields there are two curves on each side of the river of 150 acres, rich, which have been cultivated. Just below the town the Sulenojuhnene ford, the lands level on the right bank. There is a small island to the right of the ford; on the left a ridge of rocks. The lands on the left bank high and broken. Above the town there is a good ford, level, shallow, and not rocky; the land flat on both sides.

Otaulgaunene, 3 miles. This path crosses at two islands; the ford is a good one; the lands broken on both sides. There is some good land below these falls, on the left bank.

Ecunhutkenene, 4 miles. This is also called Chelucconene-auhassee, the old horse path, the first path to the Creek nation. This is a rocky ford and pretty good, the banks steep on the left bank. Here the falls terminate and the flats begin to spread out.

Cooccohapofe, 5 miles. On the right bank here was for-merly an old town; the fields were cultivated on the left bank; the swamp three miles through; on that side large sassafras.

Padjeeligau, 3 miles. The swamps are wide on the left; 3 miles high, and good canebrake on the right, near one mile through, low and flat.

Okauhutkee, 15 miles. This creek on the right bank there are five fine, flowing, reedy creeks between Padjeligau and Okauhut-kee, open pine lands with ponds, reedy flats joining the river, near a mile through. This creek is 60 feet, a bold runing creek at all times; pine land for 8 miles up, then some oak, pine again, and reedy branches. The mouth of this creek is remarkable for the resort or rock fish; they ly all the summer in the mouth of the creek. Just below there is a pine barron bluff on the river; ¼ mile this swamp again.

Opilthlucco, 1½ miles.

Timothy Barnard's, 1½ miles.

Hatchee Loome, 4 miles. 15 feet on the right bank.

Ittoopunnauulgau, 3 miles.

Crooked Wood, 15 miles.

Autussauhatche, 12 miles. 30 feet; piney.

Wecuiwau, 7 miles. 10 feet; oaky land.

Springs.

Large Creek, 11 miles. Pine barron.

Cheauhau Village, 3 miles. Situated on the river, a pine barron surrounding it. There is a ford here, opposite the town.

Tullewhoqaunau (Tucane Town), 2 miles. Pine barron. Here is another ford, the best.

Otellewhoqaunau, 7 miles. A small village of 20 familys on the right of the river; pine barron on both sides. They plant on some small swamp margins at the mouth of a little creek. These people inhabitated the village above of the same name.

Ocmulgee Village, 7 miles. There is a few families, the remains of the Ocmulgee people who formerly resided at the Ocmulgee fields on Ocmulgee River; lands poor, pine barron on both sides; the swamp equally poor & sandy; the growth dwarf scrub brush, evergreens, among which is the Cassine.

Kitchofoone (Mortar Bone Creek), 8 miles. This creek is 80 feet; the land site pine barron.

Hitcheteepro, 5 miles. Potokes Village on the left bank of the river; nice barron bluff on both sides.

Chickasawhatchee, 10 miles. 90 feet. There is some good land up this creek and some settlements of Hitchetee people. The swamps are good, large canebrakes, some ponds and oak woods; range fine for cattle.

James Burges, 100 miles. The lands poor white pine barron, sandy bluffs. Small creeks only on this course, and so badly watered that travelers encamp on the river bank for water. 25 miles to the fork of the river; the lands good, cane in the swamp and on the creeks and high lands.

EXTRACT TO MR. DINSMOOR:

8th April, 1797.

I wish you to take measures to prevent this visit of the Indians from being an expence to the government. Those who are invited must have rations; those who are visitors must, as far as is practicable, be left to their own exertions for supplies. I had yesterday a conversation with 13 chiefs; they then asked me how the visitors to the garrison were to be supplied with provisions. I replied: Those who were invited are come on public business, would be fed; those who came on private business or from curiosity must do as they saw their white neighbours—supply themselves.

No. 1. James Bosley applied to inform the Agent for Indian Affairs that some time about the year 1788 or 1789, a negro fellow of his named Sam was taken by some Creek Indians within three miles of Nashville; he was with a waggon. They took four horses out of the waggon and at the same time they fired on and killed John Hunter, and during the same day they fired on and killed Major M. Kirkpatrick and cut his head off. Mr. Bosley is informed that this negro is in possession of Stephen Sullivan, who lived where he had this information, at New York, the town of the residence of the white Lieutenant. Sam is about 45 years of age; he is a good waggoner and active plantation negro. Mr. Bosley lives within 2 miles of Nashville.

23rd May, 1797.

No. 2. George Ridley and his wife, one child, and a negro girl, returning from the Natches in 1789 or 1790, while on Duck River, at its junction with the Tennessee, making a canoe, were fired on by Indians, said by the Chickasaws to be Creeks. They killed Ridley and his wife, and it is suspected that the girl and boy were taken prisoners. The girl about 12 years old, the boy about 2 years old. George Ridley, the grandfather, lives within three miles of Nashville.

23rd May, 1797.

No. 3. Some time in 1788 or 1789, when Mrs. Williams was taken prisoner, the Creeks took from Tugalo a negro boy about 6 years old called Sam, the property of Samuel Isaacs of Pendleton County, in South Carolina. He had a burn on the right arm, on the off side, and was in the possession of McGillivray's widow.

No. 4. Edmund Gamble informs that he has a negro some where in the Creek country, taken on the 15th of April, 1790, near General Robertson's; said to be found in the woods nearly perished with hunger. The discription:

He is named Ned; about 17 years old at the time he was taken; pretty well grown, jet black, the wool on his forehead remarkably low down; was raised near Halifax, in the State of North Carolina, by Major Joel Hart.

The negro is said to be in the possession of a John James Oakley (probably a halfbreed). The application dated Nashville, 20 May, 1797.

No. 5. General Joseph Martin on Tugalo River in the fall of 1788, had a large cream coloured horse at that time about four years old, supposed to be taken by the Creek Indians. It is said he is in possession of the Mad Dog. He was branded R. C. and is heavy made.

No. 6. George Gentry, of Davidson County, near Nashville, applies on the 19th of May, 1797, for justice and states the grounds: On the 31st of January last, his brother, John Gentry, was killed by some Creek Indians; at the time he was in company with Edward Ragsdale and John Browder. His brother lost 2 blankets, saddle, bridle and meal bag; that the saddle has since been returned by the Creeks in care of Sackfield Maclin. He requests the agent to take all lawful means to cause justice to be done in the premisses.

Property lost: 2 blankets, 3 dollars each, 6 dollars; one bridle, $1.25; meal bag, $1.00; total $8.25.

No. 7. Edward Ragsdale, mentioned in No. 6, states his claim and therein corroborates the preceeding demands. He says on oath: "That on the 31st of January, he, together with John Gentry and John Browder, were on the waters of Harpeth, on the north side of the ridge dividing the waters of Cumberland from those of Duck River, and they were there fired on by persons unknown, but conjectured to be Indians; that Mr. Gentry was

wounded by a shot and died in a few minutes; it appeared that
his (Mr. Gentry's) mare was wounded by the same shot; that the
two survivors left their horses, one gun and the dead body of Mr.
Gentry and his wounded horse; that the horse which Mr. Sackfield
brought from the Creek nation is the same horse mentioned in
this statement. He further deposes that he lost a saddle, blanket,
bridle, hat and meal bag, and he believes the persons who fired
got the whole except the hat. He further deposes that John
Browder lost at the same time one horse, one blanket and a bridle.
He further deposes that John Gentry had with him at the time
he was killed, two blankets, a saddle, bridle and meal bag, and that
the saddle returned by Sackfield Maclin from the Creek nation is
the same saddle belonging to John Gentry. He further deposes
that the mare which Mr. Gentry rode and which died, as he
believes, of the wound before mentioned, was the property of Fred-
rick Browder."

Edward Ragsdale's property lost: One saddle, 8; one blanket,
3; one bridle, 1.25; one meal bag, 1.50; in all, in dollars, 13.75.

Camp near Nashville, 21st May, 1797.

Beloved Chickasaws:

I am now here for the purpose of ascertaining and marking
the boundary line between the Indian nations and the United
States. I shall finish the Cherokee and Creek lines first, and then
yours, and after that I shall visit your nation. You have heard
of an attempt of Zachariah Cox and Co. to settle the best of Tennessee; he came on to Knoxville while I was at Tuskeegee and applied
to me for permission to come and trade among you, but as he
stated his object fully, and as I am informed that the Indians were
not willing he should be among them, as they looked on him as
the precursor of those who are represented as grasping after their
lands; that he was to make the first attempt to get possession and
the rest were to follow with the train of evils so alarming to the
Indians. I have not consented to indulge Mr. Cox with the permission he applied for.

I have seen a letter from Piomingo to General Robertson; he
complains that the Creeks are stealing horses from the Chickasaws.
I know the Chickasaws to be a brave and honest people and I
hope they are wise. It is my duty to ask them for their own good
not to be drawn into a war with any of their neighbours. I wish
you to keep an account of your losses by the Creeks and inform
me of it. I will call upon the Creeks to do you justice, and if they
refuse, I will inform you of it, and then I will inform you what
to do.

George Colbert has applied to me about his claim against the Cherokees; he says he has applied to his nation and is informed in a letter from one of them that the nation have agreed to pay him for his negros; he asked me to pay him out of the annual present made the nation. If the nation are willing to pay this claim, they must get together and write to me to have it paid. If they do this, they must get together and pass the order; it must be signed by the interpreter, four of the head men and by two white men, if there are any in the nation.

Accept of my best wishes for the prosperity of the Chickasaws.

The Chiefs, Head Men
   and Warriors of the
      Chickasaw Nation.

1st June.

Received letters from Timothy Barnard, Richard Thomas, Secretary of War, William Panton, Ensign Thompson, Colonel Henley, Mr. Overton and Captain Hunter.

I sent a letter with this for the Chickasaws to John Pitchlin, interpreter among the Choctaws, to inform him of my having passed his claim, and of the measures in train of execution, which I must complete before I could visit that nation. This letter was in the care of a Choctaw on his way home.

On the dividing ridge between the waters of Duck River and Cumberland Rivers, 4 june, 1797.

Sir:

I received a few days past yours of the 20th of April, with the laws of the last session of Congress, and this day I received from Colonel Henley a copy of the intercepted letter sent on to you in care of Mr. Byers. The letter is intercepted at a time which may eventually be productive of much real service to the U. States, by an exposure of those dirty intriguers and their villanous attempts to involve the government in difficulties and distress. When I accepted the trust confided to me, I counted on much opposition, and determined to surmount the whole. I find that opposition more powerful than I expected, but I find too that my exertions outstrip it, and relying with confidence on the approbation of the

President, I will deserve success, be the consequences what they may. I received a letter of the 11th May from a confidential correspondent who has resided long in the Creek nation, who has a family and much property there, and who speaks their language accurately; he says: "Althings was quiet in the Creeks; they long much to see you, they are informed of what you are doing and they seem much satisfied at your proceedings." If embarrassments should increase, arising from unforeseen difficulties, I shall be under the necessity to ask permission to have a small fund in addition to what I am now restricted. I must have a regular intercourse between the tribes, and I contemplate an Indian post. I can get lads on whom I can rely, at a low price, to perform this service on foot.

If Chisholm, or any other man of his character, in the present conjunction of affairs, should be wicked enough to come among the Indians, he must be instantaneously removed. You have only to give directions and I will see them executed; perhaps a special instruction to me may be deemed the most advisable.

We are progressing but slowly; it is very difficult to trace the ridge. We went on south from Nashville and found the ridge somewhat short of 26 miles, and are going eastwardly as soon as we find the point. 40 miles above Nashville, we shall make more way. We are now together and no disagreement among the Commissioners. We shall finish the Cherokee line as soon as we can, and leave the Chickasaw line till the fall, when with one more of us, we can easily perform that business at that season.

I wish you would direct one of your young men to send me from time to time newspapers and such pamphlets as may be worthy of notice; I will gladly pay the expence. I am so much in the woods that I am almost cut off from society, and as I shall be doomed to this life for some time to come, they will amuse me.

I wish you to mention me respectfully to the President, to assure him of my sincere wishes for his health and happiness, and believe me yourself, with sincere regard and esteem, Sir,

Your obedient servant.

The Honourable
    JAMES McHENRY,
        Secretary of War.

From the woods on the Cherokee line, the 14th June, 1797.
Sir:

The plans contemplated in the laws and treaties for the civilization of the Indians and the preservation of their friendship requires that the agents should reside among them, and as yours informs, you could not remove to reside among the Chickasaws and the arrangement renders it unnecessary to have an agent exterior to that nation. You will be pleased to consider your commission as expired on this day.

In making this communication, I am happy to subjoin that during my agency no part of your conduct has been exhibited to me in an unfavourable point of view, and I hope should your services be wanted on any future occasion, that you will give them with readiness.

You will have your accounts made up in the usual mode and returned to the Agent for the Department of War as heretofore.

With due regard, I am, Sir,
Your obedient servant,
B. H.
P. T. A. for I. A. S. of Ohio.
GENERAL JAMES ROBERTSON,
Of Moro District.

24th June.

Major George Colbert, Captain George and three other chiefs or warriors of the Chickasaws visited me, with Mr. McClish, the interpreter; they brought dispatches from that nation informing that the Creeks appeared to have hostile intentions against them; that three Creeks had recently came into their land and killed one Chickasaw and mortally wounded another; that the murderers were pursued, overtaken and put to death; that the Creeks continued to steal their horses, and they were apprehensive of a war with that nation, unless I would interpose. They requested to be furnished with arms and military stores.

Major Colbert brought an order, in conformity with the advise of the 21st of May, to receive payment out of the annual present allowed the Chickasaws, for his negros, agreeable to the recom- mendation of the President, in Philadelphia, of 19th of December, 1796. I judged it advisable to pay the order and I requested Colonel Henley to give him the money, for which I gave this bill of exchange:

Knoxville, 6th July, 1797.
Exchange for 750 Dollars:

At sight of this, my first of exchange, the second of the same tenor and date not paid, pay to Colonel David Henley, Agent for the Department of War, or to his order, seven hundred and fifty dollars; it being for so much paid George Colbert for his negros, by order of the Chickasaw nation, of the 4th June, agreeably to the recommendation of the President, of the 19th December, 1796, and which sum is to be deducted out of the annual present made to that nation.

750 Dollars.

The Honourable
    JAMES McHENRY,
        Secretary of War.

There being four principal characters of the Chickasaw nation who visited me on the affairs of their nation, I, after consulting the Agent of the War Department, wrote to him:

Knoxville, 6th July, 1797.

Sir:

There are four principal chiefs of the Chickasaws now at Tellico; they came with dispatches to me from their nation, relating to the misunderstanding between them and the Creeks. They have requested a supply of ammunition. I am of the opinion it would be advisable to furnish them with some for present use, and if the necessity should exist, to supply them liberally. I hope to be able to accommòdate this misunderstanding between them and the Creeks. I have already interposed, and the Creek council, who met on the 5th of June, have come to a resolution to do justice to the Chickasaws.

I recommend to you, Sir, to give to these four visitors twenty dollars each, and to deduct their nation with that sum. I mean the twenty dollars each to be in goods suited to the wants of these Indians.

I am, with much esteem, Sir,
                        Your obedient servant.
COLONEL DAVID HENLEY,
    Agent for the Department of War.

Extract of a letter of 5th to the Secretary of War:

I have repeatedly had dispatches from the four nations, and with very few exceptions, every thing promises to progress as well as I had a right to expect it would. My last from the Creeks was of the 5th June. They have in public council determined to do justice to the Chickasaws. Mr. Benjamin James, a reputable inhabitant of the Choctaws, left that nation the 28th May. He has three sons, halfbreeds, men grown; one a man of some learning; the others capable of managing his commercial concerns, and all of them in a situation to know the temper and disposition of the nation, as well as the intrigues which may be carried on there by the Spaniards. He says everything was quiet when he left the nation; there had not been any interference on the part of Spain injurious to the U. S. He had heard of some idle tales and traced them, and when he mentioned them to a Spanish officer at a post on the rout to Mobile, he told him the reports were not founded. When the Spaniards consent honestly and fairly to fulfill their stipulations with us, there will be an end to these tales.

The Chickasaws have runners to me with talks of the 6th June. Three Creeks had come into their land and killed one Chickasaw and wounded another mortally. The murderers were pursued, overtaken and put to death. They have applied for aid in arms and ammunition.

They have applied also to the Spaniards and Mr. Panton to endeavour to prevail on the Creeks to be at peace. I shall dispatch a messenger in a day or two to the Creeks on this subject.

I send you Carey's examination and I shall direct my messenger to the Creeks to call on Rogers. As soon as I got out of the woods, I proceeded to Tellico to make the examination. Captain Van Ranssalaer with his troop is arrived, and Colonel Butler is on the road from Cumberland; expected to arrive in a few days, if waggons can be had in the neighbourhood of Fort Blount to transport the baggage, but it will be difficult to obtain waggons in that quarter. The arrival of these troops have a happy effect in disposing the minds of the people to submit to the laws; it exhibits a curious contrast to those who have seen the manuvers in this quarter for some time past. To Colonel Henley it is a post. I do not know whether you are personally acquainted with the Colonel, but whether you are or not, I may venture to pay him my tribute of applause for his zealous attachment to the interest of the United States, and for his honest, firm and persevering exertions to fulfill the duties enjoined by the trust reposed in him. None rejoice more than the Cherokees, and were more alarmed than they were for their situation. They have had circulated among them again the report that Zachariah Cox & Co. were still anxiously grasping after their lands, and they were apprehensive the force in this quarter was not sufficient to prevent it, and they in consequence had directed their young men to remain at home and have their moccasins ready. The Chickasaws have come to a resolution to pay Major Colbert for his negros, agreeably to the recommendation of the President of the 19th of December, 1796. I called on the nation on 21st of May to take this subject under consideration, and directed how they were to proceed in case they approved of the recommendation. They have, according to the form prescribed, drawn on me for 750 dollars, to be paid out of the annual present allowed their nation. I have requested Colonel Henley to pay that sum to Colbert, and I shall give him a bill on you for the same. The Cherokees applied to me also to adjust this matter between the parties concerned, and I shall direct the sale of the negros under the direction of Mr. Dinsmoor, and the proceeds to be divided among those who lost horses. As you had not given any direction to General Robertson, and I found he was acting as agent for the Chickasaws under his last commission, I, on my arrival at Nashville, gave notice to him to have his accounts made up in the usual mode and returned to the Agent for the Department of War, as heretofore, and that he would consider his commission as expired on the 14th June.

Knoxville, July 11th, 1797.

I have received your favour of the 4th inst. I expected you would meet much difficulty in procuring the necessary transport for your stores and baggage, and that that would necessarily detain you longer in that quarter than we had counted on.

I should have done myself the pleasure of visiting you before I left the neighbourhood of Cumberland, but I was under the necessity to proceed without delay to Tellico, to examine into the conduct of some people who seem determined to disturb the peace of our government. The inclosed copy of a letter is intercepted at a time which may eventually be productive of much real service to the U. States by the exposure of those dirty intriguers and their villanous attempts to involve the government in difficulties and distress. It has been sent to the War Office. You know, I believe that the writer is one of the Senators of this State.

I have had some points intrusted to me relative to the fixture of military posts in this frontier where they would give the most effectual protection to the Indians and to our fellow citizens. I shall be able to make a communication to you thereon when I have the pleasure of conversation with you. One of the posts, which I believe to be the most important, you will pass, S. W. Point; it is on the Indian lands, some miles south of the line of division. I am of opinion that all the posts should be on the Indian lands, and I have obtained permission from the Indians to chuse the proper places and to fix the posts so that you will have a choice all along this frontier.

General Pickins is in our neighbourhood, getting our small escort in readiness to accompany us. We shall move to the line mentioned in your letter as soon as we have the pleasure of seeing you. Everything in my department seems to be in a promising situation to do well, and I hope, with the aid of you and Colonel Gaither, that the benevolent views of the government will be carried into effect.

I am, with great respect, Sir,

Your obedient servant.

THOMAS BUTLER,
Lieut. Colonel Commanding 4 U. S. Regiment..

10th June, 1797, in the woods near the Cherokee line.

Beloved Cherokees:

Nonnetooquh has sent one of his young men to inform you what we have done in this quarter. He will inform you we have had much difficuly after we found the ridge, to trace it to 40 miles above Nashville. We have found that point and are now going northeast to Cumberland. As soon as we have done the line, I shall send you a copy of our proceedings. Your Commissioners have behaved well.

You may depend upon my taking great care of your interests and those of the white people. I know no difference between you; you live on the same land and are intitled to equal rights, and must live as friends and brothers, and it is my particular duty to see justice equally distributed among you. I must advise you on all occasions to be at peace with your neighbours and prevent your young men from doing unwarrantable acts, and to follow the advice of your friend and father, the President of the United States, and to listen to no talks but what come from him.

I am your friend,

BENJAMIN HAWKINS,
P. T. A. for I. A. South of Ohio.

KEANETOH, THE TURKEY.
OCUNNA, THE BADGER.

Holston River, in Tennessee, 13th July, 1797.

I have received several of your favours sent on by Reed; he, I suppose, sent them from some part of the Cherokee country to Tuskeegee, called with us Tellico. They bear date 9th May. You must never apologise to me for writing long letters; I wish you and all others in my department to make it a rule to inform me of every event that can in the least degree be interesting to me in the execution of the duties enjoined on me.

I am informed by the Secretary of War of the unfortunate affair you relate of the Euchees; the man's name was Brown; he lived in Washington. You have done well in demanding satisfaction, and I hope from the tenor of your letter, that the chiefs have given it. I was in hopes that from the pains taken at Colerain, and since by the government, and from the zealous co-operation of all my assistants in the Creek Department, that we should not so soon have had our sensibility roused by so unjustifiable an outrage against any of my fellow citizens in Georgia. That murderous business of Harrison is the cause of this, but as the innocent have suffered, and since the intervention of a solemn public treaty, it is indispensably necessary for the preservation of peace, and for the protection of the rights of the Indians themselves, that the guilty should suffer. If any thing has happened to prevent the chiefs from executing their interests, it becomes my duty to call on the nation and demand that the person or persons who have perpetrated this murder in violation of the treaties existing between the Creeks and the United States be delivered up. If this demand is not complied with, it will become indispensably necessary that the whole tribe to which the murderers belong should be punished by the United States in such a manner as to make them repent of an act which has given great pain to the President and rendered it extremely difficult to restrain the people of Georgia. You must take the necessary measures on the premises. I expect to be soon on the return to the Creeks. I have had much difficulty to encounter in this quarter, but notwithstanding, we progress, tho' slowly, with the line. The Cherokees have behaved well. The complaints are against the Creeks; they are stealing horses from the Chickasaws and people of Cumberland, and they have killed two Chickasaws. The Chickasaws pursued and killed three Creeks, the murderers. The Creeks have also killed John Gentry, on the waters of Cumberland. Mr. Gentry was a peaceable, orderly man. The murderers live among the upper towns and must be punished. Nothing, I see, will restrain the Creeks but the fear of punishment.

I have sent Mr. Maclin expressly to call on them to deliver the stolen property and with the orders for satisfaction for Gentry and Brown.

I am glad to hear that you are progressing right with your farming; I hope in a short time we will be able to extend it among our red brethren. I have sent by Maclin your last quarter's pay, and I shall bring money with me for the remaining objects when I return.

Remember me to your family, and believe me to be your friend and obedient servant,

BENJAMIN HAWKINS.

TIMOTHY BARNARD,
P. A. of the Creeks.

ALEXANDER CORNELL:

I wrote you last from Fort Fidins. I have been much longer employed on this line than I expected when I wrote to you. I am moving on and shall be round in your quarter next month. I was in great hopes when I visited your nation after a public treaty, that all things would in future be done according to the solemn stipulations entered into at Colerain; that the chiefs would take measures to govern the nation, and when the hatchet was buried, to punish any unruly individual who would lift it up against the voice of the nation. I have already said to you: "The chiefs of the land ought to have the right of making peace and war, and any man who acts contrary thereto must be taught to know he does rong. I actually had some doubts while I was at the Cowetas, whether I ought to apply to the chiefs or the young men, as the latter seemed determined on mischief and the chiefs unable to control them." I did not expect, when I left your nation and informed them I was runing the lines between the red and white people, that I should hear of constant complaints against the Creeks in my neighbourhood. When I was in Cumberland, they stole several horses; just before my arrival there they murdered Mr. John Gentry, a man friendly to Indians. They were stealing horses from the Chickasaws and murdered two people of that nation; the Chickasaws pursued and settled this account by killing the murderers. All this was done when the Creeks knew I was in the neighbourhood and must hear of it. The Indians who murdered Mr. Gentry live in the Upper Creeks.

The Uchees, they too, must be doing mischief; they have killed a Mr. Brown in Washington County, and much injured his wife. For this abominable act Mr. Barnard informs me he demanded satisfaction, and that the Creek nation have promised it, and I hope they have fulfilled their promise. If they have not, it is my duty to demand it. I told the Creeks that after the treaty at Colerain, all violators of the treaty at New York, on both sides, should suffer. The white people, when I left Oconee, were preparing to carry their part into effect. Colonel Gaither has faithfully done his part, but what have the Creeks done? Or what are they doing? I have sent Mr. Maclin to you with this letter, to hear from you and them on this subject:

Beloved Creeks:

When I visited your nation and informed you of the disposition of the government of the United States towards you Creeks, that a military force would be placed down on your borders to protect your rights and to keep peace between you and your neighbours, and that you might now rely on the fulfillment of all the promises made to you at the treaty of Colerain. I was in hopes that the hatchet was buried, and that the chiefs would take measures to govern their nations and to punish any unruly individual who should violate a solemn treaty.

You chiefs have the right to make peace and war, and any man who acts contrary thereto must be taught to know he does rong. When you signed the treaty of Colerain to carry the treaty of New York into effect, all was peace, and he who violated it was to suffer. This treaty was a law to the white people; it is a law also for you Creeks. The President sent his warriors and put them down on your lands to protect your rights and to keep the peace between you and your neighbours.

I directed Mr. Barnard to inform you what I was doing for the red people, and that when I ascertained and marked the lines between them and the white people, that I should return among you. I am now coming on with the Cherokee line, and when that is done, I shall come directly into your nation.

When I left you I expected your people would behave well; I sent to the Secretary of War information that the Creeks were more inclined to peace and more friendly to the white people, their neighbours, than they have ever been known to be. The President had given orders to treat you with justice and with kindness; he wished that you should enjoy all good things equally with the white people, and as you are unprovided with many of the necessaries in use among your neighbours, he has directed you should be assisted as a father assists and takes care of his children. The President, in doing this, executes the will of the American people.

While the President and his agents are doing these things for you, what are you doing for him? Hear the truth: Some of the Uchees have murdered Mr. Brown, in Georgia, and wounded his wife; some of the Upper Creeks have murdered John Gentry, on the waters of Cumberland, and your people are stealing horses from Georgia, Tennessee and the Chickasaws.

A stop must be put to these things; the guilty must be punished, that honest men may not be afraid to show their faces. The people who do such wicked things must be punished, to prevent the whole nation from being charged with countenancing such doings. The families of Brown and Gentry cry out for justice; they call upon the President to have the murderers punished. No innocent man must suffer say they; the guilty must die.

These things have happened since we made peace and took each other by the hand at Colerain. These things have happened since I told the President that the hatchet was buried and that the promises of the Creeks might be relied on. The President has heard of them, and they give him great pain; his war officer calls upon me for justice and I must demand it of you; you must give up the guilty. I say you must give up the guilty persons, and then you have nothing to fear; your people need not be afraid to go any where in our land.

Accept my beloved Creeks of my sincere wishes for the prosperity of your nation, and believe me to be your friend.

Knoxville, 14th July.

RICHARD THOMAS,
    Creek Assistant:

I have received two of your favours since I saw you. I wish that the Creeks may have given satisfaction for the murder of Brown. It must not be concealed from them that they are in a delicate situation; the disposition of our government is friendly to them in a very high degree; they must show by their acts they are deserving of our friendly attention.

Some of the Upper Creeks have murdered John Gentry, in the neighbourhood of Cumberland; he was a worthy man, friendly to the Indians. His brother has called on me to see justice done, and I have demanded it of the nation.

You and all persons in the department must be very careful of and attentive to the interests of the United States; you must omit no opportunity to be useful. There is a train of villainy which you must aid to unfold; the particulars will be explained to

you. Remember me to your neighbours, Messrs. Carr, Marshall
and Darouzeaux.   I hope for the pleasure of seeing them 'ere long.
Accept of my sincere wishes for your prosperity.

Knoxville, 10th July, 1797.

A letter from Mr. Blount to you relative to a negro of yours,
has come into my hands and I forward it to you. The Commissioners are now tracing the line from the Kentucky trace on Cumberland and the Clinch; they will then descend and commence on
the Clinch and proceed across the Holston to the South Carolina
line. You must be here in about fifteen or twenty days, that you
may make arrangements about geting possession of the ferry on
Clinch. I wrote you by the Bloody Fellow from the conference
at Tuskeegee. It will be necessary that you should be here before
I go from this into the Creeks, as I must make some arrangements
with you. Raleigh and his family are settled on the south side of
Tennessee, opposite the fort at South West Point.

I wish you may do well.

                              BENJAMIN HAWKINS.
JOHN ROGERS.

Knoxville, 16th July, 1797.

I wrote you a day or two past, inclosing you a letter from
Mr. Blount about a negro of yours and relative to the ferry. I
have directed Mr. Maclin to deliver you that letter, and this which
I now send you. You will find by a newspaper which will be shown
to you that a letter from Mr. Blount to James Carey has been
published; by this our government are appraised of the plan you
and Chisholm arranged with the British Minister last year, as he
calls it. You will see, as Mr. Blount says, that the discovery of it
would injure much the parties concerned. As you are a man with
a large family of Indian children, and I wish much they may do
well, and by your coming to Clinch you can do well for them, I
am desirous of your saving yourself if you can. You must, upon
the receipt of this, send me an exact statement of every thing,
and if your statement should be true, I will retain you in the post
assigned you, and contribute to make you and your family easy in
your circumstances. You will see it depends on yourself. We
have some other letters, and Carey and others have been examined.

I promised Carey you should have an opportunity to acquit yourself, and by this letter I fulfill my promise.

JOHN ROGERS.

Knoxville, 6th August, 1797.
Sir:

In my letter of the 4th of May I gave you freely and without reserve what occurred to me as proper relative to your project for obtaining possession of what you call the lands of the Tennessee Company. Your communication of this day, on the same subject, I have read with attention, and I confess with some degree of surprise, as it appears to me to be an attempt, and with the aid of the officers of government too, to trespass on the Indian rights under the pretext of a friendly intercourse with them, and which if in the least degree countenanced by the officers, must have the tendency to destroy that confidence which the Indians have in the justice of the United States.

If you intend legally to pass down the Tennessee, why do you want men to protect the company from savage hostilities? The savages are at this moment as friendly as we could wish, and not hostile to a legal intercourse with them. If you really mean to endeavour to secure under the authority of the United States a relinquishment of the Indian rights, why do you set out with an attempt to subvert that authority by raising troops, for that is the plain and obvious meaning of your number of able bodied men, to continue with the company, and with this force, aided by the emigrants, you contemplate an easy and pleasant mode of "securing," not obtaining, the relinquishment of the Indian rights to the soil, as you intend immediately upon the arrival at the destined place of settlement to make deeds of consequence for a part of the pay, and promise the balance at the expiration of the term of enlistment.

Is it possible Sir that a man as well informed as you are, and acquainted with the Indians, can suppose that the plan contemplated by you to seize upon their country would, if explained to them, be acceptable; and if it should be rejected on your arrival there, which I am confident would be the case by the whole nation, do you believe if you obtained the countenance of the public officers to make the trial in the way you propose, that it would be an easy task to remove your troops and emigrants after you had fixed them down armed to defend themselves?

I cannot, being much engaged with the duties enjoined on me here, say as much to you as I intended on this subject, but I think it unequivocally my duty to assure you that I deem the plan, as exhibited to me, to be unfriendly to the Indians and destructive of that confidence which I know they have in the justice of the Government, and delusive to such of my fellow citizens as would be weak enough to embark in the execution of it under the expectation of obtaining land for their service.

MR. ZACHARIAH COX.

The plan exhibited to me by Mr. Cox being in print, and I not having leisure to copy it, I submitted it to Colonel Butler and Colonel Henley, with the foregoing. I afterwards sent it to the Secretary of War and made this entry on it:

6th August.

Mr. Cox called on me and gave me this plan as the one he intended to carry into execution with the approbation of government to enable him and his associates to obtain the Tennessee Company's claim from the Chickasaws, and he requests I would examine the subject, and if there were no objections, to grant him a licence for himself and associates to trade with the Chickasaws. He said it was not material whether the licence was to trade at this place or any other on the Tennessee, tho' they greatly prefered the one they applied to the President for.

I gave Mr. Cox an extract from my letter of the 4th of May to the Secretary of War on his application to me then, and promised him I would consult Colonel Butler and Colonel Henley and give him an answer to his present application.

My letter is on the file.

I think the plan of Mr. Cox is now sufficiently explained; the embodying of an armed force capable of positive proof, and I expect to hear of his being arrested and secured with his accomplices, that they may be brought to condign punishment.

To Samuel Mitchell, Esq., Temporary Agent for Indian Affairs with the Choctaws:

Having constituted you Temporary Agent for Indian Affairs with the Choctaws, and confiding in your judgment, discretion and integrity, I charge you with the execution of the following instructions and such others as you may receive from time to time relative to the nature of your appointment:

Your first care will be to visit the towns in your agency, to examine into the disposition of the Indians, and whether any intrigues are carried on injurious to the United States, and endeavour to secure to the government the affections of the Indians.

You will write to Mr. Andrew Elliott, the Commissioner for runing our boundary line between the U. S. and Spain, and inform him of your mission and request from him a communication of his opinion on the conduct proper for you to observe towards the Spanish officers, your neighbours.

You will, immediately on your arrival, take measures to inform the officers in that quarter of your mission, and readiness to co-operate with them in carrying the plans of the government into effect.

The treaty with the Choctaws, with Spain and the "Act to regulate trade and intercourse with the Indian tribes and to preserve peace on the frontiers," you will consider as forming a part of your standing instructions, and in the exact fulfillment of all our stipulations by treaty.

To aid in the execution of the Act you will be guided by the following instructions:

1st. You will require of every citizen or resident of the United States, or other person who comes in the Choctaw nation, where you reside or of whom you have knowledge, to exhibit his pass, and you will keep a book in which you will record their names and by whom their pass is signed, and if the person has no pass or refuses to produce it, you will forthwith report his or their names to the Agent for the Department of War in Tennessee, and to the officer commanding the troops of the United States in your neighbourhood, and signify to the Indians that such person being a citizen of the United States, has violated the law and may be expelled by them from their nation, but that in driving them out, they must do him no injury or violence.

It is conjectured that the plan mentioned in the intercepted letter may be known to John Pitchlin or some others in your agency; you will take measures to sift it, and communicate the result. Pitchlin is your Choctaw interpreter; he has been long in my estimation.

You were furnished with a copy of the Choctaw conference while in Philadelphia as information, and those of the Chickasaws; these nations speak the same language with but little variation, and until I can find an active and suitable person, I must require your attention to them. I shall order Mr. McClish, the Chickasaw interpreter, to attend you to that nation, and follow your directions. He stands well in my estimation for the shortness of my acquaintance with him, and will serve the United States with zeal and fidelity.

I have directed the establishment of an Indian post from Tellico through the Cherokees and Creeks to the Oconee. You must, if practicable, send a runer with your dispatches once in three weeks to the Little Turkey's town, and couple your rout at that place. I expect you may get Indian lads who may be depended on to perform this service for 25 cents the day, or 20 miles.

I have requested Colonel Henley to advance you 200 dollars on account; as this is a contingent fund, you will in all cases, where practicable, obtain receipts for its expenditure. Your sallary will be 500 dollars per annum, to commence with your appointment.

You will keep a journal of your proceedings and transmit a copy to me quarterly. You will correspond regularly with the agent of the War Department here; these letters will go immediately from him to the war offices, and you will keep me informed of every occurrence necessary to be known.

Given under my hand this 12th of August, 1797.

B. H.,

P. T. A. for I. A. S. of Ohio.

————

Encampment near Holston, 12th of August, 1797.

Mr. Samuel Mitchell is appointed agent to the Choctaws. He is directed to proceed through the Chickasaw nation in the execution of the trust enjoined on him. You are hereby required to hold yourself in readiness to accompany him and to aid in the execution of such duties as he may enjoin on you to perform in the Chickasaw nation. I have informed Mr. Mitchell that for the short acquaintance I had with you, you stood well in my estimation, and I relied upon your serving the United States with zeal and fidelity.

I am your friend and obedient servant,

BENJAMIN HAWKINS.

MR. McCLISH,
  Chickasaw Interpreter.

Encampment near Holston, 12th of August, 1797.

JOHN PITCHLIN:

Mr. Samuel Mitchell is appointed agent to the Choctaws. He is directed to proceed immediately to that nation in execution of the trust enjoined on him. You are hereby required to be ready at all times to aid in the execution of such duties as he may enjoin on you to perform.

I have informed Mr. Mitchell that for several years you stood high in my estimation, and I relied upon your serving the United States with zeal and fidelity. Remember me on all occasions to my red brethren; assure them of my sincere attachment to their rights, and of a constant exertion for the preservation of them.

I am your friend & obedient servant,

B. H.

JOHN PITCHLIN,
Choctaw Interpreter.

Encampment near Holston, 12th August.

Richard Richardson, of Thomas County, has by these presents permission to remove his cattle from the State of South Carolina through the Cherokee nation to the place of his residence. He is to employ one Cherokee assistant to aid him.

This pass good for 1797 only.

Camp near Chilhowe Mountain.
JAMES RICHARDSON:

You are hereby, by virtue of authority vested in me, appointed to keep the ferry at Clinch until the end of the present year. The ferriage will remain as heretofore fixed during that period. The Indians are at all times to pass with their property free of expences, as well as the officers, and soldiers with the property of the U. States and in their service, and you are in all things to consider yourself as attached to the post of S. W. Point, and amenable to such regulations as are or shall be made by the commanding officer of the U. States in the State of Tennessee, for the government of that part at all times, to have the necessary boats in suitable repair.

Given under my hand this 12th of August, 1797.

Camp near Chilhowe Mountain.

SAMUEL RICHY:

You are hereby appointed interpreter of the Cherokee language. You are to conisder yourself as attached to the post of S. W. Point, and subject to the orders of Lt. Col. Butler, commanding the troops of the U. S. in Tennessee. Your pay will be 100 dollars per annum and two rations a day, to commence on the 6th of June, the time of arrival at S. W. Point, by invitation from Captain Wade.

Given under my hand this 18th of August.

Joseph McMartrey has lost a horse discribed to be black, ten years old, nearly 15 hands high, branded on the shoulder O; a bald face, the white turns over one of his eyes more than the other; a white spot on one of his sides about 2 inches square; all his feet white; a little hip shotten, and cress fallen.

He was said to be in the neighbourhood of Mitchell Sanders's in the course of the spring or about March.

William Thompson supposes his negro was taken to the Creek nation by one Newal Walton, or by his direction. He, shortly after the negro left his master, offered to purchase him.

Fort Wilkinson, 14th September, 1797.

Sir:

I have received your favour of this month by Captain Fielder, with the claims of several of your neighbours. I shall pay particular attention to all of them, and as far as it depends on me, my fellow citizens may rest assured that they shall obtain justice. From the measures adopted by the government and now in execution, I was in hopes that I should not hear of any more bloodshed on this frontier. On the 12th of this month two imprudent men crossed over the Oconee from near the mouth of Sandy Run, went up Little River, and wounded one of the chiefs of the Cusseta. It is yet uncertain whether the chief will die; he has sent to me and I have afforded him such assistance as he required. If your neighbours will conduct themselves well towards the Indians, they will have nothing to fear from this outrage.

I am Sir, with due regard,

Your obedient servant.

COLONEL WM. MELTON.

Mother Towns of the Upper Creeks, or Muscoguegee.

g has always the hard sound in Creek and j is used for the soft g.

Tallessee. James McQueen, William Powell.

Tuckabatchee. Christopher Heickle.

Auttossee. Richard Bailey, Josiah Fisher.

Othluwaulee. James Russel, Abraham, Mr. Mordecai.

Fuscehatchee. Nicholas White, William McCart.

Cooloome. Gregory.

Ecunhutkee. Copinger.

Ecunnau, earth and hutkee, white, called by the whites, white ground.

Sauvanogee. John Haigue.

Mooklausau. Michael Elhert.

Coosaude. Robert Walton, Francis Twzaut, John McLeod.

Wetumcau.

Hookchoie.

Hookchoieoochee.

Tuskeegee.

Ocheaupofau. Hickory ground; from oche, hickory, and aupofau.

Wewocau.

Tuccuntaulauhassee. May apple, old field, from oppuccau, may apple, and taulauhassee, old town. John Proctor, halfbreed.

Coosah. John O'Kelley, halfbreed.

Aubecoochee.

Nauche. James Quarls; Thomas Wilson, sadler.

Eufaulehatche. James Lessley.

Woccocoie. John Clark, John Gilliard, James Simmons.

Hillaube. Robt. Grierson, David Hay, Stephen Hawkins.

Ocfuskee. A point of land, from oc, in, and fuskee, projecting, this town being on a point of land. Patrick Donnelly.

Eufaulau. John Townshend.

Kialijee. John O'Riley.

Fort Wilkinson, 20th September, 1797.

MR. MACLIN:

Having executed the trust enjoined on you, by me, very much to my satisfaction and much to the accommodation of some of our fellow citizens, your neighbours, who had had their horses stolen by the Creeks, you will be continued in the Indian Department till further orders. You'l continue your usefulness.

I am desirous, if possible, to put a stop to the practice of horse stealing, and I believe, if our affairs are soon settled with Spain, that the plan you are in the execution of will be productive of that desirable end.

I wish you to be on all occasions attentive to the rights of Spain, and urge the necessity on the Indians of doing justice to the inhabitants of the Floridas, as well as the Indians, their neighbours. You will collect such of the horses as are in the nation on your return, and send them to their owners, if known, or to such place as you may deem advisable, upon obtaining the requisite information from the Indians relative to the place from whence they are taken.

I wish you success

                                                        B. H.

SACKFIELD MACLIN,
    An Assistant in the Indian Department.

———•———

                    Fort Wilkinson, 20th of September, 1797.
My dear sir:

I arrived a few days past at the new establishment of Colonel Gaither on the Indian lands on the south side of Oconee. The store is but just opened; the house is good and convenient; the fortification in considerable forwardness; the men healthy. Mr. Maclin, who is here, has made a favourable report of his mission; he has obtained 23 horses and sent them to the care of his father for their owners. The Creeks had collected 20 belonging to the Chickasaws, and some belonging to the inhabitants near Pensacola, and promised him they would send them immediately to the Chickasaw nation and Pensacola. They were in many towns, as friendly as we could wish, and expressed on all occasions their confidence in the justice of the United States, and determination to follow our advise and directions. He did not hear of any interference on the part of Spain.

I am much fatigued with my journey, tho' I continue otherwise well. I shall soon set out from this for the center of the Creeks to make some arrangement for the distribution of their annuity and to have a view of things myself. I wrote you and intended to send it by Crody from the neighbourhood of Captain Wear's, but he behaved improperly and General Pickins did not give him the letter. The three Indians behaved well. We were under the necessity to stop the line at the 50th mile in the mountains, which we found we could not pass with pack horses, and the season too warm and dry to attempt it with rum only. I do not know when it will be recommenced.

Two men in my neighbourhood crossed the Oconee at the mouth of Little River and went 10 miles up that river on the 12th of this month, fired upon an Indian chief and wounded him badly. I know the chief; he could have had both of the men killed, but would not have them pursued, and made his men take him to his camp, and then sent four of them to me to inform me of what had happened. His fate is uncertain, but he is determined to depend on the United States alone for justice.

I have a letter of the 20th of August from Mr. Grierson at the Hillabee, of which this is an extract: "The Spanish Government has issued orders for the different posts to be delivered up, agreeable to the tenor of their treaty with America which was received at New Orleans lately, and, I believe, complied with."

Adieu my dear sir, and believe me your friend and obedient servant.

MR. DINSMOOR.

Fort Wilkinson, 20th September, 1797.

I arrived here a few days past and am making arrangements to go among the Creeks. I am in want of money only, and am under the necessity of sending to Savannah to obtain some from Mr. Habersham; as soon as my messenger returns I shall set out. Mr. Price has shown me the account of the stipend for the Creeks. If you will examine an article of the New York treaty, which never has been published, I believe it is marked secret, you will see that the stipend is more than 1,500 dollars a year; the United States having agreed to allow each of the great medal chiefs, of certain towns therein mentioned, one hundred dollars annually each. This deficiency I must request you to order out as soon as practicable, as I wish a dividend of the stipend to be made and given out.

I send you a report of Mr. Maclin, who I sent after Rogers, and with directions to visit all the towns for the objects reported on by him. He has had a little assistance in drawing up the report, but I believe it to be strictly true, and he has executed the trust enjoined on him, much to my satisfaction.

I have just received two letters from the Creeks; one of the 20th of August, of which this is an extract: "The Spanish Government has issued orders for the different posts to be delivered up, agreeable to the tenor of their treaty with America, which was received at Orleans lately, and, I believe, complied with." The other the 16th instant. "I am informed by a man from Tombigbee, about six days ago, that the line between the United

States and Spain is begun, which information he says he has from the Spanish Commandant at Mobile, Don Pedro Olivero. He likewise says the Spaniards were about evacuating their fort on Tombigbee, which they say will be left out of their territory." He adds in a postscript: "It seems the Baron de Carondelet is on the line, and Governor Gaioso, former Governor of the Natches, commands in Orleans."

An important affair happened in our neighbourhood on the 12th of this month; two men who live in Hancock County crossed over the Oconee on the Indian lands, went up the Little River about 10 miles, fired upon and wounded a Cusseta chief who was hunting there. The men are known. The chief, altho' he had several young men with him, would not have the men pursued, but directed his people to carry him to his encampment, and from there, on the 16th, sent 4 of them to this post to inform me or Colonel Gaither how he had been treated on his own lands. I sent him some necessaries and offered to send for him to the garrison to be assisted here with whatever he might want. They told me he could not ride; they would attend to him, and bring him if necessary. I shall hear from him in a day or two. I asked the chief of the 4 who visited me, what the wounded chief expected or wished me to do for him? He answered: This chief visited you here last spring and promised you he would keep his young men from this frontier till this fall, and that when he found Colonel Gaither had crossed over and fixed himself on their lands, he would come with his young men and hunt, and remain with them and prevent their doing any mischief; that he has fulfilled this promise, and intends, notwithstanding what has happened, to rely on the United States for justice; that he knows there are bad, foolish young men on both sides who will be doing such things, but he hopes measures will be taken to restrain them; that his present talk is to be considered as asking nothing for himself, but as information. I have introduced the plough the past season with great success. I hired a farmer and sent him to an Indian village to make a crop for the principal chief of the village and to teach the Indians to plow. The experiment has succeeded; several have been learnt to plough and in the village there is much more corn made than heretofore, altho' the season has been too dry.

I have the honour to be, with great respect, Sir,

Your obedient servant.

The Honourable
JAMES McHENRY,
Secretary of War.

Sir:

Fort Wilkinson, 20th September, 1797.

I arrived here on the 12th instant from the State of Tennessee, on my way to the Creek nation. I expected on my arrival here to be able to draw some of the sallary due me for the past year's service, to enable me to proceed on, but I cannot find any one who will take a bill on Philadelphia. I am therefore under the necessity of dispatching a man to you with a bill; expecting you will find no difficulty in geting cash for me in Savannah. I wish you to send me some bank paper, in small notes, and about four hundred dollars in gold or silver.

I have daily advises from the Creeks; they are conducting themselves well. I have a letter of the 20th of August, of which this is an extract: "The Spanish Government has issued orders for the different posts to be delivered up, agreeable to the tenor of the treaty with America, which was received at Orleans lately, and, I believe, complied with." Since this, I received yesterday a letter of the 16th inst., from Flint River, of which this is an extract: "I am informed by a man from Tombigbee, about six days ago, that the line between the United States and Spain is begun, which information he says he had from the Spanish Commandant of Mobile, Don Pedro Olivero; he likewise says the Spaniards were about evacuating their post on Tombigbee, which they say will be left out of their territory."

MAJOR JOHN HABERSHAM.

————— ——

Sir:

Fort Wilkinson, 20th September, 1797.

I have this day drawn on you, in favour of Major John Habersham, for one thousand dollars, in part of any allowance for the first year of my service as Agent for Indian Affairs South of Ohio. I have been under the necessity of adopting this mode, as I cannot sell a bill on you where I am, and have sent the bills to him by my young man to obtain the money for them in Savannah; as soon as he returns, I shall, as you request, go immediately among the Creeks.

I have the honour to be, with great respect, Sir,

Your obedient servant.

The Honourable
   JAMES McHENRY,
      Secretary of War.

18th September.

Hannah Hales taken from Ogeechee, near Rogers Fort, is within four miles of Isaac Thomas, now at the Fish Ponds. She is the wife of the Far Off, a head man of that town, and has 4 children, one boy and 3 girls; has a good stock of cattle; has purchased a negro boy; has plenty of corn, butter and milk, and is industrious.

I sent her harness, slay and shuttle, and cards; the order dated the 18th September.

Fort Wilkinson, 22nd September.

William Hill, of Green County, as attorney for Joseph Cook, exhibited a claim for the undermentioned negros, now or lately in the possession of the family of the late General McGillivray, and he means, in due time, to establish proof to support the claim. Tom, his wife, Gen; a daughter, Ame; Easter; Nut, a wench; her daughter Fan; Beck, commonly called Bella; and Jince and Agg, who had a boy called Ben; a wench called Mill; her daughter Jin; a son, Bill, and another Jim; a girl, Patt; a fellow, Kitt; & Jacob and their increase.

Mr. Hill exhibits also a claim against the estate of Stephen Sullivan, late of New York, for fifty pounds, being a debt due to Joseph Cook. It is conjectured this property was left in the hands of General McGillivray.

WM. HILL.

Fort Wilkinson, 22nd September, 1797.

Iofekeh, the Cusseta chief who was wounded on the 12th, is in want of a blanket, one lb. sugar and 6 lbs. flower. I request you to deliver the same to the bearer who attends on him and charge it to the Indian Department.

EDWARD PRICE.

Town of St. Mary's, 9th January, 1797.

CAPTAIN JOHN GARIDEAUX,
        Newport:
Sir:

The bearer hereof, Simothly, is the Hitchetau Indian who purchased two of your negros in the nation, and is the same who you agreed with in my presence to pay for these negros. He has now called on me for the pay according to your agreement, and insists on having it without delay. I hope you will find it convenient to settle with this man, as he belongs to a gang who might be very troublesome on our frontiers if sent away displeased. You know that this fellow Simothly came honestly by your fellow negros, and that you agreed to pay him what he gave for them. I have no longer any direction of Indian matters, or I should endeavour to settle with this man out of the public store at Colerain. I think that if you was to write a letter to Major Freeman and to Mr. Price, the factor, requesting their settling it for you, that it would be done. Are you desiring Freeman to retain your pay in his hands for that purpose? If so, you will take care that no injury or insult is offered to Simothly or his companions whilst with you or in returning. With respect, I am,

Your obedient servant,
JAMES SEAGROVE.

P. S. I am of opinion you had best come on to Colerain with Simothly, where I think the business may be settled to his satisfaction.

24th September.

James Denley, Hiram Monger and Alex Megrew, of Tombigbee, exhibited passes from the Commandant of Fort St. Stephens, on the Tombigbee, to go to A los Estados D'America. I signed the passes to go through the Creek country.

Mr. Denley thinks there are 40 men settled on the right bank of the Tombigbee, and about 60 men on the Tensaw, on the left bank of the Alabama, and all hold their rights to their lands from Spain.

Fort Wilkinson, 25th September, 1797.

I have received several of your favours written lately. Simothly's claim against Garideaux cannot be paid here; I have advised him to apply to Garideaux himself, and perhaps he may settle it. He may go safely to Fort James, and from thence, I hope, to Mr. Garideaux's place of residence. If recourse must be had to law for this money, it seems that the proof, as stated by Mr. Seagrove, is positive, and in that case a recovery would be had. There is a beging spirit which manifests itself in every visit; it must be crushed. The annuity will be punctually paid and distributed and the Indians must expect in all other cases that they are to apply to Mr. Price and obtain from him such articles as they may want from the public store, and that they are to pay for the same.

I expect to leave this in 7 or 8 days and go from this, by your house, to the Tussekiahs and to the Cussetas. I shall remain a short while there and meet the chiefs there or at Tuckabatchee. If you do not come down, I shall call on you and take you with me. You may give a letter to Simothly for Garideaux.

26th September.

Passport granted Major John Colber to the Creek nation.

29th September.

Captain Francis Woodward has leave to pass into the Cherokee country; he is of Wrightsborough. Major John Colber certifies that he has known Mr. Woodward for 12 years and he has conducted himself well.

1st of October, 1797.

Isaac Downs, of Hancock County, states that some time in June, 1796, the Indians of the Creek nation were in his neighbourhood on the south side of Oconee; that some white men went over and stole a rifle from one of them; that he and some others exerted themselves to recover the rifle, knowing that the Indians would in all probability retaliate on some one of them; that they recovered the rifle and restored it; that in the interim a mare of his was taken, he supposes for satisfaction; that the mare was on the Indian lands nearly opposite to his dweling; he saw her the evening before she was taken, and the evening before they restored the gun, and he has since heard that Old Jacob's son was seen with such a mare just over the Oakmulgee, by two white men who came from the nation. Ransome Lee saw the two men and told them she was his mare.

The mare was a sorrel, light coloured mare, inclined to a bay, then a sorrel, with a ringing bell, of 4 or 5 value. He believes she had a little white on one of her fore feet, and some white in the face: a choice siseable saddle creature, 4 feet, 5 or 6 inches high.

October 24th this mare recovered at Cusseta and sent down to the care of Mr. Downs's son.

A bill of sale, Jonathan Holly to Joshua Howard, of Natches, 30th December, 1797, assigned to John Randon, 24th January, 1798.

1st of October.

William McKenzie, of Washington County, in the State of Georgia, states that on or about the years soon after the conclusion of the late war, John Randall, a halfbreed Creek, took from John Holley certain negros; Aley, her oldest son, Billey, and her increase, then in the possession of Paddy Carr. Carr had previously plundered two negro fellows, the property of John Randall, from his executor, Parris, who lives on Briar Creek. Parris, he recovered, at a suit of law in Burk County, these negros from Carr, and is supposed to hold them still in his possession. Randall has once had them in possession; they left him and returned to Parris. William McKenzie, he bought the negros belonging to John Holley after they were in possession of Randall, and on or about six years past, John Randall came in to the Rock Landing and there made a verbal bargain to give fifty pounds sterling for the said negros, then in his possession, belonging to John Holley, and promised pay the next fall, about 6 months from the time of purchase. He, some few days after this purchase, to bind the bargain, sent 20 dollars by John McKenzie from Booth's; this 20 dollars was to be forfeited if the money was not paid according to contract, and the property in the negros so sold was to revert to William McKenzie. John Randall never did pay the amount promised, and William McKenzie claims the said negros and their increase.

WM. McKENZIE.

Sworn before me.
BENJAMIN HAWKINS,
P.T. A. for I. A. South of Ohio.

2nd of October.

Silas Monk, of Hancock County, about six miles from Fort Wilkinson, states that a dog belonging to Meal Monk, his son, was carried to the Creek nation at the time his son was confined at this fort in the course of the spring. The dog is middle sized, yellow, with a ring round his neck, a white face, the legs white with yellow specks; his name Venture. His owner holds him in high estimation. He is valuable for tracking deer.

See counter claim, 29th November.

October 5th.

William Fitzpatrick: A negro, who run from him 7 years past, from Oconee, of a yellowish complexion; and a cream coloured horse. William Hill, his attorney, for the recovery.

No. 2. John Lang: A negro girl, about 12 years old, named Lucy, from his plantation near Oconee, the 9th May, 1787. William Hill, attorney.

No. 3. Silvanus Walker: That about 18 years past he lost 2 negros; one a lad about 12 years old, named Caesar, very black complexion; the other a wench, about 25 years old, of a yellowish complexion; had a stiff, crooked finger on one hand. They were taken from Phillip's Fort on Little River. He has been informed that the boy was in the possession of Reuben Dier. The wench had four children and they were in possession of one Grayham. William Hill, Attorney.

Saturday, 14th October.

I this day arrived at the Cussetas from Fort Wilkinson.

19th.

I visited the Coweta chiefs in their square and fixed on the 27th for a meeting of all the chiefs of the lower towns in that square, and advised that the Efau Haujo, of Tuckabatchee, and the Tallassee King should be invited. The Hollowing King gave me Mr. Dinsmoor's report of the 24th of August.

Cusseta, 20th of October, 1797.

Sir:

Two young men of the Eufaulies have called on me for a letter of introduction to you. Billy is a son of George Cousins, white king of that town. The other, Intummaule, is his cousin. Cousins has always been of good character and has lived well and been a trader; he is reduced. His son has three loads of skins and is desirous of trading; he has supported, for a young man, a good character. The old man has a few cattle left. He wishes his son to have a small credit of two pieces of Strouds. The articles: 1 keg of powder, and balls equivalent, 4 kegs of rum, half a piece of duffils and half a piece of shag blankets, white plains, a piece of handkerchiefs, and some stuff for shirts. I am requested to mention this to you by the young men, as you may not have an interpreter. He adds, there is no trader in his town or neighbourhood. On the subject of credit I have one uniform answer: That you have the regulation of the trade as intrusted to you; that credit may be the ruin of it, and of course must be discouraged; that if you would credit them at all, you would be the sole judge of the amount and they must receive your answer and be satisfied.

I expect a meeting of the chiefs at the Cowetas in a few days. I beg you to remember me to Colonel Gaither, and to believe me your friend and obedient servant.

MR. EDWARD PRICE,
U. S. Factor.

Mr. William Grey: Dr. to Thomas Lott, 1796.

One horse, called Smylie	$150.00
Two cows and calves	26.00
One steer	6.75
One horse, for Harrod	20.00
To 17 silver broches	5.00
One side of leather	3.00
Two pack saddles	8.00

$218.75

Thomas Lott complaines to me on oath that you, William Grey, are indebted to him two hundred and eighteen dollars 75 cents for the articles expressed in the above account, and that you delay or refuse payment. You are hereby required to appear before me on the 22nd of this month to answer the above complaint.

Given under my hand, at my lodging in the Cussetas, the 20th October, 1797.

To Peter Shugart, to execute and return.

Cusseta, Creek Nation, 20th October, 1797.

Hardy Reed, a resident in this country, complains to me on oath that some time in the spring last, he lent some horses to the

Leader's son, who went to hunt near the Oconee; that on the return of the Leader's son, he reported that he had been robbed of two horses, as hereby discribed, by white people, on the Indian hunting ground, he understood, by way of reprisal for some that had been stolen by the Indians from the citizens of Georgia, bordering on the north side of Oconee; one a bay pided mare branded on the mounting shoulder, H. R. on the thigh, 5.13½ hands high, with a colt, and one of them had a bell on. He further declares on oath that the said horses are now his property and that he has never parted with them or either of them.

His

HARDY ✕ REED.

Mark

Sworn to and subscribed before
BENJAMIN HAWKINS,
    P. T. A. for I. A. South of Ohio.

Cusseta, in the Creek Nation, 20th October, 1797.

MR. REED:

You are hereby authorized to go into Georgia to recover your property. I hope you will find no difficulty in the recovery, as the citizens of Georgia know how to obtain redress for stolen property, as when they confirm to the laws: "The United States, for property taken, stolen or destroyed, guarantee to the party injured one eventual indemnification."

Joshua Howard, an inhabitant of the Natches, called on me with testimonials of his being an orderly and decent man. He brought me a letter from Doctor James White to recommend him.

Mr. Howard informs me that he left the Natches on the 24th September; that he saw Mr. Ellicot just before he set out; that Mr. Knox had arrived with dispatches from the Secretary of State; that the Spaniards were still in possession of the Natches and Walnut Hills; that Major Minor commanded at the former; that Captain Ginor was at the Chickasaw Bluffs, and Colonel Howard on the opposite side of the Mississippi; that he came through the Choctaw lower settlements and passed the Spanish post of St. Stephen; that he visited Mobile on private business, and was there informed that it was not expected that the line would be run between the U. S.

and Spain; that he came through the Tensaw settlement and gives the following particulars of the murder of Jacob Townshend; that Townshend came there with powers of attorney from some persons in Georgia to claim and take possession of some negros and property in the possession of some inhabitants of the Tensaw settlement; that Gerald Burns, Adam Hollinger, John Miller and Melton, from some or all of whom he claimed property under his power of attorney. They appointed to meet Townshend at Joseph Thompson's, and while there they took him a prisoner and set out with him; that after riding in a circle, they, near the road, shot him, with two balls, through the body and through the head, and carried the body some distance and throwed it into a reedy branch; that they went to the house of Beard, where they drank freely. The horse of Townshend followed them, and it was discovered that the top of his saddle was much marked with a spur, supposed as he fell from his horse. Joseph Stiggins, the next morning, enquired of one of the murderers what had become of Townshend; he answered: He is gone to the Creek nation; that he fired at them and went off; they returned the fire, but knew not whether he was wounded. Stiggins, he replied: You have murdered him. He then retraced them to the scene of action and discovered the dead body; that an inquest had been held, who brought in a verdict of "willful, premeditated and hidden murder;" that the Commandant of Mobile had sent up an officer and an interpreter to examine into the whole procedure; that nothing had transpired from the officer, and the interpreter was heard to say at Robert Kilchrist's that Townshend had been a troublesome, bad man, and but little notice would be taken relative to him.

Cusseta, 21st October, 1797.

Hardy Reed applied for licence to trade in the Little Chehaws or Factor's Town. I have not heard any thing to his disadvantage; he is not charged with buying or trading in Georgia horses; is reported as an industrious man and one who exerts himself to obtain a remittance for what he owes. I have given him this certificate to leave with you.

MR. EDWARD PRICE.

Ochpoilthy, of Cusseta, called on me and claimed that he was sent down with dispatches from Mr. Jourdan to Mr. Seagrove; that he went opposite Fort Fidins, and from thence to that fort and delivered his dispatches; that the day after his arrival, Major Adams crossed over the Oconee, attacked the camp where his property was, and took from him three horses, one a mare; the other one two, and one a year old; a kettle, saddle and a blanket and some other things. As he was sent down on public account, he claims pay for his losses; he does not know the date, but it was when Barnard and his party were robed, and by the same party, sometime in May, 1794.

Answer to this claim.

At the treaty of Colerain the Indians received 6,000 dollars from the United States, in consideration of their friendly disposition towards the U. S., evidenced by their stipulations in that treaty, that losses of this sort were then mentioned; that the Creek nation are to receive 1,500 dollars annually from the U. S.; that application for claims of this sort must now be made to this nation, and if allowed, they must be paid out of the Creek stipend; that claims since the 19th May, 1796, are on a different footing, as the U. S. guaranty to the party injured an eventual indemnification. The chiefs of the nation are soon to convene and it will be proper to bring this claim before them.

23rd of October.

Pass to Abraham Gindrat, of Georgia, to pass through the Creek land, and special licence to buy a horse of Richard Thomas.

Joshua Howard, pass through the Creek nation.

The horse sold by Richard Thomas to Abraham Gindrat, a black horse, 14 hands high, branded on the mounting shoulder & buttock R. D.; 11 years old.

Cusseta, in the Creek Nation, 23rd October.

Sir:

I find that the information I gave you on the 20th ultimo, relative to the line between the U. S. and Spain, was premature, although it came from the Commandant of Pensacola.

I expect a meeting of the chiefs of the lower towns and some from the upper towns at the Cowetas, in my neighbourhood, on the 27th. The chiefs who attended the meeting of the 4 nations in

August, on the part of this nation, have returned; they report favourably of the whole transaction during the meeting. If their assurances may be relied on, peace is established between this nation and the Chickasaws, and the four nations have determined to aid each other in establishing peace and a friendly intercourse among themselves, and with their white neighbours. They have confidence in the justice of the United States. The plan now in execution, to better the conditions of the Indians and to preserve peace and a friendly intercourse with them, will have the effect contemplated in the establishment of it. It has already taken so deep root that I do not believe it is in the power of the enemies of the United States to destroy it.

The agents met with much fatigue, some crosses and vexations, but this was to be expected, and we met the whole with a steady and patient perseverence in fulfilling the duties enjoined on us.

You have, in the inclosed, a narrative of a recent murder at Tensaw. In that settlement there are 60 families; in that of Tombigbee there are 40. The two settlements are on our side of the line; the first on the left bank of the Alabama; the other on the right bank of the Tombigbee. They have Spanish rights for their lands. The latter settlement is the one complained of by the Choctaws in their conference with you.

You will hear from me in a few days.

I have the honour to be, with much and sincere regard, Sir,

Your obedient servant.

The Honourable
JAMES McHENRY,
Secretary of War.

Cusseta, 23rd of October, 1797.

Sir:

Several applications have been made to me to obtain credit at the store, and to some of the applicants I have given letters, but no assurances that they would on them obtain credit. I find that the skin trade is on the decline, and that the wants of the Indians are increasing. The little traders appear to me to be extravagant and improvident. I expect, in the course of the winter, the Indians who hunt on your side of Ocmulgee (Ochesehatchee) will carry their skins to you.

I shall have a meeting with the chiefs on the 27th, at the Cowetas, and I will inform you of the result. I shall endeavour to put an end to that system of beging, which has taken such deep root among them, and which manifests itself in every visitor.

I have received from Mr. Dinsmoor a report of the proceedings of the 4 nations at their meeting in August. It is very satisfactory, and if the assurances of my red brethren can be relied on, all is well. They have unquestionably unbounded confidence in the justice of our government, and I do believe it is not in the power of our enemies to disturb it.

A long continuance of the fatigue I daily experience would be more than I can bare. I must devise some mode to shift the same, and I know not what that will be. Can you and the Colonel devise one for me? Can you send Eliza Hollinger here to superintend the household? If you can, you will afford an assistant who will enable me to be more useful. If you cannot, you must write to Francis to send me one, or to Parish to send one of the Wopian sisters.

I wish you to send me, by Whitaker, 3 good blankets, 1 pc. oznabrigs, some thread and needles, binding, 2 kegs of spirits and anything that will make a load or two to buy provisions. I believe he will have two spare pack horses. I want some nails, the spade shovel, hand saw, drawing knife and grindstone. You will pay Whitaker 4 dollars a load, and I wish you to pay at that rate for any thing you may send me from time to time. I shall write you fully after the meeting.

MR. EDWARD PRICE.

I wish you to pay Davis for his service, at the rate of 10 dollars per month, from the 2nd of this month until he returns with this letter, for bringing blacksmith's tools to the nation. Let him raise a small account vs. the Indian Department, and insist on it as a voucher.

———————

Cusseta, 23rd of October.

I omited in my letter of this date to mention to you that you must attend with great caution to the execution of Section 10 of the "Act to regulate trade and intercourse with the Indian tribes, and to preserve peace on the frontiers." This trading in horses is the source of endless mischief, and unless we can check it and reduce it to the bounds of legal commerce, will totally frustrate the benevolent plans of the government. Mr. Darouzeaux's son, who offered for sale a small horse, which I ordered to be returned, was playing the rogue; he did not own the horse; and since my return, I find that a fat cheeked Cusseta fellow has sold a horse for a rifle, which did not belong to him; he was without ears and exchanged the horse for the rifle.

As you are to grant special licence, let me advise you in all cases to have a certificate from me, or from the head man of the town, accompanying the horse. This check will be sufficient, and there will be no difficulty in obtaining one or the other. I shall, at the meeting next to be had, order this plan to be promulgated through every town.

MR. EDWARD PRICE,
U. S. Factor.·

See the application of the 1st of October.

Cusseta, 24th October.
MR. DOWNS:

Your mare was taken last evening from my residence. I sent this morning to the chiefs to have her restored; they immediately exerted themselves and sent her to me. I have permited them to send a messenger after your son to deliver her to him, to take her down to you. Remember me to Mrs. Downs and the girls.

MR. ISAAC DOWNS.

John Marino, a Spaniard, arrived from St. Mary's without a pass. He says he came with an intention of living with Francis Lesslie at the Chevally's. He has an iron grey horse, 13 hands high, without brand, and an old saddle and bridle.

26th.

Permission to Joseph Bates to pass to the State of South Carolina.

Permission to George Johnston to pass to the State of South Carolina.

Coweta, 27th of October, 1797.

Mr. Hawkins met the Indians of the 12 river towns at the Coweta square, and went into a lengthy detail of the proceedings in relation to the four southern tribes under the direction of the President of the U. States; his attending to ascertain and mark

the boundary on the frontiers of the Cherokees; the conference
with the chiefs of that nation at Tuskeegee; the improper conduct
of some Creeks on the borders of Cumberland while he was there;
their stealing horses; their ill treatment of the Chickasaws, in
stealing horses and murdering the people; that the Chickasaws had
applied to him for justice, and stated their complaints in bold and
strong language; they had now lost all confidence in the promises
of the Creeks and their conduct justified the opinion that they were
a faithless, rogueish people, capable of being restrained only by
force. He replied he would use his best endeavours to cause
justice to be done; that he believed it would be proper to convene
the four nations to see if the Indians could settle the existing disputes among themselves; and if after a fair experiment, it required
his interposition, he would give it, and he trusted with great effect;
that the Chickasaws must suspend their resentments for the
present, and not charge the base conduct of some ungovernable
Creeks to the whole nation; that if after the meeting, which I
contemplated, the representatives of the nation should refuse to
do justice to the Chickasaws, then, and then only, the Creeks might
be branded with the epithet of "a faithless, rogueish people;" that
he was happy to find that the experiment succeeded, and there was
now a prospect of a happy accommodation of all past differences
among the four nations; that he, as their agent, rejoiced that his
voice, which was that of the President and the whole people of the
U. S., had been listened to. There now remained one thing more
to be done: The chiefs, who are now here, sent a deputation to
the meeting of the 4 nations; the deputies are present and have
made their report of what they heard and did, and your beloved
man, Mucclassee Hoopoi, is to go to the Chickasaws and carry the
ratification of the proceedings at the four nations to that nation,
with all the stolen horses. You must now, in my presence, take
this matter under your consideration. Here is the letter of that
chief; he says: "The Chickasaws are yet dubious of the Creeks,
altho' they don't say so." Ratify what you have done. This letter
brings you a talk from the Chickasaws, with some beads and
tobacco, the usual tokens of friendship among you red people.
Accept of them and send on your part what Mucclassee Hoopoi
wishes, what I wish, and what must be the wish of all good Creeks,
The two evidences of friendship required of you, a ratification of
the peace accompanyed with the stolen horses. You will answer on
to-morrow.

Coweta Square, 28th October, 1797.

The speach of the Cowetas, Cussetas and other lower towns to the
Chickasaws, in reply to the address of yesterday:

TUSSEKIAH MICO:

There are ten towns present, and they have seen the talks of the Chickasaws. The Choctaws and Cussetas & the three kings of these towns have sent a talk to the Chickasaws, which they have already seen. I have seen the head king of the Chickasaws and told him that they and the Cussetas were one fire; that the Cussetas and Cowetas were one fire, and all the men of these three towns were considered as one people. The talk the king and I had together, was that if his people came into our town, we considered them as our people, and when we went into their town, we should consider ourselves as at home. When I saw this king, I told him I formerly knew his chiefs, but they were gone; the chiefs now there I did not know. The king replied, I must see them and talk to them. I was appointed to talk to these head men of the Chickasaws. I was directed to take the emblem of peace and friendship and put them down before these chiefs, and talk to them; this I did. Fan Omingo, Tusscuppatapa Omingo, Whelocke Emautlau and Insuchelah, and the Chickasaw Mico; when I met these men, they told me when I went back to my nation, I must let them know that the Chickasaws had spoken with the older brothers; and accordingly, when I returned into my land, I went to the chiefs of the Abbecohatche and Tallapoosahatche and told them to mind their hunting and think of nothing but peace. I told the Chickasaws, also our young brothers, when they went a-hunting, to behave well and mind their hunting, and if they saw any of their older brothers, the Abbecoos, to treat them kindly; if either of them had meat, to share it with the other.

I talked to heads of both parties, and advised them when they went into the woods, not to injure the stock of each other. I told them likewise, if the Chickasaws or Upper Creeks visited each other, to behave friendly and to assist the visitor with corn. From that advise I expected the chiefs would prevent mischief before it was too late, but I heard the Upper Creeks did not listen to the talk, and that they have spilt each other's blood in the Chickasaw savannas. After this talk to the head men, Insuchelah said he had some reserved ground for himself, and if he discovered any Creek hunters beyond that, he would take their skins from them; that this reserve was beyond a great white rock, known to the hunters of both nations. I replied to Insuchelah, no, that they must share these things among one another and not take their's alone. The older chiefs of the Chickasaws approved of my advise and said that Insuchelah was rong; that these moves should not be made. After the talks were over, the Chickasaws handed a pipe, a red one, which the Chickasaws had received from the Quoppaws; they received it from the Ooseuchees; they directed this pipe to be delivered to the Cusseta Mico and Hoopoi Mico of Coweta, that Hoopoi Mico is still alive and the pipe is in being in remembrance of that conference we had together, as I talked to them to keep peace and quiet among them then; that talk is still in remembrance, altho' some of the men who heard it are dead, and the talk now is the same, to keep peace and be in friendship with each other, and I hope this is the wish of all, and that they will exert themselves on both sides, and the sending the horses is a proof of this.   There was a meeting called in the Cherokees of the 4 nations; I was not able to attend, but I have heard and approve of the talks concluded on there, and if they continue during this winter's hunt, I hope they will be attended by all the nations, and that there will be peace.

FUSATCHEE MICO.

The heads of the ten towns have met to give an answer. One of our chiefs has delivered a speech in behalf of all of us, and I have something to add. As the heads of different towns have met, and the two fires of the Cowetas and Cussetas, which form but one, are here, I have not much to say, but that little is to strengthen our efforts for peace. As the intention of this meeting is for the benefit of all classes of red people, old and young, I add my mite. We have met with a good intention; we have heard the Chickasaw's talks at our separate fires, and here we have met to answer them, and I hope our answers will be beneficial in future. When people meet and hear each other's talks, and they appear satisfactory, it is pleasing; this is our case and I am in hopes ours will have the desired effect.

YEAUHOLAU MICO.

My talk has lately been delivered. I and my kings have been and talked at the meeting of the nations in the Cherokees; at this meeting I spoke, and what I there said to the 4 nations I shall now repeat. At this meeting I spoke to them all, and desired all the Indian nations to be peaceable and hunt the game and be friendly to each other; this I am now to repeat: I expect the Abbeecoos are taking measures agreeable to this talk; there were some of them present, and I have the white beads in my hand and I hope they will keep peace and be quiet. I desired them to keep that talk. I considered it would be to their advantage, and that of all red people, to pursue their game, and lie down at night and sleep in peace; that by being in peace and pursuing their game, they might all live comfortable. I have sent this talk before, and I hope the Chickasaw chiefs have heard, and I now send the same advise; it was good there and is so now. I sent my talks before, and desired them to be in peace; my talk is the same now, and I must repeat, it is my opinion, it would be good for all the red people to live in peace with each other. The Pauachucklui, the Warrior King of the Cusseta, the Big King of that town, and I, who talked to them before, send this written talk to them. These white beads are a token of the paths being strait between the Chickasaws and our towns; I had these beads in my hand when I made this speech, and the Chickasaws know this is the way for us red people. I send another token, the tobacco; this is the ancient mode among red people. I have sent the talks down to the Simanolees and all the Indians in this quarter. I send this other token from the red people in this quarter, and I hope the Chickasaws and others will get together and smoke it and let all animosities vanish, as the smoke does, in the air. I sent a full talk from the Cherokees and this is a confirmation of it, and I hope it will be taken as such. The reason I send them this again is that the fall, the season for hunting, is come; they will be all in the woods. I hope they will be friendly to each other and with the return of the spring, all things will be strait.

The man who takes this talk was appointed as the ambassador of this nation, and he was to take talks of this sort and go set down and deliver them in the name of his nation; he is Mucclassee Hoopoie, Opoie Mico.

Cusseta Town, 31st October, 1797.

This day, by a power to me invested, I demand of Thomas Carr, of this town, a certain negro man by the name of Harry, which I had just reason to believe was in his possession down at Pensacola, and after stating the circumstances relative to said negro, the said Carr agreed to deliver me the said slave, Harry, on or before the 10th April ensuing, at Fort Wilkinson, on the Oconee River, in consequence of my paying him one hundred & twenty-five dollars, which sum of money he had paid to an Indian for said negro.

Given under our hands the day & date above.

G. W. FOSTER.
THOMAS CARR.

In the presence of
BENJAMIN HAWKINS,
   P. T. A. for I. A. South of Ohio.

6th November.

Mr. Carr informs me that he has made a different bargain; that he has agreed to give two hundred and forty dollars for this negro to Mr. Foster, and he did, in my presence, deliver, in part payment to William Mapp, one big horse at one hundred dollars, and the ballance is to be paid in May next, being one hundred and forty.

                                        G. W. FOSTER.

Approved by Mr. Foster and signed in presence of

BENJAMIN HAWKINS.

10th of November.

In consideration of the sum of two hundred and forty dollars, above stated, I have sold to Thomas Carr the negro man, named Harry, the property of Henry Charleton and Ludwell Evans, late deceased; and I do hereby warrant and defend the same to him and his heirs. Given under my hand & seal this 10th of November, 1797.

                                        G. W. FOSTER. (Seal).

Signed and sealed.

BENJAMIN HAWKINS.

Cusseta, 31st of October, 1797.

James Moore is hereby permited to exchange the town of Big Tallassee upper for Tuhtocaugee, Michael Welch, licenced for that town, having informed me that he is unable to carry on trade.

I have sent an Indian by Mr. Foster's to inform you what I have been doing here. There has been a meeting of some of the towns in this neighbourhood; there were ten present. I informed them of all things necessary for them to know, and gave them assurances of the determination of the President to fulfill all the promises made on the part of the United States. You understand every thing well, and you could have been of service had you been with us. The Cowetas are unwilling to understand the treaty of Colerain; the Hollowing King said a great deal on the Tulapocca being the boundary. I told him there was an end of this land business, it was well understood at Colerain and there was settled by the nation, and it was not in his or my power to alter it. I left them yesterday; I do not know what they will do, but you and I know what they ought to do. I am this day informed by the Tussekiah Mico that the Hollowing King will be here in the morning, and that all things will be strait. I think the Indians about here are growing better. I spoke to them about horse stealing, and this murdering business on the frontiers. I shall prevent the white people from buying Indian horses without a licence; this will put an end to it. I know it has been too much encouraged by white men. The Indians of these towns have sent a very good talk to the Chickasaws; it is to go by the Mucclassee Mico. I wish your towns would attend to keeping peace with the Chickasaws; it would be a disgrace to them to violate a peace made or confirmed in the presence of the 4 nations. I hope also, that your people will be more careful than they were last year, and that I shall not hear so many complaints against them for taking horses from their neighbours. I have told you before that the chiefs of your land ought to govern it, and to have the right of making peace or war; that when this is done, any man who violates the peace should be punished. Try to make your people understand this, and let us be neighbourly with our white brethren. I want to see your chiefs respectable. Your young men must be attentive to their chiefs, and then you will be a great people.

Mr. Moore called on me. I find, from him, you have had some liars in your neighbourhood; you must not let such foolish people make you do any thing injurious to your character. You are an officer in the service of the United States, and you will be respected as such. I have requested Mr. Foster to read this letter for you; he is a magistrate in Georgia, come into the nation after some of his property, and I expect you will treat him with attention. I wrote to you that I left your last quarter's sallary with Mr. Price; he will pay it to you. I cannot come into your town till things are settled here; then I shall see you. Remember me to the Mad Dog, and assist him to keep matters right in the upper towns, while I am doing so among the lower. Tell him his nephew called on me, and has heard the Coweta talks and does not like them. Farewell.

MR. ALEXANDER CORNELL,
Assistant & Interpreter among the Upper Creeks.

Cusseta, 31st of October, 1797.

John Galphin has exhibited a claim before me against William Augustus Bowles for sundries furnished him, the ballance unpaid being 868 dollars. This claim is strengthened by a certificate of

Richard Thomas. John Galphin also informs me that there is in possession of Peter Shugart some property belonging to the said Bowles, and he requests that the same may be secured to pay this debt, or so much thereof as the same may amount to. Hereupon, I have ordered this account to be registered, and I do hereby require that Peter Shugart shall exhibit an account of the property aforementioned, in his possession, and such claim as he has, if any, against the said Bowles, that justice may be done, and that he holds the said property, when returned, subject to my order.

November 2nd, 1797.

Patrick Brown, John Wheat, Kinchil Sheffield, Sampson Mounger, his wife and four children, exhibited passes to pass thro' the Creek nation, signed Com. Freeman and countersigned by Edward Price.

James Denley, Alex. Magrue and Hiram Monger exhibited passes from the Commandant of Fort St. Stephens, countersigned Henry Gaither, Lieut. Colonel Commandant.

4.

Momejuh, of the family Hotallee, was in company with 2 others, the spring of 1794, at the house of John Boothe on Oconee; they tarried there all night, and lost out of the field a small black horse. Boothe gave them no satisfaction in the morning. The horse was branded P. on the left shoulder.

Information is lodged with me that a small, slim grey horse, supposed to belong to Timothy Barnard, and stolen from him while attending the duties enjoined on him at Fort Wilkinson, was seen at the camp of Andrew Darouzeaux called Fullidgee, and he sold him to a man who kept goods for sale at John Boothe's, where the informant saw him in a pen last month, and he was stolen during that month.

5th.

Leave and permission is hereby given to Richard Thomas to purchase from Robert Walton a black gelding, 12 hands high, branded on the mounting shoulder R. W., on the thigh E. Z.; three years old and upwards. Robert Walton is a trader in the Coosadoes, and Richard Thomas is clerk in the Indian Department, residing in the Cusseta.

Cusseta, 7th November, 1797.

Joseph Thompson, an inhabitant of Tensaw, this day complained, on oath, before me that Zachariah McGirt, in the neighbourhood of Tuckabatchee, did, as he believes, on or about July last, prevail on two negros, Munday and Nancy, late the property of Samuel Moore, in his possession, and belonging to an infant and heiress to Samuel Moore, late deceased, and now the daughter-in-law of him, the said Thompson, to leave his plantation and go into the Creek nation; and in proof of this belief he states that he had been informed that this McGirt had declared his intention of geting possession of these negros under pretence of having a claim to them, but he was dissuaded from carrying his first intention into execution by Jacob Townshend; that upon missing these two negros on his return home, at the period aforesaid, he judged that McGirt, who had been lately seen in his neighbourhood, had taken them. He thereupon got two of his neighbours, James Randal and Edward King, to go with him in pursuit of them, and near Richard Bailey's they got a-head of McGirt and George Cornell, there they met, & McGirt inquired the business of his journey, and on being informed, McGirt acknowledged he had the negros in his possession.

Joseph Thompson further states that about four years past, Zachariah McGirt brought suit for this property before the Commandant of Tensaw, and failed to establish his claim; that when this suit was brought before the Commandant, this deponent exhibited, on the part of the heiress of Samuel Moore, two bills of sale, one from John Rogers, dated 11th of May, 1782, for the negro woman, Nancy, and the other, dated Dix, New Vienna, Jour de Janvier, 1787, from Charles Hall, attorney for the Sieur Spiear Christopher, for the negro, Nawnne Londy (called Mondy); that after he failed in the establishment of the claim, this deponent did expect that there was an end to the same.

The deponent further states that application has been made to the Commandant of Mobile for redress, and that he sent a writing to the Mad Dog, of Tuckabatchee, but without effect, and he now applies for justice in the premises to the Principal Temporary Agent for Indian Affairs South of Ohio.

JOS. THOMPSON.

Subscribed and sworn to before me.

BENJAMIN HAWKINS,
P. T. A. for I. A. South of Ohio.

ZACHARIAH McGIRT, in the neighbourhood of Tuckabatchee:

You are hereby required and commanded to appear before me on or before the first day of December next ensuing, to answer the complaint of Joseph Thompson and to retain the said negros in your possession till further orders. Given under my hand this 7th of November, 1797.

8th of November.

The towns recommended by the chiefs at the Coweta meeting, which convened on the 27th ultimo, as entitled to half of the annual stipend of the Creeks:

Stipend for 1796 and 1797.

Miles from
Coweta

	1, Coweta	$	250.00
2½,	2, Tallauhassee		150.00
5,	3, Cusseta		250.00
13,	4, Uchee; Agent, Uchee Will		100.00
21,	5, Ooseuchee; Opoi Haujo		100.00
21,	6, Cheauhau		100.00
25,	7, Hitchetee		100.00

November 19th.

28,	8, Palachooclee; Taykeneau	80.00

November 15th.

34,	9, Oconee; Coloktau, Agent	80.00
38,	10, Sauwoogelo	170.00

December 1st.

40,	11, Sauwoogelaochee; Tuccosau Tustunnagau	80.00
55,	12, Eufaule	120.00

Added on the 10th, Coweta		250.00
Tallauhassee		120.00
Cusseta		250.00

$2,200.00

On further deliberation, and on application of the chiefs in the Cusseta square the 10th, it was deemed advisable to add for the present year 250 dollars to the Cusseta, and as much to the Coweta dividends, and to the Tallauhassee 120 dollars. It appears that these towns are the most exposed, bordering on the frontiers, and that they have the most difficulty, trouble and expence in restraining their young men and carrying the national engagements into effect.

Cusseta, in the Creek Nation, 9th November, 1797.

Dear Colonel:

I yesterday received your favour of the 20th of September in the packet from the War Office in the care of Steele. I know well the importance of your command. You have your share of difficulties, as we all have, but let us buoy ourselves above them by a firm, patient and persevering conduct. The Secretary of War will unquestionably do whatever depends upon him to enable you to fulfill the expectations of the government in your quarter. The laws must be executed. As far as this depended on me, I have made the necessary communications and contributed my mite. The positions you have taken are well chosen.

I was of opinion when I showed you Cox's plan on the 6th of August, and consulted you and Colonel Henley on the answer proper to be given him, that the crime of embodying an armed force would subject him to arrest and punishment. I sent the plan and my correspondence with Mr. Cox to the Secretary of War, and I have expected before this to hear that Cox and his associates were apprehended.

My old friend, Campbell, has not the faculty of seeing clearly even one side of the questions he attempts so laboriously to defend. As to there being two sides, it is out of the question with him; he and his associates are right, and they have not been able to discover that their neighbours possess any rights at all. The Indians are unquestionably the rightful possessors of their own lands; they have ever been so, and there is but two ways of ousting them, conquest or compact, neither of which can be plead by Campbell. I remember your and my being together at Colonel Craig's when he urged the right of intrusion; he said he had lived there ten years, knowing himself to be an intruder, and five years of that time lived in an intrusion castle. I remember that the bare mention of intrusion as a right was new to you and me.

The dust you mention, of the 18th of September, is like the expiring blast of a lamp. While I am coupled with my honest old friend, Colonel Henley, I shall be in good company. I would not exchange one ounce of his integrity for the whole group you mention.

I am here in the midst of the Lower Creek towns, and I have been for a month on business with them; we begin to understand each other; we have black drink and talks in the day, and dancing at night. I go to bed about 12 and rise pretty early; the remainder of the time is claimed by the Indians, and I devote it to them. They will not be excluded even at meal times; they bring their private and public claims; I attend to them, and I am happy to find that by my exertions the benevolent views of the government have already taken so deep root that I may defy the malice of the enemies of it. I have lately countersigned the credentials of one of the best men in this land (Mucclassee Hoopoi), who is appointed and sent, with full powers, to ratify the peace made between the Creeks and Chickasaws. I believe the four nations are now at peace, and that they have confidence in the justice of our government.

I shall avail myself of every opportunity to let you hear from me.

I have the honour to be your friend, & dear Colonel

Your obedient servant.

COLONEL THOMAS BUTLER.

Extract to Mr. Panton:

Cusseta, 6th November.

I arrived here early last month, and have been constantly engaged in the execution of the duties enjoined on me by my appointment. This being the first opportunity I have had since the receipt of your favour by Whitaker, I avail myself of it to thank you for your friendly communication and to assure you of my persevering endeavours to merit the esteem of all good men. My task is an arduous one, as you well know, but I have the pleasure already of finding that I make some progress, and I am not without hopes that the benevolent plan of the U. S. to better the condition of the Indians will be a productive one during my agency. The cloud that hovered over us some time past is dissipated.

Cusseta, in the Creek Nation, 9th November, 1797.

Dear Colonel:

I yesterday received your favour of the 14th of September, inclosed with dispatches from the War Office in the care of Steele. I have been so long riding in a circle that I have not received any letters from your quarter since I left you before this. I have heard of the dust in your quarter of the 18th September, and that as far as the words of the infidels can affect us, we are damned. While I am coupled with you I shall be satisfied, notwithstanding, as I know our faith is that honesty is the best policy in politics as well as private life, and that our actions will correspond with our faith.

I find that Cox is obstinately bent to carry his point; I did believe when I received from him, on the 6th of August, his plan, which I submitted to your and Colonel Butler's inspection, that the crime of embodying an armed force was sufficient to subject his to arrest and punishment. I sent his plan, and my correspondence, with him to the Secretary of War, and I have expected before this, that he would be apprehended. The laws must be executed. I see that Chisholm has bestowed one solitary damn on a few of us as a last dying speech.

I have been among these lower towns for more than a month. I have obtained a ratification of the peace made with the Chickasaws, and we have sent one of the most influential chiefs in this land to take the ratification to that nation (Mucclassee Hoopoi). The Creeks have gathered a large number of the Chickasaw horses and sent them home. I cannot express to you the difficulty I have had to encounter since I left you, but I can assure you that the benevolent views of our government have been thoroughly impressed on my red charge and that it has taken so deep root that I do not believe it is in the power of its enemies to disturb it.

I must advise you not to grant a licence to any one to buy a horse from a Creek, and that when you grant a special licence, apply it to the horse and persons buying and selling, and in no case to a Creek that has not a certificate from me that the horse is his, or from the chiefs of his town, countersigned by the trader of the town. I find this horse stealing is the source of much evil in this land, and to check it without stopping the trade in horses for a while, or limiting it, as I advise, will be impracticable.

The chiefs of the upper towns have informed me that several of their young men who have gone to hunt on the borders of Cumberland have stolen horses from the traders and from the Indians with the view of selling them in that quarter. They request my interposition to prevent it, and that they may not be suffered to sell their horses at all.

I have found it necessary to retain Mr. Maclin during the hunting season at least, in the Indian Department; he has deserved well. I have ordered him to go to Tellico to visit you, and go thence to the borders of Cumberland to use his endeavours to check the improper conduct of the Indians who are gone to hunt in that quarter. His pay is a dollar a day, he finding his horse and bearing his expences. If he should apply to you for some money, I wish you would aid him.

I have the honour to be, with great and sincere regard, dear Colonel,

Your obedient servant,

B. H.

COLONEL DAVID HENLEY,
Agent of War.

Cusseta, 9th November, 1797.

I have received the packet you sent by Sandy Grierson, and I have paid him one guinea for bringing of it. The letters I send you, you must deliver yourself to Colonel Butler and Colonel Henley. I have written to Colonel Henley to advance you some money; if you should apply for it, you must go, as you propose, to the borders of Cumberland and use your endeavours to check this horse stealing. I have written fully to Colonel Henley on this subject; you must notice particularly that a licence to purchase a horse from an Indian or of any white man in the Indian territory, must be a special licence. If you hear of any man who violates the law in this particular or any other, you must report him to Colonel Gaither and to Mr. Dinsmoor; in the report fix the name of the person and his place of abode, and the witness, if any. If you buy any horse for your own use, you must report him to me, discribing the particulars; when I say your own use, I mean as a public officer, to enable you to fulfill the duties enjoined on you by your appointment; in no other light can you or any man in the department be permited to buy.

I have had much difficulty here in arranging matters to my satisfaction, and upon the whole, I have not much to complain of. The chiefs, some of them, have exerted themselves, but they want some aid to carry their decision into effect. I believe I shall be able in the course of a few months to make some examples, and they are much wanted.

As you are going on the frontiers you will hear much conversation relative to Indian transactions, and perhaps some personal abuse intended for me. I do not wish you to embark in any dispute on my account, but treat every one with attention where it is in your power, and to those that are rude, retaliate on them no otherwise than by being silent and doing your duty. I expect that you will find on your arrival at Knoxville, that Cox has been arrested on the crime of embodying an armed force; he is certainly guilty and will meet his just reward.

Mr. Blount, I hear, has arrived at Knoxville; you will be cautious to leave him and his demerits to be decided on by the proper tribunal.

Let me hear from you by every opportunity; continue as you have hitherto done, to deserve well, and you will possess the confidence of your obedient servant.

B. H.

MR. SACKFIELD MACLIN.

Cusseta, 9th November, 1797.

Sir:

After I parted with you, the General and I progressed, in all, 50 miles, and there from the concurring testimony of our experience, that of the white hunters and the Indian Commissioners, we found ourselves under the necessity to halt the line; the weather was too dry and warm to move without the aid of pack horses, and the mountains were impassable for them. I came on to the General's, and there dispatched our journal and papers and came on here by the way of Fort Wilkinson, the headquarters of Colonel Gaither, on the Oconee.

I am now in the midst of the Lower Creeks, and have been one month engaged in conversation with them. I go to bed at 12, arise early, and the remainder of the time is claimed by the Indians, and I devote it to them; they will not be excluded even at meal times, and bring their private as well as public claims, which I attend to.

I find more crosses, vexations and difficulties than falls to any officer of the government in my neighbourhood; added to this, I have had an attack of the gout or rheumatism, which was sorely afflictive for some days, but I find my mind disposed to buoy itself above the whole, and I find some amusement in the certain progress of the benevolent views of the government intrusted to my superintendency.

I have directed Mr. Maclin to hover on the borders of Cumberland and to aid me to put a stop to horse stealing from that quarter; this itch had subsided for a while, but a few white men on the frontiers have, regardless of the law, gave encouragement to the young, worthless fellows, who heretofore embarked in it, and they have begun on the traders and stockholders in the land. I have, at the request of the Upper Creeks, requested Colonel Henley not to suffer a Creek to sell a horse in Tennessee without my certificate accompanys the horse, or the certificate of some of the head men of the towns where the seller lives, countersigned by a trader.

I find no difficulty in establishing peace with the Chickasaws. The Creeks have sent one of their most respectable chiefs (Mucclassee Hoopoi) as Minister Plenipotentiary, to certify the peace, and they have also sent a number of the Chickasaw horses home.

I countersigned the talks, at the request of the chiefs, that this chief takes with him.

I shall be glad to hear from you as opportunities occur. I shall not, I fear, be in your quarter again till the close of winter.

I have the honour to be, with due regard, Sir,
Your obedient servant,
B. H.

GENERAL JAMES WINCHESTER.

Cusseta, Creek Nation, 9th November, 1797.
Sir:

Mr. Maclin, who has conducted himself much to my satisfaction, has my orders to return on your frontiers to aid me in putting an end to horse stealing. I find that many of the hunters are gone out towards Cumberland, and that they have made free with the horses of the traders and some of the Indians who have horse stands or stamps. I expect they will endeavour to sell some of these horses in your quarter or near Tellico. The law directs in this business and those who offend must be punished. At the request of the chiefs of the upper towns, I have advised Colonel Henley not to give special licence to buy, but in case that the seller has my certificate to sell, or a certificate from the head men of his town, countersigned by a trader.

I hope I have at last concluded a peace between the Creeks and Chickasaws; one of the most esteemed chiefs of this land is gone to ratify the peace; he takes with him the remains of the stolen horses and the peace talks countersigned by me. I have had much difficulty since I saw you, but I am going on. Assure your neighbours of my constant attention to their interests, and believe me yourself with due regard, Sir,
Your obedient servant,
B. H.

GENERAL JAMES ROBERTSON.

Cusseta, 9th November, 1797.

I have not heard one syllable of you since you left me; I suppose, notwithstanding, that you are well, or I should have heard your death announced in the newspapers. I find a number of my Creek family are likely to visit you this winter; they have gone towards Cumberland to hunt, and they have taken the traders' horses and some from the provident Indians who keep horse stamps.

I have written to Colonel Henley to aid me to put a stop to this abominable traffic. I have, at the request of the Upper Creeks, notified those who have horses to sell that they must have a certificate from me, or one from the head men of the town, countersigned in the last case by a trader. I expected some of these may be offered in your neighbourhood for sale, and in that case, I request you to note the purchaser and report him to Colonel Henley or our friend, Mr. Dinsmoor.

I was informed some time past that you owed your appointment to a great man, who you have had the ingratitude to undermine. I am told Colonel Henley owed his appointment to the same man; the latter I said I believed, but as for you, I said I understood that a short billet from the Secretary of War had picked you up far to the east and placed you at Tellico.

I am informed you have Mrs. Butler with you and her amiable family; I wish it may be true; you must present my love to her, and assure her that I have been anxious ever since I had the pleasure to be acquainted with her, to be nearly allied to her, but I was too old for her daughters, and for herself too, if she was a widow; but as fortune would have it, behold, she is my daughter. I must send her a chapter on the rights of my Cherokee daughters, to the end that if she has any contest with the Commandant, she may easily prove at all times she is in the right.

I would be glad to hear from the Cherokee hatter; I want a hat, and I fear I must send to Philadelphia for one. May I venture to apply to you for a chapter on gardening? Do you understand this business well? If you do not, let me inform you that the first thing to be done is to have the lot well fenced, the next place well planted, and lastly, well worked and kept free from weeds. I am, with the sincerest regard and esteem,

Your obedient servant,

B. H.

MR. JAMES BYERS,
U. S. Factor, Tellico.

Extract of a letter to Mr. Grierson, in the Hillabees:

Cusseta, November 9th, 1797.

But why will you not have your cotton spun at your own house? You have females enough to make 1,000 yds. annually, and I will assist you with cards, &c.

I sent up by Stephen, a harness, slay and shuttle for Hannah Hale; he told me that Hayes was to make her a loom; I wish you to tell Hayes to make her a good one and I will pay him for it, and to assist her to put it in motion.

November 10th.

George Clem, a trader, residing in the Weetumpkee, informs that about the 1st of September he sold Abraham Mordecai a sorrel horse, blaze in his face, one white foot, branded G. C. on his mounting thigh, three years old next spring, for sixty dollars, to be paid in goods; that on the 23rd of October he received a letter from Abraham Mordecai informing him that he had sent him his horse by Henry Wilson; that on his return he would pay him for his horse, or the hire of him, if he should think proper to take his horse back; that Wilson lost the horse about Flint River, and an Indian of the Cusseta named ———— having found the horse and now has him in possession. George Clem requests permission to take possession of his horse, which permission is granted on the terms aforesaid.

From the recorder.

13th November.

Pass to Senogechee, of the Cusseta, to cross the Oconee on a visit to Mr. John Hill.

12th November.

Power of attorney of Henry Carleton, of Greene County, in Georgia, to George W. Foster, to recover two negros in the Creek nation. Dated 30th September, 1797.

Cusseta, 12th November, 1797.
MR. TOWNSLEY BRUCE:

It being represented to me that John Mareno, a Spaniard, has come from Colerain into the Creek nation, and that he stole and brought off with him a slim, iron grey horse, thirteen hands high, belonging to Linch, now residing at the burnt fort at St. Illas, you are hereby authorized to apprehend the said John Mareno and send him and the horse aforesaid to me, to be dealt with as the law directs.

The Tygar Warrior Claims from the U. S. or some of the Citizens.
Valued in chalks,
4 to the dollar

6 Skins of Summer Deer	12
1 Tyger skin	2
1 Black Otter skin pouch	8
1 Knife	1
2 Brass kettles, one large, the other small	40

63

Cotchau Tustunnagau, 12th August, 1796, reported this loss in the Cusseta Square.

Chemauille.

10 Deer skins	20
1 Curb bridle	8
1 Club hatchet	3
1 Looking glass	2
1 Pair Wanlies	1
1 Brass kettle, small kettle of one gallon	15

49

Chemauille, on the 12th August, 1796, reported this loss in the Cusseta Square.

Whoethlau Nookesau.

1 Kettle of brass	15

Cotchau Tustunnagau, Chemauille and Whoethlau Nookesaw, all of Cusseta, reported on the 12th of August, 1796, that they were robbed of the foregoing articles, and stated that this robbery was committed just below where the hunting path to the mouth of Tulapocca crosses Little River, where there was a hurricane. There was five white men; they robbed the camp of the things above mentioned, and left the remainder of their property. Upon being robbed, they left the camp and came in five days to the Cusseta square and made their report. The day before the robbery was committed, they were out hunting and discovered much sign of white peoples' horses moving about, and they expected that some mischief had been done them by stealing their horses, as they discovered one trail which crossed theirs and that another was in pursuit of it. They intended, upon seeing this, to remove their camp the next day, but were robbed.

On coming into the town they found that the Cowetas had taken 3 or 5 horses, one a large sorrel. These horses were immediately recovered and sent back by Mr. Barnard to the care of Colonel Gaither.

That upon finding these horses in the nation, and expecting that the usurpers had plundered their camp, the claimants demanded that they might keep the horses till they were payed; but the chiefs refused the demand and sent the horses, and told them to wait, that justice would be done. They have conducted themselves accordingly and waited more than one year, and request now that they may be attended to. Their characters can be known from the square; they meddle with no property but their own, and they assist readily when called on by their head men to do justice to the whites.

Upon examining into this statement made by the chiefs, and information from William Hill, of Georgia, and others, and finding it to be true, I have judged proper to pass their claims, and to give drafts on Mr. Edward Price, U. S. Factor, to pay the same, and charge it to the Indian Department. Mr. Hill informs that the articles taken were by 2 of the party; that this robbery was disliked and exclaimed against by the officer commanding, and that the articles were reported to the superior officers in the state.

————

Cusseta, 12th November, 1797.

MR. DAVID WALKER:

You are hereby authorized, empowered and required to take into your care and possession all the property of the late Jacob Townshend. You are to make a true inventory thereof and return the same to me. Such parts thereof as may, in your judgment, be of a perishable nature, you are to sell at public sale, to the highest bidder, on a trust of six months, the purchasers to give security for the payment.

Joseph Cook has this day exhibited to me, on oath, his account with Alexander McGillivray, late deceased, and a claim for sundry negros, said by him to be left in the care of Mr. McGillivray. A part of this claim depends in part on certain papers in your care, belonging to the said Townshend. You are especially enjoined to restore to me all the papers of the deceased, to be delivered to the respective claimants whenever it may be deemed just and proper to do so. If you have any claims against the deceased, you are to exhibit them to me with an account of your expenditures in the premises, when you return an inventory of the effects of the deceased.

Given under my hand.

Cusseta, 12th November.

Came before me John Galphin and made oath that the horse that David Walker has here now in possession is the same horse that he purchased of an Indian of the Coweta town by the name of Emautly Haujo, son of the Coweta Leader, and I believe, from the information I got from said Indian at the time he was stolen, that he is the property of Peyton T. Smith, of Greene County, between Zachariah Phillips & Greene's Borough; and further saith this deponant that he sold said horse to John Mulegan, of Savannah, & Mulegan sold him to John Randolph, of Tenesaw, & Randolph sold him to Lachlin Durants, and Durants sold him to Benjamin Durants, his father.

JOHN GALPHIN.

Affirmed to be true before:

BENJAMIN HAWKINS.

13th.

Leave and permission to George W. Foster to purchase a bay horse, 14½ hands high, branded T. C. on the mounting buttock, seven years old, folded and raised the property of Thomas Carr. Also leave and permission to purchase from James Lovett, trader in the Tallauhassee, a sorrel horse, branded G. R. on the mounting shoulder, P. M. on the off shoulder, five years old, about thirteen hands & half high, and from information, raised on the Appelookee. Also one bay horse, four years old, branded T. L. on his cussion, a natural pacer, raised by said Lovett.

Cusseta, 13th November, 1797.

Leave and permission is hereby given to William Mapp to purchase from Richard Bailey, a trader in the Ottassee, a black stud horse, 15 hands high, branded on the near buttock R. B., seven years old, raised the property of said Bailey.

———

Cusseta, 13th of November, 1797.

Dear Colonel:

I have recently received dispatches from the War Office and the public officers in Tennessee. I find, by a letter from Colonel Butler, that the three companies of the 3rd Regiment in that quarter are sent down the Tennessee. The Colonel has erected a fort in Powell's Valley, within three miles of Chisholm's Spring; his cavalry are stationed at Colonel Or's as a corps of observation. He has also taken a position on the Holston, within the Cherokee line, and erected two three-gun batteries; one on an island and one on a hill above the junction of Holston with the Tennessee; in these batteries he has placed all his ordnance.

It seems Mr. Cox has continued his armament, and I find, by a letter from Colonel Henley, that he intends to make an attempt to descend the river in full force, having a large boat 60 by 23 feet, and armed with cannon. The position taken by Colonel Butler is a favourable one to compell him to respect the laws.

I have for some time expected to hear that Mr. Cox was arrested for his embodying an armed force; it is a crime for which he and his accomplices will unquestionably be punished. I sent on the 6th of August, my correspondence with Mr. Cox, my opinion of his plan, and the plan to the Secretary of War. The dispatches from the War Office are of the 12th, and the newspapers the 24th of that month.

I have two lengthy reports from Dinsmoor; among the Cherokees, every thing progresses as well as I had a right to expect it would. My daughters are spinning and weaving. He saw at one place 42½ yards of good homespun and some more ready for the loom.

I have recently received a letter from Mr. Panton; I find there are still some difficulties in the way of marking our boundary with Spain.

I am, with sincere regard and esteem, dear Colonel,

Your obedient servant.

COLONEL HENRY GAITHER.

———

3 of the pack horses are strayed or stolen; if any should be offered for sale at Fort Wilkinson, Wade, or any of the escort who

were with me on the Cherokee line, will know them; one is a sorrel horse which Richard rode; the other two are, one a grey, which carried our mess boxes; the other a horse which Patt rode.

Cusseta, 13th November, 1797.

Benjamin Rawlins, of Ogeechee, in Georgia, exhibited his pass to me, and upon being asked what his lawful business was, answered, to recover some money from the estate of General Alexander McGillivray which was due him.

I do hereby certify that I have sold to James Lovett, of Tallauhassee, one negro man, called Humphrey, about twenty-seven years of age, the property of Henry Carleton & Ludwell Evans, late deceased, which negro has been in this nation seven years, for the consideration of two hundred and fifty dollars; cash received, sixtyfive; and the remainder secured by note; and I do hereby warrant and defend the property in the said negro to him and his heirs.

Given under my hand and seal this 13th of November, 1797.

G. W. FOSTER.   (Seal)

Signed & sealed in presence of

BENJAMIN HAWKINS.

13th November.

Benjamin Rawlins, of Ogeechee, in Georgia, personally appeared before me and made oath that on or about 1783 he lost a horse, a sorrel, about 14 hands high, near Opilthlucco, on the Tuckabatchee path; that he heard that he was in the possession of George Barnard, a trader in the Ooseuchees, and on examination he found it to be true, and he kept him seven or 8 years. He applied 3 different times to Barnard for the horse, and being informed that Barnard had given a shirt and flap for the horse to an Indian, he sent and offered to repay this sum, once by Richard Bailey and once by Richard Coleman, but never could or did receive the horse or any value for him. George Barnard is now dead, and his property, if any, is in the hands of Thomas Miller. He declares that he gave, at Kennard's, fifty dollars for this horse.

He applies to the Principal Agent for Indian Affairs to cause justice to be done in the premises.

B. RAWLINS.

Subscribed and sworn to before
BENJAMIN HAWKINS,
P. T. A. for I. A. South of Ohio.

Cusseta, the 13th November, 1797.

I have received your favour of the 26th October by Mr. Hill. I send you inclosed Cook's claim as exhibited to me. You will oblige me by communicating freely what you know relative to the justness of this claim; from your letter to me there is a very great difference in his expectations and your report; as I may have to decide finally on this claim, when I shall have collected all the proof on both sides, I wish you would send me your report, on oath, with any explanations you may judge proper and which can throw light on the subject. If you wish any interrogations to be put to him, I request you to state them, and I will order him to answer them. He has returned to Georgia and prays me to give a decision in the course of the winter.

I send you some newspapers by Mr. Marshall; they are the last I have received. I have been for some time riding in a circle, and out of the way of a regular conveyance. I expect in future to be more fortunate.

Zachariah Cox and his associates seem obstinately bent on attempting to settle somewhere on the Indian lands by force; by my last advises from Tellico, I find that he intended to attempt to descend the river Tennessee by force; he had a large boat, 60 feet by 23, and armed with cannon. Colonel Butler, who commands in that quarter, has had orders to prevent him. I made a statement on this subject on the 6th of August to the Secretary of War, and I doubt not but Mr. Cox is liable to arrest and punishment for embodying an armed force.

I cannot understand from any of his Catholic Majesty's officers, what objections they have to runing the line. I have read with attention the letters which have been published on this subject, and the reasons assigned, as they never did exist, cannot be true, I think there would have been more dignity in being silent altogether, after pleading the orders of their superiors, without a comment.

I shall fulfill the duties enjoined on me, and on all occasions prove the sincerity of my orders to carry our stipulations with Spain into effect by my actions. I beg you to assure the commandant in your neighbourhood that notwithstanding the line is not marked between us, that I shall be happy to contribute any thing in my power to preserve a friendly intercourse between the people under my agency and his Catholic Majesty's subjects.

I am, with much esteem and regard, Sir,

Your obedient servant.

MR. WM. PANTON.

14th November.

Downy Leadbetter exhibited his pass, 26th of October, signed Edward Price.

14th November.

Archibald Walker exhibited his pass of the 8th of November, signed Edward Price.

Cusseta, 15th November, 1797.

Sir:

Henry Wilson, in the service of Abraham Mordecai, goes down to your fortress for the public stores left in your care, belonging to the Indian Department; he has 8 pack horses, and I request you to deliver to him the articles under-mentioned. I hope in a few days to be able to send down for the remainder.

I find I make some progress in carrying the benevolent views of the government into effect, but it is slow; the materials I have to operate on have been sadly corrupted.

I have recently received letters from Tellico; Colonel Butler has erected a fort in Powell's Valley, and taken and fortified a position on an island near the junction of the Holston with the Tennessee on the Cherokee lands. By my last account from Fort Wilkinson, your brothers in arms were well there. There is no progress made in our boundary with Spain. I have had strayed or stolen from me here 3 horses; one a white, I believe branded U. S., chunkey and used to the pack service, and has the marks on several places; the other, a chesnut, with white mane and tail, called here an eagle tail, docked; the other a slim chesnut horse with a streaked face; they had been shod about four weeks past. If you should see or hear of them, claim them and send them by the first conveyor.

I am, with sincere wishes for your happiness,

Your obedient servant.

SAMUEL ALLINSON,
Ensign Com. Fort Pickering.

Box No. 1, vs. Colonel Benjamin Hawkins for the Creek Indians.
Box No. 2, Ditto.
Box No. 3, Ditto.
Hand Case No. 14.
Canvas Valice No. 15.
2 pack portmanteaux.
1 pack saddle with the apperatus.
In hd. No. 10 there is some rope and leading line; if it should be wanted, and in one of the trunks 70 yards of wrapping. Make up the loads complete, 150 lbs. to the load, out of the iron. Send an inventory.

The Creek Nation:

To John Galphin, Chinabee Moss Mico, Ocheese Tustunnagau, Wehah Tustunnagau, Emautle Haujo, Tuskeegee Tustunnagau & Wauthlucco Haujo: You are hereby appointed, on the part of the Creek nation, to attend at such time and place as you may be required to do by Colonel Benjamin Hawkins, the Principal Temporary Agent for Indian Affairs South of Ohio, and proceed with the Commissioners of the United States to see the line ascertained and marked from the Currahee Mountain to the source of the main south branch of the Oconee River, called Tulapocca, agreeable to the treaty of New York, of the 7th of August, 1790, and the treaty of Colerain, of the 29th of June, 1796.

Given at the residence of Colonel Hawkins, in the Creek nation, this 15th of November, 1797.

YEAUHOLAU (H.K.) MICO,
Of the Coweta.
BENJAMIN HAWKINS,
P. T. A. for I. A. South of Ohio.

The Form of the Separate Commissioners:

Chinabee Moss Mico is one of the Commissioners of the Creek nation, to the line ascertained and marked, from Currahee Mountain to the source of the main south branch of Oconee River.

Cusseta, 15th November, 1797.

Cusseta, 16th November, 1797.

The bearer is Short Neck; he lives above this about 30 miles; he has a hundred cattle and some hogs; is careful and attentive, always attached to the U. S., and deemed honest; he goes down with some skins and requests that I would introduce him to you. He has more skins than he carries down; he will give you the weight, and you may safely rely on him. I have begun to draw on you for the stipend; this may draw down a crowd. I have drawn the sums hitherto negros. The towns appoint their agent, and the drafts are in his favour, as agent. I have given notice publicly in the squares that those who visit you are to carry their own provisions. The agents being but few, and such as I may deem suitable, I shall name, to be attended to; as for the rest, they must conform to the rule. I have received your favour by Michael; I shall soon address you on some points mentioned in it. The Commissioners are appointed, on the part of the Creeks, to see the line ascertained and marked. I have given them their commissions, and I shall soon address Colonel Gaither on the subject, as we shall want some of the cavalry to go up Tulapocca and to the Currahee Mountains with the Commissioners.

You may see that my paper is out, or I should not address you on this. I congratulate your good fortune; I am told you have a big fellow.

B. H.

MR. E. PRICE,
U. S. Factor.

Cusseta, 17th November, 1797.

Leave and permission is given to A. Gindrat for purchasing three head of horses of John Brown, being in part of a debt due by John Miller to William Clark: 1 gray horse, about 13½ hands high, branded on the mounting shoulder & buttock V.; 1 bay horse, 13 hands high, branded O. on shoulder and buttock, & one bay horse, 14 hands high, branded K. on mounting buttock; from George Clem, a grey horse, about 15 hands high, branded on the mounting shoulder B., and both glass eyes.

Cusseta, 17th November, 1797.

MARTIN HARDIN, Contractor for supplying the troops:

Sir:

I have received a return from you of a horse purchased by you. If you will attend to Section 10 of the Act, you will see that to buy a horse you must have a special licence; a general licence to trade does not authorize the purchase of horses.

I find this traffic so injurious to the morals of the Creeks, and so destructive in its consequences of the peace and intercourse between the Indians and citizens, that I am constrained to go to the utmost extent of my authority to crush it. I find it necessary to direct that no Creek shall sell a horse that has not a certificate from me or the head men of his town, countersigned by a trader in the town, to accompany the horse.

I am out of paper, or I would address you and the Commandant on a whole sheet. Present my respects to him, and believe me to be, with due regard,

Your obedient servant.

19th November.

John Galphin has applied for leave and permission to sell a horse, the property of his wife. The said horse is 13½ hands high, no brand perceivable, three white or frosted legs, his body almost white, & of the colour commonly called a roan; paces in general. There does not appear any objection to his being permitted to sell.

Cusseta, 19th of November, 1797.

Sir:

I wrote you on the 23rd ultimo. The meeting expected to take place on the 27th was a representation of the towns on this river. I continued the meeting from day to day till the 15th of this month, some times at the Coweta, Tallauhassee and Cusseta squares, There has been a meeting also of the upper towns at the Tuckabatchee. The result is, upon the whole, favourable to our wishes. I first took up the business of the Chickasaws and had the peace with them ratified, and one of the most influential chiefs sent to announce it to the Chickasaws, and to take with him such of the stolen horses of that nation as remained yet to be returned. I went fully and repeatedly into all the objects intrusted to my agency, and I believe I have given all possible satisfaction to the Indians on every subject in the mode originally suggested by them.

They have appointed 7 men from the towns more immediately interested to attend and see the line ascertained and marked agreeably to treaty, and I shall fix the first of the new year for the commencement of this business. I found this a difficult affair with some of the young warriors, notwithstanding the repeated stipulations heretofore made with the chiefs relative to it; but it is finally assented to and put out of the reach of any further agency in their square, as the Indian Commissioners have received their commissions and instructions, and they are to attend to my directions "till the completion of business."

Being ordered to ascertain, in the most unequivocal manner, whether the nation is disposed to sell to the State of Georgia the land between the Oconee and Oakmulgee, and from the junction of these rivers to the head of St. Mary's, I have taken time to fulfill this order, and paid that attention to it that its importance required, and I can now inform you that the nation are not disposed to sell. On the contrary, it requires that a man should be high in the confidence of the Indians to be able to mention the subject in the public square without being insulted. As the wants of the Indians are increasing and the game decreasing, they may be induced to part with their lands for an equivalent in the course of a year or two, if the Indians can be impressed with confidence in the justice of their neighbours and a friendly interchange of good offices should take place between them.

I have been constantly with the Indians at their public meetings of business or amusement, at their houses, in traveling parties, or at my own table, where I have entertained daily a number of them, and conversed with them in a free, easy, plain and friendly manner on their situation. I have pointed out, in the best manner I could, the dangers attending their obstinate perseverence in their old habits, and how necessary it is to their existence as a nation to conform in some sort to the ways of their neighbours. I pointed out the benevolent views of the government, and the pains taken to better their condition. I have pressed their attention to these things, and called on them to remember that the troops which now protected them might be withdrawn at a short notice, and they be left to their own exertions for defense; that the report I should make of the success of my mission would, in a great degree, if not wholly, influence the future operations of the government in relation to them; that the sons of America, which sent me here, must be listened to; it was not that of the French, English or Spaniards, but of their fathers and brothers, natives of the same land with themselves. The last time I addressed them in the public square, I recapitulated every thing and told them I should take my leave of them. The effect was very visible; they listened in attentive silence to the end and replied they had, for nearly a month, exerted themselves to understand me and they believed me to be their friend, and they had confidence in the disinterested benevolence of their father; and they would exert themselves to prove to me that my mission should not be fruitless; that the line and every thing should be as I wished.

Notwithstanding, I rely for the present on the assurances I have received, I must inform you that the game has become scarce; the wants of the Indians are increasing, the men too proud to labour; the distemper has destroyed their horses; the presents heretofore given by Great Britain, in quantities sufficient to cloathe all the idlers, has ceased; those given by Spain are mere baubles. The men, bred in habits proudly indolent and insolent, accustomed to be courted, and to think they did a favour by receiving, where naked, cloathes and comforts from the British agents, will reluctantly and with difficulty, be humbled to the level of rational life. It is, therefore, to be feared that they will renew their favourite practice of horse stealing again as a means of cloathing themselves, and I have already taken some precautions on this head. As the Creeks, of all the southern Indians, are the most refractory and addicted to this view, I have found it necessary to affix an additional check to this traffic. I have ordered that no person shall purchase a horse of a Creek without a certificate from me that the property is good, or from the head man of his town, countersigned by the trader of the town, and I have given information of this regulation to Colonel Henley and Mr. Price, & the chiefs of the land are pleased with it. The progress in agriculture and manufactures is slow. I have two webs spun in the nation, and I am making arrangements to have another wove. The women will labour and I will assist them. I have one smith established in my neighbourhood, and I shall, as soon as I can, establish another in the upper towns. As to presents of goods, I am of opinion they will produce no good; implements of husbandry and a plan to convert the corn raised by the women into cloathing for themselves and families, will give a spur to their industry. I find some difficulty in arranging such a plan; notwithstanding, I have experienced the good effects in the expenditure, by barter, of goods of the value of one hundred and fifty dollars a month, for corn and other provisions in my neighbourhood, whereby many poor families are made comfortable, by being cloathed.

The wounded chief and his family are very attentive to me; he is recovered, but he is unable to procure any thing for this season, and will be lame for life. I have bestowed, in all, about fifty dollars on him and his family, to cloathe them & furnish them with necessaries for the winter.

I have received your dispatches to the 4th of August, and newspapers to the 24th, with letters from Colonels Butler and Henley, and lengthy reports from Mr. Dinsmoor; he has had 42½ yards of good homespun made, and more ready for the loom. The Cherokees are far before these people in many things, and their agent is a faithful and able assistant. I must assist him to establish a school in the neighbourhood of his residence.

I sent you, in my communication of the 6th of August, Cox's plan and my opinion of it, and my correspondence with him, and I have expected to hear of his being arrested and brought to condign punishment for the crime he had committed, as soon as the executives could give the proof they possessed to the proper authority.

Mr. Dinsmoor had my directions to attempt to obtain at the meeting of the 4 nations, permission to make an establishment at the Muscle Shoals. I also have attempted it, but hitherto without success.

The hunters of this nation are all gone into the woods and not expected to return till from the first of March to the begining of September; this gives me some leisure to attend, with General Pickins, to the runing of the line, if it should be necessary.

The distance is short and the woods open, and it can be completed in a fortnight.

I have on hand almost all of the articles sent me in the care of Mr. Price; they are still at Colerain; I find it very difficult to get them brought up, and shall be under the necessity to order some of them round by Savannah to Fort Wilkinson.

The list of articles for the ensuing year will be but few: 4 doz. pair cotton cards, twine for two seines of 40 fathoms, with leads, ropes and corks; twine for ten scoope nets, two ream of fine and one of coarse paper, some garden seeds and peas.

I have begun to divide the stipend for 1796 and 1797. I am not satisfied with the plan, but it is the best I could devise for the present. Each town appoints an agent and I give a draft in his favour as agent for the portion alloted to the town. The dividend will be small and perhaps it will give as much satisfaction this way as any other. I told the chiefs they ought to consider it as a fund to enable them to fulfill their stipulations with us, rather than as capable of being divided among the whole nation; that in the first case it would enable them to do justice to those who faithfully exerted themselves for the honour and interest of their country, and in the latter it was not worth dividing.

Some of the assistants with Mr. Seagrove are unpaid for four months, and some of them more; they have applied to me, and I have put them off till that gentleman has settled his accounts. Their wants are pressing, and I shall be under the necessity of assisting them, Mr. Barnard for near five months, and Mr. Thomas from July 1st to the last of November of last year. This subject I have stated to you in a former communication; his express riders I settled with and discharged.

I sent you an account of the murder of Townshend, at Tenesaw. If you should deem it advisable for me to extend my agency over the two settlements, I can readily do so, notwithstanding the officers of Spain have taken on them to appoint some civil officers in those settlements. I find it necessary to take on me the settlement of accounts between the white people residing here and some of old standing, and judge finally on claims for property, in some cases to a large amount. The rule I have adopted is this: The plantif exhibits a statement of his claim, on oath; to this the defendant answers, on oath; the plantif replys; the defendant rejoins, and I decree, and record the whole, free of expence.

I have the honour to be, with sincere respect and esteem, Sir,
Your obedient servant.

The Honourable
JAMES McHENRY,
Secretary of War.

Cusseta, 19th November, 1797.
Sir:

I have to inform your Excellency that I have appointed the first day of January next to commence the line between the State of Georgia and the Creek nation. The Creeks have appointed Commissioners on their part, to attend the Commissioners of the United States, to see the line ascertained and marked. I intend to be at Fort Wilkinson by the 25th of December, and to proceed from thence up the Tulapocca to its source. If you should direct any gentlemen to attend on the part of Georgia, I shall be glad to see them at the fort, and of their company in the rout I shall go up the river.

I find the Indians improve a little in their efforts to maintain a friendly intercourse with their neighbours. I find no difficulty in obtaining restitution of property taken since the treaty of Colerain, and of negros who run from the State of Georgia. In the latter case, as I have no document to satisfy one that there existed any positive engagement on the part of the Indians to restore them, I have called on the nation, ex-officio, and promised a reward of twelve and a half dollars to have them restored to their owners, and there are now in my care two of them, the property of General McIntosh, of Savannah, and I request you to cause the General to be informed of this, that his negros are with the public smith at Tallauhassee, in my neighbourhood, and will remain there until he gives orders respecting them.

The Uchee who murdered Brown is under sentence of death and has fled. Mrs. Brown has exhibited a claim for losses at the time; this I shall pay on her application to Mr. Price, and deduct it out of the Creek stipend. If she applies in person to Mr. Price the first of January, I shall pass the account and direct him to pay it on that day.

I have the honour to be, with due regard, Sir,

Your obedient servant.

His Excellency,

THE GOVERNOR OF GEORGIA.

Cusseta, 19th November, 1797.

My Dear General:

This is the third time I have written to you since I left you without having had the pleasure of a line from you. I expect, by a communication from Mr. Dinsmoor, that he must have visited you by the 12th of this month; he will, of course, communicate every thing to you relative to the Cherokees and affairs in Tennessee since we left there. I have had no dispatches from the Secretary of War since the 4th of August, with newspapers to the 24th of that month. I have letters from Colonel Butler of the 20th September; he has erected one fort within three miles of Chisholm's Spring, in Powell's Valley, and has fortified the island just above the mouth of Holston, and erected a battery on the high land near it. These two fortresses have all his ordnance in them, and he has orders to prevent Cox from carrying his plans into operation.

I expect Cox is arrested before this; his plan is evidence of his guilt, and it is high time that he and his accomplices had met the punishment due to their crimes.

I have appointed the 1st of January to run the Creek boundary. The Indians have appointed men on their part; they are commissioned and are to attend to my directions. I found this a difficult affair with the young warriors, notwithstanding the repeated stipulations heretofore made with the chiefs relative to it; but it is finally assented to, and put out of the reach of any further agency in the square.

I shall give notice to Colonel Gaither to furnish an escort, and intend to leave the nation so as to be at Fort Wilkinson the 25th of December, to go from thence up to the source of the Tulapocca. I wish you would direct one of the surveyors to begin a traverse line at the point on the Tugalo; go over the Currahee Mountain towards the Tulapocca to meet us there, and that you would yourself meet me at any point you judge proper, either at the fort at Phillip's or anywhere you will direct. It will take some time to ascertain the true source, tho' not much, as the Indians are disposed to give the information we may require.

I expect several gentlemen of Georgia will attend us. I have seen some from the neighbourhood of Phillip's who have promised me to be of the party, and that we shall meet a welcome reception.

I discharged Richard at the fort; his horse and the one that Patt rode, and the grey that carried the mess boxes, I brought with me here; the three have been stolen. I have sent in all directions to detect the thieves; if they should come your way, I beg you to claim them. I had reported them to Colonel Gaither as public property, and two of them were sent with the blacksmith and some of his tools to the Tallauhassee, a town in my neighbourhood.

I cannot express to you how much fatigue and trouble I have had since I came here. I have, since the 27th ultimo to the 15th of this month, been with the chiefs of all the towns on this river, engaged in explanations and settling claims, and to add to my misfortunes, sorely afflicted with the gout or rheumatism.

I am, with much and sincere regard, my dear General,

Your obedient servant.

GENERAL ANDREW PICKINS.

                                        Cusseta, 20th November, 1797.
JOHN GALPHIN:

You will proceed, without delay, to Fort Wilkinson, and there act as interpreter until I arrive, as you are required to attend the Commissioners of the U. S. on the line to be run between Georgia and the Creeks. In the latter case, you will attend as a Creek Commissioner, with the other Commissioners; you will inform them that they are to be at the fort by the first of January, to go from thence up the river to the head of Tulapocca.

If the Creek Commissioners should be in want of some provisions before my arrival, you will apply to Colonel Gaither for some for them. You must be particularly careful of your character. The Indians who go down will be troublesome when they have received, through the agents of their town, the amount of their orders; they have got all that is allotted for them for this time; Mr. Price, having paid the orders, has nothing further to do. I know the Indians will teaze you to interpret for them; in all cases, give them decent answers, and whatever Colonel Gaither says is to them a law, and they must respect him as the Commander-in-chief. I am out of paper, or I should send your directions on a whole sheet. I must require of you to take care of your character, and you will be entitled to my friendly attention.

November 20th, 1797.

Robert Walton, a residenter of the Tuskeegees, in the Creek nation, complaineth, on oath, before me that John Galphin sold a negro, named Sterling, to William Kennard, of the Cowpen, in the Simanolees, which said negro was the property of the said Robert Walton, and he now applies for justice in the premises to the Principal Temporary Agent for Indian Affairs. The said negro is now in possession of some Indians who inhabit the village called McCullee; that he never parted from him.

Robert Walton, a resident trader of Tuskeegee, complains, on oath, that some time about three years past he left a negro fellow, his property, at the house of a daughter of Mr. Stradham; the fellow was named Sterling; he was left in the care of Mr. Stradham's daughters for their use till he should return and take him. After this, John Galphin applied to purchase the said negro and was refused; that after this, Galphin told Walton that Harrod had taken the negro and sold him to Kenard and taken one back which Mrs. Durant sold Kennard; that since this, Walton says Harrod informed him that it was John Galphin who sold this negro to Kennard. Robert Walton, he purchased the negro of Mrs. Durant; she claimed him as the property of her father, and he had been 12 or 13 years in the nation, and it is now said he is in the possession of some Indians at McCullee. He prays and applies for justice in the premises to the P. T. A. for I. A. South of Ohio.

ROBERT WALTON.

Subscribed and sworn to before
BENJAMIN HAWKINS,
P. T. A. for I. A. South of Ohio.

———————

20th November.

60 at 4 miles.

Set out down the river on a visit to Benjamin Stradham's; in 50 minutes cross Ucheehatchee, 60 feet; in 110 minutes pass Fullothoejy's village, in a pine barron; in 15 minutes cross Hitcheteehatchee, 15 feet over; in two hours cross Oconee, 60 feet; in one hour and 40 minutes cross Cochesses, 20 feet, and in 15 minutes arrive at Stradham's; here I saw one of his daughters at the spining wheel; she spins well and has, of her own growing and spining, 6 pounds of web and most as much filling. He has two daughters grown, who can spin; the youngest appears neat and attentive, very cleanly in her person and house; she attended and set the table, brought in her provisions, and kept her table furniture all clean.

The course for this distance is S. and by W. The lands to the first creek pine barron, and generally speaking it is a pine barron most of the rout. There is some flat land on the north of Fullothoejy's village, mixed with hickory and oak. The village has about twenty houses, and they commenced building a square. Beyond Hitchetee, to the left, I pass Palachooklee, situated on a poor flat joining the river; the lands off, pine barron; there are about 25 houses and a town house. On the north side of Oconee, for near two miles, the lands level, some part thick set with dwarf hickory trees. On the south side of the creek there is about 50 acres of rich land, broken, bordering on the creek; the margin of the creek in some places affords clay for pots. The branches of all these creeks are said to afford reed and some of them cane, and a fine range for cattle. The cattle go out 20 miles of this river around in the winter and return every spring to the ponds near the river. These ponds are now dry and appear, none of them, when full to have more than 4 feet water. The cattle are fond of feeding in and round them; perhaps the food is a little brakish, or more sweet than any in the adjoining lands. Stradham is on a pine barron without knowing it is so.

24th November.

Opoiuchee, of Sowgohatchee, applies for a trader in his town; he says there are thirty hunters and they will treat a white man well; that the women are in want of a man who will supply them with salt and thread for such articles of food as they can spare.

Ehopoie, of the Nocoosulgee, wife of Bowman Sutton, informs me that her brother, Secosciche, now about 40 years of age, if living, is supposed to be somewhere in the United States; he was taken just after General Wayne was surprised by the Creeks in Georgia during the late revolution war, but those who took him, knowing he was friendly to the U. S., cloathed him, and set him at liberty. He was nephew to the Cusseta King. She has heard he is still living, somewhere in the U. S. He was a man of weak understanding, of easy temper and industrious, and she requests that the Principal T. A. for I. A. South of Ohio will cause enquiry to be made after him, and to inform the family if living.

———————

Cusseta, 24th of November, 1797.

Tustunnagau Emautlau, of Tuckabatchee, called on me on business for Alex. Cornell. I had heard that he was a brave and determined man, who had often signalised himself when called on to fulfill any national engagements which required a bold and decisive line of action. I requested to know of him whether the Spaniards had made any overtures to him lately to take part with them in any enterprise they may meditate against the U. S.; that I put this question to him with this statement: That there was some objection on the part of Spain to the fulfillment of their treaty with us. I did not understand the grounds of the objections; that I had seen the correspondence between some of the Spanish officers and our artist, Mr. Elliot, on this subject, but they afforded me no satisfaction, as the purport was not true, and if true, were no just grounds of complaints against us. He replied: No, the Spaniards had not communicated any thing on this subject to him; he did not know they were hostile to the U. S.; he had heard that something which he did not understand had stoped the line runers. As you ask me whether the Spaniards are unfriendly, I will tell you a story about four or five years past: Colonel O'Neil, Governor of Pensacola, sent for him by Captain Oliver and invited him and urged him repeatedly to go and take hair from the Americans and he should be paid for it. He replied infrequently, and they as often urged him to go. He promised at length to go and bring some hair; that reflecting on his promise, he doubted the justness of it in part; he had promised hair; he never violated his word; the Spanish Governor had obtained his promise; the Americans had done him no injury. He went immediately among the Spanish settlements above the Natches and there killed one man and carried the hair to his town and informed the Governor what he had done.

The Governor was vexed at the mistake and sent up to his town and demanded his head for it; that at this time Captain Oliver, the agent, was absent from the nation, and Louis Melford, in his stead, who received the orders for his head; Melford knew the difficulty of executing this order, determined to send him to carry his head himself; he wrote a letter to the Governor and informed him: "You have demanded the head of the Indian who murdered the man above the Natches; the bearer is the man; I have sent him to you, head and all." This letter he was ignorant of the contents of. The Governor received him and treated him well, but did not mention the purport of the letter, nor did he know it till his return, when he was informed of the contents. At first he said it made him smile, and he replied to his informant that had the Governor mentioned the subject to him, he should have given him a severe reprimand for his conduct; I would have told him: It is your fault, you are to blame, you encourage us to go to war against the U. S.; at a time when you are too cowardly to avow your intentions, you call us and set us on. The people of the U. S., on the contrary, are honest and manly; when they fought the British, Mr. Galphin

constantly required of us to be silent and neuter. The British
agents called on us to help and we foolishly did so and lost many
men and some land by it. The people of the U. S. now require
of us to be quiet and in friendship with all their neighbours. You
are constantly teazing us by your agent, Captain Oliver, to fight
them. I have given them my hand; we have most of us done so,
and in future determined to listen to their friendly and manly talks;
but as you must have hair, I took it, that you might feel I took
it from one of your people; he was a sorry loking man, like myself,
of not much account; but it is a lesson for you.

Mr. Hawkins then asked if the other chiefs were invited by the
Spaniards to take up the hatchet against the U. S. He answered:
Yes, all of them, without exception, where he lived, and powder and
ball was frequently given for the purpose and they were frequently
rebuked for not using it as the Spaniards wished; if you are desirous
of knowing more, you will see some of them when you come to the
upper towns, and they will, all in general, answer you as I do.
Have you not had an invitation lately, within one year, or since
last spring, to take up the hatchet? No, I told you this before. I
believe they know the answer we should give: They may fight
their own battles. I have no love for the Spaniards, and I believe
few Indians have any love for or confidence in them.

Have you heard any thing of the difficulties which surround the
four nations, of Blount and his projects, or Cox and his, and other
intruders on the Indian rights? Yes, I was one who attended the
meeting of the four nations; there I heard all about it; the Coweta
Mico (Little Turkey) told us every thing; the difficulties you had
with the white and red people about the Cherokee line; that Fusse
Mico and Chesse Tunno wanted to get you out of the Indian
country, that they might ruin the red people; that Cox, the leader of
the Ocunnaunuxulgee, was ready to seize upon the Muscle Shoals,
but you and the officers of the government had disappointed all of
them. He told us the difficulty you had with the red people; that
you set down with them at Tuskeegee and talked to them as if
you were their father; you told them their situation; that they must
restrain their young men and make them leave off horse stealing
and medling with the white people's property; that you did not
once threaten them, but beged they would listen to your talks; that
if they did not, they were a ruined people in spite of all you and
the officers of government could do, and the Ecunnaunuxulgee
would rejoice at it and get possession of their whole country.

When you heard these things did you and your people listen
with attention? Yes, and we have talked it over since; we have
talked over your demand for satisfaction for the murder of Gentry
and Brown, and your advise to our nation to do justice to the
Chickasaws, to be at peace with the red and white people, and be

neighbourly with them; the advise you first gave us, not to meddle with affairs of the white people, but let them fight their own battles. We have talked over all these things, and our people begin to listen to them; there is now a majority in our land who have taken your talks and will abide by them, and by the spring, when wou take the same pains with the upper towns as you have with the lower, there will be a great majority, and they will follow your advise. We have talked this over several times, and we see our people grow better every day and see more into the situation of things. I am one of the chiefs who was appointed by the head of our land to assist the people of these towns to put the Uchees to death who murdered Brown; I came here for the purpose, and went with some of the warriors. He fled; I afterwards heard he was at the Little Savannas; we went there and heard he had fled to the Shawnees, and we stoped the pursuit, as we heard you had given orders not to do any injury to any innocent person of the family. Some of us talked of killing one of the family and puting and end to the business, but were restrained by your orders.

Do your chiefs see their danger arising from the misconduct of their young men? Do they see that if the troops which at present restrain the intrusions of the land speculators and others were removed, that your nation is not safe? Do they see the diffi- culty I have with the reds and whites? Do they see the wickedness of your young men, who even steal the horses of the agents who attend my orders, and are not punished? Do they see that they must help me or all is lost? Do they talk of the joy it would give the enemies of the Creeks if my lips were sealed by their bad con- duct and thereby removed, and the plan of the government defeated?

Yes, all these things have been talked over, and at the last meeting at Tuckabatchee, and the chiefs said they were determined to help us in the spring and take your talks; they saw Yauqmulgee was their true friend; they heard of the fatigue you underwent on their account, and they would help you; they said particularly, you must be helped, or if by their bad conduct they shut your mouth from speaking in their favour, the Ecunnaunuxulgee will rejoice; they will be like the dog which shakes his tail with joy.

I certify the foregoing to be faithfully translated from the Creek.

TIM. BARNARD.

Being present when this information was obtained by Colonel Hawkins from Tustunnagau Emautlau, it brings to my recollection that I then lived in the Tuckabatchee, saw Mr. Melford, and am myself a witness of the truth of the Tustunnagau's statement. The man he killed was named Williams, and the report he gave of the conversation he intended to give the Governor, he actually mentioned in his town. It was then a common thing, both in Captain Oliver and Melford, the Spanish agents, to encourage the Indians to commit hostile acts against the citizens of the United States, and the Indians disliked it. The Spaniards applied for permission to build a fort at the fork of Alabama, where the old French fort, Toulouse, stood, and said it was for the purpose of defending the Indians against the encroachments of the Georgians; the Mad Dog asked me my opinion of the answer which should be given to the Spaniards, and I advised that he should ask the Spaniards to build a fort at Oconee if they were earnest in their declarations of defending the Indian lands against the Georgia encroachments, and I believe he gave this answer to the Spanish agents.

RICHARD THOMAS.

Translations of Creek expressions used in the foregoing:

Ecunnaunuxulgee: People greedily grasping after the lands of the red people against the voice of the United States.

Fusse Mico: The Dirt King, Governor Blount; the Cherokee name of this gentleman is the Dirt Captain, and in both nations it arose from their opinion of his insatiable avidity to acquire Indian lands.

Chessecuppetunne: Captain Chisholm, the pumpkin Captain.

I will add another name; Ecunnauaupopohau: Always asking for land.

General Clerk of Georgia,

RICHARD THOMAS.

g frequently occurs in the Creek tongue and is always hard in sound: Vaujinulgee means the Virginia people, and is sometimes used for the U. S. Taullowauhutculgee: The People of the beloved town where the President resides and from whence the good talks come.

Town of St. Mary's, 6th January, 1797.

Dear Thomas:

I have now before me five of your letters unanswered, viz., 21st October, 1st November, 6th, 11th & 13th December; lost all of them. I have attentively perused, and had I time, would reply minutely to them by this opportunity, but the great deal I have to write and do will not allow; I shall in a few days. You have doubtless heard that I am no longer agent; of course I cannot answer any of your orders, but I have wrote to Mr. Price to answer them, which I hope he will do. I have received your silver watch, & I shall send it to Charleston for repair. You will see by my letters to the chiefs of the Upper and Lower Creeks the reasons for my being no longer agent; it is with the nation, if they wish my services, to call a meeting of the principal chiefs and draw up a clear and spirited remonstrance to the President, which will have the desired effect. In this you can be very useful by dressing their sentiments in a proper stile; let it be full and expressive of my services to them & my own country. There has been base foul play used against me, which will all come out in time. I shall write you again at large in a day or two.

Yours, etc.,

JAS. SEAGROVE.

I certify the foregoing to be a true copy of the original in my possession.

RICHARD THOMAS.

Cusseta, 25th November, 1797.

I thank you, my dear sir, for the hint relative to the Warrenton postoffice keeper; I accept it as an invitation for a regular correspondence monthly with him, and I pledge the faith of Istechatelige osetat chemistechaugo (the beloved man of the four nations) to be punctual on his part. I am now and have been in this town, which is on the Chattahoochee among the Lower Creek towns, (160 miles from Fort Wilkinson, the residence of Colonel Gaither, on the Oconee) for more than a month, and much engaged in the duties enjoined on me by my office. It is not necessary to detail to you the difficulties I have encountered daily in adjusting with these people the differences in the way of a friendly intercourse between them and their neighbours. They, the men, are bred in habits proudly indolent and insolent, accustomed to be courted, and to think they did confer a favour by receiving, when naked, cloathes and comforts from the British agents, and will reluctantly and with great difficulty be humbled to the level of rational life. I spend their days at their public places in conversation, or at my hut, where I have entertained a number, and the evenings I devote, till 12 o'clock, at the town house to see their dancing and amusements, or at my hut attending to their language or making arrangements to decide on disputed property, and adjusting the misunderstandings between the four nations. As business increased on me, I found my mind and exertions always ready to rise above it, or as it would be better expressed, to be equal to my wishes, and even beyond my expectations. In this situation I had one visitor sorely afflictive, a severe attack in my left leg and foot of the gout or rheumatism for 6 or 10 nights; some times not able to turn in my blankets, yet constantly crowded with visitors and obliged to attend to the head men and warriors of twelve towns, invited to convene at Coweta, a neighbouring town. I have one faithful assistant in Mr. Barnard, one of the interpreters. The white and red people are much indebted to his constant persevering and honest exertions to do justice to all applicants. It sometimes falls to the lot of one man, tho' apparently in the humblest walks of life, to render more effectual service to his creatures than thousands of his neighbours. This has been the case with this gentleman; he was a trader in this nation before the war, and remained in it during the whole progress of it, constantly opposing the cruel policy which pressed these people to war with the Americans, and urged their being neuter; he repeatedly risked his life and fortune in the cause of humanity, and remains to witness that the purity of his actions has given him a standing among the red people which could not be purchased with money.

I have, since I left you, seen much of the western country; witnessed the downfall of a character I highly valued, when I first had the pleasure of knowing you, and seen a check given, I hope an effectual one, to a base system for the destruction of the four nations, by the Ecunnaunuxulgee (people greedily grasping after all their lands), and I have the happiness to know that I have contributed much to the establishment of the well grounded confidence which the four nations have in the justice of the U. S., and that this confidence is so well grounded that the malice or wickedness of the enemies of our government cannot destroy it.

Will you assure Mrs. F. that I often wish her health and happiness; that if she is fond of grandure and will send her son to me, I will give him a queen, or if he, by her permission, prefers the custom of the Oriental country, I will give him half a dozen, with fortunes suitable to their rank, each a pestle and mortar, a sifter and riddle and fanner, an earth pot, pan and large wooden spoon, with one hoonau (half petticoat), as low as the knee, and iocoofcuttau (short shift), not so low as the tie of the hoonau; earrings surrounding each of the rims of the ears, a necklace, a string of broaches before, with one hatchetau (or blanket) and as much tucfullwau (binding) as will club the hair; they will each have a full portion of the temper of the mule, except when they are amorous, and then will exhibit all the lovely and amiable qualities of the cat.

With assurances that I shall persevere in the duties enjoined on me, and hopes that I shall better the condition of these tawney and oppressed daughters of the woods, I pray you not to forget your friend and obedient servant,

WM. FAULKENER, ESQ.

Cusseta, 26th of November, 1797.

Auwihejee, son of Lauchejee, of Tallassee, called on me for a letter to you; his father is called Crook Neck by our misnomers, and in that name I gave him a note to you. Lauchejee has 750 lbs. of deer skins, & 36 lbs. of beaver, which he takes down to you; his son, Auwihejee, and a black boy will accompany him. He leaves behind 200 deer skins and 30 or 40 small furs; these he will take down in the spring; for the value of these he wishes a credit till he can send them down.

The goods he wants are 6 pcs. Strouds, 1 pair white blankets and 1 pc. Duffils, 3 pair arm bands, 3 pair wrist bands, 2 pcs. petticoat linseys, 2 pcs. white linen for shirts, 2 pcs. black handkerchiefs, 2 or 3 pieces callico, 1 piece striped cotton homespun, 1 piece negro cloth, 50 lbs. powder and 100 lbs. of lead, 12 fine combs, 12 long knives, 12 cutteaux knives, 12 pair scissars, ribband, binding, 1 lb. white thread, 100 needles, flints, paint, 2 or 3 scarlet blankets, 3 pcs. of romals, 3 pcs. coarse check or stripe for shirts, 1 brass kettle, 7 bags salt, 1 keg of brandy, broaches, ear bobs, beads, 1 fowling piece, 1 hat, a good one, black feather; hatchets, axes, looking glasses.

I have taken the list down as the son named them; the father lives at Long Island, on this river, 35 miles above this; he is a careful, industrious man, not in debt, and seven negros, good property, and the old man does not drink, and is honest in the discharge of his debts; you will be safe in crediting him to the amount of skins and furs left at home, and beyond that relying on the truth of this statement. You will be pleased with the old man, as I have been with the information I have obtained & herein communicate to you of him and his affairs. I am,

Your friend & obedient servant.

MR. EDWARD PRICE,
U. S. Factor.

Cusseta, in the Creek Nation, 25th of November, 1797.

I have the pleasure, my most estimable friend, to acknowledge the receipt of your favour of the 10th of August; it came by Knox-ville, through the Cherokee and Creek country, to this place. Guess what could have been my feelings on the discovery of that letter which caused you to speak of one old batchelor in such hansome terms. I had not been two days on the frontiers of Tennessee before I suspected there was some thing in train of execution injurious to the United States; Colonel Henley, Mr. Dinsmoor, General Pickins and myself spoke freely to each other on the subject, and we were induced to exert all our vigilence. Mr. Byers, who was in our confidence, we know to be zealously attached to the U. S. When the letter was sent to me, I was surprised it was from an unexpected quarter; the man, my old friend, formerly very much in my estimation, and until the last year or two of my being a member of the Senate, deemed to be of the purest integrity; he is before that tribunal which has and will do him justice, and there I leave him.

I cannot express to you the difficulty and fatigue I under-went in ascertaining and marking the line, and the anxiety I had at seeing a number of my fellow citizens certain victims of their own folly by intruding on the rights of the Indians. Powell's Valley, an extensive settlement west of Clinch and south of Camp-bell's line, without any pretext to cover their intrusions; the line on the one hand being marked and known ever since 1777; on the other hand, a large river, and both expressed without any ambiguity in the treaty of Holston. A something crept into the State of Tennessee, which leaped over the bounds of decency and law, and determined to put the government to defiance; it had already taken such a growth when I arrived there as to be alarming in a high degree, and nothing but the prudent precaution of the President in sending Colonel Butler there with a respectable force, checked it.

I have been for almost a month in conversation with the chiefs and warriors of 12 of the Lower Creek towns, having directed them to convene in my neighbourhood. I have adopted a line of conduct which seems to succeed; I am firm, patient and persevering. I have pointed out, in the plainest and strongest light in my power, the situation and duty of the chiefs, and the effect has equalled my expectations. I dwelt much on the magnanimity and benevolence of the government; the anxiety of the President and the great body of my fellow citizens for their future well doing, and the difficulty I and the officers of the government had on account of the improper conduct of the young men and the want of the aid of the chiefs of the land.

Pardon me, my most estimable friend, you are not yet Secretary at War, and you may well judge from my letter it was intended for such a character. I have no regular hours for business; it is now 12 o'clock at night. I am all the day with the Indians, and have no other time than the evenings to attend to my friends. I was some few days past, sorely afflicted with the gout or rheumatism; I could not turn in my blanket, and the arrival of the Queen of Tuckabatchee was announced to me; that town is 60 miles from me. I was so sure that it was you, that the gout left me for a moment and I rose up; but alass! I invited her and her friends to spend two or three days with me, which she did. Very early one morning she came to my bed side and sat down; I awoke and she accosted me: My visit is to you, I am a widow, I have a son so high (holding her hand 3 feet from the ground), I have a fine stock of cattle, I wished them to be secured for my use and for my son; I know you are Istechatelige osetat chemistechaugo (the beloved man of the four nations); my relations are not careful of my interest; if you will take the direction of my affairs, the chiefs have told me you may settle my stock where you please and it shall be safe. When you go to Tuckabatchee you will have a home; maybe I am too old for you, but I'll do any thing I can for you. I shall be proud of you if you will take me. If you take a young girl into the house I shall not like it, but I won't say one word; maybe I can't love her, but I won't use her ill. I have brought some ausce (cassene youpon) for you. I want some cloathes for my boy and for myself; you can give them to me and make the traders take some of the cattle for pay; if you direct them, they won't cheat me. I was taken a prisoner by the Chickasaws with my boy when he was so high (about 2 feet); I run from them and was 17 days in the woods, geting to my nation. I had no provisions when I set out, and I was like to perish. When you was in the upper towns last year I came twice to see you, and drest myself; you took me by the hand and asked me to sit down; I wanted to speak to you then, but I could not. I said then I would never have an Istechate (red man).

She was about 23 years of age, plump built, not tall, of copper colour, full breasted, her face regular, with the appearance of neatness in her dress. She had the stillapica (moccasin) without stockings, the hoonau (short petticoat) just below the knee, ornamented with tucfullowau (binding); her iocoofcuttau (shift) just to the hoonauewonaugetau (petticoat string), made open before, but confined with sittaholcau (broaches); the length seemed designed to accommodate a young child, and by raising it an inch or two the child could be put to the breast; she has eight hutscotalcau (ear bobs) around the rim of each ear, and a cunnauwau (necklace), all of silver beads and bobs, and a hatchetau (mantle); her hair was clubbed and tied with tucfullowau chate (red binding).

It is not customary anywhere among the Creeks to associate with the women, and it is a curious fact that there are white men in this land who have been here five years without ever entering an Indian house. I visit them, take them by the hand and talk kindly to them, and I eat with them frequently, and this day I had four Indian women to dine with me, with some chiefs and white men; a thing, they tell me, unknown before to either of them. One thing I have noticed in all I have conversed with: They have a great propensity to be obscene in conversation, and they call every thing by its name, and if the concurrant testimony of the white husbands may be relied on, the women have much of the temper of the mule, except when they are amorous, an then they exhibit all the amiable and gentle qualities of the cat.

I have made some progress in learning their language, and its an amusement to me the few moments of leisure I have. I began with writing words, names, then dialogues; as my knowledge increased, I corrected my errors. I am preparing a treat for our friend, Mr. Jefferson. I expect in one year to give him an extensive vocabulary of the tongues of the 4 nations; the Creek will be my work, and it will be well done. I have application myself and an able assistant.

Remember me, I pray you, to Mr. Venable; I intended to write to him, but your letter has consumed my whole stock of paper, and I do not expect any more for ten days. Your son and you must be well; and you are to be settled near Mr. Jefferson; do not forget, I pray you, that I am to be your gardener and Walker the shepherd. Mrs. Easton, she is a deserter; however, as she has set up the manufactory of babes, we must forgive her; she will succeed; they will all of them imbibe the good qualities of the mamma, and make others happy by it.

And Mr. Matlock, success to his establishment; pray, bespeak the birth of godfather for me, and if I cannot attend, I hereby vest you with authority to appoint a proxy for me, who, in my name, shall have full power to renounce the devil and all his works, and the vain pomp and glory of this wicked world, &c., &c.

Pray authorize your son or Mr. Venable to give one kiss to the amiable daughters where you are in remembrance of me, and accept of one yourself from Mr. V. as the perpetual pledge of the sincere affection of your friend & obedient servant.

MRS. ELIZA TRIST.

Cusseta, the 27th November, 1797.

I have received your letter of the 14th of this month, in answer to mine of the 30th of October; it is the first I have had from you. This letter you send me I have read with attention, and if you had not informed me you were sick, I should have supposed you were deranged in mind; perhaps it is a delirium arising from sickness; in that case it is a misfortune, not a fault. If I did not believe something of this sort really to affect you, I would let you know that if you do not know your duty, I know mine. Whoever heard of your being talked of about what was done at Colerain? Nobody, but your own imagination. You were only an interpreter, and I know the Indians never fault them for doing their duty faithfully. I can tell you another thing; you over rate your standing when you say the Indians blame you; the fact is they have not blamed you, and for a very obvious reason; the Indians do not suffer the white men in their land even to mention, much less to influence them in their treaties.

Another thing, you talk of Tulapocca and the complaints of the Indians about it, and the trifle of goods; that these things must be settled before I leave the land. What do you mean by this stuff? Do not you know the Tulapocca line was settled by McGillivray and the Indians who went to New York? Don't you know that this nation appointed agents to go and run the line, and that Bowls's coming prevented it? Did you not hear the chiefs tell me this publicly at Colerain? And did you not know they told the truth?

What do you mean when you say if the Indians suffer, you must suffer? Have you not, as it was your duty to do, told them boldly and plainly what all the interpreters at Colerain were ordered to do, that the Indians have now nothing to fear, the United States has guaranteed their country to them? Did you not hear the plan of government explained at Colerain, to better the condition of the Indians? And don't you know I am here to carry that plan into execution? Don't you know the Indians took part with Great Britain against the United States and did us much injury, and that the retaliation on our part is to forgive them because they were a poor deluded people, to enlighten their understanding and to better their condition, by assisting them with tools and implements of husbandry, and teaching them the use of them; by furnishing them with blacksmiths and wheels and cards, looms and weavers? Where have you been that you have forgot these things? Don't you know that we have placed an army, at great expense, to protect the Indians in the enjoyment of their rights, and that we established two stores to supply the Indians at cost and charges?

You want me to clear you? Of what can you clear yourself, if you have not explained faithfully these things to the Indians? You cannot. You ask me to send you a certificate of what is done here, signed by two or three chiefs. What do you mean by this? Must Istechatelige osetat chemistechaugo have a certificate from three Indians? You are surely dreaming.

One piece of information I can give you; the Indians have appointed seven Commissioners to see the line run agreeably to the treaty of New York, and it will be run just after the commencement of the new year; that the Indians do not complain, but are satisfied with the measures of government, and do believe they are for their good.

The Indians, I hope, will never forget how much they are indebted to Mr. Barnard; he is the true and faithful friend of the red people; the best or worst of times he is the same, and does good for them solely from the pleasure it gives him to do so. He is true and faithful to his trust; he knows the purity of the intentions of our government, and it is fortunate for the Indians that he is the faithful interpreter of them. You must visit me about the 25th of next month at the store on Oconee, there to explain your conduct and receive your sallary.

I wish you health and happiness.

JAMES BURGES.

———

ENSIGN ALLINSON:

I wrote you on the 15th November by Henry Wilson; he went down for some of the articles belonging to the Indian Department. Michael Elhert, he goes down for the remainder. I have been told there is not much reliance on Mordecai; of course, if he has not executed the order I gave on you by Wilson, you will deliver the whole to the bearer.

I have given the list as complete as I can; I see however, that a few of the things were given out by Mr. Price. I wish you, if you can conveniently, to note such things in this invoice by a stroke as are not delivered and return it to me by him.

The Indians are mostly in the woods or on the path to Fort Wilkinson for their annuity; their conduct upon the whole is satisfactory. We shall run the line early in January from the head of

Tulapocca to Tugalo. The Commissioners, on the part of the Indians, are appointed, have received their commissions, and are instructed to attend to my orders.

25th November.

Some time in the summer past, about the latter part of July, the Uchees who inhabit the Sauvannogee Village stole two horses from some Cherokee traders. The trader, McDonnal, and his man Ross, they applied to Mucclassee Hoopoi, of Occhoiuchee, to obtain satisfaction; he went directly to the town with some warriors, and the thieves were gone, but were known, and the townspeople had taken the horses and restored them to the care of Richard Bailey. Mucclassee Hoopoi went to their houses, took three guns from them, and burnt three houses with all their property in it.

There were two negros who were guilty of thieving; he went and had them both shot, and gave notice that he would put all to death who kept disturbing the property of the white people, and kept confusion in their land. He gave notice to the negro holders that they must take care of their slaves, as he would undoubtedly put the law in force against them.

The owner of one of the negros called on him for satisfaction for executing his negro; this chief replied: You have justice in the execution of the thief, that is all you are entitled to; I have negros, if they are guilty of theft, come you and you may execute them as additional satisfaction.

Cusseta, 29th November, 1797.

This day Zachariah McGirt appeared before me in obedience to the order on the complaint of Joseph Thompson, and answers that the two negros, Monday and Nancy, claimed as being late the property of Samuel Moore, is bona fide the property of his wife, Louisa McGirt, as will appear by indenture bearing date the 4th day of January, 1797, from James McGirt, of the Province of East Florida, her father-in-law. He, at the same time, exhibits the deposition of James McGirt, stating on oath before James Sea-grove, Esq., of Cowpen County, on the 9th of August, 1797, "that about the year 1780 he purchased of George Arons, an inhabitant of Georgia, a negro man, Monday, and a negro wench, Nancy, for which he had a bill of sale from the said Arons for the said negros; that at the time of the British evacuating East Florida, the before-mentioned negros were stole and carried away from him the said night; that about 4 years after, the said negros were discovered in the possession of a man of the name of Samuel Moore, residing in West Florida; that a person named Joseph Thompson, who married the widow of the aforesaid Samuel Moore, and now resides at Tensaw, in East Florida, is now in possession of the said negros," and further, as appeareth by the said deposition.

He exhibits also the deposition of William McGirt, an inhabitant of East Florida, taken in like manner and on the day aforesaid, stating that about three years past, I eing then in West Florida, he saw in the possession of Lachlan Durant, George Aron's bill of sale to James McGirt for the two negros, Monday and Nancy, as stated in James McGirt's testimony thereto annexed. He exhibits a letter of Lachlan Durant stating that the bill of sale got destroyed at the time he and Billey McGirt came from Little River. He exhibits a paper dated July 29th, 1797, East Florida, St. Augustine, signed George (A—his mark) Arons, certifying that he gave unto James McGirt, Sr., a bill of sale for two negros named Monday and Nancy, which negros were supposed clandestinely carried out of that province by Samuel Moore.

Zachariah McGirt further states that he was informed by John Rogers that he did let Samuel Moore have the negro Nancy; that he asked Rogers how he came to sell his father's; he said he had sold her, but had not received pay for her; that this declaration of Rogers was in the presence of Charles Weatherford. He further states that he heard that Rogers was to have given Bosefield 60 dollars for the negro woman. He further states that John Rogers went to Moore's to get pay for this negro; that Moore had at the time a note against John Rogers for £30 sterling; that on hearing Moore intended to apply to the Commandant to make him pay that sum, he fled, and returned.

That he has heard that James Moore harboured the said negro six or seven months, meaning the negro Monday, before he left St. Mary's and fled with them to West Florida.

                                   ZACHARIAH McGIRT.
Subscribed and sworn before me

BENJAMIN HAWKINS.

———————

See claim of the 5th of October for this fellow by a slave.

John, claimed by William Fitzpatrick as his slave, states that he is the son of Tobe, formerly held in slavery by Joseph Fitzpatrick; he lived in Virginia, in Albermarle County; she knew him and recovered her freedom and afterwards hired herself to her quondam master and lived with him four years. She was decreed to be free in right of her mother, who was an Indian of the Delaware tribe. He states that his mother had nine children; that of these, Harry, the oldest brother, recovered his liberty, and Toby, another brother, recovered his; that is as this narrator has heard and believes. Joseph Fitzpatrick, the brother of William, sold him about of the age of 19, for two years to a Captain Wear. He has three sisters living, but whether free or not he knows not; the oldest, Tilloh, Aggey, & Phebe, named after her mother.

Cusseta, 23rd November, 1797.

I have lately been visited by the agents appointed to receive the stipend for 1796 and 1797. The conversation I have had with them you have a sample of in the inclosed. This chief has remained with me and continues to express himself in a bold, candid and intelligent manner to the agents and others, and he assures me that the chiefs on this river think of the situation of their nation as he does, and will unquestionably aid me throughout in the spring.

I deemed the conversation with him worthy of your perusal, and have had it transcribed; you will perceive by the Creek expressions I retained how capable they are of drawing a line between our government and that class of our fellow citizens who are unworthy members of it. The Ecunnaumuculgee is more expressive than any word I know of what they and we mean when we speak of that class of our fellow citizens.

I have added the letter from Mr. Seagrove to Mr. Thomas; if this gentleman keeps a copy of his letters, he must have a very peculiar turn of mind; if he cannot discover how absurd his conduct must appear to the officers of government. I sent you his address to the Creeks; therein he could not nor would not serve the government upon the terms required of him.

The officers you now have may, without exception, be relied on to fulfill the orders of the government and to serve it with zeal and fidelity at every hazard.

If that gentleman or any other believes the town of St Mary's the proper place for the residence of the Superintendent, and that the affairs of the Indians can be better managed there than by a residence in the nation, and by visiting them in their towns from time to time, or that the river St. Mary's is a suitable place for a commercial intercourse with them for the objects contemplated by the government, it would become them to be cautious how they expressed such a belief, or they might be suspected of selfishness, and of being capable of sacrificing the public good to their own ease & emolument.

There is unquestionably some difference between a seaside residence, with a handsome sallary & a large contingent fund, surrounded with one's friends, and a residence among the Indians.

I have the honour to be, with much and sincere regard.

The Honourable
JAMES McHENRY,
    Secretary of War.

———

Cusseta, November 30th, 1797.

Joseph Hardridge exhibited his licence, No. 4, for to carry on trade with the Creek Indians in the town of Eufaulee for two years, from the 21st day of October, 1797.

1st December.

James Hardridge and Joseph Hardridge called on me and stated they had in their possession a roan filly, two years old last spring, belonging to Thomas Lott; he left this filly under the care of James Hardridge and was to satisfy him for his careful attention to her. He showed the filly, and further stated that Thomas Lott was indebted to the three brothers, James, Joseph & William Hardridge the sums hereunder mentioned.

Chalks

To James, for the swap of a horse............................ 30
Paid an Indian, for hunting his horse........................ 6
Paid Forister, a debt in partnership......................... 16
                                                            ——
                                                            52

To Joseph, for 7 yds. Irish linen at 3 per yd................. 21
To an overcharge paid by James for recovering a small white
    horse 15
                                                            ——
                                                            36

To William, for a gun, 12 dollars, or a set of silversmith's tools, 48
                                                            ——
                                                            136
This charge is to be credited for five dollars paid Joseph....... 20
                                                            ——
    Ballance 116

This ballance is unpaid; they are informed that Lott is gone towards the store on the Oconee, and they pray that justice may be done them.

JAMES (JH) HARDRIDGE.
JOSEPH (JH) HARDRIDGE.

Subscribed and sworn to before

BENJAMIN HAWKINS.

Ordered that James Hardridge hold the filly hereinbefore described in his care and possession till further orders, subject to the securing of payment for the debts charged against Thomas Lott, when a final order shall be made in the premisses.

December 3rd.

Major John Colber exhibited his pass of the 26th September.

John White exhibited his pass of the 2nd of November, 1797, from Edward Price, acting for the Agent of War. He is of Green County, and State of Georgia, and on being asked his business in the nation, answered, to see a brother of his who he was informed lived on Tombigbee.

Major John Colber stated that he had brought with him three young men of good character; that he did not know that it was necessary to obtain passports, as he had one from me, and was coming directly to the town of my residence; their names William & George Tanehill, brothers, & Mathew Bilboa, all of Green County, Georgia.

I gave them permits to go to Tensaw, informing them that I should report them to the Agent of War.

Cusseta, 5th of December.

John Randon, of Tensaw, states that some time about the year 1784 he waited upon the Governor of Georgia and claimed the property of Peter Randon, his father, then deceased; that he was directed how to proceed by General James Jackson, and he obtained an order from the Governor to take his property wherever to be found in the state.

Some of the property had been sold under direction of Governor Martin under the idea that it was confiscated, but his father had never been put in the act of confiscation, and he and his brothers were all minors at the death of their father.

He proceeded as directed and recovered nine negros, little and big, and in the year 1785 set out with them to the Creek nation, and two of the negros, Manuel and George, left him and run off, and he has been informed they are in possession of Francis Paris, on Briar Creek; Paris's father was executor to the will of Peter Randon.

There are three brothers, David, John & James, now living, sons of a Creek woman of the Cotchulgee, and on a division of the negros, these two negros were alloted to David and James.

He further states that he gave a power of attorney to James Gray, of Beech Island, to sell some lands belonging to the estate; he intended at the time to sell his share only, but on examining into the power, General Jackson said it was a general power to sell all the lands; he replied to the General he was illiterate and did not mean to dispose of more than his own. General Jackson sent twice to him afterwards to come and sign the papers; he replied he could not, as he had not received value for the land, and could only sell his own share. After this the General rode up to his lodgings and urged him to go; he still refused, but the General said if he did not, it would be put into the Chancery and would cost him more than it was worth; upon this, he went and signed.

Some of the lands were left in the hands of old Nunns, the father of halfbreed Samson, for 400 and the other 180 pounds sterling.

When Peter Randon died, John Randon went with David Holms, and he understood that David Holms had all the plots and grants for their land, and he was recently informed by Jacob Townshend that the original deed was in possession of General Jackson, and Abner Hammond had offered £1,300 for the land.

This statement is made to the Principal T. A. for Indian Affairs South of Ohio by the brothers, to request his interposition in the premisses, that justice may be done them.

JOHN RANDON.

Cusseta, 5th December, 1797.

Sir:

I have received your favour from Mobile of the 13th ultimo by Mr. Randon. I shall have a meeting of the Upper Creeks some time in the spring, and intend then to decide on such cases of property as can be clearly ascertained. The mode I have judged advisable for the present is this: The plaintiff enters his claim, on oath, circumstantially detailed, taken in the usual manner at the place of his residence, or before me. A copy of this I send the defendant, with an order to answer in a given time, and if it is then deemed necessary, I send this answer, with interrogations, to the plaintiff; he replies; the defendant rejoins, and I decree.

You must state your claim in conformity with the mode adopted and send it to me.

I am, sir, with due regard,

Your obedient servant.

MR. JOHN JOYCE.

A copy sent to John Lindar, of Tensaw.

Cusseta, 6th of December, 1797.

I find I cannot wait any longer in this quarter, some business pressing my return to the frontiers for a few days. I therefore set out this day. I rode up, dined with your family, and inquired after your wheat; it is sowed.

I shall write to Colonel Batts Beard for his final answer relative to his fellow, Ned, and until I obtain it you must either pay a daily or weekly hire for him, or put him with Tyler, there to remain under public pay till I direct what will be done with him.

If you should have any commands for me, direct them to the care of Colonel Gaither; I shall be with him till the last of this month.

I have had some intelligence recently from the seacoast which gives a hope that peace is established in Europe.

I wish you well, and am,

Your obedient servant.

MR. MARSHALL.

Cusseta, 6th December, 1797.

I have this day set out for Fort Wilkinson; I imagine your pack horses have shared the common fate, and are all with the strollers or hunters in the woods. I find I shall be much pressed for time, and therefore set out with such conveyance as I can procure here. Alex has been with me for three days; the Big Warrior left me yesterday. I must suspend my visit to you till my return from the line early the next year. Wilson and Michael must leave their loads in the care of John Tyler; with him I have left directions what is to go to the upper towns. If you have a conveyance, I should be glad if you would send my tent and the two traveling trunks to meet me at Oconee by the last of this month, with two of the small blank books.

Remember me to your family, assure them of my sincere wishes for their welfare, and believe me yourself, with sincere regard & esteem,

Your obedient servant.

MR. BARNARD.

Fort Wilkinson, 13th December, 1797.

Nancy and her little girl, of the Creek nation, are on their way to Andrew Berryhill's, near Galphin's old town on Ogeechee; she is of a family friendly to white people. I request my fellow citizens to be attentive to her and treat her with kindness, and to direct her in her rout.

Fort Wilkinson, 15th of December, 1797.

Sir:

I did, on the 19th ultimo, address a letter to General Pickins, one of the Commissioners appointed to ascertain and mark the boundary line between the Indian nations and the U. S., to inform him of my having appointed the first of January to commence the runing of the Creek line. As there may be some delay in the conveyance I used from the Creek nation, I am desirous of sending a special mesenger from this to the General, to be certain of his receiving the notice I have given, and I must request this favour of you; to order an express from this place to set out to-morrow to carry my dispatches to him.

I have the honour to be, with sincere regard & esteem,

Your obedient servant.

HENRY GAITHER,
Lt. Col. Commandant.

Leave and permission is hereby given to Thomas Cage to purchase from Thomas Lott a grey mare, 13½ hands high, branded Z on the mounting shoulder.

15th December, 1797.

Hopoiche Thlucco, of Sawgohatchee, complains that some time last winter, as he was hunting on this side of Chattahoochee, some Cherokees, three of them, stole two horses and carried them into the settlement near Tugalo, and there delivered them to some white men; that it appeared, by information obtained from the Cherokees, that they had been employed to steal these horses; that at the same time, there was another horse taken from Tuckhoiqua, a Tallassee, who lives near James McQueen's. He repeats that the Cherokee chiefs informed him that their young men who stole these horses were invited to do so by the white people in Georgia, and he adds that he has not received any satisfaction for his horses, and he requests the agent of the four nations to cause justice to be done to him. One of them was a mare sorrel with a small streak of white down the face to the nose; small mare, worth about fifteen dollars. The other was a grey mare worth about forty chalks.

16th December.

My dear General:

The foregoing is a copy of a letter I sent you from the nation, and to prevent the possibility of your not having received information in due time, I have applied to Colonel Gaither for an express to convey it to you. I arrived here on the 14th; my health not yet restored, but I can attend to business. If you find it convenient to visit us at this place, we shall make your tour up the river agreeable. You can direct the surveyor where to begin the traverse line, and to extend it over the Currahee towards the Tulapocca; we can meet them up at the head of that river and return with the line.

Pray remember me respectfully to Mr. P., &c., and believe me, with the truest esteem and regard,

Your obedient servant.

GENERAL ANDREW PICKINS.

This letter alludes to one of 19th November.

Fort Wilkinson, 16th December, 1797.

Sir:

When I was in the Coweta town I saw your negro, and informed Mr. Marshall of your orders; he told me he could not give the amount you ask, and he offered me 200 dollars; perhaps

he may be willing to give fifty more. He went afterwards to
Pensacola, and did not return before I was under necessity of
coming on this frontier. I have directed your negro to be sent to
the public smith in Tallauhassee, three miles from Mr. Marshall.

I am informed he has declared that he would die before he
would be brought out of the nation, and it is believed he would
fulfill his threat. You will judge what is best to be done and write
to me; if you mean to have him removed, you must send some man
for him with your order to me, and I will cause him to be delivered.

I am, with due regard,

Your obedient servant.

COLONEL JOHN B. BARD.

17th.

Information is this day received that the report of the 4th
of November is true; that Phil Spillar, who keeps a store at John
Booth's, bought the horse.

Information is also given to me that Robert Williams, just
above Booth's, on Rocky Creek, purchased a horse of an Indian
some time in the month of September, at or near Fort Wilkinson;
a small roan. He went with the horse into the nation in company
with Daniel Spillar; he returned with the horse into the settlement,
& there has probably disposed of him. The informant adds that
he is not certain whether Robert Williams purchased or stole the
roan.

Fort Wilkinson, 19th December, 1797.

MR. CORNELL:

Immediately on your arrival at Tuckabatchee you will have a
blacksmith's shop erected near your house at some convenient
place; there must be two houses, one a shop, & another for the
smiths to live in. I want a small lott of land for a garden at them.

I have engaged Tuns, and I expect the smith at Weatherford's
to come there as soon as the shop is ready. You must direct Tuns
to attend to your black people and those of the Mad Dog; at this
season they must make the fences and clear up the land.

I have left an order with Tyler to send one smith's shop set of
tools, some iron, steel, hoes, axes, saws, augurs and drawing knives.
When you get at the Cusseta you call on Tyler and direct him to
make a pair of wedges for you. I have directed a cross cut saw to
be sent to your shop.

The smiths will want provisions; they must be bought, and I will give an order for the payment here, or there, at the same price for meat that is paid at this garrison.

You will take care that the tools and things sent up are not scattered. The large axes I sent may be lent to those who will use them. I wish they may be used well, but I want you to know where they are when we may want them all at the public work in the spring.

I shall be in your town as soon as I can get the business done here, and spend some time there. I shall expect to see all your chiefs, when they return in the spring, at your public square. I shall let you know in time to give the broken days. You must notice I shall always, when I address anything to the upper chiefs, send you notice of it first, and you will act according to that notice. As to public business, that belongs to the agents intrusted with it, and no man beside must have any medling at all. The traders must mind their business, and they are not to purchase any horses without a special licence for that purpose. I expect on the return of the hunters some of the ungovernable young men will bring stolen horses, and we can check that business if we stop the sale of them.

If any thing happens worth your notice, I shall write you fully. I wish you health and happiness.

MR. ALEXANDER CORNELL,
Assistant and Interpreter.

Opoi Haujo, of Cusseta, applies for information respecting the losses sustained when Major Adams attacked the party opposite Fort Fidins. He is informed that losses, since the Act to regulate trade and intercourse, will be satisfied on the terms of the Act, but those before that period must be provided for by the nation.

He is further informed that he must apply to Mr. Barnard for a written statement, and the letters of Governor Mathews, who it is said promised payment for these articles.

James Seagrove, Esq., Superintendent of Indian Affairs, with Richard Thomas.

1796.	Dr.	Chalks
July 29, Provisions supplied three Spanish deserters........		10
Aug. 13, Paid an Indian for going express to the Tuckabat- chee		20
14, Provisions supplied three American seamen........		10

Sept. 1, Provisions to Spanish deserters   10
      9, Ditto, to 4 ditto   18
Oct. 31, Provisions to a meeting of the chiefs   60
Nov. 2, Corn supplied Townly Bruce, who had his horse
      stole by Indians   6
      12, Provisions supplied Robert Walton, express rider...   6

      Chalks 140

140 chalks, 3 equal to 1 dollar, is........................$ 46.75
To my sallary as clerk in the Indian Department, from
      July 1st, 1796, to November 30th, 1796, both inclusive,
      at 250 dollars per annum, is......................... 104.15

                                                $150.90
                          Cr.
December 19th, 1797, by an order on Mr. Edward Price, viz:

MR. EDWARD PRICE, U. S. Factor:

      Pay Richard Thomas, Clerk in the Indian Department, one
hundred and fifty dollars and 90-100, being for his sallary from 1st
July, 1796, to the 30th November, both inclusive, and for expenditures during that period as herein mentioned, and which were
allowed, and charge the same to the Indian Department.
150 90-100 Dollars.
                          RICHARD THOMAS,
                          Clerk in the Indian Department.

                          Fort Wilkinson, 19th December, 1797.

      This day personally appeared before me Richard Thomas, a
clerk in the Indian Department, and made oath that the within
account is just and true.

                          19th.

      Andrew King, near General Mitchel's Mills, on Ogeechee, in
Warren County, State of Georgia, states that the 25th December,
1793, three negros, one a girl, a yellow girl, about 15 or 16 years

old, her colour very like that of an Indian, belonging to Wiatt Collier; Jim, called Dart Jim, the property of William Slaughter; Jim is a tall black fellow with remarkable long hair; James, the property of himself, a short well set fellow, large, very large hands and uncommon big rists, his thighs large; he is a black fellow, about 19 years old at the time they left their master.

The negros were seen a few miles on the south of Oconee, near the mouth of Shoulderbone, and it is expected they are gone to the Creek nation.

John Gregory, of Rocky Creek, near John Booth's, applies:

A horse in the possession of Mahtkee, about 14 hands high, branded on the mounting cushion and shoulder with the Oconee brand, O-C; some saddle spots, left hind foot white, below the foot a white snip and a star in his forehead, a darkish bay.

Fort Wilkinson, 20th December, 1797.

Henry Snell, of Pensacola, in the service of Mr. William Panton, is hereby permited to pass through the Creek country on his way to Savannah and to return, and I require all the agents in the Creek Department to aid and assist him, and I recommend him to the friendly attention of my fellow citizens.

Fort Wilkinson, 20th December, 1797.

Dear Sir:

I arrived here a few days past from the Cusseta town. I have had a meeting of the Lower Creeks; they conduct themselves, upon the whole, as well as I could expect, and I rely upon the assurances they have given me that they will co-operate with me in restraining their imprudent young men. The frontiers are now crowded with hunters and I have so arranged my plan that every hunting party has a prudent chief, to be answerable for the conduct of the hunters. I am much embarrassed with some of the citizens on the frontiers; they will buy stolen horses from the Indians, and this trading in horses is the source of endless mischief, and unless I can check it and reduce it to the bounds of legal commerce, will totally frustrate the benevolent plans of the government.

Timothy Lane, commonly called Paddy Lane, a trader in the Tuckabatchee, has lately left the Creek nation and taken with him some horses and skins to Savannah, and as I am informed, has sold the horses and skins and declared his intention of returning to Ireland, his native country; some of the horses were his property and some were borrowed; those who have purchased from him have violated the law.

I have a letter from a correspondent in West Florida; he writes, 23rd November: "I have heard nothing lately respecting the Spanish limits. The American troops under Captain Guyon are our neighbours at the Chickasaw Bluff, and the Spaniards hold the forts at Walnut Hills and Natches. Governor Gayoso is gone to Point Coupee to meet a General Mathew and a Judge Miller."

I wish you would have some garden seeds and peas procured in your neighbourhood and forwarded to the care of Mr. Price for the Indian Department; direct Mr. Price, agent, to pay for them and to forward them.

I am, with much and sincere regard,

Your obedient servant.

MAJOR JOHN HABERSHAM.

I have appointed the commencement of the new year to begin to ascertain and mark the line from the source of Tulapocca to the Currahee.

Fort Wilkinson, 20th December, 1797.

Personally appeared before me James Ryal, of Jackson County, being near the High Shoals of Appahatchee, and made oath that on the 16th of July last, he lost two horses, one a light bay mare about 4-10 high, a number of grey hairs in her mane and tail, two or three saddle spots, white hairs in her breast and rump, not docked or branded, well and close built.. The horse about 4-9 brown bay, branded with H on the mounting shoulder, one of the hind feet white to the pastern joint, light made. They both trot and canter well.

They were taken from Robertson Creek, and supposed by Indians. John and James Cup, they saw some Indians the night the horses were taken, but of what tribe they know not. He believes they were stolen by the Creeks, because the Creeks have been in the habit of stealing horses from that neighbourhood.

JAMES RYAL.

Subscribed and sworn before

BENJAMIN HAWKINS.

William Spencer, on Sandy Run, near the mouth; Hancock County.

22nd December, 1797.

John Galphin and Emautlau Haujo do certify that a bay mare, 14 hands high, one hind foot white, long mane and tail, branded U on the off buttock and NH on the mounting shoulder, is the right and property of Emautlau Haujo, of the Coweta.

JOHN GALPHIN.
His

Witness: EMAUTLAU (I) HAUJO.
Mark

RICHARD THOMAS.

Fort Wilkinson, 22nd December, 1797.

Personally appeared before me William Spencer and made oath that he saw a grey horse in the possession of Andrew Darouzeaux, of the Coweta, which horse was stole from Matthew Durham, of Green County, in 1794. The said horse is nine years old next spring; under the foretop he has a flesh mark occasioned by a blow, the skin was broken and at present is a small 'ump.

WM SPENCER.

Subscribed to and sworn before

BENJAMIN HAWKINS.

Fort Wilkinson, December 25th, 1797.

In the presence of Colonel Gaither, Captain Tinsley requested the Indians to name his daughter after the Creek mode; the Bird King's brother, Tustunnagau Opoie, named her Illatiga, of the Nocosolge or Bear family.

27th December, 1797.

Matthew Durham, of Hancock County, this day appeared before me and states on oath that some time in July, 1795, he had a grey horse stolen from him, between 13 and 14 hands high, branded on the near shoulder and buttock, but not recollected; has just under his fore top a knot occasioned by a stroke, about 9 or 10 years old; he was taken from Log Dam Creek, and supposed by Indians, because they were then at war with the citizens. He never sold the horse to anybody.

MATTHEW DURHAM.

Subscribed and sworn before

BENJAMIN HAWKINS.

Fort Wilkinson, 28th December, 1797.

Sir:

I received yours by your son with the packet intrusted to his care in good order, and I beg you to accept of my thanks for your polite attention to me. I paid him six dollars and he has lived as one of my family since and behaved well. I send him back to the nation on a melancholy occasion, and I give him five dollars; the letter to Yeauholau Mico will fully explain the whole business, and I must request your faithful interpretation of it to that chief. The Indians have conducted themselves on this occasion so as to place them in a high point of view to me, and will entitle them to every exertion in my power for accommodations. Your son applied for some paper; we are out here, but I have plenty at the blacksmith's, Tyler's, and you may apply there for what you want. I shall endeavour to pick up some garden seeds for you and send on by a suitable conveyance.

I am, with sincere regard and esteem,

Your obedient servant.

MR. JAMES DAROUZEAUX.

Fort Wilkinson, 28th December, 1797.

YEAUHOLAU MICO,
    Hollowing King:

Beloved Chief:

I have sent an express to you to give the following information. On the 22nd, just before sundown, Ocheese Tustunnagau and Nehah Tustunnagau, two of the Commissioners, and three others were encamped on the South Branch of Withlaccoochee and were fired on; there were four or five guns fired, and it appeared there were more in the neighbourhood who held their horses; one man was killed, Halthlo Opoie, and two wounded, Nehah Tustunnagau, one of the Commissioners, and Samoau Haujo, both nephews of Yeauholau Mico. They were eating when fired on. There were two balls thro' the dead man, and the wounded men, one with a ball, and the other a buck shot; the balls entered in near the back strippings, as the Indians call it, and seem to range thro' the body. I thought one of them mortal, but I now hope they will recover. I assisted in dressing them & the doctor has since visited them.

The murderers robbed the camp of three horses, three kettles, three hatchets, one shirt, and twenty-three deer skins. As soon as the runner came to me, I set out with a strong detachment of cavalry and infantry, visited the Indian camp, and buried the dead man with the honors of war. I then took twelve Indians and trailed the murderers to the Oconee; they crossed the South Branch of Little River and went up Little River & crossed the same; then up the Oconee & crossed at Hall's ford; here I crossed and was informed that four men had crossed the river on the 22nd instant, and went into the Indian country and returned just before day. I obtained their names and dispatched an express immediately to Colonel Lamar with the information I had obtained and requested his co-operation. I have not since heard from him. Returned thro' the settlement and crossed the Oconee at Tom's ford and returned here on the evening of the 26th instant.

The Indians have behaved well on the present occasion; several of them have visited me by invitation, and I had yesterday a conversation with them; on this occasion they seemed tranquil and determined.

I gave them no promises; I made a statement of facts and told them I had called on the citizens of Georgia to do them justice; they must give me a little time and I would faithfully state to them the result, and then give them my opinion. They answered, they relied on my doing them justice and they hoped the time I asked would not be long.

I have sent two runers up the river to the camps above to bring the relations of the deceased and wounded here and to give a faithful detail of what had been done.

I cannot express to you the fatigue and trouble I have had with my red and white brethren, but I can assure you that notwithstanding this unfortunate and abominable act, I am in hopes that by persevering to do justice to the Indians and aiding them in the manner pointed out by the President, we shall make them a happy people. To you I address myself and beg you to continue your able exertions for the happiness of the Creeks.

Accept of my sincere wishes for your happiness, and believe me always your friend.

See November 29th, 1797   The foregoing is a reply to a claim entered by William Hill, attorney for William Fitzpatrick, for a man of colour, named John, at present in the family of the Little Prince, of Tallauhassee. It is therefore necessary that the attorney, Mr. Hill, or William Fitzpatrick, be prepared to reply on oath to the foregoing statement, and give satisfactory proof of property in the negro claimed, or this statement will be taken and recorded as true.

BENJAMIN HAWKINS,
P. T. A. for I. A. South of Ohio.

WILLIAM HILL,
Attorney for William Fitzpatrick.

Fort Wilkinson, 30th December, 1797.

MR. BURNS and MR. CLEMENTS:

Gentlemen:

I have this moment received your favour of this date. The unfortunate affair of the 22nd has given me much anxiety and some embarrassment; I cannot yet say what will be the issue of it. I have been necessitated to postpone my departure from this place to the 5th of January, and I shall go from this to the junction of the Tulapocca with the Oconee. I shall be glad to see you tomorrow at dinner with Colonel Gaither and me and I beg you to believe me, with much esteem and regard,

Your obedient servant.

23rd of December, 1797.

A runer arrived this morning about 10 o'clock from Ocheese Tustunnagau, one of the Creek Commissioners, to inform me and Colonel Gaither that last evening, just before moon down, his camp had been fired on by some men supposed to be Georgians; that one Indian was killed dead and two badly wounded, one of them Nehah Tustunnagau, a Commissioner; that the white people had robed the camp of some skins, kettles and three horses; that having promised the agent of the four nations he would visit the Indian camps and impress on the young men the necessity of behaving well, he had done so, and having promised that if any misfortune should happen he would communicate it immediately to their great beloved man; he now fulfilled that promise.

I communicated this information immediately to Colonel Gaither, stating to him that there were near one thousand hunters on this frontier, and that it was important to the peace of the frontiers that I should immediately visit the Indian camps at and in the neighbourhood of the wounded Indians, and with a strong detachment of cavalry and infantry, and I requested the Colonel to order such a detachment to proceed immediately to the camp of the wounded Indians, and he gave orders accordingly. The detachment marched at 1 o'clock under the Command of Lieutenant Webb, and I accompanyed them. I dispatched runers to the neighbouring towns to inform the Indians of what had happened, and that I should go myself to examine into this unfortunate affair; that they must not be alarmed, but rely on the officers of the government to do justice; that such an abominable act must not be charged to the whole body of their neighbours, but to the wickedness of some few depraved routches; that an act of this sort on either side must not be suffered to destroy the peace and good understanding established between the U. S. and the Creek nation; that when I returned I should expect to see the heads of the neighbouring camps at this place to hear my report and to receive my advise.

We proceeded on and encamped in the neighbourhood of the Indian encampments on the waters of Little River; here I was visited, about eleven at night, by Ocheese Tustunnagau and others. That chief told me that the moment the runers informed him I was coming, he set out to meet me; that the wounded Indians and all others who were present expressed in strong terms their gratitude for this attention and their firm reliance on me to do them justice, and their determination to wait for my report and advise.

I replied, this corresponded with the opinion I had formed and given of the Creeks to the Secretary of War, and I must call on him and all the chiefs to aid me in this difficult and unpleasant affair; that his conduct had pleased me much and would entitle him and all the red people to my continued exertions for the happiness of the Creeks.

24th.

We marched in the morning before sunrise and arrived about 10 o'clock at the camp of the wounded Indians. There soon arrived some Indians from eight camps. I visited the wounded Indians, examined their wounds, and told them I had brought a doctor to dress their wounds and to assist in the care of them; that I know the customs of the Creeks on similar occasions, but they must dispense with them and suffer me to give directions for their treatment. One of them replied: "I never say no to any thing you advise." I then called on them to give me a report of the attack on their camp.

Extract sent the Governor:

Ocheese Tustunnagau, the Commissioner, made this report:

"That on the 22nd December, just before moon down, about bed time, he and Nehah Tustunnagau, the other Commissioner, and three others being encamped in the neighbourhood of the present encampment on the waters of Little River (Wethluccooche), were fired on; there were four or five guns fired, and it appeared there were more in the neighbourhood who held their horses; that one man was killed, Halthlo Opoie, and two wounded, Nehah Tustunnagau, one of the Commissioners, and Sauwauhidjee, both nephews of Yeauholau Mico; as soon as they were fired on they left the camp; they were all eating when they were fired on. The dead man was left and there were two balls through his body. The murderers robed the camp of three horses, one a little grey, branded on the mounting shoulder I. S., in good order; a sorrel horse, near 14 hands high, branded ✕; a ✕ in a circle and a white spot on the rump on the right side, in good order; the other a little bay mare, branded O. K., a handsome mare and in good order; one saddle and bridle, an old saddle, when new a good one, the stirrups plated; three kettles, of brass, such as are usual among hunters; 23 deer skins, 3 hatchets and one shirt. Information, 30th December, 1797.

They yesterday had the murderers trailed home to a flat on the Oconee; the trail divided between this place and the river; the other division has been trailed also and can be followed. The persons who did this act seemed to know well the woods, as they frequently divide and come together again. They left behind a small black horse, shod before, which they now deliver to the agent of the 4 nations; they left also an old cloth glove. As soon as this unfortunate affair happened they dispatched a runer to the fort to inform Colonel Hawkins of what had happened, to prove to him they had fulfilled their promises to him. They saw the difficulties he had to encounter with the red and white people, and were determined to aid him. They promised him to visit the encampments and aid in impressing on the hunters the necessity of conducting themselves well on the frontiers; that some days past, a middle aged man came to this camp on this horse with a deer tied behind him. They have put the dead man in the ground."

After this statement was made, I asked the other Indians if it was true, and they answered yes, that Ocheese Tustunnagau was not a man to tell an untruth; that the whole was true. I then directed that particular attention should be paid to the wounded, and that they were not to want for any thing. I gave a draft on Mr. Price for some cloathing for them and provisions and corn for the women, and directed what they should all do.

There were collected some Indians from eight camps; I required of them to give me twelve warriors to accompany me; to send two men to all the camps to inform them of what had been done, and what I was about to do. I directed them to send the wounded Indians to the neighbourhood of Colonel Gaither, to return to their several encampments, to impress on the Indians the necessity of a steady, firm, prudent line of conduct, and above all, to wait for my report and advise; that my voice was, on this occasion, that of the President, their father, who spoke the will of the U. S., and it must be listened to and obeyed. I invited the Fusatchee Mico and the old men to spend their Christmas with Colonel Gaither, and when I returned, to visit me at the fort.

They answered: We will follow your advise.

I then addressed the wounded Indians and their companions: I intend to bury your unfortunate companion with the honors of war; he was a beloved chief of the land and a good man; you must attend me if you can and see the ceremony performed. I am the great beloved man of the four nations, and it is my duty to attend to them, and I pride myself in the charge.

Nehah Tustunnagau, one of the wounded, replied: We are the children of our father, the President; you are his representative. This where I am is mother earth; yonder hill is the grave of my companion, chosen by you to accompany us on the line; he was like you, a son of the President; he is no more; I can, but my companion here cannot accompany you; he is soon to follow; let the ceremony be postponed over our fire, and it will serve as a funeral ceremony for 2, if not more of us.

I agreed and requested Captain Webb to act in conformity; to begin the ceremony where we were and march around in front of the wounded camp and perform the ceremony; this he did. I immediately marched and took the trail of the murderers that branched to the left. We soon crossed the South Branch of Little River and continued to the neighbourhood of the river; here we found that the murderers had divided, and to use the expression of the Indians, scattered. They said there was one track which could be followed, if I approved; I did so and went on wandering through the one down the river for a mile, and crossed; here four or more of them came together. We continued on and encamped near some reeds about sunset, four miles on this side of Oconee: here I saw some cattle and heard some bells.

25th December.

We set out early in the morning and when we approached within a mile of the river, the horse left at the Indian camp which we had packed, passed all of us and took the trail, which was followed with some difficulty to the river where it crossed.

I determined to go over to obtain what information I could and proceed down to Tom's ford, recross the river and return to Fort Wilkinson. The first plantation I came to, the family, alarmed, fled and left their house open. I turned down the river to the flat; here I directed the infantry and baggage to prepare to X the river, and here I found four men, and was informed that some people had been at the flat, about to X, but were alarmed at the sound of the troops they left their guns in the flat. I found here four men, and on inquiry, was informed that on Friday, the 22nd, Hardy Smith, John Reed, Pierce and Barron, and I believe Samuel, had on that day crossed over the Oconee at the place where the trail recrossed; that they recrossed about two hours before day, and it was hinted that some mischief would be soon heard of. My informants were William Taylor, David Felps, James Felps and Charles Pruith. I judged proper to send immediately to Colonel Lamar to inform him of what had happened and to request his co-operation. I wrote him this letter and sent it express.

Oconee, above the mouth of Little River, 25th December, 1797.

On Friday, 22nd instant, at night, just before moon down, some men fired on a camp of Indians south of Little River, killed one man and wounded two others badly; one I think mortally. They robed the camp of three horses, three hatchets, three kettles and twenty-three deer skins and one shirt. One of the horses, a little grey, branded on the mounting shoulder I. S., in good order; a sorrel horse, near 14 hands high, branded O., in good order; the other a little grey mare, branded O. K., handsome and in good order; an old saddle, when new, a fashionable one with plated stirrups. I am informed that some men on that day Xed the river and reXed late at night. I have had them traced from the camp to the river, and am informed that the men are Hardy Smith, who lives eight miles from this on the Augusta Road; John Reed, ——Pierce and Barron; perhaps Samuel. (Mr. Booth says he knows the name is Samuel Barron). One of the wounded Indians is a Commissioner, on the part of the nation, and had, at my request, visited the hunting camps to keep them from doing mischief. It is an unpleasant affair, and has given me much anxiety, but I have visited several of the hunting camps with a respectable armed force, and am in hopes that if my fellow citizens will exert themselves, that the Indians may be prevailed on to wait the decision of law. I must request the favour of you, Sir, to co-operate with me and aid me to bring these people to justice. They left a small black horse at the Indian camp, shod before, some saddle spots, branded, but not distinguishable.

I am, with sincere regard, Sir,

Your obedient servant.

COLONEL THOMAS LAMAR.

I shall go down to Booth's and should be glad to see you whenever it is convenient for you. I would visit you, but must return to the fort to calm the minds of the Indians.

Having written this letter, I communicated the contents to the Indians and directed them to go with me thro' the settlements, that they might have an opportunity of seeing the friendly attention of their white neighbours. I saw as I passed a number of the citizens gathered together at some houses in sight of the river to amuse themselves, it being Christmas. I informed them of what had happened, and how necessary it was for them to unite their efforts in aid of the Magistrates to bring the offenders to justice; that they saw their exposed situation and I could assure them that if they would exert themselves I would be answerable for the conduct of the Indians, but if they would not, they must be prepared for the consequences. I explained to them the difficulties I had on my part to restrain the Indians, who were in great numbers on this frontier; I believed greater than they were ever known to be. They had confidence in the assurances I had given, that they might go any where in safety, and in the measures I had adopted to prevent their being disturbed by their own disorderly young men or ours; that trade here would be free, and they would find a market for every thing.

I encamped one night among the citizens and was visited by many of them in the course of the evening and morning. I directed the Indians to take the women by the hand; they were their sisters, born in the same land, and were not their enemies. Nitta Huntlah replied: "Yes, your neighbours have done us much evil, and roused our resentment, but you I know are not our enemies; you have done us no injury, I give you my hand and my heart."

26th.

We marched very early and halted at Booth's to obtain some provisions; we had been nearly two days without, and it was difficult to obtain any till our arrival there. We recrossed at Tom's ford; the river here is about 400 yards wide, shoally, the ford a good one. We continue, and at Itchewonhatchee saw the Commandant; he told me he was then in the neighbourhood of his camp with the wounded Indians, and came to meet me. I gave him an account of what had passed and continued on to the fort.

27th.

The neighbouring chiefs convened and heard my report. They remained silent. I told them they must now help me. I find faithfully detailed every thing, and meant for the present to consult them; that in a few days I expected to see Colonel Lamar, and I should be able to give them some further information. I could assure them the peace and good understanding must not be disturbed by the mad conduct of a few, and I hoped our conduct on this occasion would be such as would give pleasure to our father, the President.

Fusatchee Mico replied, after consultation: "We have confidence in you; you are our true friend, and we see your conduct is the same in every situation. The President has sent you to take care of us and aid us; the other nations claim you equally, but you seem to devote more of your time to us Creeks; we shall rely upon you; we do not know what to do. This looks like an attack on our whole nation. The people find we were the Commissioners of our nation; we don't know what to think of it nor what to say. The dead man and the wounded are near relations to the Yeauholau Mico; you must know him, and you esteem him; they have some relations near Ocheesehatchee, and the dead man has a brother who is now up at Tulapocca; this brother is headstrong and ungovernable at times; you must see him and you must give directions on this information." I replied: "You must send a runer immediately for the two young men at Ocheesehatche; you must send two good and determined men after the brother with orders to bring him immediately to me, and to be answerable for his conduct till he comes, and you must get an Indian to go express to Yeauholau Mico; I will send him an account of every thing. These people who you send I will pay." Fusatchee Mico: "It shall be done as you advise; the brother must be brought to you, and you must advise and direct him."

28th.

Ocheese Tustunnagau called for necessarys for the wounded; told me the mother of the Commissioner, an old woman, would soon be at their camp, but it was his duty to inform me that the dead man left a wife and two small children by two mothers; they were naked and depended on the hunt of their father for cloathing. He said the chiefs had consulted together and they now come to give me this information and ask my answer. I replied it was right, they should inform me of this and every thing else interesting to their feelings appertaining to their unfortunate officer. I could not restore the dead man to life, but I could take care of the children, and if the family would follow my advise, I would be their father. Colonel Lamar visited me and spent the day; he showed me an offer of the suspected men to deliver themselves up to justice, and he wished for information, as he had not a copy of the law; we furnished him a copy, and I gave him, in confidence, the persons from whom I had obtained the information on which, in my letters to him, I named the persons who were suspected; told him and the gentleman with him that there appeared to me but little difficulty, judging from what I myself had obtained, to come at the truth. I showed him the horse.

As soon as these gentlemen left me the chiefs convened, and with much anxiety asked what news from Georgia. I informed them; they replied they expected justice would be done them; they hoped the affair would not be looked over, and that I should be able to answer them and give satisfaction in a short time.

I replied I was in pursuit of justice; I should make no distinction between the red or white people; I had demanded justice of the red people for the murder of Brown and Gentry and for other enormities, and I had and should demand justice of the whites for this outrage, as well as the former one; that while I demanded the punishment of the guilty, I would not consent that an innocent person should suffer. Ocheese Tustunnagau replied: "The ways of us red people are different; if we cannot find the guilty we pay the debt
be abolished
on any a   (Torn out)
I had
day I wa

for her losses when the Uchees murdered her husband, and direct Mr. Price to pay it. The governor informed her of it and she attended while I was adjusting her account. Ocheese Tustunnagau and all the chiefs at the fort called on me and began to inquire what expectations I had from the arrival of several gentle-

men from Georgia, that justice would be done them. I replied:
This is Mrs. Brown, the wife of the man murdered by the Uchees;
this day I invited her to come, and I am now about to pay her for
her property taken and destroyed at the time of that abominable
act. The chiefs looked earnestly at each other; one of them said:
"He has his share of difficulties with the red and white people,"
and all immediately left the room and did not visit me again for the
day.

Fort Wilkinson, 31st of December, 1797.

John and William Griffin exhibited a passport from the Governor of St. Stephen's, at Tombigbee, signed the 16th December, to
go into the U. S. They had certificates of being of good characters
signed by respectable people. They report that their treatment in
the nation was kind, and every thing bore the mark of friendship.
They are permited to pass into Georgia.

Richard Thomas, clerk in the Indian Department, complains
that in the month of June, 1796, an Indian of the Euchee town
named————stole a bay mare, about 14 hands high, from the
neighbourhood of the Cusseta town. The chiefs of the Cusseta
sent a man for the mare, who returned and said the Euchee
acknowledged that he took the mare and packed her to Flint River,
where she died.

RICHARD THOMAS,
Clerk in the Indian Department.

Auwollobedjee, of Coweta, Nehah Tustunnagau's brother, is to
take the place of his brother as Commissioner.

Fort Wilkinson, 4th July, 1798.

I wrote you a long letter on the 19th November; I was then
sorely afflicted with the gout or rheumatism in my left foot, and
under a pressure of business. As soon as the hunters had gone into
the woods, each party with a chief to be answerable for their good
conduct, according to a plan I had devised, I set out down the
Chattahoochee to view the settlements on that river, and to make

some arrangements for the good conduct of the Indians who are going towards the Floridas, and returned from thence to this place the 13th December. The precautions I had taken to preserve peace on this frontier were such as deserved success, but the detailed account of the unpleasant affair of the 22nd ultimo, herewith inclosed, will prove to you that without the co-operation of my fellow citizens, I shall be compelled to resort to expedients suited to the existing state of society in this quarter, or all my well meant endeavours will be fruitless. The affair of the 12th of September is now remembered only by the Indians. The honest chief, wounded on that day, has just visited me to offer his assistance, although he is lame for life. There never was a period in the history of the Creeks when their character exhibited itself in so estimable a point of view. The frontiers crowded with hunters; their public Commissioners fired on, one killed, and two wounded, and instead of the war whoop, their resentment is suspended for the report and advice of the agent of the four nations. What am I to advise?

When I trailed the murderers to the Oconee, I could have trailed them to their houses, but my respect for the law restrained me, and I dispatched an express to the Colonel of the County, Thomas Lamar, to co-operate with me, and I returned to calm the minds of the Indians. The Colonel has visited me repeatedly, and some of the magistrates; they express much concern, and he assures me he will exert himself to bring the murderers to trial, and I rely on his assurances, but the magistrates express doubts; the law does not depend on them for execution. The civil magistrates includes only the district judge and those of the supreme court. Mr. Van Allen, a gentleman of the law, is of the same opinion. I made my report to them and gave them my opinion, that they were in the present case the civil magistrates intended by the law. This day they were to convene and examine the suspected persons.

I have directed the wounded men to set out for the Coweta to-morrow, and I shall leave this and go up the river to ascertain and mark the Creek boundary. I have appointed, by consent of the chiefs, persons, the most respectable in the land, to replace those who go home, and I shall take them with me. I have given the wounded Indians and their attendants and the family of the murdered chief, in all, about forty dollars.

I have the honour to be, with sincere regard and esteem, Sir,

Your obedient servant.

The Honourable
JAMES McHENRY,
Secretary of War.

5th January.

Two of the Commissioners of Georgia are here, Colonel Burns and Colonel Clements. I have received a letter from General Pickins; he cannot attend, but he informs me that the surveyor and chain carriers would set out from Tugalo the 4th of this month to meet me at the source of Appalatchee. I set out this day. I have had another conversation with the Indians; I explained to them the report I make to you, with which they seem to be much pleased. They said they rejoiced that their conduct would give pleasure to their father, the President.

6th January.

Letter sent to the governor with the report of the unpleasant affair of the 22nd ultimo.

13th February, 1798.

George Gray, Hugh Horton, William Williams, all of Hancock County, visited me and informed me that on the 11th, about half an hour before sundown, Nicholas Vines, who lived at the mouth of Rocky Creek, was amusing himself on the bank of the Oconee on his own lands; was fired on by Indians from the right bank of the Oconee. It is believed that there were four or five guns fired, one of which killed him. There were found at the place where the Indians fired from, two papers, one of them a commission to Ocheese Tustunnagau, as Commissioner on the part of the Creeks to see the line ascertained and marked between them and the U. S., and another, acknowledging that this affair is for satisfaction. This chief is one of the Commissioners who were fired on and who returned to the nation.

The Commission.

Ocheese Tustunnagau is one of the Commissioners of the Creek nation to see the line ascertained and marked from the Currahee Mountains to the source of the Main South Branch of the Oconee.

BENJAMIN HAWKINS,
P. T. A. for I. A. South of Ohio.

Cusseta, 15th November, 1798.

The Address.

Friends and Brothers, as we now call you and always did, we are sorry that we are oblidged to take our due satisfaction ourselves; you have often promist to give satisfaction to us in the Licke casses, but never have done itt once. Now we have gott itt, our harts is strait and itt is all over. We are now as good friends as ever we was, and can take you by the hand in friendship again.

Fort Wilkinson, 16th February, 1798.

Sir:

I addressed a short note to you on the 12th ultimo from the Tulapocca. I proceeded up that river to its source, and completed on the 2nd of this month the line from thence over the Currahee to Tugalo. Colonel Burns and Colonel Clements, two of the Commissioners on the part of Georgia, accompanied me, and I am happy in being able to assure you that there was no diversity of opinion among us, and that the line was closed in perfect harmony. There are some families on the Indian lands on the west of this line; I believe not more than sixteen, three of them, Mr. Cunningham, Colonel Wafford and Mr. Smith, have embarked property to obtain lands, and been at some expence in making their establishments. The others are mostly tenants, and all of them with small huts, and some so recently made as not to have any cleared lands about them. Colonel Wafford, who sustains the greatest injury, has a letter of introduction from me to you of the 2nd of this month; the old gentleman will deliver it to you himself and detail to you the situation of that frontier. The settlers made their establishments under the laws of this state and with the expectation and general belief that they would be on the east side of the line. They have conducted themselves well and appeared to be a poor, decent, orderly and industrious set of people. I told them they would not be permited to make another crop on the Indian lands, and that they would do well to make arrangements to move by the spring; that in their neighbourhood, on the east side of the line, there was an extensive tract of uncultivated country, to which they could easily remove. Jackson County, which borders on this line to the west, and the Appalatchee on the south, has not more (I believe) than ten families in twenty-five miles square, of its southernmost corner.

On our return to this place, I met an express on the 6th of the month, from the Governor of Georgia, with a concurred resolution of the Honourable the Legislature of that State, of the 1st, and his order of the 3rd inst., recalling the Commissioners on the part of the State. His letter and my reply I herewith inclose. I have the honour to be very respectfully, Sir,

Your obedient servant,

BENJAMIN HAWKINS.

The Honourable
JAMES McHENRY,
    Secretary of War.

———

Fort Wilkinson, 18th February, 1798.
Sir:

I left Greensborough immediately after I wrote my letter to your Excellency of the seventh. I arrived here on the ninth. I have been since then much afflicted with the gout, but I am now on the recovery and soon to be well. On the 13th three men from Hancock County visited me & gave me the information, No. 1, and this day I received a letter from a correspondent at the Coweta that the party out were two brothers of the Indian who was killed on the 22nd of December and some of their relations.

I find that the paper was written in the nation at the request of the Indians, and they intended to put it on "the body of those they kill," and that they intended to kill two if they found them on their hunting grounds.

You will see by the enclosed, No. 2 and 3, the early steps taken to cause justice to be done in the case of Brown, pursuant to the orders of the President. I cannot now give you the whole of the proceedings on this subject, but I can assure you that the Creek nation were convened on my order; that they agreed justice should be done; that the guilty person should be delivered up, if practicable, or put to death. The guilty fled; were pursued, and it was reported they had left the Creek land & gone to the Shawnees. They were then outlawed, and some of the principal warriors of the Creeks were put under my orders to put them to death. The unfortunate chief, now in the gaol of Oglethorpe, was one appointed to execute my orders, and a more friendly, useful & determined man is not to be found in the Creek nation than he is. I have had so much difficulty in preparing the Indian mind for the new order of things in remedying former abuses and removing the old leven of Toryism which had fled into the Indian Department, that I could not do more than to try to establish peace & an interchange of good offices between them and my fellow citizens. I have, however, in aid of the pastoral life, introduced the plough, the wheel & the loom, & with success. The weaver in the department has just reported to me that he has wove fifty yards of good 500 thread at one house, the whole of which was spun by two Creek girls, and the cotton planted and raised since my appointment. While I am, by a faithful discharge of my orders, increasing the confidence of the Indians in the justness of the United States, I impress on them the necessity of doing justice to my fellow citizens, and in all cases since the treaty at Colerain, they seem determined faithfully to fulfill this stipulation; but in all cases prior thereto, they urge either a fulfillment on their part on a requisition of Mr. Seagrove, or a misunderstanding of the stipulation. They say Mr. Seagrove called on them and they delivered all the horses and negros they could get, except such as were deemed legally their property, according to the rules of war, and which they had received from the British for their services, or such negros as had fled to them, and which they were not bound to restore.

I mention their reasoning on this subject to show they seem to be intelligent, or that they have been aided in forming those observations. The 1st Article of the treaty of Colerain states that the Governor of Georgia may empower three persons to claim & receive this property under the direction of the President of the U. States. I believe there is a like stipulation in substance in the treaty of New York. I would advise that Your Excellency would, without delay, appoint persons in conformity with the beforementioned authority, & to direct them to repare to the Creek nation during the present spring or summer, under the direction of the President of the U. States, to fulfill the duties enjoined by the said treaties, and I can assure you I will, on my part, give them every aid in my power.

I receive, with pleasure, the assurances of Your Excellency that you will cordially assist in preserving peace, & I am confident, by the mutual efforts of those whose duty it is to aid us, we shall succeed, not only to obtain this desirable end, but, by an interchange of good offices, to prepare the Indian mind to accommodate the wishes of our fellow citizens in points important to the citizens of Georgia.

If this much desired period should arrive during my agency, it will afford me pleasure, and I will contribute to it with zeal and fidelity.

I have the honor to be, very respectfully, Your Excellency,

Your obedient servant.

His Excellency,
JAMES JACKSON,
Governor of Georgia.

Fort Wilkinson, February 22nd, 1798.

Sir:

I received Your Excellency's favour of the 17th this day by Lieutenant Smithers. I have written a letter to you, of the 18th, in answer to yours of the 3rd, and intended to send it by Mr. Hill to-morrow. I have detained Mr. Smithers till I could have the references copied, to send it by him. I shall write you again by Mr. Hill in answer to your last communication.

I heard, a few days past, a man was killed at Long Bluff, & I immediately called upon the Indians in my neighbourhood to inform me who of their nation were hunting in that neighbourhood; they could not give me any information, but promised to send some of the young warriors to examine into it. I have ordered the few chiefs who are now near me to attend to-morrow, & I shall unquestionably take such measures as may be proper to find out and punish the guilty.

I am this day informed that an Indian has been killed since the murder of Allen, at the same bluff. It is here reported he climbed up a tree to converse with a Mr. Oats, & was fired on while in the tree, & across the river.

It is added this was done by way of retaliation for Allen, & that in consequence of it, Mr. Oats has removed from his plantation.

I shall send down some Indians to examine into this affair on their part, & I shall call on Colonel Gaither to extend his patrole to that quarter. I have just received letters from the Upper Creeks of the 8th, and from the Lower of the 11th of this month; they are friendly.

I have appointed a meeting of all the chiefs of the former in the month of April, and of the latter the last of March, or during the ensuing month.

I have the honour to be, with sincere regard, &c.

His Excellency,
    JAMES JACKSON,
        Governor of Georgia.

Fort Wilkinson, 23rd February, 1798.

Sir:

I wrote you on the 16th. I was then, and am still, afflicted with the gout, but hope soon to be well. On the 18th I wrote, No. 1, to the governor, and yesterday I received No. 2 from him;

No. 3 is the acknowledgment and No. 4 the answer. I shall certainly cultivate, by every means in my power, a spirit of harmony with the governor, as well as the citizens on this frontier. I have been treated with much attention by all persons during my tour from this to the source of Appalatche to Tugalo, and from thence on my return through Franklin, Jackson, Oglethorpe and Green Counties to this garrison.

You have, in my letter to the governor of the 7th, the result of the proceedings relative to Tuskeegee Tustunnagau, one of the Creek Commissioners; when this unfortunate affair happened I was in the rear of the escort some miles with one of the gentleman Commissioners of Georgia who was unwell.

The escort had divided, and when I overtook them the Indians divided also, and came on directly after me on one of two roads leading to Greensborough.

I had given orders to march the Indians, under guard, through the settlements, to prevent their being insulted by any disorderly person they might meet, or giving offense to any of the citizens. I informed the chiefs of the orders, and the necessity then was for them strictly to observe my directions. They conformed immediately. Tuskeegee Tustunnagau had been long known and respected for his attention to the white people, and could never believe they would do him any injury; he was fond of strong drink and would call in to the houses we passed, in one of which he committed this outrage.

The complainant and two of his neighbours arrived directly after me; he expressed in strong terms his determination to put the offender to death.

The chief was with me, but from report, the suspicion fell on one of those on the other road. In a short time I had a crowd of visitors in arms. I fixed on the place for the junction of the escort and had dispatched an express with the necessary orders. It was nine o'clock at night before they joined and I got the Indians together. Soon after this Mr. Hilton, the injured man, arrived and repeated his determination to put the offender to death.

I replied I would examine into the affair and would cause justice to be done; that the force with me was competent to the purpose, and I should deliver the offender to the civil authority. They urged repeatedly and with much earnestness that I should deliver the whole up to them. I detailed the mode I intended to pursue, and declared my determination not to deviate from it. In the morning I convened the Indians, addressed them suitable to the occasion, and they, in ten minutes, delivered up the offender. Their first reply to me was: "Justice must be done to the white people; we can and will find out the offender." I told this chief what I was bound to do by the duties of my office, and explained

the confinement & mode of treatment and trial he might expect.
He replyed: "I will submit. I am a man. If I get a rope it is my
fate." I then made a suitable address to my fellow citizens &
ordered the cavalry to parade before my tent, & I delivered the
prisoner to the officers & he parted from me and his companions
with much firmness. The officers returned in the evening with a receipt from the gaoler of Oglethorpe County for the body of the
chief. No. 5 is the address of the Creek Commissioners to a gentleman of Green County who has promised me to attend to the
prisoner and supply his wants, and they have requested me to send
a copy of it to the Governor of Georgia in their name. No. 6 is
an account of a murder in retaliation for that of the 22nd of December. This hasty procedure arose, I am informed, from a report
received in the nation that the murderers of that day had been tried
by the magistrates and acquited with joy and firing of guns. I
have a letter from the man who wrote the address for the Indians.

The affair of the 16th mentioned by the Governor, I am now
tracing. I have some Indians from the neighbourhood of Long
Bluff who have hunted there during the season. They were encamped in a few miles of the bluff on their side of the river and
have come up from thence since the 14th. They doubt the truth of
the charge against them. I shall know the truth by April, if it has
been committed by an Indian.

I have letters from the Upper Creeks of the 8th, and the Lower
of the 11th. The hunters begin to return, and give assurances that
the complaints for the present winter will be much less than the
last. I have heard of some which I can remedy. I have two
smiths engaged, one in the Tuckabatchee, the other among the
lower towns. The Indians seem to be much pleased at this arrangement. This establishment is founded on the VIII of the
Treaty of Colerain, and I have hitherto directed the smiths not to
receive pay from the Indians, but to render to me monthly, an
account of the work done by them.

I wish you to give me your directions on the execution of this
article; are the smiths to be at the expense of the U. S.? My
present decision is that they are, and on this idea the establishment
commences; but I have reserved to myself the right whenever I
deem it advisable, to order the smiths to receive pay; and I have
it in contemplation to do all work appertaining to agriculture free
of expense, but to make the hunters pay for their guns and traps.

I have still on hand more than half of the articles which were
sent out to commence the plan for bettering the conditions of the
Indians; they are deposited with the two smiths. The Quaker
present is but just carried into the nation. There are still at
Colerain ten or 12 horse loads, and I find that Ensign Allinson,
who commands there, has sent up by the last conveyance some

articles remaining of the former establishment, as present goods; these I shall send you an account of as soon as I get into the nation. I progress in the good work intrusted to me, though slowly.

I have had fifty yards of good 500 thread wove at one house; the cotton was raised and spun by two Creek girls, the last summer and fall, and I sent a weaver to the house who fixed up a loom and wove it; he tells me he was much visited during the time he was weaving, by the women of the neighbouring towns, who expressed a determination to attend to the raising of cotton and following my directions. I have sent some cotton to the nation, and I have a quantity here, with some wheels.

I cannot express to you the difficulty I have with this proud, haughty, lying, spoiled, untoward race. I have daily occasion for an exercise of my whole stock of patience, prudence and firmness. Being determined to deserve success, my perseverance overcomes my strength of body. I have made considerable progress in learning their language; this I find is flattering to them, and it amuses me during my leisure hours, which are but few. While our affairs with France and Spain are unsettled, the expenses in my department will increase a little. I am now under the necessity of employing a young man of this country, and to assign to him to attend particularly to the recovery of property from this country. I have allotted him 220 dollars a year subscription rate.

I shall, as soon as I have made a report to you of the expences of the last year, return immediately into the nation, and this I shall be able to do in about 20 days.

I have the honour to be, very respectfully, Sir,

Your obedient servant.

The Honourable
    JAMES McHENRY,
        Secretary of War.

———————

Fort Wilkinson, 25th February, 1798.

Sir:

I shall now reply to such parts of Your Excellency's favours of the 3rd and 17th as remain unanswered. I heard of, while I was on the western frontiers of the state, the conduct of the Indians towards Captain Bowen, and I took measures immediately to ascertain the nature of the complaint, that I might cause justice to be done. No. 1 is the Captain's deposition. I have sent a copy to the agent of the Cherokees with orders to call on that nation to ascertain the offenders if the charge be true.

I examined Captain Bowen in the presence of his neighbours, and of your Commissioners, and I can assure you the inhabitants on that line unanimously declared that the conduct of the Indians, many of whom had visited them repeatedly during the winter season had been very friendly, and this charge was unexpected. No. 2 is the address of the Creek Commissioners relative to their unfortunate companion, which I send by their request.

I am informed that the court in Jackson County will be early in April. Although I have delivered up this chief to the civil authority, and it may seem I have no further agency in the case, it may be proper that I should order an interpreter to attend the trial; of this you will be the judge, and if you don't, I will send one here. I should be glad, he might meet a subpoena at this place, blank, to the care of Colonel Gaither, to be filled up by him.

Colonel William Wofford, one of the settlers on the Indian lands, has a letter of introduction from me of the 2nd inst., to the Secretary of War, to represent his situation and that of his unfortunate neighbours in person. I stated in the introduction that "I readily grant his request, as from the best information relative to him, he is incapable of making any representation that will not be true." I have no doubt that he will fulfill the expectations of his neighbours by a faithful detail of every thing interesting to them. I shall, as I now am able to attend to business, report this line to you in a few days, and submit to you, whether it would not be proper for you to proclaim it to the citizens, that they may conform to it. I told the settlers that they would not, in my opinion, be permited to make another crop, and that they would do well to look out in time, and remove as soon as they could remove their stock, which I expected they might do in the month of April, as by that time there would be a supply of grass any where. There is a great scope of unsettled land in the southwest corner of Jackson County, and much of it better than any I have seen to the southward. As most of the settlers on Indian lands are tenants, they could there be accommodated.

The President has not been inattentive to the wishes of the citizens of Georgia. I am ordered to ascertain in the most unequivocal manner whether the nation is disposed to sell the lands you were authorized to purchase at Colerain.

My first attempt has not been successful, but I shall take upon me to renew it on all fit occasions, and I am not without hopes that if the Indians can be impressed with confidence in the justice of their neighbours, and a friendly interchange of good offices should take place between them, but that I shall succeed. This depends as much on the co-operation of Your Excellency as any man I know.

In reply to the other part of your communications, I have to add that I took care the last fall not to suffer a hunting party to leave the nation without a chief who would be answerable for their good conduct, & who should be bound to report it to me at the annual spring meeting; I ordered expressly that the Indians should abstain from crossing over to the white settlements unless with a permit from me or the commanding officer on this frontier, naming the Indian & his business, and I am confident that this order would have been better attended to than it has been if it was not for the frequent invitations of my fellow citizens on the frontiers to visit them, and the illicit commerce carried on by some of them.

Notwithstanding the recent unfortunate and improper conduct on both sides, I find that I am daily making progress, and I expect at the annual spring meeting, which I shall attend, I shall be able to do much towards lessening the complaints against the Indians.

I am now tracing by 4 more Indians the affair of the 14th. I have some Indians since I wrote you, from the neighbourhood of Long Bluff, who have hunted there during the season; they were encamped within a few miles of the bluff, on their side of the river, and have come up from thence since the 14th. They doubted the charge against them. They left their women and children at their camp.

I shall know the truth by April, if it has been committed by an Indian.

Mr. Hill, my messenger, is intelligent and to be relied on; he is on his way to Savannah and will execute any of your orders.

I have the honour to be, very respectfully,
        Your Excellency's obedient servant.
His Excellency,
    JAMES JACKSON,
        Governor of Georgia.

Fort Wilkinson, 25th February, 1798.
Sir:

I am necessitated again to send to you to have my wants supplied; I cannot any where find a man who will give cash for a bill on Philadelphia, and I have sent Mr. Hill, a man now in my department, who is intelligent and much to be relied on, expecting you will find no difficulty in getting cash for one in Savannah.

I have closed the line on this frontier and am happy to assure you there was no room for adversity of opinion with the Commissioners of this state, and that the utmost harmony subsisted between us throughout the whole of it. The recall, by order of the

Legislature, met us some days after we had completed the line and
were on our return. There are but a few settlers on the west side;
three of them, Mr. Cunningham, Colonel Wafford and Mr. Smith,
have embarked property; the others are mostly tenants, and most
of them with huts so recently made as to be without any clearing.
I have letters from the Upper Creeks from the 8th, & the Lower of
the 11th; they are friendly, but having been embarrassed recently
by some worthless white people who have traveled through their
nation, they have requested me to put a stop to it till arrangements
can be made to secure the Indians from the imposition of such
characters. Mr. Hill, who has been with me for some time, will
inform you of some transactions which have happened in this
quarter which are unpleasant. I have recently had two letters from
the governor and I shall rely on his co-operation to secure peace
and establish an interchange of good offices with my red charge
and the citizens on the frontier. I have the account of your friendly attention to my request for garden seeds, but that is all; Snell
has imprudently left them at Fort James, and I have only to expect
them from thence in one month. I expect to go again into the
nation on the return of my messenger, where I shall have a
troublesome spring and summer.

I am, with much esteem & regard, Sir,

Your obedient servant.

MR. JOHN HABERSHAM.

Fort Wilkinson, 25th February, 1798.

Exchange for 1,000 Dollars:

At sight of this, my second of exchange, first of the same tenor
and date not paid, pay to Major John Habersham, or to his order,
one thousand dollars for the like sum advanced me for my sallary,
due to the 8th of September last, exclusive of my ration allowance
as P. T. Agent for Indian Affairs South of Ohio.

I am, Sir,

Your obedient servant.
1,000 Dollars.

The Honourable
    JAMES McHENRY,
        Secretary of War.

Sir:

Fort Wilkinson, 25th February, 1798.

I have this day drawn on you in favour of Major John Habersham for one thousand dollars for my sallary, due to the 8th of September last (exclusive of my ration allowance), as Agent of Indian Affairs South of Ohio.

I have been under the necessity of adopting this mode again, as I cannot sell a bill on you where I am, and have sent the bills to him to obtain the money for them. I am making arrangements again to return into the heart of the nation.

I have the honour to be, with great respect and esteem, Sir,
Your obedient servant.

The Honourable
JAMES McHENRY,
Secretary of War.

I drew on you of the second, in favour of J. C. Kilpatrick, the public surveyor, for one hundred dollars, for his services in ascertaining the line from Appalatchee to Tugalo.

27th.

Mr. Edward Brown, on Town Creek, reported that yesterday, at a log rolling in his neighbourhood, he was informed by a man who arrived there that an Indian was recently killed at or near Long Bluff. He was on the left side of the river. The person who killed him was in the woods, and he heard the bleat of a fawn and halted; he then proceeded; it was repeated, and he heard something like the snap of a gun, and on looking about he discovered an Indian, who flashed at him; he jumped behind a tree and immediately fired and killed him.

Fort Wilkinson, 5th March, 1798.

TUSSEKIAH MICO & YEAUHOLAU MICO:

Beloved Chiefs:

On the 11th of last month some Creeks fired across the Oconee and killed a white man, Nicholas Vines, on his own plantation in

Hancock County, near the mouth of Rocky Creek; they left an address to the inhabitants to inform them this was for satisfaction for the murder of the 22nd. They left the commission which I gave Ocheese Tustunnagau, as a Creek Commissioner, with the address; and on the 14th, two or more Indians murdered William Allen in Washington County, near Oats's, on Long Bluff. A short time after this, three Indians came opposite Oats's and called over, and while Oats was speaking a white man slipped up behind him and fired at the Indians across the river, but we do not know whether they are wounded or not. The cavalry has been down the river and Indians have been sent to all the Indian camps I could hear of to warn them of the danger that threatened from the bad conduct of a few wicked fellows. I have not heard of any more mischief which has happened lately. I have sent the Indian with this talk to you to inform you of it, to ask you to enquire and find out who killed Allen, and to try and make your people behave better. It appears to me that some of the Creek warriors have not the understanding of children, as when they know their people are hunting on the frontier, they have the wickedness and imprudence to come and shed innocent blood. If I was not a better friend to you than you are to yourselves, your hunting camps would have been attacked by a body of men who would be able to put all they met to the sword, & would at this moment be in your country. I shall do what I can for you, but you must help, or all I could do will amount to nothing. I am determined never to forgive any man, red or white, who sheds innocent blood, and I expect to see the day when all who shed innocent blood will be put to death, and that an honest man may go where he pleases and be not afraid.

I have directed Mr. Oats to go back to his plantation; we all know he is friendly to Indians.

Pass of 8th March, Colonel John Phillips & Charles Burk, Esq.

Fort Wilkinson, 8th March, 1798.

I have sent up by Michael's black man an anville for the Tuckabatchee shop; this makes every thing complete with you. I shall be among you next month. Mordecai will inform you that Ocheese Tustunnagau is restored to his nation; this act will, I hope, be received by the Creek nation as it ought. By the laws of the white people he has forfeited his life, but by the kind interposition of the frontier people it is restored to him.

The Indians are charged with killing one Allen at Long Bluff, the 14th of last month. The Dog Warrior tells me it was done by Uchees. I shall examine into this affair when I shall be among the lower towns.

The public goods are on the way; they were shiped early in winter, and the vessel caught in the Ice in Delaware. Bailey's and Durant's two oldest boys came out with them, and they went from Savannah to Colerain with Mr. Seagrove.

I received your complaints against white people traveling through the Creek land; if they are true, the white people must be punished. You must not forget yourself when you send a talk again and give it as the talk of the nation. I know well that the talk you sent me was made by a man at the Hickory Ground. I was myself in your land all the spring; I was with twelve towns and they never mentioned the subject to me, and at the time the talk was dated at the Hickory Ground, your chiefs were all in the woods. I say you must take care and not forget yourself; when the nation gives out a law respecting the people of a neighbouring nation, red or white, it must be done at a public meeting of all the chiefs, and I shall sign it.

I have not yet heard what boats went down the Tennessee, but I am informed they were not Coxe's; he was, by the last accounts, at Knoxville.

I wish you would have some of your corn planted the next full moon; it will be a good time, and I find the Indians all plant too late; we are begining to plant now; I have planted peas, early beans, cymblins, cucumbers and garden stuff.

Remember me to your family, and believe me to be,

Your friend.

ALEXANDER CORNELL,
Assistant & Interpreter among the Creeks.

No. 1. Tuskeegee Tustunnagau, discharged and restored to his nation.

No. 2. Address of Colonel Phillips, &c., on delivering the body.

Fort Wilkinson, 9th March, 1798.

Since my last to Your Excellency of the 25th ultimo, I have been informed by a Cusseta warrior that two Uchees were in the neighbourhood of Oats's on the 14th, and he believes they killed Allen. I have dispatched two runers to the nation on this subject; Mr. Barnard will go off to-morrow, and I shall follow, myself, by the end of the month.

On the 7th of this month several men from Green County arrived here with Tuskeegee Tustunnagau. The enclosed, No. 1 and No. 2, are copies of original papers in my possession; that chief has returned to the nation.

I omitted to inform you in my last that the store at Colerain is not a public one, & that it is in contemplation to carry on all the public trade at this place.

I have the honour to be, very respectfully,

Your Excellency's obedient servant.

His Excellency,
JAMES JACKSON,
Governor of Georgia.

Cloth for coat 200
Making coat 300
Triming, do. 100
Cloth for pantaloons 150
Making do. 150
Trimings do. 50
W. Cloth & Making 150
K. Cloth & Making 150

1250

Fort Wilkinson, 14th March, 1798.

Sir:

I send herewith inclosed to Your Excellency, in the care of Colonel Burns, a map of the line from the source of Appalatchee over the Currahee to Tugalo. I have sent forward to the Secretary of War a copy, with notes explanatory, and a journal of my whole proceedings in relation to it.

I have not heard of any occurrence since my last worthy of your attention. Mr. Barnard is gone to the nation, and I shall follow by the end of the month. I shall communicate to you from time to time the progress I make in the execution of the duties enjoined on my appointment.

I have the honour to be, very respectfully,

Your Excellency's obedient servant.

His Excellency,
JAMES JACKSON,
Governor of Georgia.

I have had the pleasure of Colonel Burns's company for two evenings; he informed me you were well. My difficulties and embarrassments have had their crisis, and my hopes are again on the wing. I was, for some days after I left you, afflicted with the gout; it deprived me of ten or twelve days, which I intended to devote to bringing up my impoverished business; and what was more distressing, it deprived me of the pleasure I contemplated in a visit I intended to Louisville to pay my respects to your governor and to spend one day with you.

I have had Mr. Barnard with me; he arrived just after I returned, and I have been able to express myself as I wished to the Indians. When the Tussekiah Mico and the other Creek Commissioners left me, they requested me to remember them to you and to tell you they would not forget your friendly attention to them; that when you and Colonel Burns first joined them at this place, after the affair of the 22nd, they viewed you with distrust and dislike, but that they trusted and lived with you until they looked on you as their friend.

Tuskeegee Tustunnagau, when he was brought here by Colonel John Phillips from his confinement, he made speech friendly in the extreme to Georgia:

"I forfeited my life and the people restored it to me; I was ashamed that I, who had delighted in doing good acts to the white people, should violate their laws. I suffered much, not from fear of death, because I am above fear, but because I had done an injury to white people in company with our great beloved man and the beloved men of Georgia, which put me to shame. If our beloved man had not taken my knife, raisor and moccasin all from me, I should have put myself to death. I now rejoice that I am alive to tell how I have been treated, that the great body of the people of Georgia are friendly to the Indians; that the Governor of Georgia sent a guard to take care of me; that this guard, tho' but few in number, faithfully obeyed their orders, and when his jail was attacked by a number of bad men, the Governor's guard saved my life; they fired on their own people and wounded two, one of them badly. My people have lost four of their beloved chiefs by white men and we never retaliated; I expected I was the fifth, but I am saved, and I hope for the good of the white people; I will now die sooner than cease to be friendly to them. If our beloved man and the chiefs of our land will restore me to my former rank, I shall be able to do much good, and I am as willing as I shall be able."

I am going on the last of this month to the nation; I have ordered Mr. Barnard and he has returned, and I am to follow. Whenever I return I hope to be your way, and until then accept of my sincere wishes for your prosperity, and believe me, with sincere regard and esteem, Sir,

Your obedient servant.

COLONEL JOHN CLEMENTS.

19th March.

David Cowden, who lives within 3 miles of the High Shoals, states that he lost a mare, a dark bay, branded T on the shoulder, on the rising, and uncertain whether branded on the buttock; 4 years old. A bright bay horse, colt, a large star and snip on his nose, 2 years old; he is branded T-H on shoulder and buttock. They were lost the 28th or 29th of January.

Isaac Handby, near the Cedar Shoals, reports that he lost a black mare about the 7th; branded A-P on the shoulder, 8 or 9 years old.

Fort Wilkinson, Creek lands.

James Shearly and Minna Brind did this day, in my presence, agree to take each other as man and wife, and having done so, they are to be considered as such and respected as such.

Given under my hand this 22nd of March, 1798.

B. H.,

P. T. A. for I. A. South of Ohio.

Charlotte Benson, taken 1780, on December 24th, then about 5 years of age; her father and grandfather were murdered the same day.

16th of April, 1798.

TUSSEKIAH MICO:

I arrived at Mr. Barnard's the fourth day after I left you. I remained there three days and arrived here last evening. In the morning I set out for the Cusseta and shall arrive there in the evening. I am unwell; I can ride, but make an awkward foot at walking, my left leg and foot being swelled and painful.

Some travelers from South Carolina, who came by Fort James and obtained passes from Ensign Thompson to go to Tensaw, have been plundered in the Cusseta by some Indians from one of the upper towns. The motives they assign for this improper conduct are that the passes were not regular, and that they were advised to do it to put a stop to white peoples' traveling through their land until arrangements can be made to secure the Indians from the imposition of worthless characters.

Some of the chiefs of the upper towns have lately taken upon themselves to give talks to the nation, and the talk I showed you in February, from Alex Cornell, was their first attempt. My reply of the 8th of March suspended their further proceeding. I sent an order to them not to forget that when the nation gave out a law respecting the people of the U. S. or a neighbouring nation, red or white, it must be done at a public meeting of all the chiefs and signed by me.

The chiefs of the lower towns have showed proper resentment upon the occasion; they have collected a considerable part of the property and restored it, and have sent an order to these and the upper town chiefs to collect and restore the remainder; as this act arose out of their improper conduct, they have also appointed two chiefs to conduct Mr. Bilbo and his party safe to their destination.

I must request you to suspend granting passes through the nation till I have had a meeting with the chiefs and inform you of the result.

Individuals coming into the nation on lawful business will be safe; property passing through will not be safe. I find the Indians are much opposed to settlements being made on the waters of the Mobile above our line, and they view every traveling party as intruders on their lands.

I opened Tussekiah Mico's letter to you at his request, as Mr. Barnard was with us, to know whether it was as he intended, and to make some additions. I readily consented to his carrying you some bacon, as I believe you are in want, notwithstanding we are in a country of improvident people, and I find it will be difficult to get provisions after I leave the inhabitants of this industrious little village. I request you to communicate this letter to Colonel Gaither; I shall write to him by the first conveyance from the Cusseta. I believe you gave 6 cents for bacon; this price is enough.

I am, with sincere regard and esteem, Sir,

Your obedient servant,

BENJAMIN HAWKINS.

MR. EDWARD PRICE.

April 21st, 1798.

Stomolutkee, of Cohau, informs that he has an old negro called Tom, his property; he exchanged a negro for him, of good property, with Noah Harrod, who had him of Benjamin Stradham and son; this negro, Tom, is now among the Cherokees, and he is desirous to sell him to Christian Russel, a trader; that Christian Russel knows where this negro is, and is willing to give 200 chalks and a rifle gun for the negro, and he, Stomolutkee, has agreed to take that price for him, and applies to have the necessary writings on the subject to confirm this bargain, and to obtain for Russel a right to get possession of and to retain the negro.

A pass to James Hubbard, his wife and two children.

———

Benjamin Hawkins, Principal Temporary Agent for Indians Affairs South of Ohio, to Hopoithle Mico:

I am come again into the Creek land. I expect a meeting in twelve days of many chiefs of the towns on this river, and after that I shall come up on a visit to the towns of the other two rivers, and I intend to pay you a visit. I want much to see you. I have a great regard for the old chiefs of this land, particularly for Hopoithle Mico, Tuskenehutkee, Efau Haujo, Yeauholau Mico, Mico Thlucco, Cusseta Mico and Tussekiah Mico. I wish much to see you all together. It is to meet & consult with such great chiefs on the affairs of the Creeks that I am sent by their friend and father, the President of the U. S., to inform them of the friendly disposition of the people of the U. S. towards them, and to assist in making the Creeks a great and happy people. You must come and see me in this town. I shall then go home with you, and we will have a meeting of your upper towns at such time as we may judge proper.

Some young people of your town have lately robed some white women and children in this neighbourhood. The chiefs who give you this letter are sent to you to have justice done to these poor people. I hope you will assist them in doing justice. I am your friend.

———

22nd.

John de Strange, a native of South Carolina, pass to Tensaw; he is one of the unfortunate travelers recently plundered in the neighbourhood by some of the red people.

25th.

Francis Killingsworth, a native of North Carolina, with his wife and three children.

William McDonald, a native of South Carolina, his wife & four children, and two brothers.

Tallauhassee, 22nd of April, 1798.

Sir:

Mr. Peg delivered me, the night before last, your favour of the 15th, and last evening I received by Mr. Marshall's servant, Limus, yours of the 17th, with the packets sent from the postoffice.

It is much to be regreted that disorder of so serious and alarming nature as those detailed by you should have taken place in the garrison. I understood from you the evening before I left you that the officers had unanimously determined to apply to the Secretary of War to adjust the misunderstanding between them and Mr. Price, and I hoped from that quarter a mandate would be sent that would put all things to rights. The departments were so distinct that there appeared to me to be nothing required from each other but an interchange of good offices, and I think that respect we owe to the source from whence we derive our appointments ought to have influenced our conduct, and the gentlemen of the military and of the factory ought to have sacrificed their party animositys on the altar of public good.

It is not incumbent on me, with the documents I possess, to say positively who has done wrong, but I have received enough by the two last conveyances to justify the following observations. If the military gentlemen have determined at all events to remove Mr. Price, that determination is an insult to the President of the United States; it is an insult to you, who have the command of the military on the southwestern frontier. The authority which placed Mr. Price, in my opinion, alone can remove him; if his conduct is improper, let it be stated to the Secretary of War.

You asked me, my worthy friend, for my advice. I am surrounded with difficulties. I have some serious misunderstandings to reconcile in my department. I have some white women and children who have been robed and striped of their cloathing, now depending on me for aid, and I meet some Spanish interposition which arose out of their first improper conduct towards us. I am surrounded with one hundred Indians daily; all of them with complaints, and my health is fast declining; yet with this pressure and my infirmities what I possess I give unto you.

The order you have given to cut off the intercourse between the military gentlemen and the factory is proper. I would advise that until the Secretary of War could give directions, that even the passage through the factory be closed, and that a communication be either near one of the blockhouses or between your hut and the factory; let Mr. Price and his department be separated and unconnected; if he wants your aid, he will ask it, and then you will give the necessary aid. As Mr. Price is the head of an important department, I think you should protect him against the combination mentioned in a former part of this letter; at all events until the Secretary of War has an opportunity to give the necessary orders. I would advise you to inform Mr. Price of the regulations you make for his protection, and invite him to return to his charge. I say I would advise you to do this, and these are my reasons: Mr. Price has been selected by the proper authority for the trust reposed in him; he has given security for the faithful discharge of that trust, and he is in the execution of it, and it is unquestionably as respectable as that of any gentleman who has only the fatigue of doing once in 4 or 5 days the honour of officer of the day.

I am, my dear sir, with much regard and esteem,

Your obedient servant.

COLONEL HENRY GAITHER.

Tallauhassee, 22nd of April, 1798.

Sir:

I have to acknowledge two of your favours, one of the 14th, which I received the evening before last; the other of the 17th, which I received last evening with several inclosures, and I lose no time in reply to them.

If the charge in the first part of Mr. Price's letter be true, it must be resisted and checked; if the military gentlemen have really combined to remove him from his station, it is an insult, in my opinion, of the first magnitude against that authority from whence we all derive our appointments, and it must be known whether they or the President of the United States has a right to judge. You ask my advice; why ask it? You yourself may be removed by the same force and combination which removed Mr. Price; I speak this positively, because he says you were an eye witness of the "violence, outrage and unprecedented conduct of the officers of the garrison." The military gentlemen have nothing to do with Mr. Price nor he with them, but to harmonize by an interchange of good offices; if they cannot do this, he has his sphere and they theirs to move in, and they will never come in contact.

I have no doubt Colonel Gaither will give the assurances required by Mr. Price, and he will be safe in returning to the duties of his appointment; if he does not return, your instructions will warrant your acting in his absence. You will, of course, have recourse to your own judgment for your conduct.

In cases where the debtors don't bring peltry sufficient to discharge the debts already created, you would do well to take, in all cases, the pack horses and put the public brand on them, and limit them to a small credit until they extricate themselves. I am an enemy to credit, but it arose before my agency, in a mistaken policy, which, as I am informed, has been since sanctioned by the Secretary of War. I will sanction it only until the parties can extricate themselves. The distinction drawn in your question I understand; if you had given the credits you could regulate them, but this is not material and you would do well, as the peltries were purchased with the goods on credit, to let them go to ballance that debt.

The points in your last letter I have answered; that is, I would let the traders in arrears have a small credit to extricate themselves, and a running account of small things only. The peltries should go to the original debt, and the remittance for the season should leave the ballance for our future deliberation; these ballances you will note particularly. I would advise you, by every exertion, to be prepared in aid of Mr. Price for the settlement of his accounts; he has had a very difficult task; the experiment was a new one and the source from which information was to be drawn not sure. I am not well and am under a pressure of difficulties; I will write you again in a few days.

I am, with much regard and esteem, Sir,

Your obedient servant.

MR. MATTHEW HOPKINS.

24th.

Tuskenepaulauchuclee called on me to inform me that a talk came into his town that 4 men of Micasuckkee had been down on St. Mary's cloplaqufcau and stole some horses. They came up and crossed Sawaupa River and encamped in a bend of the river. While they were there, one of them went out to hunt on the back trail and discovered some white men pursuing of them; he returned to the camp, gave the information, and they fled into the swamp.

The white people came, took the horses, plundered and destroyed every thing at the camp, and made much exultation. On their return, the Indians judged where the white people would cross the Sawaupa. The leader of the red party said when he set out he determined to steal horses, and it appeared he determined to shed blood, and we go and waylay the crossing place of the river; that he did so and he discovered the white people coming, one in advance, at whom he fired, and he saw him fall; the fire was returned, and the leader wounded with shot, but has since recovered, and returned to his town. Mr. Kennard has sent Mr. Homes, a negro and Indian, who is trusty, to Colerain to know the truth, and they are to return in 12 days. The man who did this says he will go again and will have blood; that he has but one life, and if that goes, there will be an end of him; that Kennard ordered two letters from Colerain, one for him and one for this town; when he gets them, he will send one up.

24th.

Received from Stunafuni a sorrel horse, 13 hands high, saddle spots & some white spots on his shoulder, blazed face, the near hind foot white, branded on the cheek C, and paid him three dollars.

Note—The horse has a broad, tanned leather collar & bell.

26th.

Sowed a variety of beans and garden seeds.

Tallauhassee, 3rd May.

David Mortimer, late a soldier of the U. S., pass to Georgia.

John White and Major Colber, return passes, see 3rd of December.

Thomas Rutledge, Edward Hagan, Joseph Jackson and Charles Burk, Jr., permission to pass into Georgia.

Plant 3 seed of a large cymblin.

4th.

Captain Joseph Carson, John Pinckard, pass to Mobile.

Coweta Tallauhassee, 10th May, 1798.

JOHN ANTHONY SANDOVAL:

Thomas Carr has called on me for justice on his complaint against you last fall for not paying your debt due him of two hundred and sixty-one dollars. You admitted the justness of his demand then, and stated that you could tell when Tarvin returned how soon you could be able to settle this account with him.

I must now require of you to settle your debt with Mr. Carr or show cause why judgment may not be given against you and your property for the sum claimed by him and admitted by you.

Given under my hand.

5th.

Planted cabbages, the season remarkably dry; I watered them and covered them. Planted corn in new ground, coultered both ways & checked. Planted potatoes. Our little crop late from necessity.

12th May, 1798.

John Anthony Sandoval this day appeared and agreed that he was justly indebted the sum charged, of two hundred fifty-six dollars, and that the mortgage now on his boy with Mr. Price should remain and be transferred to secure this debt, and that I am to give orders to that effect to Mr. Price. This debt to be paid at the Rock Landing, to the credit of Mr. Carr, and on the receipt, the negro to be returned.

Coweta Tallauhassee, 20th May, 1798.

Your messenger, Snell, having called on me, I avail myself of the opportunity to send you this note. I have had a meeting a few days past of the chiefs of all the towns on Chattahoochee, at the Coweta town to remedy some improper and unjustifiable conduct of their disorderly young hunters. I gave particular charge to the chiefs to be attentive to your messengers and your interests, and not to forget that in the hour of their embarrassment you were their friend.

I have given out the broken days for a general meeting of the whole nation at Tuckabatchee on the 23rd instant, and expect there to make effectual arrangements for bettering the condition of these people, and bringing about an interchange of good offices between them and their neighbours.

I received at the meeting at Coweta, very favourable accounts from the Choctaws, Chickasaws, Cherokees and the northern nations. A broad belt of peace arrived from all of them and was very favourably received.

I have not received from the War Office any intimations relative to your proposals on commerce. The plan of the U. S. is not as extensive as you suggest; it is intended as an instrument of peace without being a monopoly, and it will be my endeavour to make this instrument common and mutually beneficial to those trading under the authority of His Catholic Majesty and the United States of America.

Mr. Seagrove, I see from an address of his to the Creeks, has established a store at Colerain, on the St. Mary's, in partnership with Jourdan, formerly an assistant of his. They invite the Creeks to trade with them; they promise cheap goods for furs, skins and cattle.

I daily expect some important information relative to our political affairs; by the last accounts I have received, it was probable our misunderstanding with France would not be settled in the course of this season, and we should be under the necessity of taking effectual measures for self defense.

I sent you by an Indian, Nitta Huntly, the last newspapers I received, and I shall continue from time to time to forward them.

With assurances of my best wishes for your prosperity, and a desire that you would believe me, with much esteem and regard, Sir,

Your obedient servant.

MR. WM. PANTON.

10th May.

Senogeeche, pass to go to the borders of Tulapocca.

11th.

Planted pumpkins, water melons, tobacco, and transplanted cabbages and lettuce.

Coweta Tallauhassee, 12th May, 1798.

(Extract) TO COLONEL GAITHER:

My Dear Sir:

I had on the 5th a meeting of all the chiefs on this river at Coweta, to endeavour to remedy, if practicable, the improper conduct of the young hunters and horse thieves; and I found it necessary on the 7th to call a meeting of the whole nation at Tuckabatchee, on the 23rd of this month, and then I believe I shall remedy some of the evils complained of. The travelers mentioned in my letter to Mr. Price of the 16th ultimo, I have cloathed and sent on to the waters of Mobile. I was not able to recover their horses or cloathes. The people who were guilty of this outrage and some mischief makers, expecting I would call them to account, determined, if practicable, to alarm me and the people around me. Alex. Cornell and the Mad Dog came to see me, on invitation, the 3rd. In the evening an old chief called at my lodgings to inform us that a large body of Indians, armed, with hostile views were coming up the river to visit. He was soon followed by others who corroborated what the old chief said, and added they were within five miles. They then consulted together and ordered my horses to be brought from the woods and saddled. They sent runers to Cusseta and Coweta, and called on the chiefs to assemble at my lodgings without delay. They then advised me to set out immediately and go to a place they named, where I might be safe. I replied to the chiefs that if the Indians were coming here to find an enemy they would be mistaken; I was their friend; that if they were determined for war and mischief, I advised them to take a little time to collect all the rogues and rascals in the nation, and march in a body; I would conduct them to Colonel Gaither, who would soon make them sick of war and mischief; that I believed the well disposed among the Creeks, aided by Colonel Gaither and Colonel Butler, would be an overmatch for all the mischief makers, red and white; that as they called me the friend and father of the four nations, I should, in that character, judge for myself; I should order my horses to be turned into the woods and go and sleep in my tent. In the morning I found I had been guarded by some of the principal chiefs of the land. This day I amused myself with gardening and farming. The 5th I set out for Coweta; I had not entered into the square for five minutes before we heard the war whoop coming up the river after me in full speed. The town was alarmed. I retained my seat, and after the messenger arrived and made his report, the head warrior was ordered out to call the warriors together and go in force to examine into the affair. The women, they began to gather and declared their determination to defend me; they knew that there were some giddy horse thieves who wished to bring trouble on their land; to drive them and their children into the woods and swamps to perish; but they were determined to resist and would, if I would arm them, defend me. The chiefs from all the towns, being convened, they, after consultation, informed me that what had caused so much alarm and uneasiness among themselves was in fact the misrepresentations of an intention to compliment me; that the young warriors had collected below and were coming up armed to salute me, and had come within a few miles of my lodging before they were informed that a rong construction had been given to their movement, and that as soon as they were informed of the misrepresentation, they immediately determined to return, and were now on their way home. I replied I was satisfied with the explanation; they saw I showed no concern from the first, and I felt myself quite safe among the chiefs of the land.

On the next day I found that the people who expected to be called to account had in fact given the misrepresentation of the friendly intention of the young men expressly to alarm me and to prevent my demand of satisfaction.

I have received dispatches from all our friends at Knoxville, and from the northern nations and southern tribes a broad peace belt. It was read on the 7th in the square; it is strongly expressive of peace and friendship toward all nations, red and white. Yeauholau Mico said to me: "I have a talk; it is a short one; the northern tribes sent it to me; they have tried our strength and are conquered. The most of our old and best warriors now rot in the earth, or whiten on its surface. We have made peace; we have buried deep under a great lake our sharp weapons, and hope our young ones will grow up in peace and friendship with the children of our red and white brethren, and we hope you Creeks and Simanolees will follow our example, and that you will take the talk and inform us you have done so."

Honourable Benjamin Hawkins, P. T. Agent Indian Affairs.
To Thomas Carr, Dr.

1797.

To half a steer	4.00
4 lbs. of gunpowder	4.00
80 balls	.50

1798.

3 yards cotton stripe	3.00
6 white shirts	8.00
4½ yards Stroud	6.00
1 Duffil blanket	4.00
4 lbs. shot	

Dollars, 29.50

U. S. and the British were
French and Spaniards or to   (Torn out)
Governor gave the old man tw
at Tensaw or Escambie this summer with the intention of calling
again on the Governor for his talk.

I am, with much esteem and regard, Sir,

                                        Your obedient servant.
MR. EDWARD PRICE,
U. S. Factor.

Coweta Tallauhassee, 14th May, 1798

I have, in virtue of a power of attorney from John Batts Bard,
of South Carolina, sold to Thomas Marshall, of Coweta, a negro
man, named Ned, for two hundred and fifty dollars, and on the
payment of that sum into the U. S. Factory at Fort Wilkinson, and
obtaining a receipt for the same from the principal, Mr. Price or
either of the assistants there, acting for and on account of the said
John Batts Bard, the receipt to be on the back of this instrument;
then a complete title shall vest in him, the said Thomas Marshall
and his heirs forever to the said negro Ned.

Given under my hand.

16th May.

William Howel, pass from Tensaw to Georgia.

The corn is peeping out. This day planted corn and peas. Our
field first coultered both ways; the lands new, the season dry.

(Torn out)   Yellow Wood Creek, sold to John
Tarvin, trader of Coweta, a negro man, named Ceasar, for two
hundred and fifty dollars, and acknowledged receiving the above
sum in the presence of

                    TIMOTHY BARNARD,

                    RICHARD THOMAS,
                    Clerk in Indian Department.

Tuckabatchee, 26 of May, 1798.

This day the chiefs of the towns of all the upper, and a deputation from the lower Creeks and Simanolees convened at the public square.

26, in the afternoon.

The chiefs having all convened in the square, and the agent attending, they began to reply to the address made to them this day.

Efau Haujo, being selected as first speaker, addressed first the chiefs and then the superintendent.

I will give you a little talk this afternoon as a begining, and we will then go on until we have accomplished the business we have met on. The first thing I will mention is relative to the cattle ranging on our lands. They cannot be restrained well; they do not understand stipulations relative to boundaries; where they have once had good grass they will go again; we have thought much on this subject, we wish for good neighbourhood; when they come over, people who own them must have time to hunt them; bad weather or sickness may some time cause delay and the cattle thereby get a distance from their homes. When the people come over they must come without their arms. We wish you to discourage all you can the white people from driving their stock on our lands, or permiting them to come over, and we hope you will prevent it if possible. We wish not to encourage our young men to injure their neighbours; when the men come over on our lands after cattle or horses let them come without arms of any kind, guns or swords, and if they meet an Indian, let them show signs of kindness, offer their hands, and if they can speak our language, tell what they have lost and the Indian will help them to recover it. These things are mentioned as our wish, is to put things in a train for a friendly interchange of good offices; conduct like this will prevent the use of sharp weapons.

I have considered of these things with good intentions, and I call on you, as the agent of the four nations, to assist and cause the white people to be neighbourly on their parts; I mean not to omit any thing that may tend to the good of both parties. There are people of ours who go down among the people on the frontiers and there pretend to be great men, chiefs of this land, when they are not so; they go to the white people, are kindly treated, get a dram, and in return grant the privilege of cattle to run on our lands; this conduct is improper, the grants of such people are of no value; it is a national right and can only be given by the nation.

I don't mention these things to prevent a friendly intercourse among the red and white people; we wish this intercourse, but we wish no attempts may be made on our people to obtain this consent.

We wish you to send this talk from our nation to all their neighbours around, bordering on us or the Cherokees.

I have no other talk to give you; it is time for us to look about us, our land is small, game is scarce, the white people are on our hunting grounds, particularly near Cumberland and it's neighbourhood.

27 May.

The Yeauholau Mico opened the meeting with exhibiting the belt received from the northern nations at the meeting of the Lower Creeks at Coweta. He addressed himself to the agent: This belt you have seen and it has been explained to you, and I have at this meeting explained it to the chiefs, and now I call you to witness we take fast hold of the belt; the whole of the Muscogueulgee take fast hold of this belt; it is usual with us when we speak of peace, to hold this white emblem in our hands, and this is the belt we use on such great and important occasions. This mode of transacting our business was handed down to us by our forefathers; they are all dead and gone and we, their descendants, are following their ways.

This business being ended Mr. Hawkins called on the chiefs to attend next to horse stealing and encouraging negros to leave the service of their masters to come into the Creek land and there find protection from Indians who claim them and found their claims on the getting possession of them first. He stated that this evil was of a serious and alarming nature; if the young people could not be restrained from stealing horses and doing mischief to their neighbours, that the nation would be answerable for the thefts; that in the first instance a deduction would be made from the annuity paid the nation, and that even this would not be sufficient, and recourse would be had to their land; that every theft of a horse might be considered as the stealing of a plantation from the Creeks; in short, they might expect that this evil, unless checked, would bring ruin on their land.

The chiefs took this subject into immediate consideration, and Efau Haujo and Oche Haujo made two long and animated speaches to their own people. They then addressed the white traders and said you must not encourage mischief in our land, you must not circulate falsehoods, you must not disobey our laws, we are the chiefs of the land, you must respect us as such while you live with us, we will protect you and your property as long as you conduct yourself well; you have some of you been imprudent and treated us with disrespect, you must alter your conduct.

Mr. Hawkins said that it was the duty of the traders to respect the chiefs, and if any white man behaved himself in a way disagreeable to the chiefs, at their request, he would immediately remove him from the town or nation.

Hopoie, of Thlotlogulgau, informed that John Shearly, a trader in that town, was a troublesome lying man, that he almost daily brought some report of murder or battles into the square which were not true, and that by this conduct he constantly disturbed the peace of the town.

The conversation turned on the conduct of some of the traders, and complaints were stated against Richard Bailey, that he treated some of his town people with contempt, that he had repeatedly declared his determination to live on their lands without their consent, and that the limit* of the lands where he lived were his property. Mr. Bailey denied the charge and a warm altercation ensued; several of the traders entered into the conversation and it finally terminated by the interposition of Mr. Hawkins. He stated to the chiefs that this day they saw how necessary it was that the nation should convene annually, examine into the affairs of the nation, and assist by their councils to restore peace at home and abroad.

In the Evening.

Efau Haujo: I am going to talk a little to my friend the agent; there is twenty-nine towns present, four main towns absent; when we do make a law we believe we can execute it; we now address our talk to all our towns, and I believe when the sticks are cut and put into the hands of the warriors they will exert themselves; now I will try the experiment, it is for the good of our land, you have long wished it; you have a regard for our land and wish to see us in peace and quietness; I will try the experiment and I think it will succeed.

The chiefs then informed me that the Yeauholau Mico, Cusseta Mico, and Cusseta Tustunnagau, who were present, were to carry this talk to Oosuche and then spread it over all the Lower Creeks.

They said further, they wished to send it in writing, with the sticks, to be lodged with Burges for the Simanolees.

Efau Haujo: I have finished one talk and now I begin another:

The Indians who have met here are one town with the Savanukee and this belt is our mode of speaking. This is the day I present

---

* This word very uncertain in manuscript.

my token of friendship to General Washington and his children, as an earnest of a long and lasting friendship. This belt of six strans, with two white ends, two rows of blue wampams on each edge, and two rows of white wampams thro' the middle is thus explained: The two rows of white are the path of perpetual peace, leading from one white end to the other, and the two white ends are the beloved bearer, one of them, and the other the Creeks and Simanolees. It is with a view to join the hands of the people of the United States and the people of my land that I offer this belt, that they may never again be separated or at enmity. The reason I have used white for the white people is that they may set down in peace, we will be at peace on our end, and if any thing interposes to cause uneasiness let both sides strive to remove it earnestly. It is a great talk I now give and I hope that I live to see the good effects from it, and when we are dead and gone, that the young people will see and remember it and the good effects produced by it. It is true there is bad talks going sometimes thro' our land, but I do not mind them, and I hope both sides will reject the bad talks and circulate those that are good. I hope when you and the other good men who are with you do what you can and I and the good men of my land do what we can, that something good will result from it to our land. When you and we have done all we can I hope we shall immitate a happy family who have swept the yard and are siting down viewing the children who are innocently playing in it. What I say to make every thing right on both sides is sincerely my wish and intention; I wish to remove every obstruction to a happy reconciliation between the red and white. This day I hope, if I have spoken the truth, has been allowed me to give a talk for the good of our women and children. I direct this talk to the President of the U. S. and to this great man as our father, friends, and brothers, and I hope it will be reviewed as an evidence of our ernest wish for an everlasting peace with the people of the U. S.; he then delivered the belt.

The agent then delivered the address of the Quakers with their **present.**

28 May.

Efau Haujo opened the business of this day; he stated that he was appointed to deliver the voice of the nation relative to the conduct of certain white men in this land.

There is a young man here of the Ottasies, he has arrived to be a chief of that town; he, in behalf of his town, says that Richard Bailey is an unfit character to be in their land, and he must leave it. The chiefs present concur in opinion that Richard

Bailey is an unfit character and are determined he shall leave their land.

Francis Lesley, trader in Otteluwauly, known by the Indians by the name of Wotecau, is an unworthy and unfit character to be in their land, and the chiefs are determined he shall leave their land.

John Sherley, called by the Indians Sauluchee, the trader at Thlotlogulgau, is an unworthy and unfit character to be in their land and the chiefs are determined he shall leave their land.

It is not for any fears we have that these people can do us any damage that we report them and banish them, it is because they are liars and medlars and rogues; they will meddle in public affairs, are constantly circulating reports injurious to our peace, that they have information that mischief is brewing, the American troops are coming on our land, and such like stories; they disturb the peace of our land by making our young men uneasy by their false and foolish stories.

Samuel Lyons, a hireling of Francis Lesley, is an unworthy character and unfit to be in their land, and the chiefs are determined he shall leave their land.

William Lyons at Tuckabatchee, Tallauhassee, a hireling to James Moore, is an unworthy character and unfit to be in their land, and the chiefs are determined he shall leave their land.

Charles Weatherford is an unworthy character and unfit to be in their land, and the chiefs had determined he should leave their land, but in consideration of his family on the Indian side, and of a promise made by Opoie Hutke of Ocheaupofau, that he will in future attend to his conduct and endeavor to make him reform his conduct and behave well in future, the chiefs have determined to forgive the past and let him remain on his future good behaviour, and if he do's misbehave again he is then to be removed without any favour or affection.

Robert Killgore being represented as an unworthy character and a vagabond, a fugitive from justice and now in the neighbourhood of Ocheaupofau, the chiefs are determined that no such character shall find refuge in their land, and when any such arrive, the agent of the four nations shall give them notice to leave the land, and if they hesitate, he may, by an order under his hand, call on the head men, who will order out as many warriors as may be necessary to make such character respect his orders.

The chiefs request the agent to give notice to the parties concerned of their banishment and that their stay in the land be twenty-four days; that when he sends a written notice to them, he will send the broken days to the head man of the town of their residence, and when the broken days are out they are to commence their journey of banishment.

The agent will give orders where any man is banished and complains that there are debts due him, that the trader who may be licenced to such town shall collect and account for the debts, and the heads of the town will give directions and encourage their young men to pay the debts.

In the Evening.

In conformity with the determination of the representatives of the Creeks now convened, a copy of the proceedings was sent this day to Richard Bailey, Francis Lesley, John Sherley, Samuel Lyons and William Lyons with this notice:

MR. RICHARD BAILEY:

The foregoing is an extract from the proceedings of the chiefs of the land now convened in this town, and I give you notice thereof, and this day the broken days are sent to the head men of the Ottasey. If you know wherein I can be of service to you in arranging your affairs for the approaching state of things you will inform me.

An order was sent to Robert Killgore to depart from the Creek land in 24 days, not to return.

In the Evening.

Efau Haujo, in behalf of all the Creeks, declared that no families should be permited to pass through the Creek lands, that honest men of good characters who have business in the land or to pass thro' it may be permited to pass.

The Indians expressed much uneasiness at the passage of boats down the Tennessee, and wished that it could be stoped; they expressed an intention to send to the Cherokees to stop them.

Mr. Hawkins said that boats navigating the Tennessee were under an agreement made in the treaty of Holston, and that any stipulations by treaty could not be infringed or violated whether they were in favour of the red or white people.

29.

The Indians spent this whole day in explanations relative to trade, the boundary between the United States and Spain, and in arranging some differences among themselves.

In the Evening.

I called on the chiefs to be explicit on the points I submitted to them, and on which the happiness of their land depended.

Satisfaction for three murders ascertained to have been commited by some people of their land, one a Uchee who murdered Brown, one of the Upper Creeks who murdered Gentry in Cumberland, and a Simanolee who murdered Benjamin Times.

There was three other cases under consideration, a negro woman belonging to John Fielder at the High Shoals of Appalatchee, the other Nicholas Vines murdered by some Cowetas in retaliation for the Indian Commissioner murdered on the 22 of December, and the 3rd that of Allen murdered near Oats's. The first of these must be paid for; the case relative to the second had already been fully explained, and as to the third, I had not yet had proof of the murder being commited by an Indian, but they must aid me in the search.

The negros in their land and horses of every discription belonging to their neighbours must be given up, and property of every discription.

Cusseta Tustunnagau spoke in answer to these points by order of the chiefs, as follows:

I am chosen by the nation to take the sticks to the lower towns; I am to convene the chiefs at three places, to give out to them the laws given by this meeting, and I am to attend to the carrying them into execution; the task on the lower towns is an ardious one, we border on Georgia and our young people have been much in the habit of doing improper things. I shall do all I can, and if it is in the power of the chiefs, I hope we shall do much good. In one month I shall let you know if the guilty persons are in our land, and whether we can do justice to the white people; if we cannot, I am to apply to the upper towns and they are to help; I have nothing further to say.

Yeauholau Mico then addressed the agent: I leave in your care this belt which we received from the northern natives, you will return it with the answer we have put on your book, and let the messenger show it to the Coweta Mico, and then deliver it to Colonel Butler, who will send it to the northern nations.

When you was in my square I was discouraged from the gloomy prospects before me, I was fearful I could not restrain my young men and get my land in peace; I then said little, and was pleased when you ordered the broken days for the nation to meet at this square; we have been together, 29 of the largest towns in the nation, and there are only 4 of the principal towns absent. We have been several days in council and we are now unanimous in what is proper to be done for the good of our nation. I have gathered courage from this meeting; I shall return to the lower towns with the advise of these upper towns, and do all I can to cause justice to be done to the white people in restoring to them their negros, horses and property, and in the satisfaction demanded of us.

Efau Haujo then said: The chiefs here present have had much conversation on the address of the agent to them; they begin to see that the rulers of the United States are desirous of doing justice to the red people, that the men now sent by the President have had much trouble with the red people, and the land speculators; that the chiefs now listen with pleasure to the voice of the President, the man who gives it has proved to us that he is the friend to peace and justice and that he strives to help us, and we have come to the determination to help him; we wish to do justice to the white people.

An explanation was asked of the reasons for runing a line between Spain and the U. S., as this, notwithstanding the repeated explanations heretofore given, had caused much uneasiness, and perhaps the true source of this uneasiness was the improper mischiefmakers who had taken refuge in their land.

The agent took much pains to explain the whole. Efau Haujo declared himself perfectly satisfied, and said he expected now all would be satisfied, the red people had confidence in the justice of the U. S.

The chiefs of the lower towns took leave of the agent and chiefs in the square and set out on their return home.

30th.

The chiefs of the upper towns convened and Espannau Haujo exhibited a letter from Martha Ruth of Philadelphia, which was read and explained, and the Quaker address was again explained to them, and the list of presents. They directed some of the chiefs to give an answer in their name, in a friendly manner, to be sent to the Quakers.

Eufau Haujo then said: I will as soon as I hear from the lower towns cause justice to be done for the murder of Gentry.

I told the chiefs a young man at Epucenau Tallauhassee, by the name of Mayfield, must be ordered to visit his friends, and that the little girl at Occhois, daughter of Mrs. Williams, must be delivered to me.

They answered Mayfield had been long at liberty to go where he pleased and that he must go and see his friends.

This day the whole proceedings of this meeting were transcribed and forwarded to James Burges at the request of the chiefs, to be by him communicated to the Simanolees and chiefs in that quarter, with this letter:

Tuckabatchee, 30th May, **1798.**

MR. BURGES:

According to my promise and at the special request of all the chiefs here present, I send you the proceedings of the chiefs at the public meeting here.

I have taken it from the journal from day to day as the same was transacted, in the very words of the chiefs. This makes it longer than if I had sent the substance only, but I told the chiefs I would send you the whole; they wish you to explain it to your chiefs.

I am, with sincere regard & esteem,

Your obedient servant.

---

3 June.

Efau Haujo called on the agent and informed him that being appointed by the chiefs of the Creek land to return an answer to the Quakers, he had come for the purpose and would not deliver it.

Coweta Tallauhassee, Garden. 1798.

19th.

I found my garden lott of 4 acres fenced; the timber cut down, the brush burnt, but the logs not cut up or the lands grubed. I set to cleaning up, burnt all the logs and grubed the whole; then coultered it both ways, ploughed it, and commenced my planting too late, from necessity; and I planted the divisions as they were prepared.

26th April.

Sowed a variety of beans, cucumbers, radishes, beets; planted shallots and canteloup melons.

May 3rd.

Planted 3 seed of a large cymblin.

5th.

Planted potatoes. Planted cabbages. The season very dry; I watered and covered. Planted the corn at the north end of the garden; it peeped out the 16th.

11th.

Planted pumpkins; ¼ of an acre in chuks of wheat. Planted tobacco. Planted water melons, cymblins; transplanted cabbages and lettuce.

16th.

Planted corn and peas. I sent for Mr. Hill from the upper towns, who arrived and had all the lott ploughed and freed from weeds.

13th June.

Replanted the corn.

14th.

Fine rain; planted cabbages.

15th.

Ploughed, and with the corn planted the 5th, two great rains. Planted potato slips. Planted red pepper. Finished replanting corn, ploughed the pumpkins, and little corn, and ploughed corn of the 16th. The little crop looks well. Toped a few plants of tobacco.

The Indians at the Coweta Tallauhassee and Cusseta very late planting; some at it this day.

19th.

Finished ploughing and earthing our corn.

20th.

Snaps from those of the 26th of April. Planted potato slips.

22nd.

The weather continues cloudy and moist.

Orders for the Creek Stipend for the Years 1796 and 1797, Drawn
on Edward Price, Factor for the U. States.

1797.

Sept.17, No.	1, For the Dog Warrior	$ 17.00
24,	2, Big Feared of Cusseta	16.00
25,	3, Tustunnagau Haujo	4.50
25,	4, Sunalthly of Hatchetau	4.50
Oct. 2,	5, Okeleesaw of Oakchoie	10.00
2,	6, Mico Opilthocco, Big Swamp	10.00
6,	7, Efau Haujo of Tuckabatchee	30.00
	8, Mico Opilthocco, 50 lb. meal	
3,	9, Iofekah the wounded chief	20.00
	10, The Bird Tail's brother and party	10.00
30,	11, Tuskenah Hutkee	25.00
Nov. 1,	12, Tehikeh and his party	30.00
5,	13, Emauthy Hutkey	5.00
13,	14, Yeauholau Mico	500.00
	15, Enehau Thlucco	500.00
	16, Abecuh Tustunnagau	270.00
	17, Uchee Will of Uchee	100.00
	18, Opoi Mico	5.00
15,	19, Mico Thlucco	2.00
15,	20, Colohtau, agent for Oconee	80.00
16,	21, Enehau Thlucco	
19,	22, Tuskeneau of Potachooclee	80.00
25,	23, Enehau Thlucco and Holautau Tustun-	
	nagau of Hetchetu	100.00
26,	24, Opoi Haujo of Ooseuchee	100.00
	25, Catchau Haujo of Long I. Village, one	
	blanket	
30,	26, Coosau Mico of Tallauhassee	172.½
	27, Opoi Uchee of Sawgohatchee	72.½
	28, Tuccosau Tustunnagau	80.00
Dec. 5,	29, Tustunnagau Thlucco	250.00
13,	30, Coosau Emautlau	2.50
16,	31, Coosau Mico, ½ bushel of salt	
18,	32, Foosatche Mico, 1 bushel salt and 2½ yds.	
	oznabrigs	
21,	33, Chahau Mico, agent Chickasaws	100.00
1798.		
Jan. 2,	34, Opoie Howla of Tuskeegee	80.00
	35, Stumelugee of Oakchoie	40.00
June 4,	Fixico Haujo of Occhoi Tallauhassee	120.00

June 8,   Yufcau Leyja of Tuckabatchee, for a horse
             stolen at Colerain ....
9,   George Cornell, for sundries furnished by
             him for redeeming prisoners, by order of
             the chiefs 22.50
10,   Itchhos Haujo, for redeeming Colonel
             Titseward's daughter & negro............. 125.00
             Mooklausau Hopoie, for his brother, carry
             Chickasaw talks 10.00
             Ditto, for two Indians going twice with
             Chickasaw horses 15.00
             Ditto, for Josiah Francis for a horse
             restored by him 57.00
             Mooklausau Hopoie for the town of Och-
             caupofau 75.00
             Little Warrior of Coweta Tallauhassee,
             for the lone of a horse to go to Tucka-
             batchee 2.25
Dec. 25,   Salley & Patsey Headham, on E. Price.....   69.75

Fort Wilkinson, 13 December, 1797.

The Commissioners for ascertaining and marking the boundary
line between the Indian nations and the U. S.:

1797. Dr.

Dec. 13, No. 1, To two blankets and 50 lbs. of corn meal delivered
             Nohah Tustunnagau and Ochese Tustunnagau, two
             of the Commissioners of the Creeks.
         2, Emautle Haujo, ditto, 25 lbs. of meal.
         3, John Galphin, ditto, 25 lbs. of flower.
         4, John Galphin, 15 dollars.
         5, John Galphin, 10 dollars.
         6, Wauthlucco Haujo, 25 lbs. of meal & 4 quarts of
            salt.

Dec. 17,   7, Emautle Haujo, one bushel corn.
         8, Tuskeegee Tustunnagau, two bushels.
      9-10, ditto, one bottle rum.
        10, John Galphin, two dollars.
        11, Emautle Haujo, 20 lbs. beef, 25 lbs. flower.
        12, John Galphin, seven dollars.

Orders on Edward Price for the Quarterly Payment of the Assistants and Others in the Creek Department.

1797.
Mar. 9, No. 1, Timothy Barnard $233.⅓
            2, Alexander Cornell 133.⅓
            3, James Burges 133.⅓
            4, Richard Thomas 66.⅔
Aug. 3,   Cash paid by Maclin 100.00
    25,   Timothy Barnard, by ditto.............. 175.00
               Richard Thomas 50.00
Sept. 17,   5, Jeremiah Spellar, Creek farmer........... 60.00
    20,   6, Sackfield Maclin 12.34
Oct. 3,   7, Timothy Barnard 175.00
            8, Timothy Barnard, for Felix Counts....... 196.00
    6,   9, Richard Thomas 50.00
    7,   10, Alexander Cornell 100.00
    16,   11, John Galphin, express rider 37.00
Nov. 5,   12, Robt. Walton, express rider 207.00
Dec. 17,   13, Alexander Cornell 100.00
    19,   14, Richard Thomas 150.90
    28,   15, Townly Bruce 22.00
    31,   16, Richard Thomas 50.00
1798.
Jan. 1,   17, Richard Thomas 3.75
Mar. 10,   18, Timothy Barnard, to the 1st of January,
               1798 .... 175.00
1798.
May 9,   James Burges, to December 31st, 1797...... 550.00
Nov. 8,   William Beard, an assistant for 6 months... 48.00

Orders on Edward Price, U. S. Factor, for Sundries for the Creek Department as Contingencies.

1797.
Sept. 17, No. 1, Iofekeh, the wounded chief ....$ 18.00
    22,   2, ditto   ditto 23.00
    27,   3, ditto   ditto ....
              4, Captain Johney, half bushel of salt........ 1.00
Oct. 7,   5, Negro Primus 3.00
    30,   6, White Lieutenant 2.50
Nov. 1,   7, Thletaupee, 4 kegs brandy.

Nov. 4,	8, Momejuh, for the recovery of a horse.....	7.50
5,	9, Emautley Hutkey	1.50
12,	10, Cotchau Tustunnagau	15.75
	11, Chemauille	12.25
13,	12, Iofekeh, the wounded chief	25.00
	13, Yeauholau Mico, for pork for Smith's......	35.00
15,	14, Cullosabe, for McIntosh negros...........	25.00
16,	15, Eufau Tustunnagau, two bags meal.	
20,	16, Whoethlau Nookesaw	3.75
28,	17, Tustunnagau Luste, one blanket.	
Dec. 16,	18, Opoi Haujo, the old chief, one bag salt, 30 lbs. of meal.	
16,	19, Family of the agent of Tuckabatchee, 40 lbs. flower.	
20,	20, Tustunnagau Emautlau, ten lbs. of beef and fifty pounds of meal.	
	21, Lohtau Haujo, a credit of 4 dollars.	
	22, Tustunnagau Emautlau, 25 lbs. meal.	
	23, John Hoskins, five dollars.	
	24, Nitta Huntleah, 25 lbs. of meal.	
	25, Emautlau Haujo, 25 lbs. meal.	
	26, Tuskeegee Tustunnagau, 25 lbs. meal.	
	27, do do 1 quart rum.	
	28, do & Emautlau Haujo, 1 blanket each.	
21,	29, Andrew Darouzeaux, 5 dollars.	
22,	30, Yeauholau Mico, 1 bag of salt.	
	31, Opoiethly Tustunnagau, four bags of corn and two quarts of salt & 1 quart of brandy.	
	32, Ochese Tustunnagau, 25 lbs. flower, 2 lbs. sugar, one shirt, 1 silk handkerchief.	
	33, ditto, 25 lbs. of flower for 2 expresses.	
	34, Nitta Huntleah, six bushels of corn.	
	35, Mico Thlucco, one bushel corn.	
	36, Ochese Tustunnagau, one bottle rum.	
	37, Tuskeegee Tustunnagau, 2 bags corn.	
	38, Wauthlucco Haujo, 2 bags corn.	
	39, Andrew Darouzeaux, an express, 10 lbs. flower, 10 of beef.	
	40, Andrew Darouzeaux, express, 5 dollars.	
	41, Ochese Tustunnagau have one bottle of wine and one of rum and one black silk handkerchief.	
	42, Ochese Tustunnagau, 1 bottle wine, 25 lbs. flower and two bags of corn.	
	43, Suahoey, 25 lbs. flower.	
	44, Tuskeegee Tustunnagau, 2 bushels of corn	

Dec. 22, 45, John Tarvin, 1½ dollars.
Mittahose, 1 blanket petticoat, shift & tin kettle.
46, Isweauri, ½ bushel corn.

1798.
Jan. 1, 47, Mary Brown, for property taken and destroyed when her husband was murdered, 18 April, 1797.
48, Ochese Tustunnagau, 1 bottle wine & one of rum.
49, Ochese Tustunnagau, seven dollars 50 cents, for going express for the brother of the Indian killed on the 22nd December.

3, 50, Wauthlucco Haujo & Tuskeegee Tustunnagau, 10 lbs. meal, 10 lbs. beef.
51, Ochese Tustunnagau, 25 lbs. flower.
52, John Barnard, 25 lbs. flower and 20 lbs. beef or pork.
53, Ochese Tustunnagau, ½ bushel salt & 1 knife.
54, John Barnard, 1 bushel of corn.
55, Iokee, 25 lbs. meal.

4, 56, Iokee, 1 bag of salt.
57, John Barnard, 5 dollars.
58, Ohiethly Tustunnagau, 10 lbs. pork.
59, Ochese Tustunnagau, 9 bags of corn.
60, Emautlau Haujo, ½ bushel salt.
61, Tuskeegee Tustunnagau, 1 bushel of corn.
62, Suahoey, 30 lbs. bacon.
63, Indian department, 1 bushel of corn.
64, Hothletocco, 2 bags of corn & 1 bag of salt.

Private Expences.

1797.
Oct. 3, Cash to Miss Viney.....................$ 20.00
Cash paid the sadler 2.25
Nov. 9, Jacob, three dollars, 36.................. 3.36
15, Stimmahikee 16.67
17, Tunmautalkee 20.00
1798.
Apr. 26, 67, Isthlolobe of Coweta Tallauhassee, twelve and a half dollars for the recovery of a negro named Tom, the property of William Radcliff of the Cherokees.

Apr. 26,   68, Eufale Tustunnagau 16.50

27,   69, John Headham, for 73 lbs. bacon, 32 chalks, for the use of the public factory at Tallauhassee.

70, Mr. Headham's daughters, for 176 lbs. of bacon for the use of the public factory at Tallauhassee 75.½

May 10,   Yeauholau Mico, for a beef for the public meeting, 8 dollars.

Ditto, .25 dollars on the extra fund sent to my care by the Secretary of War on the —.

The wife of Yeauholau Mico for two tin kettles and a small loaf of white sugar.

***

Orders on Edward Price, U. S. Factor, for Contingencies in the Creek Department.

1797.

Sept. 18, No. 1, Hannah Hales, harness, hay, etc...........$ 4.75

Oct. 2,   2, Daniel Spiller, for seed wheat............ 3.00

1798.

Jan. 19,   William Gray, for packhorses to carry distressed familys to Tensaw.............. 10.00

19,   Mahonidjee of Cusseta, one keg of 2 gallons whiskey for a horse.

19,   Chaktulgee of Cusseta, one keg of 2 gallons whiskey for a mare and colt taken up at Taulauhatchee.

July 5,   Tuskeegee Tustunnagau, one bag salt and two kegs of whiskey for the recovery of stolen property.

6,   Towwehegee of Cheauhau, one gun for one stolen by a white person.

May 20,   Mico Thlucco of Cusseta, ten dollars, being a part of the extra fund sent to my care by the Secretary at War.

20,   Nehau Thlucco of Cusseta, twelve & half dollars.

12,   Thomas Marshall, fifteen dollars for a beef to meeting on the 5th.

Thomas Carr, twenty-nine dollars fifty cents for sundries furnished distressed travellers on their way to Mobile.

May 14,   John Tyler, public smith, ninety-seven dollars thirty-four cents for sundries.

19,   David Randon, twenty-six dollars fifty cents for provisions and board furnished distressed travellers on their way to Mobile.

June 13,   Nitta Huntleah, going on public service to Tuckabatchee 2.50

Sauwahidjau, an Indian wounded on 22 Dec. and unable to get a livelyhood............. 12.50

Aug. 21,   Chietoolgee (Jack), 20 lbs. of flower for taking and restoring a public horse.

21,   Eufaulau Tustunnagau, a public express with dispatches from the Commissioners at Tellico and from Mr. Dinsmoor.

27,   Sohtigee, a Cusseta woman, 12 lbs. of flower and 12 lbs. of beef to enable her and her son to return to that town.

Creek Stipend for 1798·

June 7, No. 1, Morgan of Wewokee, one bag of salt.......$ 1.00

23,   2, George Cornell, a chief of Tuckabatchee, for the use of the chiefs of the Creek nation, 100.00

Aug. 17,   3, Nancy, the Indian woman under protection of government 318.½

One bag with flower and 20 lbs. of beef.

21,   4, Haffocolotigee, her husband, and family, one bag salt and one bag of 20 lbs. flower.. 2.25

27,   5, Sohtigee, a Cusseta woman, one shift...... 1.50

6, Thomas Marshall, by order of Yeauholau Mico 9.50

7, Coweta agent, Nehau Thlucco Haujo, stipend for 1798 .... 125.00

8, Coweta Tallauhassee, Abbeuh Tustunnagau, agent 75.00

9, Cusseta agent Mico Thlucco, stipend for 1798 .... 125.00

10, Efau Tuckeneah & Tau Jammey, agents for Ooseuchee, 3 December, 1798............. 50.00

11, Honaubo, Emautlau Thlucco, Sahopoie, agents for Palachooch, 3rd Dec., 1798...... 40.00

12, Euohau Thlucco & Olocte Emautlau, agents for Hitchetee, 3rd Dec., 1798 .... 50.00

13, Mico Emautlau of Cheauhau, agent for that town, 5 December, 1798................... 50.00

Aug. 27, 14, Tuccosau Tustunnagau of Sauwoogeloochee, 8 December, 1798................... 40.00
15, Efau Haujo, of Tuckabatchee 25.00
16, Uchee Will & Cholateah, agents Uchees,
10 December 50.00
17, Maulechau & Yeauholau Mico, agents of Sau-
woogelo 80.00
18, Ditto, for 1796 and 1797................. 50.00
19, Euchau Thlucco of Cusseta, 14 December.. 10.00

The Indian Department.

Oct. 1, No. 1, Emautlau Haujo, for public dispatches from
F. W......................................$ 4.00
3, 2, Thomas Marshall, for a beef for the Smith's
Tallauhassee 11.00
Dec. 4, The wife of Yeauholau Mico, one bag of
flower, one of corn.
17, Stitlepica Chate, one grind stone for the
village of Tussekiah Mico.
18, Thomas Marshall, on the order of Cheauhau
Mico for the recovery of 2 negros of John
Houtton McIntosh of McIntosh County.... 25.00
25, James Lovet, trader of Coweta Tallauhassee, for sundries for the Indian department 4.37½

Creek Stipend for 1798.

1798.
No. 20, Mico Hutkee, agent of Eufaula, for 1796
& 97 ....$ 50.00
Dec. 14, 21, Ditto   ditto   for 1798 .... 60.00
22, Tussekiah Mico, for his faithful and persevering exertions in the service of his
country 50.00
23, Tuskeegee Tustunnagau, for his faithful
service in the execution of the national engagements 12.50
24, Tustunnagau Hopoie, for his fidelity and
zeal in executing his national engagements, 12.50
25, Mico of Oketeqockenne and Hopoie, agents
of Oketeqockenne, 26 December, 1798..... 25.00

Dec. 14,   26, Efau Tustunnagau, 8 April, 1799, for geting
              and restoring a stolen horse, on Mr. Hop-
              kins, U. S. Factor 2.50
1799.
Apr. 13,   27, Billey, called Longhair, one keg of whiskey
              to be charged to the Cussetas.

On W. Hawkins.

1799.
Oct. 17, No. 1, Ocheefcau of Cusseta, for a beef for the
              public meeting at Coweta..................$ 10.00
              2, Sumaule, for a beef for the public meeting
              at Cusseta 12.50
20,   3, Fullauman, for a guard with Mrs. Mc-
              Intosh's negros 3.00
20,   4, Cattoqo, for a guard with Mrs. McIntosh's
              negros 3.00
20,   5, James Forester, for a guard with Mrs. Mc-
              Intosh's negros 3.00
20,   6, James Forester, for that sum paid James
              Burges for receiving for the warriors and
              risque taken 30.00
              7, Auhulie Auhaulau, as a guard with Mrs.
              McIntosh's negros, 20 October, 1799.......   3.00
1799.
Jan. 1,   1, Fuscehatche Haujo, for bringing public dis-
              patches from Hillabee 5.00
12,   2, Stephen Hawkins, an express with public
              dispatches from Hillabee 5.00
              3, Normand Mountague, public striker at
              Tuckabatchee, 1st Sept. - 31st Dec......... 40.00
15,   4, Olohtau Haujo of Ooseuchee, for a stolen
              mare 15.00
20,   5, Townly Bruce, for a public packet brought
              from Colonel Gaither.....................   3.00
              Emautlau Haujo, 2 or 3 bags of meal or
              corn.
31,   7, Dole of Yeauholau Mico, for 1,500 rails for
              the Indian department 7.50
Feb. 27,   8, Nauothee, with public dispatches, in com-
              pany with Japtha Tarvin to Fort Wilkinson,   3.00
Apr. 9,   9, James Looch, for a horse and the hire of a
              horse to McDonald and Killingsworth, dis-
              tressed travellers 25.00

Apr. 9,	11, Lewis Rowley, a striker, to the public smith at Coweta, from 1st January to the 31st March	30.00
15,	12, John Tarvin, for horse hire and labour for public service	13.00

Tustunnagau Cochookomee.

July 31,	Efau Tustunnagau, on the stipend to the medal chiefs according to the treaty with McGillivray for 1798, ten dollars, 2, ditto...	12.00
Aug. 2,	Chief of Coweta Tallauhassee, one bushel of salt	2.50
3,	George Cornell	2.75
	Ditto	1.00
23,	Tussekiah Mico	3.00
Oct. 18,	Paid for corn at the Cusseta square	2.00
	Tussekiah Mico	5.00
Sept.24,	Paid an express from Burges to St. Mark's with letter to Mr. Utak	2.00
Oct. 20,	Paid Jack of the Green, a public express...	3.00
21,	Paid Tuskeegee Tustunnagau	9.00
29,	Paid Tyler Brothers for the recovery of a public horse	2.50
20, No.	8, Aupeithle, for three horses and sundry articles of small property taken or destroyed when Major Adams attacked the Indians near Fort Fidins; this account allowed by the chiefs out of their stipend	70.00
20,	9, Thauneco, brother of Mico Thlucco, as a guard for Mrs. McIntosh's negros	3.00
21,	10, Nitta Huntleah, for restoring two public horses	5.00
25,	11, Nehau Thlucco, of the stipend allowed the 6 medal chiefs, etc.	5.00
26,	12, Cusseta Tustunnagau Thlucco, his portion of the stipend allowed the great medal chiefs and other beloved men of that town, for 1798	10.00
28,	13, Framautlau, for his services as a guide and hunter with the Commissioners of Spain and the U. S.	7.25
28,	14, Sauwaulee, for his services as a guide and hunter with the Commissioners of Spain and the U. S.	11.00

Oct. 28,	15, Ofonitche of Coweta, for his services as a guide and hunter with the Commissioners and to accompany Mr. Robbins to St. Mark's	11.25
	16, Aupoique Haujo, for his services as a guide and hunter with the Commissioners, from 13th August to 29th October, inclusive.....	19.50
	17, Oche Haujo, for his services as a guide and hunter with the Commissioners of Spain and the U. S., from 14 September to 29 October, both inclusive	11.50
31,	18, Naukeche, marked in the certificate, No. 8, Immauthlmuke, for his services as a guide and hunter with the Commissioners of Spain and the U. S., from 13 August to 17 inst., inclusive, 66 days.................	16.50
Nov. 1,	19, Okelesee Nehau, of the Tussekiah Mico's village, for taking care of two public horses which were stolen from the Commissioner's escort and recovered.	
1,	20, Hoseputtalk Tustunnagau, for apprehending two negros of Mrs. McIntosh..........	20.00
6,	21, The son of Yeauholau Mico, four dollars for a packet on public accounts sent to Fort Wilkinson.	
8,	22, William McIntosh, for restoring a negro belonging to Mrs. McIntosh..............	10.00
9,	23, Efau Haujo, for recovery of a stolen horse, by an Uchee from near Carr's Bluff........	2.50
	24, Mico Thlucco, of the stipend allowed the great medal chief of Cusseta, etc.	20.00
	25, Tuskeegee Tustunnagau	20.00
Dec. 8,	26, Hopoiejee of Cusseta, for a canoe stolen by two negros, the property of a citizen of Georgia, who fled to Bowles..............	6.25
8,	Ofullejee of Ocfuskee, for an express to His Excellency, Governor Foch...........	7.50
10,	27, Sauwauhidjee, for recovery of a negro belonging to W. Ingram.................	12.50
10,	28, Mr. Thomas Carr, for a horse to go to Pensacola on public account.	
11,	29, Tustunnagau Emautlau, for the provisions for the national council at Tuckabatchee...	12.50
11,	30, Olohluh Mico, one blanket for butchering beef for the national council.	

Dec. 11,   31, Tustunnagau Haujo, ifor a beef for John
           Miller, the smith at Tuckabatchee 7.50
           32, Tustunnagau Emautlau and Tustunnagau
           Haujo, agents for the stipend to the medal
           chief and others of Tuckabatchee 798.00
12,   33, Tunnotalkee, for beef and bread furnished
           the chiefs at the national council at the
           annual meeting at Tuckabatchee 54.75
22,   34, Tallauman, for recovering a horse of
           Colonel Hawkins' stolen at Hatchetoochee,   7.00
22,   35, Imhulle, for provisions 66.50
           36, Tewhooche, for pork 5.12½
           37, Timothy Barnard, 1 quarter's pay, 1 July - 30
           September 175.00
           On Mr. Wright Imhulle 71.50
Mar. 13,   Mr. Barnard 175.00

Stipend for 1796, 1797 and 1798.

1799.
Nov. 14, No. 1, In favour of Tustunnagau Hopoie of
           Coweta Tallauhassee, the stipend allowed
           that town for 1798 ....$ 75.00
14,   2, In favour of George Cornell, out of the
           stipend allowed by the U. S. to the Creeks
           for the year 1798 .... 10.00
           3, Ditto, Nahomohtah Hopoie 10.00
           4, Ditto, Emautlau Jauno 10.75
16,   5, Emautlau Haujo, for delivering a horse
           stolen by a black man from George Brown,   2.10
           And Insomochuh, for carrying him to the
           fort 1.00
17,   6, Cusseta Tustunnagau Thlucco, for a horse
           taken the summer 1797 from Cotchau Tus-
           tunnagau, belonging to a citizen of the
           U. S.; this claim allowed in the Cusseta
           square 7.50
           7, Cusseta Hoithlepoie of Eufaulau, for a
           prisoner delivered up by order of the chiefs;
           payment decreed 29 November 25.00
29,   8, Summoniejee, for the recovery of a horse
           lost in Tennessee in the spring; this draft
           by order of the chiefs on loan, and if it
           appears that the horse is really stolen by
           white people, then the sum to be refunded
           to the stipend by the U. S. 33.00

Nov. 29,   9, Ooseuchee Yeauholau, a rifle gun as pay
              for one of their prisoners; this per order of
              the national council.

Dec. 11,   10, Emautlau Hutkee, for beef supplied the
              national council at the meeting in Tuckabat-
              chee, one 6, one 5 years old 27.50
              11, Olohtuh Mico, one low priced shot gun, of
              the stipend allowed by the U. S. to the
              Creeks, and $3.75 for a blanket and shirt
              worn by some citizens of Georgia.

       11,   12, Tuscoonau Haujo, the value of a low
              priced rifle, or such an one, of the stipend
              allowed the Creeks by the U. S.
              13, Tuscoonau Haujo, agent for Tuckabatchee,
              for to pay some old woman for supplies for
              the meeting at Tuckabatchee 40.00
              14, The representative of Aupoithle; see No. 8
              on Mr. William Hawkins 70.00

       14,   15, Nehau Thlucco Haujo, agent for Hillabee, 75.00
1800.
Jan. 8,   16, Tuskeegee Tustunnagau, warrior of the
              5 great towns on Chattahoochee 13.37½

                      Stipend for 1799.
1800.
Apr. 16, No. 1, Tuccosau Tustunnagau, agent for Sauwoo-
              golooche ....$ 40.00
       22,   2, Nehau Thlucco, Jauneco, agents for Cus-
              seta, stipend 1798-1799, 225 dollars; the
              whole sum being 250, from which was de-
              ducted 25 for a rifle given their late Tus-
              tunnagau Thlucco, and 20, one-third of a
              bay mare stolen by John Galphin and sold
              at Grunsborough, claimed and demanded by
              the agent in the public square of Cusseta, of
              the 3 towns, Cusseta, Tallauhassee and
              Coweta and lost by their inattention.

May 3,   3, Coweta Tallauhassee, Tustunnagau Co-
              chookome, agent 75.00

       3,   4, For the chiefs of the Creek nation about
              to assemble at Tuckabatchee, William Hill, 200.00

       5,   5, For a meeting of the chiefs, one beef, Tus-
              keegee Tustunnagau 5.00

May 17,   6, Nehau Thlucco, Necau Haujo, Ecunchate,
             Emautlau Chatejus, Coweta Tustunnagau,
             agents for Coweta 65.00
             This town was rated at 125, and 60 has
             been deducted for a bay mare stolen by
             John Galphin, demanded of the 3 towns
             by the agent and lost by their negligence.
23,   7, Efau Tuskanehau and Tustunnuc Haujo,
             agents for Ooseuchee 50.00
27,   8, Tustunnuc Hopoie, brother of Mico Thluc-
             co, one grind stone.
June 7,   Upper towns 1500.00
             Hiussetuh 20.00
17,   Messrs. Hutke & Long Tom, Talchiscau
             Mico, account of Ocfuske 100.00
July 20,   Emautlau Haujo, a messenger on public
             business from the Creek nation........... 7.50
23,   Tuskeegee Tustunnagau, for his services on
             the mission to the Simanolees 12.50
23,   Hoithle Ponorich, for like services........ 10.00
June 7,   The chiefs of the upper towns $1,500, in the
             following drafts:
9,   Abbacoochee ....$ 54.00
11,   Eufaulauhatche 75.00
14,   Hillabee 60.00
15,   Unnelluh Chapco 80.00
15,   Nuoqaucou 60.00
                                              _____
                                               $329.00
             Nauche 200.00
17,   Robert Walton 102.50
             Mr. Tygard 100.00
             Tussekiah Mico, Hutke & Tommy Cregseo,
             public dispatches 6.00
55,   John Tyler, public smith, one quarter, to
             the end of September................... 78.00
1798.
July 2,   5, Henry Wilson, assistant to the public smith
             at Coweta, one quarter's sallary, to the last
             of June 30.00
6,   12, William Hill, from 9 February to 30 June.. 85.00
June 24,   13, John Tyler, public smith, from 1st April
             to 30 June 75.00
Sept. 5,   29, William Beard, from 5 March to 5 July,
             in the service of the I. department......... 45.00
             42, Caurlu Burks, note to B. H. for the U. S.... 40.00

Sept. 5,	43, Mr. Barnard, two orders, from 1st April to last September	350.00
	45, Received Thomas Clark, 1st April - 30 September	100.00
	48, W. Tuly, smith, 1st April to 30 September..	130.00
	54, L. Raby, 26 September to 31 December, striker	30.00
	55, John Tyler, from 1 June to 30 September, as public smith	75.00
1799.		
Jan.	58, James Burges, assistant and interpreter, from 1st December, 1796 to 30 March, 1797,	133.⅓
	59, Ballance, from July 1st, 1796 to December 31, 1797	550.00
	60, Richard Thomas, 1 quarter's sallary, 31 December, 1797	50.00
	61, Timothy Barnard, 1st October - 31st December, 1799	175.00
	62, William Hill, 1st July to 31 December, 1798,	110.00
	65, John Miller, public smith, from 24 July, 1798 to 31 March, 1799, for rations..............	55.55

```
            161 days, at 2 rations.......$40.25
            322 at 12½  ................. 15.30
            ─────────────────────────────────
             90 at 17  .................$55.55
```

| | 69, Nomand Montague, from 1 September to 31st December, and 1 January to 31 March.. | 36.30 |
| | 73, Louis Renby, striker to the smith, one quarter, 1 January to 31 March, 1799....... | 30.00 |

Creek Agency, 27 December, 1799.

No. 1.

Mr. Edward Wright, U. S. Factor:

Pay Uchee Will and Cholateta, agents for the Uchees, stipend goods of the value of fifty dollars, being the portion assigned to that town of the stipend allowed by the U. S. to the Creeks for the present year, 1799.

1801.

Wheels made by Lemmons and delivered out to the Indians:

1. Peggy Sullivan.
3. Hannah Hale of the fish ponds.
1. Stimmau Whoçatlau.

John Headham has in his possession Sandy, about 45 or 50, claimed as the property of Israel Bird of Bryant, formerly Effingham. John Headham bought him of Fuakolusta of Ooseuchee; he gave fifteen head of cattle, and he gave eighty dollars for a horse which he gave to the Bason (Stimmocee). He gave also a gray horse of the value of twenty dollars, and the cattle are estimated at four dollars.

Major Jesse McCall and James Bird, the first of Bryant and the second of Bulloch County, in Georgia, demanded this negro this 13 November, 1799. The answer to the demand is a statement of the sum given by John, and he offers the negro for the payment of the sum given by him, not otherwise.

JESSE McCALL.
JAMES BIRD.
W. STIDHAM.
BENJAMIN HAWKINS,
P. T. A. for I. A. S. of Ohio,
Creek Agency, 12 November, 1799.

Joseph Thomas, formerly of North Carolina, a favourable certificate by Redman Thornton, J. P., and other reputable citizens of Green County, in Georgia, 18th February, 1801. Attested under the county seal by Thomas Carleton, Clerk, 22nd February, Inf. Court G. C. Certified by the agent 6th of April.

---

8 July, 1801.

John Woods of Adams, bound to Georgia; pass by Major John Collier, Esq., 26 June, 1801.

8 July.

John Laurence of Washington County, M. Territory, of good character, by Major J. Collier, Esq., 26 June.

8 July.

Frederick Tillen, by Captain Steaumbuosh, 24 June.

15 July.

Thomas Aikens of Bristol, in Pennsylvania, without pass, returning to his native country from New Orleans. Pass into Georgia by the agent.

22 July.

Stern and David Simmons, return pass to Georgia, 31st May, by Major Peters.

22 July.

Major John Moore of Berkley County, in Virginia, on his return from Mississippi Territory.

B. H. Pass.

7th September, 1801.

William and John Pierce of Washington County, Mississippi Territory, on their way to Savannah.

18th September, 1801.

Major Stuth Deen, Isaac Masseck and Robert Walton, from Burk County to Tombigbee, pass from David Emanuel, Governor of Georgia.

Saufochigee, opposite the fields of Cusseta, for a wheel and cards, 7 March.

Jenney Stephenson, in Coosau, has 4 children and at the house of Passcofe Emautlau. She wants to leave the Creek nation.

Salley Stephenson, in Eufaulau, has 1 child, the wife of Hillabee Mico.

Passcofe Emautlau claims Jenney for a brother of his who was killed accidently by the fire of a gun while on a corn house.

Landon of Efau Haujo, striker to the smith, 2 August to 28 November, lost 8 days.

13 days, Indian John.

Souhotina, the wife of Auttossee Emautlau, and Auhoinjee, 8 February, 1 pair No. 10 cotton cards; each a pair of cards and wheels.

A short chunky negro, 21 years old, about 140 lbs., Tom, lost one eye, near white, William Robertson, 10 days before Christmas.

Matthew Durham vs. Creeks, drawn under treaty July, 1793.

In all cases of property lost or supposed to be stolen by Indians, the applicant for payment must state his claim in writing, expressing:

1. Where the property was taken or stolen and the time.
2. Where and how situated at the time.
3. The reason why it is supposed to be stolen by Indians.
4. And whether they be Creeks or Cherokees. The applicant must describe the horses and cattle and accompany it with the best evidence the nature of the case will admit of. The whole must be certified by a magistrate and there must be two copies, one of them to be sent to the Agent of War at Fort Wilkinson.

Auhonijee, Sauhotina, each a pair of cards, delivered February 8th.

Salley and Patsey Headham, February 15, each a pair of cards.

Suckey Randon, Peggy Sullivan, Muthoie Barnard, each a pair of cards.

Sarah, the daughter of the Little Prince, Louis's wife.

F.

The United States in Account with the Indian Department.

1796.		Dr.
Nov. 29, No. 1,	Cash paid William Ralley, a pilot from Ocunna Station to Etowwah ....$	5.00
Dec. 3,	Cash paid two Cherokee pilots to the first Creek station	6.00
9,	Paid my guides at Nuoqaucou to procure provisions for the path home............	1.00

1797.

Jan. 31,   Cash paid for cloathing for Tiejee, her son
             and daughter engaged as an interpreter
             for the factory 10.00

Mar. 9,   4, Cash paid Richard Williams for his
             service from the 1st of October.......... 50.00

Apr. 15, 5, Paid Chohaddookee of Etowwah for re-
             covering a sorrel mare of the U. S....... 15.00

July 16, 6, Cash paid Sackfield Maclin in part of his
             sallary 50.00

Aug. 3,   7, Cash paid Alexander Cornell, one
             quarter's sallary, from 1st of April to 30
             June 100.00

      25, 8, Cash paid Timothy Barnard, one quarter's
             sallary, from 1st April to 30 June........ 175.00

      25, 9, Cash paid Richard Thomas, ditto........ 50.00

Oct. 6, 10, Cash paid R. Williams, going express to
             Louisville and Savannah 13.00

Nov. 10, 11, Cash paid Sandy Grierson, a halfbreed, an
             express from the U. Creeks............. 4.67

Dec. 13, 12, Cash to Autopey to enable herself and
             family to buy provisions for their home... 2.00

      16, 13, Cash paid I. Hawkins for a pair of cards
             for a halfbreed at Hillabee 1.50

      21, 14, Cash paid Darouzeaux, an express sent
             from the Creek chiefs 6.00

      30, 15, Paid John Tarvin for a pair of cards for
             a halfbreed Creek woman 1.50

1798.

Mar. 9, 16, Paid Wm. Hill, going express to Louis-
             ville and Savannah 10.00

         17, Paid ditto, for 4 green pine for Indian
             department 2.00

      10, 18, Cash paid James Darouzeaux for services
             as interpreter 3.00

May 9,   19, Paid Alexander Cornell on account of his
             sallary 100.00

      10, 20, Yeauholau Mico, part of the extra fund... 25.00

      15, 21, Paid William McIntosh, a halfbreed, for
             beef for the public meeting at Cusseta.... 12.00

      16,   Cash paid John Galphin, going express to
             Opoithlu Mico 4.00
             Paid ditto, for a horse, bridle, and saddle
             taken on the 22 December, when the
             Indian Commissioner was murdered....., 65.00

June 22,	22, Paid Thomas Lott for stocking seven ploughs and making a pair of bars.......	4.00
	Paid Nitta Huntleah and his brother for the hire of one horse and conducting the distressed families to Tenesau	15.00
		$ 730.67
1796.		Cr.
Sept. 17,	By cash received in Philadelphia.........	800.00

The United States in Account with the Commissioners for Ascertaining and Marking the Creek Boundary.

1797.		Dr.
Sept. 9,	No. 1, Paid John Batts Bard for corn for the escort returning from the Cherokee line..$	3.50
14,	2, John Linsey for ditto	3.00
	3, William Lord for 3 bushels corn........	1.50
15,	4, Shadrick Taylor for corn & fodder.......	3.00
19,	5, Wm. Edwards for sheaf oats	1.25
1798.		
Jan. 3,	5-6, David McKinney, express from General Pickins	8.00
9,	6, James Young for corn & fodder..........	.42
11,	7, George Vaughn for corn	1.14
18,	8, Joseph Wilson for whiskey	1.25
	9, John shields for bacon & corn for the surveyors	6.00
22,	10, George Vaughn, a pilot	13.00
	11, Wm. M. Stokes, a pilot	9.00
	12, John Lafferty, a pilot	9.00
30,	13, Wm. Kilpatrick, pack horseman	14.00
	14, Abraham Anderson chain carrier	14.00
	15, Rheubon Reynolds, chain carrier	14.00
Feb. 3,	16, J. C. Kilpatrick, small expences	4.50
	17, J. C. Kilpatrick, as surveyor	100.00
	The contractor, his account for supplies for the Commissioners, surveyors & assistants, certified	392.59¼
12,	John Galphin, as Creek Commissioner and interpreter to the Commissioners, a draft on E. Price, U. S. Factor	94.00

Feb. 12,	5 Creek Commissioners, one dollar each per day, a draft on E. Price..............	243.00
	Two Indian attendants, ditto, on ditto....	23.00
11,	Joel Freeman, for his and assistants services in marking the lines	13.00
	John Brown, for T. Wade for pack horse service	16.50
	J. Brown & Randal Carter, for ditto......	17.00
14,	Joseph Spillar, for attendance on Indian Commissioners	19.00

$1,024.65¼

1798.   Dr.

Feb. 16,	Phil Carroll, for self and associates in marking the line ....$	14.00
18,	Martin Swob, 3 day's labour in ditto......	.75
	Benjamin Hawkins, as Commissioner on the Cherokee line, from 11 March to 12 September, both inclusive, 186 days at $4,	744.00
	To ditto, as Commissioner on the Creek line, 41 days at 4 dollars per day..........	164.00

$1,947.40

1798.   Cr.

Feb. 2,	By a draft on the Secretary of War in favour of J. C. Kilpatrick, public surveyor,	100.00
	By sundry drafts on E. Price, U. S. Factor, as stated in the account	448.25
	By contractor's account, to be paid by J. Habersham	392.59
	By ballance due the Commissioners, to be drawn for by Benjamin Hawkins on the Secretary of War	1,006.56

$1,947.40

A.

The Indian Department to the U. States Factory.

1797.		Dr.
Sept. 5,	For 2 gallons corn for Maclin ....$	.12½
17,	Paid J. Spiller, services from 11 March to 11 September, as Creek farmer	60.00

Sept. 18,	Mrs. Hawkins, per order for cards & harness ....$4.75 ½ bushel of salt, $1; 1 lb. sugar, 25c, 1.25 4 lbs. flower for wounded chiefs... .25—	6.25
20,	Sackfield Maclin, per order ....$12.35 6 yards silk furnished Colonel Hawkins .... .60—	12.95
23,	1 stripe blanket, $2; 1 lb. sugar, 25c; 6 lbs. of flower at 6½c, 37½c, for Iofekey......	2.62½
27,	10 lbs. flower 6¼c, 62½c; 1 qt. brandy, 37½c; 1 lb. sugar, 25c, for Iofekey, the wounded chief	1.25
30,	1 bottle brandy for ditto	.37½
Oct. 1,	10 lbs. flower, 62½c; 3 lbs. sugar, 75c, for ditto. 29 lbs. corn meal, 87½c; ½ bushel salt, Captain Jon	3.24½
2,	Daniel Spiller, for 2 bushels wheat.......	3.00
3,	Timothy Barnard, assistant & interpreter, for 1 quarter's sallary, 1st July to 30 September, inclusive	175.00
	100 lbs. corn meal, $3; 28 lbs. flower, $1.75; 3 lbs. sugar, 75c, for the wounded chief, &c.	5.50
	4 club axes delivered Downs, at $1.50, ...$6.00 1 par. needle, 6¼c; 13 yds. oz., $3.25; 1 oz. thra., 25c............ 3.56¼—	9.56¼
4,	To Tim Barnard for part his draft, in favour of Hardy Reed, for 40 days going express to Cherokees ....$ 32.00 Felix Counts, Creek smith, from 21 February to 21 September, inclusive, per order .... 196.00—	228.00
	20 lbs. of flower, $1.25; 50 of corn meal, $1.50; 40 lbs. of beef for Tyler, the smith, & party going to the nation	5.25
5,	10 lbs. beef, 62½c; 10 lbs. corn meal, 4 cents ....$1.12½ 3 ¾ augers at 37½ cents........ 1.12½ 1 hand saw .... 2.00 1 drawing knife .... .62½ 1 spike gimblet, 50c; 5¾ rope at 25c .... 1.93¾ 6 oz. of wire, 37½c; 2 oz. borax, 25c, for the smith at Tallauhassee, .62½—	7.33¾

Oct.	5,	To Primus	3.00
		To Indian rope 25c, pork salt 25c.........	.50
	6,	8 yds. bale cloth to Harry Dergin, at 12½c,	1.00
		Richard Thomas, sallary, 1st July - 30	
		September	50.00
	7,	1 whip saw, 9 dollars; 2 shovels, $2.25....	11.25
		1 spade, $1; 2 bear skins, $4..............	5.00
		19 lbs. bacon, 12½c.....................	2.37½
		1 pair sisars, 25c; 1 grind stone, 2 dollars..	2.25
		4 whip saw files	.50
		1½ yds. oznabrigs at 25c	.37½
	No. 9,	2 yds. ropes, 50c; 2 yds. oznabrigs for	
		bags, 50c	1.00
		40 lbs. of nails at 25c...................	10.00
	17,	3½ gallons brandy at $1.50, per order to	
		Iofekey	3.25
		7 lbs. beef to Whitaker, 21c; 1 qr. venison,	
		25c	.46
	29,	Silas Downs, for wages from 2 to 28 Oct.,	
		at 10 dollars per month	8.38
Nov. 12,	12,	Robert Walton, express rider, 2 October,	
		1796, to 17 February, 1797	207.00
	9,	Emautlau Hutkee, for burying Down's	
		mare	1.50
		16, Thlataupee, 9 gallons brandy, 4 kegs......	13.50
	13,	28, Yeauholau Mico	35.00
Dec. 10,	1,	Clotchau Tustunnagau, for sundries	
		taken from him in August, 1796, by white	
		men	15.75
	11,	Chemauille, for sundries taken at	
		Sainahau	12.25
	12,	8, To Iofekey, the wounded chief, for his	
		support during the winter	25.00
	13,	To Nitta Huntleah, 1 bottle brandy........	.37½
		One of the Indians who was robed, 25	
		lbs. meal	.75
		Sullivan's daughters, 5½ lbs. sugar	1.37½
		1 bottle brandy	.37½
		3 lbs. coffee at 37½ cents	1.12½
	15,	To Somochee, for his services in recover-	
		ing stolen horse, 1 blanket	2.50
	16,	Wm. Wright, an Indian, 1 bottle brandy..	.37½
		The Big Warrior of Tuckabat-	
		chee, 1 bottle brandy ....$ .37½	
		One bushel corn .... .62½	
	19,	40 lbs. flower for the path home.. 2.50 —	3.50

Dec. 18,	To Opoi Haujo, 30 lbs. meal..... .90	
	½ bushel of salt................ 1.00 —	1.90
2,	Alex Cornell, sallary, 1 December, 1796, to	
	30 March, 1797	133.33
10,	ditto, ditto, 1 July to 30 September	100.00
	ditto, ditto, 1 October to 31 Dec., 1797,...	100.00
20,	16, To bill for provisions and other expences	
	at the annual meeting of Creeks at Tuck-	
	abatchee	22.00
	20, Tustunnagau Emautlau, going	
	express, 10 lbs. beef at 6¼c......$ .62½	
	50 lbs. meal at 3c, $1.50; 1 brass	
	bottle, $4.50 .... 6.00	
	22, 25 lbs. ditto .... .75 —	7.37½
	Nitta Huntleah, 1 bag salt	1.00
21,	Loctau Haujo and his party, 50 flints and	
	5 lbs. powder	5.50
	22, Tustunnagau Emautlau, 13 ft. blanket,	
	$2.67; ½ oz. thread 12½c, ⅜ yd. serge	
	18¾c, 31¼c	2.98¼
Dec. 24,	To Nitta Huntleah, 25 lbs. corn meal at 3c,	.75
	¼ lb. powder to G. Galphin in pursuit of	
	Indian murderer	.25
	Richard Thomas, clerk in the Indian de-	
	partment, his sallary, 1st July to 30	
	November, 1796, and for sundry expences,	150.90
30,	24, Yeauholau Mico, 1 bag salt	1.00
31,	To Opoithly Emautlau, 4 bags	
	corn $1.50	
	2 quarts salt, 6¼c; 1 bottle	
	brandy, 37½c .... .43¾—	1.93¾
23,	John Hoskins, 10 bushels cotton seed....	5.00
29,	A. Darouzeaux, express from the nation..	6.00
	25, For the Indians wounded on the 22nd:	
	2 2½ point blankets, $2.25.....$ 4.50	
	3 brass bottles, 18 lbs., at 75c... 13.50	
	25 lbs. flower 1.56¼	
	2 lbs. sugar, 2 quarts whiskey.. 1.25 —	20.81¼
	26, Ocheese Tustunnagau, 1 qt. spirits	.75
	John Middlebrook, 6 cotton wheels.......	13.00
	33, Ocheese Tustunnagau, 25 lbs. flower	1.56¼
	32, ditto, 25 ditto $1.56½	
	2 lbs. sugar, 50c; 1 shirt, $1.50... 2.00	
	1 black handkerchief for wounded	
	Indian .... 1.50 —	5.67½
	36, 3 pints brandy to ditto................	.56¼

Dec. 29,	37, T. Tustunnagau, 2 bags corn	.75
	35, Mico Thlucco, 2 bags ditto..............	.75
	To the old Lt. of Broken Arrow, 18 bags..	6.75
	To Efau Tustunnagau, 2 bags	.75
	39, Andrew Darouzeaux, 10 lbs. flower, 10 lbs. beef	1.25
	To ditto, going express to the nation.....	5.00
	34, To Nitta Huntleah, 6 bushels corn	4.50
27,	41, Ocheese Tustunnagau, for the wounded Indians, 1 bottle wine, 75c; one pair pants, 75c...................$1.50	
	1 black handkerchief .... 1.25—	2.75
	12 lbs. of flower, 75c; 4 qt. kettle, 62½c, for a man going after Rolley's horse......	1.37½
15,	Townly Bruce, clerk in the Indian Department, from 1st December, 1796, to 9 January, 1797	22.00
	42, Ocheese Tustunnagau, for the wounded Indians, 1 bottle wine..$ .75	
	25 lbs. flower 1.56½	
	2 bags corn .... .75 —	3.06½
30,	43, 25 lbs. flower, sallary	1.56½
	44, Tuskeegee Tustunnagau, 4 bags corn	1.50
	45, John Tarvin, for 1 pair cotton cards for a halfbreed	1.50
	46, Iswhocauna, half a bushel of corn........	.37½
	Nitta Hose, mother of the wounded Coosau:	
	1 blanket $2.67	
	1½ yds. strand 1.75	
	1¾ yds. Linen .... .87½	
	1 3 qt. bottle, 50c; ¼ tobacco, 6¼ .... .56½—	5.85
	Nitta Huntleah, 1 qt. rum	.75
	Paid the contractor for that part of his account belonging to the Indian Department, up to 15 November..............	10.64
	Tim Barnard, per order No. 1, 4 months' sallary, ending 31st March, 1797..........	233.33
	Received Thomas, order No. 4, same time,	66.67
	Tussekiah Mico, in repayment of Colonel Hawkins's draft	3.75

$1,898.73¼

Cr.

By a draft on James McHenry, Secretary
of War, for the amount of this account, 1,898.73¼

B.

**The United States in Account with Sackfield Maclin, Assistant
In the Indian Department.**

1797.		Dr.
Dec. 17,	To sundries furnished a Creek Indian for assisting in collecting and delivering 25 horses stolen from Cumberland, one rifle..$	20.00
1798.		
Feb. 24,	3 yds. furniture callico	3.00
Apr. 14,	3 yds. linsey for a shirt at 62½..........	1.87½
	¾ yds. cloth at $3.00, $2.25; 1 iron comb, 25c	2.50
	1 handkerchief, $1.00; 6 yds. binding, 54c..	1.54
18,	½ lb. powder, 50c; 1 lb. lead, 25c; 1 knife, 50c	1.25
19,	1 pc. binding, $2.00; 1 bridle, $1.50; 1 blanket, $3.00	6.50
	To the hire of a horse, Encau Thlucco, to go to the Hickory Ground, $1.00; cash paid him, $1.00	2.00
	Paid a pilot from Arthur Cordy's to Willstown	4.00
	Corn for a Cumberland horse, 6 days.....	1.00
	ditto, 4 horses, 8 days..................	4.00
	Paid a squaw for corn, $1.00; ditto, John Tarvin, $3.00	4.00
	Paid John Turner, assisting in with horses,	3.00
	Paid a squaw for corn	1.00
Nov. 6,	Paid an Indian for gathering Cumberland horses to Hillabee	3.00
15,	Paid for feeding four Cumberland horses 4 weeks	9.00
	Paid an Indian for recovering a stolen horse	3.00
	Paid Sandy Grierson for carrying dispatches to Cusseta	5.00
	Paid a pilot from the Turkey's town to the Upper Creeks	3.00

Paid for provisions and corn for three
Cumberland horses and an Indian from
Upper Creeks to Knoxville, and from
thence to Nashville 24.00
Paid for recovery of two Cherokee horses
which were stolen and returned 8.00
To my sallary as assistant in the Indian
Department, from June 8, 1797, to June
the 8th, 1798, both inclusive, at 1 dollar
per day 365.00
_____

$475.66½

Cr.

July 15,   By cash received of Colonel Hawkins:
             P. T. A. for I. A. S. of Ohio....$50.00
Sept. 20,   By Cash received at Fort Wilkin-
             son 12.00
Dec.   By ditto received of Colonel
             Henley .... 40.00— 102.00
             By a draft on David Henley for this
             ballance, Tuckabatchee, 4 June, 1798..... 373.66½
             _____

             $475.66¼

                     Signed,

             SACKFIELD MACLIN,

                 Asst. in the Indian Dept.

         Subscribed and sworn before

             BENJAMIN HAWKINS,

             P. T. A. for I. A. S. of Ohio.

         This is a duplicate account of Sackfield
Maclin; on the original I gave a draft on
David Henley, Agent of War, for the
ballance, 373.66½ dollars.

             BENJAMIN HAWKINS,

             P. T. A. for I. A. S. of Ohio.

E.

The United States in Account with Benjamin Hawkins, P. T. A. for I. A. S. of Ohio.

1798.   Dr.
To my sallary, from 8 September, 1796, to
1 January, 1797 ....$ 626.02
To allowance for the same time, 12 rations
per day at 9 96-100 cents 139.00
To my sallary for 1797 .... 2,000.00
To rations for the same period, 11 cents.. 481.80
To my sallary for the first half year 1798, 1,000.00
To rations for the same period 273.75

$4,520.50

1797.   Cr.
Sept.20,   By a bill of this date in favour of Major
             John Habersham on the S. of War.......$1,000.00
1798.
Feb. 25,   By ditto ditto ditto 1,000.00
Aug. 2,   By ditto in favour of Maj. Com. Freeman, 1,000.00
             By ballance 1,520.50

$4,520.50
BENJAMIN HAWKINS,
P. T. A. for I. A. S. of Ohio.

Account of Sundries Furnished Wm. McDonald & Francis Killins-
worth on the 29th May.

12½ yds. Russia sheeting at 62½c.........................$ 7.81½
8 skeins white thread, 25c; 4½ yds. linsey, 62½c.......... 3.06½
2 handkerchiefs, $1.25; 2 lbs. soap, 50c.................. 1.75
6 yds. Russia sheeting, 62½c 3.75
4½ yds. striped linsey, 62½c 2.81½
4 ditto 2.50
4 yds. Russia sheeting, 62½c 2.50
12 skeins white thread .... .37½
6 yds. Russia sheeting 3.75

```
2 handkerchiefs  .........................................  1.25
2 lbs. soap  ..............................................   .50
20 bushels of corn, 67c  ................................  13.33
100 lbs. bacon  .........................................  10.75
5 horse ropes  ..........................................   .93¾
3 pack saddles  .........................................  9.00
4 3 point blankets  .....................................  10.67
                                                          _____
                                                          $74.75
Freight  ...............................................  2.00
                                                          _____
                                                          $76.75
```

                    Signed,
                        His
            FRANCIS X KILLINGSWORTH.
                       Mark
            WILLIAM McDONALD.
Witness:
    RICHARD THOMAS,
        Clerk in the Indian Department.

An Account of Sundries Furnished William Hubbard, 19 May, 1798.

```
One pair of Britannias  ...............................$ 3.50
8½ yds linsey at 62½c...................................  5.31½
9 skeins of thread  ....................................   .25
6 needles  .............................................   .06¼
7 yds. brown sheeting at 62½c..........................  4.37½
4 handkerchiefs at 62½c  ...............................  2.50
2 lbs. soap  ...........................................   .50
10 lbs. bacon  .........................................  1.06½
2 3 point blankets  ....................................  5.33
                                                          _____
                                                          $22.89½
```

                    Signed,

                        JAMES HUBBARD.

                        I.

    National Council at Tuckabatchee, 6 June, 1798.

    An account of sundries paid for provisions for the chiefs of
the Creek nation convened in national council at Tuckabatchee,

May 25, 1798, by order of Benjamin Hawkins, P. T. A. for I. A.
S. of Ohio.

2 pcs. strouds at $23.33	$ 46.67
10 pcs. callico at $1.25	12.50
1 lb. thread	1.50
2 gross binding at $2.67	5.33
3 3 point blankets at $2.67	8.00
	$ 74.00
25 per cent. advance	18.50
	$ 92.50
Cash paid for 1 stear	12.00
	$104.50
By 1 for farm land $6.00	
12 broaches .... 6.00—	9.00
	$ 95.50

Provisions Consumed:
   8 beeves.
   1 hog.
   1 side bacon.
   50 baskets corn.

The United States in Account with the Creek Nation.

Dr.

To sundry expenditures, marked A	$1,898.73½
To ditto, Maclin, ditto B	475.66½
To ditto, Indian Department, ditto C	2,454.98
To ditto, Burges' assistant, ditto D	683.33
To ditto, P. T. A. for I. A., ditto E	4,520.50
To ditto, contingincy, ditto F	730.67
To ditto, sundries, ditto G	488.75
To ditto, discribed in ditto H	99.64½
To ditto, ditto I	95.50
To ditto, ditto K	450.81¾

D.

To James Burges $133.33	
ditto, sallary to 31 December, 1797.... 550.00—	683.33

1796.   Cr.

Sept.   By cash received in Philadelphia as Contingent
         Fund 800.00

1797.
Sept.20, By a bill of this date in favour of Major John
         Habersham, for 1,000.00
1798.
Feb. 25, By ditto, ditto, ditto 1,000.00
June 4, By cash paid Sackfield Maclin .....$ 12.00
         By ditto, by Colonel Henley 40.00
         By a draft on Colonel Henley for bills, 373.66½— 425.66½
Aug. 2, By a bill of this date in favour of Major Com.
         Freeman on Secretary of War 1,000.00
      6, By a bill of this date in favour of Edward
         Price, U. S. Factor, on Secretary of War, for
         debt, A 1,898.73½
Sept. 3, By a bill on ditto, ditto, for ditto, C........... 2,454.98
         By cash received and acknowledged the 22 June,
         for a special purpose 500.00

Coweta, Tallauhassee, 22 June, 1798.

Expenditure of the contingent fund of 500 dollars to be expended as therein advised by the Secretary of War, the receipt of which is acknowledged in my letter to the Secretary of War.

Paid at the request of Indian Commissioners appointed to see the Creek line ascertained and marked, sundry extraordinary expences amounting in the whole to 488.75 dollars, and which was noted and approved in the meeting of the chiefs of the Lower towns at Coweta.

Certificate of Mr. William Hill.

I do certify that Colonel Hawkins did, in my presence, and for the purposes approved of by him, at the request of the Creek chiefs, pay four hundred eighty-eight dollars 75 cents as above stated.

The document marked K, for 450.81¾ dollars, for supplies by the United States Factor, from 1797, January 1, to the 25 of April, to the Indians without authority from the agent. This document rests on the letter of Mr. Price or a voucher. If it is admited by the Secretary at War, the factory will have credit for it; or if it should be deemed a debt against the nation, provision is made for the payment of it in the treaty concluded last year at this place.

———————

Teusee—God.
Soliiste—The inhabitants of the sky.
Soli—Sky.

———————

SENIOR BURNEY:

200 Chalks   Fifty Dollars   Pay Efau Tusskeucah and Tacycinney, agents for Ooseuchee, fifty dollars, being the portion assigned to that town of the stipend allowed by the U. S. to the Creeks for the year 1798.
$50.

Form of certificate.

———————

The Creek nation have classed their towns and appointed a warrior over each class to carry the laws into effect against thieves and mischiefmakers. 1st class named Sunomomekee of Wewacau.

18 August, 1800.

Elijah Lumsden of Green County, pass into the Cherokees.

18 August.

Claiborn Foster and Samuel Dale, to trade in hogs and cattle.
John Fielder of Jackson County, to trade in cattle and hogs.
James Graham, to trade in the Creeks for cattle and hogs.
Joseph Graham, his assistant.
Major Edward Moor & J. Raston of Jackson County, to trade in hogs and cattle among the Creeks and Cherokees for the present season, to end with the month of January next. They will have tnree assistants, for whose conduct they will be accountable.

15 July, 1800.

Aquilla Scott of Georgia, to trade in hogs and cattle only.
23 July, 1800, 2 assistants.

Creek Agency, 23rd of May, 1801.

Leonard Saunders Sims of Warren County, in North Carolina, on a journey of amusement. Certificate of propriety of character, 26 February, 1801, by Wm. Falkener, J. P. Certified to be so by the clerk, under the county seal, and others.

23rd May.

Captain William Wiggins of Green County, in Georgia, desirous of traveling into the Mississippi Territory. Certificate of good character, by Adjutant General Fauchee, Colonel Melton and several other respectable characters.

23rd May.

William Hill, Esq. of Green County, in Georgia, desirous of traveling into the Mississippi Territory. Certificate of good character, by Andrew Baxter, Brice Gaither, Adjutant General Fauchee, Colonel Melton and several other respectable characters.

24th.

William Hunt, return passport from Captain Shaumburgh, 27 January, 1801. Passed thro' 8 February; repassed 24 May.

24th.

Sylvanus Walker of Green County, in Georgia, on a journey to the settlements on Tombigbee on lawful business. Certificate of good character, signed by E. Park, Clerk of that County; Wm. Greer, J. P.; James Nisbet, J. P.

24th.

Robert Hide of Green County, certified to be a young man of good report, by E. Parks, Jos. Phillips, Wm. Hill and W. Wiggins, to pass to Tombigbee.

24th.

Micajah Wall of Green County, Georgia, Certificate that he has supported a reputable character; desirous to travel to the settlements on Tombigbee. Certified by,
E. PARKS.
J. PHILLIPS.
L. SOWALL.
W. WIGGINS.
WILLIAM HILL.

24th.

Lewis Sewall, Esq., of Columbia, in Georgia, request to pass to the settlements on Tombigbee.

24th.

Thomas Simmons of Lincoln County, Georgia, to pass to the settlements on Mississippi.

24th.

William Johnson, a man of good character, and an honest citizen of this State of Georgia. Certificate by the Honourable David Emanuel, Governor of Georgia, 13th of April.

25th.

Hugh Cassady, from the Mississippi Territory to Georgia; pass by John Steel, Secretary, acting as Governor.

25th.

Nathaniel Clark Green, ditto.

25th.

Moses Modic, to pass into Georgia.

25th.

Mr. W. J. Smith of the house of Smith and Robinson, to pass thro' the agency South of Ohio.

4 June.

William George, to pass to the Mississippi Territory, 7 April, by the Governor of Georgia.

3rd June.

William Patrick Hays of Georgia, to the Mississippi Territory, by the Governor of Georgia, 7 April.

3rd June.

Robert Finley of Georgia, to the Mississippi Territory, by the Governor of Georgia, 7 April.

5 June.

Major Seth Dean and Jesse Thomas, returning from Tombigbee, 10 February, 1801, by Governor Jackson.

Joseph Kercam & John Waterson of Georgia, 8 May, by Governor Emanuel.

16 June.

Samuel Berryhill and Alexander Shaw Newman, on business in the nation, 23 May; signed David Emanuel, Governor of Georgia.

16 June.

Jonathan Arnold and James Gold, citizens of the U. S., to New Orleans, 7 June, 1801, by William Peters, Major Com.

25 September, 1801.

Isaia Brenton, his wife and family, with two negros; a certificate of propriety recommended from the officers, civil and military, of Green and Jackson Counties.

22nd October, 1801.

Lewis McLain, with his family, nine whites and one black. Pass from David Emanuel, Governor protem.

Micajah Wall and John Young, pass as above.

John Burney, with his family, nine blacks and five whites, pass as above; all from Green County, Georgia.

William Verdeman, a citizen of Mississippi Territory, pass from Captain Shaumburgh, 27th January, 1801.

22nd October, 1801.

John Grayham, from Georgia, pass from David Emanuel. With him Daniel and Wm. Burford and Touchstone with two negros with passes, 20, 1801.

24th November.

William G. Gregory, from Columbia County, by David Emanuel, President of the Senate.

John Esspy, of Columbia County, Georgia, pass from David Emanuel.

Isack Weldon, Columbia County, Georgia, by David Emanuel.

John Elijah Ofin, pass from the Governor of New Orleans.

William Griffin, pass from Louisiana.

1st December, 1801.

William Colman, pass from Governor of Georgia.

Journal of the Commissioners of the United States Appointed to Hold Conferences with Several of the Indian Nations South of the Ohio, Commenced by Mr. Hawkins, One of the Commissioners.

———

On the 18 July I received from the Secretary of War this letter, at Tuckabatchee:

———

War department, 18 June, 1801.

Sir:

The President of the United States having appointed you a Commissioner, jointly with William R. Davie and James Wilkinson, Esquire, to hold conferences with several of the Indian nations South of Ohio, you are requested to repair to South West Point, in the State of Tennessee, by the first day of August next, there to meet your colleagues, the first named of whom will be the bearer of your commissions and instructions, and commence the business of your mission.

I am Sir, with high consideration,
  Your most obedient servant,
    H. DEARBORN.
BENJAMIN HAWKINS, ESQ.

———

I made the necessary arrangements for the agents in the Creek Department, and set out on the 25th of that month, and passing through the Upper Creeks and Cherokees, arrived at South West Point on the 4th instant.

4th August.

Colonel Meigs, the agent for the Cherokees, informed me that on the 11th July he sent the following address "to the chiefs and warriors of the Cherokees:

Friends and Brothers:

The President of the United States takes you by the hand and invites you and all the nations of red people within the territory of the United States to look up to him as their father and friend; to rely in full confidence upon his unvarying disposition to lead and protect them in the paths of peace and harmony, and to cultivate friendship with his brothers of the same colour and with the citizens of the United States.

The chain of friendship is now bright and binds us all together; for your and our sakes, and for the sakes of your and our children, we must prevent it from becoming rusty; so long as the mountains in our land shall endure and our rivers flow, so long may the red and white people dweling in it live in the bonds of brotherhood and friendship.

To aid in perpetuating this highly desirable object, the President has directed three of his beloved men to meet your principal men at South West Point, in the State of Tennessee, on the first day of August next. He requests you to send such of your chiefs and principal men as you have full confidence in, then and there to meet the Commissioners; and that you will empower them to state for the consideration of the government all that you have upon your minds; to hear in behalf of your nation all that those Commissioners shall have to propose, and to accede to such proposals as the Commissioners shall make and your representatives shall conceive to be proper and useful.

Given at the War Office of the United States this 18th day of June, A. D. 1801.

HENRY DEARBORN,
Secretary of War.

Colonel Meigs delivered me two packets from the Secretary of War, containing the commissions and instructions to James Wilkinson, Brigadier General in the service of the United States; Benjamin Hawkins, of North Carolina, and Andrew Pickins, of South Carolina, or any two of them, to hold conferences with the Cherokees, Chickasaws, Choctaws and Creeks, and to conclude and sign treaties with them.

7th August.

Several chiefs from the towns on the Tennessee called on me and had a long conversation with me on the affairs of their nation. They stated the improvements made in the products of the country; that a total change had taken place in the habits of the nation since the introduction of the plan for their civilization; that a desire for individual property was very prevalent, and that the current of conversation now was how to acquire it, by attention to stock, to farming and to manufactures.

I wrote this letter to the Secretary of War:

South West Point, 7th August, 1801.

I traveled through the Upper Creeks and Cherokees, and arrived here on the 4th of this month, where I received your packet containing the commissions and instructions for the Commissioners. My colleagues have not arrived.

Colonel Meigs had taken measures to send your address of the 18 of June to the Indians. Some time after this the deputation sent by the Cherokees to the seat of government arrived; who, having agreed among themselves it was necessary that the chiefs of the nation should convene and consult prior to their meeting with the Commissioners of the United States, they communicated their opinion to the Little Turkey, the chief of the nation, who concured in opinion with them and sent runners through the nation to invite the chiefs to assemble at Oosetenauleh on the 18th of this month to consult together accordingly; but before this, the invitation sent by Colonel Meigs had been received and several of the chiefs have attended here, and with them some sent by the Little Turkey to take the Commissioners by the hand and welcome them to his land.

The meeting at Oosetenauleh will unavoidably derange the periods pointed out by you for the other conferences, as the one contemplated to be held here cannot be closed till the last of this month.

I have been very unwell for some days past; am getting better, and am just able to attend to business.

I have the honour to be, very respectfully, Sir,

Your obedient servant.

The Honourable
HENRY DEARBORN,
Secretary of War.

10th.

Weele, John Wats and Doublehead, with several other chiefs, called on me and delivered this talk in behalf of themselves and the chiefs of the river towns: "Colonel Meigs sent us the invitation of the President to come and meet his Commissioners here on the first of this month; we have come accordingly and we have with us a representation from our part of the nation. We have been here several days, waiting for the arrival of the Commissioners; you are come, but we cannot hear of your colleagues, and it appears now quite uncertain when you will have a meeting. The chiefs who are to convene at Oosetenauleh sent us no invitation to go there; of course we suppose they have no need of our council. We will return home. We have taken the talks of the President from soon after your first coming among us, and as you have come through our nation, you can see and know we have done so. We shall now return home, as we are determined to concur in every thing agreed upon between you and the old chiefs soon to convene at Oosetenauleh, there is no necessity for our remaining here, and as we have manifested our respect for the new President by our immediate attention to his invitation. One thing we mention for your information: There is a division now among ourselves; we have thought seriously of it, and it is right that you should know it. We leave to the chiefs to convene at Oosetenauleh the government of our country as they think proper, which lies on the other side of Chilhowe Mountain; we shall govern that part to the west. We have one thing to say to you as Agent for Indian Affairs, which you will hear in stile of complaint from some of the other chiefs; they say we have had more wheels and cards than our share, and in consequence are more advanced in making our own cloathing, as well as in farming, than they. The fact is this: The offer of those things was made to all of us at the same time; we accepted of it, some of us immediately, and others soon after; those who complain came in late; we have got the start of them, which we are determined to keep."

The reply: Your attention to the invitation sent by your father, the President, to meet his Commissioners here do's you credit; he is a new father for you, made so by the voice of the American people. Your first father, Washington, is dead. During his administration the plan for your civilization originated in the justice of the American people; this benevolent care of the government was confided by him to my agency. His successor, Mr. Adams, was authorized by the laws of the United States to pursue the same course, and he continued me, as he found me, the agent for carrying into effect the benevolent views of the government in relation to you red people. By the Constitution of the United States the office of President is during the term of four years. This man stood high in the estimation of the people of the U. S. when they elected him President, but on mature deliberation they have altered their opinion of Mr. Adams, and would not elect him again to that office. Mr. Jefferson is the man of their choice; he is their President and your new father. He is in every way worthy of the high trust confided to him by his fellow citizens and of your entire confidence, your love and veneration. From such a man you red people have every thing to hope and nothing to fear.

I cannot say when the Commissioners will be here; by the papers I have received since my arrival they were expected to be here ten days past, and I expect one or both of them daily. One of the gentlemen named to you declined coming, resigned his appointment, and General Pickins, your old friend, is in his stead. If one comes, two of us will proceed to execute the duties of our mission, and it will be as effectual as if we were all present. I can now only tell you you may have entire confidence in my colleagues; that you have nothing to fear from such men; that all propositions made by them to you will manifest a fair and candid attention to your rights. You will be treated as a free people, under the guarantee and benevolent care of the American people. Nothing will be asked of you without offering an equivalent, and whatever is asked of you, you are advised to weigh well before you answer, and always keep this in view: You are a free people under the guarantee of the government of the United States; that you have for several years had daily and substantial proofs of the benevolent care of the government, by the protection of your rights, by a strong and expensive military establishment, by the introduction, at a considerable expence, of the wheel, loom, and plough into your land, and that if you can accommodate a people who do so much for you, and who mean to continue their good offices to you, whether you attend to their wants or not, you ought to weigh well, to deliberate long, and to have substantial reasons to offer before you say no to any proposition made to you by the Commissioners, when none will be made without offering you an equivalent.

If you return home you must leave some men who possess your entire confidence to join the other chiefs of the nation who we may expect from the council at Oosetenauleh. Your nation must not divide, you must be one people, under the government of your old chiefs.

As to the complaint you mention, it is very agreeable to me. I am glad that the people of your towns attend early to the benefits arising from the plan for bettering your condition; that you have got the start of the other towns should not be a subject of complaint on their part, but a stimulous, as they now see your prosperity from the experiment among yourselves. When they complain, tell them come on, you are ahead of them now, but to double their diligence and they may overtake you.

14th.

The evening of this day General Wilkinson arrived.

S. W. Point, 14th August, 1801.

I wrote you on the 7th to inform you of my arrival here on the 4th of this month. I am now recovered from my late indisposition and able to attend to the duties of my mission. A waggon arrived here yesterday with some public stores for the Commissioners. We have received no accounts to be relied on respecting my colleagues.

I have the honour to be, &c.

The Honourable
    HENRY DEARBORN,
        Secretary of War.

15th.

The Commissioners proceeded to execute the duties of their mission. Being informed that some of the chiefs were opposed to meeting the Commissioners at this place, and had proposed Tellico, and that there was some discontent and division among the chiefs on the propriety of the meeting at Oosetenauleh after they had received the invitation of the President to convene at this place, they wrote and sent the following letter by an interpreter express to the chiefs about to convene at Oosetenauleh:

To the chiefs and warriors of the Cherokee Nation:

We send you under cover a talk from our beloved great chief and father, Thomas Jefferson, President of the United States. We beg of you to open your ears to listen to it attentively and let it sink deep into your hearts. It is the same speach which has been sent to you by your agent, Colonel Meigs.

The people of the United States having given you a new father, we have pleasure in assuring you that he holds his red children and his white children in the same regard; that he will neither violate your lands or suffer them to be violated while you behave as you have done, like dutiful and affectionate children, who look up to him for protection; but it is our duty also to tell you that your father, the President, will expect you to pay prompt regard to this, his first invitation to meet us at this place, which he has appointed for the purpose, and where provisions and necessaries are collected. Your father has a right to name the place where he will speak to you, and you have no right to object to his invitation, since he has for object your own good as well as that of his white children. We do therefore confidently expect you will be on your feet so soon as you receive this talk, and that we shall have the happiness to take you by the hand on the 25th of the present month, that is ten days from this day. We urge this injunction upon you because our business calls us elsewhere.

We are your friends and the representatives of your father, the President.

S. W. Point, 15th August, 1801.

***

16th.

At the special request of a deputation from the towns on the Tennessee below this, the Commissioners wrote and delivered to them, to be sent under their direction, this address:

To the chiefs and warriors of the Cherokee Nation of Indians on the Tennessee:

The talk from your father, the President, was sent you by Colonel Meigs, your agent, inviting you to send such chiefs and principal men as you have full confidence in, to meet his Commissioners at this place on the first of this month, to state for the consideration of government all that you have upon your minds, to hear in behalf of your nation all that the Commissioners shall have to propose, and to agree to such proposals as they shall make, and your representatives shall conceive to be proper and useful.

We, two of the Commissioners of the United States, are now arrived and have sent to your council, convened at Oosetenauleh, to attend here by the 25th of this month, and as we understand from some of your most distinguished chiefs, that you will not be at the meeting at Oosetenauleh, we have proposed to them to send runners to invite you to attend here on the day appointed, where we shall expect and be glad to see you, for the purposes expressed in the talk of the President.

We are your friends and the friends of your nation.

S. W. Point, 16th August, 1801.

***

Colonel Meigs, the agent for the Cherokees, communicated to the Commissioners a letter from Mr. Hooker, U. S. Factor at

Tellico, of the 15, informing that an Indian woman was killed on Stock Creek, in Knox County, on the 12th inst., refering him to Captain Flannegan, near Knoxville, for the particulars. The Commissioners requested the agent to send an express immediately to the gentleman refered to for the particulars, and they wrote to the Governor this letter:

S. W. Point, 16th August, 1801.

At the time that we do ourselves the pleasure to announce to your Excellency our arrival here as Commissioners of the United States, for the purpose of holding a conference with the Cherokees on subjects interesting to our fellow citizens, we have to lament and to regret a most wicked and barbarous murder, perpetrated on Stock Creek, in Knox County, on the body of an Indian woman who was with her young child and a part of her family on her way to Knoxville seeking a market for the products of her industry.

Your excellency knows as well the affect this will have on the minds of the Indians, as the necessity there is of a speedy exertion of the competent authority to bring, with the least possible delay, the offender to justice, and we must request your interposition to produce that desirable end. The particulars of this transaction have not reached us; we are refered to Captain Flannegan, near Knoxville, who is mentioned too as a man in estimation for them; as you are near him we presume you will have received them ere this.

We have the honour to be, &c.
His Excellency,
JOHN SEVIER,
Governor of Tennessee.

The family of the murdered woman sent a runner to the chiefs at S. W. Point to inform them of the murder and that the woman left a young child not four months old, and to request their advise after they had consulted the Commissioners of the United States how they were to act.

The Commissioners communicated what they had heard and done to the chiefs, and made such observations on the transaction as were suited to the occasion.

18th.

The Commissioners, taking a thorough view of the duties enjoined by their mission & being of opinion that the delays here would unavoidably derange the conferences contemplated to be held with the Chickasaws and Choctaws, determined to prevent all unnecessary expence to place both these conferences under their control, and for that end sent a steady Cherokee runner with the following letters to the agents of the Chickasaws and Choctaws:

South W. Point, 18th August, 1801.

General Wilkinson and Mr. Hawkins, two of the Commissioners of the United States, appointed to hold conferences, &c. with the Indian nations South of Ohio, are now here, and as they will be delayed longer with the Cherokees than was expected by the President, they cannot be at the Chickasaw Bluffs by the time fixed for the conference with that nation. I have in consequence dispatched an express to you to apprise you of it, and to inform you that you may expect the Commissioners at the Bluffs by the last of September or early in October.

I request you to communicate this, without delay, to the chiefs and warriors of the Chickasaws, and to inform them that as soon as the Commissioners can fix on the day for meeting them they will be informed of it.

I have sent you a letter for Colonel John McKee which you will forward by express to prevent a like disappointment with the Choctaws.

I am, with due regard and esteem, Sir,
Your obedient servant,
BENJAMIN HAWKINS,
Agent for I. A. S. of Ohio·
MR. SAMUEL MITCHELL,
Agent for the Chickasaws.

S. W. Point, in Tennessee, 18 August, 1801.

General Wilkinson and Mr. Hawkins, two of the Commissioners of the United States, appointed to hold conferences, &c., with the Indian nations South of Ohio, are here, and as they will be detained longer with the Cherokees than was expected by the President, they cannot be at Natches by the time fixed for the conference there with the Choctaws or at the Bluffs for that with the Chickasaws.

As the conference with the Choctaws follows that of the Chickasaws, it cannot probably take place till the last of October or early in November. I request you to communicate this, without delay, to the chiefs & warriors of the Choctaws and to inform them that as soon as the Commissioners can fix on a day certain for meeting of them they will be informed of it.

I send this by express to Mr. Mitchell with orders for him to forward it by express to you.

I am, with due regard & esteem, Sir,
Your obedient servant,
BENJAMIN HAWKINS,
Agent for I. A. South of Ohio.

COLONEL JOHN McKEE,
Agent for the Choctaws, in his absence, to John Pitchlin, interpreter, to take order.

———————

The contents of both these letters were communicated to the runner, and to prevent as much as possible a failure of the object, the letters were, in the absence of the agents, to be opened by the interpreters or chiefs; and the General, he wrote to the commandant at the Bluffs respecting supplies:

———————

Head Quarters, S. W. Point, August 18th, 1801.
Sir:

You will be pleased to inform me by the bearer what may be your actual intention in regard to provisions, and what may be your expectations, with the grounds on which such expectations are founded. You will be pleased also to inform me whether provisions could, in an extremity, be suddenly procured in your neighbourhood, taking care to designate the species and quantity.

It is proposed to hold a conference with the Chickasaws at the post of your command, towards the end of next month, and the contractor has been required to furnish rations for the purpose, but as he has failed, I am fearful he may be deficient in this instance, and I send this express to be ascertained of the fact by you, that I may, in case of his default, take measures to procure a supply before I leave the Ohio. The bearer is to return in season to meet me at the mouth of Bear Creek. I therefore request you to furnish provisions and to dispatch him without a moment's unnecessary delay. I expect to leave this place about the 5th of next month.

With consideration and esteem, I am, Sir,
Your obedient servant,
JA. WILKINSON.

CAPTAIN SPARKS.

The Commissioners then wrote this letter to the Honourable Secretary of War:

S. W. Point, in Tennessee, 18 August, 1801.

General Wilkinson arrived here on the evening of the 14th, and we proceeded immediately to execute the duties of our mission. Being informed that some of the chiefs were opposed to meeting the Commissioners at this place and had proposed Tellico, and that there was some discontent and division among the chiefs on the propriety of the meeting at Oosetenauleh after they had received the invitation of the President to convene at this place, we wrote the address, No. 1, and sent it by an interpreter to the chiefs convened in that town. After this, on a consultation with some chiefs of the towns on Tennessee, we wrote and sent under their direction, 2. The same day having received the account, 3, of the murder of an Indian woman in the neighbourhood of Knoxville, we wrote, 4, and sent it by express to the Governor of this State, and directed Colonel Meigs, the agent for the Cherokees, to take measures immediately to obtain the particulars of this transaction.

Taking a thorough view of all the duties enjoined by our mission, we find that the delays here will unavoidably derange the conferences contemplated to be held with the Chickasaws and Choctaws, and we have judged it advisable to prevent all unnecessary expence to place both these conferences under our control, and to that end have sent a careful, steady Cherokee runner with the orders, 5, 6, 7.

As we have received no information from the council convened at Oosetenauleh, we have formed no idea of the probable issue of the conference to be held here. As Colonel Hawkins came through the nation he found the chiefs had been seriously alarmed by a report circulated among them "that three gentlemen of this State were appointed Commissioners, and that it was in contemplation to endeavour to obtain a large tract of country from them;" that the Indian deputation sent to the seat of government had on their return quieted the fears of the Indians as to the Commissioners, but not altogether as to the propositions for land, and that on this subject they seemed fixed and determined not to part with any more.

On the 13th of this month a waggon arrived here with some stores for the use of the Commissioners, but no goods for the Indians. We have heard of three waggons arriving at the same time at the United States Factory at Tellico, but whether for the trade or the purposes contemplated in the conference here, we are not informed.

General Wilkinson, who came here by the way of Wilkinsonville, is of opinion that the stores, goods and provisions intended to be sent down for the conferences at the Chickasaw Bluffs and at Natches will not reach the first point before the begining of November, because of the lowness of the waters and the consequent impediments to the navigation of the Ohio.

We have the honour to be, very respectfully, Sir,
Your obedient servants,
JA. WILKINSON.
BENJAMIN HAWKINS.

The Honourable
HENRY DEARBORN,
Secretary of War.

References.

No. 1, See 15th August.
2, See 16th.
3, Mr. Hooker, 16th.
4, See letter to the Governor, 16th.
5, To S. Mitchel.
6, Colonel McKee.
7, Captain Sharp.

23rd August.

The messenger sent by the Commissioners to Oosetenauleh returned with the answer to the talk of the Commissioners, of the 15th. He reported that he delivered the talk sent by him and heard it correctly interpreted to the chiefs; that after this they consulted among themselves and prepared an answer, which was to have been sent, but on further reflection, was altered to the one sent, which he delivered to the Commissioners; that of himself he told the chiefs that provision was made at South West Point for the meeting which could not be transported in time from thence to Tellico; that he understood the first answer was not respectful or friendly.

The Answer.

Oosetenauleh, 19th August, 1801.

Brothers, the Commissioners of the United States:

Your express arrived at a time when our council was seting, and we are glad to hear from you. We suppose we have, or ought to have, a right to have something to say in choosing the place of conference. Tellico is the place where we arranged to meet, and that is the place we expect you will meet us. Our nation is much scattered and it will take up time before we can communicate to the different towns the time that may be convenient to all to meet. Tellico is our beloved ground and more convenient for our nation; besides, the range there is much better, whereas, about the Point there is nothing for horses.

Beloved Commissioners:

One of our people is missing and fell, but we expect the Commissioners will look about them and have that bad action repaired by apprehending and punishing the agressor before we meet. We expect our friends, the Commissioners, will use their best endeavours to bring the murderers to light and punishment, that the authority of leading and wise men may not be trampled on.

You will see us in twelve nights at Tellico, if that place should be agreeable to you, you will see us there. With sentiments of great regard for the Commissioners, I remain,

Your friend and brother,

THE GLASS.

In behalf and at request of the meeting.

24th.

The Commissioners communicated the answer which they had received to the chiefs from the river towns who were with them. Two of them, Chuquilataque (Doublehead), and Nanetooquh (The Bloody Fellow), seemed much concerned and said: "This is unusual and contrary to our expectations; the invitation from our father, the President, is to meet his Commissioners at this place, and here the commissaries have made the requisite provisions; to move this will cause additional and unnecessary expence. If the

Indians had provisions of their own it would be another thing;
they have not; that this place is as convenient as Tellico, and they
have food sufficient at this season for their horses; that the
meeting at Oosetenauleh, as well as the present procedure, they did
not comprehend; they hoped the Commissioners would not take
any definite steps for the present, that Nenetooquh would go himself to the chiefs about to asesmble at Tellico and advise them
to come down immediately on their arrival."

25th.

———

                                    S. W. Point, 25th August, 1801.
Sir:

        Since our last, of the 18th instant, we have received from the
Cherokees assembled at Oosetenauleh the talk you will find under
cover, indicative of a degree of presumption which must not be
indulged; this being the spot assigned by the President for the
conference and the provisions being deposited here; could we
wave the impolicy of the step, we should not consider ourselves at
liberty to change the ground, under circumstances of increased
expence and delay.
        We shall therefore mildly, but firmly, admonish the chiefs
who may assemble at Tellico of the impropriety and inadvisability
of their pretentions, and again invite them to attend the conference
here at a short day, in which measure we shall have the concurrence of Doublehead and Bloodyfellow, two of the most conspicuous chiefs, who reside near the Tennessee below and are now with
us.   We believe our business, when once begun, may be completed
in a few days, after which we shall send a runner to convene the
Chickasaws, and will proceed by water without delay to the point
of interview.
        Perhaps it may not be amiss for us to remark at this time
that we apprehend the assembling of the Choctaw nation agreeably
to your notification at the town of Natches, near the center of
population in that district, will expose the inhabitants to much
unavoidable vexation and abuse of property, and the Indians to the
debauchery inseperable from our frontier villages.
        We therefore beg leave to submit to the executive considera-
tion the expediency of naming a different place for the conference,
or of authorizing us to do so.   Should any communication to us
on this subject be deemed necessary, it can be forwarded from
Fort Washington (Cincinnati) by the commanding officer there to
the cantonment on the Ohio, and from thence, in season, to over-

take us at the Bluffs and enable us to give change to the rendezvous proposed for the Choctaws without inconvenience or delay.

We have yet no information respecting goods intended for the conference at this place, but we do not propose to halt for them, and we are sorry to add that we understand the murderer of the Cherokee woman on Stock Creek has escaped from the country; the perpetrator is generally believed to be Peter Wheeler, said to be of bad character.

We are, with high consideration and respect, Sir,
Your obedient servants,
JA. WILKINSON.
BENJAMIN HAWKINS.
The Honourable
THE SECRETARY OF WAR.

N. B.—We hear nothing of General Pickins.

30th.

Nenetooquh reported to the Commissioners that he had been at Tellico and delivered a strong talk to The Bark for the chiefs about to assemble at that place, which he enjoined on him to deliver immediately on their arrival. Among other things, he said "that at Tellico there was no provisions and those who assembled there could not expect any; that provision was made at S. W. P., and that they must go there to get their belley full; that was the place appointed by the President for the conference, that was the place where provision was made, and it was idle to expect an alteration would be made as there was no substantial reason for it and the usual course had been to attend at the place and time appointed by the President."

All the Indians who were waiting the conference with the Commissioners showed much uneasiness at the mode of procedure on their part.

31st.

Charles Hicks, an interpreter, a halfbreed, who attended the meeting at Oosetenauleh, made this report: The chiefs at Oosetenauleh conducted their business in secrecy, seemed to distrust him, as he was in the public service, and withheld every thing from him as far as in their power. It appeared to him the chiefs were desirous of assuming and attempting to exercise the right of removing the public agents and interpreters; that the evening after they received the talk from the Commissioners, they prepared an answer, in his opinion rude and improper; among other things, they said that when the Commissioners of the United States would inform them that they had the murderer of the Indian woman (murdered on the 12th, on Stock Creek, near Knoxville) in custody, and would execute him in their presence, they would attend, and not till then. The next day, reconsidering this part of the answer, they determined to alter it and send a respectful one, which was done by The Glass and one or two only. In the course of the conference, at which Major Lewis, late agent attended, there appeared an intention in James Van and some others to replace the Major in the agency; he could not, being excluded, hear the proposition distinctly, but he heard the Major reply "that he would not now accept of it." He is at a loss to know whence this conduct among the chiefs originated.

1st September.

The Commissioners sent this address to the chiefs about to assemble at Tellico:

———

Brothers:

In addition to the talk delivered to The Bark by the Bloody-fellow, we think proper to inform you that having waited here 27 days to met you in conference, agreeably to the invitation of our great father, Thomas Jefferson, President of the U. S., which was delivered to you from Colonel Meigs, the Agent of War, on the 13th ultimo, we can but express our surprise that you should not have appeared before this time.

Brothers: We are sorry that you manifest so little respect to the voice of your new father, who is as able and as desirous to foster you and to protect your interests as his predecessors. We are sorry that you should be so perverse and foolish as to set up your will against that of your father, the President of the sixteen fires, who alone is able to defend you against your enemies.

Brothers: We are your friends and we are solicitous for your happiness. We therefore hope you will no longer turn a deaf ear to the voice of your father, the President; for if you shut your ears against his councils and refuse to meet those beloved men whom he has appointed to confer with you, you will deprive him of the power to serve you, and must not expect either his friendship or his protection.

Brothers: We have given you our advise, the good and bad are before you, and you are men and can choose for yourselves. If you consider the friendship and protection of the President of the U. S. necessary to you, then come forward to this place without loss of time. If you do not need his friendship and protection and can stand alone without him, we expect you will, like men and warriors, speak out and declare it.

Brothers: We have waited long for you, and we now feel it our duty to tell you, that if you are not here within four days from this date, we shall be obligded to leave the country without seeing you and to report your conduct to your father, the President.

We are your friends and the representatives of your father, the President.

Commissioners Camp, near Coosau, 1 September, 1801.

The Commissioners of the U. S. have sent to your care a talk for the chiefs about to assemble at Tellico, and they request you to have it interpreted to them by Carey. You will find that the language is plain and impressive and by no construction intended as a threat; we mention this to put the interpreter on his guard.

You have enclosed also a short talk from the chiefs here to the people of Chilhowe, which they request you to have interpreted in like manner.

I am, with much esteem and regard, Sir,
Your obedient servant,

BENJAMIN HAWKINS.

JOHN W. HOOKER,
U. S. Factor, Tellico.

South West Point, September 1, 1801.
Sir:

To gain all the time possible for an answer to our proposition respecting the conference to be held with the Choctaws, we took the liberty to address the original of the inclosed duplicate to the President at his seat, and we are sorry to inform you an unexpected casualty will detain it at Knoxville until the departure of the descending mail, which will convey this to you.

Since writing the within we have information to justify the belief that the Cherokees are indisposed to any conference at this time; we have not yet been able to develop the causes which have produced this temper, but we suspect the interference of the discontented, we apprehend the insertion of political prejudice, we ascribe great influence to the fear of further encroachments, and we impute much to the late base assassination of a squaw near Knoxville, whose murderer has not yet been apprehended.

The Glass has illy requited the courtesies he experienced at the seat of government. He is the author of the partial and unseasonable meeting at Oosetenauleh, which has produced the delays we suffer, and gave birth, we are informed, to several violent propositions against which the discretion of the assembly finally prevailed.

To prevent the further waste of time and treasure and to test the determination of the nation, we have this day dispatched the message, of which you have a copy, under cover to the chiefs assembled at Tellico, and should it fail of the desired affect, we shall immediately embark for the Chickasaw Bluffs. In this procedure we believe we consult the essential dignity of the government's sound principles of economy and the views of the executive attached to this commission.

Should a partial assembly of the chiefs take place here, insufficient to decide on the presidential proposition, we shall make a provisional adjournment of the conference to a future day, subject to the executive control.

We are assured that the Cherokees have proposed a general council of the four nations to be convened at Willstown about the 20th instant, at which a deputation from the northern nations, said to be charged with talks, is to be present.

Colonel Hawkins is of opinion that this measure is produced by a panic terror, uprising from the apprehension that they are soon to be pressed for a further relinquishment of lands. Colonel Meigs will attend this meeting, and whether it be held in public or in private, the result must soon reach us.

We have the honour to be, with much respect,

Your obedient servants.

The Honourable
THE SECRETARY OF WAR.

———

Since writing this General Pickins is arrived.

———

S. West Point, September 1st, 1801.

Understanding from the public prints that you are on a visit to Monticello, we avail ourselves of the direct conveyance to intrude on you our communications of the 25th ult. and of this day to the

Secretary of War, and we hope you may approve of this deviation from the regular course of our correspondence, which we hazzard with the intent to secure time for the seasonable arrival of any order you may think proper to issue respecting the place for holding the proposed conference with the Choctaws. Our letter of the 25 was intended to be sent on the day it was written, in the care of a Mr. Watson of Alexandria, who informed us of his being then on the road, and that he should pass near your residence, but as we found afterwards that he would be detained, we took it back and send it by the mail. Our colleague, General Pickins, arrived last evening.

With the highest consideration and the most respectful attachment, we have the honour to be, Sir,
Your obedient servants,

JA. WILKINSON.
BENJAMIN HAWKINS.

THOMAS JEFFERSON,
President of the United States.

2nd September.

General Pickins arrived last evening.

4th.

The chiefs having informed the Commissioners they were ready to assemble whenever required thereto and to hear what they had to say to them, the Commissioners fixed on 2 o'clock, when they all convened at the conference harbour, and the Commissioners delivered the following address, by General Wilkinson:

Chiefs and Brothers:

About six moons past the people of the sixteen fires assembled in their grand national council house thought proper to elect our beloved chief, Thomas Jefferson, to be the President of the United States in the place of Adams, who had succeeded Washington.

Brothers: Open your ears. No sooner did our new father, Thomas Jefferson, find himself at the head of all the white people and sixteen fires than he turned his thoughts towards his red children, who stand most in need of his care, and whom he regards with the same tenderness that he does his white children.

Brothers: Under the influence of his attachments to his red children our great father, the President of the U. S., has appointed General Pickins, Colonel Hawkins and myself his Commissioners, to meet you in council, to assure you from his mouth of his paternal affections, and to say to you that he holds your rights as sacred and is as solicitous to promote your interests and happiness as his predecessors, Washington and Adams, were.

Brothers: Listen well and let our words sink deep into your hearts. Your new father, Thomas Jefferson, is equal in power to your former fathers, and he is entitled to as much confidence and respect as they were; he is as able to protect you as they were, and he cherishes the same disposition towards you. We charge you then to shut your ears against the thieves, lyars and mischief-makers who speak evil of him, because they mean to deceive you, in order to gratify their own views and malignant dispositions.

Brothers: Your great father, the President, is desirous to ameleorate your condition, to advance you in independence, and to provide for your permanent happiness and that of your prosperity. His ears are always open to you to listen to your complaints when you are aggrieved, and to hear the details of your wants, should you need assistance, that his good will may be exerted to redress your rongs and to relieve your sufferings.

Brothers: Two of us are known to you and we hope you have reliance on our friendship; of the third, I will only say that he has long been the friend of the red people beyond the Ohio, and that his station forbids him to deceive them or you.

Brothers: Open your ears. Your father, the President of the United States, is bound to pay the same attention to the interests of his white children that he does to he welfare of his red children throughout this great country.

Brothers: Your white brethren who live at Natches, at Nashville, and in South Carolina, are very far removed from each other and have complained to your father that the roads by which they travel are narrow and obstructed with fallen timber, with rivers and creeks, which prevent them from pursuing their lawful business with his red children and with each other.

Brothers: To remove these difficulties and to accommodate his red children as well as his white children, your father is desirous to open wide these roads, but as they pass over the lands of his red children, he first asks their consent to the measure, and is willing to pay them an equivalent for the indulgence to his white children.

Brothers: Your white brethren have also complained to your father that on these long roads they have no place for rest or accommodation, which exposes them and their horses to much inconvenience and suffering. To remove this complaint your father is desirous that his red children would consent to establish houses of entertainment and ferries on these roads, to be kept by persons appointed by himself, who shall give security for their good behaviour, and pay such annual rent to his red children as may be agreed on.

Brothers: This is a small request made by your father; it is intended not to extinguish your rights, but to give value to your land and to make it immediately productive to you, in the manner of your ferry over Clinch River.

Brothers: You have been alarmed by the songs of lying birds and the talks of foolish tongues; you have heard that your father would press you for further concessions of land, and it has been said by some, even as far as the Big River. You will know hereafter how to listen to such thieves, lyars and mischiefmakers, and will treat them as they deserve.

Brothers: Listen to us and hear the truth. We stand up in this place between you and your white brethren, and we are ready to speak from the one to the other. Your white brethren want land and are willing to pay for it; if you have any to sell they will buy it from you, if you can agree on the terms, but if you are not disposed to sell any land, not one word more will be said on the subject.

Brothers: The Commissioners are all your friends; they therefore caution you to shut your ears against all white men who are not authorized by your father, the President, or his beloved men, to speak to you.

Brothers: We intreat you not to listen to your traders, because they are skin catchers and have more regard for their own interests than to yours. Deal with them honestly, pay them punctually and take care they do not cheat you, but never admit them to your councils.

Brothers: Listen not, we pray you, to drunkards or men who spill innocent blood, because they are fools and lyars, and regard not the laws of God or man.

Brothers: Listen not, we beseech you, to those white men who run after your women, because they are dispised among their own people and seek only to gatify their lusts without regard to truth, to honour, or to your welfare, and would sell their fathers, their mothers, or their country for a wench.

Brothers: We have nothing further to write at this time; we thank the great spirit for bringing us this day together in peace and friendship, which may, we hope, last as long as the waters run & the trees grow.

Soquilataque, called Doublehead, in behalf of the chiefs replyed:

The chiefs now have heard the talks of a father, and the sun is now lowering and the same hour to-morrow we will deliver our answer, and the answer we shall give will be short, and hope there will be no more of it, and hope the Commissioners will not insist on making a reply.

The Commissioners: When we have heard what you have to say we shall know whether to reply or not.

5th September.

Doublehead, on the part of the chiefs: We shall commence to-day, notwithstanding the indisposition of one of the Commissioners (General Pickins) and some of our own.

I am now going to speak.

It is but yesterday that we heard the talk of our father, the President, and to-day you will hear ours. You are appointed by the U. S. to tell us the means to be used for our interest; this was planed eight years past for the welfare of our nation, big and small; done by our father, the President, who is now no more. It seems it is by his plan that the means have been pursued to take care of the red people, and the present President, it seems, cherishes the same good will towards us, which is pleasing to us and we hold to it.

I think that the new President ought to listen to our talks, and not throw them aside. We hope his good disposition towards us will continue, that our children may live in peace, and you who are authorized by the President have said we ought not to listen to the crooked talks of those who are about us. I, in behalf of my nation, am authorized to speak to you.

There are a number of land speculators among you who say we want to sell lands. We hope you will not pay any regard to them, as they give them out for the sake of geting property. We hope you will not listen to those talks. The chiefs, the head men of these frontiers, are themselves interested in these speculations, and they will give you fine talks, which are meant to deceive, as they are for their own interest. We think it is a shame that these land sellers should impose on the government, and say that we want to dispose of our lands when we do not. When you first made these settlements there were paths which answered for them. The roads you propose we do not wish to have made through our country. Our objection to this road is this: A great many people of all discriptions would pass them, and that would happen which has recently happened and you would labour under the same difficulties you do now.

We mean to hold fast the peace that is subsisting between you and us; to preserve this we hope you will not make roads thro' our country, but use those which you have made yourselves. I mean within your own limits. There is a road we have consented to be made from Clinch to Cumberland, and another, the Kentucky trace. I expect you will think we have a right to say yes or no as answers, and we hope that you will say no more on this subject; if you do, it would seem as if we had no right to refuse. You who are picked out by the government from among the first and best men of the U. S., we hope you will take our talks and assist us; likewise you who are placed on our borders to see our rights maintained, that we may not be plagued by those people who want land.

We consider General Wilkinson the General of the army of the U. S., and we hope he will not insist on any thing here; we look to him as children do's to their father. We remember the former talks; we were told the General was to preserve our lands, and not to let us be imposed on. I am now done speaking for this day, and I hope you will not say any thing more about the lands or about the roads.

Commissioners Reply.

What has passed between us shall be faithfully reported to the President, who knows best how to estimate it. The Commissioners, having business with other nations, will leave this as soon as the boats are prepared to take them down the river.

Chuleoah.

I will now address myself to the man, meaning Colonel Hawkins, who was appointed by our former father, the President, who was to use every exertion for our benefit. I have been to the seat of government where you came from, and I hope you will have those people removed to where they formerly lived; meaning those at the Currahee Mountain.

Those people who live on our lands deceive the government; therefore to ascertain our claims we wish to remove those people (meaning Wofford). Those lines were run by order of the government; you, yourself, run those lines, and we hope this inconvenience will be removed, as the general of the army is present. There are now upwards of 50 families settled over the lines, which you did run.

These things we mention, and we know he has deceived the government. He attended at the council at Willstown and there received orders to remove in three months. He afterwards attended the council at Oosetenauleh and received a like order. This is all I have to say to the Commissioners, and I hope things will be done as we have requested.

Chuquilatossue.

I am going to speak again, and I hope these gentlemen of Tennessee will listen well (the Governor-elect, General White, and several others being present). There is no doubt you remember the talks of Tellico, which we remember. We shall not forget the talks of the U. S., but I suppose they are forgotten by the State of Tennessee. As I have mentioned, we recollect the talks of the government; they have some of our prisoners who are not returned; whereas, on our part, we have delivered all within our bounds. As I have mentioned already, this subject, which we have given proof of, as to any thing our people have done, the debt has not remained long, and in these we give our proof of friendship. As I have said, we don't forget these debts, there are two which the whites owe us, killed in Cumberland, and these debts seem to increase, as blood has been spilt lately, near to where we have met the Commissioners. We wish the State of Tennessee would exert herself night and day, and pay that blood which they owe us. We shall therefore wait for these payments, which we will never forget, and we shall think of these debts night and day. There are great numbers of warriors (among the whites) who can soon have one person taken and executed. As we know the dispositions of those chiefs, meaning of the State of Tennessee, we do not suppose they mean to be out-done by one individual. Exert yourselves and follow our example when our people do rong, that peace may be preserved. That is all I have to say to my friends and brothers.

6th September.

———

South West Point, 6th September, 1801.

Sir:

On the morning of the 4th instant, the Cherokee chiefs announced to us their readiness to hear whatever the Commissioners might have to say. We immediately met them in council and addressed them in terms adapted to the occasion, to which their speaker, Doublehead made a laconic reply, and the conference adjourned until yesterday, when we received from the same chief the answer of the council assembled here, which induced us to break up the conference without accomplishing a single object of the commission.

We beg leave to refer to our minutes, which· are under cover, for the particular conduct of the Commissioners and for the detail of the conference, which, tho' unsuccessful, may, we hope, produce happy effects on the Indian mind, of late much bewildered and perplexed by occurrences which they did not understand, by misrepresentations, and we believe, by sinister intrigues.

We discovered several days since that the chief of the nation, the Little Turkey, had determined at the council of Oosetenauleh not to meet us, and we had received other information to justify the opinion that the measures to be pursued here had been resolved upon at that council. We had observed in all our conversations with the chiefs from the commencement of our interviews with them a strong repugnance to the idea of a commission of any kind which has relation to their lands, and it was discernable that the views and dispositions of the President were suspected, nowithstanding the kindness and friendship so recently experienced at the seat of government.

These observations determined us in opening the conference to explain the standing of the President and to asert his disposition and prerogatives in such stile as appeared best calculated to remove their doubts and distrusts and to inspire them with confidence and respect, but in unfolding the object of the commission we confined ourselves to general propositions as far as was practicable, and held the specific views of government in reserve until the temper and disposition of the council might be unequivocally demonstrated.

The decided tone of "Doublehead" on the subject of their lands, his pathetic appeal to the justice and magnanimity of the government respecting the roads, and the pressing demands which followed from himself and from Chuleoah for the fulfillment of existing treaties, and for the reparation of injuries recorded in blood, rendered it, in our judgment, unavailing and inconsistent with our instructions to press the conference further; while by disolving it, we not only oblidged the Indians, but gave them an impregnable testimony of the consideration and sincerity of the President.

It is with singular pleasure we have witnessed the advance of this people in the arts of civilization, the acquirement of individual property by agricultural improvements, by raising stock, and by domestic manufactures, seems to have taken strong hold of the nation, and we believe that a few years perseverence in the beneficent plan, which has produced these effects, will prepare them to accommodate their white neighbours with lands on reasonable terms.

We propose to embark the day after to-morrow for the Chickasaw Bluffs, where we are apprehensive we shall be detained unreasonably by the non-arrival of the goods intended for the conference at that place, as we are informed they had not reached Pittsburgh on the 31st of July, and without them we cannot promise ourselves success with the Chickasaws.

We shall continue our exertions without waste of time on our part, to carry into effect the instructions of the executive, and we beg leave to assure you that whatever may be the result, we shall labour zealously to invite your approbation and that of the President.

With great respect, we have the honour to be, Sir,
Your obedient servants,

JAS. WILKINSON.
BENJAMIN HAWKINS.
ANDREW PICKINS.

The Honourable
HENRY DEARBORN,
Secretary of War.

South West Point, 6th September, 1801.

The conference with the Cherokees having terminated yesterday without the Commissioners of the United States being able to accomplish any of the objects contemplated in their mission, I have judged it advisable to give you the impressions I have received of the affairs in this quarter to accompany the report of the Commissioners.

The Glass and his associates who were sent to the seat of government, convened the chiefs of the nation at Oosetenauleh on their return and made a detached report of their mission to them, upon which it was agreed that being then in full council, and made acquainted by The Glass & his associates from the competent authority, with the objects intrusted to the Commissioners of the United States here, they would decide on them, and accordingly they refused the whole, tho' not without some diversity of opinion as to the propriety of such a procedure. It was then agreed that a deputation from the towns should go & meet the Commissioners at Tellico, if agreeable to them, hear what they had to say, and if it corresponded with the report made by The

Glass and his associates, to refuse the whole. The chief of the nation, the Little Turkey, returned home from Oosetenauleh. It was agreed he should not meet the Commissioners, but receive accounts of the proceedings with them at the annual festival soon to be held at Willstown.

The Commissioners had received information soon after their arrival to justify the belief that the Cherokees were indisposed to any conference at this time, and it is probable the causes suggested in their letter of the 1st of this month had produced it.

I find that the pressure for land exhibited from all quarters had alarmed the chiefs of the nation. The exultation of the frontier citizens on the election of the President produced a belief that the President would favour the views of those deemed by Indians inimical to their rights. The report circulated through the nation soon after the adjournment of Congress that a treaty was soon to be held to extinguish the Indian claims to the lands on the right side of the Tennessee, and the withdrawing the troops from this frontier. All these circumstances, combined by mischief-makers, produced on the Indian mind a distrust of the President and of every thing proceeding from him. It produced a panic terror in the nation, which the chiefs have endeavoured to spread throughout the agency South of Ohio. They have consulted me as agent for the department, on the propriety of looking out west of the Mississippi for an eventual residence where this nation has a settlement of near one hundred gun men.

The correct views of our government in relation to our fellow citizens and its benevolent care manifested towards the Indians, in the fidelity and success with which the plan for their civilization has been carried into effect, will soon attract the current of opinion from error and rivit the confidence of the Indians in the justice of the President.

In the Cherokee agency the wheel, the loom and the plough is in pretty general use; farming, manufactures and stock raising the topics of conversation among the men and women, and the accumulation of individual personal property taking strong hold of the men. It is questionable with me whether the division of land among the individuals would tend to their advantage or not. In such an event, the long and well tried skill of land speculators might soon oust a whole tribe, whereas the whole country being a common, each of the community having exclusive property in their own farms only, the combined intelligence of the whole might be sufficient to resist such an evil, and secure at all times land for the cultivation of the indijent and improvident.

It is my duty to apprise you of one thing in relation to the Creeks: It is usual with the old chiefs of that nation to spend the winter in the woods and they seldom return to their towns till the last of February, and I have found March, April and May the most favourable season to gather them together. In the latter months there is grass for their horses, provisions is scarce in their towns, and they now usually return poor and hungry from their hunts. They begin their hunt late in the fall, generally in October.

I cannot close my letter without expressing to you that I am well pleased with Colonel Meigs; he is a character well suited to the affairs of this agency. I shall occasionally write to you on our tour, and as soon as I can get the materials for drawing, send you a map of my tours through the agency.

I have the honour to be, with much esteem and regard, Sir,

Your obedient servant,

BENJAMIN HAWKINS.

The Honourable
HENRY DEARBORN,
    Secretary of War.

Occochappo or Bear Creek, 26th September, 1801.

I wrote you on the 18th of August to inform you of the probable delay in the conference with the Cherokees, and that you might expect the Commissioners of the U. S. at the Chickasaw Bluffs by the last of September or early in October. I can now inform you that the Commissioners are here on their way by water, and they expect to be at the Bulffs on the 10th of October.

You will, without delay, communicate this to the chiefs and warriors of the Chickasaw nation and invite them to send such of their chiefs and principal men as they have full confidence in, to meet the Commissioners of the U. S. at the Bluffs on the 10th of October, to confer with them on objects interesting to the welfare and prosperity of the Chickasaw nation. Provision is made for all who may attend, and you will accompany them yourself, with your interpreter.

I have paid the express.

I am, with sincere regard and esteem, Sir,

Your obedient servant,

BENJAMIN HAWKINS,
    Agent for I. A. S. of Ohio.

MR. SAMUEL MITCHELL,
    Agent for the Chickasaws.

Bear Creek, 26th September, 1801.
MAJOR COLBERT:

I called here on my way to the Bluffs to see you and to inform you of the time fixed by the Commissioners of the U. S. for the conference with the chiefs and principal men of your nation at the Bluffs. It is to be on the 10th of October, provision is made for all who may attend, and as the object of the conference is the welfare and prosperity of the Chickasaws and of their white neighbours, I must request your attendance and that of your brothers and other principal chiefs and men of your nation.

I am, your friend and the friend of your nation,

BENJAMIN HAWKINS,
Agent for I. A. S. of Ohio.

Wilkinsonville, October 7th, 1801.

I wrote you from Occochappo the 26th ultimo, to inform you that the Commissioners were there and expected to be at the Bluffs by the 10th of this month. We cannot move so fast as I expected; we are now here and are to leave this to-morrow, and I do not believe we shall be able to reach the Bluffs till the 15th. Captain Roth goes off to-day and is the bearer of a letter from the Commissioners to the chiefs of your agency, announcing to them the period of our expected meeting with them.

The Indians must be supplied immediately as they arrive with provisions, and you will take order or their application for rations to prevent irregularity and waste.

I am, with sincere regard and esteem, Sir,
Your obedient servant,

BENJAMIN HAWKINS,
Agent for I. A. S. of Ohio.
MR. SAMUEL MITCHELL,
Agent for the Choctaws.

October 21st.

Minutes of a conference held at the Chickasaw Bluffs by General James Wilkinson, Benjamin Hawkins and Andrew Pickins, Esq., Commissioners of the United States, with the mingco, chiefs, and principal men of the Chickasaw nation, the 21st, and ending the 24 of October, 1801.

The parties being assembled, the following address was delivered by General Wilkinson, on the part of the Commissioners:

King, Chiefs, and Principal Men of the Chickasaw Nation:

You are now addressed by Commissioners from the United States, who have been appointed by your father, the President, to meet you in council and to confer with you on subjects interesting to your own welfare and to that of the citizens of the United States.

Your father, the President, takes you by the hand and invites you to look up to him as your friend and father, to rely in full confidence on his unvarying disposition to lead and protect you in the paths of peace and prosperity, and to preserve concord between you and your white brethren within the United States. We invite you to open your minds freely to us and to set forth nation and what you wish on the part of your father, the President, to better your condition in trade, in agriculture and manufactures, that we may state the same for the consideration of government. We invite you to open your minds freely to us and to set forth your wishes and all your wants. When we hear from you the true state of your affairs, we shall be able to assist you with our advise, our attention and our friendship.

On the part of your white brethren, we have to represent to you that the path from the settlements of Natches (thro' your nation) to those of Cumberland is an uncomfortable one and very inconvenient to them in its present unimproved condition, and we are directed to stipulate with you to make it suitable to the accommodation of those who may use it, and at he same time beneficial to yourselves.

We are your friends and the representatives of your father, the President.

After some explanations as to the accommodation to be established on the road, Major Colbert, a chief, observed that no answer could be given to-day; that they would have to consult with each other, and when they had made up their minds, they would speak to the Commissioners.

22nd.

The council being convened, Major Colbert requested the Commissioners to explain fully the views of the President with respect to the road, which was accordingly done. The Indians then went into a discussion of the subject among themselves. The

Commissioners being about to withdraw, Major Colbert observed the Indians wished to settle the business as soon as possible. After some time spent in deliberation in their own language the king spoke as follows: "I am very glad to hear the Commissioners hold such language that does not require the cession of land or any thing of that kind; I consider the propositions to be made for the benefit of our women and children."

Major Colbert being fully empowered by the council, gave its determination in the following words:

"The nation agrees that a waggon road may be cut thro' this land, but do's not consent to the erection of houses for the accommodation of travelers. We leave that subject to future consideration, in order that time may enable our people to ascertain the advantages to be derived from it. In the meantime travelers will always find provisions in the nation sufficient to carry them through."

The council then adjourned.

24th.

The council met, and the treaty being deliberately read and interpreted by sections and paragraphs, was signed by the contracting parties.

THE TREATY.

A treaty of reciprocal advantages and mutual convenience between the United States of America and the Chickasaws:

The President of the United States of America, by James Wilkinson, Brigadier General in the armies of the United States; Benjamin Hawkins, of North Carolina, and Andrew Pickins, of South Carolina, Commissioners of the United States, who are vested with full powers, and the Mingco, principal men and warriors of the Chickasaw nation, representing the said nation, have agreed on the following articles:

Article 1. The mingco, principal men and warriors of the Chickasaw nation of Indians give leave and permission to the President of the United States of America to lay out, open, and make a convenient waggon road through their lands, between the settlements of Moro District, in the State of Tennessee, and of those of Natches, in the Mississippi Territory, in such manner and way as he may deem proper; and the same shall be a highway for the citizens of the United States and the Chickasaws; and the Chickasaws shall appoint two discreet men who shall serve as assistant guides or pilots during the time of laying out and opening the said road, under the direction of the officer charged with this duty, who shall be paid a reasonable compensation for their service; provided always that the necessary ferries over the water courses crossed by the said road shall be held and deemed to be the property of the Chickasaw nation.

Article 2. The Commissioners of the United States give to the Mingco of the Chickasaws, and the deputation of that nation, goods of the value of 700 dollars, to compensate them and their attendants for the expence and inconvenience they may have sustained by their respectful and friendly attention to the President of the United States of America and to the request made to them in his name to permit the opening of the road; and as the persons, towns, villages, lands, hunting grounds and other rights and property of the Chickasaws, as set fourth in the treaty stipulations heretofore entered into between the contracting parties, more especially in and by a certificate of the President of the United States of America, under their seal of the 1st July, 1794, are in the peace and under the protection of the United States, the Commissioners of the United States do hereby further agree that the President of the United States of America shall take such measures, from time to time, as he may deem proper, to assist the Chickasaws to preserve entire all their rights against the encroachment of unjust neighbours, of which he shall be the judge; and also to preserve and to perpetuate friendship and brotherhood between the white people and the Chickasaws.

Article 3. The Commissioners of the United States may, if they deem it advisable, proceed immediately to carry the first article into operation, and the treaty shall take effect and be obligatory on the contracting parties as soon as the same shall have been ratified by the President of the United States of America, by and with the advise and consent of the Senate of the United States.

In testimony whereof the plenipotentiaries have hereunto ascribed their hands and affixed their seals at the Chickasaw Bluffs the 24th of October, 1801.

Chickasaw Bluffs, 25 October, 1801.

Sir:

We arrived on the 15th instant, and on the 21st we commenced our conference with a full and respectable deputation from the Chickasaw nation, headed by their mingco or king.

We found this people, like all others of their kind under similar circumstances, jealous of our views and alarmed for their rights of territory, but their confidence in the government had not been shaken, and we experienced little difficulty in accomplishing the treaty which we have the honour to transmit to you under cover for the consideration of the President and the Senate.

Perceiving the deputation to be strongly opposed to the proposition to introduce licenced establishments on the road, for the accommodation óf travelers, we waved that point without hesitation, because we are persuaded such accommodations will be provided by the natives themselves, or the whites among them, as soon as the highway is completed.

We enclose you the minutes of our conference for the satisfaction of the executive, and also an inventory of the goods delivered on the occasion, taken from an invoice of articles amounting to 2,696 dollars, which, with 200 gallons of whiskey and 1,000 lbs. of tobacco, comprehends all the goods and merchandize we have yet received for the purpose of our commission.

To aid and inform the officers who may superintend the construction of the proposed road, and to prevent misunderstandings, we have advised that two Indians, recommended by the deputation, should be employed to attend those officers until the guide line is established, and that the resident agent of the nation should accompany them. We are also of opinion that interpreters may be necessary with the working parties until a clear understanding of our engagements with the nation may be generally diffused; it is easier to prevent difficulties with people jealous, tenacious and ignorant, than to remove them after their occurrence.

It seems fortunate the Cherokees did not consent to open a road from Nashville to the Tennessee, because we find the proposed rout embraced by the limits of the Chickasaws, which have been clearly defined in that quarter, and explicitly recognized in a declaration of President Washington bearing date the 1st July, 1794, now in possession of the nation and corresponding with the authentic copy under cover, which has been furnished us by the mingco.

The whole deputation manifested great anxiety on this subject, and expressed a strong desire that we should acknowledge this declaration and renew the assurances attached to it, and it was on this ground, to prevent distrusts and to evince the integrity of the government, that we entered into the stipulation contained in the 2nd Article, viewing it in effect, as the mere repetition of an obligation which existed in full force.

We, with pleasure, bear testimony to the amicable and orderly disposition of this nation, whose greatest boast is they have never spilt the blood of a white man, but with those dispositions they are not so far advanced in the habits of civilization as their neigh-bours, the Cherokees, tho' they discover a taste for individual property, have made considerable progress in agriculture and in stocking their farms, and are desirous to increase their domestic manufactures.

The enclosed schedule of their wants, which the deputation have requested us to submit to the executive, strongly marks their views and their providence. "We are about to raise cotton," said a chief; "we shall want canoes to carry it to market, and azes are necessary to build them." We, with great deference, submit these claims of the Chickasaws to the consideration of the government, and were it not presumptuous, we would earnestly recommend to the council of our country a steady perseverance in that humane and beneficent system which has for its object the civilization and great salvation of a devoted race of human beings. The prospects of success become daily more flattering, but to insure it an exten-sion of the means and a reform in the application may be neces-sary.

It occurs to us that it may be salutory to compel all white persons who traverse the Chickasaw country to confine themselves to the highway proposed to be opened, for which end the authority of the National Legislature may be found expedient.

We have taken measures to convene the Choctaws at Loftus's Heights on the grounds of convenience and economy to the public and of accommodation to the inhabitants. and we expect to meet them there in council about the 20th of November

The Honourable
    HENRY DEARBORN,
        Secretary of War.

Chickasaw Bluffs, 28 October, 1801.

The Commissioners of the United States having closed their labours here, I will give you, in detail, some occurrences connected with the agency. When the chiefs first heard of the objects sup-posed to be in contemplation of the government, they expressed some fears and doubts, and with these they met the Commis-sioners. As soon as they were made acquainted with the objects intrusted to the Commission, and were assured that their lands were safe, they debated the propositions stated to them in our presence, refered the one establishing houses for the accommo-dation of travelers to the nation for their future determination, and conceeded the opening of a waggon road through their lands with a hearty good will. We could not mention the Post Occochappo without alarming the fears of the nation, and we judged it advisable to be silent on it.

The Chickasaws are setting out from their old towns and fencing their farms. They have established and fenced within two years nearly two hundred. All of these farmers have cattle or hogs and some of the men attend seriously to labour. Major Colbert, who ranks high in the government of his nation and was the speaker at the treaty here, has laboured at the plough and hoe during the last season, and his example has stimulated others. Several of the families have planted cotton, which grows well, and some of the women spin and weave. As they cannot count, they cannot warp without aid, but they know the process and perform with exactness when the threads are counted for them. They begin to have a taste for individual property, and are acquiring it by every means in their power.

Their land claims have been the theme of conversation at every meeting they have had with me. In the year 1795, at the Treaty of Hopewell, the Cherokees & these people contended about their claims, and it was generally understood that their claims, as detailed in the certificate of President Washington, were the best founded. I have once seen their old town on the Tennessee; as mentioned in the certificate, it is several miles above the Muscle Shoals and extended for 6 miles on the north side of the river.

After several years of effort the Chickasaws have been prevailed on to appoint a head to transact their business; they have now a mingco, who is the first chief of the nation, and a deliberative council.

The arrangements contemplated for the agency here is one agent, Samuel Mitchell, with a sallary of 800 dollars per annum, and 4 rations per day at the contract price for rations at the post in the agency, and one interpreter, Malcom McGee, mentioned in your favour of the 25th of March, has been appointed, by Colonel John McKee, agent for the Choctaws, interpreter, with a sallary of 30 dollars per month. I find McGee to be well qualified; he has a good memory, but cannot read; he is deemed honest; a man of great probity, and much confided in by the nation, where he has lived six and thirty years. William McClish has received pay as interpreter for several years, and now near Nashville, where there was a deposit of goods for the Indians; the whole proceedure I deem improper. I have directed McClish to be notified that he is no longer an interpreter. These lodgments have been made in the Indian Department under the auspices of people who should have no connexion with it. I equally dislike the regulations adopted at the military posts for the issue or rations, doing work for Indians, and having interpreters without the knowledge or participation of an agent. The military should move in their own sphere, and co-operate only with the Agency for Indian Affairs, when required thereto by an agent.

This rule I adopted with Colonel Gaither when he commanded on the frontiers of Georgia, and the beneficial effects resulting therefrom were soon discoverable. The Creeks, the most numerous, proud, haughty and ill behaved Indians in the agency South of Ohio, did not receive one year with another 1,000 rations, and these only to use on public business and at the request of the agent. This regulation was disliked at first; they claimed as a matter of rights, to be cloathed, fed and indulged at the military posts, and in revenge they crowded my table for the first year. I persevered in the regulation; they conformed, and now a chief who is going to the frontiers will come 20 or 30 miles to me to know if I have any commands which he can execute to get an order for provisions. An officer commanding a post cannot know any thing of Indian affairs; if complaints are made to him, he must refer them to the agent, and it would be better done in the first instance, and without the expence usually attendant, to let the complaint go to the agent; then if the injury sustained is really serious, and of a nature to require the aid of the civil or military authority, the agent has the aid of the old chiefs to prepare the mind to wait our mode of doing business, which at best is deemed slow by an Indian. On this subject you will hear again from me.

I have just received a letter from Colonel McKee; he writes 10 October: "You will have Choctaws enough, I fear more than enough, at Natches, tho' I doubt not a full representation of the nation; some of the most active chiefs could not be prevailed from going into the woods to hunt, a few of the most influential young chiefs I have prevailed on to stay; of the number is your acquaintance, Mingco Ham Massabba, and of the old kings and women and children you will have enough in number to make up for the want of weight.

The Commissioners have all had the fever of the climate and are now recovering and will soon be well.

I have the honour to be, with much esteem and regard, Sir,

                                        Your obedient servant.
The Honourable

HENRY DEARBORN,
Secretary of War.

Natches, November 13th, 1801.

Sir:

We arrived here yesterday at noon and shall proceed in a day of two to Loftus's Heights, where we expect to meet the Choctaws on the 20th instant, agreeable to our invitation forwarded to them through the proper channel from the Chickasaw Bluffs.

We have had the honour to receive the President's letter dated at Monticello, the 16th of September, and are happy to find he has been pleased to approbate our proposition respecting the change of place for holding the treaty with the Choctaws. We beg leave to assure you that we shall loose no time in terminating this conference, which we flatter ourselves may eventuate favourably.

Having closed our business with the Choctaws, we shall, after due deliberation, adopt the most feasible means for convincing the Creeks and shall regulate our movements accordingly.

JAMES WILKINSON.
B. HAWKINS.
A. PICKINS.

The Honourable
HENRY DEARBORN,
Secretary of War.

Natches, 14th November, 1801.

The Commissioners of the United States arrived here on the 12th and will leave to-morrow for Loftus's Heights. We have all had the fever of the climate and are recovering. Our tour down the pellucid Tennessee, opaque Ohio and muddy Mississippi has been tedious, and in the season unfavourable for health. Here I received dispatches from the Creek agency, the most interesting of which I communicate to you, without loss of time, by the mail of this day.

No. 1, a letter from Mr. Fateos; No. 2, from His Excellency, Henry White, His Catholic Majesty's Governor of East Florida; No. 3, from Timothy Barnard, one of my assistants and interpreters, who resides among the Lower Creeks, to Governor White; No. 4, from James Darouzeaux, interpreter, for his Catholic Majesty; No. 5, extract from the talk of the Lower Creeks and from Mr. Darouzeaux to the Upper Creeks; No. 6, report of Mr. Hill, an assistant, who resides among the Upper Creeks, & No. 7, from Timothy Barnard.

You have the character of Mr. Barnard in the sketch of the Creek country, which I forwarded to you in the course of the spring, and from his character, his long residence among the Indians, and his knowledge of their language, there can not be the least doubt but that his report to Governor White is strictly correct.

It is high time the affairs of His Catholic Majesty had taken effectual measures to vindicate the honour of their sovereign by the punishment of the Simanolees. They have long since allowed Bowles and his partizans full time to make the most of the means in his power for the accomplishment of his views. Their omission to take effectual and timely measures in these premises is likely to involve us in difficulties. The Simanolees being Creeks, their friends on our side of the Line of Limits will aid them as long as the conduct of the officers of Spain continues to be what it has uniformly been, coaxing, timid and wavering; the principle which operates most powerful on Indians is fear; this, when accompanyed with justice, secures a strong hold on the Indian mind. The officers of Spain in my neighbourhood have totally neglected the first; of course the train of evils which they experience is a necessary consequence.

I do not know whether it would be advisable for our government to complain to the Court of Spain of this remiss conduct of their officers, to urge them to do their duty and to wait the issue, or to take prompt and efficacious measures on our own part to do ourselves justice, altho' I retain the same opinion I formerly suggested to one of your neighbours on this subject in a proposition to put end to those disturbances which I stated for the consideration of the President.

In my letter of the 6th of September, I stated the custom of the old chiefs of the Creeks relative to their hunts, and that I found March, April and May the most favourable months to gather them together. In the latter months there is grass for the horses, provisions is scarce in their homes, and as they now return poor and hungry from their hunts, these will be two additional inducements to attend the treaty proposed to be held with them. I think the opinion of the Commissioners will be that some time in the spring will be the proper season to convene the Creeks, and in that case I shall return without loss of time to the Creek agency, General Pickins to his home, and General Wilkinson to the troops on the proposed road.

I have the honour to be, with much consideration & esteem, Sir,

Your obedient servant.

The Honourable
HENRY DEARBORN,
Secretary of War.

Minutes of a Conference between Brigadier General James Wilkinson, Benjamin Hawkins & Andrew Pickins, Esquires, Commissioners of the United States, and the Principal Chiefs of the Choctaw Nation of Indians, held at Fort Adams, the 12th day of December, 1801.

The conference commenced. The interpreters being called forth and warned to correct each other, & after having gone thro' the ceremonies of the pipe, General Wilkinson, in the name of the Commission, addressed them as follows:

Mingcos, Chiefs & Principal Men of the Choctaw Nation:

You have all heard of the death of your father, the great Washington, and you have no doubt wept for the loss; since we experienced that heavy misfortune the people of the sixteen fires assembled in their great national council house have thought proper to elect our beloved chief, Thomas Jefferson, to be President of these United States.

Brothers: Open your ears and listen well. Your new father, Jefferson, who is the friend of all the red people and of humanity, finding himself at the head of the white people of the sixteen fires, immediately turned his thoughts to the condition of his red children, who stand most in need of his care and whom he regards with the affection of a good father.

Brothers: Your father, the President of the U. S., being far removed from you by the intervention of deep rivers, high mountains and wide forests, finds it impossible to look upon you with his own eyes or to speak to you from his own lips; he has therefore appointed two of his beloved men, Colonel Hawkins & General Pickins, with myself, to meet you in council and to confer with you on several subjects interesting to yourselves and to your white brethren of the sixteen fires. We are happy to see you. We, on his behalf and in his name, take you by the hand and we congratulate you on your safe arrival here.

Brothers: The President of the U. S. invites you to look up to him as your friend & father, to rely in full confidence on his unvarying disposition to lead & protect you in the paths of peace & prosperity, and to preserve concord between you and your neighbours. In his name we promise you that you may at all times rely upon the friendship of the U. S., and that he will never abandon you or your children while your conduct towards the citizens of the U. S. and your Indian neighbours shall be peaceable, honest & fair.

Brothers: We invite you to state to us freely the situation of your nation, and what you wish on the part of your father, the President, to better your condition in trade, in hunting, agriculture, manufactures and stock raising, that we may represent the same for his consideration. We wish you to open your minds freely to us and to set forth all your wishes and all your wants, that we may learn the true state of your condition and be able to assist you with our advice, our attentions and our friendship.

Brothers: On the part of your white brethren, we have to state to you that the path from the settlements of Natches thro' your nation towards Cumberland is uncomfortable and very inconvenient to them in its present unimproved condition, and we are directed to stipulate with you to make it suitable to the accommodation of those who may use it & at the same time beneficial to yourselves. Your brethren, the Chickasaws, have heard our request on this subject and they have consented that we should open a road through their lands to those of your nation, and we now ask your consent that we may continue the same road through your lands to the settlements of this Territory. We propose, for the accommodation of travelers and for your interests, that houses of entertainment and ferries should be established on this road, and that they may be rented by you to such persons as your father, the President, may appoint to keep them; the ground, the houses and the money arising from the rents to be for the use of your nation and subject to its disposal, and that not more than one family be suffered to live at the same place.

Brothers: Since the King of Spain has given up this district to the United States, a necessity has arisen for frequent communications between your white brethren who live in the neighbourhood of the Mississippi and those who have settled on the Tombigbee, and it follows that people are constantly traveling across your country from one place to the other. Under such circumstances, to prevent disagreement and mischief, we leave to your confederation the expediency of having but one road of communication between these settlements, to be opened and improved after the same manner and on the same terms as that proposed from the settlements of this territory to the Chickasaw nation.

Brothers: We come not to ask lands from you, nor shall we ever ask for any unless you are disposed to sell, and your father will assist and protect you in the enjoyment of those you claim, but to prevent future misunderstandings and to confine the settlers of the territory within the line long since run between you and them, we recommend that it should be traced up and marked anew, while men can be found who were present at the survey and assisted in marking it, for if all these witnesses should die before this is done, then disputes may arise between you and your white brethren respecting the boundary and mischief may ensue.

Brothers: For several years past your father, the President of the U. S., has sent you a present of goods as a token of his friendship, which will be continued the present year, but you must recollect that you have never given any equivalent for this strong evidence of his paternal regard, and you must bear in mind that you are indebted for it to his generosity more than to his justice. Should his bounty be continued to you in future, you ought to be grateful for it, and should it be discontinued, you will have no cause to complain, as you have never given any thing to the U. S. in return.

Brothers: We wish you to let this talk sink deep into your hearts; we wish you to take time and reflect seriously on it, and when you have made up your minds, we shall listen to you with pleasure in the hope that you may enable us to make an agreeable report to our common father, the President of the U. S., and in the meantime, we shall be happy to contribute to your accommodation and the good of your nation.

Colonel Hawkins then addressed the Indians:

I was appointed, as you all know, by your father, Washington, to take care of the affairs of the four nations; I am continued in the same charge by your new father, Jefferson. I always have been the friend of the red people and relied on as such. You have heard the talk of the Commissioners who represent your father, the President, here; take it with you to your camp, examine well every point of it, and if you want any information, send for one or all of the Commissioners; we will attend you immediately. You have heard us here; make your own fire and we will hear your answer here, or at any other place you may choose. Do not hurry yourselves, we have plenty of provisions for you here and for the path home.

December 13th.

The chiefs met the Commissioners at their conference room and Tuskonahopoie, a chief of the lower towns, informed the Commissioners that there were seven chiefs from different towns, and he requested, on their behalf, that they might be heard separately, that each might speak for his own town, and that after they had spoken, that the young warriors might be heard and the same attention paid to their talks as to those of the chiefs.

The Commissioners replied: You will manage your affairs your own way, we will hear all of you patiently and with pleasure.

Tuskonahopoie then addressed the Commissioners:

To-day I meet the Commissioners here who have delivered to us the talks from the President. I am well pleased with his talks, which I have received from my brothers, the Commissioners, for the welfare of my nation. I take you three beloved men by the hand and hold you fast; you three Commissioners who have visited the Cherokees and Chickasaws. One request which you ask of my nation, the cuting of a road I grant; I grant it as a white road, as a path of peace and not as a path of war; one which is never to be stained. I understood yesterday that my father, the President, allowed me an annual present, and it should never be taken from me; it must have been a mistake of his officers, as I have not received any annual allowance. He must have given it to some other of my red brethren; I deny ever having received an annual gift. It has never been told to the chiefs of the nation through the interpreters that their father allowed them an annual present for their nation.

I forgot something when I spoke of presents, which I will now mention. We have received presents from our father, the President, part at the Walnut Hills and part at Natches. I, myself, and a few of the chiefs, with a few warriors, went to the Walnut Hills and the presents were but very small. I do not know whether these presents were concealed from us or not, but I know we got but few, not worth going after. A company of the war chiefs and warriors received the last spring past a few presents at the Bluffs, that is all. If there have been any others given, it must have been to idle Indians who are stragling about and do not attend to the talks of the chiefs of the nation.

There is an old boundary line between the white people and my nation, which was run before I was a chief of the nation. This line was run by the permission of the chiefs of the nation who were chiefs at that time. They understood when that line was run that they were to receive pay for those lands. These chiefs here present acknowledge the lands to be the white peoples land; they hold no claim on it, although they never received any pay for it. They wish the line to be marked anew and that it be done by some of both parties, as both should be present (meaning red and white people).

Tootehoomuh from the same district then spoke:

I thank the President, my father, for sending you three beloved men here to speak to me; I take you by the hand, hold you fast, and am going to speak to you. I grant the road to be cut which the chief, who spoke before me, granted. I grant the road only;

you may make it as firm, as good, and as strong as you will; there are no big water courses on it, and there is no occasion for canoes or ferries.

I speak now concerning an old line which was run when I was a boy; I wish for this line to be traced and marked anew. I do not know where the line is; I have been informed by some of the young men of my nation that there are white people and stock over it. We, chiefs of the nation, wish, if any are over our lines, that they may be moved back again by our brothers, the officers of the U. S., and that they would move them back with their stock.

Mingco Pooscoos, of Chickasawha town:

I am an old acquaintance here; I came here, with other chiefs of the nation, not to differ with them, but to join them in whatever they do. I understand this business plainly; you three siting there were sent by our father, the President, to speak to our nation. My talks are not long. I am here before you three beloved men. I am a man of but few words in my town; it is the lowest, but one, in my nation. My talks are not long; I hope this will be considered as if I had said a great deal. The first time I ever saw my friend, the General (Wilkinson), he appeared as if he wished to say a great deal; I objected; I was but one. I am a well wisher; the day will come when we head men will see each other. The road through our land to Tombigbee it is not in my power to grant; there are other chiefs who hold claims on those lands; my claim is but short. The white people travel the Line of Limits (between Spain and the U. S.); they are free to use that and any of the small paths.

Oakchume, of the upper towns:

I see you to-day in the shade of your own house. I am a poor distressed red man; I know not how to make anything; I am in the place here from the upper towns. My uncle was the great chief of the nation; kept all paths clean and swept out, long poles of peace, a number of officers and chiefs in his arms. He is gone, he is dead, he has left us behind. You three beloved men in my presence I am glad to see you; you may be my father for what I know; the Great Spirit above is over us all. I hold my five fingers, and with them I hold yours; mine are black, but I whiten them for the occasion.

I understood your great father, General Washington, was dead, and that the great council got together and appointed another in his stead, who has not forgot us and who loves us as our father, Washington, did, and I am glad to hear our father, the

President, wishes that the sun may shine bright over his red children. The Chickasaws are my old brothers; you visited them, and talked to them before I saw you here. I understand you asked them for a big path to be cut, a white path, a path of peace, and that they granted it to you as far as their claims extend. I grant it likewise. There are no big water courses; there are no big rivers nor creeks, and therefore no occasion for canoes; nor is there any occasion for horse boats. It is not our wish that there should be any houses built; the reason I give is that there is a number of warriors who might spoil something belonging to the occupiers of those houses, and the complaints would become troublesome to me and to the chiefs of my nation.

I speak next of the old line; I wish it to be traced up and marked over again. I claim part in it (meaning the line itself); those people who are over it I wish back again for fear they may destroy the line and it be lost. I have done.

Puckshunubbee, from the upper towns:

The old line that the other repeated; as far as I understood from my forefathers, I will name its course and the water courses it crosses: Begining at the Homochitto runing thence nearly a southwest course until it strikes the Standing Pines Creek, thence crosses the Bayou Pierre high up, and the Big Black; from thence it strikes the Mississippi at the mouth of Tallauhatche (Yauzoo); that line I wish may be renewed, that both parties may know their own. There are people over or on the line; it is my wish they may be removed immediately. Where the line runs along Bayou Pierre some whites are settled on this line and some over it; those over I wish may be removed; if there are none over, there is nothing spoiled.

From the information I have received from my forefathers, this Natches country belonged to red people; the whole of it, which is now settled by white people; but you Americans were not the first people who got this country from the red people. We sold our lands, but never got any value for it; this I speak from the information of old men. We did not sell them to you, and as we never received any thing for it, I wish you, our friends, to think of it and make us some compensation for it.

We are red people and you are white people; we did not come here to beg, we brought no property with us to purchase any thing, we came to do the business of our nation and return. The other chiefs have granted you this road; we don't wish the white people to go alone to make the road, we wish a few of the red people and an interpreter to go with them.

We of the upper towns district, a large district; I speak for them now; there is but one interpreter in our nation; he is a long distance from us; when we have business to do we wish to have our interpreter near. It is the wish of the upper towns to have an interpreter from among the white people who live with us, that we may do our business, with more satisfaction with the chiefs of the district. I have another request to ask of you for the distress of our nation; a blacksmith, who can do our work well, for the upper towns district. Another thing I have to request for our young women and halfbreeds; we want spining wheels and somebody to be sent among them to teach them to spin. I have nothing more to say; I have complied with the request of the Commissioners; I have done. Further, I have to ask concerning the blacksmith's tools; if the man leaves us, let him leave his tools, and they remain with us as the property of the upper towns district.

Elautaulau Hoomuh:

I am a stranger; this is the first time I ever saw the Americans; I came here; I am sorry that it appeared cloudy, but it has cleared off (alluding to the cloudy weather, which cleared off just as he began to speak). I understood by what I have heard, that you are authorized by our father, the President, to come and talk to us. I am glad to take you by the hand, which I do kindly, and am glad our father, the President, thinks of his red children. It is my wish, with the rest of the old chiefs, that the line may be marked anew. There are a number of water courses in our land and I wish the white people to keep no stock on them, or to build houses. I am done; my talk is short and I will shake hands with you.

The interpreter then stated that the chiefs directed him to inform the Commissioners the young warriors wished to be indulged with making their talks on paper at their encampment, if that would do, and to be supplied for that purpose with paper.

It was ordered accordingly, and the Commissioners adjourned.

14th December.

The young warriors sent from their camp a request that Colonel John McKee, their agent, might be allowed to attend them; he was ordered accordingly.

15th December.

The communications made from the deputation from the Choctaws, in their camp, to the Commissioners of the United States, thro' their agent, Colonel John McKee:

Bucshunabbe:

I am a factor and have been so for a long time; my merchant is in Mobile; I have traded for him until I am become old. I am a man of one heart and of one mind; white people make a number of fine things; my mind is not to be changed for these fine things, and if the people of Mobile are not able to supply us, I do not wish to look to other people to supply us; we are old, we cannot take all the supplies that may be offered to us; the trade of the Choctaw nation is my object; I do not look for any trade from this quarter. We wish that no people may from this quarter, cross the road we have granted, with trade to us; we receive our supplies from another quarter, and must make our remittances there. There are a number of people wanting to trade from this quarter; we do not wish the people of Bayou Pierre, Big Black and Walnut Hills to purchase skins from the red people. We do not apply for that trade; it is a trade interfering with ours, and stealing our property, who trade from other places. These people may introduce a trade of liquor amongst us; this may cause the death of our people, which has happened lately at Natches, for which we are sorry. I want our father to send us iron wedges, hand saws and augurs.

Mingco Hom Massatubby:

I understand our great father, General Washington, is dead, and that there is another beloved man appointed in his place, and that he is a well wisher and lover of us four standing nations of red people. Our old brothers, the Chickasaws, have granted a road from Cumberland as far south as their boundary. I grant a continuance of that road, which may be straightened, but the old path is not to be thrown away entirely and a new one made. We have been informed by the three beloved men that our father, the President, has sent us a yearly present we know nothing of; there are 3 other nations, perhaps some of them have received it. Another thing, our father, the President, has provided us, without being asked, that he would send people among us to learn our women to spin and weave. He has made us these promises; I will not ask for more; I ask for women to teach our women; these women may first go among our halfbreeds and teach them, and the thing will then extend itself; one will teach another, and the white people may return to their own people again. I want people qualified well to teach our women; not people who know nothing. I understand that such things are to be furnished as I wish, therefore as we have halfbreeds and others accustomed to work, I wish that ploughs may be sent us, weeding hoes, grubing hoes, axes, hand saws, augurs, iron wedges and a man to make wheels, and a small set of blacksmith's tools for a red man. Father (the P. of the U. S.), we have a number of warriors who use their guns for a living; I understand your goods are cheap; I wish you to send us on a supply of trade; I don't want this trade here (Fort Adams), this is a strange land; I want the store at Fort Stoddart or Fort Stephens. Father, I hold your talks strong; I hope you will hold ours fast also (i. e., grant what we ask). I wish the old marks of the line of demarkation between us and the whites to be marked over, and as our father has said, he has sent us on some thing every year; I hope it will be continued, altho' we have never received it. I hope that my father will comply with my request, as we have been informed by his beloved men that he is disposed to afford us aid.

We came here sober to do business and wish to return so, and request therefore that the liquor which we are informed our friends had provided for us may be retained in store, as it might be productive of evil.

Hoche Homo:

This is the talk of the chiefs and warriors. I am one of the children of the President who has seen him in his own house; I saw my father in the beloved council house in Philadelphia; he is now dead and I am informed there is another father to the red people, appointed to keep up the great council house. I have taken by the hand these three beloved men sent by my father, the President, to meet the Choctaws. I have received his talk by them, and put it in my heart, and send this of mine in return. With the other chiefs I have granted permission to the Commissioners to open the white road of peace asked for. Father, when you receive this, I hope you will hold it fast; the chain of friendship, like an iron chain, should never be broken. I have but a short talk and hope it will be remembered.

Shappa Homo:

I was present when my father, the President, talked with the Choctaws, Creeks, Cherokees, Chickasaws and four northern nations, and heard his good advise to his children. When I was in the beloved house all talks and all paths were whitened with every nation. I am well pleased that they are kept bright. I am glad there are some people alive yet belonging to that white house, who wish to take care of the red people. We give up the road; it is not to be settled by white people.

Edmond Folsome:

Mingco Hom Massatubby's talk is mine, except that he has forgot to ask for cotton cards. My people already make cloth; I know the advantage of it, and request that good cotton cards may be sent us.

Robert McClure:

A gin is a thing I asked for long ago; it was once offered to my nation & refused by our chiefs. I asked for it last July, but have received no answer; I now ask for it again; if this will be granted I wish to know soon. I am glad to hear it is the wish of our father, the President, to teach us to do such things as the whites can do; the sooner those things are supplied the better, for by long delay they may grow out of our young people's minds. We halfbreeds and young men wish to go to work, and the sooner we receive those things the sooner we will begin to learn. I want a blacksmith sent to the lower towns district with a good set of tools, which may not be at the disposal of the smith, but remains with us should he go away. Some of our young people may learn to use these tools, and we wish them to remain for the use of the district. My reason for asking this is that our interpreter may die and our agent be recalled by his superior and another sent us who may not live at the same place and may wish to remove the tools; we wish them to remain with us and our red children.

We red people do not know how to make iron and steel; we wish our father to send us these with the smith, &c., and when presents are sent on, we wish a true inventory of all the presents that we may know when we are cheated, and that the invoice may be lodged with one of our chiefs.

17 December.

The chiefs met the Commissioners of the U. S. in the council chamber and were addressed by the latter:

Mingcos, Chiefs and Principal men of the Choctaw Nation:

We have heard the talks you delivered to us the 13th, and we have since received your written addresses of the 15th instant; those talks and this address have sunk deep into our hearts; they give us great pleasure and must prove highly satisfactory to your father, the President of the United States, to whom we shall faithfully transmit them, because he will perceive therefrom that his red children of the Choctaw nation are wise, just, dutiful and affectionate.

Brothers: We are sorry to be informed that the goods heretofore forwarded to you by your father, the President of the United States, have been delivered to improper characters, and have not reached your hands; we will take care that those which his bounty may hereafter dispense to you shall be faithfully delivered, but to prevent misunderstanding, we think proper to repeat to you that although this bounty will be extended to you the present year, and may be hereafter continued to you, at the discretion of your father, the President, yet you must not look upon it as a right, or to claim it as a debt, because you have never given any thing for it.

Brothers: We shall faithfully report to your father, the President, your wants and your wishes, as set forth in your written address to us, and we have no doubt he will give attention to them and will endeavour to ameliorate your condition; on our own parts, we promise you every attention to your true interests, and that we will use our best exertions to promote all your laudable persuits and to advance your solid happiness.

Brothers: Your father, the President, knows as well how to reward his good children as he does to punish the bad; he has therefore authorized us to give to you at this time some arms and ammunition for your hunters and some goods for your old men & women, as a proof of his friendship and as an equivalent for your dutiful attentions to his request respecting the roads & the old line of demarkation.

Brothers: To avoid future misunderstandings, we, the Commissioners of the United States, have deemed it expedient to commit to record the agreement entered into with you, the mingcos, chiefs and warriors of the Choctaw nation at this time. By this measure we propose to prevent wicked men from encroaching upon the rights of either party, to inform those who may come after us, and to keep alive forever the good works of this council. We will now read and interpret this record to you, and we shall be ready to explain any doubts or difficulties which may arise, and a fair copy be lodged with your nation, to be appealed to should occasion ever render necessary. The treaty being then deliberately read by General Wilkinson and interpreted, paragraph by paragraph, was signed & sealed and a duplicate delivered to the head chief of the Choctaw nation.

The treaty is in the following words, viz.:

Treaty of Friendship, Limits and Accommodation Between the United States of America and the Choctaw Nation of Indians.

Thomas Jefferson, President of the United States of America, by James Wilkinson, of the State of Maryland, Brigadier General in the army of the United States; Benjamin Hawkins, of North Carolina, and Andrew Pickins, of South Carolina, Commissioners plenipotentiary of the United States on the one part, and the mingcos, principal men and warriors of the Choctaw nation, representing the said nation in council assembled, on the other part, have entered into the following articles and conditions, viz.:

Article 1. Whereas the United States in Congress assembled, did, by their Commissioners plenipotentiary, Benjamin Hawkins, Andrew Pickins and Joseph Martin, at a treaty held with the chiefs & head men of the Choctaw nation, at Hopewell, on the Koowee, the third day of January, in the year of our Lord one thousand seven hundred and eigtby-six, give peace to the said nation, and receive it into the favour and protection of the United States of America, it is agreed by the parties to these presents respectively, that the Choctaw nation, or such part of it as may reside within the limits of the United States, shall be and continue under the care and protection of the said States, and that the mutual confidence & friendship which are hereby acknowledged to subsist between the contracting parties, shall be maintained and perpetuated.

Article 2. The mingcos, principal men and warriors of the Choctaw nation of Indians, do hereby give their free consent that a convenient and durable waggon way may be explored, marked, opened, and made under the orders and instructions of the President of the United States, through their lands, to commence at the northern extremity of the settlements of the Mississippi Territory, and to be extended from thence by such routs as may be selected and surveyed under the authority of the President of the United States, until it shall strike the lands claimed by the Chickasaw nation, and the same shall be and continue forever, a highway for the citizens of the United States and the Choctaws; and the said Choctaws shall nominate two discreet men from their nation, who may be employed as assistants, guides, or pilots, during the time of laying out and opening the said highway, or so long as may be deemed expedient, under the direction of the officer charged with this duty, who shall receive a reasonable compensation for their services.

Article 3. The two contracting parties covenant and agree that the old line of demarkation, heretofore established by and between the officers of His Britanic Majesty and the Choctaw nation, which runs in a parallel direction with the Mississippi River and eastwardly thereof, shall be retained and plainly marked in such a way and manner as the President may direct, in the presence of two persons, to be appointed by the said nation; and the said nation does, by these presents, relinquish to the United States, and quit-claim forever, all their rights, title and pretension to the land lying between the said line and the Mississippi River, bounded south by the 31 degrees of north latitude and north by the Yazoo river where the said line shall strike the same; and on the part of the Commissioners it is agreed that all persons who may be settled beyond this line shall be removed within it on the side toward the Mississippi, together with their slaves, household furniture, tools, materials and stock, and that the cabbins or houses erected by such persons shall be demolished.

Article 4. The President of the United States may, at his discretion, proceed to execute the Second Article of this treaty, and the Third Article shall be carried into effect as soon as may be convenient to the government of the United States, and without unnecessary delay on the one part or the other, of which the President shall be the judge. The Choctaws to be seasonably advised by order of the President of the United States, of the time when and the place where the survey and marking of the old line, referred to in the preceeding article, will be commenced.

Article 5. The Commissioners of the United States, for and in consideration of the foregoing conceptions on the part of the Choctaw nation, and in full satisfaction for the same, do give and deliver to the mingcos, chiefs and warriors of the said nation, at the signing of these presents, the value of two thousand dollars in goods and merchandise, net cost of Philadelphia, the receipt whereof is hereby acknowledged, and they further engage to give three sets of blacksmith's tools to the said nation.

Article 6. This treaty shall take effect and be obligatory on the contracting parties so soon as the same shall be ratified by the President of the United States of America, by and with the advice and consent of the Senate thereof.

In testimony whereof the Commissioners plenipotentiary of the United States and the mingcos, principal men and warriors of the Choctaw nation have hereto subscribed their names and affixed their seals, at Fort Adams, on the Mississippi, this seventeenth day of December, in the year of our Lord one thousand eight hundred and one, and of the independence of the United States the twenty-sixth.

December 18.

In conformity with the directions of the Commissioners, the whole deputation of the Choctaw nation attended at the council chamber and received from the Commissioners the goods promised, being of the value of 2,038 dollars, exclusive of tobacco, with which the Indians appeared to be well pleased, and they parted with the Commissioners with apparent good humour. In addition to the provisions they had received, the Commissioners ordered them to be furnished with twelve rations each for the path home.

Loftus's Heights, Fort Adams, on the Mississippi, Dec. 18, 1801.

Sir:

After some unexpected delay on the part of the Choctaws, we opened our conferences with a respectable representation from the upper and lower towns, which comprehended the mass of the nation and essential representation of the six towns which continue their attachment to Spain, and are now at New Orleans, on the invitation of the Governor, as we are informed.

This humble, friendly, tranquil, pacific people offered but few obstacles to our views, and we yesterday concluded a treaty with them, which we now transmit you, for the consideration of the President & the Senate.

Our minutes, which we herewith forward to you, will explain in detail the course of the conference held on this occasion, and may we hope, give satisfaction. We forebore to press for the establishment of houses of entertainment on the road, from respect to the objections of the chiefs, and from the conviction (founded on minute enquiry) that it would be extremely difficult, if not impracticable, to give protection to each solitary, sequestered settlement (where made by citizens of the United Sates) against the rapacity and abuse of vicious, mischievous individuals, to be found in every community, civil or savage.

The obvious expediency of the thing suggested to us the proposition for opening the road to the settlements of the Tombigbee and Mobile, and we have no doubt we should have succeeded if the six towns, through which the present trace passes, had been fully represented. Having received no instructions on this subject, we did not consider ourselves authorized to reply to the objections of the council, but connected with it we will beg leave to submit to the consideration of the executive the policy and propriety, not to say necessity, of devising some plan by which the extinguished claims of the natives on the Mobile, Tombigbee and Alabama Rivers may be ascertained and fixed. Unlicensed settlements have been made on those waters; they have been formed into a county by the late Governor of the Mississippi Territory and are now progressing; they are now thinly scattered along the western banks of the Mobile and Tombigbee for more than seventy miles, and extend nearly twenty-five miles upon the eastern borders of the Mobile and Alabama; the whole population may be estimated at five hundred whites and two hundred and fifty blacks, of all ages and sexes. The land east of the Mobile and Alabama Rivers is claimed by the Creeks; that which lies west of those rivers by the Choctaws. These nations view with jealousy and inquietude the progression of the above settlements; individuals among them acknowledge that concessions of soil were made to the British Government long since, and the whole appear anxious to have the lines fairly defined and their limits established. We believe this to be reasonable, and we are persuaded it is necessary to avert mischief.

The recognition of the old line to bound our right of settlement on the east in this quarter, and the stipulations, which have been founded thereon, we consider of some moment, because it appears to be a questionable point whether that line was ever extended farther south than the Hounchitto River, which would leave a considerable proportion of the population of the territory on the lands of the Indians, and therefore to obviate eventual difficulties, we embraced the concession to obtain from the nation a formal relinquishment of their claims under specific limits. The equivalent we have given to legitimate the contract into which we have entered, has been taken from the residue of the invoice for two thousand six hundred and ninety-six dollars worth of goods, out of which we paid the Chickasaws seven hundred dollars, & we trust this allowance may not be deemed profuse.

The Choctaw nation, in point of physical powers, is at least on a level with its neighbours, and its dispositions in relation to the whites are more tractable and less sanguinary than those of its kind, yet it has been long buried in sloth and ignorance; but the destruction of years has diminished the resorts of their ancestors, and the chase has become a precarious source of the support of life; goaded by penury, and pressed by the keenest wants to which animal nature is exposed, their sufferings seem to have roused their dormant faculties, and the rising generation urged by these powerful motives and encouraged by the examples of the Creeks on the one side and the Chickasaws on the other, have rent the shakles of prejudice, and in spite of repugnance of their old chiefs, are now casting their eyes to the earth for sustenance and for comforts. A very few families have commenced the culture of cotton, and it is not manufactured by more than twelve in the whole nation whose population exceeds fifteen thousand.

At this conference, for the first time, the bounty of the United States has been implored and we were supplicated for materials, tools, implements and instructors to aid their exertions and to direct their labours. These circumstances induce us to cherish the hope that by the liberal and well directed attention of the government this people may be made happy and useful, and that the United States may be saved the pain and expence of expelling or destroying them. It is a singular fact, perhaps it is without example, and therefore it is worthy of record, that this council should not only reject a quantity of whiskey intended as a present to them, but should have requested that none might be issued before, during, or after the conference.

We have deemed it expedient to recommend that an interpreter should attend the two deputies of the nation who are to accompany the troops to be engaged on the road, and we beg leave to offer the suggestion that travelers who pass through the Indian country should be confined to this rout so soon as it is opened.

With great consideration & respect, we are, &c.,

JA. WILKINSON.
BENJAMIN HAWKINS.
ANDREW PICKINS.

The Honourable
HENRY DEARBORN,
Secretary of War.

———

Fort Adams, 21st December, 1801.

Relying on the information we have received, that it is impracticable to convene the Creek chiefs in the winter, as they are in the habit of going during that season into the woods, and returning with the spring, we have fixed on the first of May for the conference with that nation at Fort Wilkinson.

We have the honour, &c.

The Honourable
HENRY DEARBORN,
Secretary of War.

———

Fort Adams, December 21, 1801.

The Commissioners of the United States having closed their labours here, I set out in the morning, with General Pickins, to the Creek agency; there I shall remain, and he will return home till the period fixed for the conference with that nation. The quartermaster here has furnished us with the necessary camp equipage and horses to take us and our baggage through the woods. The season is uncomfortable and we have 500 miles to my residence and 280 from thence to General Pickins's.

The arrangements contemplated for the agency here is one agent, one interpreter, to reside with him and one for the upper towns. As these people border on the proposed road, it is necessary to have a man among them to watch over their conduct for their benefit & the security of travelers. Turner Brasshear resides among them; he is a native of Maryland, of good character, understands the Indian language and appears to me to be fit for the appointment. The allowance to such a character should not exceed 300 dollars per annum. On the subject of rations to the agent, I am of opinion they should be increased to six, and this will not meet his expenditures for the present, but he must be satisfied with it & regulate himself accordingly. The chiefs, on all important occasions, visit the agents, and often on slight ones, and always with dependants, and he must receive and treat them with attention. Travelers are in the habit of calling on him, and persons of all discriptions, who feel themselves aggrieved, call on him for redress. There are as yet no houses for entertainment; of course they are a tax on his hospitality.

I have repeatedly expressed my disapprobation of the practice of issuing rations to Indians at military posts without the knowledge of the agent. The idle and the worthless are generally fed thereby, greatly to the injury of the plan of civilization. Coupled with this is the custom and error from pure motives heretofore in use among the military gentlemen, of giving certificates to chiefs and others, some times of very worthless, and at best, of doubtful characters. These certificates are lent from one to another, & are used to obtain rations at the posts and accommodations on the rout thro' the settlements to those who possess them. I have been plagued with the possessors of them for several years, & restrained, by respect for gentlemen holding commissions from the same source as my own, from taking them in and destroying them. I have expressed my ideas on this subject to the General, who has repeatedly declared to me his willingness to remedy the abuses complained of. I wish the military gentlemen to move in their own sphere, and co-operate only with the Agency for Indian Affairs when required thereto by an agent.

I shall write you soon; in the meantime I pray you to believe me, with sincere regard & esteem, Sir,

Your obedient servant.

To The Honourable,
THE SECRETARY OF WAR.

Journal of occurrences at Fort Wilkinson during the conference and treaty with the Creek Indians there, by Benjamin Hawkins.

———

April 30th, 1802.

Colonel Hawkins left Tuckabatchee on the 25th and arrived at Fort Wilkinson this day.

———

Fort Wilkinson, 2nd May, 1802.

I have to acknowledge the receipt of your favours of the 19th of January, 1st of March, enclosing circular orders to the Territorial Governors, the 22nd of February, and a letter under cover fronted by you the 21st of March; the two last the 26th of April on my way to this place where I arrived on the 30th.

I send you, agreeable to your request, a copy of our negotiations and treaty with the Choctaws, and of the letter of the Commissioners. I have no copy with me of my letter on the affairs of that nation, which accompanyed the original dispatches of the Commissioners; it is at my residence at Tuckabatchee, and shall be forwarded as soon as I have it in my power.

I have been much crowded by Indians for the last three months, at my residence. The chiefs appeared greatly agitated on the affairs of their nation, and on the probable objects of the conference proposed to be held with them at this place. I gave all a hospitable reception, and availed myself of the occasion to impress on them that in the hour of their difficulties they would be safe if they relyed firmly on the justice of the United States and the friendship of the President; an opportunity now offered to state all they had on their minds for the consideration of the government, to hear what the Commissioners have to say to them, and to make such friendly regulations with them as may tend to the mutual happiness and prosperity of them and their neighbours.

I gave no detail of the objects of the commission. On occasions only when they stated their poverty, and contrasted the present scarcity of game and withdrawing of presents, with former times of plenty and British profusion, I recommended to them to sell some of their waste lands to meet the present and future wants of the old chiefs, the poor and indigent; to rely firmly on the justice and benevolence of the United States, and the friendship of the President, and for the rest to give the plan devised for their civilization a fair trial among the young and middle aged. On these conditions I promised, in the name of the President, that poverty should be a stranger in their land, and that the difficulties and perplexities occasioned by the thieves, the lyars and the mischiefmakers should be banished from it.

Being apprised in March, by some Indians in my confidence, of an attempt to be made in April by the mischiefmakers to disturb the peace of the Indians, and to draw them off towards the Simanolees, under the pretence of meeting an embassy from the Governor of Providence and a ship loaded with goods for the Indians, I determined to seize the present moment to alarm the illdisposed by an act of signal justice. I was informed of the haunt of an Indian who scalped and otherwise illtreated a Mrs. Smith on Tombigbee, about four years past, and had been absent and outlawed by the nation. I called on the three leading warriors of the upper towns to have him put to death with the least possible delay; they accordingly sent four suitable characters early in April who came up with and shot him, and one of the leading warriors came with the head of the family, a good man, who made the report to me in a solemn formal manner. The welldisposed throughout the nation rejoiced at it, and the chiefs sent to me to give them the necessary days for preparation for the path, and they would set out accordingly to meet the Commissioners here. They were to move from the upper towns on the 26th ult., and I expect many of them here on the 4th and 5th. My journal during this period and to the last of April is now copying and will be sent by the next mail when I shall write you again.

I have the honour to be very respectfully Sir.

The Honourable
HENRY DEARBORN,
Secretary of War.

General Pickins has arrived since writing this letter; we have no news of General Wilkinson, he was to be at my residence the 20th of April; I waited for him to the 25th and heard nothing of him.

May 2nd.

Being informed that there were no arrangements made to feed the Indians at the proposed conference, I sent for the contracter's agent, who informed me "they had received no orders on that head from the Secretary of War; that they had a large supply of salt provisions on hand, a plenty of salt, some flower and corn meal, and that there was plenty of flower in the country and some of it convenient to Fort Wilkinson; that the only article they were deficient in would be beef, & that Mr. Grymes, a partner of the contractor, would be here in a day or two."

3rd of May.

Mr. Grymes reported as his assistant, and added that he could supply the rations wanted if he had or could get beef; he was only deficient in the article of fresh beef, the beef in the settlements was not yet fit to eat, and he had some dependence on a supply from the Indians, and had some goods suited to the Indians, but he was in want of money, and a supply would be absolutely necessary to enable him to get beef.

Reply of Colonel Hawkins.

I expected orders here for the supply of rations; last year the Commissioners of the United States were informed that the contractor of this post had orders to furnish the necessary supplies; since then I have received no further information. If no orders should soon arrive, I shall give the necessary orders, but I expect to hear from the Secretary of War by the next mail, and until then I cannot give any directions on that head. The rations for Indians will be meat and meal only, and they will want beef.

Upon the arrival of General Pickins, the Commissioners order that the rations to Indians shall be a pound and an half of flower and a like quantity of fresh beef, and that salt and tobacco shall be issued as wanted, and under the direction of the assistant agent, Mr. Barnard.

5th May.

Received dispatches from the Secretary of War of the 12th ult., enclosing definitive instructions to the Commissioners, and information that the United States factor was to supply the necessary provisions and other accommodations for them and for the Indians who may attend the treaty.

Mr. Halstead, the United States factor, was informed of the order; he said he had not received any information on the subject, but would proceed immediately to fulfill the duties enjoined on him. Colonel Hawkins ordered that all the assistants in his department and the Indian countrymen to assist the factor, and to execute his orders during the treaty. Runners were immediately sent to the stockholders in the Creek country to send on, without delay, a supply of beef.

The following orders were issued by Colonel Hawkins: The deputation from every town must appoint one man to attend the drawing of provisions for his town; he will report the number to Mr. Barnard and receive from him a ticket for two day's provisions at a time, and Mr. Barnard will, at discretion, issue salt and tobacco. Spirits are only to be issued on the orders of the Commissioners. The white people from the Indian country will assist the white people who weigh out provisions.

Mr. Grymes was informed of the order of the Secretary of War for the supply of provisions to the Indians.

8th May.

General Wilkinson arrived. A runner arrived to inform Colonel Hawkins "that the chiefs were in motion pretty generally, and would be on as soon as they could, but not as soon as was expected, and that notwithstanding the misrepresentations of the partizans of Bowles, who were seting out for St. Mark's, the nation would be with him."

Colonel Hawkins to the Secretary of War.

Fort Wilkinson, 8th May, 1802.

I have had the pleasure to receive your favour of the 7th ult. by the last mail; the officers of his Catholic Majesty have no just cause of complaint against the Creek nation, and have received substantial and repeated proofs of a disposition here friendly and determined to carry their national engagements into effect. On the 17 September, 1799, a banditti from Talassee, in this agency of 21 only, went to the Simanolees and there, conjointly with the Simanolees, insulted the Commandants of Spain and the United States, at their encampment on the Spanish side of the Line of Limits in East Florida near the confluence of Flint and Chattahoochee. I called on the chief, being myself a witness to the fact, to punish immediately the leader and his associates in an examplary manner; they sentenced the leader to be roped and whiped, his property destroyed, and his associates whiped; and this sentence was carried into effect on him and three of his associates by 72 warriors, under directions of their great chief, and in presence of Mr. Cornell, one of my assistants and interpreters. The whole was reported to the Commissioners, to the Secretary of War, and to the Governor of Pensacola, with such assurances as were proper on my part.

Some time in May, 1800, being informed that Tussekiably, a chief on our side of the line, had been towards Pensacola and stole some horses, I, without waiting to hear from the Governor Folch there, sent nine warriors under a distinguished leader, who whiped with great severity the chief and took six horses from him which were restored. The chiefs of the nation being convened, approved highly of this act and sent two of their men to accompany the dragoons who came after the horses, to ensure their safe arrival at Pensacola, with assurances of a peaceable and friendly deportment towards the subjects of his Catholic Majesty in W. Florida, and from arrangements made and under my control, these assurances have hitherto been fulfilled.

Towards East Florida, notwithstanding the Simanolees, are Creeks, and they have their connexions among our towns on Chattahoochee; the fears of a co-operation hitherto from this quarter were imaginary. The Indians on our side have not co-operated, but in a few instances; feeble in point of number, and those outlaws and fugitives from justice only. The expectation of presents has frequently induced some of them in numbers, men, women, and children to go down towards St. Mark's on the invitations of Mr. Bowles. These expectations were founded on assurances from that quarter that he was there under the auspices of Great Britain, and would receive presents from thence for the red people; and while he promised, they continued to hope for the fulfillment of them, and this hope still makes a lively impression on their minds, as he attributes his failures to the hostility of Spain and to captures made by the privateers of that nation.

There has been no negros nor property brought within our limits and Mr. Bowles has been but twice only, and then but for a short time within our limits. His residence is at Miccosooke, about 30 miles from St. Mark's, and his effective force is generally estimated by us at not more than 60 Indians, and they are more attentive to frolicking than fighting, and more desirous of property than sheding of blood. The reward offered for Mr. Bowles was 4,500 dollars by Governor Folch of Pensacola, and at his request, I had his offer interpreted to the chiefs in a convention of the nation; and it is a trait in the Indian character worthy of record, that notwithstanding the poverty and nakedness of the Indians, no one has been found to get the reward.

I have corresponded with the Governor of Pensacola and the Governor General of New Orleans, and advised the first particularly of every occurrence in the Creek agency interesting to the subjects of his Catholic Majesty, our neighbours. I will avail myself of every apportunity to do the like with Governor White of St. Augustine; it is high time the officers of his C. M. had taken effectual measures to vindicate the rights of their sovereign.

During the war in Europe, I could attribute their continued state of preparation without action to imperious circumstnces, and I contributed all in my power to protect their defenseless borders from the predatory warfare of their Simanolee Indians, aided by the mischiefmakers within our boundary, and had the pleasure to see that to the plans devised by me and carried into effect, they owed the safety they have enjoyed in W. Florida.

Mr. Bowles has had full time to make the most of the means in his power for the accomplishment of his views, and the officers of Spain must give up the Floridas or fight for them. If the officers of Spain will not act with vigour and a show of force on their part, they need not apprehend any thing from our Indians. If on the contrary, their conduct continues as it has been, coaxing, timid and wavering, they will be embarrassed and embarrass us. Our Indians near them will join in the predatory warfare.

I have the honor to be, with much esteem & regard,

Your obedient servant.

10th of May.

The Commissioners of the United States to the Secretary of War:

Fort Wilkinson, 10 May, 1802.

Sir:

We have the honour to acknowledge the receipt of your dispatch of the 12th ult., covering instructions for our government pending our conference with the Creek nation, to which we shall pay strict regard, and you may rest assured no exertion on our part shall be omitted to accomplish the views of the executive, and to make the desired impression on the public mind of the State of Georgia.

The importance of the objects for which we are to treat, suggests difficulties to us, but we will struggle to surmount them, and in the meantime we take the liberty to recall your attention to the third article of our instructions, which directs us to obtain the consent of the Creeks, if practicable, to the extension of the present boundary between Tugalo and Apalatchee Rivers. Should we succeed in the pending negotiation to obtain the concession of the Creeks, it will be considered by the Cherokees as a trespass on their territory, and will actually include a considerable tract claimed by them and heretofore disclaimed by the Creeks, particularly to Colonel Hawkins, the Commissioners of the United

States, and the· Commissioners of Georgia, for runing the line
before mentioned. These Commissioners, begining at the Apalatchee and proceeding northwards towards the Tugalo, found the
attending chiefs of the Creeks averse to accompanying them
further than the middle fork of Oconee River, but by the pressing
insistance of Colonel Hawkins, they proceeded as far as the
Currahee Mountain beyond which they positively refused to
march a step into a country which, to use their own language,
they "neither knew nor claimed;" for confirmation of these facts,
we refer to the treaty of Hopewell and to the personal knowledge
of Colonel Hawkins and General Pickins, and we beg leave to add
that the settlement of Colonel Wofford, which consists at present
of about sixty families, is included by the claims of the Cherokees
and not by the claims of the Creeks.

We are induced to believe cash will be most acceptable to
the Indians for any concession they may make, and we are persuaded it may be rendered most useful to them. The suspension
of the negotiations for a short period will not be difficult or
unfavourable to the views of the government.

We are &c.

Fort Wilkinson, 10th May, 1802.

The Commissioners of the U. S. to Governor Tattnall of Georgia:

In obedience to the instructions of the President of the United
States, and with the most cordial disposition, we have the honour
to assure your excellency that we shall procrastinate the pending
treaty with the Creek nation at this place, to accommodate the
views of the government over which you preside, and that we
shall take great pleasure in co-operating with your excellency
to the extent of our authority for the promotion of the good
people of the state.

With high consideration and perfect respect, we have the
honour to be,

Your Excellency's obedient servants.

May the 11th.

The Commissioners having determined to move out and encamp with the Indians, they chose a suitable place, visited the
Indian encampment, and communicated their intention to the

chiefs; the chiefs were pleased with the communication of the Commissioners, & ordered two of their Micos to go and examine the ground pointed out to them, that they might encamp in a body together and have their council house in a central position.

Colonel Hawkins informed the chiefs that he had provided such things as he had promised them for the ceremonies usual on such occasions among the Indians, which he would deliver to the chiefs at any time; that they were on their own ground and must make their own arrangements for their camp and council house; if for the latter they required the aid of the white people it would be furnished on the application of the chiefs; that on this occasion the Commissioners would attend and confer with them in their own council house, and at their own council fire, as they looked on the red and white people as people of one great family under one chief, the President of the United States, for all national objects.

Mr. Cornell informed Colonel Hawkins that the partizans of Bowles had moved on towards St. Mark's, and did every thing in their power to frustrate the proposed conference, but without effect, as he hoped and believed, and that he expected the representation would be numerous and respectable, but would not arrive as soon as was expected when the invitation was first given out.

Colonel Hawkins directed Mr. Cornell to inform the chiefs that they must take time for their arrangements; there was no necessity for hurrying any thing; the Commissioners had provided every thing for their accommodation and they must rest themselves and wait for their brethren.

12 May.

General Wilkinson informed the Commissioners that he wished for an opportunity to visit Louisville, and as they were now, by their instructions, to retard the proposed conference, if his colleagues approved of his going, he would be the bearer of their letter to the Governor and contribute what they might deem advisable to promote the views of the government; after some deliberation on the subject, it was determined that the General should go as soon as should be convenient for him, & that his colleagues should address another letter to the Governor suitable to the occasion.

Received information from Fort James that a party of Spanish horse, 12 or 13 in number, had attacked the Muskette town, a small one belonging to the Simanolees, killed one Indian, burnt the town, and took some horses, skins, &c., with the loss of one man and one horse; and from Oketeqockenne, a town on Chattahoochee, that some Indians of that town had been towards Pensacola, plundered some property, and brought off some horses belonging to the subjects of Spain, and among them five horses belonging to Tom Miller, a citizen of the United States, who for the present is at the residence of his late brother Jack Miller, on the east side of Koonecuh, in West Florida, and having discovered some of the horses were Miller's the thieves sent them back.

Upon the requisition of Colonel Hawkins the chiefs dispatched runners to the lower towns to cause justice to be done.

16 May.

Colonel Hawkins to the Secretary of War:

Owing to some alteration in the transportation of the mail I am informed that my communications intended to be sent the last mail will go by this; you will see in my journal the mode adopted by me to prepare the Indian mind to dispose of some of their lands, as well as a sketch of some of the difficulties with which I am surrounded.

We have now the most numerous and respectable representation I have ever seen of the Creek nation; they are forming their encampment and mean to conduct their affairs with great solemnity. We shall encamp out with them two or three miles from this garrison.

I cannot give you as yet any opinion how our mission will eventuate; the chiefs are importunate for presents, and have repeatedly urged me, and some times rudely so, to accommodate their wants or to introduce them to the Commissioners that they may, conjointly with me, accommodate them; I have not deviated from the course detailed in my journal. I shall avail myself of the existing state of things to further by every means in my power the objects of the government; and if the disturbances among the Simanolees had subsided, being compelled to yield to a dignified and energetic conduct on the part of Spain, the time would have been a favourable one.

I am informed that a party of Spanish horse surprised and destroyed a small town of the Simanolees, killed one and took some horses, skins, etc., with the loss of one man and one horse; and that a party of Indians from Oketeqockenne, a town low down on Chattahoochee, in this agency, have been towards Pensacola and brought off some horses, and that the adherents to the system of plunder devised by Mr. Bowles have pretty generally gone down to St. Mark's on an invitation of his.

The expenditures in this agency for the last year were drawn for as reported to you in favour of Mr. Edward Wright, U. S. factor; at 10 days sight, he had no opportunity of selling them here, and after keeping them by him for a long time, sent Mr. Hill with them, for the first and two last quarters, to Savannah and Charleston, to the collectors of the revenue there, to take them up or to sell them. Mr. Hill has returned; the collectors had no orders to take them up; he could not sell but on credit, and he has brought them back. The assistants in the department are much inconvenienced by the delay, as they are all needy and have no other dependence but their pay for their support. I must request the favour of your interposition to secure a regular payment in such way as you may judge proper.

Fort Wilkinson, 17 May.

The Commissioners of the United States addressed a letter to your excellency the 10th of this month; since then the Creek representation have arrived, more full and respectable than we have ever known them to be.

As we are sensible of the real & sincere disposition of the general government to make every exertion in its power for the accommodation of Georgia and citizens of Georgia in whatever may depend on the conference proposed to be held at this place with the Creek Indians, we have judged it advisable for General Wilkinson to wait on your excellency to have a personal conference with you to obtain such advise, aid or agency as may be considered useful and proper by your government. We wish we could ourselves accompany him, but it is necessary we should remain with the Indians at this crisis, to use our best exertions to promote the views of the government, and we wish it may be convenient for you, and that you would do us the favour to visit and aid us yourself during the conference; let it eventuate as it may, we trust such a measure would be beneficial to the State of Georgia.

We have the honour to be, Sir,
Your obedient servants,

BENJAMIN HAWKINS.
ANDREW PICKINS.

To the Governor of the State of Georgia.

May the 19th.

Tussekiah Mico, with Mr. Cornell, the interpreter, called on Colonel Hawkins and made this communication: "The chiefs are embarrassed in an affair that requires the advise and assistance of Colonel Hawkins, and they have sent us to inform him that the warriors sent after the murderer of Moreland have returned, and without success; the murderer is concealed and protected near Kennard's, and it appears that the failure may be attributed to Yeauholau Mico, of Coweta, Tustunnagau Hopoie, of Coweta Tallauhassee, and Jack Kennard. In this state of things the chiefs know not what to do; it has occured to them to make two representations to Colonel Hawkins, the one that the murderer being out of reach, they can and will, if required by him, give, according to the Indian rule, one of the family, a bad man and somewhat instrumental in his escape (Succuh Haujo); this man is now here and can be executed immediately, or delivered up, as Colonel Hawkins will direct. As this offer is made with some apprehension from the doctrine of Colonel Hawkins on guilt and innocence, that it will not be approved of, the other is that Colonel Hawkins will permit the chiefs, in a body, to bring and deliver this man, fast bound, to him, and that he will send him off and keep him closely confined in iron, if he will so order, until the guilty one can be come at. The chiefs are of the opinion that when this man is sent off, if Colonel Hawkins will permit them to report that he is executed, that the murderer will return and they will put him to death. The conduct of the chiefs in the satisfaction demanded in the present case has placed them in the present crisis of their affairs in a situation painful and humiliating, as they know what they have promised and Colonel Hawkins knows that they have failed to fulfill their promise and he knows how they have come to have failed.

Their friend and father Washington is dead, and they see but one of his men alive, who brought the beloved talks into their land; he is now sickly and if he should die before they get their affairs settled, they should be in a miserable situation. Colonel Hawkins has been long with them, knows their ways, and is, by his conduct, an old chief of their land; they come to him, he must order in this case and the chiefs will obey."

Colonel Hawkins's Reply.

I know the whole of this transaction as well as the chiefs themselves. Before the murderer was found out I had assurances given me by the chiefs of the lower towns, in a body, that the murderer should be executed as soon as discovered, and the four men were named who were to fulfill this promise. These assurances were made with so much solemnity that I had no right to doubt them and sent accordingly to the Governor of Georgia. They have not been fulfilled, and I shall speak on this affair in the square of all the chiefs as soon as they are ready to meet the Commissioners. On one point I can speak positively, I will have no innocent man punished, and I shall not hold those innocent who have suffered the guilty to escape, and who's duty it was to aid in punishing him.

The proposition relative to confining a man as you propose, I will refer to my colleagues; as for myself, I am a man of plain dealing and dispise duplicity. I will ask you a question which you will carry to the old chiefs for them to reflect on and for them to answer: How is it that the old chiefs who send you to me, who are wise and honest men, should think of offering Succuh Haujo because he is a worthless man and one of the family of the murderer, and not the three great chiefs to whom they attribute the failure?

If your confidence is really placed in me, in this and on all other affairs, open your minds freely to the Commissioners of the United States, and put your heads together with theirs and enter into such arrangements as will be for the present and future welfare of the Creeks.

Tussekiah Mico rejoined: "I am greatly troubled, and the old chiefs with me; we have now our two friends who met us at Colerain and entered into a treaty with us for the good of our land. I was greatly in hopes we should be able to meet them like men, but we must hang our heads and we shall never meet them again, and have not done what we promised in our treaty with them."

20th May.

Ordered in future that the issues shall be to towns and not to camps, that the tickets be made out in the public square on the report of the chiefs there, and that Mr. Hill and Mr. Barnard attend to the execution of the order; tobacco and salt to be issued in like manner as provisions. The Indians coming on business, or who may arrive in small parties, to be supplied till the regular issue to their town, in which they will be included.

Colonel Hawkins visited the public square of the chiefs and spent the day with them; there were present 150. The conversation turned generally on the internal affairs of the nation, and of the other three nations. Colonel Hawkins read to them a talk from the Choctaws claiming the lands of Tuscaulusau (black warrior), the main east fork of Tombigbee, and told them to take this claim into consideration, to make their minds up on it and to return a friendly answer; that in this as in every other case of contention between them and their red neighbours he wished a thorough investigation and an amicable adjustment and would contribute all in his power to produce it.

He stated to them "that the war between the Simanolees and subjects of Spain in the Floridas would scorch the Creeks unless the old chiefs turned their attention seriously to it, and adopted such measures as might meet the approbation of their friends and were suited to their particular situation.

The United States were bound to compel us to respect the rights of Spain, and they were able and willing to fulfill all their treaty stipulations as well with Spain as the Creek nation, and in the present case it was particularly enjoined on him by the President of the United States to watch over and attend to the execution of these treaties. He must of course make it a serious affair with them at some convenient time during our conference. They will of course revolve in their minds what we have already done, and what remains yet to be done to keep our thieves and mischiefmakers within bounds."

The chiefs replied: "We shall do what we can to get our affairs right and to keep them so."

23rd.

General Wilkinson returned from Louisville and informed the Commissioners about being informed of the agreement entered into between the Commissioners of the U. S. and those of Georgia for the adjustment of their conflicting claims to the lands bordering on the Mississippi and the southern boundary of the United States.

———

Zoholo Haujo of Oketeqockenne lost a black horse two miles from Milledgeville up Tesling Creek, branded X on the thigh and rump. Year 1806.

———

Directions for Taning, by Mr. Brown.

Green Hides.

Take them immediately from the carcase to the pond, and let them remain 12 hours; then put them in lime. One peck of black-jack ashes to a hide if large, or half a bushel to 3 hides.

The season being warm, in 3 or 4 days the hair will come; as soon as it will come, take it off; the first and second & 3rd day work them well in the lime; do this by taking them quite out, and replace them; if necessary add ashes and always water enough to cover them. After they are haired take them to the pond; the second and 3rd day work each side well till the water or lime appears to be out the hide, of a dyish cast. The 4th day put them in beaten bark, so as at that no part of the hide lies on another case; here they are to lie 9 days, and replace them in a second bark; 6 weeks replace them in fresh bark and let them remain in the tan.

Dry Hides.

7 days in warm weather; 9 days in March to soke in the pond; 7 days in lime, and 7 to take it out for warm weather, in March 9 or 10—every thing else the same.

The Reserve at the Ocmulgee Old Fields.

Surveyed by John Thomas, February, 1806.

Begining at the mouth of Oakchoncoolgau and runing thence N. 5 W., 34 pole.
> N. 55 W., 132 to the road, an offset, S. 49 W., 34 pole.
> 280 to a branch runing to the left.
> 380 to a small branch.
> 420 to a point.

W. 28 pole.
N. 33 W., 44 to a large branch runing to the left.
> 70 to the old trader's path, offset to the river, S. 79 W., 42 pole.
> 240 pole to a branch to the left.

S. 85 W., 60.
N. 40 W., 52 to a branch to the left.
> 114 to the mouth of a branch.
> 126 to the river bank.

N. 27 W., 80.
N. 75 W., 46.
S. 28 W., 28.
S. 36 E., 10 to an ash on the bank of the river 3 miles above Oakchoncoolgau.

From the mouth of Oakchoncoolgau and for miles down the river:
S. 71 E., 156 pole.
S. 19 W., 48.
S. 55 E., 24 to a dark creek runing to the right.
> 270 pole to a small creek.
> 292 to a trail.
> 340.

S., 80 to the dark creek runing to the left.
S. 45 W., 92 to the river bank.
S. 51 E., 32.
S. 10 E., 60 pole.
S. 50 W., 8 to the river.

These courses give for the river or guide line, N. 44 W. for five miles. Begining at the point 3 miles above Oakchoncoolgau at an ash on the river bank and runing:
N. 46 E., 182 pole to a branch to the right.
    368 to a path.
    416 to a branch to the left.
    512 to a branch to the right.
    523 to a branch to the right.
    664 to a branch to the right.
    700 to Oakchoncoolgau.
    960 to the corner, being 3 miles.
S. 44 E., 150 to a branch to the left.
    150 to a branch to the left.
    310 to a branch to the right.
    370 to the same branch, going down with it.
    630 a branch to the right.
    732 to the road.
    1040 to a branch to the right, fine flowing.
    1600 to a hill, a pine on the north side of a large branch, being 5 miles.
S. 46 W., 800 to a large creek to the left.
    960 or 3 miles to a maple on the river bank and up the same to the begining.

Courses within this survey to fix some points for the information of the Secretary of War.
Begining at the "offset of S. 79 W. on the old trading path:"
N. 73 E., 16 pole to a branch to the right.
    80 pole to the old path to the right.
N. 23 E., 66 to the hill.
S. 88 E., 78.
N. 84 E., 30 the ridge of 3 mounts.
    54 to the 1st mount.
    60 to the 2.
    64 to the 3.
    72.
S. 49 E., 48 to the Commandant's quarters.
    78 to the 4th mount.

S. 80 E., 26 to a branch to the right.
   60 to the road.
   72 to a branch to the right.
   96 to mount N. 5, the ridge from it S. 57 E.
S. 45 W., 34 to a branch to the left.
   62 to the 6th mount ✕ing the road.
S. 20 E., 50 to mount N. 7, 30 by 30 yards.
   84.
S. 34 W., 22 to the curve of the hill.
   50 to a deep valley.
   88 to mount N. 8, 11 by 9 pole square at top.
N. 20 W., 20 to mount N. 9.
N. 39 W. 26 to a branch to the left.
   34.
N. 65 W., 32 to mount N. 10.

———

It will be some time before the Creek young will get rid of the remains of that alloy which debased the agents and refugeed their associates, who fled to them and took up their residence among the Indians during the Revolution War, and it may be deemed unbecoming in a public character at this period of our history to drag into light occurrences of that period unfavourable to the moral character of one of the parties, but it is due to the character of the Indian to state some of these occurrences, as they are the clue to unravel the improper ideas formed by the Indians of the white character. The agents were instructed to turn loose the Indian fury against the frontiers, and some of them accompanyed the war parties and urged them to an undistinguished destruction of all ages and sexes. The American refugees, fugitives from justice in the United States, joined in this warfare, accompanyed as guides, and when too cowardly to fight, formed parties for predatory warfare, took to themselves wives, and instructed and encouraged all the connexions of their wives in every species of cuning and theft. By the return of peace they had become such adepts in the most cuning traits of villiany, that the restraints heretofore in use among the chiefs were but cobwebs to them. From the declaration of peace to the introduction of the plan of civilization in 1796, these white people pretty generally continued their predatory warfare; at that period some of the worst fled, some died, and some promised to reform; their red associates stole horses and they found a market for them, and it is a remarkable fact that the plan, since it begins to develop itself and to be understood, takes root every where better among the Indians who have had no white people connected with them than where they have; the Indian country man, with but few exceptions, is a lazy, idle, craving, thievish animal, so much degraded in the estimation of the Indians that they are considered a slave of their family and treated accordingly; if a red man has a wife, he can put her away or she can put him away, and after the annual festival the claims on each other cease; not so the white man, he is a tenant at will so far as wives' promises are concerned, but permanently bound in his property, and moreover, if she commits whoredom it is no offense against a white husband and only makes him a subject of rediculé, but towards a red husband it is a crime (murder excepted) of the deepest die; she forfeits, and the adulterer also, their cast.

That the evidence of any person, red, white or black, shall be allowed and admited in all cases, the right of which evidence being seriously considered and compared with all other circumstances attending the case, shall be left to the court.

Taning.

Put the hides in soak in the water pool, draw them daily and brake them first lengthways, then crossways until they become quite soft and pliant, then put them into lime; the first operation will be from 4 to 6 or 8 days, according to the season and dryness of the hides.

Limery.

Put the lime in the vat the day before used, churn up and put the hides in, draw daily, and add occasionally lime until the hair comes freely, then draw them, take hair off, and put them in the water pool; this operation is from 3 to 10 days, according to the season. A bushel of lime is usually enough for 20 hides.

When returned to the water pool work them daily, first on the grain side, then flesh them till the lime is out, which is ascertained by the feel, they will not be slippery; then into the handler.

The handler is a vat of ooze to colour the leather; draw them daily, handle them, hang them over the vat in smooth order and four or two at a time until coloured, then into the tan vat.

Pack them in tan bark for 40 or 60 days, then take them up and pack them away in a sufficiency of bark and let them be.

Small Skins.

These, when limed, should be put into lime drying, handled daily until they appear slimey, then into the water pool free from slime and into ooze.

Note on Liming in the Winter, 1804-5.

I put hides in ashes on the 30 December and some of them remained till 26 January before the hair came off, they raised the 1st, 2nd and 3rd day; in the same vat fresh hides came in 5 and six days; hides dried on a pole 10 to 15, and worked hides 15 to 27.

Colonel Hawkins will much oblige J. Lyon by forwarding, along with the plants collected and introduced into his garden at the Flint River establishment, a number of the smallest plants of Illicium Floridanum (Bergamot Bay) from Tuckabatchee, also seeds of the Hydrangea, Quircifolia, Haboia Tiptera, Collonsoniasp (French Tea) and any others that he may judge uncommon or curious that he can conveniently procure.

Direct the packages to John Lyon, to the care of Mr. David Landreath, corner of Market & 12th Streets, Philadelphia. Per favour of Dr. Brickell, Savannah.

24th June.

The chiefs assembled at Tuckabatchee sent an invitation to Colonel Hawkins, General Meriwether and the Commissioners of Georgia to attend their square to-morrow to partake of the ceremonies usual on the reception of dignified strangers and to dine with them.

25.

The gentlemen invited attended and were treated with very great attention; the ceremony of the black drink was given with the usual solemnity, and Efau Haujo addressed the chiefs on the occasion. "This," says he, "is not a new thing, our first acquaintance commenced with the English at Charleston, Coweta first took them by the hand, and this town next, and this ceremony was in use then and has been repeated on all like occasions; after the English, our next acquaintance was with the French, then the Spaniards, and lastly with the United States; so that what you see is only the ceremony used by our grandfathers in old times at their first acquaintance with and reception of the representatives of the white nations. We are a poor people, this we cannot help; every thing around us bespeaks our poverty, but such as we have we give freely; these visitors are born in this land with us, they are our older brothers, come from the head of their nation to aid us, a poor people; you must receive and treat them as your clan brothers and give them a hearty welcome during their stay among us."

26.

General Meriwether and Colonel Hawkins arrived in town and took up their quarters as assigned them by the chiefs; the Colonel directed the chiefs to appoint suitable persons to value the cattle and to superintend the issues of provisions to the Creeks, all cattle to be paid for by age, at two dollars and half per year, six years old to be highest for cattle; above that age the cattle are being killed, to be reported to Mr. Hill who will pay for them.

Mr. Cornell, the agent and interpreter, informed Colonel Hawkins that the speaker felt himself greatly embarrassed by the non-arrival of many towns in the opposition, and desired him to mention this to the Colonel and to inform him "that he would immediately send an express to Hopohielthle Mico, the head of the opposition, to know from him what he meant, and that he would make one of his principal supporters in mischief the messenger; that this would of necessity create some delay, but it was unavoidable and he intended it for the best, and probably to-morrow or next day he would be able to receive the Commissioners and hear what they had to communicate to the chiefs of the nation; that the chiefs of the upper towns, with the exception of Ocfuskee, were all arrived, and he should in the mean time sift the reports relative to the murders on the Mississippi; he had examined one of the Indians and was not satisfied, and he had ordered the other to attend; when they come he would endeavour to get the truth and then consult the agent upon what was best to be done."

Colonel Hawkins told Mr. Cornell to keep constantly in the council, attend all the debates, and take part in such parts only as was connected with the objects of the government and leave every thing else to the council of the speaker to be managed in such way as they might deem proper.

28.

Mr. Cornell stated that the chiefs were greatly perplexed about their affairs and were apprehensive some thing was coming upon them which would alarm their nation, and they requested to have a conference with Colonel Hawkins and General Meriwether before they addressed them on the subject of their mission; "the speaker said he would call on the Colonel and appoint the time." Mr. Cornell added, the chiefs were very generally vexed with the opposition and seemed desirous, if they knew how, to take some decisive measure with them; that on this subject they expected from him what he gave them, his opinion at great length; he told them, "on a former occasion when the Commissioners of Spain and the United States were insulted, he was called on by Colonel Hawkins to turn out the warriors and punish the leader; this he did at the apparent risk of his and the Colonel's life, but the effect was such as all like conduct will produce, and was predicted by the Colonel, the opposition being their heads."

29.

The speaker requested the agent to attend the national council to assist them by translating a talk from the western nations addressed to the four nations; the purport was "that they had resolved on a war with the Ozauzee, that their friends and fathers, the white people, had recommended to all red nations to be at peace with one another and with the white people; that all red people had come into this talk except the Ozauzee, these wared with all people, red and white, and they had united themselves against this nation. Our kings and warriors have spoken; our kings say: "Keep your legs ready, be at your homes;" the Ozauzee say: "We are their wives, and in four moons we will go and see our husbands; be ready to rise up and meet us at New Madrid."

This talk was accompanyed with four strans of red beeds, in the center of one stran were 14 white beeds, the number of nations who had taken the talk, but no names mentioned, and on the paper the name only of the others; the verbal talk accompanying the talk was that the Cherokees, Chickasaws, Choctaws, Delawares, Shawnees and other nations had taken this talk, and that the Creeks would hear from the Cherokees the day and place for the rendesvous.

In the Evening.

General Meriwether and Colonel Hawkins had a conference with a secret council of the chiefs at the request of the speaker;

he began by stating that he felt himself under obligations to General Meriwether and his father the President, for his visit to the nation; they were a poor people and he would see them as such, he might expect that they were better off than he found, but much of their present embarrassments were to be attributed to their folly, not of their young people, but of some of their old chiefs who might know better; he had been at New York and seen and taken Washington by the hand, and he remembered the beloved talks he received from him and was glad to hear what he believed to be true, that the same friendly disposition still existed towards the red people on the part of the present President and the great council of the American nation. He knew and regreted that his people were jealous and foolish, and of course he must observe caution; he was desirous to hear what the gentlemen had to say in a friendly way, but it was necessary, for him to prevent this jealousy, to confine, for the present, this conference to points connected only with the mission, and he wished in the first place to have what the gentlemen had relative to the murders commited by the red people or white people on the Mississippi.

The gentlemen replyed they would now or at any other time disclose to him the objects of their mission, they had reduced the whole to a small compass; it was to be regreted that a jealousy did exist among the chiefs, but while we regreted it, we might rejoice at there being no grounds for this jealousy; we had come, not to find fault, but to give them a correct view of the connexion between the red and white people, to point out what appeared to us indispensable to their future weldoing, and what appeared, in the opinion of the President, to be necessary on their part for the present, what he declared to be his opinion of the conduct of the American Government was true, and there was no question but the President was their friend and anxious for their weldoing; he was born among them and friendly to the rights of man from his infancy; that the gentleman here, General Meriwether, who was a member of the great council of the American nation, could well assure them of this, and the impression of such a man was an evidence of the anxiety of the President for our weldoing. They communicated the letter of 22 February from Governor Harrison, giving an account of the murder of five Creeks; the speaker said it appeared to be true in all its circumstances, and he would state what he had collected, but he was not satisfied with the report he had received and he had sent for the reporters to be examined in the square of the nation; he would get the truth if he could and then see what was to be done. Two of the Indians had returned and their story is this: "They went to war with the Quoppaumookee (Delaware) against the Ozauzee, and when they were on the enemy's ground, they discovered some men which were traced to a camp, this they surrounded in the evening and fired on in the morning and killed three of the party which they found to be a Frenchman and two of his sons by a Quoppaumookee; his wife was of the party and fled with a small child which she left in the woods where it perished. This man lived at Quoppaumookee, was a trader, and had been with the Ozauzee trading, and on the return in the beaver hunt, catching beavers, they found they had commited a mistake, that they had killed their friends; upon this they returned to Quoppaumookee and to the house of the murdered man, where they saw his wife and where the whole circumstances were related; the Quoppaumookee said it was a mistake, the Creeks were their friends going to war, and had commited a mistake in killing some of their friends. The brother of the Frenchman demanded satisfaction, but the Quoppaumookee said the white man and his sons were under white laws and those laws must give it; the man himself was white and his sons wore the garb of white people and not of Indians, and they in consequence looked on them as white also; that the brother was not satisfied, and some time after, at Pancore, they went to a man who is interpreter for many nations, this man told them to go off; the murdered man's brother was there and was determined to kill all the Creeks he could meet with; that he said he had applied to the Spanish governor for satisfaction, who said it was a mistake, but he persisted that he would kill all he saw; they, two of the Creeks, in consequence attempted to leave the town, but this man fired on them and killed one, his companion; he applied for satisfaction and for information why such a thing should be done; he came down some distance where a party of his comrades were fired on and five of them killed, this irritated him and determined him to take revenge; he got together the few that remained and saw a boat with three men he determined to kill them; some of the party said no, they were not the guilty people, and the rule now was "to put the guilty alone to death;" however he went and fired on the boat, killed the two men at the oars, the gun pointed at the man at the helm snaped, and he called out he was a friend to red people, they knew him, he had been useful to them, was a Frenchman, and had assisted them in their trade and could interpret their language; they told him their story, that he and his property was safe, and as they had lost their guns and silverware when their five men were killed, they would take the property of the two dead. men; this he pointed out, and they carried him home and came to their country."

30th.

Mr. Cornell called on the Commissioners to state to them that the chiefs manifested a considerable degree of uneasiness at the situation of their affairs and did not know well how to conduct themselves in the present state of their affairs, that they were sensibly impressed with the obligations they were under to the President and people associated with him for their friendly attention to the red people and would receive the Commissioners to-day and hear what was intended to be communicated to them.

General Meriwether and Colonel Hawkins communicated to Mr. Cornell the whole object of their mission and requested him to conduct himself in every thing in conformity with the spirit of it; they then attended the square and delivered this address:

Hopoie Mico and you chiefs of the Creeks assembled in the national council:

Since our last meeting some difficulties have occured among us which seemed to threaten to disturb the peace of the agency; the division among the chiefs is the cause of this and we must unite ourselves to put an end to such divisions and dissentions for the future. Here the nation are assembled and you Hopoie Mico are the great chief, and must be obeyed as such. Every man, red, white or black, must look here and to you and pay attention to the orders of this assembly delivered by you as the law of the land; if the thieves, lyars and mischiefmakers will not listen to us and obey you, we must use force and compel them to do it; no man or town must take the law from us and if they attempt to disturb our peace or to deprive this assembly of the right to govern the land, they must be punished with death. In the course of the spring a case of this sort occurred; although I received repeated promises on the part of the red people to complete the line from Altamaha to St. Mary's, and the last from the opposition themselves, who gave me the broken days in your presence, yet they not only refused to attend the time appointed by themselves, but threatened to rob or otherwise to injure the people on this service. Mr. Freeman, the surveyor, sent one of your chiefs (Olohuth Hathee) to me to know what was to be done; I was too far from Hopoie Mico to consult you, and I sent Mico Thlucco to Tuskenehau Chapco with directions for him to go to Hopoie Haujo to take measures to fulfill the promises of the nation, and for fear that they could not take measures in time, I called on the chiefs of Cusseta and Coweta to aid us and they sent Tuskenehau Thlucco and Tuskegee Tustunnagau with twelve men to go on with the line. Mico Thlucco gave them their orders and they told me to tell you they would obey your orders at the risque of their lives.

Among other things to prevent the finishing of the line they threatened the public establishment at Flint River, to break it up and to spill blood; they threatened Tuskenehau Chapco with the war stick. I paid no regard to their threats, being determined if they made the attempt to call on you, Hopoie Mico, to come with the warriors of the upper towns.

In the Evening.

Efau Haujo called on General Meriwether and Colonel Hawkins to invite them to a conference with the chiefs; the old man told them the subject under consideration was tangled and perplexing, but for himself he was not inclined towards it.

In the conference the speaker stated that they had seriously deliberated on the communication made to them in the name of the President and felt all its importance, the communication was of that sort as to carry conviction in their minds and they wished to consult the Colonel and General on some points; these were two, the "Road and Ocmulgee," here from the division among them, they deemed it proper to appoint some of the most distinguished men among them to go to the towns in opposition and communicate freely to them what they had received from the Commissioners, and they were certain it would open their ears; and to this end they contemplated having a meeting at Ooseuchee as soon as possible and it could be convenient for the General to attend previous to his departure for Congress; they thought at that meeting one or both of the points would be granted by the nation, and they wished to consult the gentleman on this mode of procedure; here they thought it impracticable to do any thing with effect, but it was their opinion one or the other, or perhaps both, would be done so as to meet the wishes of the President. Of this mode of procedure they requested freely the opinion of the General and Colonel, the first as a friend coming from the council of the American people, and the other as their agent and as an old chief of the land.

After some conversation among the chiefs and between the gentlemen, General Meriwether addressed the chiefs: "I feel for your situation, and my friendship for you and anxiety to contribute towards your prosperity induces me to make a sacrifice of every personal consideration in the present instance, and if you deem it indispensably necessary, of which you are the best judge, I will make my arrangements so as to meet you any where from the 20 to the last of August; I feel a sincere friendship for your rights and am very desirous that you would make such a use of the present offer of service on our part as will enable me to report you to the President as favourably as I wish, and may we, consistent with truth; I possess the disposition and will certainly do all I can for you, from this you will readily see my willingness to conform myself to whatever your judgment may deem for the best."

Colonel Hawkins said he would make some observations on past transactions as their friend and speak freely   in mind on some points. He did not expect any good from a mutiny at Ooseuchee and in his opinion it would be giving a negative to both the propositions and it would be better to say no at once here, than to ask the General to come there and to receive that answer; they well knew the insult offered to us last year in the square of Ooseuchee, it was to the speaker of the nation, to the head warrior, to Efau Haujo and all of us, the President did not escape, he was charged with cunning, with duplicity, and what were we to expect in such a square, where we were told they would adhere to old times, they prefered the old bow and arrow to the gun; I have no opinion that it would be right for us to commit ourselves again among such a people; here are the chiefs assembled, and in some of the old and usual squares it would be proper to meet; if a delay was necessary, we could send 5 or more good men to the towns in opposition to bring them to us, but it was not our business to be runing after thieves and mischiefmakers and to be influenced in our conduct by that of a people who act like spoilt children. If these people will not attend on the orders of their chiefs, we must make them, our warriors must make them, and if it is necessary, your father, the President, will aid you in men and money; he has both men and money at your service, and the first point of our address was the necessity of geting into one talk and supporting you, Hopoie Mico, as the head and this assembly as the great body of the nation; you, surrounded with these chiefs, are the nation, and here is the place to act as such. We shall not do our duty to place ourselves in a situation where your authority will be treated with contempt, I never can consent to this; there are some good men in Ooseuchee and some of them are here, but the town behaved ill; we have six towns from that river, Coweta, Tallauhassee, Cusseta, Uchee, Ooseuchee and Oconee, five of them may be relied on, and they must unite with us and let us do what our judgment dictates. From the manner in which you have invited the General he may think, & of right, that when he comes it is to receive a favourable answer to the two propositions, and I am certain it is giving this trouble for nothing, if you conduct him to that square. You have rightly estimated the friendly expressions in our address, and I must request you to reflect on what I have said and what you have learned from the General, and in the morning you will be able perhaps to form a different and more correct decision. I repeat, if you must first confer with the opposition, do it by a deputation of 5 or 6, and order them here, and here conclude on the business I have laid before you.

1 July.

Hopoie Mico informed General Meriwether & Colonel Hawkins that he had appointed the men to set out and confer with the chiefs of the lower towns, and that he, after consulting his chief, had determined to have a meeting at Coweta which he would attend himself, with some chiefs of the upper towns, that he had allowed in all about eighteen days for this business, and he wished it to be a meeting among themselves, not attended by white people at all, and he would see what could be done, he would try these people once more before he would throw them off.

In the Evening.

Hopoie Mico requested Colonel Hawkins "to inform the Commissioners of Georgia he would to-morrow hear what they had to say," and he communicated it accordingly.

2 July.

The gentlemen, Commissioners from Georgia, attended, and General Clark, first named in the Commission, addressed the chiefs; he first communicated the resolution of the Legislature of Georgia and their appointment in conformity therewith, and made the demand in conformity with the resolution and quoted extracts from the treaties, 1st of Augusta, 2nd, Galphinton, and 3rd, Shoulderbone, and urged a fulfillment of them, and demanded that all negros, prisoners, horses, cattle and other property taken from the citizens of Georgia should be restored. His speach was signed and left with the chiefs together with a digest of the laws of Georgia containing the treaties refered to. They had some halfbreeds with them who could read and they spent the day in deliberation thereon.

The Commissioners of Georgia having determined to introduce the treaties of Augusta, Galphinton and Shoulderbone, the agent, having given decidedly his opinion that they were not made by competent authority and of course of no validity, determined not to interfere so far as they were insisted on, and to leave this to the Commissioners to negotiate in their own way, and in like moment on these points, not to interfere unless asked thereto by the Indians.

9 O'clock in the Evening.

Hopoie Mico sent Mr. Cornell to General Meriwether and Colonel Hawkins to communicate the result of their deliberations on the communication made to them this day, to ask their opinion of a part of it, and to inform them of some discoveries made by the chiefs which was one great cause of present embarrassments. On the first he stated "that the speaker himself was at New York when the treaty was made there and he recollects well what passed between the President, General Washington, and his old chiefs; he was not then a man himself, but he was there and remembers it, and the old chiefs who were there also remember it, such of them as are alive. "General Washington told us that we had joined the British in their war against him, that he did not blame us for it, it was not our own hearts that were prevailed upon by the British and we joined them, but now it is peace between us and the British; at that time if you have taken any property from the whites we have no demand for these things, it was in time of war, but after the English & we laid down our arms and made peace, if you have taken any negros and property we look to you to return it; the white prisoners in your land must all come back, if any of them want to remain among you, let them come and see their friends and then they may return and live with you if they choose." We are willing to conform to this treaty as we believe it binding on us, we are willing to abide by the talks of Washington, and this is the opinion of all of us; we want however the advice on this point of General Meriwether and Colonel Hawkins, and we wish them to tell us whether what we have agreed upon in answer to our brothers of Georgia is right; we know nothing about the other talks mentioned by the gentlemen of Georgia, those who they say made them are people who never attend here, who never explained them in our public meetings, and who had no right to make talks for the nation." This is all I was ordered to communicate to you on this point and to wait your answer.

Reply.

You may tell the speaker and chiefs assembled that the treaties of New York and Colerain are binding on them, and that by these treaties they are bound to deliver up the negros and property where as expressed in those treaties, that we know nothing of the treaties mentioned by the gentlemen of Georgia.

Mr. Cornell continued: The discoveries made by the Indians, and which is a great cause of their present embarrassment, is this: When General Wilkinson was coming up here after the meeting at Ooseuchee had broke up, he met some of our people going to Pensacola, he inquired and they told him the talks were done; upon this he requested them to take a letter from him to a gentleman in Pensacola, which he rote and they took with them; on their way, being anxious to know the contents and having a white person with them who could read, they got him to open the letter with his penknife and read it to them; the purport of it was to explain the course of procedure in acquiring lands from the Indians; that Forbes must press them for lands at the mouth of Apalatchecola and up that river to the fork of Flint River, there must be a bay or place for shiping, which he would fortify and garrison with troops, and the stores must be near the fork of that river, and from thence roads to St. Mary's and St. Augustine's; that the first pressure was to be made for land to Ocmulgee and the next to Flint River, and then the white people would own all on the east side of that river. This was the purport of the discovery which, combined with other things, disturbed the Indians greatly; there was somebody trying to get lands that way, some of Mr. Forbe's clerks, and it appeared as if what they had heard was soon to come to pass. The Indians were greatly disturbed at this business, they saw what the white people were driving at; that in that quarter he for some time had discovered a disposition to oppose every thing that was for the good of the nation, these Indians, who were a wild people, seemed determined to bring trouble upon themselves and us, that he should try once more to bring them to reason, and if they persisted in their bad doings, he had one resource and would have recourse to it; the four nations had resolved on peace, and if the Simanolees wanted war he would give it to them, the other three nations had promised to help and he would give it to them; if land was to be parted with it must be by the will of the nation and not by a few wild people.

15 July.

Hopoie Mico to Colonel Hawkins:

"I have some chiefs with me on the way to Coweta, and I wish you to repeat to me what you and General Meriwether said to us in the national council, and that you'd add whatever you may deem suitable; the chiefs with me are well disposed and desirous of being armed by you with the strongest reasons in your power in aid of your propositions. I make this request to you in the presence of all the old chiefs with you here, and I hope you and they will be a council for me on the occasion and advise me for the best."

In reply, I recapitulated the whole address and added such observations on every part as occured; I stated that I believed he would find an opposition to every thing, that the chiefs who were negotiating with land jobbers for the land below the fork of Flint River were determined on their object and would not, if they could help it, admit him to interpose one word in opposition or even in co-operation, that as they had heretofore acted in opposition to the will of the nation and violated every promise they had made us it was in vain to expect them to aid us in any of our plans for bettering ourselves; we had already tasted the sweets of civilization, we began to know the value of property and the necessity of defending it, we were in a fair way of having plenty in our land and enjoying it in peace, we could spin and weave, we could plough, and had recently begun to settle out from our old towns for the benefit of stock, of new and rich lands, convenient to firewood and to fence rails; we had now four smiths at work, and four tons of iron, and this fall we were to sow wheat, I had for them of my own stock, raised on their lands, 150 bushels of seed wheat which I should present to those who would sow it, and I should add from my own resources six ploughs completed, filed with persons who could use them for the seed time this fall, and I should superintend the whole myself.

We all know one fact, that from our continuing to cultivate the old towns from year to year where the land was tired, we had scanty crops, and that for three months, that is from the middle of April to the middle of July, some of our women and children were actually starved and many so reduced by hunger as to be unfit for any business and a pray to disease; we all know this, and I know, Hopoie Mico, who is to blame; it is you, it is I, it is these old chiefs, we should blame ourselves, and not the poor and ignorant women, we have been in the United States and we know how to remedy this and we ought freely to unite our councils, we can all set examples and we can compel some to follow and some we know are well disposed and will gladly follow when once an example is made by such people as we are, and this is one of the first duties of all people who are placed at the head of a government. How often have we in this town (Tuckabatchee) wared against our services when I recommended to our people to go out and settle on new lands; an order was passed to bring them or lock them in, the latter was obeyed and hunger punished us severely. When I was vested with the authority of a chief, I spoke as a chief, and Ooseuchee Emautlau obeyed me, he moved seventy miles on Pertawau Hatchee, and has increased his settlement to 70 souls and has informed us that while we are starving he is surrounded with plenty of bread and meat. One observation which I made the other day upon being told that two little girls had perished with hunger near us, has haunted my mind; these little girls are murdered, who murdered them? It is you Colonel Hawkins and the old chiefs of the land, you know and they know how to prevent this; if a bear was about to murder them, if an Indian or white person was about to murder them, how willingly would you take your arms and at the expence of your own lives save their's, and yet you know this enemy called hunger, and you will not unite in destroying him to save many of our little ones from being murdered.

It is time for us to look about ourselves and to act according to our judgement for the good of our country; let us accommodate the President in whatever he asks of us and thereby enable him to accommodate us and to perfect our plan of civilization which will be our salvation; great changes are daily taking place around us for the happiness of men and we alone seem, of choice, still to grope in the dark, we must either associate with our neighbours in our intercourse with them as a people who know and can respect their rights or forfeit all claim to their justice, in short, we must associate with them or the wild beasts of the forest, and in the latter case we must fly our country and go to the wilds in the west; we must swap some of our lands here for lands there; you will be opposed, and seriously opposed, by many of the chiefs who you seem to confide in, but you must take courage, try once more to bring them to act with us, point out every thing to them in your own way when you are in secret council with them, and keep constantly in view before them that Ocmulgee must be our boundary, that the value for it is indispensable to our weldoing; that in accomodating the President in this, we shall have a strong claim to his future attention to us, that we cannot yet protect ourselves and must depend on the frienship of the President and justice of the American people; we must have their troops or aid otherwise, to protect our rights as well from our own unruly people as from lawless neighbours, when such should obtrude themselves on us, a line of marked trees cannot be a line of peace; where the land is good and admits of thick settlements, stock will come over, our young people will destroy it, their owners will destroy them, and thus this source of confusion will overwhelm us with distress. If, in your management of this affair, you should find it necessary to sacrifice one of the two great objects, let it be the road, we may do a little longer without that, but hold to Ocmulgee at all events, the other must follow in a little while, and the first recourse is in our claim to the friendship of the President.

I must repeat again you will be opposed, strongly opposed, you will be threatened; I know one of their weapons they intend to pull on me, they intend to break up my establishment at Flint

River, out of resentment for the loss of their favourite leader (Bowles); be it so, we can remedy that, we can take time and let it affect me as it may personally, I sacrifice all to the acquisition of Ocmulgee. I know they well know how high I stand in the estimation of the chiefs of the nation, and they think by threatening me to intimidate us; our course is plain, if we find these people will not unite with us and obey their old chiefs and you as their head, let us act without them, let us exercise our judgments and leave them to mouthe for a while and follow the course we shall shape for them. I have heard they say "they have done rong in robing and plundering of their neighbours and mean now to do an act of justice by giving land for their debts and robberys." To pay a just debt is right, to repay an injury is an act of justice, laudable in all who do so, but to pay land for this without the voice of the nation, who owns it, is doing injustice to the nation, is in fact, to commit a robery to patch up a robery. The nations alone have the right to dispose of their lands, and they have the right of appointing proper persons to liquidate the claims against themselves and to pay them, in fact they have told Mr. Forbes they mean to pay the just debts of their traders. If they forget us let us not forget ourselves, let us cleave to the friendship of the President, accommodate him in all he wants for the value which he will give, and ask of him all aid we require in our present difficult and embarrassing situation. Let us go on to get our affairs right and these wild sons of ours must 'ere long become tame and follow in our steps; if they are determined to ruin themselves and to involve us, let us take care of ourselves and punish in good time some of their leaders, and for this purpose turn out our warriors and use force; this experiment of using force has turned out well hitherto.

The old chiefs assembled assented to every thing and each give us his opinion "that we should try them once more before we left them to themselves, and accommodate the President if we can."

One difficulty presented itself to all who spoke relative to the road, "when waggons and property pass, our people may steal and we be involved in difficulties, yet as it is right our white friends should pass thro' our country, if they will use such paths as we have they are welcome, the risque to be to themselves; we promise on our part to do what we can to protect them and their property."

Hopoie Mico to Colonel Hawkins:

I have one report you will hear with pleasure: Four men of Wewocau went on a thieving party to the Cherokees, stole some horses and killed some cattle; just as they returned, one of the warriors sent up to punish a fellow for theft having heard of it just after he had collected his warriors, went immediately and executed the law on them; they croped both ears from the leader and whiped him, and cut off one ear from each associate and whiped them; the sticks and ears have just arrived and I shall take them to the lower towns.

Reply.

This was well timed and well done, it is to be regreted that we are under the disagreeable necessity of having recourse to such remedies to cure our people of the itch for horse stealing, but to be secure ourselves in our lands and other property, it is rendered now indispensable, and in my opinion, we must soon go further and make provision for hardened offenders, all leaders of thieving parties for a second offense must suffer death.

Being on this subject, I will make one observation on our fears relative to a road through our country: The same precautions we take to keep our people honest towards the Cherokees, Chickasaws, Choctaws, the people of the United States and our neighbours of Spain, seing what a wide range our traders and hunters take, will serve to protect the traveller in our land.

Another: Our people know and practice the rights of hospitality better than the Creeks, and I think we can exhibit this amiable trait towards the traveller.

I am certain if our old chiefs at the head of our annual festivals, and those appointed to initiate youth into manhood, would make it a cardinal point to instruct them to protect the traveller and strangers in our land, that when the impression is once made on infant minds, the pleasure resulting from such estimable conduct would free us from any apprehensions on this head.

28th.

Hopoie Mico sent to the agent that we were under the necessity to add 4 days to the time appointed to get a distinguished chief from the Cherokees (Cusseta Mico) to aid him.

30 July.

Okelesau informed Colonel Hawkins that the meeting at Coweta was such an one as the chiefs never had before; the opposition held a council among themselves and had an answer written to Colonel Hawkins; it was such an one as made the speaker ashamed, in it was a determination to move the agent over to Georgia or to the upper towns, they did not want him or any white people among them. The speaker told them that this was a meeting among the Indians themselves and he had not heard of any speach from Colonel Hawkins to them, of course the answer or talk to him would not be understood by him; he had called the meeting himself to consult the Indians about the sale of some lands to pay their debts, the white people did not want land, they wanted money, we owed them money and they must and should be paid; the President did not want land, he had, from the recent purchase of Louisiana, more land than he had people to settle, but was nevertheless willing to buy some from us to accommodate us in the payment of our debts and providing for us such things as we wanted; for his part he was determined to sell as much as would do for this purpose, and he came here to meet the chiefs to consult them upon the business. He wanted no written talk for Colonel Hawkins, he should give him his talk when he saw him in his own way with his interpreter; "that Ocmulgee should be the line or he would loose his life." To which Tuckeuchau Chapco replied: "It should not, if it was, he would loose his life." Hopoie Mico said he did not understand his own colour and he did not know how Colonel Hawkins should. It was agreed at Ocheubofau, in presence of the four nations, that land should never be sold but in a meeting of all the chiefs of the nation, and he has heard that the Simanolees are selling land to Forbes's clerks to pay debts and damages done to the store at St. Mark's; he did not understand this, it was rong, and would be resisted by the chiefs.

Hopoie Mico replied that all concerned in this must meet at Tuckabatchee in ten days to give an answer there to an address given there by the representatives of the President to the chiefs of the nation, and there also to account for this land selling without the voice of the nation. Hopoie Haujo replied he would not attend there, he would go immediately down "to meet the ship and establish the store and the lands he had sold to pay debts and which he would suffer no one to undoe."

The speaker then added: I came here to meet Indians, to talk with them, and now I shall go to talk with the representatives of the President in ten days, I will see them, talk with them, and do what I think is for the best; if you come it is well, if you do not, I know what to do.

CAPT. STEPHEN CLARK,
    Plainfield,
        State, Connecticut.

Orders on *————

Eufaula, for beef, order to T. Tustunnagau, $200.
Ingers Brothers, for transport of bellows, $10.
John Oriley, his account, $224.
Efau Haujo, $25.
Intatchhoe Sullivan, $300.
Cusseta Mico of the Cherokees, $100.
Mr. Grierson, for four loads iron, $600.
Tustunnagau Thlucco, ✕ties, 100, $450; steel, $50.

---

1. Sehochaja, one bag.
2. Sauhoithle, one bag.

Price, large at 4 cts.; that of 120 and under, 3 cts.; live, at ¼ less.

| 1804. Nov. | Provisions for 1805. |

16. Bacon, 225 lbs., new made, at 5 cents, $11.25.
17. Pork, alive, 140 lbs., at 3 cents, $4.20.
19. Pork, 119 lbs., at 4 cents, $4.76.
20. Pork, 69 lbs., at 3 cents, $2.07.
22. Pork, 273 lbs., at 3 cents, $8.79.
22, Pork, 95 lbs., $3.00.
22. Pork, 162 lbs., at 4 cents, $6.48.
22. Live Pork, 680 lbs., at 3 cents, $20.40.
Dec.
27. Pork, 350 lbs., $7.50.

Creek Agency, 16th January, 1805.

Tom, who called himself Johnson in the Cherokees, 36 years old, wt. abt. 140, very black, brought from Africa when young and speaks tollerable plain, small holes in his ears, the property of William Banks, of Patrick County, Virginia, when he run off in June, 1802. He is now the property of Elijah Banks, of Patrick County. While in the Cherokees he was with James Vann, and left him in November last. He run off in company with Israel, a light complected fellow about 35 years old, the property of George Anston, of Henry County Virginia, the post town Henry Court-house. Colonel George Anston had run from about 13 years past, a negro carpenter about 53 years old at this date, play on the violin and fond of drink; named Vole, alias William Johnson.

---

*Word in manuscript illegible.

R. THOMAS,

His Book,

Begun November 21st, 1796.

William Addis, London, No. 2496, capped & jewelled.
Dr. Brodum's botanical syrup & nervous cordial, at £1.2.
From M. E.: 3 yds. Stroud's for John Randall.
Barrow's mare, mounting check 2 S.
Do. cushion, A. F.
Strawberry roan, bald face, 4 white legs.
From Pensacola: Thompson's note, frying pan, pump, tacks, 1,000; ketchup, shirts, salt.
July 28, 1796: 3 shawls, $3.75; 2 romals, $1.00; 3 yds. calico, $1.75; 3 yds. calico, $1.25; 2 oz. thread, 25c; 3 yds. calico, $1.50; 3 romals, $1.50.
July 29th, provisions to three Spanish deserters, $10; John Galphin, 2 rings, $4.
August 13th, paid the Rat, for going express to the Tuckabat-chee, $20.
August 14th, provisions supplied three American seamen, $10; M. Elhert, 2 pair ear bobs, $4.
September 1st, provisions to Spanish deserters, $10.
September 9th, provisions to 4 Spanish deserters, $18.
9th June, John Thompson, 1 ring, 1 pr. ear bobs.

Cusseta, 21st November, 1795.

Dear Sir:

I arrived at this place on the 19th instant, from Knoxville; I am happy to have it in my power to inform you that the Creeks who visited Governor Blount have returned satisfied, and speak

Note: Richard Thomas was the clerk of Colonel Benjamin Hawkins, stationed at Cusseta, an Indian town on the eastern bank of the Chattahoochee River, a few miles below the present city of Columbus.

Colonel Hawkins, during most of the time included in these letters, was at Fort Wilkinson, on the Oconee River, a few miles below Milledgeville.

in high esteem of the kind treatment they received. I now inclose you the Choctaw and Chickasaw talks, with the Baron De Carondelet's letter to the Mad Dog, and a letter from Governor Blount to Alex Cornell. I have been constantly on the move ever since my return from Beard's Bluff, being obliged to attend the calls of the chiefs in the upper towns as well as here. Mr. Barnard left this place to-day for Flint River, having interpreted your talks and Wayne's treaty with the agreeable news I brought from Knoxville to the chiefs of the Lower Creeks here assembled. They have all promised to lay still and receive satisfaction from the laws of the United States, but you are no stranger to the dependence that can be placed in Indian promises. To-morrow morning I return to the Tuckabatchee to attend a meeting of the Cherokees & chiefs of the upper towns for the purpose of informing them of what has been done at Tellico Blockhouse, and to endeavour to restore peace between the Chickasaws and this nation, & explain your talk. A Captain Chisholm is to be at the meeting, with whom Governor Blount has promised to send a copy of the journal of the conference at Tellico Blockhouse when it arrives, if the paper can be procured I will send you a copy of it. Every part of this nation appears disposed to preserve the peace so happily concluded, and the frontiers have nothing to fear from the Creeks, & if the Euchees do but lay quiet until the fate of Harrison and his party is decided, I am in great hopes that the peace will long continue.

After the meeting is over I shall return to this place, but if I am wanted in the Upper Creeks, I shall go up, so that your business has not suffered by neglect, altho' I have both the Upper and Lower Creeks to attend to.

I wish you would send me by the bearer, Jno. Tarvin, one piece of Stroud's, 4 large London duffels, 6 3-point blankets, 40 lbs. sugar, 20 lbs. coffee, 1 lb. of good tea, 4 groce binding, 3 yards oznabrigs for bags, & if Mr. Tarvin can bring it, one three gallon keg of good Jamaica rum. You will also pay Mr. Tarvin twelve dollars for the hire of his horse to bring up my things. I shall write you again in a few days from the Tuckabatchee, till when I remain, with great respect,

> Your most obedient and honourable servant,
>
> R. T.

J. SEAGROVE, ESQ.

_____

Cusseta, 5th December, 1795.

Dear Sir:

Contrary to my expectations, John Tarvin is not yet ready to proceed to St. Mary's, but I suppose will cross this river some time to-morrow, and I have embraced this interval to acquaint you of what has passed since my letter to you of the 21st of November.

On my return to the Tuckabatchee, I found the chiefs of the Upper Creeks assembled, but as the Cherokees had not arrived, I thought proper to wait two days before I read your letter. At the meeting the chiefs, one and all, agreed to make a peace with the Chickasaws & receive satisfaction from the laws of the United States for the death of the men killed by H. & his party; viz., one Creek, 4 L. Creeks & 12 Euchees, but I am obliged to add that since my arrival here, runners have come in with an account of the murder of two Cussetas & one Coweta by the people high up the Oconee.

The nation has determined to wait 3 moons for satisfaction, which, if not given by that time, they are determined to take.

I could not write you as fully as I wished from the Tuckabatchee without creating a jealousy in the breast of your deputy; from the appearance of affairs, I believe you will hear from me but seldom, for if I should have any important intelligence to communicate, you have put it out of my power to send you a letter by not giving me power to send an express when I should think it absolutely necessary. The Mad Dog strongly insists on my residing at the Tuckabatchee, or else that you must send him a man capable of reading your letters & writing their talks. I told him I would inform you of it, but that they should recollect the reasons why I left the Tuckabatchee, but on the return of Fisher I would be up there to read your letters to them & they should hear what you said on the subject.

I expect before this reaches you that Mr. Clark has informed you of his narrow escape; he has a negro boy named Dick, the son of Scipio, one of the negros he got from Grierson; I wish to purchase the boy & will thank you to write him on the subject & let me know his price.

Before long, a Colonel James White, of Knox County, in the Territory S. W. of the Ohio, will, I have reason to believe, make intercession with you for Obadiah Low to be appointed your deputy agent in the Upper Creeks. The Cherokees & the gentleman G. Blount promised to send in has not yet arrived; what can detain him I know not. With Tarvin comes one of the leading men of the Cowetas, to talk with you concerning the settlement of Choulapake; he talks English and has the character of a good Indian.

I am Sir,

Your obedient servant,

R. T.

P. S. I would have come down to see you, but my present state of health prevents my undertaking so long a journey at this time. I wish you to procure for me two flannel shirts and two pair of flannel drawers; if Tarvin cannot stay for them to be made, send me as much flannel as will make them.

Flint River, February 19th, 1796.

Dear Sir:

I have been here anxiously waiting the return of Tarvin & the other traders & Indians who went to St. Mary's; their long detention makes me uneasy, and I much fear some Georgians have made free with their horses, if not with their persons. Should any accident have happened to the Indians, I expect the lives of some white people in the nation may be taken for it, & probably those who are the greatest friends to the United States.

Captain Chisholm has lately returned from the Chickasaws without making a peace, being only able to obtain a cessation of arms until the chiefs of the Chickasaws & Creeks meet in the presence of Governor Blount at Knoxville; from Knoxville I understand the Creek chiefs are to proceed to Congress. This affair was talked of when I was last in the Tuckabatchee, but I told the head men that if they wished to go to Congress they should have embraced the offer you made them when you was in the nation; that their father, General Washington, had appointed three beloved men and yourself to meet them some time in the spring, in some part of Georgia, for the purpose of settling all disputes with them, and to regulate matters for the mutual benefit of both nations.

I am now ready to proceed for the Tuckabatchee, and if I should hear of any thing worth communicating, I shall embrace the first opportunity that offers of writing you again.

I have drawn an order on you in favour of Laughlin Durant for sixty dollars, which you will please pay; it is for a horse I bought of him to carry me to the Tuckabatchee. The only one I brought here a heavy fresh carried off; it has cost me 150 dollars in horse flesh since I last saw you. By this time I hope you have heard from the Secretary of War respecting my salary; I wish you to let me know what it is. I have been at some expence on the public account, which I suppose will be allowed. I gave the account to Mr. Barnard to show you; it amounts to 130 chalks; if it passes, give me credit for the amount. Refering you to Mr. Barnard for the news of the nation, I remain, &c, &c.

R. T.

P. S. On the 31st, drew on you in favour of Abm. Mordecai for 34.87½.

J. SEAGROVE, ESQ.

Cusseta, April 8th, 1796.

Dear Sir:

In my letter to you of the 23rd of March, by the Red Warrior, I informed you that Mordecai made a bad use of what came to his knowledge, & from the conversation I had with you at Flint River, I was induced to believe that you placed no confidence in him. I am now under the disagreeable necessity of informing you that M. has published the contents of my letter to you respecting him, as also the contents of my letter to Mr. Seagrove, with what view is best known to himself. I have to request that by the first opportunity you send my letter on to Mr. Seagrove. If such men as Mordecai is to see my letters, either to Mr. S. or yourself, I must decline having any thing further to say in public affairs.

The blacksmith I talked with you concerning of, means to reside with me, & until you can settle matters with Mr. S. for his accommodation, is willing to repair the Indian's guns for pay; such tools as I have fit for his use, I shall willingly lend him, & if you think proper, you can lend him your vice, tongs & screw plates, for which I will be answerable whenever called on.

The Cowetas are still quiet, waiting your arrival; Kennard I hear nothing of; Galphin is at the Cowetas.

Alex Cornell, I hear, has made those men who come from St. Mary's sell their goods much under prime cost; when you see Leslie, Moore & Simmons you will know the truth of this matter.

I have no news worth relating; my house goes on after the old manner; not a stick of wood cut as yet. When you come in, if I cannot get a house built here, I must go over to the Broken Arrow for a house; I will have some place or other.

Wishing you a speedy recovery and many years of health & happiness, I remain,

Yours, &c.,

R. T.

T. BARNARD, ESQ.

Cusseta, September 19, 1796.

Sir:

I expect this will be handed to you by Mr. G., who carrys with him a few horses that were stole from Georgia during the treaty at Colerain. It is with great difficulty & some expence that these have been collected, as you will see by the order of the Little Prince, Hollowing King & Long Lieutenant in favour of John Tarvin for fifty dollars; I was witness to the three Indians signing the order.

On the 14th inst. there was a meeting of the chiefs of the Upper Creeks at the Oakfuskee. The second man of this town, who returned from the meeting on the 17th, informs me that a Mr. Chisholm was there, & told the Indians that the Commissioners of the United States & yourself were liars, & that the Commissioners & yourself had stole their mouths & land, & I understand that your deputy in the Upper Creeks approved of Mr. Chisholm's behaviour & is going to Knoxville with the chiefs of the Upper Creeks to take the chiefs of the Chickasaw nation by the hand, & from Knoxville they are to go to Philadelphia to see their father, General Washington & to represent the conduct of the Commissioners of the United States. This morning an Indian came here with a verbal message from A. C., requesting my immediate attendance at the Tuckabatchee to go this journey with him; I refused to go & advised the chiefs here to send him a talk for to stay at home & pay no attention to any talks but what come from you; what influence it may have with him I cannot say. Joseph Stiggins is to be employed as interpreter on this business. This fickle disposition of your deputy you are no stranger to, but the longer you repose a confidence in him the less will be his thanks for the kindness you have showed him. Some Euchees are now out on the old trade of horse stealing; the Cusseta king has promised to take the horses away if they should bring any in. The Indians appear much confused at present, and I believe your presence here would be of great service in quieting the minds of those stupid, ignorant savages, & it would also prevent their turning out to steal horses, a practice that will bring destruction on their nation of they continue it.

James Seagrove, Dr.

Dr.

To my salary, from Jan. 1st, 1794, to Dec. 31st, 1794.....$250.00
To my salary, from Jan. 1st, 1795, to June 30th, 1796..... 375.00
To two horses lost on public service................... 55.00
To sundries, paid by orders of your deputy............. 33.75

$463.75

Cr.

By sundries at Beard's Bluff..........................$250.00

February 13, 1796.

By sundries, as per bill............................... 79.73
By cash, per Ab Mordecai............................. 34.37½

19.

By Dr., per Laughlin Durant.......................... 60.00

June 27.

By sundries, as per bill from Mr. Price................. 92.01¼
By 6 groce binding at $2.50........................... 15.00
By 40 lbs. sugar at 25c............................... 10.00
By 20 lbs. coffee at 40c 8.00
Cash 50.00
By 1 piece calico 9.00
By 1 silver watch 40.00
By due bill 65.13¼

                                                    $463.75

Mr. Thomas Carr, Dr.

January 23, 1796.
                                                       Dr.
To balance ....$ 15.00

April 1st, 1796.
                                                       Cr.
By balance due ....$ 22.00
By 1 shirt 6.00
By 3 yds. linen for the Mr. Cattle.................... 6.00
By 1 deer skin 2.00

August 10.

By 1 shirt 5.00
By 1 covering black list blanket..................... 14.00

May 2.

By balance 141.00

Cusseta, March 21st, 1797.
Sir:

Inclosed you have my account against I. T. for $171.64, also an order of Colonel Hawkins for $60 & ⅔, dated March 9th. By the receipt on the back you will find a balance on this order due me of twenty-six and ⅔ dollars, which, added to my account against Mr. S. makes the amount $198.28. As Mr. S. has informed me that you have paid the orders, I have drawn on him. I have give you credit for the amount as per account inclosed. The balance in my favour I find is 92.28 chalks. Since my return from Fort Fidins I have been informed that you sent me some articles by Mr. Bruce; I have never received any thing from Colerain since I saw you in June last. By the return of Mr. B.'s son I will be obliged to you to inform me what articles were sent, by whom, & to what amount. I have a particular use for sixty dollars in cash; if it should be convenient, you can send it by Mr. Barnard's son. Mr. S. has sent a silver watch of mine to Charleston for repair; it is capped and jewelled, maker's name Wm. Addis, London, No. 2496. I have wrote Mr. S. if it is repaired to deliver it to you; the bill for repairing I wish you to discharge, and keep the watch until I see you on the Oconee.

There has been some fraudulent doings on the part of some of the traders who deal with you; I cannot enter into the particulars for want of paper. When Colonel Hawkins returns, I will endeavour to get the necessary proofs of this transaction. For the future, I would advise to take no deer skins without drying them well. The scarcity of paper compels me to conclude, and I remain, with respect,

Yours, &c., &c.,

R. T.

P. S. Please present my account to Mr. S. for his mark of approbation.

MR. EDWARD PRICE.

Cusseta, March 21st, 1797.
Sir:

Yours of January 6th I received on the 19th inst. Your letters to the chiefs of the Upper and Lower Creeks I have not seen; neither did you inform me who you sent them by. There will be a meeting of the chiefs before long, and I shall know what they determine on. If my watch is repaired, I wish you to give her to Mr. Price, who I have directed to pay for repairing. My account from July 1st to December 31st, I have sent to Mr. Price to present; as you cannot answer my orders, you can give my account your mark of approbation, as it is for services in your time. This makes the second letter I have received from you since I was at Colerain. I will thank you for a few newspapers, and I believe you forgot the pamphlets & books you promised me long ago. I could not draw my account out in the usual form for want of paper; five months is now past since I sent for three quires, but have never received a single sheet.

Wishing you health, I remain, &c., &c.,

R. T.

J. S., ESQ.

_____

Cusseta, March 21st, 1797.

Dear Sir:

You will see what I have wrote Mr. Price and J. S. Put a wafer in the letters and send them on. Darouzeaux refused to interpret what I had to say to the Indians, but he is excusable, as there was rum in the town. I have made the Little Prince sensible of the state of affairs, as well as the Cussetas. The horses stole by the Cowetas are sold, three to the Talleres and one to the Cherokees, and I am told a party of Cowetas is still out looking for a few more. I have told them not to be surprised if the Light Horse should pay them a visit; & George Cornell, I hear, has threatened to kill Colonel Hawkins and the young man with him for his brother and boy. The Tuckabatchees I shall talk to in two days, and I shall inform them that their threats will not deter Colonel Hawkins from entering this land to execute his orders, & if they do him an injury, they may expect to have their nation destroyed. I have sent you what paper I can get, and remain,

Your sincere friend & well wisher,

R. T.

T. B.

_____

Cusseta, March 28th, 1797.

Sir:

The bearer, James Hardridge, has called at this place to inform Colonel Hawkins of his intention to proceed immediately to Colerain with 1,443 lbs. of deer skins to pay off his debt and receive a further credit. When Colonel Hawkins returns, he means to apply to him for a licence. I have nothing new to acquaint you of, but remain, with due respect,

Yours, &c., &c.,

R. T.

MR. ED. PRICE.

Cusseta, March 30th, 1797.

Sir:

On the 22nd inst., as I was ready to proceed for the Tuckabatchee, your letters & broken days arrived for a general meeting at the Tuckabatchee. I immediately requested the chiefs to lose no time in sending the broken days down the river as far as possible, & a man to Mr. Barnard's. Yesterday I received an express from T. B. informing me of his laying very ill with the Bloody Flux, so that he cannot be expected at the meeting. I have talks of consequence to the nation, which I shall bring up with me. Expecting soon to see you, I remain,

Yours, &c.,

R. T.

A. CORNELL.

Cusseta, April 1st, 1797.

Dear Sir:

In your letter of the 27th March, now before me, you say "if the Tussekiah Mico would go up with you he would be a good hand, as he would do more good than all the rest." This request of yours I informed him of, & he promised to go, but you may judge my surprise when he sent for me this morning and told me that you had sent him a message by the man that brought me your letter requesting him to stay at home & collect the stolen horses, and you would come to his house & write a letter and send the horses down. Why write me one thing & tell an Indian to the contrary? You have placed me in a disagreeable situation; the Warrior King says the Indian could not tell a lie, but I am the liar. Consider, my friend, the consequence; you cannot be too particular with Indians. It is needless for you to write me if your talks to the Indians and your letters do no agree. Wishing you a speedy recovery, I remain,

Yours, &c.,

R. T.

T. BARNARD.

Cusseta, April 12th, 1797.

Sir:

The chiefs of the Lower Creeks have appointed the 19th inst. for a meeting at the Broken Arrows, and they request your attendance, as they intend to arrange matters in respect to the line. Mr. Burges attended the meeting in the Tuckabatchee; I cannot give you the particulars for want of paper. Adieu.

R. T.

T. BARNARD, ESQ.

Cusseta, April 24th, 1797.

Sir:

On the 6th the chiefs of the Upper and Lower Creeks had a meeting at the Tuckabatchee; Mr. Burges and myself was present; Mr. Barnard was, by sickness, detained at home. A Mr. Maclin, from the State of Tennessee, presented a letter from General Robertson informing the chiefs of a number of horses stole from that part; twelve has been found in the possession of the Creeks, and the chiefs promised that they should be returned. The Mad Spaniard presented a letter from Martha Routh to the Creeks; I desired the Mad Spaniard to keep it until you returned, it will be a work of some difficulty to have it rightly interpreted. The chiefs have gave out strong talks to their young people, advising them to refrain from horse stealing and deliver up what horses they have lately brought in. The Lower Creeks have delivered up a few horses, and the chiefs are trying to get the rest, and if the Georgians do no injuries to the Creeks who are hunting on the frontiers, I am in hopes that horse stealing will cease.

The chiefs at the meeting wished much to have seen you, and I have been informed that the head warrior of the Tuckabatchees expects you will give him satisfaction for David Cornell. I send you by this opportunity a letter I received from Mr. Darouzeaux, who told me Whitaker brought it from Pensacola. Mr. T. Carr has left with me, for you, an old licence which he received from Sir James Wright in 1774; I now inclose it. Mr. Barnard will write you fully on the present situation of the nation; as he is master of the language, he may inform you of what does not come to my knowledge. Having nothing further to communicate, I remain, with due respect,

Yours, &c., &c.,

R. T.

HONOURABLE BEN HAWKINS.

Cusseta, April 25th, 1797.

Sir:

On my return to this place, I acquainted the female mentioned by Colonel Hawkins of his wish for her to proceed to your garrison. She informed me that it was a bad time of the year to go a-visiting, as she had her corn, pease, &c., to attend to, but if she continued in health, she would pay you a visit in the fall. I have not been able to procure you the different seeds I promised, as the Indians had reserved no more than what was necessary for their own planting. The ensuing harvest will enable me to procure you a sufficient quantity. The Indians appear peaceably inclined, and the chiefs are collecting the horses late stole to have them returned. Last evening an Indian who had been hunting returned and says the white people have a great quantity of cattle on Little River and frequently fishes on the creeks on their land; that they have been told these was to have been removed, but they doubt it.

The bearer of this letter wishes you to give him permission to purchase a keg of rum or whiskey; he has promised not to drink it until he returns home. He will thank you to supply him with some Indian meal. I send with him two letters for Colonel Hawkins; I have not the least doubt but he will deliver them safe. I shall be happy to hear from you and will be much obliged to you for a few newspapers.

R. T.

COLONEL GAITHER.

Cusseta, April 29th, 1796.

Dear Sir:

Yours of the 25th I received on the 26th with one quire of paper, 6 quills and a paper of ink powder. Yesterday there was a meeting of the chiefs at the factor Fullateegee's; the result of their consultation I have not heard. I wish you to enquire of your son if he has no letter for me from Mr. Price, as I wrote him & Mr. Seagrove by your son. Grey goes for Colerain in a few days; if you wish to write, you can send your letter in by Mr. Elhert and I will give them to Grey. If you have any late newspapers, I will thank you to lend them to me. Expecting to hear from you by return of Mr. Elhert, I remain, with respect,

Your most obedient honourable servant,

R. T.

T. B., ESQ.

Cusseta, May 2nd, 1797.
Dear Sir:

This moment Mr. Thomas Powell arrived here, and informs me that the federal troops had taken four men citizens of the State of Georgia a fire hunting on the Indian land; these men were confined in the garrison, and Colonel Lamar came with 100 men to demand them, but they were not replaced, and Captain Webb had orders to conduct these men to Savannah with his troop of horse & a party of rifle men, & the people in the country were determined to give the federal troops battle. Should the Georgians be so imprudent as to attack the troops, we may expect to hear of hanging before the business is settled.

Mr. Powell is very sorry that he missed the path to your house, and as he brought two letters for you, I thought proper to send the bearer.

The result of the meeting at the ———— is to kill the Euchee, but I do not believe they will do any thing.

Mr. Powell did not see Mr. Clark & has brought the order back which your nephew drew on account of Counts. Mr. P. has left the order with me, & if C. should leave your house, expects he will leave 25 dollars in your hands, being the amount of the order drawn by your nephew. Expecting to hear from you by return of the bearer, I am,

Yours, &c.,

R. T.

T. B., ESQ.

————

Cusseta, S. C., May 7th, 1797.
Sir:

On the 21st of March I wrote you by Mr. B.'s son, who has returned some days ago, but I have not heard of his bringing any letters. By the return of Mr. Grey, I will be obliged to you for my account.

————

House Expences.

————

Oct. 26, Corn ....$ 30.00
Beef 30.00
Fowls 5.00
Potatoes 1.00
Ground Nuts 2.00

Oct. 27,	Butter	15.00
	Pans	3.00
	Hireling	12.00
	Fowls	1.00
	Corn	9.00
	Rice & bread	2.00
Nov. 2,	Corn	4.00
	Do	10.00
	Bacon	8.00
	Bread & pumpkins	2.00
6,	Potatoes	2.00
	Bread	1.00
7,	Corn	5.00
10,	Pumpkins & bread	2.00
	4 yds. stripe	16.00
11,	Bread	2.00
13,	Do	4.00
	Potatoes	1.00
15,	Do	1.00
	Corn	3.00
	3 yds. linsey	12.00
	2 Shawls	8.00
16,	A hog	8.00
17,	Potatoes	1.00
22,	Bread	3.00
23,	Corn	1.00
	Eggs	1.00
30,	Bread	1.00
	Pumpkins	
	Eggs	1.00
	Bacon	33.00
	Butter	9.00
Dec. 1,	Beef	30.00
	Fowls	1.00
12,	Bread	1.00
16,	Corn	20.00
	Bacon	100.00
17,	Potatoes	4.00
	Hog	10.00
18,	Corn	4.00
20,	Rice	12.00
	Hog	12.00
25,	Bread	4.00
	Hatchet	5.00

```
28, Corn  ..........................................  4.00
    Bread  .........................................  1.00
30, Peas  ..........................................  2.00
    Fowls  .........................................  4.00
                                                    _____
                                                    $447.00
```

Memorandum of Sundries Sent For By Wm. Grey, May 10th, 1797.

1 frying pan, 2 pewter plates, 2 basons, 1 lamp, 4 coffee cups & saucers, 1 trowel, 1 gridiron, 2 dishes, 2 smoothing irons, 6 3 square files.

Cusseta, 12th May, 1797.

Sir:

Yesterday at the Ball Ground, I received from the Little Prince a black mare, near fifteen hands high, branded I. A., the property of a Mr. Phillips. I have sent her to you by Challee; at the same time two Cumberland horses taken out of a waggon were delivered up to be sent to A. C. Your letter to Mr. Price I gave to Grey, and he promised to take great care of it & safely deliver it; he sets off on Saturday next. I shall be happy to hear from you by return of Joe. Having nothing new, I remain,

Your most obedient honourable servant,

R. T.

T. B.

Cusseta, May 12th, 1797.

Dear Sir:

I received yours this moment of the 9th inst., & to-morrow there will be a meeting of the chiefs at the Coweta, at which I shall attend. I shall write Alex, but I hear he is not at home, being in the woods with a young wife, & when he arrives, he has nobody to read for him. Your daughter's silverware is in hand, & as soon as finished I shall send it by the first safe opportunity. I have heard that the Euchees intend going out to do more mischief; the truth of this report I am not certain of. Adieu.

Yours sincerely,

R. T.

T.B.

Cusseta, May 12th, 1797.

Sir:

I wrote you on the 24th of April, but as the Indians was crossing the river, I received information of the Euchees having done mischief on the Oconee. I detained your letters in consequence of this news until now. Mr. B. having hired H. Reed to go express to you in the Cherokees, I have intrusted him with this letter and the letter of the 24th of April. The chiefs of the Lower Creeks determined last week to kill the Euchees, who had spilt blood on the Oconee. As yet nothing has been done, & to-morrow there is to be a meeting at the Cowetas, at which I shall attend. I cannot say how this business will end. The Euchees, I hear, are determined to act on the defensive if the Creeks should insist on their giving satisfaction. Horses brought from the frontiers are delivering up slowly. I wrote Mr. S. & Mr. P. on the 21st of March, but have never received any answer.

Your letters to Mr. Wm. Carr, Bailey & Grierson were safely delivered, and I read your letter to A. C. and gave him your order on Mr. Price for his salary in presence of Mr. Burges.

I heard yesterday that more of the Euchees intended going out to do mischief; should this be their intention, it would be doing them justice to retaliate. Wishing you health and expecting soon to see you in this nation, I remain, with great respect,

Yours, &c., &c.,

R. T.

HONOURABLE B. H.

Cusseta, May 18th, 1797.

Sir:

On the 11th inst. I received from T. B. a letter dated Flint River, 9th, in which he has desired me to inform you that his negro Joe returned from Fort Fidins on the 6th, having delivered to Colonel Gaither 6 head of horses which had been delivered by the Lower Creeks to be restored to their owners. The Colonel also informs him that he sent four citizens of the State of Georgia (who were found with guns on Indian land) to Savannah gaol, there to be tried by the Federal Law; these men were sent under the charge of Captain Webb and 48 dragoons. The Euchees have lately killed one white man and one white woman, burnt three houses and the fences on the frontiers about 12 miles above Carr's Bluff. It is time for the chiefs to seriously think on the situation of their nation, and to recollect the long account which was against them at Colerain. This conduct of the Euchees only adds to their former score. The determination of the chiefs of the Lower Creeks respecting the Euchees, the bearer can fully inform you of, as he had a conversation with the Cusseta king last evening. The white people are now kept by the troops from coming over the line. It is necessary for the chiefs to exert themselves and restrain their young people from killing, stealing, &c., &c. Having nothing further to communicate, I remain,

Yours, &c.,

R. T.

A. C.,
Tuckabatchee.

Cusseta, May 25th, 1797.

Sir:

The bearer, John Thompson, (a free black) wishes you to let him have to the amount of twenty dollars; if it will suit you to let him have to that amount on my account, let me know by him, as he intends to return here to-morrow & I will give him an order on you. When convenient I shall be glad to see you at my hut.

R. T.

W. T. MARSHALL.

Cusseta, June 1st, 1797.

Sir:

As the bearer was crossing this river on the 24 of April, I received information of the Euchees having killed a man at Long Bluff, and not knowing what other parties were out, I thought it best to detain him until I was certain what depredations had been committed. The letters I mentioned in my last, which I had intrusted the Indian with for Colonel Hawkins, I have sent to him by an express, which left this place on the 14th of May. The chiefs of the nation have determined that if Colonel Hawkins, on his return to the nation, should insist on satisfaction for the man killed at Long Bluff, to kill the Indian who led the party, and one of the women, the plea of the Indian is that he lost his son by Harrison and never received satisfaction, altho' he had waited a long time.

By a residenter in the Cherokees, who came to the Cowetas on the 26th of May, I am informed that Colonel Hawkins did not set out for the point where they were to begin runing the line until the 12th of May; this was owing to some misunderstanding between the chiefs.

The Choctaws, I hear, are much averse to the runing the line thro' their nation agreeable to the treaty between the United States & Spain.

The Indians in general appear disposed for peace, and the chiefs have gave up some horses which their young men had stole, and promises fair to return all that their people shall in future bring in, but you are no stranger to Indian promises.

A party of the Cowetas who had been a-hunting, returned a few days ago with the loss of three horses, which they say the people of Georgia took from their camp; that they had done the white people no injury. The chiefs have heard that some Indians belonging to the Halfway House have stole horses for the white people, & they suppose that the white people who took the horses from the Cowetas were in pursuit of the horse thieves. As soon as these horses come in, the chiefs will take & send them to Mr. Barnard for to be restored to their owners, & when that is done, they expect the horses taken from the Cowetas will be returned.

R. T.

LIEUTENANT COLONEL GAITHER.

June 5th, 1797.

Dear Sir:

On the 3rd, Reed came here and informed me that he returned to the Cowetas on the 1st inst., having delivered the letters for Colonel Hawkins to a Mr. Robert Brown in the Cherokees, who gave him a receipt for them and promised to send them on to Tellico Blockhouse. Mr. Dinsmoor was with Colonel Hawkins. Confusion was so great among the whites, who rose and opposed the runing of the line, as it went thro' their plantations, that Colonel Hawkins & the other Commissioners were obliged to quit and go to the other end of the line to begin; in his return, it will of course return thro' their plantations. Reed has no other news but that corn is very scarce. I have nothing new to write you. Adieu.

Yours, &c.,

R. T.

T. BARNARD, ESQ.

June 12th, 1797.
Dear Sir:

Yours of the 6th I received on the 11th, with the garden seeds
& newspapers. I wrote you 2 letters on the 12th, which I sent
by Oswullge & a mare, and on the 5th inst., informing you of
Reed's return. There is no person going out of the Cowetas to
steal horses but Reed; as the horses which were taken from the
Cowetas by the Georgians belonged to him, the horses which you
mention being in the Cowetas I never saw, but on the 20th of last
month, Nick Black's nephew came to me for pay for three horses
belonging to him, which he said he had been informed I had sent
into Georgia. I refered him to Mr. D. for information, & 1 of
the horses has Nick Black's brand, & the Cowetas intend giving
the horses up to the Indians that own them, when that they are
paid for their trouble of bringing them in. The Eufale Creek
people has brought in a Chickasaw scalp. I am very glad to hear
you are coming in; when you arrive, I will conduct you to Carr's
county seat, where you shall hear bloody news from Pensacola;
thirty thousand Spaniards defeated by the British, all killed but
one; this from Carr's Gazette.

Adieu,

R. T.

T. BARNARD, ESQ.

Drew is with A. C.

Cusseta, June 15th, 1797.
Sir:

Yours of the 26th I received yesterday, and a letter for Colonel
Hawkins by Mr. Grey, who had a bad time to return in, being without water on the road three days.

I saw Mr. Donnelly last month, and he told me Mr. Seagrove
had accepted my order but did not pay it, and that he has it at
his house.

Horses that have been stole from the frontiers have been
returned & the chiefs promise to take and return all that shall be
taken from the frontiers of any part of the United States. If
Colonel Hawkins, on his return, insists for satisfaction for the
man killed & woman wounded, but since dead, they will give it.
There is a report in circulation that some of the Upper Creeks
have brought in a Chickasaw scalp.

Cusseta, June 17th, 1797.

Sir:

Since my last, of the 1st of June, I have to inform you that the Creeks are very troublesome to the Spanish Government, and there is a report in circulation that the Eufale Creek people has brought in a Chickasaw scalp.

Such information as I send you respecting the situation of this nation, I will thank you to communicate to Colonel Hawkins. Wishing you health and happiness, I remain,

Your most obedient honourable servant,

R. T.

LT. COL. H. G.

MR. ED. PRICE:

I am destitute of paper & sealing wax; will thank you for a supply. I have drawn on you, for eleven dollars and 24 cents, in favour of Thomas Marshall, & for twenty-one dollars, in favour of John Thompson, which I hope you will accept & charge to

Yours, &c.,

R. T.

JOS. LOCKWOOD, Charleston, No. 2432. Lockwood on the plate.

Cusseta, July 7th, 1797.

Sir:

My letters of April 25th, June 1st & 17th I hope you have received. The Creeks in general appear peaceably inclined; as for the Euchees, there is no dependence in any thing they say; was I to hear them promise peace to-day, I should not be surprised at their doing mischief before next spring. It will be great satisfaction to me to see Colonel Hawkins in this nation. I am in hopes that when he has had a meeting with the principal chiefs in their own land, and they hear his talks, that they will be sensible of their situation, and for the future cultivate peace and friendship with the people on the frontiers. Permit me to introduce Mr. Marshall to your acquaintance; he is a trader in the Coweta town, very well off in negros, cattle, &c.; now the store he is fixing. I am in hopes that the run of trade will take its course to the Oconee. I wish to write to Colonel Hawkins, but as Mr. Price has sent a letter directed to him in this nation, probably he expects him by the way of the Cherokees. If you have heard what time the Colonel may be expected, I will thank you to let me know, as numbers of the Indians are daily asking of me when they are to see him in this nation. We have had very dry weather for this some time past, and without a plenty of rain the Creeks will be very hungry next year.

Yours, &c.,

R. T.

LT. COL. H. GAITHER.

_____

Cusseta, August, 23rd, 1797.

MR. ED. PRICE:

Sir:

Yours of the 19th of July I received on the 25th, by Mr. Marshall, with my watch, the glass broke. Mr. M. had the misfortune to lose my salt in the Flint River; I got one bag from him, which will do me for the present. Yours of the 5th of August, by the Tussekiah Mico, came to hand on the 19th, with the paper & wax. Peter I have not seen, nor the Coweta Indian. I hear Peter is at the Bird King's, very unwell. I expect Colonel Hawkins will not be long before he is in this nation. I have met with a misfortune in my riding saddle; will be glad if you would send me one by H. Reed, & let him chuse it, as he knows what kind of a saddle will fit my horse. If you have salts, I want 1 lb., & ¼ lb. of ginger in the clove & two lancets.

Yours, &c.,

R. T.

_____

Cusseta, August 26th, 1797.

Sir:

Agreeable to the request you made me when at Fort Fidins, I demanded of Tobler the rifle he had stole from your garrison. His reply was he had stole no rifle, but that one of the soldiers belonging to the fort gave him one, which he had sold long ago, & that he never intended to return it. I hope Mr. Martin & your family is in health, and I remain, with sincere esteem,

Yours, &c.,

R. T.

T. MARTIN.

August 26th, 1797.

Sir:

A number of the traders would have been with you before this, but by Mr. Marshall they are informed that you have not goods. As soon as goods is at your store, it would be well to inform the traders, or else those indebted to you will take their skins to Mr. P. You will find ready made great coats & trowsers of cloth a saleable article, if not too high, & a few plated half curbs with good reins. Morgan, who is in your debt, I am informed is leaving the nation and intends settling at Tenesaw. We have nothing new in this part; the bearer, Mr. Maclin, can inform you when Colonel Hawkins will be at Fort Wilkinson. Wishing you a continuance of health in your new situation, I am,

Yours, &c., &c.,

R. T.

MR. PRICE.

Cusseta, August 26th, 1797.

Sir:

Yours dated Knoxville, 14th July, I received on the 12th inst., and yesterday Mr. Maclin came here & gave me fifty dollars. There was a meeting of the chiefs of the Lower Creeks at the Hitchities on the 20th. Mr. Barnard interpreted your talk. John Kennard opposed the giving satisfaction for Brown until you had Harrison brought to the Fort & executed. I plainly see these Creeks will do nothing until you have had a meeting with them.

From the Georgia Gazette I received the account of the plan formed by the late Governor Blount and others. I had no idea of the existence of such a plan. I never approved of Chisholm's conduct, as you will see by the following extract of a letter from me to Mr. Seagrove, dated 19th September, 1796. (Extract.)

Yesterday I copied a letter from Mr. S. to Colonel John Kennard; Mr. Barnard will send it to you. My account against the U. S. Mr. S. has not paid. Mr. Price informs me that Mr. S. has no fund. I am in debt to Mr. Price 132.8. I wish much to discharge it, but it is not in my power until I receive what is due in Mr. S.'s time.

You may rest assured of my paying attention to the interest of the United States, and if I was master of the language, it would enable me to be of more service than I am at present.

Yours, &c.,

R. T.

H. B. H.

Cusseta, 26th, August, 1797.
Sir:

Yours of July 20th I received on the 25th, & by the arrival of a Mr. Maclin from Knoxville, I am informed that Colonel Hawkins will be at your garrison some time next month. The Indians wish much to see him.

The female cannot leave the nation until her crop is under cover.

We have had favourable rains of late, & I have some hopes that the Indians will make a tolerable crop. There is no news a-stirring here. Mr. Maclin can give you information respecting the western waters, & I remain,

Yours, &c., &c.,
R. T.
L. C. H. G.

Cusseta, August 31st, 1797.
Sir:

Mr. Barnard, who left this on the 27th, desired me to inform you that the bearer, J. Forrester, has come down to purchase a rifle from Mr. Price & to beg a bag of salt from you. Accept of my wishes for your health & prosperity, & I remain,

Yours, &c.,
R. T.
L. C. H. G.

Cusseta, September 16th, 1797.
Sir:

On the 29th of last month Mr. D. crossed this river with his horses, traded with D. skins, & informed me that he saw a letter in the Upper Creeks signed G. C., informing the traders that you did not want them down until the month of November. Morgan, who is in your debt, has left the nation & carried his property with him. The traders & Indians are preparing to come & see you; I should have been down myself, but am waiting the arrival of Colonel Hawkins in this part of the nation. Have wrote Colonel Hawkins by this opportunity, but if he has left Fort Wilkinson for the nation, will thank you to return the letter directed to him.

Wishing you health, &c.,
R. T.
MR. PRICE.

Cusseta, September 16th, 1797.

Sir:

Since my last of the 26th of August by Mr. Maclin, I have been informed that the Euchees who lost their relations by Harrison are very cross; it is probable they may do mischief. They have been talked to by the head men of the towns around them; what effect their talks may have, time only can discover. By a resident of Tombigbee I have been informed that the Spaniards had evacuated the fort at the Natches & that the Commissioners were runing the line. Having nothing further to communicate at this time, I remain, with due respect,

Yours, &c.,

R. T.

HONOURABLE B. H.

————

September 18th, 1797.

Sir:

On the 17th I was sent for to the Cowetas by the H. K'g., who requested me to write a leter for him to you, & he would send it by John Galphin. I told him I was willing to write any thing he should request, but to send it by Galphin I could not, as Galphin was not employed to carry letters, and the last time he was at Colerain, the Coweta Indians stole horses, killed cattle & hogs. The Hollowing King then requested me to inform you that it was his wish to see you in this land before the head men had turned out a-hunting, but should you be detained after your arrival at Fort Wilkinson, he wished you to inform him of the time when he might expect to see you and he would detain the head men until your arrival. He has a letter for you from Mr. Dinsmoor, who told him to deliver it into your hands, & he says he will keep it safe until he sees you. Galphin has desired me to inform you that he has behaved well, never urged any Indians to Colerain, or was the occasion of horses being stole or cattle & hogs killed. On the 6th an Indian belonging to the Broken Arrow brought in two negros; he says he found them between the Oconee & Oakmulgee. They say they belong to a General McIntosh, & the plantation they came from was near Savannah, their names Billy and July. I demanded these negros, but was told that they should stay where they were until you come into the nation, when they should be delivered up. I hear that runers are sent after the Euchees who went to spill blood, commanding them to return.

R. T.

H. B. H.

Cusseta, September 18th, 1797.

Sir:

Yours by Russel I received yesterday. When you are better acquainted with the traders in this nation, you will find that they speak large. Mr. Marshall, by saying you had no goods, meant that you had not a suitable assortment for the trade. It gives me great satisfaction to find your goods arrived, and I expect the demand will be large this winter, as the last accounts from Pensacola say Mr. Panton's ship is not arrived. I shall inform the traders in the upper towns by the first opportunity that offers, so that in 5 or 6 weeks you may expect a number of traders down. Bailey, Schoy & Durant will be among the first. I have wrote Colonel Hawkins. I also wrote you and the Colonel on the 16th, but I suppose you will receive this first. The Indian who comes with Mr. Daniel is my squaw father-in-law. I will esteem it as a favour, if you will give a small supply of provisions to return home. Mr. Daniel is to give him 5 dollars for conducting him to Fort Wilkinson, and the Indian, who is well known in your neighbourhood by the name of Tom, has requested me to desire you will see him paid.

R. T.

E. P.

Cusseta, September 25th, 1797.

Sir:

Last night an Indian belonging to this town returned from Little River shot thro' the thigh by two white men. The wound, I believe, is not dangerous. I cannot give you the particulars of this transaction, as I have not seen the Indian and the bearer of this is in a great hurry. Hoping to have the pleasure of soon seeing you in this part of the nation, I remain, with great respect,
Your most obedient servant,

RICHARD THOMAS.

H. B. H.

Cusseta, October 1st, 1797.

Sir:

This morning I received a letter from Colonel Hawkins informing me that he would be in the Cussetas about the 5th of this month.

I now send you a letter I have had some time in my house, but an opportunity did not offer before. I am,

Yours, &c.,

R. T.

A. C.

_____

Cusseta, 22nd October, 1797.

Sir:

David Randal, who resides in this town, has called for the purpose of obtaining a letter of credit. He has been informed that you have the direction of the store & will judge if credit should be given and to what amount. He brings with him 120 deer skins.

R. T.

MR. E. PRICE:

Colonel Hawkins requests you will let him have, or procure for him, one pair of cotton cards & charge the amount to the Indian Department.

R. T.

_____

Cusseta, 24th October, 1797.

Sir:

By this time I hope you have had my great coat & overhauls made; if ready, send them by Reed, and get me made six shirts, half trimmed of linen, at 60 or 70 cts., 2 pair flannel drawers and one pair of blue overhauls; the salts & ginger, if to be had. I wish to receive 3 yards of your chintz and 4 yards of calico, one women's riding saddle, two large blankets and a few strings of your cut garnet & white beads, & a few black wampum; one pair of shoes, 9½ in. in length, and one pair 10½ in. The great coat, overhauls & shirts I wish you to send as soon as made, by the first opportunity that offers, as the cold weather is advancing fast; the other articles by whoever will take them; probably Reed or Whitaker. Shall write again in a few days, & remain, with respect,

Yours, &c.,

R. T.

MR. ED. PRICE.

Coweta, January 9th, 1814.

Remember that day the talk assembly at Cusseta. You may act as well as you will, but you can't please an Indian, for there is no pleasing them until they are all whipt.

Monday, 8th. At 12, crossed the Oakmulgee & camped. (Page in pencil obliterated.) They sent me 1 shoulder, 1 leg, 1 backbone of a fat buck. Rainy night.

Tuesday, 9th. Fair morning, horses missing; at M. found the horses, went on at 1 o'clock and took up camp at ½ past 3. In the evening a young hunter brought me a leg of a doe.

Wednesday, 10th. All the hunters turned out at daybreak, & at M. returned. One of them wounded a buck & went with his dog after it. At ½ past 1 P. M., moved on, and at three took up camp. A young Indian turned out & killed a buck; brought in nothing but the skin. High wind, N. & N. E. Severe frost at night.

Thursday, 11th. Fine morning, horses safe. Two Indians turned out & 40 after 8 A. M. heard two bears. The old Indian dreamed that the Indians had killed white people. At 11 A. M. Tom returned with one turkey.

40 minutes after 11 the young hunter brought in a young buck & sent me two thighs and two shoulders. At M. the venison was all cut up and on the scaffold; at 20 minutes after 2 the venison barbecued. The Indian who went with his dog after the deer he wounded returned, having at last struck the path 3 miles ahead, with the skin & back strip. At ½ past 3 moved on; at 4 crossed Tukosaukey; at 6 took up camp.

Friday, 12th. Fine morning.

Note. The Indians remarked that the weather being fair & calm was the relations of the dead Indian had taken satisfaction & that his spirit was at rest. At 10 moved on; at 11 o'clock crossed Chuckuauna; at 4 P. M. camped. Oakstrovia Othuthlo Opvey went to the Talina Encathlsio & procured a bag of lye homoney.

Saturday, 13th. Cloudy morning, the horses missing; found at 11; at 10 minutes after 11 moved on, and in 30 minutes after 2 o'clock, came to Flint River, opposite the Buzzard's Roost; sent the horses over at the ford & carried our baggage in a canoe made out of an old rotten oak with a log lashed on each side. We found several Indians crossing; one of them had a large gang of hogs in good order, 30 returning home; they had been in the wood between Flint & Oakmulgee. It was dark when we had got all over and camped on the bank. I sent our horses down the river to a cane brake; this is excellent land and the Indians seem disposed to return & settle it.

Sunday, 14th. Cloudy morning; two of the men crossed the river, which detained us till ½ past 11. Went on to Padga Liga & camped. Rain all night.

Monday, 15th. Rainy morning; the black mare missing. Left our camp at ½ past 3, saw no sign of the black mare; at ½ past 5 came close to a large reedy branch full of water. The loss of the mare obliged me to put one saddle and my saddle bags, tent & 2 turkeys on my black colt; took up at dark on a large reedy branch full of water that crossed the path.

Sunday, 16th. Frosty night & fair, & I moved on; found the large creeks; swerving, took up on the big creek at 30 after 3, loosing our baggage in crossing.

Wednesday, 17th. At 9 moved on the big creek, swimming, carried over & at night arrived at my own house. Found 5 of my pigs had died thro' neglect in not feeding; heard that Michael Elhert had crossed the day before; that Mr. Howard & Colonel had crossed three days ago, & that two white men had gone for Fort Wilkinson.

Thursday, 18th. Went to the Tallauhassee at Tyler's. Mr. Darouzeaux, Tyler & Michael was taking an account of what Michael had brought & the Indians very troublesome in pilfering. On my arrival they kept at a distance, saying the cross white man was come. Assisted in counting what was delivered to Tyler, & received from Tyler 2 quire of paper, 1 pewter ink stand & 1 stick of sealing wax. At the request of Mr. Carr, I gave him one dose of salts for a negro wench that was sick & returned by his house. Notified Lovat & Carr that I had licences for them when they brought me the necessary security.

Friday, 19th. The Indians drunk. Reed & Shugart called on their way to the blacksmith's.

Saturday, 20th. David Randon & Wancy applied for ploughs. Mr. Darouzeaux came down. Gave him some wafers & a stick of sealing wax. Wrote T. B. & sent him 27 silver beads by his nephew, John Cloudy.

Sunday, 21st. Killed my large hog, weight 250 lbs. Peter Shugart & Hardy Reed applied for ploughs.

Monday, 22nd. Rain all night & very sultry. The Bird King called for a note to the blacksmith to make him a bell. He has a piece of an old saw & a piece of an old brass kettle. The Bird King is in want of a drawing knife, a saw & a plane.

Beaumont Sutton applied for a plough, drawing knife, chisel, gouge, augur, ax, hand saw.

Tuesday, 23rd. Went to the Broken Arrow with the Bird King & second man. Received from Tyler one blank book, a list of goods brought up by Michael & Wilson & a paper of needles. High wind & severe frost at night.

Wednesday, 24th. Thomas Carr came & on settling accounts find a balance of fifteen dollars due me. Patrick Donnely called here. Mr. Carr wants the lend of a cross cut saw & grind stone. Find by the Indians that Galphin did not rightly interpret what the Cowetas had to say, who lost their relations; his conduct much disapproved by the Indians.

Thursday, 25th. Reed called. Grey came on settling accounts. Find a balance due Grey of twelve dollars; promised him silver & to go down to his house on Thursday next. Grey has forty silver broaches at Sukey's to purchase corn. Went to Sukey's, who is a-spinning; transplanted two peach trees.

Friday, 26th. Cloudy, heavy rain & high wind at night.

Saturday, 27th.

Sunday, 28th. Grey called; I gave him silver to the amount of eight dollars. Gave Mingco an order on Mr. Carr for two chalks & gave him some seed.

Cusseta, January 28th, 1798.

Sir:

From accidents which have happened on the path I did not arrive here until the evening of the 17th, and was informed that Michael Elhert had crossed on the 16th, his horses much fatigued; two he left at this place, one of them since dead. On the 18th, I went to the Tallauhassee, and at Tyler's found Michael Elhert (assisted by Mr. Darouzeaux) counting the articles he had brought. I assisted. Michael was obliged to leave at Wancy's (Bellows) hatchet, 2 camp kettles, 4 tin kettles with 3 covers, 3 pewter plates, 2 long handle frying pans & two horse collars & harness. The kettles, plates and frying pans I have brought over to my house; the tin kettles much bruised and one of them useless. All the articles were in good order, except a few pieces of ribband, the paper cases of the burning glasses and the needles, which were wet. I requested Tyler to have them dryed. The anvil that came up, Tyler kept, & Michael declined carrying the blacksmith's tools until your arrival, as his horses was much fatigued. He took with him 1 $\times$ cut saw, 16 ploughs, 3 dozen of hoes & 1 grindstone. Wilson had previous to the arrival of Michael taken to the upper towns for the Singer, 2 axes, 1 hand saw, 1 drawing knife, 2 augurs, 2 hand saw files. McFerson: 1 hand saw, 1 drawing knife, 6 hand saws, 6 drawing knives, 12 axes, 4 shovels, 6 hand saw files.

David Randon, Juan Anthony, Sandoval, Hardy Reed & Peter Shugart have requested me to inform you that they will cultivate large fields of corn if they can be assisted with ploughs. Mr. Carr has his negros at work and will be thankful for the lent of a grindstone & a cross cut saw. On the 25th cotton spun by the wife of David Randon of the Cusseta; the women approve much of the plan for introducing the culture of cotton & the spinning wheel and I have had several applications for cotton seed, cards & wheels. The reply I make is that there is plenty of seed at the factory, free of expence to those that will plant it, & by the time the cotton is fit to pick the beloved man will have the cards and wheels to distribute to those that will use them. If you should have an opportunity to send some cotton seed, I will distribute it in such quantitys as you shall think proper. Soohahoey brought two gallons up, but will not spare to any of her neighbours a single grain; she is determined to plant the whole, & requests me to tell you not to forget the small wheel and cards. The turkeys are doing well. Some of the Indians grumble & groul about the trees that are cut down round the blacksmith's shop; they say a fort is to be built there & they are to be made slaves of. Some of them has talked with me on this subject; I freely told them the blacksmith could not eat old hatchets and hoes; that the walls of the fort would be rails & the garrison would consist of cabbage, collards, turnips, beans, peas, &c., &c. I always find the Indians averse to a white man's clearing a field and having a stock of cattle, but they never appear dissatisfied when asked to partake of beef, hogs, or the produce of the garden. The negro Ned that is at Marshall's has never been with Tyler, who tells me he is much at a loss to know how to get the plank Downs has left him, & he has employed Henry Wilson to blow and strike for him. The Indians carry him a great deal of difficult jobs. He is very industrious, does all he can, but is much dissatisfied with his situation, as the Indians are very troublesome. I have just been informed that the Cowetas intend turning out to-morrow to take satisfaction. The Indians often talk of taking satisfaction when they least intend it; it is very probable they will wait until they hear from you. I hope your troublesome companion, the gout, has bid you adieu. Accept of my best wishes for your health & happiness, and I have the honour to be, with due respect,

Yours, &c.

H. B. H.

Cusseta, January 28th, 1798.

Sir:

The females of this nation approve much of Colonel Hawkins's plan of introducing the culture of cotton and the spinning wheel; it may, in the course of a few years, induce the young men to throw away the hungary flute. They all appear satisfied with the Colonel's orders for the factor to purchase such articles as they have to dispose of, and if proper encouragement is given, a few years may transmiogrify a nation of hunters into farmers. When the females are able to cloathe themselves by their own industry, it will render them independent of the hunter, who in turn will be obliged to handle the ax & the plough, and assist the women in the laborious task of the fields, or have no wife. This the men already begin to perceive, which makes them backwards to encourage what will in time be for their mutual benefit. I enclose you a letter for Colonel Hawkins and one for Mr. Barnard, who I expect is with you. I have heard nothing lately from the westward, and this is a barron country for news. I was informed that the Cowetas intended turning out to-morrow to take satisfaction, but it is probable they will wait until they hear from Colonel Hawkins. Accept of my best wishes for your health and prosperity, and I remain, with due respect,

Your most obedient honourable servant,
RICHARD THOMAS.
LT. COL. HENRY GAITHER.

Monday, 29th. Women on this side turned out to clear up their ground & prepare for planting. Went to the Broken Arrow and delivered Lovat his mare, & received from Tyler 1 spade, 1 grubbing hoe & 1 drawing knife.

Tuesday, 30th. John came & covered the house. Peter brought me, in all, 17 peach trees, which I set out, & paid him 4 rings.

Wednesday, 31st. The last day of March.

Thursday, February 1st. John came & split boards to make me a cabin; settled with him & gave him an order on Mr. Carr for the balance, twenty-two dollars.

Friday, 2nd.

Saturday, 3rd.

Sunday, 4th. Went to the Tallauhassee. The Cowetas turned out for satisfaction. Bruce came from the Upper Creeks & wrote a letter to Colonel Hawkins & Colonel Gaither, & informed me that Cox had descended the Tennessee with 8 boats full of men;

that Byers had determined to quit the factory at Tellico, & that the Eufaules had brought in 4 & the Kyatuijes two horses.

Monday, 5th. Wm. Tooley arrived from the Tuckabatchee with letters from Alex Cornel for the blacksmith's tools.

6th. Brought the bellows from Wancy's.

7th. Gave Tooley the blacksmith's tools for the Upper Creeks.

8th. Wm. Tooley went for the Tuckabatchee. Wrote Alex Cornell & Obadiah Lowe.

Friday, 9th. Received a letter from Peter Shugart. 50 yards spun at Steadham's.

MR. RICHARD THOMAS:

Sir:

I heard an Indian say it was very good to take Mr. Reed's goods; that they were Virginia goods; that Samuel Parmer told him so, tho' I don't know whether it is the truth or a lie, as I have not seen him. So no more, but remain,

Your friend,
PETER SHUGART.

Saturday, 19th. Weighed David Randon's bacon, 77 lbs.

Sunday, 11th. Hardy Reed came and informed me that he intended to go for Fort Wilkinson in the morning. Wrote H. B. H., H. G. & T. B.; Reed being in a hurry, took no copies. In the evening received a packet from A. C. directed to H. B. H. or H. G.; sent it by D. Randon.

Monday, 12th.

Tuesday, 13th.

Wednesday, 14th. Planted carrots, raddish, cabbage, &c. Lott came & looked at the garden.

Friday, 16th. Went to the Broken Arrow, ground the club ax & borrowed a froe. Tyler destroyed his keg of rum.

Saturday, 17th. Transplanted scallions. At evening heard that the Cowetas had taken satisfaction.

Sunday, 18th. At evening Lott came.

Monday, 19th.

Tuesday, 20th. John Galphin brought a letter from Colonel Hawkins. McGirt crossed, supplied him with bacon & paid him a dollar. The Cussetas very cross.

Friday, 23. Cabbage, carrots, raddishs, &c. a-springing. Planted pumpkins & musk melons.

Thursday, March 1st.

Saturday, March 3. Received from D. Randon some lettuce seed which I planted immediately.

Sunday, 4th. Went to Tyler's; gave him the seed.

Monday, 5th. The Spaniard named Nappia tyed by six Indians from the Ottasseys.

Saturday, 10th. Received a letter from Colonel Hawkins, with a talk for Yeauholau Mico and Tussekiah Mico. Sent for Mr. Darouzeaux & appointed the 12th for a meeting at the Broken Arrow.

Sunday, 11th. At night received a talk for the Tussekiah Mico informed him that Tuskeegee Tustunnagau was liberated.

Monday, 12th. Read Colonel Hawkins's talk to the Indians, who requested me to copy the talks and send them to A. C. Wrote H. B. H. & sent a packet by Andrew.

Saturday, 17th. Received a letter from H. B. H. brought by Mordecai.

Thursday, 22nd. Received a letter from H. B. H. and T. B. by Whitaker, & received from Whitaker 4 kegs full & 2 bags of salt.

Sunday, 25th. Attended a meeting at the Tallauhassee, read a talk from the Chickasaws & acquainted the Indians that they might expect Colonel Hawkins in 18 days.

Wednesday, 28th. Messrs. Hubbard, Killingsworth & McDaniel arrived, produced their passports & gave me a letter from T. B. The Indians behaved very ill; plundered the unfortunate travelers of two whips and several bridles. I advised them to go to Mr. Carr's, & I went there in a few minutes after them. Found the Indians very unruly; they took more bridles & halters, & one bell. In the evening Tom came home.

Thursday, 29th. Sent Tom over to the square with a talk to the chiefs, to advise their young men to be peaceable & return what had been stole. I went to Mr. Darouzeaux, who promised me to come down in the morning. On my return to Mr. Carr's, I found the Indians had restored part of what they had taken, but were still very insolent.

Friday, 30th. Went to T. C.'s. Mr. Darouzeaux came to my house with Mr. Hubbard. Roguery's sons, John & Ausege, & young Haye agreed to go with the travelers to Miller's.

Saturday, 31st. The travelers left Mr. Carr's, expecting their guides to overtake them; Mr. Carr put them in the road and returned. At 12 the travelers took up on a reedy branch. About 1, seven Indians with guns & 1 with a tomahawk in his hand came to their camp, and after using some words which was not understood, they plundered the unfortunate people.

James Hubbard lost three horses, one man's riding saddle & one woman's saddle, & one pack saddle with all their cloathing and three blankets.

William McDaniel, six horses, 3 men's saddles & 1 woman's saddle, 1 pack saddle, five blankets, 2 guns, 2 bags with cloathing. The unfortunate people returned to Mr. Carr's at night.

Sunday, April 1st. Sent for to Mr. Carr's. Brought the distressed travelers to my house, & received from Mr. Carr 6 shirts & 3 yards stripe. At night received from David Randon one side of bacon.

Monday, 2nd. John returned with one horse, 3 pair women's shoes & 3 books.

Tuesday, 3rd. Young Haye returned with one horse. In the afternoon the Cusseta King, Bird King and head men came to my house and after receiving an account of what was lost, they agreed to send three men in the morning to the Halfway House, where the property is.

Wednesday, 4th. Wrote T. B.:

Dear Sir

Yours by Whitaker I received and stored Colonel Hawkins's strong water & salt in my house, where he will find it safe on his arrival. On the 28th ult. I received yours by Mr. Hubbard, who with his fellow travelers were much insulted on the banks of the river by the unruly youths of this town, who plundered them of two whips and three bridles. I sent for the king, who did not attend, but sent word for the travelers to cross over to my house; as the young men talked of outraging the women, I advised them to go with Mr. Carr, who was on the river bank. Expecting they would be safe at his house in a few minutes, I followed & found the young men insufferably insolent, & cutting the bridle reins, took bridles, halters and one bell. I staid with them until I had seen their horses put in the care of Indians who promised to return them in the morning. At daybreak I returned to Mr. Carr's, found the Indians still insolent & Long Tom's nephew attempting to take a horse, Tom looking on & appeared well pleased. Previous to my going to Carr's, I sent the old man of the house to the square with a talk to the head men advising them to talk to their young people & make them restore the property they had taken; to prevent Tom's nephew taking the horse he had a liking to, I put my saddle on and went to Mr. Darouzeaux, who promised me to come to Carr's in the morning. On my return, I found the youths had restored part of what they

had taken & that the old men was angry with them for their
conduct. Roguery's two sons & young Haye promised to see
them safe to John Miller's.

The travelers were now in hopes of seeing their friends without any further molestation, and on the morning of the 31st, Mr.
Carr advised them to saddle their horses and move on & their
guides would soon overtake them. Mr. C. went a few miles with
them. After Mr. C. had left them, they nooned it on a reedy
branch on the ridge path; they had not rested above an hour when
eight Indians belonging to the Halfway House came to their camp,
shook hands with them, plundered them of twelve horses, bridles,
saddles, blankets, guns & cloathing & scattered their provisions
on the ground. These unfortunate people were now compelled to
return to Mr. Carr's with two old horses, all they had left. In the
morning they sent for me; I brought them to my house, where
they now remain. I have supplied them with provisions & do the
best I can to make their situation comfortable. Yesterday
Roguery's son & young Haye returned with two horses. The
head men came to my house and after receiving an account of
what was lost, promised to send three men to the Tame King. This
morning the horses & saddles may be recovered, but the other
articles I expect will be much scattered. If Colonel Hawkins
comes by your house, remember me respectfully to him and accept
of my wishes for your health and prosperity, and I remain,

Your most obedient servant,

R. T.

T. B., ESQ.

The Cross Fellow, Mad Dog's nephew, came on Booth's mare,
with a bridle belonging to Mr. Killingsworth. Tom & young
Haye took the bridle from him. In the evening the Fellow
returned, took Strange by the hair & throwed a stick at John McD.

Thursday, 5th.

Friday, 6th. Darouzeaux's son returned from the fort with
rum. At night the Indians sent to the Tame King, returned with
2 horses, two guns, 3 saddles, 2 saddle bags & one bag with
cloathing.

Saturday, 7th. Wrote T. B. and sent it by Ausege. Ausege
crossed the river & was stopt by the King. In the afternoon
Bailey's son & Mr. Holmes arrived from St. Mary's; Mr. H.
brought a letter from Mr. Seagrove acquainting the Indians that
he had opened a store at St. Mary's. Long Tom insulted the
white people & broke open my house.

Sunday, 8th. Messrs. Holmes & Bailey went for the Upper
Creeks & John for T. B.'s.

Report the Governor of Havana has informed the Indians that in the spring of the year they shall be supplied with arms & ammunition to fight the British & Americans.

Long Tom's nephew came and took Stephen McDonald's horse. Grey informs of three horses brought in by the Ooseuchees, who says they borrowed them.

Tuesday, 10th. In the evening Mr. G. Foster arrived and informs me that Colonel Hawkins had gone to T. B.'s.

Wednesday, 11th. Long Tom brought S. McDonald's horse. Wrote to Mr. Price for the Warrior King.

Thursday, 12th. Mr. Foster went for the Tuckabatchees, accompanied by the Scratch-face Fellow. Wrote Mr. Darouzeaux to supply me with bacon.

Friday, 13th. Received a letter from T. B.

Saturday, 14th. Matthew Bilbo, Emanuel Chancy & Wm. Vaanderman, with thirteen negros, produced their passports to pass thro' the Creek nation. Two cheeses left here by Pringle on account of Harrod's wife.

Monday, 16th. Long Tom's nephew came, requested me not to scold him, but shake hands with him. I killed a hog, which I bought of Roguery's son's wife for a Stroud blanket. The white hen has hatched seven young turkeys. A severe frost last night, which killed some of the beans. Joseph Hardridge called to see Colonel Hawkins; he says he bought a negro called Summer, of Noah Harrod for three hundred dollars & paid him, but has since been informed by Harrod that the negro is mortgaged to Mr. Edward Price, U. S. Factor at Fort Wilkinson. Peter Shugart informs that the Ooseuchees has brought in two fine horses from Georgia.

Tuesday, 17th. Colonel Hawkins arrived at Tyler's; went & saw him.

Wednesday, 18th. Mr. Foster arrived from the Tallapousie.

Saturday, 21st. Wrote Colonel Gaither by Mr. F.

Monday, 23rd. James Hubbard, his wife & family, accompanied by David Randon, went for Tenesaw.

Saturday, 28th. Messrs. McDonald & Killingsworth & family went for Tenesaw, accompanied by Goodday & his brother. Colonel Hawkins supplied them with provisions & cloathing.

Monday, 30th. Russel says the Ooseuchees drove him off on account of his having a cross cut saw.

Thursday, May 1st.

Saturday, May 12th. Wrote Mr. Price, by Mr. Marshall, for two pieces romal handks. & the balance of my last quarter's salary.

Wednesday, 16th. Purchased of Tuskeegit 107 lbs. bacon at 6 d. sterling per pound, and gave him an order on Mr. Edward Price for 11.75.

June 13th. Returned from the Tuckabatchee & went to Marshall's, and received from him 66.67, my salary from January 1st, to March 31st.

18th. Purchased from Marshall 10 bushels corn at 1 dollar per bushel; paid Marshall twenty-three dollars, in full to this day.

19th. Paid Opithley four dollars.

20th. Settled with Simmons and gave him an order on T. Marshall for twenty chalks, the amount of the balance due him.

Cusseta, June 20th, 1798.

MR. J. W. DEVEREAUX:

Sir:

Please send me by the bearer, Christian Russel, 20 lbs. brown sugar; if you have no brown, send me 10 lbs. of loaf sugar, and 2 lbs. of your best tea; if out of tea, a few pounds of coffee, and half a pint, or a pint of Huxham's Tincture of Bark by the return of Russel. I thank you for the bill of what I am indebted to you, that I may make arrangements to pay it. If I can obtain leave of absence, I will be down some time in September or October. Have nothing new worth communicating, and remain,

Your obedient servant,

R. T.

Cusseta, June 20th, 1798.

Sir:

Colonel B. Hawkins has had a meeting of the chiefs of the Creek nation at Tuckabatchee; they continued in council for several days, banished six white men, passed a law for punishing horse thieves, & promised fair as to other matters. It will give me pleasure to find that they fulfill their promises. Major Freeman passed thro' the nation and went in by the way of Fort James. He called on Colonel Hawkins at Tuckabatchee & staid a night, and the next morning went on. I am happy to hear that the Spaniards have gave up the fort.

The Creeks have nearly finished planting; the prospect of a crop is small. They have so many friends in Georgia that supply them with corn, that they think it hardly worth while to plant at home. You have often talked of visiting the nation; I wish you could make it convenient to come up at the Busk. The Indians will be all in their towns, and you will have an opportunity of seeing all the belles and beaux dressed in their finest cloathes, dancing bare headed in a hot summer's day, & if you should be inclined to visit the other towns in the neighbourhood, I will accompany you and do every thing in my power to render your situation comfortable while you are with the savages; altho' termed savages, you will find some very good natured, civil Indians, and I have not the least doubt but the females will do their mite to make you comfortable with such as they have. I expect by this that France has invaded England & declared war with all the world. There is a flying report that the Tuckabatchees have killed and scalped a woman at Tombigbee. Wishing you every happiness this world affords, I remain, with due respect,

Your most obedient servant,

R. T.

HENRY GAITHER.

24th. Purchased from Marshall 1 piece of binding, 1 woman's flap & 1 knife. Mr. T. B. Singleton, a gentleman from Coosahatche, came to my house.

25. Indians drunk; Colonel Hawkins went to Tussekiah Mico's.

26th. Indians drunk; very peaceable, not one came to the house.

27th. Went to Randall's; he says he goes to the fort in 2 days more to write for 15 pieces coarse calico, & 1 keg of whiskey for Tom & 1 almanac from Colonel Hawkins. Cooked a mess of carrot 14 in. long.

Sunday, July 1st. Yesterday Wancy's horses came from Fort Wilkinson. The Indians drunk & threaten to come over & beat me.

Cusseta, July 1st, 1798.

Sir:

The Indians appear to me to be playing the old game of double, promising and never performing. The Ooseuchees have sent the horses they brought from Georgia to St. Augustine for sale, & from the knowledge I have of Indians, I am confident the Spaniards will find it no difficult task to set them a-plundering & killing on the frontiers, and I much doubt the sincerity of the chiefs in their promises to you. Should a rupture take place between France and America, & Spain join in the contest, you will please give me information as early as possible, and instructions how to conduct myself towards those Creeks, (for I firmly believe until they have had a dose of steel, they will listen to the advise of those who are the enemies of the U. S. Patience, and not a small quantity, is very necessary at this time. The Indians grumble at the scarcity of powder, & the traders' pack horses returning from Pensacola light, induces them to suppose that the time is not far distant when the Georgians will take pay for the stolen horses, cattle & negros).

The intended meeting of the four nations at the Tuckabatchees is for the purpose of preventing (if possible) the runing of the line between Spain and the U. S. (and to stipulate (say beg) for a constant & regular supply of ammunition).

David Randon will deliver you this; his wife begs you will send her one pair of cards, No. 7, some indigo & copperas. (Such newspapers as you wish to send to Mr. Panton, will be obliged to you to send them to me to forward.)

I have also sent you a packet which I received from Mr. Darouzeaux, & one that Michael brought, who wished much to see you; he says Mr. Price does not give the traders a fair opportunity to sell their horses, & that he sold him two at half their value. He will in two months be ready to go to Colerain for the iron & steel that is there, & that he has 4 sleds to make. He hopes you will allow him something extra.

Tuesday, 3rd. Sent a packet brought by Mr. Darouzeaux, & 1 brought by M. E. by David Randon. At night a heavy squal with large hail stones & severe lightning. At night a man arrived from the Eufale & brought from James Burges a letter for Colonel Hawkins, which I gave to D. R., a talk for the Hollowing King of the Coweta & Cusseta King.

Wednesday, 4th. Went to the square & informed the chiefs of the talk. Mr. T. B., Singleton, & D. R. went for Fort Wilkinson. Settled with Mr. S., and gave him an order on Mr. Edward Price, U. S. Factor, for five dollars.

Saturday, 7th. Borrowed of James Lovat 2 quarts salt.

Cusseta, July 7th, 1798

MR. GEORGE CLEM:

You will, on the receipt of this, assist the bearer in finding out a certain white man, name unknown, who passed here yesterday in company with Thomas Lott, and informed Henry Wilson at the Tallauhassee that they were going to your house. If the man has left your house you will inform the bearer where he went, but if he is with you, you will advise him to come peaceably with the Indian that delivers you this, to prevent trouble. I remain,

Your most obedient servant,
RICHARD THOMAS.

Cusseta, July 8th, 1798.

MR. ALEX. CORNELL:

Sir:

Two days ago a man passed here, and by his not calling, I suspect him to be a bad man, and it is the duty of the officers of the U. S. to prevent such characters traveling thro' this nation. I sent after him; the messenger is just returned, not being able to overtake him. You will do well to look after him; I hear he is going to Charles Weatherford's & Bailey's, & if he has not a proper passport from the officers of the government, it will be good to send him to Fort Wilkinson by the way of my house.

July 9th. Went to the square & wrote Colonel Joseph Phillips. Gave Tahigee an order on Mr. Thomas Marshall for twenty chalks for pursuing a white man, name unknown.

Wednesday, 11th. Received from Emautlau Haujo a letter for Colonel Hawkins. Went to the square. Lent Hardy Reed two dollars.

Friday, 13th. John Tyler informed me Colonel Hawkins is to be soon in the nation. Lent him two pieces of beef; drunk in town. Went to Grey's & returned.

Sunday, 15th. Went to Joseph Island's and received from him Mr. Hubbard's saddle. He informs me that a Halfway House man brought an old bay mare & two side saddles; the mare died close to his fence.

Monday, 16th. Sent for to the square and informed that the Cowetas had brought in four horses found this side the line, & Ooseuchees had stole five; one had been bit by a snake and died, the remaining four brought in. Paid Peter Shugart two dollars, being in all, five & half dollars for a shot gun; 50 cents yet unpaid, & paid him 1 dollar for Thomas Lott.

July 17th, 1798.

Sir:

A letter from Mr. Burges to me, without date, which I received on the 3rd, has the following line: "Matters is in pritey good litter here as yet," and I have since heard of some talks that are circulating among the Meccasukeys that there is talks from the Choctaws that the white people are taking their land, & that their friends, the northern tribes, will assist the four southern nations in defending their lands; that the Creeks, after the Busk, are to visit the Spaniards and get a supply of ammunition, & after their return, to turn out and steal horses twice, & then the Simanolees & the lower part of the nation are to fall on St. Mary's and the neighbouring part; the upper part of the nation are to attack the frontiers high up; the Cherokees are at the same time to attack the white people on their line, and the Choctaws and Chickasaws are to co-operate by attacking the settlements on the Mississippi, &c., and the northern tribes are to fall on at the same time. The Little Prince is returned from Pensacola, and says he went there to get advice; that he did not think you was doing what was right, but Mr. Panton had informed him you was a good man; that he must hold you fast and pay attention to the advice you gave, as it was for the good of the red people. The Spanish Governor told him to take you by the hand; that he expected that the Spaniards and Americans would soon be at war; that then he should have talks for his friends, the Creeks, who he had not forgot.

On the 6th Thomas Lott, who had been to Grey's, returned and passed my house without calling, having in company a white man. He called at the Tallauhassee & informed Wilson that the white man & him had called at my house & staid about fifteen minutes; that the man's business was urgent, as he was going to Weatherford's and had been robed by the Chehaws, & should that night go to George Clem's. On receiving this information, I suspected him to be on unlawful business, I sent an Indian after him, but Lott, instead of going to Clem's, had taken him to Joseph Island's, where he slept, and the next morning went on. The Indian returned without overtaking him, and I immediately wrote to the Tuckabatchees, informing Mr. Cornell of his passing here, requesting him to keep a lookout for him, & if he had not proper passports, to send him back. On making inquiry, I find the Chehaws had not robed a white man.

With pleasure I announce to you that the law enacted by the chiefs at the Tuckabatchee, with respect to the horse thieves, has been put in force by Efau Tustunnagau and his warriors and one of the sticks that was made use of to inflict the punishment sent to the Cowetas and the Tallauhassee. The next day the Cowetas brought in four horses; they say they found them this side of the line. Another of the sticks has been sent down the river to the towns below. The Ooseuchees stole five horses from the white people; four is brought in and one died by the bite of a snake. If the chiefs are peaceably inclined, they will certainly punish the horse thieves and deliver up the horses, but if they should be only waiting a supply of powder from the Spaniards, they will not think of fulfilling their promises to you. I shall keep a good lookout, and if any talks or invitations arrives from the Spaniards, will immediately inform you of it.

My garden comes on well; I have cut cabbage with fine heads and carrots 18 in. long. A few days before Tyler's return, 6 old women, escorted by two old men of the Tallauhassee, stormed your fence and cut down and carried off 80 head of your cabbage. I am preparing a piece of ground for turnips and intend sowing some wheat; will be obliged to you for the seed that produces early food for penned up hogs. I have preserved plenty of radish, mustard, lettuce and endive seed. The Cussetas are very attentive and polite to me, & have frequently sent for me to the square. The Busk is now begun at the Hitchitys, & Tustunnagau Opoi (Little Prince) has just called to inform me that he is going to the Busk and intends calling the Ooseuchees to see what the chiefs of that town intend to do with the horse thieves.

19th. I have this moment received your letter of the 14th, and as two days only remain for the chiefs to meet, I set out in the morning for Tuckabatchee, and as my horse is poor, I shall walk. The chiefs of the Lower Creeks are collecting the horses lately brought in, and I expect will send you a talk. I have requested Mr. Darouzeaux to write for them if they should request it. Nothing shall be omitted by me that will serve the U. S., & you may rely on my exertions. Will thank you for a supply of paper, as this is the last sheet I have.

Tom dead. Sent this letter by Emautlau Haujo.

August 6th.

Sir:

On the 20th ult., as I was setting off for Tuckabatchee, David Randon offered to sell me a horse; I made the purchase and moved on, and on the morning of the 22nd arrived at Alex. Cornell's. Water was scarce on the path, only one stream between the Natural Bridge and Tuckabatchee. I observed that the lobelia was withered.

22nd. Heard that the Spaniards have sent a talk to Opoethly Mico; that they had guns, powder & ball for the Indians; that the

Governor of Pensacola would send Anthony Garcon, his interpreter, to the nation in one month to invite the Indians to Pensacola.

23rd. Richard Bailey returned from Tenesaw.

24th. Went to Bailey's; he informed me that Mr. Turnbull had come from the Mississippi, who reported that the line between the U. S. and Spain was begun; that 250 Spaniards and 250 Americans were employed as pioneers; that they had made a good road & bridged and causewayed as they came on, & that waggons followed with provisions. After some days a variation was observed between the Commissioners' instruments; that they halted until Governor Gayoso came from Orleans, who took the medium between the two instruments for the true line; that on Mr. Turnbull's leaving the Mississippi, they had come on 15 miles further; that a Pink Morel came to Tenesaw a few days after Mr. Turnbull, who reported that the line was stopped, and that Mr. Ellicot had gone to Philadelphia. The Commandant of Tenesaw informed Mr. Bailey that he had received a letter from the Governor of Pensacola that there was eighteen thousand dollars in guns, powder, ball, &c., for the Indians at Pensacola; that he did not think it would be peace long.

Mr. Bailey's son is gone to see if the line is stopped or not.

25th. All the men, women and children of Tuckabatchee turned out a-fishing; their seine was made of cane platted, 160 feet long, 30 feet at each end, tapering, and the middle about 4 feet broad. Men & women, boys and girls swimming and supporting the seine, & about 30 strong men at each end, hauling it with grape vine; they caught a few.

26th. From the different reports in circulation respecting the conduct of the Spanish Governor, I thought proper to ask Mr. Cornell one question: You have heard all the talks the Spaniards have gave to the Indians, what do they advise with respect to runing the line between the U. S. & Spain? They say we are fools to suffer the Americans to do as they please with our land; that they do not want any line run. It appears to me, from what I have heard, that the conduct of Don Manuel Gayoso de Lemor, the Governor of Louisiana, is friendly towards the citizens of the U. S., but that the Commandants of the outposts, and the Spanish interpreters & emissaries are secretly preparing the Indians for acts of hostility against the citizens of the U. S.

29th. William Colbert and three Chickasaws arrived.

30th. The chiefs sent for Mr. Cornell and myself to come to the square; on our arrival at the square, after taking a drink, Efau Haujo called the chiefs of the different towns to the war cabbin; as soon as they were seated, Efau Haujo, of Tuckabatchee, addressed the chiefs:

"Thirty-five days were broke to call a meeting of the chiefs of the four nations to this town; when they were near expired, I made an addition of five days more; these being expired, I have waited three days in the square, to give the chiefs sufficient time to attend this meeting, and it is now 43 days since I broke the sticks. Our friends, the Chickasaws, are here, and I expected the beloved man of the four nations, but he is not come; I see his clerk is here; I expect he has something to say to us."

After a pause of a few minutes I begun: Two days before the first of your broken days was expired, I received a letter from the beloved man, in which he requested me to attend your meeting at this place. On the morning after I received his letter, I left the Cusseta, and on the 22nd, in the morning, I arrived at the house of Mr. Cornell, and this day I have the pleasure of seeing the Chickasaws and Creeks smoke the pipe of peace in friendship, under one roof. After you have convened together on the important business for which you called this meeting, I shall return to the square, and should you have any thing to communicate to Colonel Hawkins, it is my duty to pay attention to your request, and I shall do it with pleasure. The President of the U. S. has a great regard for all his red children, and it is his wish that you should have an unbounded confidence in the justice of the U. S. The beloved man has undergone a great deal of fatigue on your account. I have been a witness to many of his restless days and nights. You may rest assured he will do all he can for the red people, but the chiefs must assist him. The assistance that he requires is for you to punish your horse thieves & mischiefmakers, red or white, & the beloved man cannot prevent encroachments on your land if you do not assist him in restraining your wild young men.

I then read a letter from Thomas Perryman & James Burges.

Tussekiah Mico of Cusseta then spoke: "You have heard the talk, and I perceive you pay attention to it; it is time for us to act like men; the talk has been made and it has gone thro' our land that horse thieves should be beat; if beating will not tame them, something else must be done, & peace must be preserved between us and the white people; it will not do for us to lose our land for a few mad men."

I then informed the chiefs that I heard their white brothers had removed the cattle from their land, but the water being low, they recrossed at times; that they then stopped the crossing places, but until the water was higher, their cattle would be apt to stray and they would have to come over and hunt them. The chiefs said they were satisfied with the conduct of the white people in that respect, and well knew it would take time to keep the cattle from recrossing. Mr. Cornell was now informed his wife was speechless and he left the square. The chiefs sat up all night and finished their business.

31st. I went to the square. Efau Haujo addressed the chiefs. This day I intended to have had a talk wrote to the Simanolees, but our interpreter is detained at home by his wife's indisposition; if the breath does not leave her body, it will be wrote to-morrow. The chiefs, after consulting each other, agreed to return to their respective towns, & that Efau Haujo should, at Mr. Cornell's, tell me what to write to the Simanolees.

August 2nd.

Efau Haujo, of Tuckabatchee, to his friends, the Simanolees:

Friends & Brothers:

At the meeting there was only two nations present, Creeks & Chickasaws; the Choctaws & Cherokees were not at the talk.

We wished the four nations to have been at the talk, but the Chickasaws only came and talked over all the matters the same as if all had been present, and considered the land was small that we live on.

We took the Chickasaws fast by the hand and hope that the master of the breath will assist us in preserving an everlasting peace. We have talked over all matters the same as if all had been present, and hope our warriors, women and children will live in peace. The path between the two nations is now made, white, long & broad, and it is our sincere wish that it may never be bloody.

We have talked a great matter over, respecting our land; it is small and the four nations must preserve their land and prevent encroachments on their country. We must look around us and inform each other respecting the situation of our nations.

After we have looked around us, it is necessary to be on our guard against intruders and land speculators, who will attempt to cheat our people out of their land. We well know it is the wish of the President & the Government of the U. S. that we should preserve our land, but we must all be on our guard against speculators of every nation.

The four nations know that the talks made at this town are the laws of the nation, and we hope the Simanolees will take our talk and preserve their land and be all of one mind.

We have considered that no one nation shall part with any of their land without the head men of the four nations are present and give their consent.

We are surrounded by white people of different nations, and if they give us guns and ammunition or cloathing, we shall esteem them, as our friends, wear the cloathing and hunt with the guns, but if any nation wishes us to go to war, we must not take their talk, but set down in peace.

We have made a talk here and we hope you will pay attention to it, that no nation will dispose of their land, but pay respect to this talk, & do nothing without the consent of the other nations.

Some of our people are ignorant and the speculators will attempt to impose on them and bring trouble on us. We make this talk that the whole nation may know that no individual can part with any of our land. We are all red, altho' our languages differ; we must be at peace and assist each other. If the white people around us should go to war, it is our determination to be at peace and keep in friendship with all the white people around us, but not take any part in their wars.

We have agreed if any thing happens on the frontiers, that the Choctaws and Chickasaws will settle all misunderstandings that may arise near them, and that the Creeks and Cherokees will do the same.

There are men among the white people that distract our people by giving them advice. The four nations have considered that if the Spaniards or Americans have any thing to say to us, that they will send a beloved man, to whom we will listen as to a friend.

We have appointed one man in the Chickasaws, William Colbert, to remove the land speculators in their neighbourhood; not to make any disturbance, but to keep the white people within their line.

The four nations of red people ought to be as one, and if any of the younger brothers should go astray, we have appointed the Chickasaws to set matters to rights.

The chiefs of the four nations will strictly guard their frontiers, to prevent encroachments, and exert themselves to prevent their young people stealing any thing belonging to their neighbours. The Choctaws will pay due attention from Tombigbee to Natches, the Chickasaws will guard their frontier, & the Cherokees will, on their part, guard as far as Appalache, and the Simanolees will guard the frontiers towards the Spaniards. We all met and agreed to bury all past grievances and settle all matters with our neighbours and friends, & in token of our everlasting friendship, we have cut up a large piece of tobacco, filled our pipes, and made a white smoke in token of friendship with all our neighbours, red and white, & as the smoke ascended to the skies never to return, so we hope to remain in peace with red and white as long as the sun rises. The Chickasaws came here, and having heard our talks, agreed to them, and we find we are of one mind. The Simanolees must mind and not take any step without the consent of the four nations, but look that no encroachments are made near St. Mark's, St. Augustine & the Spanish settlements.

You must all look on Colonel Benjamin Hawkins as the agent for the four nations, and you must do nothing without the consent of the four nations.

We sent for Colonel Hawkins to come and assist us, as he is one of our brothers, but he is a good way from us. Colonel Hawkins was appointed for the four nations, and as we did not wish for him to ride all over the land, we thought fit to send for the heads of the four nations to one place, that we might see each other face, to face, and if any one was in the rong, that they might be set to rights. He is not here; he is at Fort Wilkinson.

We have thought proper to permit Richard to remain at the Ottasseys.

Efau Haujo requested me to come over to his house in the evening, as he wanted to talk a little before I returned. In the evening Mr. Cornell and myself went to the house of Efau Haujo; after being seated and smoking a pipe, Efau Haujo began: The beloved man is not here, but you are; I sent to the beloved man to buy me a horse; as I have the public business to attend to, I want a strong horse. Has he not wrote you any thing about the horse? He has not. Since he has wrote you nothing about it, it is probable he means to get one for me among the white people. My former friends told me to get plates, knives & forks, that I might treat a friend decently if he comes to see me. I wish you could tell me any thing about the horse. Probably the old Mark Maker (Bruce) did not mention it to the beloved man, or I should have had an answer by this. Colonel Hawkins would not treat his friends so ill as not to answer his letter; it is customary for one friend to answer the other friend's talks. The scarcity of paper will not permit me to give you his dialogue at length.

He informed me he intended to set off in three days to visit the Governor of Pensacola. He heard there was great presents at Pensacola for the Indians, & that the Spaniards wished to set the Indians to war. He intended to tell the Governor that they were poor people & would gladly accept any thing he would give them; that he could not think of going to war, and that the Governor must not call the nation to Pensacola if war was his motive.

I replied, you are right to exert yourselves in preserving peace, but you must not forget that if you take the Spanish talk and go to war, that you may lose your land and many of your warriors. When the British sent you to war, you lost many of your warriors and a great piece of land; you well know the Spaniards only want to involve you in difficulties. For this seven years past, the Spaniards promised great presents when they expected war, and when they found they could preserve peace, they paid you with promises or vague excuses. The beloved man that the President of the U. S. has now sent will take great care of the red people under his charge, but you must assist him, for if your conduct should induce him to leave you, the next beloved man you see will be a general. He replied that he well knew the white people could not put up with the bad conduct of the Indians, but he was in great hopes that the Indians were reforming, and that the time was not far distant when horse stealing would cease on both sides, and red & white live as friends and brothers.

I found the smith's shop shut on my arrival at Tuckabatchee. I inquired why the smith was not at work. Tooley informed me Mr. Cornell gave him orders to shut up the shop, as he was not able to support the Indians that came with work; that the coal was expended, Tune's time was up, and the Tuckabatchee Indians had killed the long negro you left there, for a wizzard; the Indians complaining that they want their guns mended, &c. I told Tooley if he expected to receive pay he must work, and as Mr. Cornell did not chuse for him to work in his yard, he must have a shop built. As I did not know where you would have the shop fixed, I directed Tooley to examine the spring above and the branch below Mr. Cornell's. He reported that the branch below was the best situation for coal, wood, and ground for a garden and field. I then applied to Zachy McGirth, and in five days had twenty cords of coal wood cut, and by this time, I expect the Indians have built a shop, and that the coal is burning. Yours of July 26th I have received, and shall pay strict attention to your orders. The Indians are preparing here for breaking. I shall embrace the first opportunity that offers to send Miller up to Mr. Cornell. Tyler wished to go up and help to fix him; I have stopped him on account of the public store under his charge. As I have discovered that Wilson has embezzled the public property during Tyler's absence at Fort Wilkinson, I have directed Tyler to keep a strict eye on Wilson, but on no account to let him perceive that I am acquainted with his conduct. Porter, who was at Tallauhassee when you left Marshall's, sold to the amount of 100 chalks, to different people in the upper towns, looking glasses, knives, razors, thimbles, cards, paint, &c. Porter is gone toward the Cherokees, or I would have had him sent to you. Tooley informed me that when Wilson was in the upper towns, he purchased a box of paint, a pair of plated spurs, & some needles from him; it is probable I shall discover more before long. The white horse thieves are censuring my conduct, and say it is no business of mine who steals horses or who comes in or goes out without passports, but I shall do my duty regardless of their threats or frowns. Had I paper, I would blacken another sheet; this I got from your friend Carr. Accept Sir of my wishes for your health and prosperity, and respectfully remember me to your friend, Colonel Gaither, and I remain, with due respect,

R. T.

H. B. H.

6th. Purchased from T. Marshall 3 yds. seymour, 2 yds. ribband, & received from him one lb. loaf sugar & 2 lbs. tea, 1 letter from H. B. H., 1 from W. H. & 1 from D. & C., brought by C. Russel.

8th. Received in the square a letter from T. B. & one from Colonel Phillips, & on the 5th received 1 from Colonel Phillips & a note from E. Park, with the Constitution of Georgia & dispatches from the envoys in France. Exchanged horses with T. Carr; gave him my bay & 40 dollars for a Spanish black.

Cusseta, Saturday, August 10th, 1798.

Sir:

The Indians are a-Busking, and I hired the bearer to carry you this packet. I have told him, as you are at Fort Wilkinson, that you will pay him. I expect Mr. Barnard here to-day; after he has had a talk with the chiefs, shall write you by Emautlau Haujo, who informs me that Mr. Seagrove has told the Indians that you want their land. At present only four Indians are acquainted with Mr. Seagrove's talk; when he comes down, he will give you the particulars. Will be obliged to you for a few of your last papers, and I remain, with due respect,

R. T.

H. B. H.

By Spanish Jim, alias James Ortegas.

Sent the letters by James Ortegas and gave him an order on Mr. Edward Price for six dollars, for rails which he has to split on his return.

15th. Received in the square, from Tuskeegee Tustunnagua, a letter for T. Barnard, & his bill of sundries. Eufale Tustunnagau arrived with a letter & broken days for Colonel Hawkins.

August 16th, 1798.

Sir:

Yesterday morning Eufale Tustunnagau arrived here from the Cherokees. He is a chief of his town, but has resided many years in the Cherokees. He informed me he had a letter for you; that he intended to carry it to Fort Wilkinson; he requested me to accompany him to the square, where he gave out a talk from the Little Turkey or Coweta Mico, and this day we went to the Tallauhassee square, where he delivered his talk; the purport of it was to inform the Creeks that they had been called by the white people, who wanted to purchase more land from them; that the Cherokees refused to part with their land, and that the line run by you and the other Commissioners should be the boundary. He says the Cherokees are well pleased with the conduct of Colonel Butler and Mr. Dinsmoor.

Having heard that some of the Tallauhassee Elgis had crossed the line and plundered some of the inhabitants of some household utensils, children's cloathing, &c., I took this opportunity of informing the chiefs that you had a firm reliance on their exertions for restraining the marauding parties. Tustunnagau Opoi gave his warriors & young men a long talk; he disapproved of their conduct and informed them that he now intended to put a stop to thieving of every description, and on my leaving the square, he told me I might depend on his exertions for preserving of peace. Gun powder & Strouds are very high at Pensacola; the powder 30 dollars for 25 lbs., Strouds 30 dollars per pair. The high price of goods at Pensacola being often the theme of conversation with the chiefs, I observed to them that it was probable that goods might be dearer & that they should omit no opportunity of exerting themselves in restraining their marauding parties and cultivating peace and friendship with their brothers, the citizens of the U. S.; that peace on their part would always entitle them to your attention.

A few of the Simanolees have gone over to Providence, sent by Mr. Leslie, of St. Augustine. The Indians, they are to bring the British to Ocatuyocane to build a town and settle stores. I cannot yet discover what the Indians really intend; they appear friendly and talked as if they wished to preserve peace; it is probable this may be a mercantile speculation of Mr. Leslie's.

Mr. Barnard is not yet arrived; I fear he is unwell, as on the 8th inst., I received a letter from him dated the 1st; he says he will be at the Busk. The letter you sent by Big Feard I shall send him this day; the Indians detained it in the square, expecting his arrival.

Eufale Tustunnagau requests me to introduce him to you; he came here last year to see you, but you was not in the nation. He is an influential chief in this town, and much thought of as a great warrior. He has been a great traveler; has in his time seen Philadelphia, Savannah, Augusta, St. Augustine, Pensacola and New Orleans. He wishes to have a great deal of conversation with you. In the Cusseta square he pointed to the chiefs the bad conduct of their young people in not paying proper attention to your talks. He explained to them the advantages they would receive from an upright conduct; that the Cherokees had profited by it; that some industrious men made saddles, silverware, &c.; that the women spun and wove their own cloathing, and if the Indians would exert themselves, they might soon be able to sell riding saddles to the white people for dollars. The use of the plough and worm fences was not forgot in his talk.

R. T.

H. B. H.

August 16th, 1798.

Dear Sir:

Yours of the 1st I received on the 8th, and have daily expected to have had the pleasure of seeing you. On the 10th I sent Spanish Jim to Colonel Hawkins; should have sent him by your house, but expected you by the way of the Warrior King's. The Spaniards are preparing to set the Indians on the frontiers, and have eighteen thousand dollars in presents at Pensacola. Report says the line between the U. S. & Spain is stopped and Mr. Ellicot gone for Philadelphia. I have not paper to give you a copy of my report to Colonel Hawkins; it was three sheets; as I soon hope to see you here, you will see it in my book. The Mad Dog is gone to Pensacola to tell the Spanish Governor he must not call the nation if war is his motive. Wilson has plundered the store of several articles and disposed of them. Colonel Hawkins has sent Miller to take Tooley's place in the upper towns. Roguery's son same here yesterday, express, with a letter for Colonel Hawkins. The Cherokees have refused to part with any more of their land, but they are well pleased with Colonel Butler and Mr. Dinsmoor. 15 days now remain for a meeting in the Cherokees, & they wish Colonel Hawkins to be there. Roguery's son goes off in the morning for Fort Wilkinson. Yesterday I received in the square the letter & account; I now send the Indian; detained it, expecting you every day. If you cannot conveniently come in, as soon as Jim returns I will come out and see you. My horses are poor. It is probable it will not be long before we see Colonel Hawkins. Wishing you every happiness the Indian soil can afford, I remain, with due respect,

Your most obedient servant,

RICHARD THOMAS.

T. BARNARD, ESQ.

Cusseta, August 17th, 1798.

MR. WILLIAM TOOLEY:

I am directed by the Honourable Benjamin Hawkins, P. T. Agent of Indian Affairs South of Ohio, to inform you that he has employed John Miller as public smith at Tuckabatchee, and that your pay will cease on Miller's arrival. You will give Miller all the tools, iron and steel under your charge, and make out your account against the U. S. to the day of Miller's arrival.

R. T.

Cusseta, August 17th, 1798.

Dear Sir:

Colonel Hawkins has sent you the bearer, John Miller, as a public smith in the place of William Tooley; he hopes he will give satisfaction to the chiefs and yourself. I have wrote Tooley that his time expires on Miller's arrival. It will be proper for you to see that Tooley delivers Miller all the tools, iron & steel that belongs to the shop, and as he is a stranger, you will oblige Colonel Hawkins by making his situation as comfortable as possible.

R. T.

MR. ALEX. CORNELL.

Gave Miller a list of the tools delivered Wm. Tooley for the use of the smith's shop at Tuckabatchee.

August 18th, 1798.

MR. EDWARD PRICE, U. S. Factor:

Sir:

The head warrior of this town has gave me information respecting a horse you purchased of Hardridge, of this nation. The horse strayed from Fort Wilkinson, was taken up in the woods by his former owner, who had received from Hardridge only half the purchase consideration. He has paid Hardridge cattle for the goods he received from him, and sold the horse to an Indian of this town.

R. T.

Inclosed this note in Colonel Hawkins's letter, sent by Eufale Tustunnagau.

Purchased of Limerick 12 lbs. of soap and gave him an order on Mr. Thos. Marshall for $3.25.

The Adjutant died at 2 in the morning.

22nd. Received from T. B. a letter dated the 17th, and one inclosed for Mr. Hill.

Cusseta, 22nd August.

Sir:

Emautlau Haujo takes with him 2 women's petticoats, 1 woman's jacket, 3 girl's gowns, 1 coffee pot & 1 quart, 2 bells and some tanned leather that was stole from some of the inhabitants near Tulappoca. Emautlau Haujo requests you to send by him to the person who lost these articles, as he intends going up to Mr. Phillips's with them. He wishes the owner to give him a list of what was stole, as the chiefs suspect the Tallauhassee Indian that brought these in has not told them the truth. He says he bought them for five deer skins. He stole also a bay mare and colt that was brought in last summer; they were taken from the neighbourhood of Tulapocca.

R. T.

H. B. H.

INDEX